Probate Records of the Province of New Hampshire

(Volume VI) 1757-1760

Editor

Otis G. Hammond

Alpha Editions

This edition published in 2020

ISBN : 9789354016905

Design and Setting By
Alpha Editions
email - alphaedis@gmail.com

As per information held with us this book is in Public Domain.
This book is a reproduction of an important historical work. Alpha Editions uses the best technology to reproduce historical work in the same manner it was first published to preserve its original nature. Any marks or number seen are left intentionally to preserve its true form.

PROBATE RECORDS

OF THE

PROVINCE OF NEW HAMPSHIRE

VOL. 6
1757–1760

STATE PAPERS SERIES
VOL. 36

Edited by
OTIS G. HAMMOND
*Director of the
New Hampshire Historical Society*

PUBLISHED BY
THE STATE OF NEW HAMPSHIRE
1938

JOINT RESOLUTION

Relating to the preservation and publication of portions of the early state and provincial records and other state papers of New Hampshire.

Resolved by the Senate and House of Representatives in General Court convened:

That His Excellency the Governor be hereby authorized and empowered, with the advice and consent of the Council, to employ some suitable person — and fix his compensation, to be paid out of any money in the treasury not otherwise appropriated — to collect, arrange, transcribe, and superintend the publication of such portions of the early state and provincial records and other state papers of New Hampshire as the Governor may deem proper; and that eight hundred copies of each volume of the same be printed by the state printer, and distributed as follows: namely, one copy to each city and town in the state, one copy to such of the public libraries in the state as the Governor may designate, fifty copies to the New Hampshire Historical Society, and the remainder placed in the custody of the state librarian, who is hereby authorized to exchange the same for similar publications by other states.

Approved August 4, 1881.

LIST OF ESTATES

Adams, William, Hollis, 1757	148
Akerman, Benjamin, Portsmouth, 1757	208
Allen, Robert, Londonderry, 1757	144
Ambrose, Jonathan, Nottingham, 1759	475
Ames, David, Newmarket, 1757	29
Anderson, John, Londonderry, 1757	179
Archdeacon, Peter, Portsmouth, 1758	330
Ayers, James, Londonderry, 1759	397
Samuel, Portsmouth, 1760	507
Babb, Joshua, Portsmouth, 1758	351
Bagley, Orlando, Amesbury, Mass., 1757	60
Barnes, Joseph, Portsmouth, 1758	274
Batchelder, Daniel, Kensington, 1758	355
Jonathan, Newmarket, 1757	67
Joshua, Brentwood, 1757	114
Josiah, Hampton Falls, 1759	479
Nathaniel, Kensington, 1757	131
Page, Chester, 1757	22
Samuel, Kensington, 1757	149
Bean, Ruth, Exeter, 1758	356
Berry, James, Greenland, 1758	249
Bickford, John, Dover, 1757	160
Blair, David, Londonderry, 1759	372
Blanchard, Joseph, Nashua, 1758	238
Boynton, Samuel, Stratham, 1757	204
Brackett, John, Greenland, 1758	226
Brown, Jeremiah, Hampton Falls, 1758	229
Pearson, Hampton Falls, 1760	515
Bruce, William, Durham, 1759	368
Burbank, Jonathan, Hopkinton, 1759	500

LIST OF ESTATES

Burditt, Daniel, Malden, Mass., 1760	529
Burnside, David, Londonderry, 1757	162
Buss, Lydia, Portsmouth, 1758	293
Butterfield, John, Nashua, 1758	246
Buzzell, Samuel, Kingston, 1757	130
Canney, Thomas, Dover, 1758	240
Carty, Daniel, Exeter, 1760	510
Cate, Tucker, Greenland, 1757	83
Caverly, Moses, Barrington, 1758	275
Chaddock, William, Somersworth, 1758	283
Challis, Enoch, South Hampton, 1759	369
Chase, Nathaniel, Londonderry, 1757	165
Ruth, Londonderry, 1758	237
Thomas, Stratham, 1757	30
Childs, Richard, Durham, 1757	40
Choate, Benjamin, Kingston, 1758	297
Jonathan, Kingston, 1757	38
Clark, Enoch, Greenland, 1759	360
George, Portsmouth, 1759	395
Clement, Daniel, Sandown, 1758	261
Clements, James, Somersworth, 1758	315
John, Salem, 1757	70
Clifford, Samuel, Kensington, 1760	516
Clough, Ann, Brentwood, 1758	301
Cochran, Joseph, Bedford, 1758	284
Peter, Amherst, 1758	323
Colby, Nathan, Concord, 1759	441
Theophilus, Sandown, 1758	320
Cole, Simeon, Durham, 1759	490
Conant, Josiah, Hollis, 1757	81
Connor, Meribah, Kingston, 1757	138
Corliss, David, Salem, 1760	537
Cotton, John, Portsmouth, 1759	457
Timothy, Portsmouth, 1759	487

LIST OF ESTATES vii

Cram, Jonathan, Hampton Falls, 1759	501
Creighton, Ann, Exeter, 1758	342
Crockett, Jonathan, Portsmouth, 1758	352
Crockford, Daniel, Portsmouth, 1757	99
Cummings, Eleazer, Hudson, 1757	150
Leonard, Londonderry, 1758	333
William, Hudson, 1757	182
William, Nashua, 1758	335
Cunningham, John, Londonderry, 1757	48
Currier, John, Kingston, 1757	191
John, Plaistow, 1758	243
Cutt, John, Portsmouth, 1759	483
Davis, Benjamin, Plaistow, 1758	334
Daniel, Durham, 1759	381
Joseph, Chester, 1759	477
Timothy, Portsmouth, 1758	221
Dinsmoor, Asa, Hollis, 1758	283
John, New Ipswich, 1758	282
Doe, Andrew, Newmarket, 1760	512
Dole, Parker, Plaistow, 1758	330
Dow, Daniel, Salem, 1758	220
Jonathan, Plaistow, 1759	496
Simon, Hampton, 1757	93
Downs, Gershom, Rochester, 1757	51
John, Somersworth, 1757	30
Dresser, Jeremiah, Concord, 1760	512
Drew, Joseph, Dover, 1757	78
Dudley, Samuel, Exeter, 1758	242
Dustin, Jonathan, Londonderry, 1757	204
Dwinell, Amos, Hampton Falls, 1757	110
Eastman, Thomas, Danville, 1760	556
Eaton, Jabez, Hampton Falls, 1760	570
Emmons, Samuel, Kingston, 1757	49

LIST OF ESTATES

Fassett, Peter, Goffstown, 1760	507
Fifield, Joseph, Kingston, 1757	103
Flagg, Eleazer, Hollis, 1757	111
Flanders, Jeremiah, South Hampton, 1757	77
Philip, Chester, 1758	221
Samuel, Brentwood, 1758	320
Fogg, Daniel, Rye, 1757	170
Forbush, Benoni, Amherst, 1758	353
Foss, Isaac, Stratham, 1759	456
Foster, Abijah, New Ipswich, 1760	525
French, James, Salem, 1759	499
James, Salem, 1760	566
Samuel, Jr., South Hampton, 1757	139
Gage, William, Methuen, Mass., 1757	8
Gale, Jacob, Kingston, 1760	554
Garfield, Benjamin, Hinsdale, 1759	388
Garland, Jonathan, Hampton, 1760	532
Gault, Matthew, Chester, 1759	393
Gilman, Andrew, Brentwood, 1757	166
Jacob, Kingston, 1757	105
Stephen, Kingston, 1758	278
Timothy, Newmarket, 1759	359
Gilmore, James, Windham, 1758	257
Glines, John, Canterbury, 1757	42
Godfrey, Simon, North Hampton, 1758	327
Gooding, James, Newmarket, 1757	46
Gordon, Thomas, Exeter, 1757	186
Gould, Joseph, South Hampton, 1757	90
Nehemiah, Mason, 1759	373
Gove, Enoch, Hampton Falls, 1759	444
John, Hampton Falls, 1759	460
Graham, Arthur, Londonderry, 1759	389
Graves, John, Kensington, 1757	73

LIST OF ESTATES

Griffin, Isaac, Kingston, 1757	147
Grow, Ebenezer, Greenland, 1760	568
Hadley, Joseph, Hampstead, 1758	327
Samuel, Hampstead, 1759	411
Haines, Samuel, Greenland, 1760	534
William, Greenland, 1760	538
Hale, Thomas, Plaistow, 1757	8
Hamilton, Samuel, Newmarket, 1758	357
Hanson, Isaac, Somersworth, 1757	91
Isaac, Dover, 1758	304
Joseph, Dover, 1758	315
Hardy, Dudley, Exeter, 1757	130
Samuel, Stratham, 1759	381
Theophilus, Durham, 1757	184
Hazelton, John, Chester, 1758	324
Heath, Richard, Plaistow, 1757	174
Richard, Plaistow, 1758	277
Hill, William, Madbury, 1760	590
Hilliard, Jonathan, Hampton Falls, 1758	301
Hills, Benjamin, Chester, 1759	413
Henry, Hudson, 1759	150
Hinsdale, Ebenezer, Deerfield, Mass., 1760	521
Hobbs, Benjamin, North Hampton, 1757	44
Humphrey, Wilton, 1757	57
John, Hampton, 1760	580
Stephen, Kensington, 1757	87
Holland, John, Jr., Exeter, 1758	282
Holmes, John, Portsmouth, 1760	518
Honey, Gideon, Nashua, 1757	91
Hopkins, William, Portsmouth, 1760	535
Horney, David, Portsmouth, 1757	85
Houston, John, Nashua, 1759	389
Hoyt, Daniel, Epping, 1757	189
Hubbard, Jonathan, Charlestown, 1760	551

LIST OF ESTATES

Hunt, Nathan, Sandown, 1759	436
Huntoon, Josiah, Newmarket, 1758	323
Huntress, Samuel, Newington, 1758	232
Jackson, Dorothy, Portsmouth, 1758	331
Elisha, Portsmouth, 1760	526
Joshua, Portsmouth, 1758	211
Samuel, Portsmouth, 1758	253
William, Durham, 1757	27
Jenkins, William, Greenland, 1757	76
Johnson, James, Charlestown, 1760	510
Jones, John, Durham, 1759	430
Jonathan, Amesbury, Mass., 1759	401
Jonathan, South Hampton, 1759	406
Jose, Ebenezer, Portsmouth, 1760	518
Judkins, Joel, Brentwood, 1758	222
Kelly, Richard, Salem, 1757	178
Kidder, Benjamin, Bedford, 1757	38
Benjamin, Bedford, 1759	368
Kimball, Aaron, Hopkinton, 1760	546
Joseph, Hampstead, 1758	234
Richard, Salem, 1757	163
Thomas, Jr., Exeter, 1757	37
Ladd, Daniel, Epping, 1758	334
Lancey, William, Nashua, 1757	137
Lang, Daniel, Portsmouth, 1757	101
Robert, Portsmouth, 1757	105
Ruth, Greenland, 1759	392
William, Portsmouth, 1759	395
Leavitt, Daniel, Exeter, 1760	511
Elisha, Stratham, 1758	356
Ephraim, Stratham, 1757	106
Jeremiah, Exeter, 1758	279

LIST OF ESTATES

Leavitt, Moses, Hampton, 1758	264
Leslie, Daniel, Londonderry, 1759	501
Libby, Jeremiah, Portsmouth, 1757	70
Liggett, James, Londonderry, 1759	394
Light, John, Exeter, 1757	86
Little, George, Plaistow, 1758	247
Littlehale, Isaac, Pelham, 1757	167
Locke, Ward, Kensington, 1758	281
Lord, Jonathan, Ipswich, Mass., 1757	51
Love, John, Londonderry, 1757	95
Lovering, Samuel, Kingston, 1760	518
Lunt, Daniel, Greenland, 1757	54
McCargin, Philip, Hampstead, 1760	527
McConechey, John, Bedford, 1757	26
Mace, Betty, Dover, 1758	291
Mack, William, Londonderry, 1760	589
McMurphy, John, Londonderry, 1757	29
McNeil, Abraham, Manchester, 1757	121
John, Londonderry, 1759	418
Main, Amos, Rochester, 1760	529
Mann, Nathan, Windham, 1758	341
Mannering, John, Portsmouth, 1757	5
Marsh, Ephraim, Londonderry, 1760	591
Marston, Daniel, North Hampton, 1757	176
Martin, Nolar, Portsmouth, 1758	211
Mason, Robert, Durham, 1760	560
Mattoon, John, Newmarket, 1760	543
Mead, Thomas, Portsmouth, 1759	428
Meader, Nicholas, Durham, 1759	424
Melvin, Patrick, Chester, 1758	262
Merrill, John, Jr., Bow, 1758	236
Joseph, Stratham, 1760	547
Samuel, Jr., Hudson, 1758	346
Meserve, Hanson, Portsmouth, 1759	483

LIST OF ESTATES

Meserve, John, Portsmouth, 1760	514
Mary, Portsmouth, 1759	489
Nathaniel, Portsmouth, 1758	289
Nathaniel, Portsmouth, 1759	386
Mills, William, Chester, 1758	348
Mitchell, George, Londonderry, 1759	430
Morgan, Timothy, Epping, 1757	158
Morrison, David, Nottingham, 1757	71
David, Londonderry, 1760	538
James, Londonderry, 1757	87
John, Epping, 1758	266
William, Nottingham, 1758	319
Morse, Jacob, Kingston, 1758	266
Moulton, Abraham, Kensington, 1757	135
Neal, Joshua, Stratham, 1760	558
Samuel, Newmarket, 1760	569
Nealey, Matthew, Nottingham, 1757	123
Nelson, James, Portsmouth, 1759	386
Matthew, Portsmouth, 1757	154
Nesmith, Arthur, Londonderry, 1758	259
Newmarch, Thomas, Portsmouth, 1757	114
Newton, John, Kingston, 1757	17
Nutt, John, Chester, 1757	182
Ober, John, Jr., Salem, 1758	328
Osgood, James, Concord, 1757	13
Otis, Stephen, Madbury, 1759	418
Packer, Ann, Portsmouth, 1759	437
Page, David, Epping, 1757	18
Joseph, Plaistow, 1757	58
Onesiphorous, Kingston, 1758	354
William, Brentwood, 1757	194
Paine, John, Portsmouth, 1758	292

LIST OF ESTATES

Palmer, Joseph, Pembroke, 1759	390
Samuel, Jr., Hampton, 1759	442
Park, Alexander, Windham, 1760	525
Parker, William, Litchfield, 1760.	508
Pattinson, Mary, Portsmouth, 1757	47
Pease, Zebulon, Hollis, 1759.	415
Peavey, William, Portsmouth, 1759	442
Pecker, John, Haverhill, Mass., 1757	25
Perham, Samuel, New Ipswich, 1760	543
Perkins, Joseph, Durham, 1759	359
Joseph, Hampton Falls, 1760	561
Perryman, Nicholas, Exeter, 1757	120
Philbrick, Caleb, Epping, 1759	416
Joses, Rye, 1757	45
Pierce, Ebenezer, Hollis, 1759	490
Pomeroy, ———, Goffstown, 1759	388
Powers, Peter, Hollis, 1757	143
Prescott, Jonathan, Hampton Falls, 1759	367
Samuel, Hampton Falls, 1758	270
Pritchard, Christopher, Newcastle, 1758	348
Purmort, John, Exeter, 1758	335
Putney, Henry, New Ipswich, 1757	173
Quinby, Daniel, Brentwood, 1759	421
Redman, John, Nottingham, 1758	349
Joseph, Hampton, 1758.	260
Reed, Philip, Portsmouth, 1759	444
Richardson, Seth, Wilton, 1757	183
Timothy, Hollis, 1757	81
Roberts, David, Plaistow, 1758	264
Francis, Somersworth, 1758	307
Stephen, Dover, 1758	286
Robinson, John, Merrimack, 1757	165
Jonathan, Brentwood, 1757	97

LIST OF ESTATES

Rowe, Benjamin, Newington, 1758	273
Charles, Hampton Falls, 1758	232
Robert, Hampton Falls, 1757	116
Robert, Kensington, 1757	205
Rowell, Job, Salisbury, Mass., 1758	279
John, Epping, 1757	175
Russell, Pelatiah, Litchfield, 1758	247
Peter, Litchfield, 1759	488
Sanborn, Abraham, Kensington, 1757	151
Ezekiel, Newmarket, 1757	137
Israel, Newmarket, 1758	256
Jonathan, Kingston, 1760	563
Sanders, Avery, Haverhill, Mass., 1759	366
Sargent, Zebediah, Haverhill, Mass., 1757	69
Saylor, John, Nashua, 1760	567
Scribner, Joseph, Exeter, 1757	169
Searles, Samuel, Nashua, 1758	209
Seavey, Samuel, Rye, 1760	541
Severance, Ephraim, Jr., Kingston, 1757	97
Seward, George, Portsmouth, 1759	367
Seymour, Henry, Portsmouth, 1757	183
Shaw, Benjamin, Nottingham, 1757	6
Shedd, John, Nashua, 1757	52
Sherburne, Hannah, Newcastle, 1759	478
Henry, Portsmouth, 1757	195
Nathaniel, Portsmouth, 1757	191
Smith, Andrew, Londonderry, 1757	146
Benjamin, Haverhill, Mass., 1758	290
Elizabeth, Kingston, 1757	145
Oliver, Brentwood, 1757	96
Oliver, Exeter, 1759	432
Priscilla, Portsmouth, 1759	421
Samuel, Exeter, 1760	513
Stackpole, Samuel, Somersworth, 1758	220

LIST OF ESTATES

Stark, Archibald, Manchester, 1758	276
Stevens, ——, 1758	281
David, Hampstead, 1757	122
James, Portsmouth, 1759	484
John, Chester, 1757	153
Nehemiah, Hampstead, 1757	152
Peter, Plaistow, 1759	428
Phineas, Charlestown, 1760	550
Stickney, Moses, Hampton Falls, 1758	353
Stinson, Samuel, Dunbarton, 1759	414
Stoneman, Charles, Portsmouth, 1760	515
Stoodley, Jonathan, Portsmouth, 1759	375
Swain, John, Hampton Falls, 1757	118
Swett, Benjamin, Hampton Falls, 1757	173
Taylor, Joseph, Exeter, 1757	175
Willoughby, Exeter, 1758	268
Thing, Jonathan, Brentwood, 1760	535
Thomas, Benjamin, North Hampton, 1758	312
Thompson, Benjamin, Londonderry, 1759	374
William, Windham, 1757	75
Tibbetts, Ephraim, Dover, 1760	593
Tidd, Joseph, Hollis, 1759	415
Titcomb, Daniel, Dover, 1758	339
Towle, Benjamin, Hampton, 1758	212
Ebenezer, Brentwood, 1757	204
Trussell, Moses, Plaistow, 1759	492
Tuckerman, Nathaniel, Portsmouth, 1758	311
Underwood, Phineas, Merrimack, 1757	151
Urin, Peter, Salem, 1760	534
Varney, Moses, Dover, 1759	403
Samuel, Dover, 1759	439

LIST OF ESTATES

Vaughan, Elliot, Portsmouth, 1758	329
Vennard, John, Newcastle, 1759	460
Walker, ——, Concord, 1757	76
Alexander, Jr., Londonderry, 1759	429
Walton, Benjamin, Amherst, 1760	566
Ward, Dorcas, Portsmouth, 1760	553
Warren, George, Portsmouth, 1760	528
Watkins, Andrew, Newcastle, 1759	380
Watson, Isaac, Dover, 1757	64
Samuel, Dover, 1757	34
Watts, John, Plaistow, 1759	422
John, Salem, 1759	419
Weare, Mary, Kensington, 1757	160
Nathaniel, Hampton Falls, 1758	357
Weeks, Joshua, Greenland, 1757	1
Walter, Jr., Greenland, 1758	245
Welch, David, Kingston, 1757	96
Wentworth, Ebenezer, Portsmouth, 1757	21
Ezekiel, Dover, 1757	95
Gershom, Somersworth, 1758	286
Mark, Somersworth, 1757	69
Samuel, Somersworth, 1758	280
Thomas, Somersworth, 1758	349
West, William, Portsmouth, 1757	41
Weston, Ebenezer, Amherst, 1759	398
Weymouth, Samuel, Somersworth, 1759	373
Wheeler, Abner, Salem, 1758	267
Whidden, John, Greenland, 1757	35
Whiting, James, Hollis, 1760	560
Whittier, Abner, Amesbury, Mass., 1757	53
Wiggin, Bradstreet, Stratham, 1757	157
Simon, Stratham, 1757	107
Williams, Benjamin, Danville, 1759	493

Wilson, ——, Londonderry, 1759	360
John, Plaistow, 1757	168
Winchester, Ebenezer, Portsmouth, 1757	6
Winslow, Elisha, Kingston, 1760	569
Wood, Joseph, Charlestown, 1760	552
Worcester, Jesse, Newbury, Mass., 1758	289
Worthen, Samuel, Plaistow, 1757	19
Wyman, Thomas, Pelham, 1760	508
York, Benjamin, Durham, 1760	512
Young, John, Kingston, 1758	318
Jonathan, Rochester, 1759	419

NEW HAMPSHIRE WILLS

| JOSHUA WEEKS | 1757 | GREENLAND |

The Last will and Testement of Joshua weeks of Greenland in the province of Newhampshire Gentlman Being of Sound Mind and Memory but Calling to mind the mortality of my Body Do Therefore this Second Day of November anno: Domini one thousand Seven hundred and fifty Two make and ordain this my Last will and Testement * * *

Item I Give and Bequeath unto my beloved wife Comfort weeks the use & Improvement of one Third part of all my Real Estate also that half part of my Dweling house which Shee Shall Chuse and also all my household Stuff Dureing her Natueral Life as also the use of my negro woman Named Hannah and the Improvement of Two Cows Six Sheep one horse my Rideing Chair and pew in the meetinghouse in Greenland afore Said So Long as Shee Remains my widow (Exepting one bed that my Son william weeks now has in his possesion and my will is that my Son william weeks Shall maintain the Said Two Cows Six sheep and horse winter and Summer Dureing my Said wives widowhood —

Item I Give Devise and Bequeath unto my Son John weeks and to his heirs and assigns for Ever one half of my Lower flats Bounding against my marsh Commonly Called and Known by the name of furbors and Shackfords Marsh in Greenland afore Said I also Give Demise and Bequeath unto my Said John weeks his heirs and assigns for Ever Ten acres of Land Laying in Greenland afore Said be it more or Less adjoyning the Land he now has in his possesion Runing northwardly upon the Road that Leads from my Said Son John⁸ house to my own untill it Coms to a Brook and from Said Brook to Run South Till it

Coms to James Cats Land and So Bounding on Said Cats Land and Land Belonging to John watson Till it Coms to my Said Son John weekes' Land that he alrady has also I give and Bequeath unto my Said Son John weeks his heirs and assigns my Negro whose Name is Neptune

Item I Give and Bequeth unto my Granson Joshua weeks the Son of my Son Joshua weeks Deceased Twenty Shillings Lawfull money in full of his portion in my Estate to be paid by my Son william weeks within Two years next after my Decease —

Item I Give and Bequeath unto my Daughter mary the wife of Jonathan Chasley one hundred and ten pounds old tenor: Thirty pounds thereof to be paid by my Son william weeks Emeadatly after my Decease the other Eighty pounds thereof to be paid by my Said Son william weeks within two years next after my Decease —

Item I Give and Bequeath unto my Daughter Martha Hilton the wife of wintroup Hilton one hundred and ten pounds old tenor Thirty pounds thereof to be paid by my Son william weeks Emeadatly after my Decease the other Eighty pounds to be paid by my Said Son william Two years next after my Decease —

Item I Give and Bequeath unto My Granson Joshua Wiggin Son of my Said Daughter Martha Hilton one Three year old haffer to be Delivered him Emeadatly after my Decease by my Son william weeks —

Item I Give and Bequeath unto my Daughter Comfort the wife of walter weeks one hundred and Ten pounds old tenor Thirty pounds thereof to be paid by My Son william weeks Emeadatly after My Decease the other Eighty pounds thereof to be paid by Said Son william weeks within Two years next after my Decease —

Item I Give and Bequeath unto my Two Gransons (viz) George Marshal and John Marshal Sons of my Daughter Thankfull the wife of George Marshall (who is Lately Deceased) Eighty pounds old tenor Equally to be Devided between them

Said George Marshal and John Marshal when they arive to the age of Twenty one years to be put to Intrust by my Said Son william weeks within two years Next after my Decease and by him be paid to them Said George marshal and John marshall with the Intrust thereof when they arive to the age of Twenty one years

Item I Give and Bequeath unto my Two Grandaughters Margret Marshal and Comfort marshal the Daughters of my Daughter Thankfull Marshall Deceased who was the wife of George marshall the fifth part of my household goods to be Taken Care of by my Executors at my own and my wives Decease and by them be put to Intrust untill the Said Margret and Comfort arives to the age of Eighteen years and then be Equally with the Intrust thereof Delivered unto them by my Executors —

Item I Give and Bequeath unto my Daughter Margret Smith the wife of Ebenezer Smith one hundred and ten pounds old tenor Thirty pounds thereof to be paid Emeadatly after my Decease by my Son John weeks and the other Eighty pounds thereof to be paid by my Said Son John weeks within Two years next after my Decease I also Give and Bequeath unto my Said Daughter Margret Smith her heirs and assigns my Negro woman Named hannah Emeadatly to Recive her at my own and my wives Decease I also Give my Said Daughter Margret my lorne Jack

Item I Give and Bequeath unto my fouer Daughters (viz) Mary Chasley Martha Hilton Comfort weeks and Margret Smith all my house hold Stuff that is not alrady or hereafter Desposed of Equally to be devided between them Emeadatly after my own and my wives Decease —

Item I Give and Bequeath unto my Son william weeks his heirs and assigns for Ever all my Dweling house Barns and out houses to Emeadatly possesed of at my own and my wives Decease Togather with all my Lands Madows pasturs thatch Ground and Salt Marsh Laying in Greenland afore Said or alce whare Exepting what I have alrady herein and Before Desposed of I also Give and Bequeath unto my Said Son william weeks all my horses Sheep Swine Stock of Catle of Every Sort and Kind Exepting what is and Shall be other waies Desposed of and one Bad that he have alrady Received and all my Emplements of husbandtarry all So my Guns Sword Case and the works of Mr Manton and Dr Mathers Church histrey and al my Right in a negro man Named Seizer that is not al Rady Desposed of togather with all my Real and personal Estate Not Desposed of the Batter to Inable him to pay my Debts and my own and my wives funeral Charges —

Item I Give unto my Son John weeks and my Son william weeks all my money Bills Bonds and Notes for payment of money Equeley to be Devided Between them —

Aand I Do hereby Constitute and ordain and apoint My Said Sons John weeks and william weeks Executors * * *

Joshua Weeks

[Witnesses] James Brackett, Marthy Brackett, Richd Young.

Beit Known unto all men by These presents That whereas I Joshua weeks of Greenland in the province of Newhampshire Gentlman have made and Declared my Last will and Testement in writing Bareing Date the Second Day of November anno: Domini one Thousand Seven hundred and fifty Two I the Said Joshua weeks: by This present Codicil Do Ratifie and Confirm my Said Last will and Testement only by This Codicil Do Explain my True Intent and meaning how and in what manner my household Stuff Shall be Devided that is Given to my four Daughters: (viz) Mary Chasley martha Hilton Comfort weeks and Margret Smith after the fifth part thereof be Tacken Care of by my Executors as mentioned in my Said Last will and Testement for my Two Grand Daughters (viz) margret marshal and Comfort marshall and That is to Say my Two Executors that I have apointed in my Said Last will and Testement Shall and are hereby ordred to Devide my Said household Stuff that Remains into four Equal parts for quantity and quality and and my Said four Daughters To Draw Lots for them —

I Give and Bequeath unto Joshua weeks my Granson The Sun of my Son william weeks My upper Case and Bottles Lock and Kee Belonging there unto and to my household Stuff Belongs the Suttle in the Corn Barn and what therein is: the Cask in my Sellers are not ment household Stuff: Nor any thing that in them is —

further I Give unto my Granson Said Joshua weeks Son of my s^d Son william weeks my Truny that I usely puts my Close In Confirmation whereof I Do here unto Set my hand and Seal the Elaventh Day of January in the Thirtyeth year of his majestys Reign Anno: Domini 1757 —

Joshua Weeks

[Witnesses] Nathanel goss, Richd Young, Rich^d × Goss.
his mark

[Proved June 28, 1758.]

JOHN MANNERING 1757 PORTSMOUTH

[Administration on the estate of John Mannering of Portsmouth, mariner, granted to his widow, Sarah Mannering, Jan. 12, 1757.]

[Probate Records, vol. 20, p. 83.]

[Bond of Sarah Mannering, widow, with Stephen March, blacksmith, and John Cutt, cooper, as sureties, all of Portsmouth, in the sum of £500, Jan. 12, 1757, for the administration of the estate; witnesses, Abraham Trefethen, Joseph Alcock.]

[Inventory, Jan. 13, 1757; amount, £397. 9. 0; signed by Joseph Alcock and John Cutt.]

EBENEZER WINCHESTER 1757   PORTSMOUTH

[Administration on the estate of Ebenezer Winchester of Portsmouth, physician, granted to Jonathan Gibbs of Framingham, Mass., gentleman, Jan. 15, 1757.]

[Probate Records, vol. 20, p. 85.]

[Bond of Jonathan Gibbs, with Samuel Hale and Seth Ring, yeoman, both of Portsmouth, as sureties, in the sum of £500, Jan. 15, 1757, for the administration of the estate; witnesses, William Parker, Samuel Haven.]

[Inventory, Jan. 19, 1757; amount, £501. 14. 0; signed by Samuel Hale and Daniel Rogers.]

BENJAMIN SHAW   1757   NOTTINGHAM

In The Name of God Amen the sixteenth Day of January 1757 I Benjamin Shaw of nottingham In ye provvence of new Hampshire In new England yeoman being weak in Body * * *

Item I Give & bequeath to my well beloved wife Ester Shaw the use & Improvement of all my Real Estate untill my Son Benjamin shall arive to ye age of Twenty one years with my stock & buldings and after that my s^d wife to have & pecably to Injoy the one third part of my land with the fore Room In the easterly end of my Dewelling house & one half of my Celler with a priviledge In my barn she to have Tow Cows Three sheep and a Riding hors she to have all my Debts by bills or nots my wife to have & to hold the above mentioned premisses During her Widow hood — further more my will is that my wife shall make sale of all my lands & marsh In the Towon Ship of hampton the first oppertunity after my Decease and If In Case she shall stand In need of Expending that money for the support of her & my three Children In their minority she shall Expend it other wise my will Is that my wife shall pay to my son Benjamin one forth part of the Remainder of It & the Rest to be at my wifes Disposing

Itm I Give & bequeath to my son Benjamin Shaw when he shall arive at the age of twenty one years Two thirds of all my Lands in nottingham To Gather with all my Buildings & stock which I have not all Ready Disposed of in ye with in will with the whole of all my out Lands & If in Case my wife shall marry again Then my son Benj^{mn} to Com Into possession of the whole of my Estate to him & to his heirs for Eveir In Case he shall pay those Lagesies I shall here after specifie —

It^m I Give & bequeath to my Daughter sarah shaw one hundred pounds old Tenor — one Cow & Two sheep to be paid by my son Benjamin when he shall arive at ye age of Twenty one y^{rs}

It^m I Give & bequeath to my Daughter Ester shaw one hundred pounds old Tenor one Cow & Two sheep to be paid by my son Benjm^n when he shall arive at full age —

Lastly I Do Constutetute & appoint my wife Ester Shaw to be sole Executrix * * *

his
Benjamin × Shaw
mark

            his   her
[Witnesses] John × Shaw, Susanna × Shaw, Joseph Draper.
          mark   mark

[Proved June 27, 1757.]

[Warrant, June 29, 1757, authorizing Thomas Simpson and John Mason, both of Nottingham, yeomen, to appraise the estate.]

[Inventory, attested Aug. 25, 1757; amount, £3165. 1. 0; signed by John Mason and Thomas Simpson.]

WILLIAM GAGE 1757 METHUEN, MASS.

[Deborah Gage renounces administration on the estate of her husband, William Gage, Jan. 19, 1757; witnesses, Daniel Jaques, Samuel Cole.]

[Warrant from Daniel Peaslee, Justice of the Peace, Jan. 19, 1757, authorizing John Sargent, Samuel Cole, and Daniel Jaques to appraise the estate in New Salem of William Gage of Methuen, Mass.]

[Inventory, Jan. 19, 1757; amount, £267. 10. 0; signed by John Sargent, Daniel Jaques, and Samuel Cole; land in Salem.]

[Administration on the estate of William Gage of Methuen, Mass., granted to his brother, Benjamin Gage of Bradford, Mass., cordwainer, July 27, 1757.]

[Probate Records, vol. 20, p. 237.]

[Bond of Benjamin Gage, with Jacob Treadwell and George Moses, both of Portsmouth, tanners, as sureties, in the sum of £500, July 27, 1757, for the administration of the estate; witnesses, William Parker, John Fernald.]

[Account of the settlement of the estate; receipts, £70. 10. 0; expenditures the same; allowed Aug. 30, 1758.]

THOMAS HALE 1757 PLAISTOW

In the Name of God amen This nineteenth Day of January In the year of our Lord one Thousend seven Hundred and fifty Seven I Thomas Hale of Plastow in the Province of New Hamshire in New England Husbandman * * *

Imprimis I Give unto my Dearly Beloved Wife Mary the use and Improvement of one half of my Dwelling House and one Third part of all my Real Estate all Dureing the Time that she shall Remain my widow

Item I Give unto my said Wife all my Household goods and my Books and one Third part of my stock of Creatures and Two Hundred Pounds in Bills of Credit of the old Tenor to be paid by my Executors

Item I Give and Bequeath unto my Daughtor mary noyes or her Heirs whatsoever she hath allready Received of me and I Give unto her my said Daughter mary or her heirs the sum of four Hundred Pounds in Bills of Creadit of the old Tenor more or other Bills or money Equivelent to be paid by my Executors within one year aftor my Decease

Item I Give unto my Grand Son Thomas Hale Son to my Son Thomas Disceased my House and Barn and all my Lands in Hampstead which I Bought of Mr William Eastman his heirs and Assigns if he arive to the age of Twenty one

Item I Give unto my Two Sons Benjamin Hale and Ebenezer Hale their heirs and assigns to be Equelly Divided Between them all my Housing Lands and meadows in Plastow aforesaid which I Have not otherwayes Disposed of in and by this my will and all my Lands in the Township of Chester in the Province Aforesaid

I Give unto my Daughter Hannah Hale Eight Hundred Pounds old Tenor to be paid by my Exetors within one year after my Decease

I Give unto my Daughter Sarah Hale Eight Hundred pounds old Tenor to be paid by my Executors within one year after my Decease

furthermore I Give unto my Two sons Benjamin Hale and Ebenezer whome I Constitute and apoint to be my Executors Two thirds of my Stock of Creatures and utencels for Husbendry and my Gun and my Tooles for Cooper and weaver Trades and my furniture for Horss Excep so much as their mother Shall have ocation to use Dureing Her Widohood and all my wareing apparill and my will is that my Executors Equally Receive all my money and my Debts that are Due to me and shall Equally Discharge all my Just Debts Legacies and Funeral Expences and my will is if after my Debts Legacies and funeral Expence and Cost of settling my Estate at the Court of Probate are fully Discharged there should be any of my Estate left not Disposed in this my will it Shall be Disposed of Equally Among my Children and those that Shall Legally Represent them and this is my Last will and Testament Having my present memory and understanding as witness my hand and seal this nineteenth day of January Anno Domina seveteen Hundred and fifty seven

Thomas Hale

[Witnesses] Abel Merril, John Knight, Joshua Merrill.
[Proved Sept. 26, 1759.]

[Mary Hale of Plaistow, widow, accepts the terms of the will Sept. 24, 1759.]

[Warrant, Sept. 26, 1759, authorizing Nathaniel Knight and John Knight, both of Plaistow, housewrights, to appraise the estate.]

[Inventory, Dec. 19, 1759; amount, £27391. 10. 0; signed by John Knight and Nathaniel Knight.]

[Mary Hale of Plaistow makes choice of Capt. Jonathan Carleton of Plaistow as guardian of her youngest daughter, Sarah Hale, March 3, 1761.]

[Hannah Hale of Plaistow makes choice of Benjamin Hale of Plaistow as her guardian March 3, 1761.]

[Guardianship of Hannah Hale, minor, aged more than 14 years, daughter of Thomas Hale, granted to Benjamin Hale of Plaistow March 6, 1761.]

[Probate Records, vol. 22, p. 42.]

[Bond of Benjamin Hale, yeoman, with Jonathan Carleton of Plaistow, gentleman, and Benjamin Baker of Chester, cooper, as sureties, in the sum of £500, March 6, 1761, for the guardianship of Hannah Hale; witnesses, William Parker, Lydia Parker.]

[Guardianship of Sarah Hale, aged less than 14 years, daughter of Thomas Hale, granted to Jonathan Carleton of Plaistow March 6, 1761.]

[Probate Records, vol. 22, p. 42.]

[Bond of Jonathan Carleton, gentleman, with Benjamin Hale of Plaistow, yeoman, and Benjamin Baker of Chester, cooper, as sureties, in the sum of £500, March 6, 1761, for the guardianship of Sarah Hale; witnesses, William Parker, Lydia Parker.]

[Warrant, Sept. 8, 1768, authorizing Jonathan Carleton of Plaistow, gentleman, Joshua Sawyer of Hampstead, yeoman, Samuel Little, gentleman, Humphrey Noyes, yeoman, and John Knight, housewright, all of Atkinson, to set off the widow's dower.]

Province of New Hampshire } We the Subscribers (Persuant to a warrant to us Directed) have Set off to mary Hale of Atkinson widow & Relict of Thomas Hale Late of Plaistow in said Province Gent Deceased her Right of Dower in the Real Estate of the s^d Deceased (viz) of the Buildings & Land in s^d Atkinson the west end of the Dwell House the upright Part so far as the entry way & the Back room below adjoyning with the cellar under s^d part of the House with free Liberty of Passing through s^d entry to all her Parts of the House & cellar when occasion shall Require & to pass at the fore Door with the priviledge of the well by s^d House & to pass to it the best way & of watering cattle at the usual Place below the orchard & the use of the Spring of water near the Tann House, also Eighteen feet of the N^o East end of the Barn with one Rod of Land adjoyning her part of S^d Barn on the Back side & one Rod & one half at the end with the priviledge of the Barn yard with those that Shall use the other Part of the Barn also one third of the garden before the Barn the s^o East side the same wedth up to the way that go into the Barn yard & the Land adjoyning the west end of the House to the way that go into s^d yard two Rods by s^d way also the N^o west Part of the orchard Bounded at the s^o east corner of s^d

House & Runing s° easterly half one Rod to the s° west of the southermost apple tree in the tenth Row from the upper end to a stake & stones midway between the s^d tenth & Eleventh Rows then N° Easterly between s^d Rows Down to the edge of a meadow then N° westerly by s^d meadow Leaving out two small apple trees to a fence that Part enclose s^d orchard then by s^d fence as it now stands to the N° East corner of s^d House giving Liberty for those that Shall live in the East Part of s^d House to Pass Round this part & with a team when occasion shall Require also about ten Acres of field & mowing Land out of the Great field Bounded at a stake & stones the N° west side of the Barn or way that go into s^d field a litle below the way up to s^d House thence Runing S° Easterly by a Road Leading from Hampstead by s^d House to Haverhill about forty five Rods then s° westerly by Land of Nath. Knight about forty five Rods then N° westerly about thirty five Rods to a Stake & Stones all by a stone wall fence then about forty Rods to the Bound by s^d Barn also Pasture & wood Land about Sixty Acres Bounded at a Large white oak tree Standing in s^d Road about twenty Rods above s^d Barn thence Easterly in the Dividing line between the two Sons of the s^d Deceased as they first Divided about one Hundred & three Rods to a stake & stones then Northerly by Lands of Benj. Pettingall s^d Knight & Stephen Noyes about seventy Rods to a stake & stones then westerly by Land of Asa Page about Eighty four Rods to a stake & stones by s^d Road then Southerly about thirty Rods Down s^d Road to a stake & stones on the west side near opposite to a Rocky ledge then west to a meadow fence then s° westerly by s^d meadow fence to Land of Jon. Page then southerly by Land of s^d Jon. about thirty five Rods to a stake & stones then N° Easterly to a stake & stones by a stone wall the s^d field fence then Northerly about fifteen Rods then N° Easterly Still by s^d wall to a stake & stones by s^d Road then Northerly about Eight Rods to s^d white oak tree

we Likewise have Set off to s^d widow of the Buildings & Land in Hampstead in s^d Province the N° east end of the Dwelling

House to the Parting about twelve feet also one third of the wedth of the Barn on the southerly side with free Liberty & convenient Room Round the Same to use them also about Eighteen Acres of Land one third in Quantity of the Premises on which the Last s^d Buildings Stand the N° westerly side adjoyning on land lately John Chase's about two Hundred Rods so Runing S° East from s^d Chases Land about fourteen Rods on Each end of s^d Land to stakes & stones

Atkinson March 28th 1769   Jonathan Carleton
                                        Samuel Little
                                        John Knight

JAMES OSGOOD   1757   CONCORD

In ye Name of God Amen I James osgood of ye Plantation called Rumford in the Province of New Hampshire in New England being now in the full exercise & enjoyment of my Rational Powers tho under great bodily weekness   * * *

I give to my well beloved wife Hannah the Improvement of my Homestead with ye buildings thereon standing & also of the Pasture contigious thereto on ye westerly side of ye High way by my dwelling House so long as she shall remain my widow & if she should at any Time marry again then that she continue entitled to the one Half of ye s^d Improvement during her natural Life & ye other Half of sd Improvements to goe to these my sons to whom ye Reversion of those Lands is ordered also liberty to cut her fire wood off my Land lying on ye southerly side of ye mill Road adjoyning to Jacob Hoyts Land during her Natural Life & the following articles I give her in Fee viz my Indian man Servant named George also my Negro woman Servant named Lucy also ye two youngest children she now has — also ye whole of my Houshold Goods of all sorts also my mare & one of my cows at her choice also the one Half of my Flax swine Grain &

Provisions y^t shall be in ye House at my decease also sixty Gallons of Rhum & one Hundred weight of sugar also the Piece of all wool cloth which is now at mr Robert Calfs to be dressed & y^t in consideration of ye above articles my s^d wife shall bring up my youngest son Hazzen without any charge to my estate untill he shall arrive at ye Age Ten years —

Item I give to my son samuel my Negro Girl named Phillis which together with ye Land I have given him by Deed of gift at a place called suncook I proprose as ye whol of his Portion

Item I give to Daughter Anna Stickny five shillings which together with ye Household goods I have already given her is to be the whole of her Portion

Item to my Daughter Elisabeth webster I give ye sum of five shillings which together with ye Household stuff she has already received is to be ye whole of her Portion —

Item I give to my Daughter Hannah ye sum of Eighteen pounds sterling money of great Britain to be paid her when she shall arrive at ye Age of Eighteen years or upon marriage Day if She should be married before that Age the s^d Legacy to raised out of my personal Estate at ye descretion of my Executrix if that shall suffice after my Just Debts & Funeral charges are discharged & if that shall fall short then such deficiency to be made up out of ye Lands I have given to my four youngest sons and if my s^d Daughter Hannah should die before she is Eighteen years old & leave no lawful Issue then it is my will that ye s^d Legacy should be divided between my four youngest sons in such Proportion as is hereafter provided y^t the Residue of my Estate should be divided

Item I give to my sons James, Benjamin, John & Hazzen ye whole of my estate both Real & Personal not already disposed of to be Equaly divided amongst them save that in regard my son James has an Expensive Trade he should have but Half so much as one of his three Brethren and it is my will that if either of my Four last mentioned sons should die before he shall arrive at ye Age of twenty one years & leave no Lawful Issue then his share shall be divided in the proportion last mentioned among his surviving Brethren exclusive of their oldest Brother samuel but if ye deceased son shall leave any lawful Issue then such offspring to be equaly entitled as if their Parent was living —

and I constitute & appoint my s^d wife Hannah to be the sole Executrix of this my last will & Testament In witness where of I have set my Hand & seal hereto this twenty fourth Day of January Anno Domini 1757 and in the Thirtieth year of his majesties Reign

James osgood

[Witnesses] Benj^a Rolfe, Ezra Carter, Timothy walker Juner.

[Proved May 25, 1757.]

[Warrant, May 25, 1757, authorizing Ezra Carter and Timothy Walker, Jr., both of Rumford, to appraise the estate.]

[Inventory, filed Aug., 1757; amount, £7179. 3. 0; signed by Ezra Carter and Timothy Walker, Jr.]

Know all Men by these Presents That James Osgood our Honoured Father late of Rumford in the Province of Newhampshire deceased did by his last Will and Testament give sundry Tracts of Land in Rumford aforesaid unto his sons James Osgood, Benjamin Osgood, John Osgood, and Richard Hazzen Osgood to be divided betwixt them in the Proportion following (vizt) one seventh part thereof to his son James Osgood and two seventh parts thereof to each of his other said sons Benjamin, John, and Richard Hazzen Osgood Furthermore Know ye that we the said James & Benjamin being of full age in Behalf of ourselves and Hannah Osgood relict widow of the said James Osgood deceased in Behalf of the other two sons John and Richard Hazzen Osgood both minors have agreed upon the Division of the said Tracts of Land as follows (vizt) That the said James Osgood shall have one of said Tracts of Land that contains ninety five Acres be the same more or less being the forty first

Lott in the Eighty Acre Division that was laid out to the Right of John Pecker which Land together with the sum of Thirty three pounds six shillings and Eight Pence old Tenor paid to him by his Brother the said Benjamin Osgood and sixty six pounds thirteen shillings & four pence paid to him by the said Hannah Osgood for & in behalf of the two said minors making in the whole the sum of one hundred pounds old Tenor the said James Osgood accepts of as his full share in this present Division That Benjamin Osgood shall have another of said Tracts of Land containing Ninety five acres be the same more or less being the forty fifth Lott in the said Eighty Acre Division that was laid out to the Right of John Austin Also One acre of Interval more or less laying in the Fann (so called) being laid out to the Right of the said Austin which two Pieces of Land together with the sum of two hundred Pounds old Tenor paid to him by the said Hannah Osgood in Behalf of the said two minors (himself having paid to his Brother James Osgood the sum of Thirty three pounds six shillings & Eight pence as above expressed) the said Benjamin Osgood accepts of as his full share in this present Division. That John Osgood & Richard Hazzen Osgood shall have a six acre Lott of Interval more or less the seventeenth Lott in the great Plain (so called) which Lot was drawn by said John Pecker. Also fifty three acres of Land more or less laying on the northerly side of the Mill Road leading to Flanders Mill being laid out to the Rights of said Pecker and Astin for their Twenty acre Grants. Also Twenty acres of Land more or less laying on the southerly side of said Mill Road being laid out to the Right of said John Pecker for Emendation to his Interval Lotts Also five acres of Land more or less laying at the middle plain (so called) bounded as follows (vizt) westerly on Merrimake River southerly on Land of the Reverend Mr Timothy Walker Easterly on the mountains and northerly on the Land of Mr Stephen Farington. Also Fourteen acres more of Land more or less laying at the Great swamp (so called) which was laid out for Emendation to the Right of John Mattis bounded Easterly & southerly on an high way westerly on Land of Aaron Stephens and northerly on Land of George Abbot which five pieces of Land are (after the sum of Two Hundred and sixty six pounds thirteen shillings & four pence paid as abovementioned by the said Hannah Osgood is deducted) to be accounted the whole shares of the said John and Richard Hazzen Osgood in this present Division N: B: The several Tracts or pieces of Land above mentioned excepting the two last pieces are all Butted & Bounded as particularly expressed in the proprietor's Records of said Rumford Reference thereunto being had In Witness whereof We have hereunto sett our hands & seals this fifth Day of Aprill Anno Domini One thousand seven hundred & sixty two

         James Osgood
         Benjamin Osgood
         Hannah Osgood

[Witnesses] Stephen Farrington J^r, Paul Burbeen.
[Province Deeds, vol. 70, p. 115.]

JOHN NEWTON   1757   KINGSTON

[Administration on the estate of John Newton of Kingston, yeoman, granted to his son, John Newton, Jan. 26, 1757.]
[Probate Records, vol. 20, p. 94.]

[Bond of John Newton, with Jeremiah Hubbard and Benjamin Swett as sureties, all of Kingston, in the sum of £500, Jan. 26, 1757, for the administration of the estate; witnesses, Cutts Shannon, John Fernald.]

[Inventory, Jan. 22, 1757; amount, £1008. 19. 0; signed by Benjamin Swett and Jeremiah Hubbard.]

[Account of the settlement of the estate; receipts, the personal estate; expenditures, £180. 17. 6; allowed Feb. 25, 1761.]

DAVID PAGE 1757 EPPING

[Administration on the estate of David Page of Epping, yeoman, granted to Jonathan Moulton, Jr., of Hampton, gentleman, Jan. 26, 1757.]

[Probate Records, vol. 20, p. 94.]

[Bond of Jonathan Moulton, Jr., with Israel James of Kingston, yeoman, and Simon Pottle of Stratham, blacksmith, as sureties, in the sum of £500, Jan. 26, 1757, for the administration of the estate; witnesses, William Parker, John Fernald.]

[Warrant, Jan. 27, 1757, authorizing David Lawrence and Ebenezer Fiske, physician, both of Epping, to appraise the estate.]

[Inventory, April 22, 1757; amount, £1228. 7. 6; signed by David Lawrence and Ebenezer Fiske.]

[Warrant, July 18, 1757, authorizing David Lawrence of Epping and Noah Emery of Exeter, gentleman, to receive claims against the estate.]

[Warrant, July 22, 1757, authorizing Capt. James Norris, Jonathan Rundlett, Ezekiel Brown, Abraham Perkins, and Samuel Smith, all of Epping, to set off the widow's dower.]

Province of } Eppin Nov[r] 10th 1757. Pursuant to the New Hampshire within Warrant to us Directed We have Sett off to Abigail Page widow Relict of David Page late of Eppin in Said Province Deceas'd Intestate for her Dower which happens to her of the Real Estate which was the Said Davids & of which he Dyed Seiz'd, Two Acres of Land in Eppin aforesaid at the South Westerly Corner of that which was the Said David's home place with the Dwelling house Standing thereon, & have Set forth the Same by Metes & bounds as followeth viz[t] begining at the highway at a Stake at the North Westerly Corner of John Page's Home place now in his Possession & from thence to run South Eighty Degrees & an half East forty Six rods thence North

Nineteen Degrees West Seven rods & an half, thence North Eighty Degrees & an half West forty Six rods to the highway, thence South nineteen Degrees East Seven rods & an half to the bounds first mentioned, Which Premisses So bounded we Sett of to the Said Abigail in full for her Dower of the Said Real Estate To hold to her in Severalty During the Term of her Natural Life, as Witness our hands the day & year aforesaid —

James noris
Abr^m Perkins
Samuel Smith } Commitee
Ezek^el Brown
Jonathan Runlit

[List of claims against the estate, Jan. 18, 1758; amount, £1260. 7. 3; signed by David Lawrence and Noah Emery.]

[Account of the settlement of the estate; receipts, £1403. 7. 6; expenditures, £528. 17. 0; allowed Dec. 18, 1760.]

[Settlement of claims; amount of claims, £1260. 7. 3; amount distributed, £874. 10. 0; allowed Jan. 13, 1761.]

[Additional account of the settlement of the estate; receipts, £401. 7. 0; expenditures, £216. 7. 0; allowed 1764.]

[Second apportionment to the creditors; amount of claims, £1260. 7. 3; amount distributed, £234. 7. 0; allowed April 8, 1767.]

SAMUEL WORTHEN   1757   PLAISTOW

In the Name of God Amen I Samuel Worthen of Plastow in the Province of New Hampshire in New England Yeoman * * *

Item I Give and Bequeath to my Beloved Son Thomas Worthen the Sum of five Pounds old Tenor to be Paid him Out of my Estate by my Executor —

And in Consideration that I have heretofore Given him his Proportion I Give him no more out of my Estate

Item I Give and Bequeath Unto my Grandson Samuel Worthen Son of my Beloved Son Samuel Worthen Deceas'd the Sum of five Pounds old Tenor to be paid him out of my Estate by my Executor

And in Consideration that I have heretofore Given my said son his Proportion I Give him no more out of my Estate

Item I Give And Bequeath Unto my Beloved Son Moses Worthen the Sum of twenty Pounds old Tenor to be Paid him out of my Estate by my Executor, and in Consideration that I have heretofore Given him his Proportion I give him no more out of my Estate

Item. My Will is that all my Estate both Real & Personal that is not heretofore Disposed of shall be Divided into three Equal Shares or Parts: And the first Share or Part I Give and Bequeath Unto the Children of my Beloved Daughter Mary Buzzel Deceas'd vizt My Beloved Grandaughter Annah Brown My Beloved Grandaughter Deliverance Clifford and My Beloved Grandaughter Judith Buzzel

And I do Give And Bequeath unto my Beloved Daughter Judith Dow the Second third part or Share of my Estate Divided as aforesaid

And I Give and Bequeath to My Beloved Daughter Hannah Gove the last third part or Share of my Estate Divided as aforesaid

Lastly I do by these Presents Constitute and appoint my Well beloved Son in Law Jonathan Gove of Hampton falls in the Province aforesaid Yeoman, to be Sole Executor of this my last Will And Testament: And my Will is that my Executor shall Equally Assess the three parts of my Estate Divided as abovementioned to Pay and Satisfy him for his Expence and trouble in the Discharge of his trust as Executor According to Law and Justice — And further it is to be understood that my Will and Meaning is That my Daughters and Grandaughters Abovementioned Come into Possession of what is Given them at my Decease * * *

And for Confirmation of all aforegoing I have hereunto Set my hand and Seal the twenty Seventh Day of January in the thirtieth Year of his Majestys Reign Annoque Domini One Thousand Seven hundred and fifty Seven

Saml Worthen

[Witnesses] Meshech Weare, Daniel Gove, Jonathan Dow. [Proved April 30, 1760.]

[Warrant, April 30, 1760, authorizing Moses Stevens and Joseph Harriman, both of Plaistow, yeomen, to appraise the estate.]

[Inventory, July 7, 1760; amount, £2378. 11. 4; signed by Joseph Harriman and Moses Stevens.]

[Petition of Timothy Dow, Israel Clifford, Thomas Critchett, and Judith Buswell, children and grandchildren of Samuel Worthen, May 27, 1763, that administration be granted to the widow of Jonathan Gove, he being deceased.]

EBENEZER WENTWORTH 1757   PORTSMOUTH

In the Name of God Amen. The Twenty Seventh day of January in the year of our Lord Jesus Christ one Thousand Seven hundred and fifty Seven I Ebenezer Wentworth of Portsmouth in the Province of New-Hampshire Shopkeeper being Sick and weak in Body * * *

Item I Give devise and bequeath unto my Daughter Rebecca and her Heirs & assigns for ever all my Estate both real and Personal wheresoever and whatsoever But in Case my said Daughter shall dye without Issue lawfully begotten of her Body I Give bequeath and devise the same unto my Brother Samuel Wentworth and his Heirs and assigns for ever — And I do hereby

Constitute and appoint my Brother Samuel Wentworth to be Executor * * *

Ebͬ Wentworth

[Witnesses] Marmaduke Browne, Robᵗ Traill, Wᵐ Drake.
[Proved March 30, 1757.]

[Inventory, May 25, 1757; amount, £11711. 7. 0; signed by Hunking Wentworth and Robert Traill.]

PAGE BATCHELDER   1757   CHESTER

[Administration on the estate of Page Batchelder of Chester, yeoman, granted to Andrew Craige and John Underhill, both of Chester, yeomen, Feb. 1, 1757.]

[Probate Records, vol. 20, p. 104.]

[Bond of Andrew Craige and John Underhill, with Joseph Batchelder of Hampton Falls, gentleman, and Robert Campbell of Londonderry, yeoman, as sureties, in the sum of £1000, Feb. 1, 1757, for the administration of the estate; witnesses, William Parker, Jonathan Hopkinson.]

[Warrant, Feb. 1, 1757, authorizing John Roby, tanner, and John Webster, innholder, both of Chester, to appraise the estate.]

[Inventory, Feb. 7, 1757; amount, £2635. 15. 0; signed by John Roby and John Webster.]

[Account of the settlement of the estate; receipts, £1456. 0. 0; expenditures, £1345. 17. 3; allowed Nov. 29, 1758.]

[Guardianship of Mary Batchelder, minor, aged more than 14 years, daughter of Page Batchelder, granted to Joseph Lynn Aug. 27, 1766.]

[Probate Records, vol. 24, p. 280.]

[Bond of Joseph Lynn, yeoman, with Edward Presson, housewright, as surety, both of Chester, in the sum of £500, Aug. 27, 1766, for the guardianship of Mary Batchelder; witness, William Vaughan.]

[Guardianship of Isaiah Batchelder, minor, aged more than 14 years, son of Page Batchelder, granted to Edward Presson Aug. 27, 1766.]

[Probate Records, vol. 24, p. 401.]

[Bond of Edward Presson, housewright, with Joseph Lynn, yeoman, as surety, both of Chester, in the sum of £500, Aug. 27, 1766, for the guardianship of Isaiah Batchelder; witness, William Vaughan.]

[Warrant, Aug. 27, 1766, authorizing Samuel Emerson, John Underhill, gentleman, Jacob Chase, Andrew Craige, and Joseph Clark, yeomen, all of Chester, to divide the real estate.]

Province of } Where as we the subscribers Were appoynted by the Hon[le] John Wentworth Esq[r] Judge of the Probate &c for said Province to Divide the Reall Estate of Page Bacheldor of Chester Deceased Intestate among the widow and children of said Intestate Have Don it in the following maner: all that was shown to us —

first We set of to the widow Elisebath as her Right of Dower in said Estate about Twenty one acres of Land Laying on the Easterly side of the Homesteed: bounded as followeth: first at the South Easterly Corner at a stake and stones being a Bound of Cap[t] Underhills Land then west nor west by the High way Eighteen Rods to a stake and stones: then North north East one Hundred and Eighty Rods to a stake and stones: then East South East 18[tn] Rods to a stake and stones: Then by Cap[t] Underhills Land streight to the first bounds mentioned —

2[ly] We Have Set of to Isaiah Bacheldor the Eldest son a Duble share Containing thirteen acres and a half of Land: adjoyning to the widows thirds bounded first at the South Easterly corner a stake and stones then west nor west by the High way Twelve Rods to a stake and stones then North nor East: 180: Rods to a Beech tree marked then East South East twelve Rods to a stake and stones then by the widows third streight to the first bound mentioned

3^{ly} We have Set of to Abigail Bacheldor in her Right one single share containing about Six acres and three Quarters bounded first at the South Easterly corner at a stake and stones being the South Westerly bound of what Land we set of to Isaiah Bacheldor then west nor west by the High way Six Rods to a stake and stones then north nor East : 180 : Rods to a Hemlock tree marked then East South East six Rods to a Beech tree marked then by the Land we set of to Isaiah Bacheldor streight to the first bounds mentioned

4^{ly} We have set of to Elisebath Bacheldor in her Right one single share containing about seven acres and a Quarter bounded first at the South Easterly corner at a stake and stones being the south westerly bounds of the Land we set of to Abigail Bacheldor: then west nor west by the High way six Rods and a Half to a stake and stones then north north East : 180 : Rods to white pine tree marked then East South East by Carrs Land six Rods and a Half to a Hemlock tree marked then by the Land we set of to Abigail Bacheldor Streight to the first bound mentioned —

5^{ly} We Have set of to mary Bacheldor in her Right one single share containing about Seven acres and a Quarter bounded first at the South Easterly corner at a stake and stones being the South Westerly bound of what Land we set of to Elisebath Bacheldor then west nor west six Rods and a Half by the High way to a stake and stones then north north East : 180 : Rods to a stake and stones then East South East by Carrs Land six Rods and a Half to a white pine tree marked then by the Land we set of to Elisebath Bacheldor streight to the first bound mentioned —

6^{ly} We have Set of to Susanah Bacheldor in her Right one single share containing about Seven acres and three Quarters bounded first at the South Easterly corner at a stake and stones being the South westerly bound of the Land we set of to mary Bacheldor then west nor west by the High way seven Rods to a stake and stones then north north East by Pressons and Heaths Land : 180 : Rods to a stake and stones then East South East by Carrs Land Seven Rods to a stake and stones then by the Land we set of to mary Bacheldor streight to the first bound mentioned —

And thus we make our Return this Eighth Day of December 1766

Sam^{ll} Emerson
Joseph Clark
Jacob Chase

JOHN PECKER   1757   HAVERHILL, MASS.

[Hannah Pecker renounces administration on the estate of her husband, Capt. John Pecker of Haverhill, Mass., March 1, 1757, because of age and infirmity; witnesses, Elizabeth Pecker, Nathaniel Peaslee Sargent.]

[Administration granted to James Pecker of Haverhill, Mass., physician, Feb. 5, 1757.]

[Probate Records, vol. 20, p. 162.]

[Bond of James Pecker of Haverhill, Mass., physician, with Samuel Watts, gentleman, and John Watts, Jr., husbandman, as sureties, in the sum of £1000, Feb. 5, 1757, for the administration of the estate of his father, John Pecker, gentleman; witnesses, Thomas Little, Daniel Little.]

[Warrant, Feb. 5, 1757, authorizing Thomas Little, tanner, and John Watts, yeoman, both of Plaistow, to appraise the estate.]

[Inventory, attested April 18, 1757; amount, £3061. 19. 0; signed by John Watts and Thomas Little.]

JOHN McCONECHEY 1757 BEDFORD

In the Name of God Amen the 15th day of February in the year of our Lord one thousand seven hundred and fifty seven I John m^{c}Conechey of Bedford in the Province of New Hampshire Husband-man being sick and weak in Body * * *

Imprimus I Give and bequeath to Mary my dearly and well beloved wife the Improvement of one third part of my Real Estate during her life allso one mare, and one third of all my Personall Estate except Cattle to be at her disposeal at her death allso one bond from John Patten and Ninian Cochran of Londonderry to me of one hundred and twenty pounds old tenor payable Novb^r 5th 1758 allso one Cow

Item I Give to my well beloved Sons Samuel & John McConechey all my Real Estate Except the third before Exprest which I likewise Give at their mothers Deceas to them their heirs and assigns for Ever in equall shairs — Itim I give to the S^d Sam^{ll} one Pair of oxen & to the s^d John one pair of Steers Coming in two years old, allso all my Emplyments of Husbandry in Equal Shairs between them — Item I Give to my well beloved son Alex^r Orr & daughter Jannet Orr forty pounds old tenor out of my money Estate to be paid as here after Exprest within Six months after my decease or to their heirs — Item I Give to my wellbeloved Daughter Martha m^{c}Conechey one bond from Patten & Cochran afore^{sd} of 120 pounds old ten^r Payable Novb^r 1st 1757 allso one brown Cow with some white on her Rump and one year old that Came of said Cow & one bed & bedsted & bolster with half of the Cloaths belonging to s^d bed and one foot wheel — Item I Give to my Daughter Mary m^{c}Conechey one bond from the s^d Patten & Cochran to me of 120 pounds payable Novb^r the first 1759 and one Cow that was bought from Hugh Gillis & the other half of the bed & bed Cloaths before Exprest and one foot wheel Item I Give to my Sons Samuel & John McConechey all and Every other articule and thing in Equal Shares not before willed & bequeathed they paying all my proper debts and the before mentioned forty pounds to Alex^r Orr & Jannet Orr or their heirs also my funeral Charges and Expences of administeration and Charges attending it — And I do Constitute and make and ordain Samuel Patten of Bedford and Province afore Said Husband man my only & Sole Executor * * *

his
John X m^{c}Conechey
mark

[Witnesses] James Moor, William Moor, Daniel Moor.
[Proved June 29, 1757.]

[Mary McConechey, widow, and Alexander, Janet, Martha, Mary, Samuel, and John McConechey, children, accept the terms of the will June 27, 1757; witnesses, William Moore, Daniel Moore.]

[Inventory, June 27, 1757; amount, £1963. 0. 8; signed by William Moore and Daniel Moore.]

[Bonds of Daniel Moore, with Samuel Patten and William Moore as sureties, all of Bedford, in the sum of £500 each, June 29, 1757, for the guardianship of Samuel and John McConechey, minors, aged more than 14 years, sons of John McConechey; witnesses, William Parker, John Fernald.]

WILLIAM JACKSON   1757   DURHAM

In the Name of God Amen the Eighteenth day of February In the year of our Lord God One Thousand Seven hundred and fifty Seven I William Jackson of the Town of Durham in the Province of New Hampshire in New England being aged and well Stricken in years * * *

Imprimis I Give unto Mary my Dearly Beloved Wife one Pair of Black Silk Gloves —

Item I will and Give my Sons William Jackson and Benjamin

Jackson Their heirs and Assigns all my Real and Personal Estate where I now live and Possess with the Priviledges and Appurtenances thereof Lying and being in Durham And Partly in Dover in the Province Aforesaid with the Messuages and Tenements Thereon with My Marsh thatch bed and flatts to be Equally Divided between them According to Quantity and Quality to be had and held by them and their heirs Forever Immediately after my Decease; Likewise I Give my said Son William my Right and property in the Second Division of Lands in the Township of Rochester In the Province Aforesaid. It is my Will Likewise that my Son Benjamin Shall Have My Right in the third Division of Lands in Rochester in the Province Aforesaid To them and their Heirs forever —

I Also Give my Daughter Meribah Huckins wife of Robert Huckins Ten Pounds to be paid to her or her heirs or Assigns by my Executor within the Term of one year after my Decease —

Item as to the Remainder and Residence of my Real and Personall Estate Wherever the same is: I will and Give my Said Son William and his heirs forever, whom I do Constitute and Appoint to be my Sole Executor * * *

his
William X Jackson
mark

[Witnesses] Samuel Stiles, Job Demeret, William Bruce.
[Proved Jan. 30, 1760.]

[Warrant, Jan. 30, 1760, authorizing Stephen Jones, gentleman, and Thomas Chesley, Jr., both of Durham, to appraise the estate.]

[Inventory, April 28, 1760; amount, £4724. 10. 0; signed by Stephen Jones and Thomas Chesley, Jr.]

JOHN McMURPHY 1757 LONDONDERRY

[Administration on the estate of John McMurphy of Londonderry, yeoman, granted to his brother, Alexander McMurphy, Feb. 22, 1757.]

[Probate Records, vol. 20, p. 104.]

[Bond of Alexander McMurphy of Londonderry, yeoman, with Robert Clark of Londonderry, yeoman, and James Dwyer of Portsmouth, truckman, as sureties, in the sum of £500, Feb. 22, 1757, for the administration of the estate; witnesses, William Parker, John Fernald.]

[Inventory, March 30, 1757; amount, £266. 6. 0; signed by Samuel Barr and Thomas Craige.]

DAVID AMES 1757 NEWMARKET

[Bond of Josiah Hilton and his wife, Sarah Hilton, with Edward Hilton and Josiah Huntoon as sureties, all of Newmarket, in the sum of £500, Feb. 23, 1757, for the administration of the estate of David Ames of Newmarket, yeoman, former husband of Sarah Hilton; witness, William Parker.]

[Warrant, Feb. 23, 1757, authorizing Thomas Young and Joseph Sanborn, yeoman, both of Newmarket, to appraise the estate.]

[Inventory, attested June 20, 1757; amount, £336. 9. 0; signed by Joseph Sanborn and Thomas Young.]

[Warrent, Dec. 28, 1757, authorizing Thomas Young and Joseph Sanborn, physician, both of Newmarket, to receive claims against the estate.]

[Notice of the commissioners, May 29, 1758, of a time limit for filing claims; signed by Joseph Sanborn and Thomas Young.]

[Warrant, June 28, 1758, authorizing Thomas Young and Walter Bryent, both of Newmarket, to receive claims against the estate.]

JOHN DOWNS   1757   SOMERSWORTH

[Administration on the estate of John Downs of Somersworth, yeoman, granted to Ichabod Rollins of Somersworth, gentleman, Feb. 23, 1757.]

[Probate Records, vol. 20, p. 119.]

[Bond of Ichabod Rollins, with Cutts Shannon of Portsmouth, gentleman, and John Perkins of Dover, yeoman, as sureties, in the sum of £1000, Feb. 23, 1757, for the administration of the estate; witnesses, William Parker, John Fernald.]

[Inventory, March 9, 1757; amount, £1102. 9. 0; signed by Moses Stevens and William Wentworth.]

[Account of the settlement of the estate; receipts, £70. 16. 3; expenditures, £76. 12. 5½; mentions "Paid the Wid^w Downs for ye Bringing up 2 of Her Childring Being under age when ther fathe Dide Viz Gershom Downs was 4 years old John 1 year"; allowed Nov. 28, 1776.]

THOMAS CHASE   1757   STRATHAM

[Administration on the estate of Thomas Chase of Stratham, yeoman, granted to his widow, Love Chase, Feb. 23, 1757.]

[Probate Records, vol. 20, p. 111.]

[Bond of Love Chase, widow, with Andrew Wiggin and Samuel Leavitt, yeoman, as sureties, all of Stratham, in the sum of £1000, Feb. 23, 1757, for the administration of the estate of Thomas Chase, innholder; witnesses, William Parker, Cutts Shannon.]

[Inventory, March 8, 1757; amount, £5234. 8. 0; signed by Joshua Neal and Theophilus Smith.]

[Account of the settlement of the estate; receipts, £1965. 15. 0, personal estate; expenditures, £1602. 8. 0; mentions "Supporting my Children that were Under Seven Years old at their Father's Decease Viz Dudley 76 Weeks Mary 156 Weeks Anna 342 Weeks"; allowed September 25, 1765.]

[Warrant, June 13, 1799, authorizing Benjamin Barker, Jonathan Wiggin, gentleman, and Thomas Veasey, yeoman, all of Stratham, to appraise the income of two thirds of the real estate while it was in possession of the widow; report, June 24, 1799, at $802; signed by Benjamin Barker, Jonathan Wiggin, and Thomas Veasey.]

[Warrant, Aug. 22, 1799, authorizing Paine Wingate, Jonathan Wiggin, gentleman, Thomas Veasey, Joseph Durrell, and John Light Piper, yeomen, all of Stratham, to divide the real estate.]

Pursuant to the annexed Warrant we the Subscribers have made partition of the real estate of the said Thomas Chase deceased, and do hereby set off the widow's dower and the respective shares as therein directed, having regard to the quality as well as quantity of said land, And to the said Love Chase we set, as her full thirds in said Estate, the great room at the northerly end of the house with the entry way to the outer door, also the Chamber over the said room and the cellar under the same, also the scaffold over the stall at the easterly end of the barn & the priveledge of keeping her stock in the stall under said scaffold & of passing & repassing from said barn and likewise of using the well and out buildings appurtenant to the house as occasion may require — And further we set off to the said Love Chase about three acres and eighty six rods of land bounded as follows — namely beginning on the northerly side of land hereafter described as set off to the right of Sarah Piper at a point twelve rods & five links from the country road thence running north twelve degrees East twelve rods & three quarters of a rod on the westerly line of the share hereafter described as set off to the said Love Chase as the share which belonged to her daughter Anna deceased, thence running westerly in a strait line paralel to said Pipers northerly line thirty one rods & twenty two links until it strikes the land which Phinehas Merrill bought of Jonathan Hoit & came out of the Thurston place (so called) thence southerly by the Thurston line (so called) seventeen rods & six links to land of Thomas Veazey thence by said Veazey's land easterly until it comes to the land hereafter described as set off to the right of Sarah Piper, thence northerly by said Pipers land five rods & a half rod, and thence Easterly by said Piper's land seventeen rods & twenty links to the point first mentioned. —

To the right or share of Sarah Piper we set off a room adjoyning to the room set to the widow's thirds & adjoyning to the room hereafter described as set to the share of Anna deceased with the priveledge of using a fire place & oven somewhere in the house, also the use of the scaffold over the barn floor and of the well & out buildings, And farther we set to the said Sarah's share one acre & five rods of land bounded as follows namely, beggining at the southeasterly corner of said land adjoyning to land of Thos Veazey and to the country road thence running by said road five rods & a half rod to a stake, thence westerly by the northerly side of said Veazeys land and carrying the full width of five rods & a half rod to extend Thirty rods westward to stakes at the southerly & northerly corners of said land.

To Love Chase in the right of her daughter Anna we set off as her share the room at the northwesterly corner of the room set to her, as her thirds, with the priveledge of the cellar under that part of the house & of the scaffold at the northwesterly corner of the barn & of the well & out buildings as occasion may require, And further we set off to the said Love Chase as the share of the said Anna One hundred & fifty rods of land, bounded as follows, namely, Beginning on the road at the northeasterly corner of Sarah Piper's share, thence running northerly on the road six rods & a half rod thence north seventy four degrees west five rods & two links, thence north two degrees west fourteen rods & ten links to land hereafter described as set off to Phinehas Merrill, thence south eighty seven degrees west three rods, thence south twelve degrees west nineteen rods & five links to the first mentioned boundary of the widows thirds & thence easterly on the northerly line of Sarah Piper's share twelve rods & five links to the bound first mentioned.

To Phinehas Merrill as his four shares in said Estate we set off all the buildings and appurtenances of the same not in the foregoing shares & thirds set off to others, And further we set off to the said Merrill about four acres & one hundred & forty one rods, not herein before described and not set off to others, being all the remaining part of the said Thomas Chases Estate to us directed to set off.

Given under our hands this Twenty third day of August Anno Domini Seventeen hundred & ninety nine

       Paine Wingate
       Jonathan Wiggin
       Thomas Veasey
       Joseph Durell
       John Light Piper

[Warrant, March 22, 1803, authorizing Paine Wingate, Jonathan Wiggin, gentleman, Thomas Veasey, yeoman, Jonathan Piper, gentleman, and William Barker, clothier, all of Stratham, to divide the widow's dower.]

Pursuant to the annexed Warrant we the Subscribers do hereby make Partition of the Dower of the said Love Chase situate in said Stratham, in the manner following. That is to say To the Share of Sarah Piper, for her one Sixth part of said Dower, we set off eighty eight rods and one half rod of land, bounded as follows, namely. Beginning at the northwesterly corner of the share formerly set off to the share of the said Sarah Piper, out of the estate of Thomas Chase, her late father, deceased thence running

Easterly by said share eight rods and fourteen & a half links to a stake & stone, thence running North twelve degrees East, ten rods & eight links, to a stake & stone, thence running north Seventy four degrees West eight rods & fourteen & a half links to a stake & stone, thence running Southerly ten rods & eight links to the bound first mentioned.

To the share of Andrew Chase, for his sixth part of said Dower, we set off eighty eight rods & one half rod of land, bounded as follows, namely — Beginning at the Southeasterly corner of the land herein set off to Sarah Piper & thence running Easterly by said Sarah Piper's former share eight rods and Fourteen & a half links to a stake & stone at the southwesterly corner of that which was set off to the share of Anna Chase out of her late father's estate, thence northeasterly on said Anna's share ten rods & eight links to a stake & stone, thence running northwesterly eight rods & fourteen & a half links to the northeasterly corner of the land herein set off to Sarah Piper, & thence running southerly by said Sarah Piper's line to the bound first mentioned.

To the share of Phinehas Merrill for his four sixth parts of said Dower we set off all the residue of the dower of said Love Chase situate in said Stratham, lying northerly & westerly of the shares herein set off to Sarah Piper & to Andrew Chase reference being had to the former seting off of said dower for a particular description of the boundaries of said Merrills share — Given under our hands at Stratham this 6th day of April A D 1803 —

       Paine Wingate
       Jonathan Wiggin
       Thomas Veasey

SAMUEL WATSON   1757   DOVER

[Administration on the estate of Samuel Watson of Dover, yeoman, granted to James Kielle of Dover, tailor, Feb. 23, 1757.]

[Probate Records, vol. 20, p. 123.]

[Bond of James Kielle, with Benjamin Mathes and Eliphalet Daniell, mariner, both of Durham, as sureties, in the sum of £500, Feb. 23, 1757, for the administration of the estate; witnesses, William Parker, John Fernald.]

[Warrant, Feb. 23, 1757, authorizing Joshua Wingate and Joseph Roberts, both of Dover, yeomen, to appraise the estate.]

[Inventory, May 16, 1757; amount, £316. 15. 6; signed by Joshua Wingate and Joseph Roberts.]

[Commission to Joshua Wingate and Joseph Roberts, gentlemen, March 29, 1758, to receive claims against the estate.]

[List of claims, attested Feb. 28, 1759; amount, £485. 3. 8; signed by Joshua Wingate and Joseph Roberts.]

[License to the administrator, March 6, 1765, to sell the widow's dower, she being deceased.]

JOHN WHIDDEN   1757   GREENLAND

In the Name of God Amen I John Whidden of Greenland In the Province of New Hampshire Gent. being Aged & Infirm * * *

Item I Give & Devise to my Son John Whidden that Part of my Land in Greenland which lies Westerly of a Line runing from the Country Road or high Way begining three Rods Easterly of the Barn which he now Improves and from thence running on a Strait Line (being near North West) to a Red oak Stump standing at or near the Creek by Deacon Cates Marsh being about Sixteen Rods Easterly of the Land of Thomas Sherburne and begining on the other Side of the Said High Way on the Westerly Side of my Little Orchard and from thence Runing on a Strait Line to the Southerly End of the Stone Wall my Land & the Land of Said Sherburne as Said Wall now Stands the Said

John to have the Land lying on the Westerly Side of this Line also these Pieces of Land being part of my home place I also give him ten acres of my Pasture Land to be taken next to the Land Lately Capt James Johnsons now Said to be John Banfields to run from the High Way over to the Land of Clement March Esqr and to be the Same number of rods in breadth next to his Land that it is at the High Way I also give him one half of that Tract of Land I Purchasd of James Jeffrey lying in Portsmouth to be taken next to the Land of Samuel Cate to have and hold all the Said Parcels of Land with all the Buildings and Appurten^s to him my Said Son John his Heirs and assigns. I also give him a Cow

Item I give & Bequeath to my Daughter Ann Jones the Wife of John Jones the Sum of Fifty Pounds old Tenor according to the Present Value to be paid by my Son Samuel within two year after my Decease this is besides what She has already had — I also give her a Bed & beding thereto belonging

Item I Give to my Daughter Hannah Jenkins the Wife of William Jenkins the Sum of Fifty Pounds old Tenor to be paid by my Said Son Samuel as aforesaid at the Same Value besides what She has already had

Item I give to the Children of my Daughter Mary Deceased the Sum of Fifty Pounds as aforesaid to be paid by my Son Samuel within the time aforesaid & to be Equally Divided between them my Grand Children

Item I give & bequeath to my Daughter Sarah Hains the Wife of Samuel Hains the Sum of Fifty Pounds old Tenor at the Value aforesaid to be paid by my Son John within two years as aforesaid

Item I give & bequeath to my Daughter Elizabeth the Like Sum at the said Value to be paid by Said John within two Years as aforesaid I also give her Six Sheep & one Cow and a Bed & Furniture one of those now in my house to be Delivered by my Son Samuel within a Year after my Decease I also give her the use of a Convenient Room in my House which She Shall

Chuse & to have her Fire Wood Provided by my Son Samuel at the Door and he to find her all necessary & Comfortable Provision the Said Room wood & Provision to be so Provided during the time she Shall live unmarried and during that time to maintain her Cow & Sheep aforesaid Summer & Winter I also give her all the Rest of my moveables within Doors meaning my household Furniture as Pewter Pots Kettles & Chairs

Item all the Rest Residue and Remainder of my Estate Real & Personal I give to my Son Samuel his Heirs Executors & admin[rs] forever and I appoint him Sole Executor of this my Last Will & Testament & Revoke all other wills by me in any manner heretofore made — In Witness whereof I have hereunto Set my hand & Seal the 26th Day of Feb[ry] Anno Domini 1757

John Whidden

[Witnesses] William Parker, Elezar Cate, William Cate Juner. [Proved May 27, 1767.]

[Bond of Joseph Whidden, blacksmith, with Samuel Langdon, gentleman, as surety, both of Portsmouth, in the sum of £500, May 27, 1767, for the execution of the will; witnesses, William Parker, Robert Parkes.]

THOMAS KIMBALL, JR.   1757   EXETER

[Joanna Kimball renounces administration on the estate of her husband, Thomas Kimball, Jr., of Exeter, bricklayer, March 1, 1757, in favor of Jeremiah Leavitt; witnesses, William Parker, John Fernald.]

[Administration granted to Jeremiah Leavitt of Exeter, innholder, March 1, 1757.]

[Probate Records, vol. 20, p. 131.]

[Bond of Jeremiah Leavitt of Exeter, innholder, with Jeremiah Bean of Exeter and Benjamin Leavitt of Stratham, yeomen, as sureties, in the sum of £500, March 1, 1757, for the administration of the estate; witnesses, John Fernald, John Langdon.]

[Warrant, March 1, 1757, authorizing Ephraim Robinson, gentleman, and John Purmort, joiner, both of Exeter, to appraise the estate.]

[Inventory, March 4, 1757; amount, £892. 9. 0; signed by Ephraim Robinson and John Purmort.]

BENJAMIN KIDDER 1757 BEDFORD

[Administration on the estate of Benjamin Kidder of Souhegan East, yeoman, granted to Benjamin Kidder of Derryfield, yeoman, March 4, 1757.]

[Probate Records, vol. 20, p. 134.]

[Bond of Benjamin Kidder of Derryfield, yeoman, with John Goffe of Derryfield and Thomas Parker of Litchfield, gentleman, as sureties, in the sum of £500, March 4, 1757, for the administration of the estate; witnesses, Noah Emery, William Parker, Jr.]

[Administration on the estate of Benjamin Kidder granted to his son, John Kidder of Derryfield, Feb. 8, 1759.]

[Probate Records, vol. 21, p. 171.]

[Bond of John Kidder, yeoman, with John Goffe and John Moore, gentleman, as sureties, all of Derryfield, in the sum of £500, Feb. 8, 1759, for the administration of the estate of his father, Benjamin Kidder; witnesses, Benjamin Smith, Matthew Patten.]

JONATHAN CHOATE 1757 KINGSTON

Elizabeth Bridgham renounces administration on the estate of her former husband, Jonathan Choate, March 8, 1757, in favor of Lieut. Trueworthy Ladd; witnesses, John Ladd, Elizabeth Ladd.]

[Administration granted to Trueworthy Ladd, gentleman, March 8, 1757.]
[Probate Records, vol. 20, p. 134.]

[Warrant, June 6, 1757, authorizing Jeremy Webster, Ebenezer Stevens, Elisha Swett, Samuel Fifield, gentleman, and William Calfe, cordwainer, all of Kingston, to set off dower to Elizabeth Bridgham, wife of Jacob Bridgham of Kingston, cordwainer.]

[Inventory, June 14, 1757; amount, £1323. 0. 0; signed by Jeremy Webster and Samuel Fifield.]

Province of } To the Honble Wibird Esqr Judge of the Pro-
New Hamps: } bate of Wills &c for the Province of New Hamps:

Pursuant to your Hon^{rs} Warrant: Authorizing us the subscribers to sett off to Elizabeth Bridgham now the wife of Jacob Bridgham: widow & Relict of Jonathan Chote late of Kingstown in s^d Province Deceased her Right of dower in the Estate of her s^d Late Husband: we have proceeded & set off to the s^d Elisabeth for her thirds in the Estate of her Late Husband: the s^d Jonathan Chote: Bounded as followeth beginning at a Pine Stump the south westerly Corner of the whole Tract & running Easterly on the southerly Line thereof to the River & so on over the River as far as the s^d Chotes Land goes to a Pitch Pine tree marked: then Back again westerly by meadow or Swamp ground of David Goodwin & Daniel Goodwin till it Comes to a Red Oak stump the south westerly Corner of s^d Goodwins meadow Ground: then Northerly to the River to a stake the North westerly Corner of s^d Goodwins meadow: then over the River & so down the River about thirty Rods to a stake by the River: thence westerly to the westerly end of s^d Chotes Land to a small white oak tree: then southerly 24 Rods to the place where it first began twelve acres be the same more or less: with the Dwelling House thereon:

said premisses set off & Described as above mentioned by us this 24th day of June Annoq domini 1757.

Jeremy Webster
Elisha Sweet
Eben^r Stevens

[Warrant, March 31, 1758, authorizing Jeremy Webster and Samuel Fifield, gentleman, both of Kingston, to receive claims against the estate.]

[List of claims, Oct. 12, 1758; amount, £103. 3. 6; signed by Jeremy Webster and Samuel Fifield.]

[Account of the settlement of the estate; receipts, £672. 0. 0; expenditures, £463. 8. 0; allowed May 16, 1759.]

[Account of Elizabeth Bridgham against the estate; amount, £893. 0. 0; receipts, £233. 6. 8; balance due, £559. 13. 4; mentions "Keeping Abigail from the 9th of January 1752 til may the 26th 1755. . . . D° for Eliz^a from the 9th of January 1752 till the 11th of December 1756. . . . D° Anna from the 9th of January 1752 till the 3th of Jany 1758."]

[Petition of the widow, Elizabeth Bean, Kingston, Sept. 21, 1773, to the court that Capt. Trueworthy Ladd may be summoned to show cause for not paying her a balance due.]

RICHARD CHILDS   1757   DURHAM

This may Certify that on or about the 25 Day of Janu^y Last I heard Hannah a Woman who has for Some years last past Lived with Richard Childs Late of Nottingham in New Hampshire Laborer Dec^d Confess that she was not the Wife of the Said Deceased and She told me they were never Married Witness my hand the 11th Day of March 1757

John Shephard

[Administration on the estate of Richard Childs of Durham, laborer, granted to Nathaniel Peirce of Portsmouth March 16, 1757.]

[Probate Records, vol. 20, p. 135.]

[Bond of Nathaniel Peirce of Portsmouth, with Daniel Peirce of Portsmouth and John Chamberlain of Merrimack, gentleman, as sureties, in the sum of £500, March 16, 1757, for the administration of the estate; witnesses, William Parker, Jeremiah Carleton.]

[Warrant, March 31, 1758, authorizing Eleazer Russell and Samuel Penhallow, shopkeeper, both of Portsmouth, to receive claims against the estate.]

[List of claims, Nov. 27, 1758; amount, £205. 16. 4; signed by Eleazer Russell and Samuel Penhallow.]

[Account of the settlement of the estate; receipts, £122. 15. 8; expenditures, £46. 10. 0; allowed Dec. 19, 1758.]

WILLIAM WEST 1757 PORTSMOUTH

[Administration on the estate of William West of Portsmouth granted to his widow, Love West, March 14, 1757.]

[Probate Records, vol. 20, p. 135.]

[Bond of Love West, widow, with Philip Reed, mariner, and John Ayers, gentleman, as sureties, all of Portsmouth, in the sum of £1000, March 14, 1757, for the administration of the estate of William West, mariner; witnesses, Henry Seymour, John Coultes.]

[Warrant, March 14, 1757, authorizing Samuel Waters, joiner, and George Marshall, sail maker, both of Portsmouth, to appraise the estate.]

[Inventory of the estate of Capt. William West, attested May

25, 1757; amount, £1228. 0. 0; signed by Samuel Waters and George Marshall.]

[Warrant, June 14, 1757, authorizing Eleazer Russell and William Knight, merchant, both of Portsmouth, to receive claims against the estate.]

[List of claims, July 25, 1758; amount, £612. 6. 5; signed by Eleazer Russell and William Knight.]

[Account of the settlement of the estate; receipts, £1286. 8. 0, personal estate; expenditures, £732. 9. 6; allowed Sept. 19, 1759.]

[Settlement of claims; amount of claims, £642. 6. 5; amount distributed, £542. 18. 6; allowed Sept. 28, 1759.]

JOHN GLINES   1757   CANTERBURY

In the Name of God, Amen. This 16th Day of March, 1757. I John Glines of Canterbury, in the Province of New-Hampshire in New-England, Husbandman, having inlisted my self in his Majesty's Service to go against his Majesty's Enemies,   *   *   *

Imprimis, I give & bequeath to Mary my dearly beloved Wife (if she outlives me) the Use & Improvement of All my Home Place so long as she shall be & remain my Widow — And also the use of all my Creatures, & Tools for farming, as well as all the Houshold stuff, which Houshold Stuff she shall have the use of during her natural Life.

Item, To my beloved Daughter Anne, I give & bequeath what she has already had of Creatures, & the keeping of them for several years past which is all the Portion I can give her out of my Estate — Except as hereafter specified.

Item, To my beloved Son Israel I give & bequeath my hundred-acre Lot which he already has a Deed of, which is all that I can give him out of my Estate — Except as hereafter specified.

Item, To my beloved son John, I give & bequeath, (beside a pair of Steers which he has already had,) All that I own in the Interval which lies between Canterbury Township & Merrimack River; & also all that I own of the Pine Plain which lies between the said Interval & the Line of Canterbury Township; and also one half of an hundred acre Lot at Contoocook, which I bought of Thomas Eastman.

Item, To my beloved sons William & Richard I give & bequeath all my Home place, when their Mother has done with it to be equally divided between them except that they are to pay out of it two hundred pounds old tenor to their younger sisters Mary & Elizabeth when they shall come to the Age of twenty one years.

Item, To my beloved son James I give & bequeath one half of my hundred acre Lot at Contoocook, above mentioned.

Item, I give & bequeath to my beloved Son Nathaniel all the present undivided Land belonging to the original Right of Samuel Smith jun^r Except that he is to pay out of it forty pounds old tenor to his two younger Sisters Mary and Elizabeth when they shall come to the Age of twenty one years, as abovesaid —

Item, To my beloved Daughters Mary & Elizabeth I give and bequeath, to each of them one hundred & twenty pounds in Bills of Credit of the old tenor, to be paid to them by their Brothers, William, Richard & Nathanael when they the said Daughters come to the Age of twenty one years: That is, by William & Richard, to each of them one hundred pounds. And by Nathanael, to each of them twenty pounds.

Moreover, My own original Right (what is still my own of it) I give & bequeath to be equally divided among all my Children — And also what stock of Creatures I leave at my Decease, to be divided in like manner: —

My Tools for farming I bequeath to be equally divided among my Sons; & Houshold stuff to be equally divided among my Daughters, when their Mother has done with them all

Lastly, I do constitute, appoint, & ordain my beloved Sons William & Richard to be jointly the Executors * * *

his
John X Glines
mark

[Witnesses] John Gibson, Richard Blanchard, James Scales. [Proved Aug. 31, 1757.]

[Inventory, Aug. 26, 1757; amount, £629. 0. 0; signed by Ezekiel Morrill, Jeremiah Clough, and Ephraim Hackett.]

BENJAMIN HOBBS   1757   NORTH HAMPTON

In the Name of God, Amen. The Seventeenth Day of March 1757, I Benjamin Hobbs of Northampton in the Province of New Hampshire in New England, Gent^n Being very Sick & weak in Body * * *

Imprimis I give & bequeath to my dearly beloved Wife Mercy Hobbs, one third of all my real Estate during her Natural Life after which her Thirds are to be equally divided between my Son Nathaniel Hobbs & my son in Law John Shepard and also I give & bequeath to my Said Wife all the Moveables in my House forever & one Half of all my Dwelling House, & Sufficient Fire wood till Marriage

Item I give & bequeath to my son Benjamin Hobbs, the sum of five hundred pounds old Tenor, to be paid, one half by son in Law John Shepherd at the time my said son Benjamin leaves College & the other half by my son Nathaniel Hobbs When my sa^d son Nathaniel shall come to the Age of twenty one years, And also that my Sa^d son Benjamin be supported comfortly & conveniently at College by my Sons Nathaniel Hobbs & John Shepherd —

Item I give & bequeath to my son Nathaniel Hobbs the one half of all my Estate both real & personal to him & his Assigns forever —

Item I give & bequeath to my Daughter Mary Hobbs the Sum of three hundred pounds old tenor to be paid equally by my Son in Law the said John Shepherd & my son Nathaniel, When she arrives at the age of eighteen Years & also I give & bequeath to her a Cow & four sheap to be deliverd at said Time by said sons John Shepherd & Nathaniel Hobbs and also Sufficient Fire wood & one half of my House till marriage

Item I give & bequeath to my son in Law John Shepherd the one half of all my Estate both real & personal to him & his Assigns forever —

Item I give & bequeath to my Grand Daughter Mehitible Marston the sum of five pounds old tenor to be paid by said sons John Shepherd & Nathaniel Hobbs

I likewise make & ordain & constitute my Friend John Weeks Esqr my sole Executor * * *

benjamin hobbs

[Witnesses] William Moulton, Joseph Hobbs, Joseph Knowles. [Proved Sept. 27, 1758.]

[Warrant, Sept. 27, 1758, authorizing John Wingate, gentleman, and Jonathan Wedgwood, yeoman, both of North Hampton, to appraise the estate.]

[Inventory, Oct. 19, 1758; amount, £11870. 5. 0; signed by John Wingate and Jonathan Wedgwood.]

JOSES PHILBRICK   1757   RYE

In the Name of God Amen: I Joses Philbrick of the Perish of Rye in New Castle in the Province of New Hampsh^r yeoman; being Sick and apprehensive of my approaching Dissolution * * *

Item I hereby Constitute & appoint my well beloved wife Abigail Philbrick my Sole Executrix of this my last will & testament —

Item I hereby will & ordain, that out of my Estate all my Just debts be duly paid in a reasonable time by my Executrix —

Item I Give to my four Sons, (viz) Joseph & Ruben & Daniel & Jonathan Each & every of them five pounds New Ten[r] to be paid by my afores[d] Executrix

Item I give to my four Daughters (viz) Hannah & Triphena & Abigail & Sarah; Each & every of them five pounds new Ten[r] to be paid out of my Estate by my afores[d] Executrix —

Item I Give to my well Beloved wife all the remainder of my Estate real & personal wheresoever of right it Shall appear; to be improved by her as She Shall think best; and by her to be disposed off, when and at what time She Shall think fit; to my afores[d] Children to them & their heirs & assigns for Ever * * *

Dated this twenty Second day of March 1757 & in y[e] 30th year of his Majestyes Reign

Joses Philbrick

[Witnesses] Anthony Emery, Richard Jennes Jun[r], noah Moulton.

[Proved April 27, 1757.]

[Bond of Abigail Philbrick, widow, with Richard Jenness, Jr., and Noah Moulton, yeomen, as sureties, all of Rye, in the sum of £1000, April 21, 1757, for the execution of the will; witnesses, William Parker, John Fernald.]

JAMES GOODING   1757   NEWMARKET

In the name of God aman the 23[d] Day of march in the year of our Lord Christ one thousand Sevn hundred and fifty Seven. I James Gooding of Newmarket in the Province of New Hamp[r] in New England, Being Sick and week in body * * *

Itom I Give to my beloved Son James Gooding all my husbanddry tools and utencals for ever also one pair of annd Iorns after his mothers Deces also one Gon to my Son James Gooding

Itom I give to my gran Son Robert Gooding all my waring Close and one Gon

Itom I Give to my well beloved wife Susanna Gooding all my Stock of Catle and Sheep horses and Swine and the movable Goods in my house that is not before Disposed off During hir natroul Life. Itom I Give to my Daughter Susanna Palmer ten Shillings. Itom I Give to my Granson John York five Shilling. Itom I Give to my Grandaughter Susanna York five Shillings

Itom I Give to my well beloved Daughter Zeviah Gooding all my Stock and moveables that is Left in hir mothers hands at the Deceas of hir Said mother and Lastly my will and meaning is that what Debts is Due to me that my Son James Gooding is to Receve them be the sam of what kind soever

and I Do apointe my above named Son James Gooding to be my Sole Executor   *   *   *

his
James + Gooding
mark

[Witnesses] Andrew Wiggin, Wm Welsh, Joseph Smith.
[Proved May 25, 1757.]

[Bond of James Goodwin (so signed) of Newmarket, yeoman, with Joseph Smith of Newmarket and Thomas Davis of Dover as sureties, in the sum of £500, May 25, 1757, for the execution of the will; witnesses, Ephraim Davis, John Fernald.]

MARY PATTINSON   1757   PORTSMOUTH

[Administration on the estate of Mary Pattinson of Portsmouth granted to her husband, Joseph Pattinson, March 24, 1757.]

[Probate Records, vol. 20, p. 136.]

[Bond of Joseph Pattinson, yeoman, with Cutts Shannon, gentleman, and Joseph Alcock, shopkeeper, as sureties, all of Portsmouth, in the sum of £500, March 24, 1757, for the administration of the estate; witnesses, Hunking Wentworth, William Earl Treadwell.]

JOHN CUNNINGHAM   1757   LONDONDERRY

In the name of God amene I John Cunnangham of Londonderry In the province of Newhampshire In New England being now bound to Go to the war this Inshowing Summer * * *

Itam I Give and bequith to brother Robart Cunninham five pounds old tenor or bills of Credet equall ther too —

Itam I Give to John Cunningham: son to my brother Robart five pounds Like tenor —

Itam I Give to Robart Cunningham son to my brother Robart five pounds Like tenor —

Itam I Give to James willson and his wife five pounds each old tenor or bills of Credette equal therunto —

Itam I Give to James tagart my Cosien twintey pounds old tenor or pasabill Bills of Cred equall therunto —

Itam I Give to my Cosien John tagart twintey pounds old tenor or pasable Bills of Credet equall therunto —

Itiam Give to Co^{ll} andrew toodd twintey pounds old tenor or pasabel Bills equall therunto —

Itam I Give to the Rev^t David macGregore teen pounds old tenor or pasable Bills equall therunto —

Itam I Give to Jannet tagart Daughter to John tagart the sume of three Hundred pounds old tenor: she paying the Corst that may aries on the administeration and Coast of Exac^{trs}

and I Do appoint make and ordain petter petterson and John Clark both of the Town and province aforesaid to be Exac^{trs} * * * In wittnes whear of I have hearunto Sett my hand and Seal this twintey fifth Day of march In the thirtey year of his majestys Rign anno Dom on thousand Seven hundred and fiftey Seven

his
John + Cunningham
mark

[Witnesses] Thomas Willson, Samuel Barr, John Barr.
[Proved Dec. 31, 1760.]

[Warrant, Sept. 11, 1760, authorizing William White and Robert Boyd, both of Londonderry, yeomen, to appraise the estate.]

[Inventory, attested Dec. 30, 1760; amount, £690. 10. 0; signed by William White and Robert Boyd.]

SAMUEL EMMONS   1757   KINGSTON

[Maria Emmons, widow, and Joseph Emmons, son, renounce administration on the estate of Samuel Emmons of Kingston March 28, 1757, in favor of Ebenezer Long.]

[Administration on the estate of Samuel Emmons, yeoman, granted to Ebenezer Long of Kingston, yeoman, April 27, 1757.]
[Probate Records, vol. 20, p. 154.]

[Bond of Ebenezer Long of Kingston, yeoman, with Ebenezer Stevens of Kingston and Daniel Little of Plaistow, gentleman, as sureties, in the sum of £500, April 27, 1757, for the administration of the estate; witnesses, Cutts Shannon, John Fernald.]

[Warrant, April 27, 1757, authorizing Jeremy Webster and Jonathan Greeley, gentleman, both of Kingston, to appraise the estate.]

[Inventory, May 19, 1757; amount, £863. 15. 0; signed by Jeremy Webster and Jonathan Greeley.]

[Warrant, July 18, 1757, authorizing Jeremy Webster and

Jonathan Greeley, innholder, both of Kingston, to receive claims against the estate.]

[Warrant, Dec. 28, 1757, authorizing Jeremy Webster, Jonathan Greeley, gentleman, Peter Sanborn, John Judkins, gentleman, and Thomas Elkins, blacksmith, all of Kingston, to set off the widow's dower to Maria, wife of David Colby of Kingston.]

Province of New Hamps: } To the Honble Richard Wibird Esqr Judge of the Probates of wills &c for s^d Province

Pursuant to your Hon^{rs} Warrant to us directed Authorizing us the subscribers to set off to Moriah Now the wife of David Colby of Kingstown in s^d Province her Right of Dower which happens to her of the Real Estate of her Late Husband Samuel Emmins deceasd &c we have set off the same as follows viz: Beginning at the upper or westerly End of the Deceased land taking the whole width thereof & Extending Easterly as the land lays to the Path or High way: & so having Land of Jabez Page on the west & on the North the s^d Path or High way on the East & Land of Sam^{ll} Sanborn on the south: with the Dwelling House & Barn thereon five acres be the same more or Less

Kingstown february the 23^d 1758 Jeremy Webster
Jonathan Greeley
Thomas Elkins

[List of claims against the estate Jan. 24, 1758; amount, £706. 16. 0; signed by Jeremy Webster and Jonathan Greeley.]

[Account of the settlement of the estate; receipts, £860. 15. 0; expenditures, £234. 10. 0; allowed July 26, 1758.]

[Settlement of claims; amount of claims, £706. 16. 0; amount distributed, £626. 5. 0; allowed Aug. 7, 1758.]

GERSHOM DOWNS   1757   ROCHESTER

[Administration on the estate of Gershom Downs of Rochester, yeoman, granted to Joseph Walker and his wife, Margaret Walker, March 29, 1757.]

[Probate Records, vol. 20, p. 136.]

[Bond of Joseph Walker, Jr., and wife Margaret, with Joseph Walker and Barnabas Palmer, yeomen, as sureties, all of Rochester, in the sum of £500, March 29, 1757, for the administration of the estate; witnesses, Theodore Willey, Theodore Willey, Jr., William Parker.]

[Warrant, March 29, 1757, authorizing John Bickford and Stephen Berry, both of Rochester, yeomen, to appraise the estate.]

[Inventory, June 16, 1757; amount, £1278. 14. 0; signed by John Bickford and Stephen Berry.]

[Account of Joseph Walker and his wife Margaret of the settlement of the estate of her former husband, Gershom Downs; receipts, £558. 14. 0; expenditures, £711. 12. 0; mentions "keeping Gershom a minor son of the Dec[d] 16 months"; allowed Aug. 8, 1758.]

JONATHAN LORD   1757   IPSWICH, MASS.

[Guardianship of Thomas Lord, aged less than 14 years, son of Jonathan Lord of Ipswich, Mass., granted to Jonathan Lord of Exeter March 29, 1757.]

[Probate Records, vol. 20, p. 136.]

[Bond of Jonathan Lord, tailor, with Joseph Lougee, tailor, and Edmund Lougee, joiner, as sureties, all of Exeter, in the sum of £500, March 29, 1757, for the guardianship of Thomas Lord, son of Jonathan Lord of Ipswich, Mass., glazier, deceased; witnesses, John Fernald and John Langdon.]

[Esther Lord, minor, aged more than 14 years, daughter of Mrs. Hannah Lord of Exeter, deceased, makes choice of her brother-in-law, Edmund Lougee of Exeter as her guardian Feb. 21, 1757; witnesses, James Thurston and Theophilus Smith.]

[Guardianship of Esther Lord, daughter of Jonathan Lord, granted to Edmund Lougee of Exeter March 29, 1757.]

[Probate Records, vol. 20, p. 136.]

[Bond of Edmund Lougee, joiner, with Jonathan Lord, tailor, and Joseph Lougee, tailor, as sureties, all of Exeter, in the sum of £500, March 29, 1757, for the guardianship of Esther Lord, daughter of Jonathan Lord of Ipswich, Mass., glazier, deceased; witnesses, John Fernald and John Langdon.]

JOHN SHEDD   1757   NASHUA

[Administration on the estate of John Shedd of Dunstable, yeoman, granted to his widow, Hannah Shedd, March 30, 1757.]

[Probate Records, vol. 20, p. 195.]

[Bond of Hannah Shedd, widow, with Thomas Lund and Ephraim Lund, husbandmen, as sureties, all of Dunstable, in the sum of £500, March 30, 1757, for the administration of the estate of John Shedd, housewright; witnesses, Peter Horney, Rachel Lund.]

[Warrant, March 30, 1757, authorizing John Butterfield and Ephraim Lund, both of Dunstable, yeomen, to appraise the estate.]

[Inventory, April 3, 1757; amount, £2784. 10. 0; signed by John Butterfield and Ephraim Lund.]

[Account of the settlement of the estate; receipts, £1414. 10. 0, personal estate; expenditures, £1219. 8. 5; mentions "maintenance of the children of the Deceased under the age of 7 years"; signed by Hannah Shedd; allowed Nov. 2, 1759.]

[Additional account by Samuel Roby and his wife Hannah Roby, administratrix; receipts, £41. 2. 6; expenditures the same; mentions "maintenance of John Shed a child of the said Deceased under the age of 7 years 197 weeks since the Exhibit^g ye former acc^t"; allowed Oct. 31, 1765.]

[Additional account by Samuel Roby and wife Hannah; receipts, £56. 13. 0; expenditures, £46. 19. 0; signed by Samuel Roby; allowed July 30, 1777.]

ABNER WHITTIER   1757   AMESBURY, MASS.

[Administration on the estate of Abner Whittier of Amesbury, Mass., yeoman, granted to his son, Abner Whittier, March 30, 1757.]

[Probate Records, vol. 20, p. 136.]

[Bond of Abner Whittier of Amesbury, Mass., yeoman, with Samuel French of South Hampton and John Challis of Salisbury and Amesbury District, yeomen, as sureties, in the sum of £1000, March 30, 1757, for the administration of the estate; witnesses, William Parker, John Fernald.]

[Inventory, March 28, 1757; amount, £1280. 0. 0; signed by Joseph Peaslee and Moses Peaslee.]

[Account of the settlement of the estate; receipts, £202. 0. 0, personal estate; expenditures, £44. 18. 0; allowed April 26, 1758.]

[Warrant, April 26, 1758, authorizing Enoch Brown, Sargent Heath, Nathan Hoag, Moses Peaslee, and Robert Stewart, all of Newton, yeomen, to appraise the real estate for settlement on the oldest son.]

[Return of appraisal, June 12, 1758; thirty two acres of land in Newton, £325. 0. 0; signed by Enoch Brown, Nathan Hoag, and Moses Peaslee. Order of court May 2, 1759, settling the estate on Abner Whittier, oldest son.]

[Bond of Abner Whittier, cordwainer, with Joseph Peaslee and Moses Peaslee, husbandmen, as sureties, all of Newton, in the sum of £650, May 2, 1759, to pay to each of the other children £83. 9. 2⅔, to the oldest two within one year, and to the other males at 21 years of age and the females at 18 years; witnesses, William Parker, David Sewall.]

[Administrator's additional account; receipts, £272. 12. 4; expenditures, £85. 0. 0; allowed May 2, 1759.]

DANIEL LUNT   1757   GREENLAND

In the name of God amen, I Daniel Lunt of Greenland in the Province of New Hampshire in New England, being in Body weak * * *

Imprimis I give and Bequeath unto my wife Mary Lunt one Third part of my Real Estate During her natural Life afterwards to Return to those hereafter named —

Item I give and Bequeath unto my Daughter Mary Lunt one Hundred Pounds old tenor to be paid when She comes of age —

Item I give and Bequeath unto mary Williams wife of Benjamin Williams the use and improvement of that House and Six acres of Land I Bought of John Allen as the Deed Shall make appear Dureing her natural life and after her Decease, to Return to Daniel Durgan her Son to him his heirs and assigns for Ever.

Item I give and Bequeath unto Abraham Lunt of York one Hundred Pounds old tenor to him and his heirs for Ever —

Item I give and Bequeath unto the Children of my Brother

Henry Lunt Deceased one Hundred pounds old tenor to be Equally Divided among them —

Item I give and Bequeath unto Samuel and Job Lunt of Falmouth one Hundred pounds old tenor to be Equally Divided among them —

Item I give and Bequeath unto the Children of my Sister Drake Deceased one Hundred pounds old tenor to be Equally Divided among them —

Item I give and Bequeath unto my Brother James Lunt of Newbury one Hundred pounds old tenor to improve During his natural life after his Decease to go to the Children of my Brother John Lunt to be Divided among them —

Item I give and bequeath unto my Sister mary wingate two Hundred pounds old tenor to her and her heirs and assigns for Ever —

Item I give unto Love Gookins one Hundred pounds old tenor to her her heirs and assigns for Ever

Item it is my will that whatever of my Estate whether Real or personal Remains after my just Debts and Funeral Charges and the above said Lagacies are Paid the Rest of my Estate to be Equally Devided Betwixt my Brothers and Sisters or those that Legally Represent them, to them their heirs and assigns for Ever.

Lastly I Constitute make appoint and ordain my Cousin John Wingate Executor * * * in witness whereof I have hereunto Set my hand and Seal this Thirty first Day of March Anno Domini one Thousand Seven Hundred and Fifty Seven —

Daniel Lnt

[Witnesses] Mathias weeks, Simeon Dearborn, Levi Dearborn. [Proved Oct. 17, 1757.]

[Inventory, Sept. 13, 1757; amount, £9403. 3. 7; signed by Enoch Clark and Levi Dearborn.]

[Summons, Feb. 17, 1759, to Benjamin Williams of Greenland, weaver, and his wife Mary, Sarah, wife of Abner Haines of

Greenland, husbandman, and Sarah wife of Matthias Weeks of Greenland, yeoman, to appear and give evidence in relation to concealment or embezzlement of the estate.]

Benj'a Williams & Mary his wife and Sarah Weeks appeared Pursuant to this Sumons and were Sworn & Benj^a Williams Testified that he knew there was the warp of a Linen Web in the House of Mr Daniel Lunt when he Died near Enough to make twenty five yards and Mary his wife Says the same and that there was two 19^s of woollen yarn in Said House and near fillen Enough to fill it which two 19^s of woollen yarn with filling Sufficient woud make about 25 yards Mrs Weeks Says Mr Lunt warped at her House a Warp of Linen yarn but how much she woud not Say but Judgd there was enough for 20 yards tho is not certain

[Account of the settlement of the estate; receipts, £8300. 9. 7, personal estate; expenditures, £3336. 17. 3; allowed Feb. 27, 1760.]

[Petition, April 24, 1760, of Gershom Griffith of Hampton, innholder, and his wife Mary, formerly widow of Daniel Lunt, by their attorney, Cutts Shannon, for the setting off of the widow's dower.]

[Warrant, Aug. 27, 1760, authorizing Capt. William Weeks, John Folsom, William Haines, Jr., Joshua Pickering, and James Brackett, all of Greenland, to set off the widow's dower.]

[Probate Records, vol. 23, p. 118.]

[Executor's additional account; receipts, £460. 0. 0; expenditures, £1732. 11. 3; allowed Nov. 13, 1761.]

Agreable to an order from Richd Wibirt Esqr Judge of Probets for the Province of New Hampshire &c To us the Subscribers, three of the five men, apointed as a Committee to Set off the thirds of Mary Griffeth wife to Gershom Griffeth her thirds of the Real Estate that falls to her that was her former husband

Dan¹ Lunt Deceased — We who have hereunto Subscribed have proceeded & done it in the following manner viz of the twenty acres that said Lunt Bought of Nathan Johnson we have Set off to the Said Mary the East side of the said twenty Acres the said thirds to Run the whole Length of said peace of Land & to be Seven Rods wide at the Road and ten Rods wide at the lower end toward the great Bay & likewise all the Right that the Said Dan¹ Lunt had in yᵉ house & Barn that he Bought of Said Nathan Johnson we have Set of to the said Mary all which the said Mary to Injoy as her Dower or thirds —

Given under our hand at Greenland the 12ᵗʰ of May 1763

James Brackett
John Folsom
Joshua Pickering

[Executor's additional account; receipts, £4076. 1. 1; expenditures, £3518. 5. 8; allowed March 6, 1764; mentions payments, evidently legacies, to Jonathan and Priscilla Allen, Joseph and Jane Pallet, children of Nathaniel Drake, children of Robert Drake, Abraham Drake, Samuel Lunt, Joshua and Mary Wingate, Simon and Mary Marston; Capt. Little for John and James Lunt.]

HUMPHREY HOBBS   1757   WILTON

[Anna Hobbs renounces administration on the estate of her husband, Capt. Humphrey Hobbs of Number Two, deceased at Fort William Henry, April 4, 1757, in favor of her brother, Joseph Simonds.]

[Administration granted to Joseph Simonds of Middleton, Mass., yeoman, April 6, 1757.]

[Probate Records, vol. 20, p. 146.]

[Bond of Joseph Simonds, with Nathan Hutchinson of Monson and Nathan Blanchard of Number Two, yeomen, as sureties, in the sum of £500, April 6, 1757, for the administration of the estate; witnesses, John Langdon, John Fernald.]

[Inventory, attested Sept. 22, 1757; amount, £1291. 2. 9; signed by John Shepard and Nathan Blanchard.]

[Warrant, Nov. 24, 1757, authorizing Joseph Blanchard, Jr., of Merrimack and Joseph French of Dunstable, gentleman, to receive claims against the estate.]

[List of claims; amount, £1730. 6. 7½; attested May 20, 1758, by Joseph French and Joseph Blanchard.]

[Account of the settlement of the estate; receipts, £1239. 6. 3; expenditures, £611. 8. 9; mentions "p^d the Widow for Support of her youngest Child 7 months"; allowed June 7, 1759.]

[Settlement of claims; amount of claims, £1779. 1. 7½; amount distributed, £627. 17. 6; allowed June 7, 1759.]

JOSEPH PAGE   1757   PLAISTOW

In The Name of God amen The Last will and Testament of Joseph Page of Plastow in the provence New hamsher in New england yeaman. Being Very Sick and weak in Body * * *

Itam I give to Mary my Dearly Beloved wife one Haf of my Dweling hous and to be cape in Repare by my Exectuer and also hav Choice of two Cows out of my stock and to be Capt well winter and sumer by my Excetor also I give her six cord of wood corded up at the dore also four gallons of rum and Twenty bushels of Ingan meal and four bushels of rye meal and two bushels of wheet meal and fower Barrels of sider brought and put into the Seller and Eight pound of flex teer and Six pound of Sheeps wool and one pound of Cotten wool and one bushel of molt and Six pound of Suger and two gallons of mallasses and also one hundred weight of good beaf and one barrah pig of a month old in the month of march and one pack of oatmeal al these artickles to be paid yearly by my Excuter also I give her at my Deceas one hundred and fifty wait of good poark to be paid by my Executer and also I give her the priviledge of being carried to metting by my Excuter as ofen as she pleasseth and also to pay his mother as much money yearly as shal pay the hier of a good maid to wait on her and also I give her all my within doars houshold stuf such as Bidding Chears bras Iron wood and tin all these to her and at her Disposing of as Long as She Remain my widdow —

Item I give unto my Son Timothy Ten pounds in money of the old taner as it now passeth or Bills of the provence aforesaid to be paid to him with in one year after my Deceas which money to be paid by my Excetor which together with what Land I have here tofore made sure to him by deed is as I say his full portion out of my whole Estate both Real and parsonal —

Itam I give Unto my son moses Ten pound in money or blls of craddet of the provence aforesaid of the old taner as thay now paseth to be paid to the said moses or his heires within one year after my Deceas this money with what Land I have made Sure to him by deed when paid by my Excetuer is as I Say his full portion out of my Estate Both Rael and parsonal —

Itam I give Unto my Daughter Mary Herriman Decest that is to Say to her Heires Ten pounds in money or bills of credet of the provence afore said of the old taner as thay now passeth to be paid by my Exeter with in one year after my Deceas which Money together with what she has had done or given her heretofore is her or thaire full potion as I Say out of my rael and parsonal Estate —

Itam I give Unto my son Joseph with paying my Just debts and what I have given by will all my Rael and parsonal Estate which I have not Expresly disposed of in this my Last will and testament finally I do hereby Nominate and a point My said son Joseph to be sole Exectuer * * *

In testimony I do here Unto Set my hand and affix my seal

the fift Day of Aprel in the year of our Lord one Thousand seven hundred and fifty seven and in The Thirtuth year of his Mejesties Reign also I order my Exceituer to Bury his mother in a desent Christan buriel —

Joseph page

[Witnesses] Israel Webster, Daniel Peasle, Daniel Poor. [Proved Aug. 27, 1760.]

[Mary Page, widow, accepts the terms of the will Aug. 26, 1760.]

[Bond of Joseph Page, with Israel Webster and Daniel Poor as sureties, all of Plaistow, in the sum of £1000, Aug. 27, 1760, for the execution of the will; witnesses, William Parker, Solomon Loud, Jr.]

ORLANDO BAGLEY   1757   AMESBURY, MASS.

[Administration on the estate of Orlando Bagley of Amesbury, Mass., granted to Orlando Bagley of Kingston, gentleman, April 6, 1757.]

[Probate Records, vol. 20, p. 143.]

[Bond of Orlando Bagley, with Benaiah Colby of Chester, gentleman, and Benjamin Baker of Epping, yeoman, as sureties, in the sum of £500, April 5, 1757, for the administration of the estate; witnesses, William Parker, Cutts Shannon.]

[Inventory, May 23, 1757; amount, £5086. o. o; signed by Jeremy Webster and Ebenezer Stevens.]

Province of New Hamps: } To the Hon[ble] Richard Wibird Esq[r] Judge of the Probate of Wills &c for the Province of New Hamps: —

Pursuant to your Hon[rs] Warrant appointing us the subscribers & Com[tee] to Divide the Real Estate of Orlando Baglie Late of Almsbury in the County of Essex in the Province of the Massachusetts Bay Esqr Deceas^d Intestate to & among the Children of the s^d Deceas^d Being scituate in the Province afores^d of New Hamps: We haveing met & viewed & valued the Premisses have divided & set off s^d Estate as follows

Imp^s To Orlando Eldest son of the deceasd the first & second shares being scituate partly in Kingstown in s^d Province & partly in Newtown in s^d Province as followeth viz One piece scituate in s^d Kingstown being mill Pond Right (so called) in the upland division & Bounded as it Lays & haveing a High way on the south easterly part & Land of Rowels & Goulds on the south westerly part & Land of Ralph Blasdel Ter^s in part on the Northerly part & partly on a High way; and then North Easterly & North westerly on Land or Meadow Ground of the s^d orlando Baglies; and then North Easterly on Powow River (so Called) forty five Acres and Three Quarters be the same more or Less; and another piece being mill Pond Rights in the flowed Ground (so Called) Containing fourteen Acres be the same more or Less & was Laid out to the original Right of Thomas Stevens & Bounded as it Lays, having a High way on the straight side, & Lays partly on Land or meadow of Samuel Jewel: & also meadow ground of the s^d orlando Baglie, & otherwise Bounded Chiefly on the aforementioned Powow River; and two Acres & three Quarters more or Less being part of the Deceasds Farm at Newtown aboves^d which shall be hereafter described

3dly The Third share to David Baglie Laying on the Westerly side of the s^d Farm at Newton aboves^d & Bounded as followeth viz: Beginning at the North Westerly Corner of s^d Farm & from thence Running south westerly on the westerly side of s^d Farm to Davids other Land in s^d Farm which he had of his father (the deceas^d in his life time) then Easterly or south Easterly on s^d Davids s^d other Land about Twenty Nine Rods & Thre Quarters to A stake & stones then North Easterly to the Northerly side of the s^d Farm to a stake & stones then North Westerly 29 Rods & about 12 feet to the place where it first began Nine acres more or Less

4ly The fourth share to Thomas being also part of the above s^d Farm at s^d Newtown beginning at the North Easterly Corner of the 3^d share & running south westerly on the s^d 3^d share till it comes to the south Easterly Corner thereof to the s^d Davids s^d other Land; then south easterly on the s^d Davids s^d other Land 30 Rods & about three Quarters to a stake & stones; then North Easterly to the Northerly side of s^d Farm to a stake & stones, then North westerly 29 Rods & about 13 feet ½ to the place where it first began Nine Acres more or Less then the forementioned two Acres & Three Quarters to the fore Named orlando to make up his shares forementioned: Beginning at the North Easterly Corner Bounds of the 4th share & running south westerly on s^d 4th share to the south Easterly Bounds thereof to the s^d Davids other Land, then south Easterly on s^d Davids s^d Land Ten Rods & about 13 feet to a stake & stones then North Easterly to the Northerly part of the Farm to a stake & stones; then North westerly Nine Rods & about 13 feet ½ to the place where it first began, Two acres & Three Quarters be the same more or less

5ly The fifth share to Dorothy Now the wife of Jacob Morril being also part of s^d Farm & Beginning at the North Easterly Corner of the Piece Last mentioned & running south Westerly thereon to the s^d Davids other Land; then south Easterly on s^d Davids Land to the North Easterly Corner thereof, then south south westerly on the s^d Davids Land till it Comes to Land of Coll^{ll} Jonathan Baglie (another of the sons) in the same Farm Conveyed to him by the deceas^d in his life time, then south Easterly on s^d Jonathans s^d Land 16 Rods & about one foot & a Half to a stake & stones then North Easterly to the Northerly side of the s^d Farm to a stake & stones then North westerly 25 Rods ½ & about 1½ feet to the place where it first began Nine acres more or Less

6ly The Sixth Share to Jonathan (before Named) Beginning at the North Easterly Corner of the 5th share & running south Westerly on the s^d 5th share to the south Easterly Corner thereof then southeasterly on the s^d Jonathans other Land above mentioned & also partly on Henry's other Land Given him by the deceas^d in his Life time Twenty Rods & about Ten feet & ½ to a stake & stones then North Easterly to the Northerly side of the s^d Farm to a stake & stones then North Westerly Nineteen Rods & about ten feet & a Half to the place where it first began Nine acres more or Less

7^ly The seventh share to Henry (before Named) Beginning at the North Easterly Corner of the 6th share & running south westerly thereon to the s^d Henry's other Land forementioned to the south Easterly Corner of s^d 6th share then south Easterly on s^d Henry's other Land Twenty Two Rods & about one Quarter of a Rod to a stake & stones, then North Easterly to the Northerly side of the s^d Farm to a stake & stones, then North westerly Twenty Rods three Quarters & about 1½ feet to the place where it first began Nine acre more or Less

8^ly The Eighth & Last share to Sarah widow & Relict of Moses Sargent Late of Almsbury deceas'd Beginning at the North Easterly Corner of the 7th share & running south Westerly thereon to the south Easterly Corner thereof to the s^d Henry's s^d other Land, then south easterly on s^d Henry's s^d other Land Twenty one Rods Three Quarters & about ten feet to the easterly Line of the whole Farm then North easterly on the s^d easterly Line to the North Easterly Corner thereof, then North Westerly Twenty one Rods & about one foot & a Half to the place where it began Nine Acres more or Less —

and it is to be understood here that we reserve a Priviledge one Rod wide from ye Easterly end of the whole Farm to the westerly end thereof, on the Northerly side through all the forementioned shares, from an open High on the easterly side, to another open way on the westerly side, for a drift way for the use & benefit of the s^d shares for ever

August the 3^d day 1757   Jeremy Webster
              Eben^r Stevens
              Jonathan Greeley
              Jonathan Blasdel
              William Rowell

ISAAC WATSON   1757   DOVER

Mr Dudley Watson Says that he often heard his Uncle Isaac Watson Say that he had made a Deed of Conveyance to his Son Samuel of a Tract of Land which he Said was more than his Proportion of his the Said Isaacs Estate besides what he paid for it & that he did not Design he Should have any more for that was more than his Share and has often heard the Said Samuel Say that he had given his father a Quittance and Discharge from any farther Demand for his Part of Said Estate

Mr Joseph Hall Says that he heard Isaac Watson Say that he purpos'd to Execute a Deed of a Certain Tract of Land lying near the Dep^{ts} Land at Tole End that it was more than his part of Said Watsons Estate & that he Designd to make him pay a Sum of money for it and after that he heard the Said Isaac Watson say that he had Executed Such a Deed to his Said Son & made him pay two hundred pound for it because that 'twas more in Value than his Share tho' he had a Double portion the Land he had Conveyd to him was more than his Double Share & that Samuel told the Depon^t he had Such a Deed & had given an Acquittance to his father of any farther Demand on his Estate and did not Expect any more and afterwards when the Said Isaac was asked why he did not make a Conveyance to Samuel of a Little nuke or Gore of Land adjoining to the other the Said Isaac Said he woud not do it because Saml had got more than his proportion of his Estate already and the Said Isaac said the £200 he designd to put the Said Sum out to Interest for his Son Isaac which he Designd to put out to a Trade & the Dep^t understood what the said Isaac had so Convey'd he Designd to be his Said Samuels Share of his Said fathers Estate

Mr Joseph Young says that he heard Saml Watson Say that the Acquittance which he had Signd to his father to Acquit the Estate of any father Demand he had got it & Burnd it with his Own hand & took it off of the table at Mr Cushions when his father Signd the Deed he gave to him the Said Samuel said that he took it and M‍ʳ Cushion never had tho' it was thot to be Left with him

James Rogers Says that he heard Samˡ Watson Say that the Land that was Conveyd to him by his father was Intended by his father as his full portion & he never Expected any thing more and after that he the said Samˡ Sold it the Depoᵗ in Conversation with the said Samˡ Said to him he was unwise to Sell it the Said Samˡ answerd twas no matter he woud do well Enough why Said the Depᵗ you have given an Acquittance have you not yes Says he why how will you do then why Says he if I have Given it let them find it and added that he designd to get a Double Portion yet out of his fathers Estate.

[Endorsed] taken 11 Apr. 1757

[Warrant, April 13, 1757, authorizing William Shackford, Moses Wingate, gentlemen, Richard Scammon, Joseph Hanson, Jr., and Otis Baker, yeomen, all of Dover, to divide the real estate of Isaac Watson of Dover, yeoman, the oldest son, Samuel Watson, being deceased.]

Province of New Hampshire } Whereas We the Subscribers being Chosen and appointed by The Honᵇˡᵉ Richard Wibird Esqʳ Judge of Probate for Said Province to Divide the Real Estate of Isaac Watson Late of Dover Decᵈ to and among the Relict Widow and the Children of sᵈ Deceased Which we find will be Predicial & hurtfull to the whole Estate to Lot out Every Childs part by it Self and In as much as it appears that Samuel the Eldest Son of Said Decᵈ hath been heretofore advanced by Settlement Therefore we agree and Conclude to Divide & Settle the Same as followeth vizᵗ We order & Set off to Joanna Watson widow of Sᵈ Deceased the two Lower Rooms in the Southerly End of the Dwellinghouse of sᵈ Deceased and also the South west Chamber over the Largest of Said Rooms together with one third of the Cellar under yᵉ house also the west End of the barn as far as the barn floor with a Prividge of the floor to bring in & Carry out hay or any other fodder whatsoever or for any other use We also

Set off to Said Joanna fifteen acres of Land being part of Sheffields Grant (So Call^d) and bounds westerly partly on the Lands of George Hanson & Partly on the Land of Isaac Hanson Southerly on the Land of the Dec^d northerly on the Land of Joseph Hanson Esqr or however otherwise the Same be bounded It being that Same fifteen acres which the Said Isaac Watson Purchased from Charles Baker and is to be agreeable to the Bounds mentioned in a Deed of the Same on Record and Nine acres and one hundred & forty four Rods of Land more Joyning to the former and begins at the Southerly Corner of S^d fifteen acres then runing by Hansons Land forty four Rods then northeast Thirty Six Rods Then north forty two Degrees west forty four Rods to s^d fifteen acres then by s^d fifteen acres to the afores^d Corner with a free and full priviledge to pass and Repass any where through Said Estate as She may have occasion for transporting her affects & no further So as not hurt or Damage the Estate by any Extravegancy thus far for her right in the homsted farm. We also order to the said Joanna five acres of Land more being part of a Lot of Eighteen acres heretofore Improved by s^d Decased for a mowing field Lying on the northerly side of the Road Leading to Littleworth (so Call^d) and is on the westerly side of said field & Bounds on the Lands of Ens Joseph Roberts and the Lands of Ichabod Hayes and is Seven Rods by the Road and is to Run notherly one hundred & Seventeen Rods holding the bredth of Seven Rods to the notherly End of Said Eighteen acres being untill Said five acres be fully Compleated which Compleats her Dower

And In as much as it appears to us to be hurtfull to Said Estate to Set off Each Child their meats & bounds We apprize and value the Residue of Said Estate in manner & form following vizt The two thirds of the house Exclusive of that part Set off to the widow Six hundred pounds old Tenor the barn Exclusive of D^o two hundred pounds old Ten^r The homsted farm Containing fifty four acres Exclusive of that part Set off to the widow at fifty five pounds old Tenor ℔ acre two thousand nine hundred &

Seventy pounds old Ten^r also thirteen acres more on the notherly side of the Road Leading to Little worth being part of Eighteen acres being part of the Estate of s^d Dec^d and is Exclusive of five acres Set off to the widow at Seventy pounds old Ten^r ⅌ acre nine hundred & ten pounds old Tenor —

We further order that the widow and heirs Shall Submit and Give way to Each other through Each of their parts of the whole premisses for Improvement thereof as far as is needfull not to hurt Each other any further then Necessity requires and that They have hold and Enjoy the Same in manner and form as the Same is above Expressed —

Given under our hands the Twenty third Day of April Anno Dom 1757 —

N B we find that there is 136 acres in the Second Division in Rochester & Some other wilderness Lands that we Cant view & apprize at Present —

Wm Shackford
Moses Winget
Richard Scam'on
Jos: Hanson j^r
Otis Baker

[Additional inventory, April 25, 1758, of land in Rochester, £1360. 0. 0; signed by William Shackford, Moses Wingate, and Joseph Hanson, Jr.]

[Bond of Joseph Watson, yeoman, with John Gage, Jr., innholder, and David Watson, blacksmith, as sureties, all of Dover, in the sum of £4000, 1758, to pay the other heirs their shares of the estate, there being thirteen children in all; witnesses, none.]

JONATHAN BATCHELDER 1757 NEWMARKET

In the name of God amen The Twelveth day of april in the year of our Lord one thousand seven hundred and fifty seven I

Jonathan Batchelder of newmarket in the province of newhampshire in newengland husbandman being about to go into the present war * * *

Item I give and bequeath to my Son willian Batchelder Ten pounds in old Tenor to be paid in one year after my decease by my Executor Iten I give to my Son Jathro Batchelder fifty pounds old Tenor bills Credit to be paid in three years after my decease by my Executor Item I give to my daughter Elisabeth Batchelder ten pounds old Tenor to be paid by my Executor in four years after my decease: Item I give to my daughter mary Batchelder Ten pounds old Tenor to be paid by my said Executor in five years after my decease: — Item I give to my Daughter Sarah Batchelder Ten pounds old Tenor to be paid by my Executor in five years after my decease Item I give to my daughter hannah Batchelder Ten pounds old Tenor to be paid in six years after my decease by my Executor and further my will is That my Executor Keep a Cow winter and sumer well for my Loveing wife Elizabeth Batchelder and deliver to her Ten bushels of good Indean Corn a year yearly and also Two bushels of malt a year annualey as Long as she Remains my widdow Item I give and bequath to my Son Jonathen batchelder all my Land in notingham in the province aforesaid to gather with all my Stock namly Two oxen Two Cows Eight sheep with their Lambs To gather with the swine and also all The utencales belonging to the farm To have and To hold To him and his hairs for Ever and I do hearby mak and ordain and appoint my Said Son Jonathan Batchelder my Sole Executor * * *

                           his
            Jonathan X Batchelder
                         mark

[Witnesses] Elias Critchett, Nath[ll] Doe, Thomas Young.
[Proved June 24, 1761.]

[Bond of Jonathan Batchelder, with Benjamin Piper and Samuel Weeks as sureties, all of Newmarket, in the sum of £500,

June 24, 1761, for the execution of the will; witnesses, William Parker, Solomon Loud, Jr.]

ZEBEDIAH SARGENT 1757 HAVERHILL, MASS.

[Warrant, April 13, 1757, authorizing Daniel Shepard, Jonathan Watson, and Jonathan Kimball, all of South Hampton, yeomen, to appraise the estate of Zebediah Sargent of Haverhill, Mass., to be exhibited by Charles Sargent and Aaron Sargent, brothers of the deceased.]

[Inventory, April 19, 1757, land in South Hampton and two rights in Perrystown, £1540. 0. 0; signed by Daniel Shepard, Jonathan Watson, and Jonathan Kimball.]

MARK WENTWORTH 1757 SOMERSWORTH

[William Wentworth, Benjamin Wentworth, and Ebenezer Wentworth renounce administration on the estate of their brother, Mark Wentworth of Somersworth, "whose Desire it was that John Wentworth should administer with his wife on his estate & she having Lately Deceased & Left five Children all minors"; dated Somersworth, April 16, 1757; witness, Bartholomew Wentworth.]

[Administration on the estate of Mark Wentworth, yeoman, granted to John Wentworth of Somersworth, gentleman, May 22, 1757.]

[Probate Records, vol. 20, p. 167.]

[Bond of John Wentworth, with James Garvin of Somersworth, mariner, and Stephen Jones of Durham, gentleman, as sureties, in the sum of £1000, May 22, 1757, for the administration of the estate; witnesses, William Parker, Jeremiah Libby.]

[Inventory, May 5, 1757; amount, £6305. 17. 6; signed by Moses Stevens and Moses Carr.]

[Account of the settlement of the estate; receipts, £3345. 17. 6, personal estate; expenditures, £3820. 19. 5; mentions "p^d Ebenezer Wallingford for keeping a Child from the first Day of May 1757 to the first Day of May 1764. . . . To myself keeping one Child under Seven years old 1 Year & half. . . . p^d two Daughters out of the moveables"; allowed Feb. 23, 1769.]

JOHN CLEMENTS   1757   SALEM

[Administration on the estate of John Clements of Salem, yeoman, granted to his widow, Ruth Clements, June 29, 1757.]
[Probate Records, vol. 20, p. 201.]

[Bond of Ruth Clements of Salem, widow, with William Sanders of Salem and Ebenezer Gile of Hampstead, yeomen, as sureties, in the sum of £500, June 29, 1757, for the administration of the estate; witnesses, William Parker, John Fernald.]

[Inventory, April 25, 1757; amount, £470. 10. 6; signed by Obadiah Eastman, and Obadiah Dustin.]

JEREMIAH LIBBY   1757   PORTSMOUTH

[Administration on the estate of Jeremiah Libby of Portsmouth, gentleman, granted to his widow, Sarah Libby, May 11, 1757.]
[Probate Records, vol. 20, p. 167.]

[Bond of Sarah Libby, widow, with Jeremiah Libby, gentleman, and George Libby, mariner, as sureties, all of Portsmouth, in the sum of £500, May 11, 1757, for the administration of the estate of Jeremiah Libby, Jr.; witnesses, William Parker, John Fernald.]

[Warrant, May 11, 1758, authorizing Hunking Wentworth and John Shackford, gentleman, both of Portsmouth, to appraise the estate.]

[Inventory, July 26, 1758; amount, £4845. o. o; signed by Hunking Wentworth and John Shackford.]

[Guardianship of John Libby and Jeremiah Libby, aged less than 14 years, sons of Jeremiah Libby of Portsmouth, deceased, granted to Joseph Simes of Portsmouth, painter, May 21, 1759.]

[Bond of Joseph Simes, with Jeremiah Libby, housewright, and George Hart, blacksmith, as sureties, all of Portsmouth, in the sum of £500, May 21, 1759, for the guardianship of John and Jeremiah Libby; witnesses, Thomas Packer, David Sewall.]

[Administration on the estate of Jeremiah Libby, Jr., of Portsmouth, gentleman, granted to Joseph Simes April 25, 1763.]

[Probate Records, vol. 22, p. 545.]

[Bond of Joseph Simes, painter, with Moses Noble, blockmaker, and Michael Whidden, Jr., joiner, as sureties, all of Portsmouth, in the sum of £500, April 25, 1763, for the administration de bonis non of the estate; witnesses, James Grouard, T. Greenwood.]

DAVID MORRISON   1757   NOTTINGHAM

In the name of God Amen the fourteenth Day of may Anno Domini 1757 I David Morrison of ye town of Nottingham in ye Province of New Hampshire in New England Husbandman being Indisposed of Body * * *

Imprimis I Give and Bequeth to my Daughter Mary Ray Wife of Wm Ray five shillings money to be Levyed out of my Estate and paid by my Executors within twalve monthes after my Decease

Itim I Give & bequeath to my Grand son David Ray one Half of the ten acre Lot N° 6 in fishstreet in ye township of Notting^m afores^d to be ye Inheritance of my Said Grand Son David his Heirs & assigns for ever

Item I Give & bequeath to my Daughter Margret Morrison all my Home Place where I now Live with all ye Buildings standing thereon it being ye lot N° 38 in fish street in ye Township of Nottingham & ye one half of ye Lot N° 6 in fish street aforesaid to be the Inheritance of my Said Daughter margret her Heirs and assigns for ever and also I Give & bequeath to my said Daughter Margret the whole of my Goods Chattles Debts & movebale Effects she paying out of ye same the Legacis hereafter mentioned my Just Debts & funeral Charges

Item I Give and bequeath to my Grand son Wm Ray Junr my Gun and one Horse Colt 2 years old to be his property for ever only his father Wm Ray to have the use of them till such time as my said Grand son Wm Ray shall arive at ye age of 21 years

Item I Give & bequeath to my Grand son John Simpson son of Sarah Simpson Deceased which was Wife of Thos Simpson of Notting^m aforesaid ten pounds old tenor to be Levyed out of my Estate and paid by my Excutors at such time as my said Grand son shall arive at ye age of twenty one years

Item I Give & bequeath to my Grand Daughter Elisabeth Simpson ten pounds old tenor to be Levyed out of my Estate and paid by my Executors at such time as my said Grand Daughter Elisabeth shall arive at ye age of Eighteen years

Item I Give & bequeath to my Grand Daughter Sarah Simpson ten pound old tenor to be Levyed out of my Estate and paid by my Executors at such time as my said Grand Daughter Sarah shall arive at ye age of Eighteen years

Item I Give & bequeath to Wm Ray all my Body or wearing Clothes to be his forever

Item I Do hereby Constitute appointe & ordain my Brother

William Morrison of Notting^m & my Daughter Margret Morrison aforesaid to be Executors   *   *   *

his
David + Morrison
mark

[Witnesses] James Morrison, Andrew Simpson Ju^r, Robert Harvey.

[Proved Dec. 12, 1758.]

[Warrant, Jan. 31, 1759, authorizing Robert Harvey, gentleman, and Andrew Simpson, Jr., yeoman, both of Nottingham, to appraise the estate.]

[Inventory, April 17, 1759; amount, £2288. o. o; signed by Robert Harvey and Andrew Simpson, Jr.]

JOHN GRAVES   1757   KENSINGTON

In the Name of God Amen I John Graves of the Parish of Kensington in the Province of Newhampshire in Newengland Yeoman being weake of Body   *   *   *

1ly I Give and Bequeath to my wellbeloved wife Elisabeth Graves all the household Goods that shee Brought with her and all my stock of Cratuers of all Sorts to Depose of as Shee Shall See Cause and I Give my Said wife the improvement of one halfe of my Dwelling house and the improvement the one halfe of my Barn and the improvement of all my Land laying in Kensington untill my son John Graves arives to the age of twenty one years and then my Said son is to Come into possession as I shall order in this my will — and then my Said wife Shall have the improvement of but one halfe of my home place and halfe the house and halfe the Barn During her widowhood and no longer and at her Death or marriage Day then the land and house and Barn to go to them that I Shall order in this my will

2ly I Give and Bequeath to my son John Graves forever all

my land laying in the Parish of Kensington with the house and Barn on said land only his mother is to have the improvement as is above mentioned in Every particular and no other wise and I Give my Said son John Graves my Chast of Draws and a hanging Cubbard my looking Glass and one Tramill and my loom and Table and one Kittle

3ly I Give and Bequeath To my son william Graves forever the one half of my land laying in the Parish of Brintwood in New hampshire my son william to have the East End so Runing westerly Carrying the whole Breadth of said land untill it Contains the one halfe of Said piece of land and I Give my Said son one Bead and Tramill and one Iron pot two Chasts and one Box and my warming pan and one Bason and one puter platter

4ly I Give and Bequeath to my son Jacob Graves forever the one halfe of my land laying in the parish of Brintwood the westerly halfe of Said piece of land

5ly and I order my wife to bury me in Desent Christian manner and to pay all my Just Debts and I Do Constitute and appoint Dea^n Jonathan Dow to be my Executor * * * In Witness whereof I the Said John Graves have hereunto Set my hand and seal this Eighteenth Day of May anno: Domini: 1757 and in the thirtieth year of the Reign of King George the second &c

John Graves

[Witnesses] Samuel Clifford Ju^r, Nathan Dow, Ezekiel Dow. [Proved Oct. 26, 1757.]

[Warrant, Oct. 26, 1757, authorizing Theophilus Page and Samuel Clifford, Jr., both of Kensington, yeomen, to appraise the estate.]

[Inventory, Dec. 22, 1757; amount, £5779. 4. 6; signed by Theophilus Page and Samuel Clifford, Jr.]

[John Graves, aged 14 years, son of John Graves, makes choice of his uncle, William Marston of Hampton, yeoman, as his guardian March 22, 1758; witnesses, Jabez Smith, John Smith.]

[Bond of William Marston, with Ezekiel Moulton of Hampton and Joseph Draper of Kensington, yeomen, as sureties, in the sum of £1000, April 10, 1758, for the guardianship of John Graves, minor, aged more than 14 years, and William Graves, aged less than 14 years, sons of John Graves; witnesses, William Parker, David Sewall.]

WILLIAM THOMPSON   1757   WINDHAM

[Agnes Thompson renounces administration on the estate of her husband, William Thompson, in favor of her son, Samuel Thompson; dated Londonderry, May 20, 1757; witnesses, Samuel Barr, John Barr.]

[Administration on the estate of William Thompson of Windham, yeoman, granted to his son, Samuel Thompson of Windham, May 25, 1757.]

[Probate Records, vol. 20, p. 169.]

[Bond of Samuel Thompson yeoman, with Samuel Barr and James Wilson, yeoman, both of Londonderry, as sureties, in the sum of £500, May 25, 1757, for the administration of the estate; witnesses, William Parker, John Fernald.]

[Inventory, attested May 15, 1759; amount, £1184. 10. 0; signed by Samuel Barr and James Wilson.]

[Account of the settlement of the estate; receipts, £1184. 10. 0; expenditures, £1459. 3. 3; allowed March 12, 1760.]

——— WALKER   1757   CONCORD

[Isaac Walker, aged about 16 years, being fatherless, makes choice of Joseph Hall of Rumford as his guardian; dated Rumford, May 21, 1757.]

[Elizabeth Walker petitions for the appointment of Joseph Hall as guardian of her son, Isaac Walker; dated Rumford, May 21, 1757.]

WILLIAM JENKINS   1757   GREENLAND

In the Name of God Amen I William Jenkins of Greenland in the Province of New Hampshire Yeoman being in Health * * *

Item I give & bequeath to Mary my beloved wife the use and Improvement of that part of my Dwelling House & Cellar which I now Improve for her Sole use during her natural Life and I also give her two Hundred weight of good Pork Six Cord of good firewood hald & Cut at her Door Six Barrells of Cyder to be Deliverd & put into her Cellar or deliverd to her Order yearly fourteen Bushells of Indian Corn and as many apples as She Shall have Occasion of for her own use all these to be deliverd to her Yearly during her natural Life by my Son William in Consideration of what I herein give to him I also give my Said Wife One good Cow to be at her Disposal and also the support of Said Cow Summer and Winter to be well kept by my said Son all the year so long as she Shall keep Said Cow for her own use & shall live in my Said House I also give her all the Goods & Effects which she brought to me and were her own before our marriage together and all the money and Bills of Credit which I shall leave.

Item I give & bequeath to my Daughter Allice Grove the Sum of Ten pounds old Ten^r I having given her already her full Portion & part of my Estate

Item I give and bequeath to my Daughter Mary Ayres the

Sum of One Hundred Pounds old Tenor I also give her my Bed and all the Beding & Furniture belonging I also give her One good Cow & six Sheep the Said Hundred pounds to be paid with in two Years after my Decease by my Said Son — and the Bed Cow & Sheep to be Deliverd Immediately after my Decease and it is my will that the said Sums herein given to My Said Daughters shall be Equal in value to the Respective Sums herein given to them at this time —

Item all the Rest & Residue & Remainder of my Estate Real & Personal both in Possession and Reversion with the Remaind[r] & Reversion of the Real Estate herein given to my wife I give & Devise to my Son William Jenkins his Heirs and assigns and also Constitute & appoint him my Said Son to be Sole Execut[r] of this my Last Will and Testament hereby ordering him to pay all my Debts funeral Charges & all the Legacies aforesaid and my meaning is that he shall have all Money & bills of Credit due to me at my Decease & not in my House but that which Shall then be in my House I give to my wife as aforesaid and I Do hereby Revoke all other wills by me heretofore made In Witness whereof I have hereunto Set my hand & Seal the 23rd Day of May 1757

willam Jenkens

[Witnesses] W[m] Parker, Samll Weeks, John Furnald.
[Proved Nov. 27, 1765.]

[Bond of William Jenkins of Greenland, with Winthrop Pickering of Newington as surety, in the sum of £500, Nov. 27, 1765, for the execution of the will; witness, William Vaughan.]

JEREMIAH FLANDERS   1757   SOUTH HAMPTON

[Mehitabel Flanders renounces administration on the estate of her husband, Jeremiah Flanders, May 24, 1757, in favor of her son, Jeremiah Flanders; witnesses, Richard Collins, Christopher Gould.]

[Administration on the estate of Jeremiah Flanders of South Hampton, yeoman, granted to his son, Jeremiah Flanders of South Hampton, yeoman, May 25, 1757.]

[Probate Records, vol. 20, p. 181.]

[Bond of Jeremiah Flanders, with Richard Collins and Christopher Gould as sureties, all of South Hampton, yeomen, in the sum of £500, May 25, 1757, for the administration of the estate; witnesses, William Parker, John Fernald.]

[Inventory, July 14, 1757; amount, £7009. 19. 0; signed by Jeremy Webster and Richard Collins.]

JOSEPH DREW   1757   DOVER

[Administration on the estate of Joseph Drew of Dover, yeoman, granted to his widow, Tamson Drew, May 25, 1757.]

[Probate Records, vol. 20, p. 173.]

[Bond of Tamson Drew of Dover, widow, with Thomas Davis of Dover and Ephraim Davis of Durham, yeoman, as sureties, in the sum of £500, May 25, 1757 for the administration of the estate; witnesses, Ezekiel Greeley, John Fernald.]

[Inventory, Aug. 29, 1757; amount, £5897. 0. 0; signed by James Davis and Joseph Sias.]

[Guardianship of Francis Drew, minor, aged more than 14 years, son of Joseph Drew, granted to John Gage, Jr., of Dover, gentleman, May 31, 1758.]

[Probate Records, vol. 20, p. 517.]

[Bond of John Gage, Jr., of Dover, with Benjamin Watson of Dover and Cutts Shannon of Portsmouth, gentlemen, as sureties, in the sum of £500, May 31, 1758, for the guardianship of Francis Drew; witnesses, none.]

[Guardianship of Abigail Drew and Joseph Drew, minors, aged

more than 14 years, and Tamson Drew, aged less than 14 years, children of Joseph Drew, granted to Hubbard Stevens March 31, 1762.]

[Probate Records, vol. 22, p. 329.]

[Bond of Hubbard Stevens of Durham, tanner, with Ephraim Davis of Durham, yeoman, and Moses Stevens of Somersworth, tanner, as sureties, in the sum of £500, March 31, 1762, for the guardianship of Abigail Drew, Joseph Drew, and Tamson Drew; witnesses, William Parker, Joseph March.]

[Warrant, March 31, 1762, authorizing Ephraim Hanson, Joseph Roberts, Howard Henderson, all of Dover, Moses Emerson of Durham, and Solomon Emerson of Madbury to set off the widow's dower to Tamson, now the wife of Paul Hayes of Dover, gentleman.]

Province of } Pursuant to a Warrant directed to us the New Hamp[r] } Subscribers By the Hon[ble] Richard Wibird Esq[r] Judge of the Probate of Wills &c for said Province to view the Real Estate of Joseph Drew late of Dover deceas'd and to sett off to Tamson now the Wife of Paul Hayes of Barrington in said Province Gent[n] her Dower and the remaining two Thirds to Divide among all the Children, or make an impartial Appraisement of the same according to the present Value in Order to a Settlement thereof on y[e] eldest Son We have accordingly sett off as follows Viz[t]

To the said Tamson for her Thirds; part of the Homestead Beginning at the N. E. Corner of the House & Runing North Twenty Feet, then South 70° East to the lower End of the Farm then Southerly by the Fence to the Road, then Westerly by the Road Sixty one Rods, then upon a strait Course to the Corner of the House first mentioned — Also part of the upper End of said Farm Beginning by the Road at the Southerly Corner of Sam[ll] Hayes's Land, and run'ing by said Road 34 Rods, then N. 52° East 89 Rods then North 40° W. to the High Way leading from Dover to Durham, then by said High Way to Land of Sam^ll Hayes's, then by said Hayes's Land as the Fence now stands to the Bounds first mentioned. Also one Third part of the Dwelling House vizt, the Lower Room & Garrett of the East End & One Third part of the Barn with Liberty to pass & repass to & from said Buildings

The Remaining Two Thirds we find can't be Divided among the Children without prejudice to, or spoiling the whole, therefore have apprised it as follows Viz^t —

55 Acres of the Homestead @ £70	£3850
25 ditto at a place called the Dry Pines @ £80	2000
11 ditto at Madbury @ £120	1320
1 ditto of Thatch Bed at a place call'd Johnson's Creek	130
⅔^ds of the Dwelling House	132
⅔^ds of the Barn	66
old Ten^r	£7498

Witness our Hands this 30th of June 1762

Sol^o Emerson
How^d Henderson
Joseph Roberts
Moses Emerson

[Bond of Elijah Drew, yeoman, with Shadrach Hodgdon, gentleman, and James Nute, yeoman, as sureties, all of Dover, in the sum of £3750, Nov. 19, 1762, to pay the other children their shares when the daughters, Abigail and Tamson, shall be 18 years of age, and the son, Joseph, 21 years, the oldest son, Francis, having sold his share to Elijah; witnesses, William Parker, William Vaughan.]

[Account of the settlement of the estate by Paul Hayes and wife Tamson; receipts, £1427. 0. 0, personal estate; expenditures, £1261. 12. 0; allowed Oct. 26, 1763.]

TIMOTHY RICHARDSON 1757   HOLLIS

[Administration on the estate of Timothy Richardson of Hollis, yeoman, granted to Joshua Wright of Hollis May 25, 1757.]
[Probate Records, vol. 20, p. 173.]

[Bond of Joshua Wright, with Daniel Emerson of Hollis, clerk, and David Hobart of Dunstable, yeoman, as sureties, in the sum of £500, May 25, 1757, for the administration of the estate; witnesses, William Parker, John Fernald.]

JOSIAH CONANT   1757   HOLLIS

[Bond of Catherine Conant, widow, with Daniel Emerson, clerk, and Joshua Wright, yeoman, as sureties, all of Hollis, in the sum of £500, May 27, 1757, for the administration of the estate of Josiah Conant of Hollis, yeoman; witnesses, Samuel Cummings, Stephen Ames.]

[Inventory, April 5, 1757; amount, £5084. 6. 6; signed by Samuel Cummings, Francis Worcester, Jr., and David Hobart.]

Province of New Hampshire } We the Subscribers, being a Com^{tee} to set off to the Widow Katharine Conant, her Dower, or thirds that happens to her, out of the Estate of Josiah Conant late of Hollis in said Province Joiner Deceased Intestate which is as follows, vizt

About Eight Acres of woodland being in said Holles, be the same more or less, bounded as follows beginning at a Stake & Stones which is the westerly corner of the Premises, thence North easterly by Benjamin Wrights land Seventy Eight Rods to a Stake & Stones, thence South Forty one Rods, to land lately owned by Enoch Hunt to a Stake & Stones, thence west by said Hunts land Sixty Eight Rods to the first Bound Mentioned.

Also about nine acres of Land more, be the same more or less being part of the Homestead being in said Holles, Bounded as follows beginning at a stake & stones, which is the northeast corner of the Premises, the same being the northeast corner Bound of the Homestead, thence South by land of Benjamin Blanchard, Twenty Six Rods to a Stake & Stones, thence west Forty one Rods to a Stake & Stones, thence North Seventeen degrees west Thirty Eight Rods to a Stake & Stones, thence East three degrees North Six Rods to a Stake & Stones, thence north about three Rods to the Highway, thence Easterly by the Highway Forty Six Rods to the Bound first mentioned, Reserving liberty to pass across the Pasture by Benjamin Blanchards fence to the other land with putting up the fence or bars, also the whole of the Dwelling House standing by the Premises last mention'd, meaning all that part of the Dwelling House that was built by the Deceased, in his lifetime, (Excepting & Reserving a Small Bed Chamber, in the Northeast Corner of the House) from the Bottom of the Celler to the Top of the House, together with the Liberty of two Rods of Land round the west, South, & East Ends of the said House for a Priviledge of Leying wood passing & repassing round the said House in all respects, with Liberty also, of using the well that is nigh the South End of the House; Also one third part of the Barn standing nigh the said House, vizt the Easterly End of said Barn, vizt the one half of the stable room under the long scaffold, being the northerly end thereof, & the whole of the said long Scaffold up to the top of the Barn with liberty of the said Barn floor to cart in Fodder, or any thing Else, & liberty to thrash out grain &c together with the Liberty of two Rods of Land round the North, East, & South Ends of said Barn for a Priviledge of carting yarding or any thing else that shall be necessary & convenient. the above Articles we have set off to the said widow, as her full Dower or thirds, out of the Real Estate of the said Josiah Conant Deceased. Holles April 14th 1769 —

Saml Cumings
Jon^a Philbrick
Noah Worcester
Amos Fisk

[Appraisal of the remaining two thirds of the real estate at £103. 10. 8, April 14, 1769, with the recommendation that it be settled on the oldest son; signed as above. Order of court, April 26, 1769, settling the remainder on Josiah Conant, the oldest son, he paying the others their shares.]

[Account of the settlement of the estate; receipts, £2983. 1. 6, personal estate, expenditures, £2463. 12. 1; mentions "Maintain^g Boarding Clothing & providing for Katharine, daughter of the Deceased from Decem^r 16th 1756, untill she arived to the age of seven years, being 195 weeks. . . . ditto Maintaining &c Abel, from December 16th 1756, untill he arrived to the age of seven years, being 303 weeks"; allowed April 26, 1769.]

[Guardianship of Catherine and Abel Conant, minors, aged more than 14 years, children of Josiah Conant, granted to Daniel Emerson Dec. 27, 1769.]

[Probate Records, vol. 5, p. 232.]

[Bond of Daniel Emerson, clerk, with Stephen Jewett and Ephraim Burge as sureties, all of Hollis, in the sum of £500, Dec. 27, 1769, for the guardianship of Catherine Conant and Abel Conant; witnesses, John Hale, Samuel Hobart.]

TUCKER CATE   1757   GREENLAND

In the Name of God Amen the Twenty Eighth Day of May anno Domini one Thousand Seven hundred and fifty Seven I Tucker Cate of Greenland in the province of New hampshire Yeoman Being very week of Body * * *

Imprimis My Debts and funeral Charge being paid I Give and Bequeath unto my Dutyfull and Loveing Son Joshua Cate all my Esteate Boath Real and personal in Greenland afore Said and where alce any part thereof may be found to him his heirs and assigns Excepting what I Shall herein after Despose of —

Item I Give unto my Three Daughters viz Abigail Cate Rachel Cate and Sarah Cate the use and priveladge of one half of my Dweling house Sellar and Barne while thay Remain unmarried and a Sufficiency of wood for fire to Burn in Said house Dureing Said Terme

Item I Give and Bequeath unto my well Beloved wife all my moveable Estate oxen Cows Sheep Swine horse Kine and all my Indore household Goods

Item I Give unto my Granson Jonathan Allen five Shillings old Tenor to be paid unto him by my Executor herein after mentioned within one year after my Deceas —

item I Give unto my Daughter mary Allen five Shillings old tenor To be paid unto her by my Executor herein after mentioned within one year after my Decease —

ittem I Give unto My Daughter Lydia Haines five shillings old Tenor to be paid unto her by my Executor herein after mentioned within one year after My Decease —

Item I Give unto my Daughter Cumfort Sevey five Shillings old Tenor to be paid unto her by my Executor herein after Mentioned within one year after my Decease —

Item I Give unto My Daughter Martha Thing five Shillings old Tenor To be paid unto her by my Executor herein after mentioned within one year after My Decease —

Ittem I Give unto my Daughter Margret Johnson five Shillings old Tenor to be paid unto her by my Executor herein after mentioned within one year after my Decease —

Ittem My will is that if my Said Son Joshua Cate Shall Die without a Lawfull heir Lawfully Begoten of his own Body that my Estate Given as afore Said unto him Shall Return unto my Two youngest Daughters their heirs and assigns viz Rachel Cate and Sarah Cate —

Ittem I Do Constitute make and ordain my afore Said Son Joshua Cate the Executer * * *

Tucker Cate

[Witnesses] nathan Goss, Debroah + Goss, Richd Young.
her
Mark

[Proved Dec. 28, 1757.]

[Bond of Joshua Cate of Greenland, yeoman, with Richard Young and Joshua Hill, both of Stratham, yeomen, as sureties, in the sum of £2000, Dec. 28, 1757, for the execution of the will; witnesses, David Sewall, Daniel Gilman.]

DAVID HORNEY 1757 PORTSMOUTH

In the Name of God Amen. The second day of June in the year of our Lord Christ one Thousand seven hundred and Fifty Seven — I David Horney of Portsmouth in the Province of new-Hampshire Mariner being Sick * * *

I Give and Bequeath unto my Son John Horney, if alive, the sum of Ten shillings New Tenor.

Item. I Give unto my wife Hannah the use and Improvement of my Dwelling House Garden and Barn in Portsmouth afores^d during her natural Life in full of her Dower and Thirds of my Estate —

Item I Give and Bequeath unto my Daughter Prudence the wife of John Gerrish of Newbury in the County Essex in the Province of the massachusetts Bay Blacksmith one feather Bed one Bolster Two Pillows Two Pillow Bears Two sheets and Two bed Blankets —

Item. I Give unto my Daughter Honour the wife of Joseph Hixon of Portsmouth aforesaid the sum of Ten Pounds New Tenor —

Item I Give unto my Daughter Mary Horney the sum of Twenty shillings new Tenor —

Item I Give unto my son Gilbert Horney the sum of Thirty shillings New Tenor —

Item I Give Bequeath and Devise unto my Daughter Betty Horney a Chince Gown also the one Half of my Personal Estate Funeral Charges Debts and Legacys being paid — I also Give Bequeath and Devise unto my said Daughter Betty the one half of my real Estate (after the Death of my wife Hannah) and to her Heirs and assigns forever —

Item I Give unto my Daughter Prudence Gerrish the wife of John Gerrish the Rest and Residue of my Estate both real and personall wheresoever and whatsoever and to her Heirs and assigns for ever Funeral Charges Debts and Legacys being paid —

Item I Do hereby Nominate Constitute and appoint Matthew Livermore of Portsmouth aforesaid Esqr to be my Executor of this my last will and Testament — And I do Give unto him the said Matthew Livermore the Sum of Five Pounds new Tenor to buy him a Ring to Remember me by — * * *

David Horney

[Witnesses] Clem^t Jackson, Saml Griffith, John Beck.
[Proved June 18, 1757.]

[Hannah Horney accepts the terms of the will July 6, 1757; witnesses, James Kielle, Nathaniel Fellows.]

[Inventory, June 18, 1757; amount, £4806. 11. 0; signed by Eleazer Russell and Samuel Penhallow.]

[Additional inventory, Sept. 16, 1757; amount, £121. 10. 0; signed as above.]

[Account of the settlement of the estate; receipts, £2861. 17. 6, personal estate; expenditures, £2215. 4. 8; filed June, 1765.]

JOHN LIGHT 1757 EXETER

[Administration on the estate of John Light of Exeter, gentleman, granted to his widow, Deborah Light, June 9, 1757.]
[Probate Records, vol. 20, p. 195.]

[Bond of Deborah Light, widow, with Theophilus Smith and Noah Emery, gentleman, as sureties, all of Exeter, in the sum of

£1000, June 9, 1757, for the administration of the estate; witnesses, Thomas Deane, Daniel Tilton.]

[Inventory, June 28, 1757; amount, £3592. 1. 9; signed by Benjamin Thing and Nathaniel Folsom.]

[Petition of the administratrix, Aug. 1, 1758, for license to sell real estate; license issued Sept. 13, 1758.]

JAMES MORRISON   1757   LONDONDERRY

[Administration on the estate of James Morrison of Londonderry, yeoman, granted to Samuel Morrison of Windham June 9, 1757.]

[Probate Records, vol. 20, p. 194.]

[Bond of Samuel Morrison, with John Morrison and Thomas Morrison, both of Londonderry, as sureties, in the sum of £500, June 9, 1757, for the administration of the estate; witnesses, William Parker, John Hogg.]

[Warrant, June 9, 1757, authorizing Moses Barnett and John Weare, both of Londonderry, gentlemen, to appraise the estate.]

[Inventory, attested June 26; 1758; amount, £2235. 10. 0; signed by John Weare and Moses Barnett.].

STEPHEN HOBBS   1757   KENSINGTON

In the Name of God Amen: The 14th day of June 1757 I Stephen Hobbs of Kensington in Hampton in the Province of New-Hamps: in New England Husbandman: * * *

Imp^s I Give and Bequeath unto Patience my now dearly beloved wife the one third part of all my Lands for her use & Improvement so long as she remains my widow: and also the fore Room in the Easterly End of my dwelling House: only it is my true Intent & meaning here, that in Case my Son Samuel desires it he shall have liberty to dwell in the s^d Room till he can otherwise provide for himself also the one third part of my Barn: viz: at the westerly End: and also that she has sufficient fire wood provided for her & bro't Home to the House (as shall be hereafter mentioned) all these priviledge my s^d wife to have & Enjoy so Long as she remains my widow: further I Give & Bequeath unto my s^d wife one Cow & two sheep and all my Houshold stuff within doors for ever & to be at her dispose —

Itim I Give & Bequeath unto my well beloved son Samuel Hobbs Twenty acres of Land in my Home place Bounded as followeth viz — to Lay on the westerly side of my s^d Home place the whole Length thereof & to Extend Easterly into my s^d Land till it Compleats twenty Acres and also the forementioned priviledge as beforementioned: Then further my will is & I do hereby order that the residue of my S^d Lands (that is to say) the residue over & above the forementioned twenty acres Given to the s^d samuel & also twenty acres before Given to my son Noah Hobbs I say all remaining above these two twenty acres, my s^d two sons viz: Samuel & Noah to be Equally divided between them as Convenient as Can be: but it is to be understood here that my s^d sons shall not Interrupt their mother in her Enjoyment of what I have hereby given her: and so my s^d sons to Come into the Immediate possession of my s^d Lands & Building at my decease (saveing their Mothers thirds as above mentioned) and then at her marriage or death to Come into the possession & Enjoyment of all as aboves^d; and all this Estate as above mentioned my s^d sons To Have And To Hold to them their Hiers & assigns forever —

Item I Give & Bequeath unto my wellbeloved Daughter Hiphzibah one Cow & two sheep to her, her Hiers & assigns and also one feather Bed & Comfortable bedding & furniture therefor, to her Hiers & assigns as the other further I Give to my s^d daughter one Hundred pounds money Equal to the Old Ten-

our; to be paid as shall be hereafter mentioned and I do aso will
& ordain that the forementioned Cow & two sheep be kept &
supported for my s^d Daughter yearly & every year summer &
winter so long as she lives a single life & remains unmarried and
that together & as Convenient for her as may be as also shall be
further mentioned — and also that she Enjoy the liberty &
priviledge of the Back Room in the Easterly End of the House —

Again I Give to my s^d son Samuel all my stock of Cattle
Horse sheep swine &c (saveing what is before Disposed of) also
all my tools and Implements for man & Beast to work with I
order to be Equally divided between my s^d two sons also the
fire Arms which is now Called theirs Each to have & Enjoy his
own — further after the marriage or decease of my s^d wife &
Daughter my Will is that my s^d son Samuel shall have & Enjoy
the whole Easterly End of my s^d dwelling House: and the Gun
which is now Called mine I Give to the s^d Samuel also my s^d
son Samuel at my wifes decease to have Barn as the House furthermore I Give & Bequeath to my s^d son Noah his Hiers and
assigns for ever all my Right & Interest in a share of salt marsh
so Called being scituate in Hampton before mentoned at a place
Commonly Called the Glade: which s^d share of marsh my
Brother Nehemiah Hobbs died siezed of: And to my s^d son
Samul I Give and Bequeath all my Right & Interest in another
share of salt marsh so Called Layin in Hampton aboves^d by
Sergeants Island way (so Called) which s^d Last share was also
my s^d Brother Nehemiah's: and yet further all the Right Interest
& demand which I now have may or ought to have of in or to
the Estate of my s^d Brother Nehemiah deceasd my will is that it
be Equally divided between my s^d two sons their Hiers & assigns
forever

Item I Give to my well beloved son Stephen Hobbs his Hiers
& assigns the sum of Twenty shillings (New tenour) to be paid
by my Executors as shall be hereafter mentioned he haveing had
his portion out of my Estate

And I do hereby Constitute make & ordain my two sons viz

Noah & Samuel to be sole Executors of this my Last Will & Testament and I do hereby Will & order that my s^d Executors provide & bring home to my s^d wife her fire wood yearly & every year as before mentioned and keep & maintain the Cow & two sheep before mentioned for my s^d Daughter as before mentioned, & also pay the forementioned sum of one Hundred pounds old tenor to my s^d Daughter at the End of one year after my decease; and also the forementioned Legacie to my s^d son Stephen: And in all these duties & Legacies my s^d Executors to be Equal in Doing & paying: and also to pay all my Honest Debts, & be at the Cost of my funeral * * *

his
Stephen + Hobbs
mark

[Witnesses] Jeremy Webster, Abraham Smith, Elizebeth webster.

[Proved Nov. 30, 1757.]

[Warrant, Nov. 30, 1757, authorizing Abraham Prescott and Jeremiah Sanborn, both of Kensington, yeomen, to appraise the estate.]

[Inventory, Feb. 1, 1758; amount, £5692. 10. 0; signed by Abraham Prescott and Jeremiah Sanborn.]

JOSEPH GOULD   1757   SOUTH HAMPTON

[Administration on the estate of Joseph Gould of South Hampton, yeoman, granted to Thomas Pike of Newbury, Mass., and his wife, Abigail Pike, June 16, 1757.]

[Probate Records, vol. 20, p. 243.]

[Bond of Thomas Pike and wife Abigail, with Samuel Currier and Abner Morrill, both of South Hampton, as sureties, in the sum of £1000, June 16, 1757, for the administration of the estate; witnesses, Jeremy Webster, Thomas Morrill.]

[Warrant, June 16, 1757, authorizing Samuel Currier and Abner Morrill, both of South Hampton, yeomen, to appraise the estate.]

[Inventory, June 23, 1757; amount, £1594. 2. 4; signed by Samuel Currier and Abner Morrill.]

[Account of the settlement of the estate; receipts, £955. 2. 4; expenditures, £754. 8. 3; allowed Aug. 30, 1758.]

GIDEON HONEY   1757   NASHUA

[Administration on the estate of Gideon Honey of Dunstable granted to his widow, Hannah Honey, June 18, 1757.]

[Probate Records, vol. 20, p. 275.]

[Bond of Hannah Honey, widow, with Thomas Blanchard and Thomas Blanchard, Jr., husbandmen, as sureties, all of Dunstable, in the sum of £500, June 18, 1757, for the administration of the estate; witnesses, Hannah Dow, Jonathan Lovewell.]

[Warrant, June 18, 1757, authorizing Jonathan Lovewell and Ephraim Adams, both of Dunstable, yeomen, to appraise the estate.]

[Inventory, attested Sept. 2, 1757; amount, £1547. 17. 10; signed by Jonathan Lovewell and Ephraim Adams.]

[Account of the settlement of the estate; receipts, £998. 17. 10 personal estate; expenditures, £1350. 12. 1; allowed Oct. 2, 1767.]

ISAAC HANSON   1757   SOMERSWORTH

In the Name of our Lord and Saviour Jesus Christ Amen— Now I give to my well beloved Wife Sarah Hanson, all my homestead Lands, and Buildings thereon, and mills and Marsh together with all the movables appertaining thereto, During Her Widowhood State, and She to pay all Honest Debts, and when She marryeth to carry nothing off from the S^d Estate only what the Law allows Her, and the Sick Child to be taken Care of at the Cost of the S^d Estate So long as he Shall Remain Sick, and I Give to my three Daughters, each fifty Pounds old Ten^r out of the Same Estate, And Isaac Hanson Junr (Now being out in the Kings Service) if he Shall return, to be heir of the same and if not then John Hanson to have it and his Heirs, and hold it forever, And Ebenezer Hanson to have all I own in Berwick old Town except the wood below: and All the Rest of my out Lands, or all that ever Shall appear to be mine to be Destributed equally amongst the Rest of my Children, and John to come in with them if Isaac shall Return

Somersworth June 25th 1757   Isaac Hanson

[Witnesses] Nathanal Downes, Daniel Hanson, William Mark
+ Jons.
his

[Proved Jan. 25, 1758.]

[Bond of Sarah Hanson of Somersworth, widow, with Daniel Hanson of Somersworth, yeoman, and Nathaniel Downs of Berwick, Me., as sureties, in the sum of £1000, Jan. 25, 1758, for the administration of the estate with will annexed; witnesses, Meshech Weare, William Parker.]

[Warrant, Jan. 25, 1758, authorizing Moses Carr, physician, and Moses Stevens, tanner, both of Somersworth, to appraise the estate.]

[Inventory, April 5, 1758; amount, £5475. 15. 0; signed by Moses Carr and Moses Stevens.]

SIMON DOW   1757   HAMPTON

In the Name of God Amen this twenty seventh Day of June Anno Domini 1757 in the thirty first year of his Majestys Reign Georg the second King over Grate Britain &c I Simon Dow of Hampton in the Province of new Hampshier in new england yeoman * * *

Itam I Give and bequeath to my son Noah Dow my Lettle Lot of land Laying in the plains in said Hampton bounding northly on land that was Peter Johnsons southly on land of the Parsonage, eastly on the Road Westly on land that was layed to the falls men in the first of the five Divisions being one acre more or less with one acre of Marsh near Sargent Island Path on the ox common in said Hampton bound southly on said Path that leads to Sargents Island northly on the Mill Creek Eastly on marsh of Browns westly on marsh of Dearbons I also Give to my said son Noah Dow a Privilidg of Pastouring one Cow in my Pastour that lays Joining to Tucks Mill Pond with a privilidg of getting fier wood on my wood land northly of Lettle River in said Hampton yearly and every year sufficiant for one fier I also give to my said son Noah Dow a Privilidg to Live in the westly end of my Dwelling house untill he has Provided him self to Live other whare I also give to my said son Noah one Eighth Part of the apples that grows in my orchard yearly and every year I also give to my said son Noah one Gun all that I give to my said son Noah as above said I give to him and his heirs excepting only the privilidg of liveing in the westly end of my Dwelling house which he is to have no longer than till he has Provided him self a place other whare to live

Itam I give and bequeath to my Daughter Sarah Johnson the wife of Peter Johnson my Lettle Lot of land Laying in the Ring swamp which said Johnson hath within fence

Itam I give and bequeath to my Daughter Hannah Jannas the wife of Nathaniel Jannes Eighty shillings in money old tenour to be Paid to her by my sons Simon Dow and Jeremiah Dow equilly between them

Itam I give and bequeath to my Daughter Mary Dow one Eighth Part of the Apples in my orchard and one milks Cow and nessecery fier wood and sufficiant bread Corn and Meat all as afore said to be found and provided for her yearly and every year by my sons Simon Dow and Jeremiah Dow equilly between them so long as she Remains unmarried I also give to my said Daughter Mary a privilidg to Live in the westly end of my Dwelling house so long as she Lives unmarried

Itam I give and bequeath to my said Simon Dow my Dwelling house saveing onely the Privilidgs in it that I gave to my said son Noah Dow and mary Dow my said Daughter to live in as before is expressed in the westly end of my Dwelling house I also give to my said son Simon one gun

Itam I give and bequeath also to my said son Noah Dow and my said Daughter mary Dow to Each of them one fether bed with the beding and furniture of one bed with all other the moveables in my house which I have not here in other ways Disposed of to be equilly Devided between them

Itam I give and bequeath to my Said son Jeremiah Dow the house he Lives in

Itam I give and bequeath to my said sons Simon Dow and Jeremiah Dow all my land and marsh and meadow Ground and Pastour Ground which I have Laying in said Hampton (which I have not here in other ways Disposed of) to be equilly between them to them and to their heirs with all other my buildings which I have not here in other way Disposed of I also give to my said sons Simon Dow and Jeremiah Dow all my stock of Cattle and husbandry Implements and moveables out of Doores to be equilly Devided between them it is my will that my said son Jeremiah Dow Shal have one Gun I Do Like wise Constitute Make and ordan my said sons Simon Dow and Jeremiah Dow to be Executors   *   *   *

Simon Dow

[Witnesses] John Lamprey, Samuel Palmer 3ᵈ, Robert Moulton 3ᵈ.

[Proved Feb. 29, 1764.]

[Bond of Simon Dow and Jeremiah Dow, with John Lamprey and Samuel Palmer as sureties, all of Hampton, in the sum of £500, Feb. 29, 1764, for the execution of the will; witnesses, James Dwyer, William Parker.]

JOHN LOVE   1757   LONDONDERRY

[Administration on the estate of John Love of Londonderry, yeoman, granted to Patrick Douglas of Londonderry, yeoman, June 28, 1757.]

[Probate Records, vol. 20, p. 199.]

[Bond of Patrick Douglas, yeoman, with Robert Boyes and Thomas Wilson, yeoman, as sureties, all of Londonderry, in the sum of £500, June 28, 1757, for the administration of the estate; witnesses, Thomas Westbrook Waldron, Joshua Wilson.]

[Warrant, June 28, 1757, authorizing Thomas Cochran and Thomas Wilson, both of New Boston, to appraise the estate.]

[Inventory, attested Aug. 1, 1757; amount, £580. 0. 0; signed by Thomas Cochran and Thomas Wilson.]

EZEKIEL WENTWORTH 1757   DOVER

[Administration on the estate of Ezekiel Wentworth of Dover, yeoman, granted to his widow, Elizabeth Wentworth, June 29, 1757.]

[Probate Records, vol. 20, p. 206.]

[Bond of Elizabeth Wentworth, widow, with Benjamin Austin and Benjamin Austin, Jr., as sureties, all of Dover, in the sum of £500, June 29, 1757, for the administration of the estate; witnesses, none.]

[Warrant, June 29, 1757, authorizing Nathaniel Horne of Somersworth and Samuel Austin of Dover, yeomen, to appraise the estate.]

[Inventory, Aug. 27, 1757; amount, £2587. 15. 0; signed by Nathaniel Horne and Samuel Austin.]

DAVID WELCH 1757 KINGSTON

[Administration on the estate of David Welch of Kingston, yeoman, granted to Samuel Welch of Kingston June 29, 1757.]
[Probate Records, vol. 20, p. 206.]

[Bond of Samuel Welch, yeoman, with Joseph Fellows, yeoman, and Benjamin Swett as sureties, all of Kingston, in the sum of £500, June 29, 1757, for the administration of the estate; witness, John Fernald.]

[Inventory, attested Nov. 30, 1757; amount, £454. 6. 6; signed by Samuel Winsley and John Stevens.]

OLIVER SMITH 1757 BRENTWOOD

[Bond of Jane Smith, widow, with John Sleeper and Jonathan Smith, yeomen, as sureties, all of Brentwood, in the sum of £500, June 29, 1757, for the administration of the estate of Oliver Smith of Brentwood, husbandman; witnesses, Israel Smith, Enoch Bean.]

[Warrant, June 29, 1757, authorizing John Sleeper, gentleman, and Jonathan Smith, yeoman, both of Brentwood, to appraise the estate.]

[Inventory, July 6, 1757; amount, £531. 6. 0; mentions "half the house the other half Being his Brother Thomases"; not signed.]

[Account of the administratrix; receipts, personal estate as inventoried and £137. 0. 0; expenditures, £866. 16. 0; mentions "Abigail maintained 26 weeks. . . . Hannah 104 weeks. . . . Jeremiah & Oliver 410 weeks Each & not 7 years old now"; allowed Oct. 28, 1761.]

EPHRAIM SEVERANCE, JR.   1757   KINGSTON

[Bond of Elizabeth Severance, widow, with Benjamin Swett and Jacob Severance, yeomen, as sureties, all of Kingston, in the sum of £500, June 29, 1757, for the administration of the estate of Ephraim Severance, Jr., of Kingston, yeoman; witnesses, Joseph Fellows, Anna Swett.]

[Warrant, June 29, 1757, authorizing Samuel Winsley, yeoman, and Joseph Fellows, gentleman, both of Kingston, to appraise the estate.]

[Inventory, attested Sept. 16, 1757; amount, £1416. 3. 0; signed by Samuel Winsley and Joseph Fellows.]

JONATHAN ROBINSON   1757   BRENTWOOD

[Administration on the estate of Jonathan Robinson of Brentwood, yeoman, granted to his widow, Alice Robinson, June 29, 1757.]

[Probate Records, vol. 20, p. 199.]

[Bond of Alice Robinson of Exeter, widow, with Ephraim Robinson of Exeter, gentleman, and Josiah Shaw of Hampton, yeoman, as sureties, in the sum of £500, June 29, 1757, for the administration of the estate; witnesses, none.]

[Warrant, June 29, 1757, authorizing Benjamin Veasey and Elisha Sanborn, yeoman, both of Brentwood, to appraise the estate.]

[Inventory, July 18, 1757; amount, £6321. 18. 3; signed by Benjamin Veasey and Elisha Sanborn.]

[Additional inventory, Dec. 25, 1758; amount, £2850. 0. 0; signed as above.]

[Account of the settlement of the estate; receipts, £2247. 13. 0, personal estate; expenditures, £991. 7. 1; allowed June 27, 1759.]

[Warrant, March 7, 1770, authorizing Samuel Dudley, Elisha Sanborn, Joseph Shaw, yeomen, all of Brentwood, Joseph Greeley, and Elisha Sanborn, Jr., to divide certain real estate.]

Province of } To the Honble John Wentworth Esqr Judge New Hampsh^r } of the Probate wills &c for said Province Pursuant to the appointment or warrant to us the Subscribers as a Commettee to Devide a certain piece of Land named in Said warrant or appointment belonging to the Heirs of Sd Jonathan Robinson Deceas'd & James Robinson Gent: Deceas'd, we have Done the Same according to the best of our Judgment faithfully & Impatially in manner following Viz^t

to Heirs of Capt James Robinson in ye peace or percel of land afore mentioned begining at Daniel Sanborns north west corner bounds at a stake & stones So runing north by Leu^t Jonathan Veasey's Land ninety Eigh Rods & one half a rod to a stak & stones then Runing East forty five Rods to a Stake & Stones from thence to run South ninty Eight rods & ½ keeping the Equal bredth of forty five rods to a Stake & Stones then west forty five rods binding on Sd Daniel Sanborns Land forty five rods to the bounds first mentioned

To the Heirs of Jonathan Robinson before named to begin at the northwest corner bounds of Said James's heirs Shair or part in said peice of land before mentioned to run north ninty

Two rods & one half rod to a certain pile or heap of Stones by Said Veasey Line & being Robart Rows bounds of a certain Peice of Land which S^d Rowe bought of cap^t Leavit then runing Easterly forty five rods to a stake and Stones, then runing South ninty Two rods & a half rod to a stake & stones from thence runing west forty five rods to the first mentioned bounds in the Last Division

Elisha Sanborn
Joseph Shaw
Jos. Greely

[Attested March 24, 1770.]

DANIEL CROCKFORD   1757   PORTSMOUTH

[Administration on the estate of Daniel Crockford of Portsmouth, barber, granted to his widow, Isabella Crockford, July 12, 1757.]

[Probate Records, vol. 20, p. 235.]

[Bond of Isabella Crockford, widow, with Ephraim Ham, blockmaker, and Samuel Evans, cordwainer, as sureties, all of Portsmouth in the sum of £500, July 12, 1757, for the administration of the estate; witnesses, Robert Drought, T. Greenwood.]

[Warrant, July 12, 1757, authorizing Samuel Waters and John Marshall, both of Portsmouth, to appraise the estate.]

[Inventory, July 13, 1757; amount, £1022. 2. 0; signed by Samuel Waters and John Marshall.]

[Warrant, July 3, 1758, authorizing Eleazar Russell and Samuel Penhallow, shopkeeper, both of Portsmouth, to receive claims against the estate; mentions John Noble and wife Isabella as administrators.]

[Warrant, March 29, 1758, authorizing Thomas Peirce, gentleman, John Marshall, boat builder, William Lewis, carver,

Ephraim Ham, blockmaker, and Samuel Waters, joiner, all of Portsmouth, to set off to Isabella Noble her dower in the estate of her former husband, Daniel Crockford.]

Province of } Portsmth Novr 30 1758
New Hampsh^r } Wee the Subscribers appointed by the Honble Richard Wibird Esqr Judge of Probate for S^d Province to Set of to Isabella Noble her Dower which happens to her of the Estate of her former Husband Daniel Crockford Deceased have Set of to Sd Isabella her Dower in Sd Estate Bouned as followeth Begining at the North West Corner of the Mains^n house Runing Southerly on the Street twenty four feet then to Run Through the House or Shop twenty feet Back from the Street then to Run twenty four feet to Land of Mr John Marshals then twenty feet by Sd Marshals Land up to the Street that is the Land within the above Bounds and that Part of the House from Bottom to Top Standing within Sd Bounds

Thos Peirce
Willm Lewis
John marshall
Sam^{ll} Waters
Ephraim Ham

[List of claims, Jan. 31, 1759; amount, £872. 3. 0; signed by Samuel Penhallow and Eleazer Russell.]

[Account of the settlement of the estate; receipts, £289. 4. 4, personal estate; expenditures, £225. 3. 6; allowed Jan. 31, 1759.]

[Settlement of claims; amount of claims, £872. 3. 0; amount distributed, £64. 0. 10; allowed Feb. 1, 1759.]

[Additional inventory, May 20, 1762; amount, £61. 13. 6; signed by Samuel Waters and John Marshall.]

[Administrators' additional account; receipts, £1271. 13. 6; expenditures the same; allowed May 26, 1762.]

DANIEL LANG   1757   PORTSMOUTH

In the Name of God Amen I Daniel Lang of Portsmouth in the Province of New Hampshire Marin^r being Sick and Weak * * *

Item I give & Devise to Martha my beloved wife the use and Improvem^t of all my Estate Real & Personal (Excepting what is herein otherwise disposed of) to hold to her During the time of her Remaining my widow until and as my Children shall arrive at Lawful age viz the Boys to the age of twenty One & the Girls to the age of Eighteen then they shall have their Respective Portions But upon my wifes marrying after my Decease then she is to have only her thirds & Dower according to Law and if She Remains a Widow after the Youngest of our Children Shall be of full age to Receive his Portion then she to have her Dower & thirds as aforesaid and if she Continues a Widow as aforesaid She is to take the Care of bringing up and Educating our Children till the Respective Ages aforesaid and to have the use & Improvement of my Said Estate for that End till the Respective times aforesaid But upon her Marriage as afores^d then my Executors are to have the Care & Charge afore said & the Income of my Estate for that End (Except what the Law gives my Said Wife) till the time their Respective portions are to be Delivered & paid to them as afores^d

Item I give and Devise to my Son Daniel Lang all that Land and Buildings I Purchasd of my Grandfather Nathl Lang and that Ten acres of Land I purchased of Stephen Jones to hold to him my Said Son and the Heirs of his Body Lawfully Begotton but he is not to Enter nor have the Profits until he Comes to full age but the Said Profits in the mean time are to be Applied as above Declared — But if my Said Son Shou'd Die without Such Heirs then the Said Premises are to go to his Brother Moses and the Heirs of his Body Lawfully Begotten and if my Said Son Moses Shou'd Die without Such Heirs then the said Premises shall be Equally Divided among my three Daughters Catherine Martha & Sarah to hold to them their Respective Heirs &

Assigns & the Representatives of Such of them as shall then be Deceased

Item I give and Devise to my Son Moses Lang the Land & Buildings thereon Standing where I now Dwell Standing near the Mills to hold to him his Heirs & assigns but not to Enter nor take the profits untill he arrives at full age as afores^d but Such Profits are to be applied as afores^d But if my Son Moses shoud Decease before he shoud attain to full age without Lawful Issue the Said Premises herein last mentioned Shall go his Brother Daniel if he Shall be then living or to his Male Issue if my Said Son Daniel shall be then Deceased in fee Simple

Item I give & Bequeath to Each of my Daughters aforesaid the Sum of three hundred pounds old Tenor according to the Present value thereof or other Currency Equal thereto that shall be passing at the time of payment which is to be as they shall Respectively arrive at the age of Eighteen years yet I hereby give my Executors Power in Case either or all of them my Said Daughters Shoud marry before that age Liberty to pay Said Legacies at said Marriages if said Executors shall Judge it proper & Convenient —

Item I hereby give & Grant to my Executors herein after named full Power to Sell all my Right Interest & property in my father Robert Langs Estate at a Place in Portsm^o afores^d Called Ellinses Point and all my Estate in Rye in said Province and to Apply the money that Shall be Raised thereby to the Support of my Children all the Rest Residue & Remainder of my Estate I give Devise & Bequeath the same to and among my said Children Equally and the Legal Representatives of Such as shall be Deceasd when Such Estate Shall Come to be Divided —

Lastly I hereby Constitute & appoint my Hon^d father in Law James Moses & my Uncle John Griffeth Jointly to be Executors of this my Last Will & Testament & Revoke all other Wills by me heretofore made In Witness whereof I have hereunto Set my hand & Seal the 16th Day of July Anno Domini 1757 —

Dan[l] Lang

[Witnesses] Rich[d] Evans, Thomas Bickford, W[m] Lewis.
[Proved Aug. 10, 1757.]

[Warrant, Aug. 10, 1757, authorizing Samuel Penhallow and Andrew Clarkson, both of Portsmouth, merchants, to appraise the estate.]

[Inventory, Aug. 23, 1757; amount, £8033. 1. 8; signed by Andrew Clarkson and Samuel Penhallow.]

JOSEPH FIFIELD   1757   KINGSTON

In the Name of God Amen I Joseph Fifield of Kingston In the Province of New Hampshire Yeoman Being in Health of Body & of Sound mind & memory but being also Aged   *   *   *

Item I give and bequeath to Sarah my beloved wife all my Household Goods meaning my Furniture and necessaries for housekeeping within Doors to her own use & to be at her Disposal as she Shall judge Proper. I also give her One Hundred Pounds Weight of Pork Sixty Pounds of Beaf the keeping of One Cow & Five Sheep with their Produce yearly, and Eight Bushels of Indian Corn one of Rye One Bush[l] of Malt one of wheat One Pair of Shoes Six pounds of Flax as many apples as she can use for her Self One Barrel of Cyder Ten Cords of Wood to be hald & Cut fit for use at her Door two Gallons of Molasses & Nine Pounds old Tenor bills of Public Credit of the Old Tenor or Equal thereto in other Currency all the aforesaid Articles are to be provided & Deliverd by my Executor herein after Named Yearly to my Said Wife I also Give her the use of One Convenient fire Room in my Dwelling House During her Life all which is to be in Lieu & In Full of her Dower and thirds of my Estate I also give her One Milch Cow

Item I give & bequeath to my Son Samuel five pounds old Tenor he having already had his part & Portion of my Estate

Item to my Daughter Sarah Stevens the Wife of Benjamin Stevens I give Twenty Shillings old Tenor

Item I give to my Daughter Margaret the wife of Peter Dearborn the like Sum of Twenty Shillings I having already given my Said Daughters their Portion of my Estate

Item I give & bequeath to Each of my Grand Children Timothy Eastman Joseph Eastman & Samuel Eastman the Children of my Daughter Shuah Eastman Deceasd the Sum of five Shillings new Tenor bills of Credit I having given their mother my Said Daughter in her Life time what I Designed to give her of my Estate—

Item all the Rest Residue and Remainder of my Estate Real & Personal wheresoever the Same is and may be found I give bequeath and Devise the Same to my Son John his Heirs & assigns forever And I hereby Constitute and Appoint my Said Son John Sole Executor * * *

In Witness whereof I have hereunto Set my hand & Seal the 25th Day of July Anno Domini 1757 —

Joseph Fifield

[Witnesses] John Hunton, Tristrum Sanborn junr, John Tucker.

[Proved July 6, 1761.]

[Sarah Fifield, widow, acknowledges receipt from her son, John Fifield, executor, of the moveables left to her by the will of her husband, Joseph Fifield, July 6, 1761, and waives inventory; witnesses, Ebenezer Stevens, Ephraim Elliot.]

[Bond of John Fifield, with John Huntoon and John Tucker as sureties, all of Kingston, in the sum of £500, July 6, 1761, for the execution of the will; witnesses, William Parker, Richard Cutts Shannon.]

ROBERT LANG   1757   PORTSMOUTH

[Administration on the estate of Robert Lang of Portsmouth, mariner, granted to his widow, Abigail Lang, July 25, 1757.]

[Probate Records, vol. 20, p. 237.]

[Bond of Abigail Lang, widow, with Philip Reed, mariner, and William Earl Treadwell, merchant, as sureties, all of Portsmouth, in the sum of £500, July 25, 1757, for the administration of the estate; witnesses, John Fernald, David Sewall.]

[Warrant, July 25, 1757, authorizing Jacob Sheafe, merchant, and John Griffith, shop keeper, both of Portsmouth, to appraise the estate.]

[Inventory, Jan. 6, 1758; amount, £1340. 14. 0; not signed.]

JACOB GILMAN   1757   KINGSTON

[Administration on the estate of Jacob Gilman of Kingston, husbandman, granted to Abigail Gilman of Kingston, widow, July 27, 1757.]

[Probate Records, vol. 20, p. 277.]

[Bond of Abigail Gilman, with James Young of Brentwood and David Clifford of Kingston, yeomen, as sureties, in the sum of £500, July 27, 1757, for the administration of the estate; witnesses, James Bean, James Dudley.]

[Warrant, July 27, 1757, authorizing James Bean and James Dudley, both of Brentwood, yeomen, to appraise the estate.]

[Inventory, Oct. 21, 1757; amount, £968. 0. 0; signed by James Bean and James Dudley.]

[List of claims against the estate; amount, £165. 18. 0; filed Feb. 28, 1759.]

[Account of the settlement of the estate; receipts, £1103. 0. 0; expenditures, £1486. 5. 6; mentions "Cloathing Lodging & Boarding my Son Peter Gilman 25 Weeks. . . . Ditto for my son Jonathan Gilman 160 . . . . Ditto for my Son Stephen Gilman 364 weeks . . . . Expenses in my Lieing in with my son Stephen Gilman"; account submitted by James Proctor, executor of the will of Abigail Gilman, deceased, and allowed Aug. 28, 1765; signed by James Proctor and David Clifford.]

[Bond of David Clifford, with Joseph Wadleigh and Daniel Clark as sureties, all of Kingston, in the sum of £10,000, June 5, 1765, for the administration of the estate; witnesses, John Moody Gilman, Ann Wadleigh.]

EPHRAIM LEAVITT 1757 STRATHAM

In the Name of God Amen, the fifth Day of August in the year of our Lord God, one Thousand Seven Hundred and fifty Seven; I Ephraim Leavit of Stratham in the Province of New Hampshire Yeoman; Being weak in Body * * *

Imprimis. I give and Bequeath unto Sarah my well Beloved wife, all my Cattle Sheep and Swine, and all my Household Stuff, and all other my Personal Estate, Excepting wearing Cloaths; also I give unto my Said wife, the whole Use and Improvement of all my Lands and Marsh in Said Stratham, so Long as She Continues my widdow, She paying my Debts and funeral Charges.

Item. I give unto my Son Samuel Leavit all my Wearing Cloaths, Besides what I have given him in time past.

Item. I give unto my Son Jonathan Leavit, and to my four Daughters vizt Sarah Wadley, Elizabeth Bickford, Martha Dolloff & Hannah Dudley one Hundred Pounds in old Tenor Money to be Equally Divided Between them; and paid as hereafter mentioned.

Item. I give unto my Son John Leavit, and to my two

Daughters Abigael and Susannah, their Heirs and Assigns, all my Land and Marsh and all the remaining part of my Estate in Said Stratham, to be Equally Divided between them; they to come into Possession of the Same when the aforesaid Term of my Said wives improvement is Expired; and also at the time when they come into possession thereof, to pay Equally Between them the aforesaid Sum of one Hundred Pounds old Tenor Money to my Son Jonathan, and to my four Daughters aforementioned.

Item. I give unto my four Grand Children vizt Martha Leavit, Samuel Leavit, Jonathan Leavit, & Stephen Leavit, all my Right of Lands in Gilmantown (that I have not already Disposed of) to be Equally Divided between them.

And further my Will is, and I do hereby Constitute appoint and ordain my Said Wife, my Sole Executrix * * *

Ephram Leavit

[Witnesses] Joshua Neal, Sam^{el} Cate, Saml Lane.
[Proved Aug. 31, 1757.]

[Guardianship of Samuel Leavitt, minor, aged more than 14 years, granted to William Pottle, Jr., March 29, 1764.]

[Probate Records, vol. 23, p. 201.]

[Bond of William Pottle, Jr., blacksmith, with Jonathan Wiggin and Samuel Wiggin as sureties, all of Stratham, in the sum of £500, March 29, 1764, for the guardianship of Samuel Leavitt; witnesses, William Parker, William Vaughan.]

SIMON WIGGIN   1757   STRATHAM

In the Name of God Amen the fifth Day of august, Anno: Dom: one Thousand Seven hundred and fifty Seven I Simon Wiggin of Stratham in the province of New hampshire Gent Being very week in Body * * *

I Give and Bequeath unto my well beloved wife Susannah the

use Improvement and Incom of all my Reail Estate of Lands madow Ground and Buildings Laying and being in Stratham afore Said untill my Son Joseph Wiggin arives To the age of Twenty one years and after that Time one Third part there of Duering her Natueral Life—

Also I Give and Bequeath unto my Said wife all my personal Estate of what Kine So Ever and Six acres of Land Laying in Eppin in Said province which I Bought of John hains to her and her heirs and assigns to Inable her to pay My Just Debts and funeral Charges—

Item I Give and Bequeath unto my Son Joseph wiggin Twenty acres of Land and madow Ground in Stratham afore Said a the South-East End of my Land Joyning to Land Now in the possion of Samuel Clark and from thence to Run aboute west Nor west the whole wedth of my Land So farr as to Make up Said Twenty acres to him my Said Son Joseph his heirs and assigns for Ever—

Ittem I Give and Bequeath to my Said wife Liberty to Sell So much Land at the west nor west End of the Land I have Given to my Son Joseph as Shall be Sufficent to Inable her to pay my Debts and funeral Charges if what is above mentioned to her Should prove Insufficent

Ittem I Give and Bequeath unto welbeloved Son Simon wiggin all my farme of Land and madow Ground that I have in Stratham afore Said with all the Buildings Standing thereon that is not alrady and hereafter Desposed of by this my Last will and testement to him his heirs and assigns for Ever and all Right to the Grist mill Standing on the Crick Joyning to Said premesses and to Com into the possion thereof at the End of the Time that my Said wife have the Improvement thereof—

allso my Said Son Simon his heirs & assigns Shall have Liberty to pass and Repass to and from Said premesses through the Land Given To My Said Son Joseph he and thay Shating Gate and Barrs after them

Ittem I Give unto my Daughter Sarah perkins fifty pounds

old Tenor To be paid her by my Son Simon wiggin within one year next after my Decease Shee haveing alrady Receved most of her portion

Ittem I Give unto my Daughter Susannah wiggin five hundred and fifty pounds old tenor to be paid to her by my Son Simon wiggin three hundred pounds thereof within three years next after my Decease and the other Two hundred and fifty pounds thereof within Six years next after my Decease and priveladge of Liveing in my Dweling house Till her marage Day —

Ittam I Give unto My Daughter Mary Wiggin five hundred and fifty pounds pounds old Tenor to be paid to her by my Son Simon wiggin three hundred pounds thereof when Shee arives To the age of Twenty years and the other Two hundred and fifty pounds thereof when Shee arives to the age of Twenty Three years and priveladge of Liveing in my Dweling house Till her marrage Day —

Ittem I Give and Bequeath unto my Two Sons Henry Wiggin and Thomas wiggin the Land I have in Eppin in Said province that I Bought of Moses Thurstin and francis Durgin which Contains aboute fifty acres be it more or Less to them their heirs and assigns Equally to be Devided Between them for quantity and quality —

I also Give unto my Said Sons Henry and Thomas a peace of Salt marsh Containing aboute Two acres and a half be it more or Less Laying in Stratham afore Said on the noth East Side of the Bass Crick So Called to them their heirs and assigns for Ever Equaly to be Devided Between them the Said henry & Thomas and to Com into possion thereof at the End of the Time my wife is to have the Improvement thereof

Item I Give unto my Said Two Sons Henry and Thomas Each of Them one hundred pounds old Tenor to be paid Them by my Son Simon Wiggin when Each of them arives to the age of Twenty one years Either in Labor on the Land Given them In Eppin afore Said by this my Last will and Testement or in passable Bills of Credit —

Item I Do Constitute make and Ordain my well beloved wife Sussannah Wiggin the Soul Executroix * * *

Simon Wiggin

[Witnesses] John Clark, John Neal, Ephraim Barker. [Proved Oct. 26, 1757.]

[Bond of Susanna Wiggin, widow, with John Clark, yeoman, as surety, both of Stratham, in the sum of £500, Oct. 26, 1757, for the execution of the will; witnesses, William Parker, John Smith.]

[Guardianship of Joseph Wiggin, minor, aged more than 14 years, son of Simon Wiggin, granted to Simon Wiggin Aug. 31, 1763.]

[Probate Records, vol. 23, p. 79.]

[Bond of Simon Wiggin, husbandman, with William Pottle, Jr., blacksmith, as surety, both of Stratham, in the sum of £500, Aug. 31, 1763, for the guardianship of Joseph Wiggin; witnesses, William Vaughan, Joseph March.]

AMOS DWINELL   1757   HAMPTON FALLS

[Administration on the estate of Amos Dwinell of Hampton Falls, physician, granted to Abigail Dwinell, widow, Aug. 11, 1757.]

[Probate Records, vol. 20, p. 277.]

[Bond of Abigail Dwinell, widow, with Jacob Smith and Nathaniel Gove, yeomen, as sureties, all of Hampton Falls, in the sum of £1000, Aug. 11, 1757, for the administration of the estate; witnesses, Meshech Weare, Caleb Sanborn.]

[Warrant, Aug. 11, 1757, authorizing Nathaniel Gove and Jacob Smith, both of Hampton Falls, yeomen, to appraise the estate.]

[Inventory, Aug. 29, 1757; amount, £282. 15. 0; signed by Jacob Smith and Nathaniel Gove.]

[Warrant, Jan. 26, 1758, authorizing Meshech Weare and Jonathan Swett, yeoman, both of Hampton Falls, to receive claims against the estate.]

[List of claims, Dec. 18, 1758; amount, £49. 12. 9; signed by Meshech Weare and Josiah Batchelder.]

[Account of the settlement of the estate; receipts, £375. 15. 0, personal estate; expenditures, £414. 0. 0; mentions "Bringing up (Anna) a Child of said Intestate from the Time its Father Died (in october 1756) till March 1759. . . . D° (Molly & Susannah) 2 other Children of said Intestate yet under Seven from the 29th Day of october 1756 till this Time"; allowed April 25, 1759.]

ELEAZER FLAGG   1757   HOLLIS

In the Name of god Amen The twelth Day of august: A: D: 1757 I Eleazer Flagg of Holles in the Province of New Hampsheir in New England yeoman — being very Sick and weak in Body * * *

Imprimis I give and bequeath to Hannah my Dearly beloved wife the Improvement of the one third of my Estate During her Naturrall life

Item I Give to my well beloved Son Jonas Flagg whom I likewise Constitute Make and ordain my Sole Executor of this my Last Will and Testament, for five years sarving of me scence he was Twenty one years old Two full Shears of all my Estate —

Item it is my will that my beloved Son Eleazer Flagg have but one Single Shear of my Estate

Item it is my will that my beloved son John Flagg that is gon in to his Majesties savis if he Returns home again if he gives up in to my Estate all his wages that he have one shear of my Estate and if he Refuses and will not give and Deliver up in to my Estate his wages my will is that he Shall have five Pound of my Estate and no more

Item my will is that the Rest of my beloved Chaildren have Equell Shears of my Estate and those of them that are marriad that what they have had to be so muth of their Shears * * *

his
Eleazer × Flagg
Mark

[Witnesses] Daniel Emerson, John marshall, Sam[ll] Cumings. [Proved Sept. 28, 1757.]

[Inventory, Sept. 21, 1757; amount, £6654. 0. 0; signed by Samuel Cummings, Samuel Farley, and Stephen Ames.]

[Warrant, Sept. 28, 1757, authorizing Samuel Cummings, gentleman, Stephen Ames, Samuel Farley, Benjamin Abbott, and Zachariah Lawrence, all of Hollis, to set off the widow's dower.]

Province of } By Vartue of authority to us from the New Hampshire } Honorable Richard Wibird Esq[r] Judge of probate for said Province, to Set of to the widow Hannah Flagg Relict of The late Eleazer Flagg of Holles Decesed the one third part of the Decest Reall Estate we have Set of to the said widow Hannah Flagg at the North End of said Decesed farm thirty three acres of land Concesting of plowing mowing pastering and wood land with the one half of the Dwelling House being the East End of s[d] House with prevelidge of the well and all so one half of the East Barn being the East End of said Barn all which is Discribed in this plan but resarving to the Children of the said Decesed prevelidge of passing and repassing as the path is now trod from the Barn throw the widows paster land to their own land — and all so we have Set of to the said widow two acres and three quarters of an acre of orcharding near to the South East Cornor of the Said Farm as it is likewise Discribed in said plan and the said widow is likewise to have

NEW HAMPSHIRE WILLS

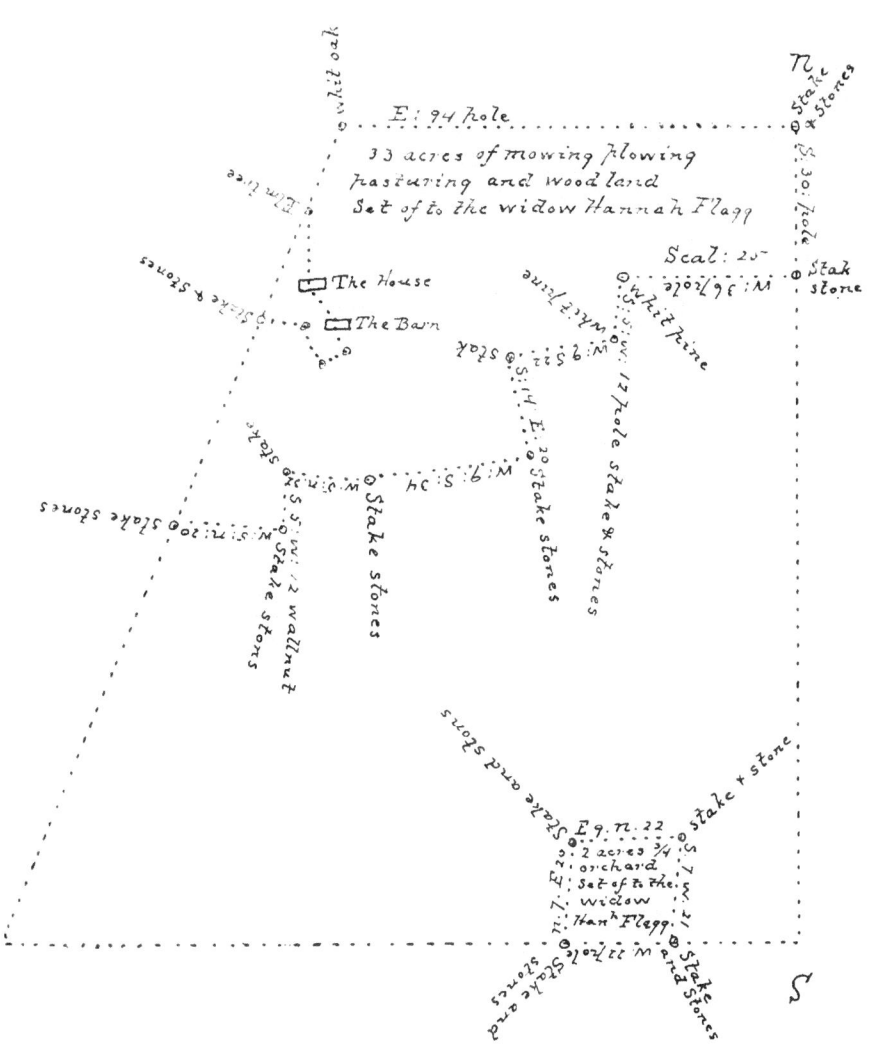

prevelidge of passing through peart of the Childrens land to her orchard

Holles November the 29th 1757 —

       Sam[ll] Cumings
       Benj[n] Abbot
         His
     Zaceriah × Larrence
        Marck

THOMAS NEWMARCH   1757   PORTSMOUTH

[Sarah Newmarch of Portsmouth renounces administration on the estate of her husband, Thomas Newmarch, in favor of her son, Benjamin Newmarch, Aug. 17, 1757.]

[Bond of Benjamin Newmarch, blacksmith, with Joseph Cotton, boat builder, and John Cutt, cooper, as sureties, all of Portsmouth, in the sum of £500, Aug. 17, 1757, for the administration of the estate of Thomas Newmarch of Portsmouth, blacksmith; witnesses, William Parker, John Fernald.]

JOSHUA BATCHELDER   1757   BRENTWOOD

[Mary Batchelder of Brentwood renounces administration on the estate of her husband, Joshua Batchelder of Brentwood, blacksmith, Aug. 29, 1757, in favor of his brother, Nathaniel Batchelder of Kensington; witnesses, James Merrill, Samuel Batchelder.]

[Administration granted to Nathaniel Batchelder, yeoman, Aug. 31, 1757.]

[Probate Records, vol. 20, p. 271.]

[Bond of Nathaniel Batchelder, with Samuel Batchelder, wheelwright, and William Parker, gentleman, as sureties, all of

Kensington, in the sum of £500, Aug. 31, 1757, for the administration of the estate; witnesses, William Parker, John Parker.]

[Inventory, Nov. 10, 1757; amount, £2574. 0. 6; signed by John Judkins and James Merrill.]

[Administration granted to William Parker, Jr., of Kingston, April 10, 1767.]

[Probate Records, vol. 24, p. 391.]

[Bond of William Parker, Jr., with Noah Emery of Exeter and John Pickering of Greenland, gentleman, as sureties, in the sum of £50, April 10, 1767, for the administration de bonis non of the estate; witnesses, Hunking Wentworth, William Parker.]

[Warrant, April 22, 1771, authorizing Zaccheus Clough, gentleman, Nathan Brown, Daniel Sanborn, yeomen, all of Poplin, Dyer Hook, gentleman, and Phineas Sanborn, yeoman, both of Hawke, to divide the real estate.]

Province of } Pursuant to a Warrant from the Judge of New Hampsh } the Probate of Wills &c for said Province appointing us a Committee to Divide the real Estate of Joshua Bachelder late of Brintwood in Said Province blacksmith Deceased among his Children —

1 We have Set off to Joshua Bachelder the oldest son of said deceased for his two shares in said Estate that tract of land in Poplin in said Province which said deceased purchased of Elizabeth Glidden containing Nine Acres as in the Deed thereof to said deceased it is bounded —

2 We have set off to Sarah the Wife of Phinehas Beede for her share in said Estate three acres & fifty Rods of land in a tract of Land in said Poplin which said deceased purchased of Jonathan Thing beginning at the Northwesterly Corner of Nathan Browns land thence to run northerly on the highway Seven Rods & an half then Easterly by said Browns Land keeping the breadth of Seven Rods & an half till it comes to Exeter River

3 We have set off to Mary Bachelder for her share in said Estate three acres & fifty Rods of Land in that tract purchased of Jonathan Thing & adjoining to the share above set of to Sarah to begin at the Northwest Corner of the said share set off to Sarah & to run Northerly on the highway Eight Rods & carrying the breadth of Eighth Rods to run Easterly by Sarahs said share till it comes to Exeter River —

4^{ly} We have set off to William Bachelder for his Share in said Estate three acres & fifty Rods in the aforementioned tract purchased of Jonathan Thing beginning at the Northwesterly corner of the Share above set off to Mary & thence runing Northerly on the highway Eight Rods & an half & carrying that Breadth to run Easterly by Marys said Share to Exeter River —

5^{ly} We have set off to Cornelius Bachelder as his Share in Said Estate three acres & fifty Rods of Land in the aforementioned tract purchased of Jonathan Thing to begin at the Northwest Corner of the Share above set off to William & to run thence northerly Nine Rods on the highway & carrying that breadth to run Easterly by Williams said Share to Exeter River — April 27th 1771 —

          Zaccheus Clough
          Dyer Hook
          Phineas Sanborn

ROBERT ROWE   1757   HAMPTON FALLS

In the Name of God Amen this thirtieth Day of August Anno Domini Seventeen Hundred And fifty Seven in the thirty first year of his Majestys Reign &c: I Robert Row of Hampton falls in the Province of New Hamps^r in New England Yeoman being Aged and Infirm in Body   *   *   *

Item I Give And Bequeath to my well beloved Wife Mehetable All my Stock of Creatures & Moveables within Doors And without I also order her a Comfortable Maintenance Out of my Estate by my Son Pain Row As hereafter Mentioned.

Item I Give and Bequeath to my Son Daniel Row his heirs and assigns a Piece of Land in Kingstown where his Dwelling House is Containing about four Acres

Item I Give And Bequeath to my Son Pain Row his heirs And Assigns my Home Place Containing About Sixty Acres be the Same more or less Lying on both Sides Drinkwater Rode so Called with the Buildings thereon Excepting that my Son Nathan Row is to have the Improvement of that Part of my Dwelling House which he has Liv'd in And Usually Improved for the term of two Years after my Decease and no Longer —

I Also Give to my Said Son Pain Row a Piece of Land of About two Acres lying at the Burnt Swamp so Called. And I Order my Said Son Pain Row to Keep for his mother Mehetable Row both Winter And Summer A Horse and two Cows and two Sheep And Also find And Provide for her firewood, Corn, Meat, And All necessaries for her Comfortable Support And Maintenance During her life And Pay the Charges of her Funeral at her Death I Also Give my said Son two Acres of Marsh —

Item I Give And Bequeath to my Son Nathan Row his heirs and Assigns All my Land in Kingstown in the Province aforesaid not before Disposed of

Item I Give and Bequeath to my Daughter Elizabeth Taylor Fifty Pounds old Tenor to be Paid her within two years after my Decease by my Executor

Item I Give and Bequeath to my Daughter Mary Blake Fifty Pounds old Tenor to be Paid her by my Executor within two years after my Decease

Item I Give and Bequeath to my Grandson John Row Son of John Row Deceas'd fifty Pounds old Tenor to be paid by my Executor within four years after my Decease

Lastly I Do Appoint my Son Pain Row Sole Executor * * *

                                his
                          Robert + Row
                              mark

[Witnesses] Meshech Weare, Richard Nason, William Swain. [Proved Sept. 28, 1757.]

[Warrant, Sept. 28, 1757, authorizing Samuel Prescott and Richard Nason, both of Hampton Falls, to appraise the estate.]

[Inventory, Nov. 23, 1757; amount, £8254. 14. 0; signed by Samuel Prescott and Richard Nason.]

JOHN SWAIN   1757   HAMPTON FALLS

In the Name of God Amen this thirtieth Day of August Anno Domini Seventeen hundred and fifty Seven in the thirty first year of his Majestys Reign &c: I John Swain of Hampton falls in the Province of New Hampshire Yeoman being tho' Aged and Infirm in Body * * *

Item I Give and Bequeath to my well beloved wife Martha the Use Incom and Improvement of One half of my House and Barn and of my Home Place lying on Each Side of Drinkwater Rode so Called and a Piece on the Notherly Side of the way by Coll^o Prescutts During her Natural life Also the use of All my Household Goods for the same term Except what I have Given to my Daughter Abigail Swain and to my Grandaughter Mary Blake as hereafter mentioned And after my wifes Decease All my Houshold Goods shall go to my Daughter Abigail Except what I Give to my s^d Grandaughter I also Order that my said Daughter Abigail shall have the liberty for to live in the House with her Mother so long as my said Daughter shall Remain Unmarried & if her mother should Dye yet my said Daughter to have the liberty of Living in the House so long as she Remains Unmarried. I also Give to my said wife two Cows And four Sheep and my Swine

Item I Give and Bequeath to my Son Stephen Swain to him his heirs and assigns four Acres of Land where his Dwelling House now is Bounding as follows vizt at the westerly End of a Pair of Bars by the Rode near his House thence Running Notherly so as to leave one Rod in wedth from the Westerly End of his House And then to Run so as to take one Row of Apple trees on the Easterly Side of my Orchard: And from the Place where it first Began to Run Easterly by the Road till it Comes within One Rod of the Land of Robert Row And so to Run back from the Rode so far as to make four acres.

Item I Give And Bequeath to my Son William Swain his heirs and assigns a Certain Piece of Land Adjoyning to the Land where he now lives on the Easterly Side thereof Beginning at the Northeasterly Corner of the Garden he now has where there is now a Spruice tree And from thence Running on a Strait line to the Southeasterly Corner of his land then by his land to the Rode and then by the Rode to the Bounds first mentioned also my Right in a piece of marsh lying at Gouges Wigwam

Item I Give and Bequeath to my Son Jonathan Swain Fifty Pounds old Tenor to be Paid him within One year after my Decease by my Son John Swain. I Also give to him his heirs & assigns All my Right in a Lott of Land which was Sold by William Swain Deceas'd to Francis Page Lying at the Little River so Called

Item I Give and Bequeath to my Son Nathan Swain his heirs and assigns a Certain Piece of Land in the Township of Exeter which I bought of Nathanael Bartlett by Estimation twenty five Acres be the same more or less being the one Moiety or half part of a tract of land Containing fifty Acres Granted unto Richard Glidden As I Purchased the same Also a Yoke of Steers Coming in three years old which have been Called And Reputed as his Also one Acre of my Marsh Lying at the Clambanks so Called to be Equal as to Quality with my other Marsh Lying there

Item I Give and Bequeath to my Daughter Abigail Swain One feather Bed and Beding And one Cow, Also a weavers Loom with all the tackling belonging therto Also all my Houshold Stuff after her mothers Decease which was given to her mother

Item I Give and Bequeath to my Grandaughter Mary Blake the Bed which was her mothers And a Chest of Draws that was her mothers Also a Plain Chest & three Pewter Platters Six Pewter Plates three Porringers which were her Mothers to be Delivered her by my Executor when she shall Come to the age of Eighteen Years I also Give her one Cow.

Item I Give to my Son in Law Israel Blake five shillings old Tenor to be paid by my Executor

Item I Give and Bequeath to my Son John Swain to him his heirs and Assigns All my home Place And Salt Marsh And all my land in Hampton not before Disposed of And All my Stock of Creatures and Husbandry Tools And Personal Estate not otherwise Disposed of And I do hereby Constitute my said Son John Sole Executor * * *

John + Swain
his mark

[Witnesses] Meshech Weare, Pain Row, Caleb Swain.
[Proved Jan. 25, 1758.]

[Warrant, Jan. 25, 1758, authorizing Samuel Prescott and Nathaniel Healey, yeoman, both of Hampton Falls, to appraise the estate.]

[Inventory, March 23, 1758; amount, £9159. 13. 0; signed by Samuel Prescott and Nathaniel Healey, Jr.; attested by Col. Samuel Prescott and Lieut. Nathaniel Healey.]

NICHOLAS PERRYMAN 1757 EXETER

[Administration on the estate of Nicholas Perryman of Exeter granted to Noah Emery of Exeter, gentleman, Aug. 31, 1757.]

[Probate Records, vol. 20, p. 272.]

[Bond of Noah Emery, with John Gilman, Jr., of Exeter and Cutts Shannon of Portsmouth as sureties, in the sum of £500,

Aug. 31, 1757, for the administration of the estate; witnesses, William Parker, Jr., John Parker.]

ABRAHAM McNEIL   1757   MANCHESTER

In the Name of god amen I Abrham m^{c}Niell of Derry field in the Province of Newhampshire In New Ingland Wifeor Being wicke of bodey * * *

Item my will is that my Beloved wife Gian m^{c}Nieall Shall Have one Hallfe of all my Rell and Persnol Estat —

Item my will is that my Beloved Son Robert m^{c}Niell Shall have twentey Shillens paied him out of my Estat by my Exatours with what he has alredy goet —

Item my will is that my Beloved Doughter marey m^{c}Neall Shall have twentey Shillens paied hir out of my Estat by my Exators with what She has alredy got

Item my will is that the Remandien peart of my Estat Rell & persnoal Be Equelly Divied By my Exators Be twixt my belovd Childeren Elisabeth m^{c}Niell & Ginat m^{c}Nieall and William m^{c}Nieall & Richieal m^{c}Nieall

Item my Will is that all my Rell and Persnol Estate Shall Be Sold By my Exators In order to peay the Sumes Before minesioned —

Item and I Do Hereby Nominate Counstute & appoint my Beloved wife Gian m^{c}Nieall and John Clark of London Derry Exautors * * * In Witeness where of I Have here unto Set my Hand and Sell this thirtey firest Day of August in ye thirteyeth year of His majestes Rigen anno Dom 1757

                                             Abraham McNeill

[Witnesses] Abraham Merrill, Ebenezer stevnes, John Hall.
[Proved July 26, 1758.]

[Warrant, Sept. 23, 1757, authorizing John Hall of Derryfield, gentleman, and Peter Patterson of Londonderry, weaver, to appraise the estate.]

[Inventory, Oct. 10, 1757; amount, £1072. 0. 0; signed by John Hall and Peter Patterson.]

[Commission, Sept. 14, 1758, to James Taggart and Samuel Dickey, both of Londonderry, yeomen, to receive claims against the estate.]

[Depositions of Thomas Hall, March 24, 1759, and of the widow, Jean McNeil, March 26, 1759, as to certain lands and liabilities of the estate.]

[List of claims against the estate; amount, £708. 17. 1; signed by James Taggart and Samuel Dickey, and attested March 26, 1759.]

[Account of the settlement of the estate; receipts, £988. 10. 6, personal estate; expenditures, £533. 10. 0; allowed March 28, 1759.]

[Settlement of claims; amount of claims, £708. 17. 1; amount distributed, £465. 0. 6; allowed March 31, 1759.]

DAVID STEVENS   1757   HAMPSTEAD

[Administration on the estate of David Stevens of Hampstead, yeoman, granted to Mary Stevens, widow, Aug. 31, 1757.]

[Probate Records, vol. 20, p. 277.]

[Bond of Mary Stevens, widow, with Stephen Emerson, yeoman, and John Mills, cordwainer, as sureties, all of Hampstead, in the sum of £500, Aug. 31, 1757, for the administration of the estate; witnesses, James Graves, John Muzzey.]

[Warrant, Aug. 31, 1757, authorizing Thomas Wells and John Muzzey to appraise the estate.]

[Inventory, attested Oct. 18, 1757; amount, £3874. 3. 0; signed by Thomas Wells and John Muzzey.]

[Account of the settlement of the estate; receipts, £1624. 3. 0, personal estate; expenditures, £996. 15. 0; mentions "maintaining 3 Children under 7 years to this time from the time of the dec⁸ of the Intestate July 29, 1757"; allowed Sept. 26, 1759.]

[Guardianship of David Stevens and Benjamin Stevens, aged less than 14 years, children of David Stevens, granted to Benjamin Stevens of Goffstown March 27, 1760.]

[Probate Records, vol. 21, p. 407.]

[Bond of Benjamin Stevens, with John Muzzey and Stephen Johnson, both of Hampstead, yeomen, as sureties, in the sum of £1000, March 28, 1760, for the guardianship of David Stevens and Benjamin Stevens; witnesses, William Parker, Solomon Loud, Jr.]

MATTHEW NEALEY 1757 NOTTINGHAM

[Administration on the estate of Matthew Nealey of Nottingham, yeoman, granted to Thomas Simpson, yeoman, and Margaret Nealey, widow, both of Nottingham, Aug. 31, 1757.]

[Probate Records, vol. 20, p. 272.]

[Bond of Thomas Simpson and Margaret Nealey, with John Nealey of Nottingham, yeoman, and Joseph Young of Newmarket, gentleman, as sureties, in the sum of £500, Aug. 31, 1757, for the administration of the estate; witnesses, William Parker, Jr., John Parker.]

[Inventory, attested Dec. 28, 1757; amount, £24,641. 12. 0; signed by John McCrillis and Francis Harvey.]

[Account of the settlement of the estate; receipts, £9702. 3. 2; expenditures, £9720. 14. 6; mentions "To the widow margaret Nealy for bording the Intestates youngest Child being under Seven Years old from the seventh of august 1757 to the seventh of august 1760"; allowed Sept. 24, 1760.]

[Warrant, Sept. 24, 1760, authorizing Benjamin Whitcher, Abraham True, James Kelsey, all of Nottingham, yeomen, and Capt. James Norris and Abraham Perkins, both of Epping, yeomen, to divide the real estate.]

Province of New Hamps^r } Persueant to a Warrant from the Honble Richard Wibird Esqr Judge of the Probate of wills for Said Province To Benjamin Witcher Abraham True James Kelsey all of Nottingham in Said Province and Capt James Norris Abraham Perkins both of Epping in Said Province to Divide the real Estate of Matthew Neley Late of Nottingham in Said Province Deceased Intestate and according to Said Warrant We Benjamin Witcher Abraham True James Kelsey James Norris and Abraham Perkins aforesaid have Divided Said Estate and are Set forth by meets and Bounds each one his or her Proportion or Share as is hereby Described and Set Down in the following Manner viz: To margaret the widow of Said Intestate one full third Part of Said Estate as her Dower for term of Life and is as followeth viz: twenty acres of Land more or Less Lying on the North Side of Bow Street in Said Nottingham belonging to the home Lotts together with the house & Barn Standing on the Same and Likewise forty acres be it more or Less lying the South Side of Bow Street and the west Side of fish Street Bounding upon Said Bow Street & fish street excepting two acres that we Set off to Margaret Neley Daughter of the Intestate Said forty acres Lyes in the home Lotts in the first Division and also Eighty acres of Land more or less lying in Lott N° 2 in the Second Division in Bow Street in Said Nottingham and also one Quarter Part of a Sawmill known by the Name of Drowns mill in Said Nottingham —

To matthew Neley Eldest Son of Said Intestate we Set of as a Double Share Sixty Six acres more or less Lying in Lott N° 13 in Summer Street and twenty acres of Land Lying in Lott N° 11 in Said Summer Street in the Second Division in Said Nottingham and also one Eighth Part of a Sawmill known by the Name of the great falls mill —

To Joseph Neley Second Son of Said Intestate we allow a full Single Share one hundred & Six acres of Land more or less Lying in Lott N° 21 in the Seventh Range in the third Division in Said Nottingham and also one Quarter Part of that Lott N° 4 in the Sixth Range in Said third Division beginning at the Northeasterly end of Said Lott and run Southwesterly carring the Whole Weideth of Said Lott So far as will Contain Just one fourth Part of Said Lott N° 4 —

To Andrew Neley third Son of the Intestate we allow as a full Single Share three Quarters of the Lott N° 4 in the Sixth Range in the third Division in Said Nottingham Beginning at the Southwesterly end of Said Lott and run Northeasterly So far as will Contain Just three fourths of Said Lott and also three Quarters of that tract of Land Lying in that Lott N° 5 in the Said Sixth Range that belonged to the Said Intestate at his Decease begining at the Southwesterly end and run Northeasterly as Said Lott runs So far as will Contain Just three fourths of Said tract —

To Jean Samborn Eldest Daughter of the Intestate we allow as a Single Share all that Lott of Land Lying in Bow Street N° 25 in the Second Division in Said Nottingham and also twelve acres of Land Lying in Lott N° 8 in winter street in the said second Division and is to begin at the southeast end of said Lott and run Northwesterly Carring the whole weideth of said Lott so far as will Contain Just twelve acres of Land and also one Quarter Part of a Sawmill known by the Name of Fowlers mill in said Nottingham —

To Mary Mason Second Daughter of the Intestate we allow as a Single Share all that tract of Land Lying in the Lott N° 20 in the Seventh Range of Lott in ye third Division in Said Nottingham that Lyes the southwest side of Pleasant Pond So Called and also one Quarter Part of that tract of Land Lying in Lott N° 5 in ye sixth Range of Lotts in Said third Division that belonged to the said Intestate at his Decease and is to begin at the Northeast end of said tract and run southwesterly carring the whole weideth of Said tract so far as will Contain Just one fourth

Part of said tract and also thirty acres of Land Lying at the Southeast end of Lott N° 10 in winter street in the Second Division in Said Nottingham —

To Sarah Neley third Daughter of the Intestate we allow as a Single Share all that tract of Land Lying in Lott N° 8 in Winter Street in the second Division in said Nottingham that belonged to the Intestate at his Decease excepting twelve acres that we have allowed to Jean Samborn eldest Daughter of the Intestate —

To Margaret Neley youngest Daughter of the Intestate we allow as a Single Share all that tract of Land Lying in Lott N° 10 in winter street in the Second Division in said Nottingham that belonged to the said Intestate at his Decease excepting thirty acres which we allow to mary mason which Lyes at the Southeast end of Said Lott and also one hundred acres of Land Lying in Lott N° 10 in the Nineth Range of Lotts in the third Division in Said Nottingham and also two acres of Land Lying in Lott N° 3 in fish Street in the first Division in Said Nottingham and Bounded as followeth begining at the Northeast Corner of Said Lott upon Sd fish Street and run Southwesterly as said street runs till it Contains half the weideth of Said Lott then run westerly carring one half the weideth of Said Lott till it contains Just two acres of Land —

To the Division as is above mentioned we the Subscribers do hereunto Set our hands this 25th Day of December Anno Que Domini one thousand Seven hundred and Sixty &c

Benjamin Witcher
Abraham True
James kelse } Committee
James noris
Abraham Perkins

[Guardianship of Joseph Nealey, minor, aged more than 14 years, son of Matthew Nealey, granted to Joseph Sias of Lee Jan. 15, 1767.]

[Probate Records, vol. 24, p. 331.]

[Bond of Joseph Sias, with Joshua Burnham of Lee and John Nealey of Nottingham, yeomen, as sureties, in the sum of £500, Jan. 15, 1767, for the guardianship of Joseph Nealey; witnesses, William Parker, Reuben Hill.]

[Bond of Joseph Nealey, with Asa Gile and Joseph Hodgdon as sureties, all of Nottingham, in the sum of £1000, Aug. 16, 1782, for the administration de bonis non of the estate; witnesses, Jonathan Flanders, William Parker.]

[Inventory, attested Oct. 12, 1782; amount, £301. 10. 0; signed by Rice Rowell, Thomas Bartlett, and Jonathan Gove.]

[Warrant, Oct. 30, 1782, authorizing Rice Rowell, John Harvey, gentleman, Jonathan Gove, gentleman, Andrew Simpson, yeoman, and John Ford, blacksmith, all of Nottingham, to divide the real estate.]

State of New Hampshire Rockingham ss } Pursuant to a Warrent to us Directed by the Honourable Joseph Gilman Esqr Judg of Probate of Wills &c for the Said County of Rockingham we have Divided the Estate of Mathew Nealey Not already Divided Late of Nottingham in Said County Yeoman Deceased Intestate in Manner following viz To Each of the Children and the Representatives of Such as are Dead a Single Sheare Each which is buted and bounded as followeth viz

To Joseph Nealley Son to Said Deceas'd for his Single Share of Said Estate Not already Divided Begining at the highway on the Line between Said Deceas'd Estate and Land of Thomas Bartlett and Bounded Easterly & Southeasterly on Said Bartlets and Said Bartlets Mothers Land Northwesterly and Land Set of to Andrew Nealey out of Said Estate and Southwesterly on Said highway Containing four acres of Land Presiesly with the Mansion House Standing thereon

To Andrew Nealey Son to Said Deceas'd Not already Divided we have Set of all the Remainder of Said Deceas'd Estate Laying on the North Side of the highway Commonly Call'd Bow Street belonging to the home Stead Bounded Southeasterly on Land Set of To Joseph Son to Said Deceas'd Easterly on the widdow Love Lunts Land Northwesterly on Rice Rowell Land and Southwesterly on Said highway

To the Hairs of Jena Samborn Daugtor of Said Deceas'd we have set of out of his Estate Not already Divided as followeth a Certain Peice of Land bounded as followeth viz begining on fish street at the bounds between the Lots N° 4 & three in Said Fish Street and Bounded by Said fish street untill it Comes to Two acres of Land formerly set of to Margrit Norris in a former Division of said Deceas'd Estate then Northeasterly on Said Two acres untill it Comes to the Miter Line So Call'd then on a Parrelel Line with fish Street untill it Comes to the Divideing Line between the third and fourth Lot in fish street then by Said line between said third and fourth Lots in fish street untill it Comes to the bounds first Mentioned and also Part of the Lot N° 2 in Bow street Hundred acres Lots Laying on the North Side of the highway that Leads from Nottingham to Deerfield Bounded Southeasterly on Land belonging to Ebenezer and Ezra Barker Northeasterly on bow Street Northwesterly on Land Sold out of said Lot to James Morrison and Southwesterly on the said highway that goes from Nottingham to Deerfield

To Mary Hodgdon Daughter of Said Deceas'd we have set of for her share of said Deceasd Estate Not heretofore Divided a Certain Peice of Land out of said Lot N° 2 in bow street Hundred acre Lots on the Southwesterly side of the highway that Lead from Nottingham to Deerfield and is bounded Southeasterly on Lands belonging to Ebenezer Barker and Ezra Barker and to Extend the full of one half of the width of Said Lot in Every Part Except what has been sold out of Said Lot to Morrison and to Run to the Southwesterly End of said Lot

To Sarah Gile Daughter of Said Deceasd for her share of said Estate Not already Divided we have Set of all the Remaining Part of Said Lot N° 2 in bow street Hundred acre Lots on the Southwesterly side of the highway that Leads from Nottingham to Deerfield Except what has already been set of to Mary Hodgdon and what has been Sold to Morrison.

To Margrit Norriss Daughter of Said Deas'd for her share of said Estate Not before Divided we have set of a Peice of Land in Nottingham Bounded as followeth viz Begining on Bow street at Place Called Back Street then by bow street to the Corner of the Squaire Near the Meeting House then by the Squaire to a Peice of Land Sold out of the Lot N° 2 in bow street ten acre Lots to Jonathan Longfellow then by said Land Sold to Said Longfellow to the Miter Line So Called to the South westerly Corner of the Two acres Set of to the Said Margrit in a former Division of said Deceas'd Estate then by Land Set of to the hairs of Janey Samborn in this Division untill it Comes to the line between the third and fourth lots in fish street then by the line between Said third and fourth Lots to Back Street then by Said back street to the Place first Mentioned

The four going is a Just and Impartial Division of said Deceas'd Estate Not before Divided to the best of our Judgments Nottingham Decemb^{r} 5th 1782

Rice Rowell
John Harvey
Jonathan Gove } Committee
And^{w} Simpson
John Ford

[Bond of Matthew Nealey Sanborn, with Joseph Hodgdon and Joseph Nealey as sureties, all of Nottingham, in the sum of £200, April 12, 1783, to receive the real estate of his mother, Jane Sanborn of Nottingham, he being the oldest son, and to pay the other children their shares; witnesses, Nathaniel Parker, William Fogg.]

DUDLEY HARDY   1757   EXETER

[Administration on the estate of Dudley Hardy of Exeter, yeoman, granted to his widow, Mary Hardy, Aug. 31, 1757.]
[Probate Records, vol. 20, p. 272.]

[Bond of Mary Hardy of Exeter, widow, with Biley Hardy of Exeter and Jeremiah Hubbard of Kingston, yeomen, as sureties, in the sum of £500, Aug. 31, 1757, for the administration of the estate; witnesses, William Parker, John Parker.]

[Inventory, attested Oct. 25, 1757; amount, £6903. 9. 0; signed by James Gilman and John Odlin.]

[Administration de bonis non on the estate of Dudley Hardy granted to John Giddings March 29, 1769.]
[Probate Records, vol. 25, p. 369.]

[Bond of John Giddings, with Robert Hardy and Eliphalet Gilman, yeomen, as sureties, all of Exeter, in the sum of £500, March 29, 1769, for the administration of the estate; witnesses, William Parker, Samuel Hale, Jr.]

SAMUEL BUZZELL   1757   KINGSTON

[Administration on the estate of Samuel Buzzell of Kingston, yeoman, granted to William Buzzell of Kingston, yeoman, Aug. 31, 1757.]
[Probate Records, vol. 20, p. 272.]

[Bond of William Buzzell, with Jeremiah Hubbard and Samuel Roby as sureties, all of Kingston, yeomen, in the sum of £500, Aug. 31, 1757, for the administration of the estate; witnesses, William Parker, John Parker.]

[Warrant, Aug. 31, 1757, authorizing Samuel Winsley and Ebenezer Sleeper, both of Kingston, yeomen, to appraise the estate.]

[Inventory, attested Nov. 28, 1757; amount, £744. 2. 4; signed by Samuel Winsley and Ebenezer Sleeper.]

[Account of the settlement of the estate; receipts, £744. 2. 4, personal estate; expenditures, £744. 2. 1; allowed May 30, 1759.]

NATHANIEL BATCHELDER 1757   KENSINGTON

In the Name of God Amen: I Nathaniel Batcheldor of the Parish of Kensington in the Province of Newhampshire in New England yeoman being week of Body * * *

1ly I Give and Bequeath to my well beloved wife margaret Batchelder all my Stock of Creatures of all sorts excepting one Cow and I Give my Said wife all my moveables within Doars all to Despose as Shee shall See Cause and I Give my said wife the improvement of all my Real Estate untill my two sons Nathaniel and Joseph Shall Come to the age of twenty one years then my wife is to have the improvement of but one third of my Real Estate as long as Shee lives and at her Death then her thirds to go to those that I Shall Give it to in this my will and I Give my said wife my east fore Room to improve So long as Shee Continues my widow and no longer —

2ly I Give and Bequeath forever unto my two Sons Nathaniel Batchelder and Joseph Batchelder my house and Barn and all my land laying in Kensington and in hampton falls parish and allso all my salt marsh laying in partnership with Nathan Batchelder Said marsh lays at hampton Twon all my land above mentioned and marsh and house and Barn to be Equally Divided between them when they Come to the age of twenty one years only there mother is to improve as is above Exprest my two sons paying as I Shall order them in this my will

3ly I Give and Bequeath to my son John Batchelder all my land laying in the township of Nottingham forever it being one third of a two hundred acre lot

4ly I Give and Bequeath to my son Ephraim Batchelder

three hundred pounds money old tenor Bills of Credit or Equal there unto in silver at Dollars Six pound apiece to be paid to him by my two sons Nathaniel and Joseph to pay Equally alike and to be paid to my Said son Ephraim when he Shall Come to the age of Twenty one years

5ly I Give and Bequeath to my son Josiah Batchelder two hundred pounds money old tenor Bills of Credit or in Silver Equal thereunto Dollors at Six pound apiece to be paid to him by my two sons Nathaniel and Joseph Equelly alike to be paid to him when he Shall Come to the age of twenty one years

6ly I Give and Bequeath to my son Thomas Batchelder two hundred pounds money old tenor Bills of Credit or in Silver Equal thereunto in Dollors at Six pound apiece to be paid to him by my two sons Nathaniel and Joseph and to be paid to him when he Shall Come to the age of twenty one years

7ly I Give and Bequeath to my mother Sarah Batchelder one Cow and three sheep to be paid to her by my wife at my Decease and I Do Constitute and appoint my wife margeret Batchelder and my Brother Thomas Batchelder to be my Executors to this my last will and testament Rattifying and Confirming this and no other to be my Last will and testament In witness whereof I the Said Nathaniel Batchelder have hereunto set my hand and seal this seventh Day of september: anno: Domini: 1757 and in the thirty first year of the Reign of King George the second &c

           Nathaniel Batchelder

[Witnesses] Joseph Tilton, Nathan Batchelder, Benjamin Batchelder.

[Proved Aug. 9, 1764.]

[Warrant, Aug. 9, 1764, authorizing Jonathan Dow of Kensington, yeoman, and Jonathan Gilman of Exeter, innholder, to appraise the estate.]

[Inventory, Sept. 27, 1764; amount, £14,876. 10. 0; signed by Jonathan Dow and Jonathan Gilman.]

[Administration, with will annexed, granted to Winthrop Rowe March 27, 1765.]

[Probate Records, vol. 23, p. 410.]

[Bond of Winthrop Rowe of Kensington, with Nathaniel Healey, Jr., of Kensington, gentleman, and Thomas Rand of Hampton, gentleman, as sureties, in the sum of £5000, March 27, 1765, for the administration of the estate; witnesses, Joseph Pattinson, William Vaughan.]

[Guardianship of Josiah Batchelder and Ephraim Batchelder, minors, aged more than 14 years, granted to Joseph Tilton May 23, 1769.]

[Probate Records, vol. 25, p. 551.]

[Bond of Joseph Tilton of Kensington, with Timothy Tilton of Kingston as surety, in the sum of £500, May 23, 1769, for the guardianship of Josiah Batchelder and Ephraim Batchelder, sons of Nathaniel Batchelder; witnesses, John Wentworth, Jr., William Parker.]

Province of New Hamp^r } Pursuant to a Warrant to us directed from the hon^{ble} the Judge of the Probate of Wills &c for said Province authorizing & appointing us a Committee to divide a Lot of Land belonging to the heirs of Nathaniel Bachelder late of Kensington Deceased, and Sherburne Tilton of said Kensington lying in Common & undivided being the Lot originally granted to Aaron Morril Numbered thirteen in the Sixth Range in the third Division of Lots in Nottingham — We have proceeded And Set off to the Said Sherburne Tilton for his Third part of Said Lot one hundred & fifty Acres more or less off the Northeasterly End of said Lot, beginning at the Northeasterly End of said Lot & carrying the whole Breadth of Said Lot to run Southwesterly into Said Lot two hundred & thirty Rods & twelve feet —

2dly To Timothy Bachelder one of the sons of the Said Nathaniel Bachelder Deceased for his Share in the two thirds of said Lot we have set of four Acres & three Quarters more or less bounding on that part of said Lot set off to Sherburne Tilton & thence running Southwesterly carrying the whole breadth of Said Lot Seven Rods one Quarter & one foot —

3dly We have Set off to Samuel Bachelder another of the Sons of said Deceased four Acres & three Quarters more or less bounding on the part above mentioned to be set off to Timothy Bachelder & taking the whole breadth of said Lot to run Southwesterly into Said Lot Seven Rods one Quarter & one foot —

4ly We have Set off to Thomas Bachelder another Son of said Nathaniel Bachelder Deceased four Acres & three Quarters more or less bounding on the part abovementioned to be set off to Samuel Bachelder & Carrying the whole breadth of Said Lot to run thence Southwesterly into Said Lot Seven Rods one Quarter & one foot

5th To Josiah Bachelder another Son of Said Deceased we have set off four Acres & three Quarters more or less bounding on the Part Set off to Nathaniel Bachelder abovementioned & taking the whole breadth of Said Lot to Run thence Southwesterly into Said Lot Seven Rods one Quarter & one foot —

6th To Ephraim Bachelder another of the Sons of Said Deceased we have set off four Acres & three Quarters more or less beginning at the Share above set off to Josiah Bachelder & thence running Southwesterly into Said Lot carrying the whole breadth thereof Seven Rods & a Quarter & one foot —

7ly To Joseph Bachelder another Son of Said Deceased we have likewise set off four Acres & three Quarters more or less beginning at the Share set off to Ephraim Bachelder as before mentioned & Carrying the whole breadth of said Lot to run thence Southwesterly into Said Lot Seven Rods one Quarter & one foot —

8th To Nathaniel Bachelder another Son of Said Deceased we have set off Nine Acres & an half more or less bounded on the Share above mentioned to be set off to Joseph Bachelder & carrying the whole breadth of Said Lot to run thence Southwesterly fourteen Rods and an half & two feet —

9 To John Bachelder another of the Sons of Said Deceased all the Remainder of Said Lot we have set off bounding Northeasterly on the Share above mentioned to be set off to Nathaniel Bachelder & then running Southwesterly (Carrying the whole breadth of said Lot) to the Southwesterly end thereof being forty Acres more or less — Memorandum that thro all the Shares above mentioned to be Set off to the heirs of the said Nathaniel Bachelder deceased we have reserved & set off a Drift Way on the Northwesterly Side of Said Lot for the Said Tilton his heirs & Assigns to pass thro to his Said Share of Said Lot forever — Witness our hands the first Day of November Anno Domini 1769 —

       Joseph Wadleigh jr
       David Green
       winthrop Rowe

[Administrator's additional account; receipts, £91. 6. 8; expenditures, £93. 4. 4¾; allowed Sept. 26, 1781.]

ABRAHAM MOULTON 1757 KENSINGTON

In the Name of God Amen I Abraham Moulton of Kensington in the Province of New Hampshire yeoman being infirm in body * * *

Item As it has pleased God in his holy Providence to deprive my two Daughters Mary & Elizabeth of the Exercise of their Reason, I give Each of them only five Shillings old Ten^r to be at their Disposal, & for the further Maintaining them I Will & order that my Daughter Huldah Hilyard take the Care & be at the trouble & Charge of maintaining & keeping the one of them vizt my Daughter Elizabeth, and that my Daughter Dorothy Page take the Care & be at the Charge & trouble of keeping & maintaining the other vizt my Daughter Mary — for which purpose, & on Condition of the faithful performance whereof I Give Devise & bequeath unto my said Daughters

Huldah Hilyard (the wife of Joseph Chase Hilyard) & Dorothy Page (the wife of James Page) & to the Heirs & assigns of them my said Daughters respectively forever, All my Real Estate wherever the same is or may be found, to be equally Divided between them —

I further will & order that in Case one of my Said Daughters mary & Elizabeth, die before the other that the surviving one be equally maintained by my said Daughters to whom I have given my real Estate —

Item I Give & bequeath to my Daughter Dorothy Page her heirs & assigns my Riding Mare & one Cow & five Sheep and all my Implements of husbandry, two feather beds & bedding, a brass kettle, & great Iron Pot & a small one, with a fire shovel & Tongs, & a warming pan, & all my Chairs & my Round Table & largest & square Table & one Dozen of pewter plates and three pewter Platters not the largest, all my wooden Trays plates & Dishes & my moveable pine Closet or Cupboard, & all my wife's (her mother's) wearing apparrel, & my Great Bible —

Item all the rest & residue of my Estate of what nature or Kind soever I give & bequeath to my Daughter's Huldah Hilyard & Dorothy Page their heirs & Assigns to be equally Divided between them

Item I will & order that my Daughter Hilyard have & hold to herself her heirs & Assigns the westerly half of my Dwelling house And my Daughter Page her heirs & Assigns the Easterly half of my said Dwelling house The Division of every other thing herein bequeathed them I leave to be made by them —

Item I hereby constitute & appoint my Sons in Law Joseph Chase Hilyard & James Page Executors * * * In Witness whereof I have hereunto set my hand & Seal the Tenth day of September Anno Domini one thousand Seven hundred & fifty Seven —

            Abraham Moulton

[Witnesses] John Page, Caleb Shaw, Wm Parker j^r.
[Proved Dec. 17, 1761.]

WILLIAM LANCEY 1757 NASHUA

[Administration on the estate of William Lancey of Dunstable, yeoman, granted to William Lancey of Souhegan West, husbandman, Sept. 12, 1757.]

[Probate Records, vol. 20, p 425.]

[Bond of William Lancey, with Samuel Lamson and Ebenezer Lyon, both of Souhegan West, husbandmen, as sureties, in the sum of £500, Sept. 12, 1757, for the administration of the estate of his father, William Lancey; witnesses, Benjamin Wright, Jonathan Lovewell.]

[Warrant, Sept. 12, 1757, authorizing John Alld and Nehemiah Lovewell, both of Dunstable, yeomen, to appraise the estate.]

[Inventory, Jan. 11, 1758; amount, £1049. 3. 0; signed by John Alld and Nehemiah Lovewell.]

[Commission to John Alld and David Hobart, both of Dunstable, yeomen, to receive claims against the estate.]

[List of claims, Oct. 3, 1758; amount, £2650. 6. 2; signed by John Alld and David Hobart.]

[Account of the settlement of the estate; receipts, £1554. 6. 0; expenditures, £226. 8. 3; allowed Nov. 17, 1758.]

[Settlement of claims; amount of claims, £2650. 6. 2; amount distributed, £1327. 17. 9; allowed Dec. 2, 1758.]

EZEKIEL SANBORN 1757 NEWMARKET

[Elizabeth Sanborn renounces administration on the estate of her husband in favor of her son, Jonathan Sanborn, Sept. 14, 1757; witnesses, Samuel Weeks, Moses Coffin.]

[Administration on the estate of Ezekiel Sanborn of Newmarket, yeoman, granted to Edward Sanborn and Jonathan Sanborn, both of Newmarket, husbandmen, Sept. 15, 1757.]

[Probate Records, vol. 20, p. 288.]

[Bond of Edward Sanborn and Jonathan Sanborn, with Josiah Burleigh and John Pike as sureties, all of Newmarket, husbandmen, in the sum of £500, Sept. 15, 1757, for the administration of the estate; witnesses, William Parker, Edward Eastman.]

[Warrant, Sept. 15, 1757, authorizing Jonathan Gilman of Exeter and Moses Coffin of Epping, yeomen, to appraise the estate.]

[Inventory, Nov., 1757; amount, £12,107. 14. 0; signed by Jonathan Gilman and Moses Coffin.]

[Account of the settlement of the estate; receipts, £3605. 2. 0, personal estate; expenditures, £1498. 4. 0; allowed Sept. 27, 1758.]

MERIBAH CONNOR   1757   KINGSTON

In the Name of God, Amen. I Meribah Conner of Kingston in the Province of New-Hamshire Widow * * *

Secondly I give & bequeath to my nephew Amasa Dow of s^d Kingston & the Children which He now hath, all my Estate Personal & Real to be at His & their disposal, to His & their use & Behoof forever.

Thirdly, I constitute & appoint s^d Amasa Dow to be my Sole Executor to this my Last Will & Testament * * *

In Wittness whereof I have hereunto sett my Hand & Seal this twentieth Day of September in the Year of our Lord one thousand seven Hundred & fifty seven

             her
          Meribah + Connor
             Mark

[Witnesses] Sanders Carr, Edward Sleeper, Micah Brooks.
[Proved Nov. 30, 1757.]

[Bond of Amasa Dow, with Edward Sleeper and Micah Brooks as sureties, all of Kingston, in the sum of £500, Nov. 30, 1757, for the execution of the will; witnesses, William Parker, David Sewall.]

SAMUEL FRENCH, JR.   1757   SOUTH HAMPTON

In the Name of God Amen. I Samuel French Junr of South-Hampton in the Province of New Hampshire in New-England Husbandman being under bodily Weakness * * *

Item — Secondly I give to my Well beloved Wife Mary French the use and Improvement of my Home Lots with the buildings thereon. I also give her the use and Improvement of my Stock and moveables of all kinds untill my son Samuel French shall arrive at the Age of Twenty one years, and then my Son Samuel Shall have Liberty to live in the House with his mother if he sees fit. Then I give her the use of part of the House, the Barn, and one third Part of my home Lots, she taking her third on the North Side of the High way where the Buildings now stand, these I give her the Improvement of so long as She remains my Widow. I also give her the use and Improvement of my Lands in Kingston untill my Son Henry French Shall arrive at the age of Twenty one years. I also give her, her Fire Wood, So long as she remains my widow, she taking it off of my Kingston Lands. I also give her all my Household Goods, Household Stuff, and household Moveables to dispose of how and when she sees fit. My Will also is that she maintains my son Ezekiel French till he arrives at the age of Twenty one years, and my Daughter Mary French till she arrives at the age of Eighteen years.

Item — Thirdly I give to my Son Ruben French Fifty Pounds old Tenor Money, Bills of Credit, retaining its present Value to be paid him by my Son Samuel French hereafter named, any time within three years after he arrives at the Age of Twenty one years

Item — Fourthly I give to my Son Green French Fifty Pounds old Tenor Money Bills of Credit, retaining its present Value to be paid him by my Son Samuel French hereafter named, any time within three years after he arrives at the Age of Twenty one years.

Item   Fifthly, I give to my Daughter Ruth French Fifty

Pounds old Tenor Money Bills of Credit, retaining its present Value to be paid her by my Son Samuel French hereafter named, any time within three years after he arrives at the Age of Twenty one years.

Item — Sixthly. I give to my Daughter Deborah French Fifty Pounds old Tenor Money, Bills of Credit, retaining its present Value to be paid her by my son Samuel French hereafter named, any time within three years after he arrives at the Age of Twenty one years.

Item — Seventhly. I give to my Daughter Hannah French Fifty Pounds old Tenor Money, Bills of Credit, retaining its present Value to be paid her by my son Samuel French hereafter named, any time within three years after he arrives at the age of Twenty one years.

Item — Eighthly. I give to my Daughter Mary French Fifty Pounds old Tenor Money, Bills of Credit, retaining its present Value to be paid her by my Son Samuel French hereafternamed, any time within three years after he arrives at the Age of Twenty one years.

Item — Ninthly. I give to my Sons Henry French and Ezekiel French my Lands in Kingston after my Debts are paid, Excepting fire wood which I before reserved for the use of my Wife so long as she remains my Widow. That is to Say, I Give to my Son Henry French the use and Improvement of my Lands in Kingston, after he Shall arrive at the age of twenty one years. This I give him the use and Improvement of until my Son Ezekiel French Shall arrive at the Age of Twenty one years, and then my Will is that the Said Kingston Lands are Equally divided between them that is to say between the Said Henry and Ezekiel French. This I give to them, their Heirs and Assigns for Ever.

Item — Tenthly I give to my Son Samuel French the Liberty of living in my House with his mother as long as he sees fit. My Will also is that my son Samuel French pays the foregoing Legacies which I have bequeathed and given to my Children within the Time beforementioned, that is to say To Ruben, To

Green, To Ruth, To Deborah, To Hannah and to Mary French Fifty Pounds Each. And when he arrives at the Age of Twenty one years I give him the use and Improvement of two Thirds of my Home Lots, during my wifes Widowhood. I also give to him his Heirs and Assigns forever and Liberty to dispose of the Same, when and to whom he pleases, after he arrives at the age of Twenty one years, that part of my home Lot upon the South Side of the High Way, And that Part of my home Lot upon the North side of the High Way with the Buildings thereon I give him the use and Improvement of, After the Decease or marriage of my Wife, during his natural Life, and then to his Eldest Heir and assigns for ever. I also give him all my stock of Cattle and Husbandry utensils after he arrives at the age of Twenty one years, to dispose of, how, when and to whom he pleases.

Finally — I do make Ordain and Constitute my Well beloved Wife Mary French to be sole Executrix * * * In Witness Whereof I have hereunto Set my Hand and Seal this Twenty Second Day of September Anno Domini One Thousand Seven Hundred and Fifty Seven, and in the Thirty First year of the Reign of George the Second King Over Great Britain &c.

         Samuell french Juner

  his
[Witnesses] Henry + French, Benjmin morrill, James French.
  Mark

[Endorsed "presented for Proof the last Wendsday in October proof was suspended on & again & at Length Disallowed for want of Proof."]

[Warrant, Oct. 27, 1757, authorizing Samuel French, gentleman, and Abner Morrill, yeoman, both of South Hampton, to appraise the estate.]

[Inventory, Nov. 5, 1757; amount, £3064. 11. 0; signed by Samuel French and Abner Morrill.]

[Administration on the estate of Samuel French, Jr., granted to his widow, Mary French, Dec. 28, 1757.]

[Probate Records, vol. 20, p. 435.]

[Bond of Mary French, widow, with Samuel French, gentleman, and Joseph Whiter, yeoman, as sureties, all of South Hampton, in the sum of £1000, Dec. 28, 1757, for the administration of the estate; witnesses, Reuben French, Moses French, Joseph French, Hannah French.]

To the Honor[ble] Judge of Probate in y[e] Province of New Hampshire

Hon[rd] S[r]   I Being with m[r] Sam[el] French Late of South Hamton And Haveing y[e] Care of him as a Phisition frequently visited him in his Last sickness am fully of y[e] opinion that he was Not for some Month before his Death in a Capacity of acting or Transacting Any Bisness of Importance Rationally being to Impared in his Reason

Amesbury Decemb[r] y[e] 23rd 1757   Nehemiah Ordway

South-Hampton Dec: 31, 1757

S[r] I am informed you are desirous of having my Thoughts concerning Samuel French late of this Town deceas[d], whether he was a Person of Sound Judment and of Perfect Mind and Memory when he made his Will.

To which I Say, that I do not Imagine that he was a Person of sound Judgment And I also believe his Powers to be much Weakned by Reason of his long Sickness. I visited him often in his Sickness, Especially in the latter Part of it, and some times thought him some thing Delirious. He insisted much upon my writing his Will, And when I wrote, I asked him some Questions concerning his Will why he made it as he did? And he gave me his Reasons which I thought had some Weight in them. But notwithstanding his Reasons, it is doubtful with me, whether he was so capable of disposing of his Estate as he was before his Sickness

From your Humble Serv[t]   William Parsons

PETER POWERS   1757   HOLLIS

[Administration on the estate of Peter Powers of Hollis, gentleman, granted to Stephen Powers of Hollis, yeoman, Jan. 6, 1758.]

[Probate Records, vol. 20, p. 411.]

[Bond of Stephen Powers of Hollis, with Jacob Bailey of Hampstead, gentleman, and Abel Webster of Hollis, yeoman, as sureties, in the sum of £3000, Jan. 6, 1758, for the administration of the estate; witnesses, David Sewall, Elizabeth Adams.]

[Warrant, Jan. 6, 1758, authorizing Benjamin Blanchard and Abel Webster, both of Hollis, yeomen, to appraise the estate; mentions Stephen Powers as son of the deceased.]

[Inventory, Sept. 23, 1757; amount, £2166. 15. 3; signed by Jeremiah Lawrence, Benjamin Blanchard, and Abel Webster; an addition of £40. 18. 6 was made June 12, 1758.]

[Warrant, Sept. 14, 1758, authorizing Jonathan Lovewell of Dunstable, gentleman, Francis Worcester, and Benjamin Blanchard, yeomen, both of Hollis, to set off the widow's dower.]

Province of } Pursuant To a Warrant from the Hon[ble]
N. Hamp[r] } Richard Wibird Esq Judge of the Probate of Wills &c for Said Province — Directed to us the Subscribers with Jon[a] Lovewell Esq appointing us a Committee to Value appraise & Set off to Anna Powers of Hollis In Said Province Widow Relict of Peter Powers Late of Hollis aforesaid Gent. Deceased Intestate (her former husband) her Dower which happens to her of the Real Estate of the Said Intestate & of which he Died Seized & to Set forth the same By metes & Bounds to hold to her In Severalty as her thirds In Said Estate and the Premises hereafter Described we Adjudge to be Equal to One third part of the Real Estate of the Said Deceased which we Set off to her as follows — Begining at a Stake & Stones the Northwest Corner of the Premises w[ch] is Deacon Worsters Corner &

Runing from thence East Seventy two Rods & an half to a Stake & Stones by the Road Leading from Josiah Bloods to the Widow Conants thence Southerly by Said Road one hundred & four Rods To a Stake & Stones by Josiah Bloods Land thence West Seventy two and an half Rods To a Stake & Stones thence West by the Revd Mr Joseph Emersons Land & Land of Benjamin Blanchard one hundred & four Rods to the Bounds first mentioned with the One half part of the house & Barn Standing on Said Prem^s which was part of the homestead of the Said Dece^d as also ye Pew In ye meetinghouse In Hollis

Novr 7th 1759 — Benjamin Blanchard Jun.
                        Francis Worcester Juner

[List of claims against the estate; amount, £15,570. 3. 6; signed by Matthew Thornton and Francis Worcester; attested July 31, 1759.]

[Account of the administrator; receipts, £15,405. 7. 4; expenditures, £5048. 6. 8; allowed Jan. 30, 1762.]

[Settlement of claims; amount of claims, £15,070. 5. 6; amount distributed, £10,357. 0. 8; allowed Feb. 2, 1762.]

[Additional account of the administrator; receipts, £274. 11. 4; expenditures, £188. 16. 6; allowed Aug. 27, 1773.]

[Additional distribution of £1714. 16. 8 to the creditors; allowed Sept. 9, 1773.]

[Bond of Francis Powers of Hollis, cordwainer, with Joseph Bailey, joiner, and John Dwinell, yeoman, both of Londonderry, as sureties, in the sum of £1000, April 21, 1791, for the administration de bonis non of the estate; witnesses, Nathaniel Parker, John Nesmith, Jr.]

ROBERT ALLEN   1757   LONDONDERRY

[Margaret Lee of Boston, Mass., renounces administration on the estate of her son, Robert Allen, who "dyed Comming down from the Camp", in favor of William Clendenin, Sept. 26, 1757.]

[Administration on the estate of Robert Allen of Londonderry, husbandman, granted to William Clendenin, gentleman, Sept. 27, 1757.]

[Probate Records, vol. 20, p. 298.]

[Bond of William Clendenin, gentleman, with James Wilson, yeoman, and David Hopkins, cordwainer, as sureties, all of Londonderry, in the sum of £500, Sept. 27, 1757, for the administration of the estate; witnesses, William Parker, David Sewall.]

[Warrant, Sept. 27, 1757, authorizing James Wilson and Matthew Reid, both of Londonderry, yeomen, to appraise the estate.]

[Inventory, Oct. 6, 1757; amount, £198. 12. 0; signed by James Wilson and Matthew Reid.]

[Account of the settlement of the estate; receipts, £570. 2. 0; expenditures, £239. 15. 6; allowed Nov. 1, 1758.]

ELIZABETH SMITH   1757   KINGSTON

[Administration on the estate of Elizabeth Smith of Kingston granted to Nathaniel Smith Sept. 26, 1757.]

[Probate Records, vol. 20, p. 296.]

[Bond of Nathaniel Smith of Epping, with Daniel Smith of Kingston and Nathaniel Gordon of Exeter as sureties, yeomen all, in the sum of £500, Sept. 26, 1757, for the administration of the estate of his mother, Elizabeth Smith; witnesses, William Parker, Benjamin Rolfe.]

[Warrant, Sept. 26, 1757, authorizing Theophilus Smith of Exeter and Biley Lyford of Brentwood, yeoman, to appraise the estate.]

[Inventory, Oct. 11, 1757; amount, £2354. 8. 0; signed by Theophilus Smith and Biley Lyford.]

[Additional inventory by the administrator of "Debts Due to The Estate of my Houn^d Father Nathaniel Smith & mother Elisabeth Smith both Late of Kingstown Deceased", Aug. 29, 1758; amount, £2040. 11. 0.]

[Account of the settlement of the estate; receipts, £3381. 8. 10; expenditures, £77. 0. 0; allowed Aug. 30, 1758. Additional account, Aug. 12, 1760, of receipts of £88. 4. 0, and expenditures of £12. 16. 0.]

ANDREW SMITH 1757 LONDONDERRY

In the name of God amene I Andrew Smith of Londonderry in the province of Newhampshire in New england being sick and wekly of bodey * * *

Itam my will is that my aged and Honred mother shall have and Injoy all my personal estate in fee to hir and hir assigns for ever she Cliring and paying my funnral Charges

Itam I Give and bequith to my Sister Susanna Smith one quarter parte of my Reall estate with the quarter parte of the buldins and Improvements ther on in fee Sempel which is in full for all Legesies and bequithments that I the testator was in any ways to Give hir by my fathers Last will and testement

Itam I Give and bequith unto my brother in Law James petterson who is married to my sister Rachel one hundred and fiftey pounds old tenor to be paid by my brother william smith hear after mentioned as also the one half of my part of the Saw mill Iorns

Itam I Give and bequith unto my brother In law Jonathan Adams who is married to my Sister Sarah Smith one hundred and fiftey pounds old tenor to be paid by my brother william smith hear after mentioned

Itam I Give and bequith to my brother william smith all the

other three quarters of my Reall estate with the buldins and Improvements ther on in fee simpel to him his heirs and assigns for ever and my part of the Saw mill with the one half of the Iorns of the Same he paying the before mentioned Legises and performing and full filling all the Deuteys to my Honr'ed mother that I the testator was oblidged to Do and perform by my Honr'ed fathers Last will and testement: and also to pay to my sister Sarah Smith wife to Jonathan Adams three hundred pounds old tenor that I the testator was oblidged to pay by my said fathers testement

and I Do appoint make and ordain my brother william smith of the Town and province aforesaid to be my exacutore * * * in wittnes whear of I have hear unto Sett my hand and Seal this twintey six Day of September in the thirty first year of His majisty's Rign ann Dom: on thousand Seven hundred and fiftey Seven

Andrew Smith

[Witnesses] James Nodd, John Bell, Samuel Barr.
[Proved March 11, 1760.]

[Administration on the estate of Andrew Smith, yeoman, granted to William Smith of Londonderry, yeoman, March 11, 1760.]

[Probate Records, vol. 21, p. 395.]

[Bond of William Smith, yeoman, with Samuel Barr and John Bell, yeoman, as sureties, all of Londonderry, in the sum of £500, March 11, 1760, for the execution of the will; witnesses, none.]

ISAAC GRIFFIN   1757   KINGSTON

[Administration on the estate of Isaac Griffin of Kingston granted to Mary Griffin, widow, Sept. 28, 1757.]

[Probate Records, vol. 20, p. 308.]

[Bond of Mary Griffin, widow, with Abraham Smith, gentleman, and John Darling, yeoman, as sureties, all of Kingston, in the sum of £500, Sept. 28, 1757, for the administration of the estate of her husband, Isaac Griffin; witnesses, Jeremy Webster, Mary Blake.]

[Warrant, Sept. 28, 1757, authorizing Jeremy Webster and Josiah Tilton, both of Kingston, to appraise the estate.]

[Inventory, Oct. 3, 1757; amount, £4372. 10. 0; signed by Jeremy Webster and Josiah Tilton.]

[Account of the settlement of the estate; receipts, £1512. 10. 0, personal estate; expenditures, £1744. 5. 0; mentions "Support of two Children both under Seven from the Death of Said Intestate to this Day being 73 Weaks Each"; allowed Jan. 15, 1759.]

WILLIAM ADAMS   1757   HOLLIS

[Administration on the estate of William Adams of Hollis granted to Mary Adams, widow, Sept. 28, 1757.]

[Probate Records, vol. 20, p. 304.]

[Bond of Mary Adams, widow, with Samuel Cummings, gentleman, and Jonas Flagg, yeoman, as sureties, all of Hollis, in the sum of £500, Sept. 28, 1757, for the administration of the estate; witnesses, William Parker and John Pendexter.]

[Inventory, Sept. 21, 1757; amount, £3120. 13. 0; signed by Samuel Farley and Stephen Ames.]

[Administratrix's account of the settlement of the estate; receipts, personal estate, £970. 13. 0; expenditures, £1656. 9. 6; allowed July 28, 1762; mentions "maintaining one of the dec^d Children und^r 7 years of age 3½ years . . . another of his Children 4 years ¾ and three Weeks."]

[Guardianship of Mary Adams, daughter of William Adams, granted to Stephen Ames Aug. 12, 1762.]
[Probate Records, vol. 22, p. 433.]

[Bond of Stephen Ames, with Stephen Powers and Jonas Flagg as sureties, all of Hollis, in the sum of £500, Aug. 12, 1762, for the guardianship of Mary Adams; witnesses, William Vaughan, William Parker.]

[Administratrix's additional account; receipts, £546. 0. 0, or £27. 6. 0, lawful money; expenditures, £44. 7. 10; allowed Oct. 26, 1768.]

SAMUEL BATCHELDER   1757   KENSINGTON

[Administration on the estate of Samuel Batchelder of Kensington granted to Mercy Batchelder, widow, Sept. 28, 1757.]
[Probate Records, vol. 20, p. 308.]

[Bond of Mercy Batchelder of Kensington, widow, with Phineas Batchelder and Ebenezer Batchelder, both of Kingston, yeomen, as sureties, in the sum of £500, Sept. 28, 1757, for the administration of the estate; witnesses, William Parker, Benjamin Rolfe.]

[Warrant, Sept. 28, 1757, authorizing Phineas Batchelder of Kingston and William Parker of Kensington, gentleman, to appraise the estate.]

[Inventory, Nov. 10, 1757; amount, £5760. 5. 0; signed by Phineas Batchelder and William Parker.]

[Account of the settlement of the estate; receipts, £2020. 5. 0, personal estate; expenditures, £421. 5. 0; mentions "Maintaining a Son of the Deceased named Samuel under 7 years of age 52 Week . . . . maintaining a Daughter of the Deceased named Sarah 36 Week"; allowed Oct. 4, 1758.]

ELEAZER CUMMINGS   1757   HUDSON

[Administration on the estate of Eleazer Cummings of Nottingham West granted to Martha Cummings, widow, Sept. 28, 1757.]

[Probate Records, vol. 20, p. 298.]

[Bond of Martha Cummings, widow, with John Marsh and Thomas Marsh, yeomen, as sureties, all of Nottingham West, in the sum of £1000, Sept. 28, 1757, for the administration of the estate; witnesses, Richard Greeley, William Parker.]

HENRY HILLS   1757   HUDSON

[Dorcas Hills of Nottingham West renounces administration on the estate of her husband, Henry Hills of Nottingham West, Sept. 21, 1757.]

[Administration on the estate of Henry Hills, yeoman, granted to Ezekiel Hills, yeoman, Sept. 28, 1757.]

[Probate Records, vol. 20, p. 308.]

[Bond of Ezekiel Hills of Nottingham West, with Henry Hills of Nottingham West and Ebenezer Richardson of Pelham as sureties, yeomen all, in the sum of £500, Sept. 28, 1757, for the administration of the estate; witnesses, William Parker, John Wingate.]

[Warrant, Sept. 28, 1757, authorizing Samuel Greeley and Samuel Hills, both of Nottingham West, yeomen, to appraise the estate, administration being granted to Ezekiel Hills, son of the deceased.]

[Inventory, attested Oct. 17, 1757; amount, £2453. 10. 0; signed by Samuel Greeley, Jr., and Samuel Hills.]

ABRAHAM SANBORN 1757 KENSINGTON

[Administration on the estate of Abraham Sanborn granted to his widow, Dorothy Sanborn, Sept. 28, 1757.]

[Probate Records, vol. 20, p. 309.]

[Bond of Dorothy Sanborn, widow, with Theophilus Smith of Exeter and Jonathan Prescott of Kensington, blacksmith, as sureties, in the sum of £500, Sept. 28, 1757, for the administration of the estate of Abraham Sanborn of Kensington, gentleman; witnesses, Ebenezer Light, John Nelson.]

[Warrant, Sept. 28, 1757, authorizing Samuel Prescott of Hampton Falls and Joseph Tilton of Kensington, gentleman, to appraise the estate.]

[Inventory, Nov. 24, 1757; amount, £17,016. 8. 0; signed by Samuel Prescott and Joseph Tilton.]

PHINEAS UNDERWOOD 1757 MERRIMACK

[Administration on the estate of Phineas Underwood of Merrimack granted to Mary Underwood, widow, Sept. 28, 1757.]

[Probate Records, vol. 20, p. 309.]

[Bond of Mary Underwood, widow, with Joseph Blanchard, Jr., and Jonathan Cummings, gentleman, as sureties, all of Merrimack, in the sum of £500, Sept. 28, 1757, for the administration of the estate; witnesses, Samuel Cummings, Jotham Blanchard.]

[Warrant, Sept. 28, 1757, authorizing Joseph Blanchard, Jr., and Jonathan Cummings, gentleman, both of Merrimack, to appraise the estate.]

[Inventory, Oct. 27, 1757; amount, £6692. 1. 0; signed by Joseph Blanchard, Jr., and Jonathan Cummings.]

[Account of the settlement of the estate; receipts, £2140. 13. 6, personal estate; expenditures, £1470. 19. 6; mentions "Bringing up two Children under 7 from the Intestates decease to this Day being 176 Weeks for one"; allowed June 7, 1759.]

NEHEMIAH STEVENS   1757   HAMPSTEAD

[Administration on the estate of Nehemiah Stevens of Hampstead granted to Anna Stevens, widow, Sept. 29, 1757.]

[Probate Records, vol. 20, p. 309.]

[Bond of Anna Stevens, widow, with John Muzzey and Stephen Johnson, Jr., yeomen, as sureties, all of Hampstead, in the sum of £500, Sept. 29, 1757, for the administration of the estate; witnesses, Stephen Emerson, John Mills.]

[Warrant, Sept. 29, 1757, authorizing Thomas Wells of Chester, gentleman, and John Muzzey of Hampstead, yeoman, to appraise the estate.]

[Inventory, attested Oct. 18, 1757; amount, £1922. 18. 0; signed by Thomas Wells and John Muzzey.]

[Account of the settlement of the estate; receipts, £722. 18. 0, personal estate; expenditures, £1093. 19. 0; mentions "there being 3 Children, 2 under Seven . . . . maintainance of two Children of the Intestate under 7 years Nine years"; allowed Oct. 17, 1769.]

[Citation to the administratrix, April 7, 1773, to appear and account for the income of the estate.]

[Additional account; receipts, £27. 3. 4; expenditures, £21. 2. 0½; allowed April 28, 1773.]

JOHN STEVENS   1757   CHESTER

[Administration on the estate of John Stevens of Chester, yeoman, granted to John Stevens of Chester Sept. 29, 1757.]

[Probate Records, vol. 20, p. 309.]

[Bond of John Stevens, husbandman, with Samuel Emerson and Thomas Wells, gentlemen, as sureties, all of Chester, in the sum of £500, Sept. 29, 1757, for the administration of the estate of his father, John Stevens; witnesses, Jethro Sanborn, Elizabeth Sanborn.]

[Warrant, Sept. 29, 1757, authorizing Samuel Emerson and Thomas Wells, gentleman, both of Chester, to appraise the estate.]

[Inventory, Oct. 6, 1757; amount, £3118. 19. 0; signed by Samuel Emerson and Thomas Wells.]

[Timothy Stevens, aged more than 14 years, son of John Stevens, makes choice of Stephen Johnson, Jr., of Hampstead as his guardian Dec. 21, 1757; witnesses, John Kezar, Benjamin Little.]

[Guardianship of Timothy Stevens granted to Stephen Johnson Dec. 28, 1757.]

[Probate Records, vol. 20, p. 394.]

[Bond of Stephen Johnson, Jr., yeoman, with John Hogg, gentleman, and John Muzzey, yeoman, as sureties, all of Hampstead, in the sum of £500, Dec. 28, 1757, for the guardianship of Timothy Stevens; witnesses, William Parker, David Sewall.]

[Account of the settlement of the estate; receipts as per inventory; expenditures, £357. 17. 6; filed May 27, 1761.]

MATTHEW NELSON   1757   PORTSMOUTH

[Administration on the estate of Matthew Nelson of Portsmouth granted to Deliverance Nelson, widow, and John Nelson, husbandman, Oct. 1, 1757.]

[Probate Records, vol. 20, p. 309.]

[Bond of Deliverance Nelson, widow, and John Nelson, husbandman, with Henry Sherburne, gentleman, and Walker Lear, yeoman, as sureties, all of Portsmouth, in the sum of £500, Oct. 1, 1757, for the administration of the estate of Matthew Nelson, cordwainer; witness, Hunking Wentworth.]

[Warrant, Oct. 1, 1757, authorizing Henry Sherburne and George Waldron, both of Portsmouth, gentlemen, to appraise the estate.]

[Inventory, attested Nov. 30, 1757; amount, £6441. 6. 0; signed by Henry Sherburne and George Waldron.]

[Additional inventories of £170. 10. 0, Oct. 23, 1758, and £19. 0. 0, Nov. 29, 1758; signed as above.]

[Account of the settlement of the estate; receipts, £1971. 16. 4, personal estate; expenditures, £1380. 0. 7; allowed Feb. 28, 1759.]

[Warrant, April 15, 1762, authorizing William Shackford, John Shackford, Joseph Langdon, gentleman, George Waldron, yeoman, all of Portsmouth, and Richard Jenness, 3d, of Rye to divide the real estate.]

Province of New Hamp[r] } We the Subscribers by a Warrant to us from the Hon[ble] Rich[d] Wibird Esq[r] Judge of the Probate of Wills &[c] for Said Province have Divided the Real Estate of Matthew Nelson Late of Portsmouth Deceased intestate in the manner following Viz

to the wedow Deleverance Nelson all the Land & marsh on the East Side of the high way being 12 acres also half an acre where

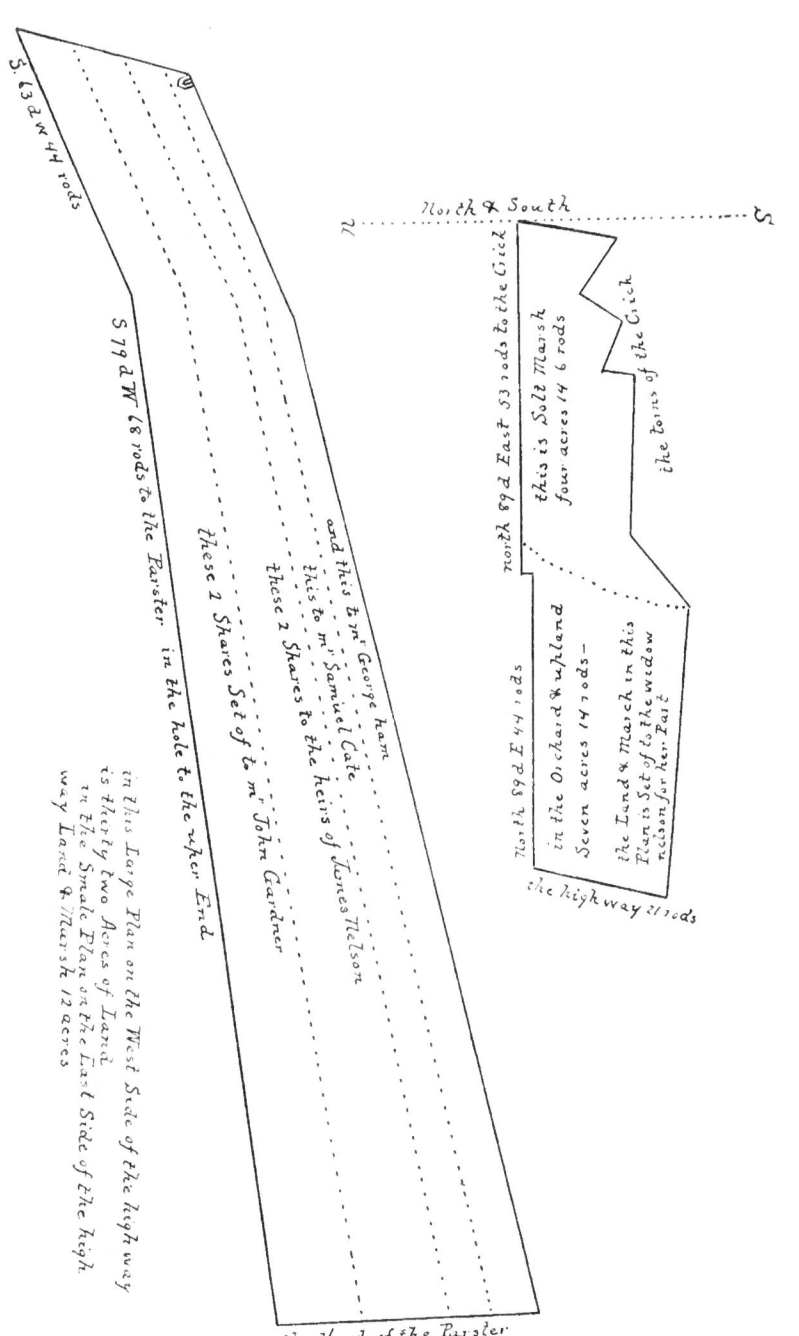

the house Stands as it is bounded out by Stacks also the west End of the house as fur as the Chimney & Doer the East End of the Seler with Leberty to Pase to & from Said Seler also one third of the barn at the west End

the Remander we have Divided in the following maner

1   2 Parts that m^r John Gardner bought of John Nelson as his Part and Philip babb in the Right of his wife on the North Side being aboute thirteen acres and halfe Eight Rods & 12 feet by the high way at the torn of the fence in the feld Eight Rods one foot and halfe and at the head of the Parstor thirteen Rods & Six feet to Staks in the Ground

2   2 Shares to the heirs of James Nelson Late of Portsmouth Deceased Said James being the oldest Son of the afore Said Matthew Nelson bounding northerly on the afore Said John Gardner Eight Rods & 12 feet by the above Said high way at the torn of the fence in the feld Eight Rods one foot and halfe and at the head of the Parster thirteen Rods & Six feet to Staks in the Ground with that Part of the barn Standing on Said Land Exsept that Part of the Barn Set of to the wedow as above Said

3   one Share to m^r Sam^{ll} Cate with the 2 Shares Set of to the heirs of the Oldest Son on the North Side that the Said Cate bought of George Nelson bounding four Rods and Six feet on the afore Said high way four Rods & one foot at the torn of the fence in the feld and at the head of the Parster Six Rods and 12 feet to Stakes in the Ground

4   the Remander being the Sixth Share we have Set of to George ham in the Right of his wife She being the youngest Daugester Lying on the South Side of the above Said Land

it is further agread that the wedow Deleverance Nelson Shall have the whole of the above said house to make Good her third Duering her Life the 11 day of May 1762

                        W: Shackford
                        Joseph Langdon
                        John Shackford
                        Richd Jenness 3^d

BRADSTREET WIGGIN 1757   STRATHAM

In the Name of God Amen The fifth Day of october Anno Domini one Thousand Seven hundred and fifty Seven — I Bradstreet wiggin of Stratham in the province of Newhampshire in Newengland Yeoman Being very Sick and week in Body * * *

Ittem I Give and Bequeth unto my apprentice Joseph Dennet one hundred acres of Land in a place Called New Salam in the province afore Said in the Second or Third Devison to him his heirs and assigns provided he Sarves out his Time Till he arives to the age of Twenty one years and aquits the oxen and a Trade mentioned in his Indenturs —

Ittem I Give and Bequeath unto my Three Sons Coker wiggin winterop wiggin and Chace wiggin all my Land and medow Ground Thatch Ground orchard and Buildings in Stratham afore Said and all my Land in the Township of Bow in Said province and in New Salam in Said province or any other place (Excepting the hundred acres Given to Joseph Dennet) after My Debts and funeral Charges are paid Equally to be Devided amongst them the Said Coker Winterop and Chace for quantity and quality —

Ittem I Give unto My Daughter Martha wiggin fifty pounds Money Equal to Dollers at Six pounds apeace To be paid her by my Son Coker wiggin when She arives to the age of Twenty years

Ittem I Give unto my Daughter Comfort wiggin fifty pounds Money Equal To Dollers and Six pounds apeace to be paid her by My Son winterop wiggin when Shee arives to the age of Twenty years —

Ittem I Give unto My Daughter Anna Wiggin fifty pounds Money To be paid Equal to Dollers at Six pound apeace to her by my Son Chace Wiggin when Shee arives to the age of Twenty years — and in Case My personal Estate prove Insufficent to pay my Debts and funeral Charges I Give My Executors here after named full power to Sell So much of my Real Estate as

Shall be Sufficent to pay the Remainder where thay Shall Think most proper

Ittem I Constitute Make and ordain my unkle Thomas wiggin Jun[r] and my Brother Chace wiggin the Executors * * *

Bradstret Wiggin
his

[Witnesses] John piper, Sam[ll] + piper Jun[r], Rich[d] Young.
Mark

[Proved Oct. 26, 1757.]

[Inventory, Oct. 27, 1757; amount, £11,638. 5. 6; signed by Stephen Boardman and Andrew Wiggin.]

[Account of the settlement of the estate; receipts, £2945. 17. 6; expenditures, £4486. 18. 0; mentions "Maintainance of Nancy one of the Dec[d] Children 8 Months .... Maintainance of Comfort another Daughter 21 Months .... Maintainance of Martha another Daughter three years .... Funeral Charges of two of the Deceasds Children viz Nancy & Comfort"; allowed Jan. 30, 1765.]

[Guardianship of Chase Wiggin, Winthrop Wiggin, and Coker Wiggin minors, aged more than 14 years, sons of Bradstreet Wiggin, granted to Winthrop Hilton Jan. 30, 1765.]

[Probate Records, vol. 23, p. 375.]

[Bonds of Winthrop Hilton of Newmarket, gentleman, with Chase Wiggin of Newmarket, yeoman, and Thomas Wiggin of Stratham, gentleman, as sureties, in the sum of £5000 each, Jan. 30, 1765, for the guardianship of Winthrop Wiggin, Chase Wiggin, and Coker Wiggin; witnesses, William Eastman, William Vaughan.]

TIMOTHY MORGAN   1757   EPPING

In The name of God Amen the Eighth Day of october 1757 I Timothy Morgan of the parish of Epping in the province of New-hampshire yeoman Being very Sick and weak in Body * * *

Imprimis I Give and Bequeath to Bette Morgan my Dearly Beloved wife whom I Likewise Constitute make and ordain my Sole Executrix of this my last will and Testament the whole Improvement of my Estate Both Reall and personal untill my two Sons are twenty one years of age that is to Say when my Eldest Son is arrived to twenty one years my will is that he Enjoy his part & the other to be Enjoyed By my wife untill my youngest Son is of the age of twenty one years as abovesaid.

Item I give and bequeath to well beloved Sons Reuben and Benjamin all my Lands Lying and being in the Parish of Epping By them freely to be possessed and Enjoyed and to be Equally divided Between them with the Buildings and appurtenances

Item I give to my well beloved Daughter Hannah forty pounds old tenor to be paid by my son Reuben in one year after he Shall Come in possession of the above said Land. Item I Give to my well beloved Daughter Abiah thirty pounds old tenor to be paid out of my Estate by my son Reuben in two years after he Shall come in possession of the Said Land. Item I Give to my well Beloved Daughter Elizabeth Thirty pounds old tenor to be paid out of my Estate the one half By my son Reuben and the other half by my son Benjamin in three years after my Son Reuben Shall Come into possession of the above Said Lands. Item give to my well beloved Daughters Anna & Susannah thirty pounds old tenor apiece to be paid out of my Estate the one half to my Daughter Anna, By my son Benjamin in one year after he shall Come into possession of the above Said Land, and the other half to my Daughter Susannah in two years after he shall Come in possession of the above said Land * * *

Timothy Mgan

[Witnesses] Ezikiel Brown, Jeremiah Prescut, frances Jennes.
[Proved Nov. 30, 1757.]

[Inventory, attested May 31, 1758; amount, £3828. 19. 6; signed by Ezekiel Brown.]

MARY WEARE   1757   KENSINGTON

[Guardianship of Nathaniel Weare, aged less than 14 years, granted to his father, Joseph Weare of Kensington, Oct. 10, 1757.]

[Probate Records, vol. 20, p. 310]

[Bond of Joseph Weare, yeoman, with Nathaniel Gordon of Exeter, yeoman, as surety, in the sum of £500, Oct. 10, 1757, for the guardianship of Nathaniel Weare, his son by his wife, Mary Weare, deceased; witnesses, William Parker, Samuel Parker.]

JOHN BICKFORD   1757   DOVER

In The name of God amen. The Tenth Day of October Anno Domini one Thousand Seven Hundred & fifty Seven, I John Bickford of Dover in yᵉ Province of New-Hampsʳ in New-England Weaver, being exercised with great Bodily Infermities, & weakess   *   *   *

Imprimis, I Give & Bequeath unto my Beloved Wife Judith Bickford the one fourth Part of yᵉ Produce of all my Land, both of Tillage Mowing Pasturing Land & Orchard; The fences about sᵈ Land to be kept in Repair, the Several Crops to be Seasonably Gathered in Secured & Housed, by my sᵈ Executor, or at his Cost & Charge, at thier Respective Harvists, Yearly & every Year, that is to Say, yᵉ one fourth Part of Sᵈ Crops for yᵉ use of my Sᵈ Wife, During the Term of her Continuing my Widow. But in Case She Shall Marry, then my Will is that She Shall have her Proper Dowry as by Law Allowed. I also Give to my sᵈ Wife yᵉ free full & Sole use of one Lower Room in my Dwelling House namely that Room which I Commonly Lodg in, and Such Improvement of yᵉ Chamber over it, & yᵉ Celler under it as She Shall have occation for: And also yᵉ use & Improvement of Such a Part of my Barn as Shall be needful to House her Cattle Sheep & fodder. My Will also is that my Said Executor Shall Procure & Provide good fire Wood for yᵉ use of my sᵈ Wife, at yᵉ Door of her Dwelling House Sufficient to Support one Comfortable fire Yearly & every Year During ye afores'd Term: I also Give unto my s^d Wife the Sole use & Improvement of all my Household Goods, Beds & Beding During ye afores'd Term of her Continuing my Widow; But in Case She Shall Marry, then her Thirds of s^d Household Goods Beds & Beding, & at her Marriage, my Will is that the other Two thirds of my s^d Household Goods Beds & Beding Shall be equally Divided among my three Daughters, namely Elisabeth Bickford Martha Tibbets & Abigail Bickford, and also what of S^d Household Goods Beds & Beding Shall Remain at ye Decease of my S^d Wife Shall be Divided among my S^d three Daughters as aboves'd. I also Give unto my S^d Wife to her own Disposal one Cow three Sheep & one Pigg.

Item. I Give unto my Son Jonathan Bickford, whom I Constiute make & Ordain Sole Executor of this my last Will and Testament, & to his Heirs & Assigns for ever all my Land Orchards & all my Buildings Standing & Being upon S^d Land; Except ye use of Such Part of ye S^d Buildings, & Such Part of ye Produce of S^d Land as I have in this Will Given to my s^d Wife I also Give to my s^d Son Jonathan Bickford all my Live Stock of Cattle Horse Kine Sheep & Swine, Except Such of them as I have in this Will Given to my s^d Wife, & Daughters, viz: Elisabeth & Abigail. I also Give to my s^d Son Jonathan Bickford all my farming Tackling & utencels, and all my Wareing Apparel; And also all such Estate that doth Properly belong to me, of what Kind Soever, or where soever ye Same may be found tho' not mentioned in this Will.

Item, I Give to Each of my two Daughters, viz: Elisabeth and Abigail Bickfor, one Cow to be Delivered unto them by my Executor, when & So Soon after my Decease, as they Shall Demand them. I also Give unto my S^d Daughters Elisabeth Bickford Martha Tibbets & Abigail Bickford, one Hundred Pounds, old Tenor, Each, to be Paid them by my S^d Executor within ye Term of one Year after ye Deceas of my S^d Wife. * * *

John Bickford

[Witnesses] Joseph Bickford Juner, Ephraim Bickford, Elizabeth Canne.

[Proved Sept. 29, 1762.]

[Warrant, Sept. 29, 1762, authorizing William Twombly, gentleman, and Joseph Hanson, yeoman, both of Dover, to appraise the estate.]

[Inventory, Nov. 9, 1762; amount, £7118. 10. 0; signed by William Twombly and Joseph Hanson.]

DAVID BURNSIDE   1757   LONDONDERRY

[Administration on the estate of David Burnside of Londonderry granted to James Paul and his wife, Margaret Paul, Oct. 14, 1757.]

[Probate Records, vol 20, p. 310.]

[Bond of James Paul and Margaret Paul, with Benjamin Thompson and John Doak, yeomen, as sureties, all of Londonderry, in the sum of £2000, Oct. 14, 1757, for the administration of the estate of David Burnside, trader; witnesses, William Parker, David Sewall.]

[Warrant, Oct. 14, 1757, authorizing Samuel Barr, John Weare, gentleman, and Benjamin Thompson, trader, all of Londonderry, to appraise the estate.]

[Inventory, Nov. 21, 1757; amount, £5086. 18. 5; signed by Samuel Barr, John Weare, and Benjamin Thompson.]

[Account of the settlement of the estate; receipts, £10,087. 15. 2, personal estate; expenditures, £5415. 6. 10; filed Aug. 29, 1759.]

[Additional inventory, Aug. 29, 1759; amount, £4986. 15. 1.]

[Administrator's additional account; receipts, £5357. 2. 4; expenditures, £645. 8. 8; allowed Sept. 28, 1763.]

RICHARD KIMBALL   1757   SALEM

[Jemima Kimball requests administration on the estate of her husband, Richard Kimball of Salem, Oct. 17, 1757, and the appointment of Daniel Gage of Pelham and John Hall, Jr., of Salem as appraisers; witnesses, William Richardson, Joseph Rowell.]

[Administration on the estate of Richard Kimball, gentleman, granted to his widow, Jemima Kimball, Oct. 26, 1757.]

[Probate Records, vol. 20, p. 317.]

[Bond of Jemima Kimball, widow, with Daniel Peaslee and Daniel Muzzey as sureties, in the sum of £500, Oct. 26, 1757, for the administration of the estate; witnesses, William Richardson, Benjamin Wheeler, Jr.]

[Warrant, Oct. 26, 1757, authorizing William Richardson of Pelham, gentleman, and Richard Dow of Salem, yeoman, to appraise the estate.]

[Inventory, attested Nov. 12, 1757; amount, £6284. 14. 0; signed by William Richardson and Richard Dow; mentions the intestate as Capt. Richard Kimball.]

[Account of the settlement of the estate by John Webster and his wife Jemima, administratrix; receipts, £2152. 14. 0, personal estate; expenditures, £762. 7. 3; allowed Oct. 25, 1758.]

[Warrant, Nov. 15, 1758, authorizing John Hall, Daniel Massey, Ralph Hall, John Johnson, yeomen, and Obadiah Eastman, gentleman, all of Salem, to divide the real estate.]

Provance of } To the Honnerable Judge of probates of Newhampshier wils for the Provance of new hampshier in obediance to a warrent from your honner to Settel the Estate of Capt richard kimbal Late of Salem Deceas'd we have settled it in the folling manner viz

1^{ly} we have set of one third part to Jemima webster of plastow who was the wife of said intestate as hir Dowry and boundded as followeth Beginning at a white oak tree at the west end of the house thence running Easterly by the road to Land of Even Jonses thence southerly by Land of Jonses to the Corner bound thence to the bounds first mentioned and also the west End of the house and also the East Scaffold and Lento in the barn 2^{ly} we have set of to richard kimbal minor the home place with the hous and barn his mothers thirds Excepted and also a peice of meadow ground about seven acres Lying apon Spicket river and also a peice of wood Land Lying betwen nathannel merriels and peter merriels Containing about twenty acres 3^{ly} we have set of to Easter whealer one of the heirs of the intestate four acres of Land it being one half of an Eight acre Lot Laing apon Land of Daniel marcies and Steven whelers and a Country road and bounded as followeth beginning at a Red oak tree marked by the road thence running westerly by sd road about twenty poles to a stake and Stones thence Southerly about thirty three pols to a Stake and Stons thence Southeasterly about twenty poles to a stake and stons thence Northerly to the bounds first mentioned and also four acres and an half of meadow ground Laing upon hittetete brook it being one half of nine acre Lot beginning at the East end of the Lot a Stake and Stones and a pitch pine being the tow Corner bounds So running westerly apon both sides of the brook to Contain four acres and a half 4^{ly} we have Set of to hannah wheler one of the heirs of the intestate four acres of Land it being one half of an Eight acre Lot Lying apon Land of Daniel marcies and apon Steven whelers and a Country road and boundded as followeth beginning at a Stake and Stons by sd road thence westerly by sd road about twenty pols to a swamp white oak thence southerly thirty three pols to a red oak marked thence Southeasterly twenty poles to a Stake and Stons thence northerly to the bounds first mentioned and also a peice of meadow ground about four acres and a half it being on half of a nine acre Lot begining at the westerly end of Said Lot the tow Corner bounds being a whit oak and a pitch pine so running

Easterly apon both sids of the brook to Contain four acres and a half

         John Hall Jun
         Daniel Massey
         Rapha Hall
         John Johnson
         Obadiah Eastman

[Guardianship of Richard Kimball, minor, aged more than 14 years, son of Richard Kimball, granted to Timothy Ladd June 30, 1763.]

[Probate Records, vol. 23, p. 46.]

[Bond of Timothy Ladd of Plaistow, yeoman, with Joseph Wright of Salem, gentleman, as surety, in the sum of £500, June 30, 1763, for the guardianship of Richard Kimball; witnesses, Cutts Shannon, William Parker.]

JOHN ROBINSON   1757   MERRIMACK

[Bond of Timothy Wilkins of Concord, Mass., yeoman, with Asa Spaulding of Billerica, Mass., yeoman, as surety, in the sum of £500, Oct. 17, 1757, for the guardianship of John Robinson, minor, in his fifteenth year, son of John Robinson of Merrimack; witnesses, Andrew Boardman and Reuben Prentice.]

[Middlesex Co., Mass., Probate Files.]

NATHANIEL CHASE   1757   LONDONDERRY

[Administration on the estate of Nathaniel Chase of Londonderry, yeoman, granted to James Chase Oct. 18, 1757.]

[Probate Records, vol. 20, p. 317.]

[Bond of James Chase of Londonderry, yeoman, with Edward Clark and Nathaniel Merrill, yeomen, both of Salem, as sureties, in the sum of £500, Oct. 18, 1757, for the administration of the estate; witnesses, Rebecca Peaslee, Elizabeth Peaslee.]

[Warrant, Oct. 18, 1757, authorizing Samuel Greeley and Samuel Hills, both of Nottingham West, yeomen, to appraise the estate; mentions James Chase as son of the deceased.]

[Inventory, attested Nov. 12, 1757; amount, £648. 4. 6; signed by Samuel Greeley, Jr., and Samuel Hills.]

[Warrant, March 3, 1758, authorizing Joseph Blanchard of Merrimack and Samuel Greeley of Nottingham West, gentleman, to receive claims against the estate.]

[List of claims; amount, £440. 16. 4; mentions "Due to Abigill Webster for Rates her late Husband Was to have Collected from said Chase"; signed by Joseph Blanchard and Samuel Greeley, Jr.]

[Account of the settlement of the estate; receipts, £648. 4. 6, personal estate; expenditures, £499. 0. 3; mentions "my Self & my Wifes attendance on the Deceas^d & his Wife in their last Sickness 10 Days each . . . . keeping a Child of said Intestate under seven for one year"; allowed Nov. 29, 1758.]

[Settlement of claims; amount distributed, £148. 15. 3; allowed Dec. 1, 1758.]

ANDREW GILMAN   1757   BRENTWOOD

[Administration on the estate of Andrew Gilman of Brentwood granted to Jeremiah Gilman of Brentwood, yeoman, Oct. 19, 1757.]

[Probate Records, vol. 20, p. 317.]

[Bond of Jeremiah Gilman, with Daniel Leavitt and Nicholas Dudley as sureties, all of Brentwood, yeomen, in the sum of £500, Oct. 19, 1757, for the administration of the estate of Andrew Gilman, gentleman; witnesses, Samuel Dudley, Biley Dudley.]

[Warrant, Oct. 19, 1757, authorizing John Gilman, Jr., of Exeter and Biley Dudley of Brentwood, yeoman, to appraise the estate; mentions Jeremiah Gilman as son of the deceased.]

[Inventory, Oct. 24, 1757; amount, £6985. 15. 0; signed by John Gilman, Jr., and Biley Dudley.]

[Account of the settlement of the estate; receipts, £1545. 15. 0; expenditures, £2079. 4. 7; allowed Oct. 31, 1759.]

[Additional account: receipts, £1740. 0. 0; expenditures, £1238. 0. 6; allowed Oct. 31, 1765.]

[Guardianship of Mary Leavitt, Stephen Leavitt, and Gilman Leavitt, children of Daniel Leavitt by his wife, Anna Leavitt, daughter of Andrew Gilman, granted to their father Oct. 31, 1765.]

[Probate Records, vol. 24, p. 24.]

[Bond of Daniel Leavitt, with Levi Morrill and Jeremiah Gilman as sureties, all of Brentwood, in the sum of £500, Oct. 31, 1765, for the guardianship of Mary Leavitt, Stephen Leavitt, and Gilman Leavitt; witnesses, William Parker, Samuel Hobart.]

ISAAC LITTLEHALE   1757   PELHAM

[Hannah Littlehale renounces administration on the estate of her husband, Isaac Littlehale, Oct. 22, 1757, in favor of Capt. William Richardson; witnesses, James Hobbs, Daniel Hutchinson.]

[Administration on the estate of Isaac Littlehale of Pelham granted to William Richardson of Pelham, gentleman, Oct. 26, 1757.]

[Probate Records, vol. 21, p. 28.]

[Bond of William Richardson, with Amos Richardson and Levi Hildreth as sureties, all of Pelham, in the sum of £500, Oct. 26, 1757, for the administration of the estate; witnesses, Joseph Hamblett, Josiah Hamblett.]

[Warrant, Oct. 26, 1757, authorizing Joseph Butler and Levi Hildreth, both of Pelham, yeomen, to appraise the estate.]

[Inventory, March 27, 1758; amount, £2698. 15. 0; signed by Joseph Butler, Levi Hildreth, and Hannah Littlehale.]

[Account of the settlement of the estate; receipts, £2390. 6. 7; expenditures, £1932. 19. 8; mentions "163 Weeks a Child of the dec^d born Septr 1, 1758"; allowed Nov. 4, 1761.]

[Additional account; receipts, £627. 12. 11; expenditures, £88. 0. 0; allowed June 29, 1763.]

[Guardianship of Isaac Littlehale, aged less than 14 years, son of Isaac Littlehale, granted to Daniel Hutchinson June 28, 1763.]

[Probate Records, vol. 23, p. 191.]

[Bond of Daniel Hutchinson, with Daniel Gage and Joseph Butler as sureties, all of Pelham, in the sum of £500, June 28, 1763, for the guardianship of Isaac Littlehale; witnesses, Ephraim Cummings, John Ferguson.]

JOHN WILSON   1757   PLAISTOW

[Margaret Wilson renounces administration on the estate of her husband, John Wilson of Plaistow, miller, Oct. 25, 1757, in favor of her brothers, James Waddell of Chester and John Waddell of Londonderry; witnesses, John Johnson, John Morrill.]

[Administration granted to James Waddell and John Waddell of Londonderry Oct. 26, 1757.]

[Probate Records, vol. 20, p. 317.]

[Bond of James Waddell and John Waddell, with Thomas Johnson and John Barnett as sureties, all of Londonderry, in the sum of £500, Oct. 26, 1757, for the administration of the estate; witnesses, William Parker, Jr., Cutts Shannon.]

[Warrant, Oct. 26, 1757, authorizing John Hogg of Hampstead, gentleman, and Thomas Little of Plaistow, tanner, to appraise the estate.]

[Inventory, attested Oct. 28, 1757; amount, £2341. 19. 0; signed by John Hogg and Thomas Little.]

[Commission to John Tolford of Chester, gentleman, and John Hogg of Hampstead, March 8, 1758, to receive claims against the estate.]

[List of claims, attested Sept. 27, 1758; amount, £569. 9. 6; signed by John Tolford and John Hogg.]

[Account of the settlement of the estate; receipts, £3004. 10. 0; expenditures, £1391. 10. 11; mentions "p^d Margaret Wilson her acco^t for the Support of 2 Children & the charge of the Last Sickness & Funeral Charge of one of them"; allowed Sept. 27, 1758.]

[Settlement of claims; amount of claims, £569. 9. 6; amount distributed, £403. 4. 9¼; allowed Oct. 15, 1758.]

[Administrator's additional account; receipts, £3. 13. 4; expenditures, £8. 10. 8; mentions decease of the widow; signed by James Waddell; allowed April 19, 1786.]

[Additional distribution of £3. 13. 4 to the creditors; allowed May 17, 1786.]

JOSEPH SCRIBNER 1757 EXETER

[Lydia Scribner renounces administration on the estate of her husband, Joseph Scribner of Exeter, and of his son, Joseph

Scribner, Jr., Oct. 25, 1757, in favor of her son-in-law, Joseph Lougee of Exeter, tailor; witnesses, Theophilus Smith, John Glidden.]

[Bond of Joseph Lougee, with John Steele and John Glidden, yeomen, as sureties, all of Exeter, in the sum of £500, Oct. 26, 1757, for the administration of the estate; witnesses, John Smith, William Parker, Jr.]

[Inventory, Nov. 1, 1757; amount, £3227. 11. 0; signed by Caleb Kimball and Theophilus Smith.]

[Account of the administrator; receipts, £2183. 13. 0; expenditures, £1837. 7. 0; allowed April 17, 1760.]

DANIEL FOGG 1757 RYE

[Administration on the estate of Daniel Fogg of Rye, yeoman, granted to his widow, Hannah Fogg, Oct. 26, 1757.]

[Probate Records, vol. 20, p. 317.]

[Bond of Hannah Fogg of Rye, widow, with Samuel Knowles of Rye and Josiah Batchelder of Hampton Falls, yeomen, as sureties, in the sum of £500, Oct. 26, 1757, for the administration of the estate; witnesses, William Parker, Jr., William Parker.]

[Warrant, Oct. 26, 1757, authorizing Samuel Knowles, yeoman, and Richard Jenness, 3d, gentleman, both of Rye, to appraise the estate.]

[Inventory, attested Jan. 25, 1758; amount, £10,044. 10. 0; signed by Richard Jenness, 3d, and Samuel Knowles.]

[Guardianship of Daniel Fogg, minor, aged more than 14 years, son of Daniel Fogg, granted to Jeremiah Fogg of Kensington, clerk, Oct. 26, 1757.]

[Probate Records, vol. 20, p. 317.]

[Bond of Jeremiah Fogg, clerk, with Jonathan Dow and Samuel Clifford, Jr., yeomen, as sureties, all of Kensington, in the sum of £500, Oct. 26, 1757, for the guardianship of Daniel Fogg; witnesses, William Parker, Jr., William Parker.]

[Warrant, Aug. 5, 1760, authorizing Richard Jenness, 3d, Reuben Moulton, yeoman, both of Rye, Samuel Knowles, Enoch Sanborn, and Stephen Batchelder, yeomen, all of North Hampton, to divide the real estate.]

Province of } By order from the Honble Richd Wibird New Hampshire } Judge of the Probate of Wills for Said Province &c appointing us a Commettee to Divide the Real Estate of Daniel fogg Late of Rye yeoman Deceased — after a Careful Suervey of Said Estate we have agreed & Set of to Each Party their Respective Shares & parts of Said Estate in the Manner following Viz —

to hannah fogg Wedow Relick of Said Intestate one full third Part thereof viz the East Lower fore Room the west fore Chamber one third of the Garrat at the East End and one third of the Celler at the East End also twelve feet of the west End of the Barn the whole weadth also Seventeen acres of Land in Rye in the home Place Laying on the west side of the high way that Leads from Rye to hampton and the north End by the high way that Leads from Rye to North hampton and from Said high way on the west 34 rods to a tree Marked and by the high way on the East Side 27 Rods to a Stake in the Ground taking one 3^d part of the orchard as it is Laid out and Bounded also the third Part of thirteen acres at north hampton in the 12 Shares So Called on the west Side as it is Laid out and Bounded also one third Part of the Salt marsh at hampton on the South Side as it is Laid out and bounded also all the Salt Marsh at Little River So Called also the third Part of five acres of Land at the Little Boars head as it is Laid out and Bounded

to Daniel fogg the Eldest & only Son of the said Intestate a Doble Share of the Remaining two thirds viz the East fore

Chamber Parte of the Kitchen Celler & Garret as makes up his full part of the house afore Said also 20 feet the full Breadth of the East End of the Barn — Also about Eight acres of Land at ye East End of the house Bounding on the high way from hampton to Rye on the west & the way to the Sea on the north the wedow Elken's Land on the East and on the South Land of Nehemiah Moultens Also aboute 13 acres of Land at the west Side of the high way that Leads to hampton afore Said at the South End of the home place & to Extend Northerly into Said Place on the East & west to Stakes Set up for Bounds also aboute 5 acres of wood Land in the North Division Shares on the South Side to marked trees also his Part of 13 acres at Northampton on the East Side also his Part of the orchard Joyning to the wedow also his full part on the north Side of ye Marsh at hampton as it is Bounded out also his part of five acres of Land at Little Boars head on the west Side also one acre of thach Ground in Rye

to Sarah fogg the only Daughter a single Share of ⅔ of Said Estate the west Lower fore Room with all the house & Barn not before mentioned in this instrement also about 19 acres of the home place on the west Side of the afore Said way to hampton Bounding northerly on the wedows part & southerly on Daniels part as it is Staiked out also her Part of the 13 acre the midle Share as it is bounded out also her part of 5 acres at Boars head the midle Share also her part of Salt marsh at hampton the midle share as Bounded out also halfe an acre of thach Ground in Rye to Gather with about 3 acres of the Remander of wood Land afore Said Except one acre of wood Land to the wedow hannah fogg for her to Cutt wood on when She Cant Geet wood Convently on the Land before Laid out to her

Rye august 26th 1761

Richd Jenness 3^d
Samuel Knowles
Enoch Sanborn

BENJAMIN SWETT   1757   HAMPTON FALLS

In the Name of God Amen the twenty Sixth Day of October Anno Domini Seventeen hundred And fifty Seven — I Benjamin Swett of Hampton falls in the Province of New-Hampshire in New England Blacksmith being Infirm in Body * * * I do Constitute and Appoint my friend Meshech Weare of Hampton falls aforesaid Esq[r] to be Sole Executor of this my will to make a Just Settlement of my affairs to Receive all Debts Due to me and to Discharge Such as I owe so far as my Estate will be Sufficient And to Pay himself a Debt for which he Stands Ingaged on my account to Mark Hunking Wentworth Esq[r] for Something more than five hundred Pounds old Tenor And if there shall be Any Remainder after my Debts as abovementioned And necessary Charges shall be Paid, It shall be Disposed of As follows Namely to my Sister Deliverance Coleman of Nantuckett twenty Pounds old Tenor and to my Sister Huldah Coleman of Nantuckett thirty Pounds old Tenor they not having had their full share of their fathers Estate as others have had. And all the Remainder of my Estate I Give to my Son Jonathan Swett * * *

Benj[a] Swett

[Witnesses] John Green, Nath[a] Healey Junr, Daniel Cram.
[Proved Feb. 23, 1758.]

[Warrant, Feb. 23, 1758, authorizing Joseph Worth and Jonathan Swett, both of Hampton Falls, yeomen, to appraise the estate.]

[Inventory, Feb. 28, 1758; amount, £1902. 7. 4; signed by Joseph Worth and Jonathan Swett.]

HENRY PUTNEY   1757   NEW IPSWICH

[Administration on the estate of Henry Putney of New Ipswich granted to Martha Putney, widow, Oct. 26, 1757.]
[Probate Records, vol. 20, p. 471.]

[Bond of Martha Putney, widow, with Reuben Kidder, gentleman, and Aaron Kidder, yeoman, as sureties, all of New Ipswich, in the sum of £500, Oct. 26, 1757, for the administration of the estate; witnesses, William Clary, Joseph Blanchard.]

[Warrant, Oct. 26, 1757, authorizing Reuben Kidder and Aaron Kidder to appraise the estate.]

[Inventory, attested Nov. 10, 1757; amount, £62. 3. 11; signed by Aaron Kidder and Reuben Kidder.]

[Warrant, May 20, 1758, authorizing Reuben Kidder and Aaron Kidder to receive claims against the estate.]

[Martha Putney's account against the estate, May 21, 1759; amount, £218. 15. 8; mentions "Bringing up a Child from Decr 1755 to the Day of Date hereof Said Child is Seven years old Next Sept^r"; allowed May 22, 1759.]

[List of claims against the estate; amount, £59. 19. 0; signed by Reuben Kidder and Aaron Kidder.]

RICHARD HEATH   1757   PLAISTOW

[Caveat of Stephen Harriman of Haverhill, Mass., Oct. 26, 1757, against granting administration on the estate of Richard Heath of Plaistow, husbandman, without notice to the widow, who has eight small children.]

[Administration on the estate of Richard Heath of Plaistow, yeoman, granted to Thomas Hale and Benjamin Richards of Plaistow Nov. 29, 1758.]

[Probate Records, vol. 21, p. 110.]

[Division of the estate among the creditors; claims, £1327. 1. 10; paid, £445. 2. 3; allowed Nov. 30, 1759.]

[Probate Records, vol. 21, p. 341.]

JOHN ROWELL   1757   EPPING

[Administration on the estate of John Rowell of Epping, joiner, granted to his widow, Sarah Rowell, Oct. 26, 1757.]

[Probate Records, vol. 20, p. 329.]

[Bond of Sarah Rowell, widow, with Joseph Chandler and John Dow, yeomen, as sureties, all of Epping, in the sum of £1000, Oct. 26, 1757, for the administration of the estate; witnesses, William Parker, Jr., John Smith.]

[Warrant, Oct. 26, 1757, authorizing Jacob Freese, yeoman, and Ebenezer Fiske, physician, both of Epping, to appraise the estate.]

[Inventory, Jan. 20, 1758; amount, £3869. 2. 0; signed by Jacob Freese and Ebenezer Fiske.]

JOSEPH TAYLOR   1757   EXETER

[Administration on the estate of Joseph Taylor granted to John Taylor Oct. 28, 1757.]

[Probate Records, vol. 20, p. 329.]

[Bond of John Taylor of Brentwood, yeoman, with Zaccheus Clough of Brentwood and Willoughby Colby of Exeter, yeomen, as sureties, in the sum of £500, Oct. 28, 1757, for the administration of the estate of Joseph Taylor of Exeter, yeoman; witness, William Parker, Jr.]

[Inventory, Nov. 15, 1757; amount, £3424. 0. 0; signed by Caleb Kimball and Ephraim Robinson. Additional inventory of £182. 0. 0, April 28, 1760.]

[Anna Taylor and Catherine Taylor, daughters of Joseph Taylor, "One of us ninteen Years & the other Sixteen Years of Age & without father or mother", make choice of their brother-in-law, Moses Lovering, as their guardian March 31, 1761.]

[Guardianship of Anna Taylor and Catherine Taylor, minors, aged more than 14 years, children of Joseph Taylor, granted to Moses Lovering of Exeter, yeoman, April 8, 1761.]

[Probate Records, vol. 22, p. 69.]

[Bond of Moses Lovering, yeoman, with Jonathan Gilman, innholder, and Noah Emery, attorney at law, as sureties, all of Exeter, in the sum of £500, April 8, 1761, for the guardianship of Anna Taylor and Catherine Taylor; witnesses, Richard Sutton, John Taylor.]

[Account of the settlement of the estate; receipts, £458. 14. 8; expenditures, £278. 15. 6; allowed April 8, 1761.]

DANIEL MARSTON   1757   NORTH HAMPTON

In the of God Amen I Daniel Marston of North Hampton in the Province of New Hampshire in New England Yeoman being in poor state of Body * * *

Item I Give and Bequeath unto my Beloved wife Sarah Marston the improvement of one third part of all my Estate dureing her Naturel Life and all My Household stuff I give to her to be at her Disposell my weareing Cloaths and Tropeing furniture Excepted —

Item I Give and Bequeath unto my three Sons Daniel Samuel and Robie Marston All my lands in the Township of Nottingham to be Equelly Divided between them to them their hiers Exectr[s] Administ[r] and Assigns forever Samuel to have his part on the Easterly Side Daniel to have his part in the middle and Robie to have his third part on the westerly side of s[d] Land and I also Give to Each of my s[d] Sons Daniel Sam[ll] and Robie all my part of a Saw Mill in Nottingham aforesaid each of them to have one third of my part when they arive to the Age of twenty one Years.

Item I Give and Bequeath unto my Son Theodore Marston all my Lands in the Township of Bow and also all my Right of land in a place Call[d] Buckstreet to him his Heirs and Assigns forever.

Item I Give and Bequeath to my Daughter Anna Marston three Hundred Pounds old Tenor to be paid at the Age of Eighteen Years or at the time of her Marriage if Sooner —

Item I Give and Bequeath unto my Daughter Meriam three Hundred Pounds old Tenor to be paid at the age of Eighteen Years or time of Marriage if Sooner —

Item I give to my Daughter Sarah Three hundred Pounds old Tenor to be paid at the Age of Eighteen Years or at the time of Marriage if sooner.

Item I Give unto my Son David Marston three Hundred Pounds old Tenor to be paid to him at the Age of Twenty One Years All the above Legicies to be paid by my Executor hereafter named.

Item I Give unto my Beloved Wife Sarah and my three Daughters above named the Improvement of one half of my Dwelling House from the Seller to the Garritt (the East end) to my Daughters with their Mother so long as they remain unmarried and to my Wife Dureing her Naturel Life — I Also Give to my five Sons Daniel Sam[ll] Robie Theodore and David all my Cloaths (my Trooping Cloaths Excepted) to be equally Divided between them

Item All the Rest and Residue of my Estate both Real and Personel wherever it may be found I Give and bequeath unto my son Simon Marston to him his Heirs and Assigns forever with all my Debts Dew to me at my Decease, He paying all my Just Debts and funeral Charges with all the Above Mentioned Legicies.

Lastly I do hereby Constitute and Appoint my well Beloved wife Sarah Marston and My son Simon Marston to be my Exector[s] * * * In Witness whereof I have hereunto set my Hand and Seal this Ninth Day of November Anno Dom: Seventeen Hundred & fifty seven & in the 31st Year of the Reign of George the Second by the Grace of God King &c

Daniel maston

[Witnesses] John Taylor, John M^{c}fee, Levi Dearborn. [Proved Nov. 30, 1757.]

[Bond of Sarah Marston, widow, with Simon Marston, yeoman, Levi Dearborn, both of North Hampton, and John McFee of Rochester, as sureties, in the sum of £500, Nov. 30, 1757, for the execution of the will; witnesses, Thomas Westbrook Waldron, William Parker.]

[Guardianship of Samuel Marston, minor, aged more than 14 years, son of Daniel Marston, granted to Ebenezer Sanborn May 21, 1763.]

[Probate Records, vol. 22, p. 545.]

[Bond of Ebenezer Sanborn, gentleman, with Simon Page, yeoman, as surety, both of North Hampton, in the sum of £500, May 21, 1763, for the guardianship of Samuel Marston; witnesses, Jonathan Pinkham, William Vaughan.]

RICHARD KELLY 1757 SALEM

[Judith Kelly, widow, and William Kelly, oldest son, renounce administration on the estate of Richard Kelly, who died Sept. 9, 1756, in favor of Peter Merrill; witness, Peter Merrill.]

[Administration on the estate of Richard Kelly of Salem, yeoman, granted to Peter Merrill Nov. 23, 1757.]

[Probate Records, vol. 20, p. 352.]

[Bond of Peter Merrill, yeoman, with Andrew Balch, gentleman, and Edward Clark, yeoman, as sureties, all of Salem, in the sum of £500, Nov. 23, 1757, for the administration of the estate; witnesses, Susanna Copp, Caleb Balch.]

[Warrant, Nov. 23, 1757, authorizing Richard Dow and John Hall, Jr., both of Salem, yeomen, to appraise the estate.]

[Inventory, Dec. 6, 1757; amount, £512. 12. 0; signed by Richard Dow and John Hall, Jr.]

[Warrant, Feb. 14, 1758, authorizing Joseph Wright, gentleman, and Richard Dow, yeoman, both of Salem, to receive claims against the estate.]

[List of claims, attested Sept. 4, 1758; amount, £364. 1. 3; signed by Joseph Wright and Richard Dow.]

[Account of the settlement of the estate; receipts, £392. 3. 0; expenditures, £364. 16. 0; allowed Sept. 6, 1758.]

[Settlement of claims; amount of claims, £364. 1. 3; amount distributed, £27. 6. 2; allowed Sept. 7, 1758.]

JOHN ANDERSON   1757   LONDONDERRY

[Janet Anderson renounces administration on the estate of her husband, John Anderson of Londonderry, Nov. 14, 1757, in favor of her brother, James Anderson, and Samuel Fisher; witness, Robert Wallace.]

[Administration granted to James Anderson, Jr., and Samuel Fisher of Londonderry, yeomen, Nov. 15, 1757.]

[Probate Records, vol. 20, p. 352.]

[Bond of James Anderson and Samuel Fisher, both of Londonderry, yeomen, with Robert Anderson of Derryfield and Robert Wallace of Londonderry, gentlemen, as sureties, in the sum of £1000, Nov. 15, 1757, for the administration of the estate; witnesses, James Wallace, Robert Campbell.]

Londonderry February the 25th 1760
To the Honourable Judge of Probates
The humble petition of Jannet Anderson Widow Humbly Sheweth that your petitioner humbly Begs for y[r] Patience to

hear my Complaints and Difficulties which I Laboured under and now Labours under first when my Husband was taken from me I was in Difficult Circumstance for in thirteen Days after the Decease of my Husband I was Deliver'd of a Child and then was taken ill with a fever which held me ill for two months which Render'd me Incapable of Carrying on the Administration and under these Difficult Circumstances I gave way to my Brother James Anderson and my Brother Samuel Fisher to administer but I wanted to be in along with my Brother Anderson but he hurried on the administration and told me that I Could not be one with him Because I was not able to go to your Honour to take out the Letters of administration and I think I Could do Better for the Children than what he does and now I wou'd Desire the favour of your Honour to give me Liberty to act in the Room of my Brother Anderson and to be Ex^{tr} in his Stead for I think it wou'd not be so Chargeable to the Estate if I had the managment of the Whole of it So I hope your Honour will Consider me in my Difficulty and grant your petitioner my Request, and for you I will Ever pray —

Jannet Anderson

[Account of the settlement of the estate; receipts, £1477. 13. 0, personal estate; expenditures, £1658. 13. 11; allowed Feb. 27, 1760.]

Agreeable to the within warrant we the Subscribers have Gone and Veiw^d the Estate of John anderson Late of London Derry Dec^d therein Mentioned — and according to the Best of our Judgments have Set of the widdows thirds of Said Estate as therein Directed and the Bounds thereof is as follows Viz Begining at a Red oak tree a few Rods South west of the house that belongs to S^d farm thence North fivefty four Degrees East Eight Rods to a Stake thence North twenty four Degrees west ten Rods to a Stake thence North sixty one Degrees East ten Rods and an half to a heap of Stones thence South thirty four Degrees East Eight Rods to a stake thence North fivefty four Degrees

East to a Broken Red oak tree Marked Standing in the Line Betwen S^d farm and Land Belonging to Mathew Thornton Esqr South East twenty Six Rods to the Leading Rhoad to Litchfeild thence South west and Bounding on Said Rhoad to the Cross Rhoad through Said farm thence North westerly to the Bounds first Mentioned Containing about twenty Acres and one hundred Rods be the Same More or Less — as also another part of Said farm Bounded as follows Begining at a heap of Stones on the South west Side of the Cross Rhoad Before Mentioned about Ten Rods Distant from the house belonging to S^d farm and Due Southwest from S^d house thence Runing Southwest by Marked trees to the Line of John Clarks Land to a Red oak tree Marked thence South East and Bounding on S^d Clarks Land about fourty four Rods to a heap of Stones upon the afores^d Leading Rhoad to Litchfeild thence Northeast and bounding on S^d Rhoad to the before Mentioned Cross Rhoad thence North westerly Bounding on S^d Rhoad to the bounds first Mentioned Containing about Sixteen acres be the Same More or Less as also one half of the house and one third of the Barn Belonging to the premises and also a Common privilige for Both the widdows thirds and the Rest of S^d Estate from the North west Corner of the House to the North East Corner of the Barn and to the High way —

Given Under our hands at Londonderry ye 20th of March 1766
      Edward Aiken
      Henry Campbel
      James MacGregore

[Additional account of the settlement of the estate; receipts, £73. 10. 0; expenditures, £98. 3. 7½; filed March, 1767; mentions widow and three children.]

[Guardianship of Jane Anderson, Matthew Anderson, minors, aged more than 14 years, and John Anderson, aged less than 14 years, children of John Anderson of Londonderry, granted to Samuel Fisher April 7, 1770.]

[Probate Records, vol. 26, p. 405.]

[Bond of Samuel Fisher, with Robert Wallace and Thomas Wallace as sureties, all of Londonderry, in the sum of £500, April 7, 1770, for the guardianship of Jane Anderson, Matthew Anderson, and John Anderson, children of John Anderson; witnesses, Thomas Wallace, Jr., Robert Wallace, Jr.]

JOHN NUTT   1757   CHESTER

[Bond of Mary Nutt of Chester, widow, with John Ramsey of Londonderry, gentleman, and Nathaniel Lynn of Chester, yeoman, as sureties, in the sum of £500, June 17, 1760, for the administration of the estate of John Nutt of Chester, yeoman; witnesses, John Cummings, Robert Clark, Agnes Lynn, Ann McCarrell.]

[Warrant, Nov. 15, 1757, authorizing Robert Craige and James Crossett, both of Chester, yeoman, to appraise the estate.]

[Inventory, Aug. 2, 1760; amount, £1194. 5. 0; signed by Robert Craige and James Crossett.]

[License to the administratrix, Mary Greer, Aug. 20, 1760, to sell real estate.]

[Guardianship of Jane Nutt, minor, aged more than 14 years, daughter of John Nutt, granted to Joseph Lynn Aug. 27, 1766.]
   [Probate Records, vol. 24, p. 280.]

[Bond of Joseph Lynn, yeoman, with Edward Presson, housewright, as surety, both of Chester, in the sum of £500, Aug. 27, 1766, for the guardianship of Jane Nutt; witness, William Vaughan.]

WILLIAM CUMMINGS   1757   HUDSON

[Administration on the estate of William Cummings of Nottingham West granted to Sarah Cummings Nov. 24, 1757.]
   [Probate Records, vol. 29, p. 531.]

[Inventory, Dec. 2, 1757; amount, £4284. 3. 6; signed by Samuel Greeley, Jr., and Henry Hale.]
[Probate Records, vol. 20, p. 541.]

SETH RICHARDSON   1757   WILTON

[Administration on the estate of Seth Richardson of Number 2 granted to Sarah Richardson, widow, Nov. 24, 1757.]
[Probate Records, vol. 20, p. 353.]

[Bond of Sarah Richardson, widow, with Samuel Greeley, Jr., and Ezekiel Hills, yeoman, as sureties, all of Nottingham West, in the sum of £500, Nov. 24, 1757, for the administration of the estate; witnesses, Elliot Vaughan, William Parker.]

[Inventory, attested Nov. 14, 1757; amount, £1520. 16. 0; signed by Ephraim Butterfield and Jacob Putnam.]

[Account of the settlement of the estate; receipts, £411. 16. 0, personal estate; expenditures, £492. 15. 6; mentions "maintenance of Susannah the Daughter of the said Deceased under the age of seven years 192 weeks in the whole deceased ye 15th of Novr 1759"; allowed Jan. 24, 1761.]

HENRY SEYMOUR   1757   PORTSMOUTH

[Administration on the estate of Henry Seymour of Portsmouth, shopkeeper, granted to Ann Seymour, widow, Nov. 30, 1757.]
[Probate Records, vol. 20, p. 360.]

[Bond of Ann Seymour, widow, with Mark Langdon, gentleman, and John Sherburne, merchant, as sureties, all of Portsmouth, in the sum of £500, Nov. 30, 1757, for the administration of the estate; witnesses, William Parker, David Sewall.]

[Warrant, Nov. 30, 1757, authorizing Eleazer Russell and John Shackford, both of Portsmouth, to appraise the estate.]

[Inventory, Feb. 20, 1758; amount, £2097. 3. 6; signed by Eleazer Russell and John Shackford.]

[Warrant, Sept. 11, 1758, authorizing Eleazer Russell and Samuel Penhallow, shopkeeper, both of Portsmouth, to receive claims against the estate.]

[List of claims, May 30, 1759; amount, £1052. 17. 9; signed by Eleazer Russell and Samuel Penhallow.]

THEOPHILUS HARDY 1757 DURHAM

[Sarah Hardy renounces administration on the estate of her son, Theophilus Hardy, and his wife, Love Hardy, who left several minor children, in favor of Mark Jewell of Durham, husbandman, Nov. 30, 1757; witnesses, Joseph Sias, Miles Randall.]

[Administration on the estate of Theophilus Hardy of Durham, yeoman, granted to Mark Jewell, husbandman, Nov. 30, 1757.]
[Probate Records, vol. 20, p. 375.]

[Bond of Mark Jewell, with John Davis and Thomas Simpson of Nottingham, yeomen, as sureties, in the sum of £1000, Nov. 30, 1757, for the administration of the estate; witnesses, Simon Randall, David Sewall.]

[Inventory, Dec. 31, 1757; amount, £5600. 17. 0; signed by Joseph Sias and Miles Randall.]

[Guardianship of Theophilus Hardy, Mary Hardy, Sarah Hardy, Love Hardy, and Nathaniel Hardy, minors, children of Theophilus Hardy, granted to Joseph Sias Feb. 28, 1759.]
[Probate Records, vol. 21, p. 199.]

[Bond of Joseph Sias of Durham, trader, with Jeremiah Burnham of Durham, yeoman, and Josiah Ladd of Exeter, gentleman, as sureties, in the sum of £1000, Feb. 28, 1759, for the guardianship of Theophilus, Mary, Sarah, Love, and Nathaniel Hardy; witnesses, William Parker, John Hoag.]

[Account of the settlement of the estate; receipts, £3099. 0. 0; expenditures, £3085. 19. 1; allowed June 4, 1765.]

[The guardian being dissatisfied with the account, he and the administrator agree, July 13, 1767, to submit the same to Moses Emerson, merchant, John Smith, schoolmaster, and Ebenezer Thompson, physician. They report, Aug. 15, 1767, that the administrator is indebted to the estate £20. 15. 8.]

Province of New Hampshire } January the 25th Anno Domini 1768 Pursuant To an order from The Honourable The Judge of Probate of Wills &c for the Province of New Hampshire Appointing us the subscribers a Committee to view the Real Estate of Theophilus Hardy late of Durham in said Province yeoman Deceas^d Intestate & to Consider whether the same might be Divided into five shares (allowing a Double Portion or share to the Eldest Son) without prejudice to or Spoiling the whole and in Case it might be so divided To make the Division and if not To Appraise the same According To the Present value in order to make a settlement of the whole on the Eldest Son as the Law of said Province in such Cases Provided Directs — We have met & viewed the Real Estate of the Said Intestate & upon due Consideration do adjudge That the Same Cannot be Divided as aforesaid without prejudicing & spoiling The whole: whereupon we have appraised The same as follows viz The House Barn & one acre & a Quarter of Land Near Durham Falls at sixty five pounds Lawful money and the Twenty Acres of Land adjoining To Lands of Capt Thomas Chesle which the Said Intestate bought of Col^o Joseph Smith of Newmarkett at Sixty pounds Lawful money in the whole Amounting to one hundred & twenty five pounds which we apprehend to be the present value thereof Witness our hands the Day & year above mentioned

                Moses Emerson
                Hubbard Stevens
                Jn° Sullivan
                Ephraim Folsom

[Bond of Theophilus Hardy of Durham, yeoman, with John Sullivan of Durham and Walter Bryent, Jr., of Newmarket as sureties, in the sum of £500, July 26, 1769, for the payment of their shares to Mary Hardy, Sarah Hardy, Love Hardy, and Nathaniel Hardy; witnesses, Stephen Cogan, Susanna Varrell.]

[Bond of Antipas Gilman of Gilmanton in the sum of £50, Oct. 20, 1785, as guardian of Nathaniel Ladd and wife of Gilmanton, to prosecute a suit on the bond of Theophilus Hardy to pay his co-heirs their shares; witnesses, Samuel Parker, William Parker.]

THOMAS GORDON   1757   EXETER

In the Name of God amen the Second day of december annoque domini one Thousand Seven hundred and fifty Seven I Thomas Gorden of Exeter in the Province of Newhampshire in New England yeoman being ancient * * *

Item I Give and bequeath to my Son Thomas Gorden his heirs and assigns for ever aboute Six acres of land be the same more or less lying in the Parish of Brintwood in the Province aforesaid on the Southerly Side of Jonathan Gliddens land and the Northerly Side of James Beans land and on the Westerly Side of the litle River So Called and to be bounded on the westerly End by land which I Shall Give to my Son Daniel in this my Will and I also Give to my Said Son Thomas fifty Pounds Equal to Silver Coine at the Rate of four Pounds old tenor per ounce to be Paid to him within three years after my decease, I having Given him the Greatest Part of his Portion already by deed.

Item I Give and bequeath to my Son Daniel Gorden his heirs and assigns forever fourteen acres of land be the same more or less lying on the Westerly side of that way which Leads from the way that Goes from the Great hill So Called to the mill Commonly Called the black Rock mill to my Son Thomas Gordens dwelling house it being that fourteen acres of land which was allowed to me by the last Committee which Proportioned the Comon and undivided land in Said Exeter and also Seven acres of land lying on the East Side of land heretofore belonging to Nathaniel Smith deceased and on the Northerly End by land in Possession of James Bean and on the Southerly End by land which I Shall Give to my son Benoni Gorden in this my will and to be at that End as the fence now Stands between my Said Sons viz daniel and Benoni and also Twenty Pounds Equal to Silver Coin at the Rate of four Pounds old tenor bills of Publick Credit per ounce

Item I Give and bequeath to my Son Benoni Gorden his heirs and assigns forever five acres of mowing land more or less bounding Northerly by land which I Gave my Son Thomas by deed Westerly by land lately belonging to Nathaniel Smith deceased and Southerly as the fence now Stands between my Said Sons viz: daniel and Benoni and Easterly by Jonathan Glidens land, and also one hundred Pounds to be paid to him his heirs and assigns within one year after my decease at the Rate of Silver Coin at four Pounds per ounce I haveing Given him Part of his Portion heretofore by deed. I further Give him my wareing appariel.

Item I Give and bequeath to my Son Timothy Gorden his heirs and assigns for ever Twenty Pounds old tenor bills of Publick Credit Equal to Silver Coin at the Rate of four Pounds per ounce to be Paid within two years after my decease he having Received the Greatest Part of his Portion already.

Item I Give and bequeath to my Son James Gorden his heirs

and assigns forever Thirty Pounds old tenor bills of Publick Credit Equal to Silver Coin at the Rate of four Pounds per ounce to be Paid within two years after my decease he having Received the Greatest Part of his Portion already.

Item I Give and bequeath to my Daughter Dinah Mugoon her heirs and assigns forever one hundred Pounds old tenor bills of Publick Credit Equal to Silver Coin at the Rate of four Pounds Per ounce to be paid by my Son Benjamin Gorden out of what I Shall Give to him in this my will within four years after my decease and also a Suite of mourning Cloaths at my decease and a Cow and a Tramiel and a Pot hooks and three Puter Plates and a fether bed and beding it being the bed and beding which I now use my Self to lodge in.

Item I Give and bequeath to my daughter Abigail Robards her heirs and assigns forever Seventy five Pounds old tenor bills of Publick Credit Equal to Silver Coin at the Rate of four Pounds per ounce to be paid by my Son Nathaniel Gorden out of what I Shall Give to him in this my will within one year after my decease, and a Cow and a Smaul pot and a Tramel and a Pot hook and three Puter Plates to be delivered to her as Soon as may be Conveanantly after my decease.

Item I Give and bequeath to my daughter Hannah Smith her heirs and assigns forever, fifty Pounds old tenor bills of Publick Credit Equal to Silver Coin at the Rate of four Pounds per ounce to be paid by my Executors Equaly out of what I shall Give them in this my will within four years after my decease, and a fether bed which was her mothers and beding and three Sheep and three Puter Platters to be delivered to her as Soon as Conveanantly may be after my decease.

Item I Give and bequeath to my two Sons viz: Benjamin Gorden and Nathaniel Gorden their heirs and assigns forever all my homestead and my dwelling house and barn and other buildings thereon Excepting half an acre of land to be Reserved for a burying Place as Convenant as may be where my last wife was buryed and Several of my Children & Grand Children and also a Conveanant way to Pass and Repass to and from it to the Cuntry Road leading from Exeter to Kingstown. I also Give and bequeath to my Said Sons Benjamin and Nathaniel all my medow adjoyning to Benjamin Graves & Henry Steels land and land which I Sold to Joseph Kimbull of Exeter aforesaid. I also Give them all my Stock of Creatours and all my Usenteals of Husbandry and all other of my Personal Estate which I have not alredy disposed of in this my Will, the Said Premises to be Equally divided between them

Finaly I do hereby Constitute appoint and ordain My Two Sons viz: Benjamin Gorden and Nathaniel Gorden of Exeter afore Said my Executors * * *

his
Thomas + Gorden
mark

[Witnesses] Josph Kimball, Daniel Smith, Sam^{ll} Gilman. [Proved May 27, 1761.]

[Bond of Benjamin Gordon and Nathaniel Gordon, both of Exeter, with Joseph Kimball of Exeter and Joseph Smith of Kingston as sureties, in the sum of £1000, May 27, 1761, for the execution of the will; witnesses, Cutts Shannon, Solomon Loud, Jr.]

DANIEL HOYT 1757 EPPING

[Administration on the estate of Daniel Hoyt of Epping, husbandman, granted to Joseph Cilley of Nottingham, gentleman, Dec. 3, 1757.]

[Probate Records, vol. 20, p. 376.]

[Bond of Joseph Cilley, with Robert Harvey of Nottingham, gentleman, and Joseph Burleigh, Jr., of Newmarket, yeoman, as sureties, in the sum of £500, Dec. 3, 1757, for the administration of the estate; witnesses, William Parker, David Sewall.]

[Warrant, Dec. 3, 1757, authorizing Joseph Chandler and Simon Drake, both of Epping, yeomen, to appraise the estate.]

[Inventory, Jan. 9, 1758; amount, £1652. 7. 6; signed by Joseph Chandler and Simon Drake.]

[Warrant, April 26, 1758, authorizing John Bartlett of Nottingham, Joseph Chandler, Ebenezer Dow, Simon Drake, and Jonathan Elliot, all of Epping, yeomen, to set off the widow's dower.]

Province of } Pursuent to the within Preceipt I John Bartlett of Nottingham & we Simon Drake & Jonathan Elliet of Epping within Named have Sott of to Juda Hoit Widow Relict of Daniel Hoit Late of Epping Deceasd Seven acres of Land and the House & Barn theiron to be her full Right of Dower and is Bounded as followeth viz Begining at the northeast Corner of the Said Daniel Hoit Land and run South 29 Degrees West twenty Rods and Sixteen feet to a stake then run west and be north fifty seven Rods to a stake then run North 29 Degrees East twenty Rods & Sixteen feet from thence east & be South fifty Seven Rods to the Place first mentioned as Witness our hand this 22nd Day of June at Epping 1759

       John Bartlett
       Simon Drake
       Jonathan Eliot

[Warrant, July 26, 1758, authorizing David Lawrence and James Norris, gentleman, both of Epping, to receive claims against the estate.]

[List of claims, July 31, 1759; amount, £1108. 12. 9; signed by David Lawrence and James Norris.]

[Account of the settlement of the estate; receipts, £1732. 7. 6; expenditures, £570. 12. 0; allowed Feb. 22, 1760.]

NATHANIEL SHERBURNE 1757   PORTSMOUTH

[Administration on the estate of Nathaniel Sherburne of Portsmouth, shopkeeper, granted to Mehitabel Sherburne, widow, Dec. 5, 1757.]

[Probate Records, vol. 20, p. 377.]

[Bond of Mehitabel Sherburne of Portsmouth, widow, with William Pearson of Portsmouth, shopkeeper, and Joseph Sherburne of Boston, Mass., merchant, as sureties, in the sum of £1000, Dec. 5, 1757, for the administration of the estate; witnesses, Nathaniel Mendum, William Parker.]

[Warrant, Dec. 5, 1757, authorizing Eleazer Russell and Samuel Penhallow, shopkeeper, both of Portsmouth, to appraise the estate.]

[Inventory, Jan. 23, 1758; amount, £8680. 16. 10; signed by Eleazer Russell and Samuel Penhallow.]

JOHN CURRIER   1757   KINGSTON

In the Name of God Amen I John Currier of Kingston in the Province of Newhampshire in New England Yeoman being Ill & weak in body * * *

Item To my beloved Wife Ruth Currier I Will & bequeath forty Dollars to be her own As also my Negro Servant Named Sego to be at her dispose I also give her all that is owing to me by Notes Bills bonds or book debts & all my moveable & personal Estate (Excepting what shall hereafter in this my will be disposed of otherwise by me) she paying the Legacys to my Children that I shall in this my will Appoint her to pay. I also Will her the Improvement of One half of my Dwelling house & the one half of the Cellar that is in it & the Improvement of my New barn so long as she shall remain my Widow I also will her the Improvement of all my Lands & real Estate that I Shall in this my will bequeath to my two Sons Ezra & John the whole of their respective parts till they shall respectively Come to be of Age and after that the Improvement of the one half of Each of their parts in my Lands As long as she shall remain my widow I also give her of the things in my house one Bed & furniture half a dozen of Chairs & a Case of draws to be her Own to use & dispose of as she shall please I also will her the Improvement of the whole of my live stock of Cattle horse sheep & swine she keeping the Same good till my Children to whom they shall in this my will be given shall respectively come of Age to receive them of her or as long as she shall remain my Widow

Item To my three Daughters Mary, Rhoda, & Judith I will And bequeath to Each & Every one of them Ten Acres of land to them & their heirs which said ten acres of land to Each of them is to be taken out of a Certain forty Acre lot of land which I purchased of John Fifield of Kingston & at or near A place Called Beech plain in s^d Kingston

Item To my Said three Daughters Mary, Rhoda & Judith I will & Bequeath the Sum of two hundred Pounds money According To the old Tenour to Each & Every one of them to be paid them by my Executrix hereafter Named As soon as they shall arrive to the age of Eighteen years or at marriage I also give & bequeath to Each of my said Daughters a Cow to be receivd by them at the age of Eighteen years or at marriage

Item To my Son Ezra I will & bequeath to him & his heirs my Dwelling house & all my homestead Land Adjoyning & lying On Each side the way together With the Orchard & buildings standing thereon As also a piece of land which I purchasd of Tristram Sanborn of Kingston Containing about fifteen acres & lying between the Land of Joshua Woodman & Cap^n Orlando Bagly of said Kingston Woodmans on the North & Bagly's on the south of it As also a Piece of salt marsh which I purchased of John Casman of South hampton Containing about two acres & an half lying in South hampton Near Gatchels rocks So called I also give him the Sum of two hundred Pounds money According to the old Tenour to be paid him by my Executrix as soon as he shall arrive to the age of Twenty one Years

Item To my Son John I will & bequeath to him & his heirs all that tract of land that I purchased of Samuel Emmons Late of Kingston deceas'd Containing one or two & thirty Acres or thereabouts having Land of Joseph Bean of said Kingston on the west & land of Deacon Nathan Bacheller deceasd on the East as also all that tract of land which I purchased of Ebenezer Webster of Kingston where said Webster some Years Ago lived Said tract of land Containing twenty Seven acres or thereabouts As also the remainder of the forty Acre lot forementioned which I Purchasd of John Fifield of Kingston after the thirty acres which I have already bequeathd to my three Daughters is taken out of it As also a piece of Salt Marsh which I purchasd of Joseph Greeley Junr Containing about two Acres lying in South hampton & near Gatchels rock so Called As also the Sum of four hundred Pounds in money According to the old Tenour to be paid him by my Executrix as soon as he shall arrive to the age of twenty one Years

Item To my Son Ezra I Will & bequeath to him & his heirs a Peice of land which I purchasd of my Brother Eliphalet Currier lying in South hampton & joyning to land of Lawrence Straw said piece of land Containing Seven Acres or thereabouts

Item my Wearing Apparel I give to my two sons Ezra & John to be Equally divided between them

Item I Give to Each of my Said Sons a bed & bedding in my house

Item To my son Ezra I give my Desk

Item as to the rest of my houshold goods that I have not already in this my will disposd of my will is that they be Equally divided between my three Daughters Each to receive her part as soon as she arrives to the age of Eighteen years or at marriage

Item to my two Sons Ezra & John I also give & bequeath all my Stock of Cattle & horse sheep & swine (Excepting the three Cows already bequeathed to my three Daughters) to be Equally divided between them as also all my tools of husbandry & Implements for work abroad such as Carts & sled Yokes & Chains Axes hoes & the like to be Equally divided between them likewise

Item all my right & Interest in the Iron Works Saw Mill & Grist mill at Trickling falls so Called I give & bequeath to my two Sons Ezra & John to be Equally divided between them

Item my will is that the ten Acres of land which I have In this my will bequeathed to Each of my three daughters to be taken out of the forty Acre lot which I purchased of John Fifield as before mentioned shall be set off to them in the following manner Vizt Mary's to be taken off of the West Side Extending the whole length of the said lot Rhoda's ten Acres adjoyning to her's & Judiths ten Acres Adjoyning to hers Each to Extend the whole length of the lot likewise.

Item my will is & I do hereby Constitute & Appoint my beloved wife Ruth Currier to be Sole Executrix * * * In testimony whereof I have hereunto set my hand & seal this seventeenth day of December Anno Domini One Thousand seven hundred & fifty Seven & in the thirty first year of his Majisties Reign

John Currier

[Witnesses] Peter Coffin, Jeremiah Currier, Theophilus Clough.

[Proved March 1, 1758.]

[Warrant, March 1, 1758, authorizing Jeremy Webster and Ebenezer Stevens, both of Kingston, to appraise the estate.]

[Inventory, April 5, 1758; amount, £21,268. 5. 9; signed by Jeremy Webster and Ebenezer Stevens.]

WILLIAM PAGE   1757   BRENTWOOD

[Elizabeth Page renounces administration on the estate of her husband, William Page of Brentwood, Dec. 26, 1757, in favor of Sargent Currier of South Hampton.]

[Administration granted to Sargent Currier of South Hampton, yeoman, Dec. 28, 1757.]

[Probate Records, vol. 20, p. 404.]

[Bond of Sargent Currier, with Abner Morrill and Ephraim Carter as sureties, all of South Hampton, yeomen, in the sum of £2000, Dec. 28, 1757, for the administration of the estate; witnesses, David Sewall, William Parker.]

[Warrant, Dec. 28, 1757, authorizing Samuel Currier and Eliphalet Merrill, both of South Hampton, yeomen, to appraise the estate.]

[Inventory, Feb. 15, 1758; amount, £635. 17. 9; signed by Samuel Currier and Eliphalet Merrill.]

[Citation to Sargent Currier of Hopkinton, April 13, 1778, to appear and render an account of the estate.]

HENRY SHERBURNE   1757   PORTSMOUTH

In the Name of God Amen I Henry Sherburne of Portsmouth in the Province of New Hampshire Esq' being aged & weak of Body * * *

Item I give and Devise to my Sons Samuel Sherburne & Henry Sherburne all my Lands lying between the Roads or high Ways Commonly Called the middle Road & the Mill Dam Road joining to the Said Middle Road the Land of Thomas Packer Esq' the Land of Mark Langdon Thomas Wibird & Daniel Warner Esq'ˢ Equally Divided between them my Said Sons their Heirs & Assigns

Item my Farm at Greenland and all my Lands there I give & Devise to my Sons Samuel & John & if either of them Shall Dye without Lawful Issue then the whole shall be for & go to the Survivor of them & his Heirs & assigns but if they both leave Lawful Issue then to go to Such Issue & their Heirs & Assigns

Item I give and Devise to my Son Henry all that Land I have joining to his Land on the Southerly Side of the Road leading to Rye or on the left hand of the said Road as one goes to Rye to him his Heirs & Assigns & my Land lying on the other Side said Road near the Same & so runing up to the Cedar Swamp being Sixty Acres more or Less I give & Divise to my Grandson Henry the Son of my Said Son Henry his Heirs & Assigns. I also give my Said Son Henry that Seventeen acres of Land which joins to or is near his Land which was Set off to me from Rye aforesaid I also give to my Said Son all my Land & marsh and Buildings at the Place called Little Harbour whether it lies in New Castle or Portsmouth or falls within the Bounds of Rye aforesaid all to him his Heirs & assigns — and my fresh Marsh lying at the head of the Creek so called near the Marsh of Hunking Wentworth & Elliot Vaughan Esq^{rs} I give with my Said Farm at Greenland & to go in the Same manner as I have ordered That as aforesaid —

Item all my Lands in Kingston Haverhill Kittery and all my Rights & Lands in the New Townships in the Province of New Hampshire or Else where not herein otherwise disposed of I give the Same Equally Divided between my Sons Henry and John their Respective Heirs and Assigns — I also give to my Son Henry the House & Land thereto belonging where my Late Son in Law John Eyre Lived near the Dwelling House of Samuel Wentworth in Portsmouth aforesaid to him his Heirs & assigns —

Item I give to my Grandson John the Son of my Son John all the Land I own between the Said House & the School House and the Street & mr Packer's Land to him his Heirs & Assigns

Item I give to Each of my Daughters Ann Langdon & Dorothy Gilman the Sum of One hundred pounds old Tenor to be paid to them by my Executor

Item I give Devise & Bequeath to my Son John my Mansion House & Land thereto belonging and all other my Real Estate Lying on the North Side of Crafford's Lane or Daniel Street So Called to him his Heirs & assigns and all the Rest of my Estate Real and Personal not herein otherwise Disposed of I give &

bequeath to him my Said Son John his Heirs & assigns & hereby Constitute & appoint him to be Sole Executor of this my Last Will & Testament & order him to give up without any Demand to the Reverend Mr Samuel Langdon the Bond I have of his & the Debt he Owes me and to Pay to the Reverend Mr Arthur Brown & the Revd Mr Samuel Haven the Sum of twenty pounds Each old Tenor as a token of my Regard & Respect for them * * * In Witness whereof I have hereunto Set my hand & Seal the 27th Day of Decemb^r Anno Domini 1757

H Sherburne

[Witnesses] Saml Langdon, Saml Haven, William Parker. [Proved April 29, 1758.]

[Decree of court, April 29, 1758, proving and allowing the will against the protest of Samuel Sherburne, oldest son, who claimed that the testator was not of a sound and disposing mind.]

[Bond of Samuel Sherburne of Portsmouth, with Joseph Langdon of Portsmouth, gentleman, and Peter Gilman of Exeter as sureties, in the sum of £100, June 6, 1758, to prosecute an appeal of the probate of the will; witnesses, Jonathan Longfellow, Joshua Crockett.]

[Administration de bonis non granted to Henry Sherburne of Portsmouth, gentleman, Nov. 29, 1758.]

[Probate Records, vol. 21, p. 102.]

[Bond of Henry Sherburne, gentleman, with George Waldron, husbandman, and Samuel Cate, yeoman, as sureties, all of Portsmouth, in the sum of £3000, Nov. 29, 1758, for the administration de bonis non of the estate; witnesses, David Sewall, William Parker.]

At a Court of Supreme Probate held at Portsmouth within & for the Province of New Hampshire on the 27th Day of Octob^r 1763 his Excellency the Governor having Transmitted to the Council a Copy of a Judgment of his Majesty in Council on the appeal of John Sherburne of Portsmouth aforesaid Merch^t against Saml Sherburne Esqr & others Relating to the Probate of the Will of Henry Sherburne Late of Portsm^o aforesaid Esqr Deceased Reversing a Judgment of this Court concerning the Same and affirming a Decree of the Judge of Probate of wills for said Province touching the said Will &c with which his Excellency Recommended that they woud do what was proper to be done in the Case upon which it is considered that as the Decree of the Judge of Probate is affirmed & that of this Court Reversed the Said Copy ought to be Sent down to the said Judge to be carried into Execution

A True Copy attested

₱ T Atkinson Junr Sec^y

From this Probate & Decree an appeal was Asked & Granted to the Supreme Court of Probate where the Probate of the Will as to the Real Estate was Reversed Two of the Witnesses being Disallowed as Incompetent and as to the Question of the Testators Sanity the Court was Divided from which Decree An appeal was Asked And Granted to his Majesty in Counsel Whose Judgement is as follows Viz^t

At the Court at Saint James's the 5th of April 1762
    The Kings most Excellent Majesty

Lord President	Erl of Powis
Lord Chamberlin	Earl of Hardwicke
Duke of Rutland	Lord Bathurst
Duke of New Castle	Mr Vice Chamberlain
Earl of Bute	

Upon reading at the Board a Report from the Right Honourable the Lords of the Committee of Council for hearing Appeals from the Plantations dated the 16th of last Month in the Words following Viz

Your Majesty having been pleased by your Order in Council of the 2^d of January last to refer Unto this Committee the humble Petition And Appeal of John Sherburne Gentleman, Youngest Son of Henery Sherburne late of New Hampshire Esqr deceased Setting forth Amongst other things that the Said Henery Sherburne being Seized of a Considerable Real Estate in the Said Province And also of some Personal Estate And having Several Children And no Wife And being minded to dispose of his Said Estate Amongst his Said Children in Such a manner as he Saw fit did duly make his last Will and Testament in Writing And therein taking Notice of his being Aged Weak of Body but of Sound and Disposeing Mind And Memory willed that all just Debts Should be paid out of his Personal Estate by his Executor — Item he desvised to his Sons Samuel Sherburne And Henery Sherburne Certain Lands therein Mentioned equally between them their Heirs And Assigns Item his Farm at Greenland And Certain other lands there he devised to his sons the Said Samuel And the Appellant, John Sherburne, And if Either of them shou'd Die without Issue then to the Survivor of them And his Heirs but if they both left lawful Issue then to go to such Issue — Item he Devised to his Son Henery Certain other Lands to him his Heirs And Assigns — And Certain Other Lands he Devised to his Grandson Henery Son of his Son Henery And his Heirs And Assigns And devised to his Son Henery Certain other Land — And his Fresh Marsh lying at the head of the Creek, he gave with his Said Farm at Greenland And to go in the Same manner as he had given that — Item all his Lands in Kingston Haverhill Kittery And all his Rights And Lands in the New Townships in New Hampshire or Elsewhere not in his Said Will otherwise disposed of he gave the Same equally to be divided between his Said Son Henery And the Appellant John Sherburne — He gave to his Said Son Henery his Heirs And Assigns a Certain House and Land — And Devised to his Grandson Son John Son of the Appellant John Certain Lands therein Mentioned to him his Heirs And Assigns — He gave to each of his Daughters Ann Langdon And Dorothy Gilman One hundred Pounds old Tenor to be paid by his

Executor He devised to his son the Appellant John Sherburne his Mansion House And Land thereto belonging And all other his real Estate Laying on the North Side of Craffords Lane or Daniels Street to him his Heirs And Assigns And all the rest of his Estate Real And personal not therein Otherwise Disposed of he gave to his Said son John the Appellant his heirs And Assigns And Appointed his Said Son John Sole Executor of his Will And the Testator ordered his Executor to give Up without any Demand to the Reverend Samuel Langdon the Bond he had of his And the Debts he owed him And to pay to Arthur Brown And the Reverend Samuel Haven Twenty Pounds Each old Tenor as a Token of the Testators Regard And Respect from them. And he revoked all other Wills by him thentofore made which Will was signed And Sealed by the Testator in the presence of three Witnesses Viz Samuel Langdon Samuel Haven And William Parker who Attested the Same to be Signed Sealed And Declared by the Said Testator to be his last Will And Testament in their Presences who Subscribed as Witnesses in his Presence — That the two first Subscribing Witnesses are two of the Small Legatees in the Will And the Testator soon After making his Said Will without Revokeing or Altering the Same. That the Appellant John Sherburne the Executor of the Said Will And one of the Devisees therein After the Testators Decease propounded the Said Will before Richard Wibard Esquire the Judge of Probate of Wills in the Said Province: But the Said Samuel Sherburne tho' he had been very amply provided for by the Testator in his life time yet with a Vew to Defate the Appellant of the Provision that had been made for him by his Father in his Said Will thought fit to enter a Caveat against the Proveing thereof Alledging And Pretending that there was Some inequality in the Dispositions therein Contained And that the Will being but a Short time before the Testators Death he was not Capable by Reason of his Sickness of making any Reasonable And Just Settlement of his Estate: whereupon the Parties proceeded to make Proofs And Examine Witnesses in the Court of the Said Judge of Probates touching the Validity of the Said Will And the three Subscribing Witnesses being all Examined as to the fact of the Execution of the Will Samuel Langdon & William Parker Two of them deposed that they Saw the Testator Sign & Seal & heard him Declare the Same to be his last Will & Testament, And that at the time of Doing thereof he was to their best Discernment of Sound disposing Mind And Memory And that they with the Other Subscribing Witness Samuel Haven Subscribed the Same as Witness in the Testators Presence. And the Said Samuel Haven made Oath to the Same Saving that he Said he Cou'd not Swear that the Testator was or that he was not at that time Capable of Disposeing of his Estate but that at that time Whilst he Discoursed with the Testor the Testator discoursed rationally — That there was Also Several other Witnesses Examined touching the Sanity of the Testator And the Disposition of his Estate And on the 29th of April 1758 the Cause came on for Sentence before the Judge of Probates, who after hearing Counsel for both Sides And the Depositions of the witnesses read was of Oppinion the will was good for that it appeared by the Oaths of the Witnesses to the will that it duly Executed According to the Law of the Province for preventing Frauds & Perjuries; That the Testator had then the Use of his Reason And Two of the Witnesses were Express as to his Capacity at that time And the other Seemed only to be Uncertain of the proper meaning And Extent of the Words Used on the Occasion of disposing mind And Memory And the Proof was Sufficient to Satisfy the Statute; besides there was Several other Witnesses proveing the Testator to have the Use of his Reason during his Sickness to the last day of his life And that there was not any Evidence to the Contrary; And as to the Objection of an Enequal Disposition of the Estate by the Will the Testator might have Reason to make it And there was Evidence to that Purpose Therefore the Judge Pronounced for the Will And Decreed a Probate thereof to be Grated to the appelant That the Said Samuel Shereburne the Eldest Son of the

Said Henery Shereburne the Father Deceased being Dissatisfied with that Sentence and having been joined by Peter Gilman Esqr And Dorothy his wife And Joseph Langdon And Ann his wife which Said Dorothy And Ann are the two Daughters of the Said Henery Shereburne Deceased who intervened for their Interest they prayed and were allowed an Appeal therefrom to the Governor And Council of the Said Province Sitting as a Court of Supreme Probate — That the Parties went into New And further Proofs in the Said Suprame Court And there were Several Other Witnesses Examined to the Number of Eight or Nine who Corroborated the former Proof of the Testators Sanity And Also of his Declaration in favour of the Appellant his son John And his having before made Provision for his other Children that Two Receipts were Exhibited Dated the 1st of March And the 5th of April 1758 from Two of the Subscribing Witnesses Samuel Langdon And Samuel Haven to the Appellant as Executor of the Testator that is to say Langdon for his Note of £80. 0. 0 Old Tenor Delivered Up to them According to the Will And the Other for his Legacy of £20. 0. 0 given him thereby: And also a General Release from the Appellant to them of all Actions that on the 29th of June 1758 the Cause Coming on to be heard again in the Said Supreme Court an Objection was taken to the Competency of the two Subscribing Witnesses to the Will Viz Samuel Langdon And Samuel Haven for that they were Legatees in the Will And the Said Supreme Court was pleased for that Cause to over Rule their Evidence And to Adjudge them to be disqualified to be Witnesses to prove the Said Will And therefore did Adjudge that the Said Will so far as it Related to the Real Estate of the Testator Should be Disapproved and Disallowed And as to the Sanity of the Testator the Judges having been divided in their oppinion gave no Judgment thereon that the Petitioner Conceiving himself aggrived by the Said Sentence of the Supreme Court in disapproving And Disallowing the Said so far as it Relates to the Said Real Estate And Also by the Said Supreme Courts not proceeding to a Sentance in Affermance of the Probate decreed of the Said Will by the Said Judge of Probate prayed And was Allowed an Appeal to your Majesty in Council from that part of the Said Sentance that Adjudges the Said Will so far as Relates to the Said Real Estate be disapproved And disallowed, The Petitioner therefore prays that the Same may be reversed And that the Said Final Sentence of the Judges of probate pronounced in favour of the Said Will And Decreeing Probate thereof to the Appellant may be Affirmed — The Lords of the Committee in Obedience to your Majestys Said Order of Reference this day took the Said petition And Appeal into their Consideration And heard all partys therein Concerned by their Counsel Learned in the Law and do thereupon agree humbly to Report as their oppinion to your Majesty that the Court of Probate has no jurisdiction so far as the Will Relates to Real Estates And if they had, that Samuel Langdon And Samuel Haven are Competent Witnesses And ought Not to have been Rejected And that therefore the Sentence given by the Supreme Court of Probates on the 29th of June 1758 Shoud be reversed And Upon the Rest of the Cause the Judgment given by the first of Probates on the 29th April 1758 Affirmed —

His Majesty this day took the Said Report into Consideration And was pleased with the Advice of His Privy Council to Approve thereof And to order as it is hereby Ordered that the Sentence given by the Supreme Court of Probates on the 29th of June be reversed And Upon the Rest of the Cause that the Judgment by the first Court of Probates on the 29th of April 1758 be Affirmed — Whereof the Governer or Commander in Chief of his Majestys Province of New Hampshire for the time being and all others whom it may Concern are to take Notice And Govern themselves Accordingly.

Hen ffane

[Probate Records, vol. 23, p. 25.]

EBENEZER TOWLE   1757   BRENTWOOD

[Warrant, Dec. 28, 1757, authorizing Joseph Godfrey and Daniel Beede, both of Brentwood, yeomen, to appraise the estate of Ebenezer Towle of Brentwood, yeoman, administration of which is granted to his widow, Alice Towle.]

[Inventory, Feb. 5, 1758; amount, £2080. 19. 0; signed by Joseph Godfrey and Daniel Beede.]

[Account of the administratrix; receipts, £615. 19. 0, personal estate; expenditures, £277. 10. 0; mentions "maintaining two Children under 7 years of age from Augt 24, 1757 to May 30th 1759"; allowed May 30, 1759.]

SAMUEL BOYNTON   1757   STRATHAM

[Administration on the estate of Samuel Boynton of Stratham, blacksmith, granted to Sarah Boynton, widow, Dec. 28, 1757.]

[Probate Records, vol. 20, p. 409.]

[Bond of Sarah Boynton of Stratham, widow, with Joshua Hill of Stratham and Joshua Cate of Greenland, yeomen, as sureties, in the sum of £1000, Dec. 28, 1757, for the administration of the estate; witnesses, William Parker, David Sewall.]

[Warrant, Dec. 28, 1757, authorizing Joshua Hill and Nathan Hoag, both of Stratham, yeomen, to appraise the estate.]

[Inventory, Jan. 19, 1758; amount, £2416. 1. 0; signed by Nathan Hoag and Joshua Hill.]

JONATHAN DUSTIN   1757   LONDONDERRY

[Administration on the estate of Jonathan Dustin of Londonderry, yeoman, granted to Sarah Dustin of Londonderry, widow Dec. 28, 1757.]

[Probate Records, vol. 20, p. 396.]

[Bond of Sarah Dustin, widow, with John Dow of Plaistow, yeoman, and James Paul of Londonderry, husbandman, as sureties, in the sum of £1000, Dec. 28, 1757, for the administration of the estate; witnesses, William Parker, David Sewall.]

[Inventory, Jan. 7, 1758; amount, £93. 19. 9; signed by Obadiah Eastman, Seth Pattee, and Abraham Dow.]

ROBERT ROWE   1757   KENSINGTON

In the Name of God Amen I Robert Row of the Parish of Kensington in the Province of Newhampshire in newengland yeoman * * *

1ly I Give and Bequeath to my well beloved wife Apphia Row the improvement of the East End of my Dwelling house and the seller under said end of said house and the one third part of my Barn and the one third part of all my land laying on the west Side of the Road that goeth from Kensington to Exeter it being five halfe Shears my said wife to have the improvement of what is above mentioned so long as Shee Continues my widow and no longer and at her Death or Day of marriage then what I have Given to my wife to go to those that I shall Give them to in this my will; and I Give my said wife the one halfe of all my Stock of Creatures of all Sorts and all the house hold Goods shee Brought with her when I married her and all that we Got since wee lived together that Shall be in the house at my Decease my said wife to have to Despose of as Shee Shall think proper

2ly I Give and Bequeath to my son Joseph Row forever the one halfe of a sixty acre lot laying in the Township of Chester he haveing had his portion mostly Given him by Deed

3ly I Give and Bequeath to my son Jonathan Row forever my Dwelling house and seller under it and my Barn and the one halfe of my five halfe Shears laying in the parish of Kensington laying on the west Side of the Road that leadeth from Kensington to Exeter and I Give my said son the one halfe of my salt marsh laying in the falls parish and the one halfe of all my stock of Creatuers of all sorts and all my implyments of husbandry

and I Give my said son Jonathan Row all the moveabls that was in the house when I married my last wife that I have not otherwise Desposed of Before only his mother is to improve as Before mentioned he paying as I shall order him in this my will

4ly I Give and Bequeath to my son moses Row forever the one halfe of a sixty acre lot laying in the Township of Chester he haveing his portion Given him by Deed.

5ly I Give and Bequeath to my son Jeremiah Row five pounds money old tenor Bills of Credit to be paid to him By my Executors within one year after my Decease he haveing had his portion Given him by Deed

6ly I Give and Bequeath to my son Benjamin Row forever the one halfe of my five half Shears laying in the Parish of Kensington laying on the west Side of the Road that goeth from Kensington to Exeter and the one halfe of my salt marsh laying in the falls parish only his mother is to have the improvement of what is before mentioned her widowhood and no longer he paying as I Shall order him in my will

7ly I Give and Bequeath to my son Robert Row forever all my land laying at Dearhill so Called in the Township of Exeter be it more or less Excepting fourscore acres that I have Given my son Jeremiah Row by Deed

8ly I Give and Bequeath to my son Winthrop Row forever one hundred acre lot laying in the Township of Chester Buting on the north Branch of Exeter River

9ly I Give and Bequeath to my son Caleb Row forever a hundred acre lot so Called laying in the township of Chester it being number 43 which lot his father Bought in the year 1757

10ly I Give and Bequeath to my Son John Row forever an hundred acre lot in the Township of Chester and laying in that Division Called the second hundred acre lots and a meadow lot so Called

11ly I Give and Bequeath to my son Ephraim Row forever a fourscore acre lot laying in the Township of Chester

12ly I Give to my four sons namely winthrop Row and Caleb Row john and Ephraim Row forever all my part in the Common or undivided land in the Township of Chester to be Equally Divided Between them and if any one of my above mentioned four youngest sons Dye without an heir then the other named to have what I have Given him in this my will

13ly I Give and Bequeath to my five Granchildren the Children of my Daughter Jane Sweat namely Joseph Josiah Jonathan mehetable and sarah Sweats one hundred pounds money to paid in Dollors at three pound apiece or in Bills of Credit Equal there unto to be paid to them within three years after my Decease By my son Jonathan Row

14ly I Give and Bequeath to my Daughter Ruth fellows one hundred pounds money in Dollors at three pounds apiece or in Bills of Credit Equal thereunto to be paid to her By my son Benjamin Row within one year after my Decease

15ly I Give and Bequeath to my Daughter Elizabeth fellows one hundred pounds money in Dollors at three pounds apiece or in Bills of Credit Equal thereunto to be paid to her By my Executors within one year after my Decease my Executors to pay fifty pounds each

16ly and if there be any thing that I have not Desposed in this my will I Give it or them to my Executors and I order my Executors to bury me in Decent Christian manner at their Charge

and I Do Constitute and appoint my two sons namly Jonathan Row and Benjamin Row to be my Executors * * * In Witness Whereof I the Said Robert Row have hereunto set my hand and Seal the Twenty Eighth Day of December: anno: Domini: 1757 and in the thirty first yeare of the Reign of King George the second &c

              Robert Row

[Witnesses] Ezekiel Dow, Benja prescott, Joseph Tilton.
[Proved March 25, 1761.]

[Inventory, March 31, 1761; amount, £35,108. 2. 4; signed by Philemon Blake and William Parker.]

BENJAMIN AKERMAN   1757   PORTSMOUTH

In the Name of God, Amen. The last will and Testament of Benjamin Akerman I Benjamin Akerman of Portsmouth in the Province of New Hampshire being Sick and Weak in Body * * *

Item To my Beloved wife Mary I give the house I now live in with the Slaughter house and Gardens with all my moveables during her naturall life which is to be in Steed of her thirds —

Item To my son Benjamin his heirs and Assigns I give my house Orchard Lands and Tanyard At Islington so Called that was Kirks, togather with that Lot of Land at Barrington that was my Origanal Right —

Item To my Son Simeon and his heirs and Assigns I Give my lot of Land on Pickerins neck that Lays between a Lot belonging to Thomas Packer Esqr & Capt Luke Mills

Item To my Two Sons Nahum and Josiah, their heirs & Assigns I Give after the decease of my wife the house I now live in With the Gardens & Land adjoyning my Slaughter house and Garden and the Land thereto adjoyning to be Equally between them.

Item To my Three Sons vizt Simeon Nahum and Josiah and their heirs and Assigns I Give all my Orchard Mowing Land and pasture Land in Portsmouth Laying towards or near Sagamores Creek — In Equal Shares between them togather with all the Residue of my Lands at Barrington in Equal Shares —

Item To my Four daughters vizt Mary, Elizabeth, Sarah, and Hannah I Give One hundred Pounds old Teno Each to be paid by my Executors —

Item, All the Rest Residue and Remainder of my Estate after the payment of my Debts Legacies and bequests, I give to my

Two Sons viz Nahum & Josiah their heirs and Assigns in Equal Shares —

And I do Appoint My Two Sons Benjamin and Simeon to be Executors * * * And for the Confirmation of all before written I have hereunto Set my hand & Seal the Thirty first day of December in the 31st Year of his Majestys Reign Annoque Domini 1757.

Benj^a Akarman

[Witnesses] Robt Stokell, John Marshall, Cutts Shannon.
[Proved Jan. 25, 1758.]

[Warrant, Jan. 25, 1758, authorizing John Shackford and Cutts Shannon, gentleman, both of Portsmouth, to appraise the estate.]

[Inventory, attested May 31, 1758; amount, £16,801. 6. 9; signed by John Shackford and Cutts Shannon.]

[Account of the settlement of the estate; receipts, £1228. 6. 9, personal estate; expenditures, £1097. 9. 0; allowed Dec. 26, 1759.]

SAMUEL SEARLES   1758   NASHUA

In the Name of God Amen. the Seventh Day of January anno Domini 1758 I Samuel Searl of Dunstable in the Province of New Hampshire Yeoman, being very sick & weak of Body * * *

Item; I Give & Bequeath to my dearly beloved wife Lydia Searl the use & improvement of one full third Part of all my Real Estate during her natural Life; & all the Household goods & furniture that my said wife brought with her to my Estate, & a good milched Cow in the room of that Cow that she brought with her to my said Estate, the s^d Goods to made as good as when I received them.

Item I Give & Devise to my Son Samuel Searl & his Assigns forever all my Real Estate Lands Meadows & Buildings; Except the use & improvement given to my Wife as afores^d he my said Son paying all my Just Debts & Funeral Charges & Legacy herein after given to my Daughter Mary Searl; and I also give my said Son the rest & Residue of my personal Estate, besides what is given to my wife afores^d —

Item I Give & Bequeath to my Daughter Mary Searl the Sum of twenty five Pounds Sterling money of Great Briton, the one half of the s^d Sum to be paid to her at her age of Eighteen years & the other half, at her age of twenty one years; and I also give to my said Daughter all the Household Goods & Furniture that her own Mother Mary Searl brought to my Estate & also such as belonged to her Grand Mother Elizabeth Butterfield that her said Mother Mary Searl had; notwithstanding the Personal Estate before herein given to my said Son;

And I do make Ordain & appoint Ephraim Adams of Dunstable in the Province of New Hampshire my sole Executor * * *

his
Samuel + Searl
mark
his

[Witnesses] Benjamin Thomson, John fletcher, John + Searl.

Mark

[Proved June 7, 1758.]

[Mary Searles, widow, accepts the provisions of the will May 26, 1758; witnesses, Eleazer French, Jacob Adams.]

[Inventory, attested May 31, 1758; amount, £4445. 6. 0; signed by Phineas Lund, Daniel Searles, and William Lund.]

[Mary Searles of Dunstable, minor, makes choice of Thomas Lund of Dunstable as her guardian Nov. 24, 1758; witnesses, John Searles, Jonathan Lovewell.]

[Guardianship of Mary Searles, minor, aged more than 14 years, daughter of Samuel Searles, granted to Thomas Lund of Dunstable Dec. 4, 1758.]

[Probate Records, vol. 21, p. 123.]

[Bond of Thomas Lund, with John Lovewell and John Searles as sureties, all of Dunstable, in the sum of £1200, Dec. 4, 1758, for the guardianship of Mary Searles; witnesses, Joseph Whiting, Jonathan Lovewell.]

JOSHUA JACKSON   1758   PORTSMOUTH

[Administration on the estate of Joshua Jackson of Portsmouth granted to Nathaniel Jackson, cordwainer, and Samuel Jackson, joiner, Jan. 13, 1758.]

[Probate Records, vol. 20, p. 416.]

[Bond of Nathaniel Jackson and Samuel Jackson, with Jeremiah Libby, housewright, and Mark Hunking, mariner, as sureties, all of Portsmouth, in the sum of £1000, Jan. 13, 1758, for the administration of the estate of Joshua Jackson, their brother; witnesses, William Parker, David Sewall.]

[Inventory, attested March 27, 1758; amount, £1902. 4. 6; signed by George Marshall and Thomas Peirce.]

[Account of the administrators of the estate of Joshua Jackson, blacksmith; receipts, £839. 15. 4, personal estate; expenditures the same; mentions a son; allowed Dec. 31, 1760.]

NOLAR MARTIN   1758   PORTSMOUTH

[Administration on the estate of Nolar Martin of Portsmouth, mariner, granted to Elizabeth Martin, widow, Jan. 24, 1758.]

[Probate Records, vol. 20, p. 417.]

[Bond of Elizabeth Martin, with William Hooker, joiner, and John Banfill, yeoman, as sureties, all of Portsmouth, in the sum of £500, Jan. 24, 1758, for the administration of the estate; witnesses, David Sewall, Elizabeth Adams.]

[Warrant, Jan. 24, 1758, authorizing Thomas Bickford, schoolmaster, and William Hooker, joiner, both of Portsmouth, to appraise the estate.]

[Inventory, April 20, 1759; amount, £579. 19. 0; signed by Thomas Bickford and William Hooker.]

[Claims of the administratrix against the estate from Dec. 14, 1754, to Dec. 20, 1758; amount, £1310. 16. 0; mentions board of two children for four years.]

BENJAMIN TOWLE   1758   HAMPTON

In the Name of God Amen the Thirteenth day of February 1758 I Benjamin Towle of Hampton in the Province of New-Hampshire in New England Husbandman being Weak in Body * * *

Imprimis I Give & Bequeath unto my Beloved Wife Sarah Towle the Improvement of the East half of my Dwelling House And Barn dureing Life, and all my moveables in my House And one half of my Stock of Cattle horses Sheep & Swine forever And also one Third of my Real Estate dureing Life

Item I Give & Bequeath to my Son Benjamin Towle the West half of my Dwelling House And one half of my Barn And the Other half of my Said House & Barn I give unto my Said Son After the Deceas of my Said Wife And one half of all my Estate in Hampton Both real & Personall to Improve dureing Life and then to go to Rebeckah Towle the Wife of Said Benjamin to Improve till my Grand Son Jacob Towle Shall come to the age of Twenty one Years And then to go to Said Jacob & to Assigns forever

Item I Give & Bequeath to my Son Elisha Towle my House &

Barn where he now lives & one Half of All my Estate in Hampton both Real & Personall to him & his Assigns forever

Item I Give & Bequeath to my Grand Son John Sleeper my right of Land in Cantabury to him & to his assigns forever —

Item I Give & Bequeath to my Daughter Mary Page Thirty Pounds Old Tenor to be raised & levied out of my Estate & Paid by my Son Benjamin

Item I Give & Bequeath to my Daughter Tabathy Tuck Thirty Pounds Old Tenor to be raised & levied out of my Estate and paid by my Son Elisha

Item I Give & Bequeath to my Daughter Patience Hobbs Thirty Pounds Old Tenor to be raised & levied out of my Estate And Paid by my Son Benjamin

Item I Give & Bequeath to my Daughter Hapzabah Page Thirty Pounds Old Tenor to be raised & levied out of my Estate & Paid by my Son Elisha

Item I Give & Bequeath to my Daughter Sarah Clifford Thirty Pounds Old Tenor to be raised & levied out of my Estate & paid by my Sons Benjamin & Elisha

I give & Bequeath to my Sons Benjamin Towle & Elisha Towle All my Estate that is not mentioned in this Will

I Likewise constitute make & ordain my Sons Benjamin Towle & Elisha Towle and my Son in Law John Page to be my Executors * * *

his
Benjamin + Towle
Mark

[Witnesses] John Weeks, James Leavit, Sambon Chandler.
[Proved June 27, 1759.]

[Warrant, June 27, 1759, authorizing Joshua Lane, cordwainer, and James Leavitt, yeoman, both of Hampton, to appraise the estate.]

[Inventory, attested Aug. 29, 1759; amount, £7110. 1. 0; signed by Joshua Lane and James Leavitt.]

Province of New Hamps^r

Whereas by an Act of the General Assembly of Said Province Entitled "An Act for making Partition of Certain Lands therein mentioned" among other things it is Enacted that there be five freeholders in this Province appointed and authorized they or any three of them to make Partition of Said Lands; Part of which Lands Refered to in said act are Certain Lands in Hampton Devised to Elisha Towle, and Benjamin Towle in Common by their father Benjamin Towle late Deceas'd —

In Pursuance of which Act we the Subscribers have Undertaken to make Partition And Division of said Lands between the said Elisha and Benjamin, and having given Due Notice to all Parties Concern'd Agreeable to the Direction in said act, We have made the Partition And Division to Each to hold in Severalty as follows vizt of that tract of Land which lyes on the Notherly Side of the Road where the Dwelling Houses of the said Elisha and Benjamin Stand Containing in the whole about one hundred forty three acres we have set off to the Said Elisha the Easterly Part where his Dwelling House Stands to begin at a Stake set up by the Road near a pair of Barrs and from thence to Run to the Southeasterly Corner of Elkins's land and the Said Elisha to have all to the Eastward of this line which is about fifty acres & three quarters: also we have set off to the Said Elisha a Piece on the Notherly Side of the Spruce Swamp Containing About thirteen acres — being fifty four Rods and three Quarters on the Easterly Side and fifty one Rods and one Quarter on the Westerly side Bounded on the Westerly Side by a Red Burch Spotted and on the Easterly Side by a Spruce tree Spotted as is Described in the Plan herewith annexed; also a Small Lott or Share Containing About three quarters of an acre lying at the Northwesterly Corner of the abovementioned Piece at the Spruce Swamp. — and all the Remainder of that tract of Land lying on the Notherly Side of the Road aforesaid we have set off to the said Benjamin Towle in Severalty and also a Small Lott or

Share Containing about one acre on the Notherly side of the Spruce Swamp. —

Also we have Divided One Other Piece of Land lying on the Southerly side of the aforesaid Road Containing in the whole forty Six acres and a half and twenty one Rods as follows vizt We have set off to the said Elisha the Northeasterly Part Containing twenty Eight acres and twenty one Rods; and to the said Benjamin the Southwesterly part Containing Eighteen acres and a half, The Dividing line between said parts is as follows to begin at a Stake set up Sixteen Rods and a half from the Corner by the backway And from said Stake to Run across said land to a Red Burch Spotted at the Southeasterly Side of said Piece of land as Described in the Plan herewith annexed. Also we have Divided Sundry Pieces of Marsh between the said Elisha and Benjamin as follows vizt To the said Elisha a small Piece near the Beach Containing two acres and thirty two Rods Described in the Plan by the letter A Also one other Piece near Browns mill Containing two Acres and thirty two Rods Described in the Plan by the letter D, also one Other piece near Pine Island Containing One acre Described in the Plan by the letter F, also one other piece on the Beach Containing about three quarters of An Acre Described in the Plan by the letter G And to the said Benjamin we have set off a Piece of Marsh near the Beach Containing one acre and three quarters being one half of what is Described in the Plan by the letter B the other half belonging to Other persons, also one other piece of marsh near the beach Cassway Containing three acres and four Rods Described in the Plan by the letter C also one other Piece near Browns mill Containing one hundred and one Rods Described in the Plan by the letter E. And this we make as Our Return of the Partition and Division of the Sundry Pieces of land and Marsh beforementioned this fourth Day of June Anno Domini 1760 —

Meshech Weare
Jonathan Tilton
James Leavit

Whereas the whole of The Lands belonging to the Said Elisha and Benjamin Towle, Devised to them in Common by their father Benjamin Towle Deceas'd which are Refer'd to in the beforementioned act Are Not Contained in the foregoing Return; and James Leavett, who assisted in making the Division of what is beforementioned being unable to assist in Dividing the Remainder; We the Subscribers three of the Committee Appointed by the aforesaid Act Have Divided the Remainder (haveing Given Due Notice to all Parties Concern'd) which is part of a Lott or Share In the Second North Division so Called In Hampton lying on the Easterly Side of the Road near the Dwelling House of m^r Jonathan Page five Acres of which Lott having before been Sold to said Jonathan Page at the Notherly End the whole width of the Lott: we have Divided the Remainder of said Lott Containing thirteen Acres and twenty Seven Rods to the said Elisha and Benjamin Equally to hold to Each in Severalty Namely to the Said Elisha the Westerly half and to the said Benjamin the Easterly half the Division being made Lengthways of the Lott And the bounds of the Division being a Red Ash tree Spotted on four Sides in the middle of the Lott by said Page's five Acres at the Notherly End and a Stake in the middle of the Lott at the Southerly End. And This we make as Our Return this fourth Day of September Anno Domini 1760 A Plan of which Lott and Division is herewith Returned. —

Meshech Weare
Josiah Sanborn
Jonathan Tilton

[Account of the settlement of the estate by Elisha Towle; receipts, £1607. 7. 9½, personal estate; expenditures, £1560. 14. 1; mentions "paid to Jonathan Tuck his Legacy .... John Page his D° .... Thomas Page his D° .... Patience Hobbs her D° .... William Clifford his D°"; allowed Feb. 27, 1765.]

NEW HAMPSHIRE WILLS

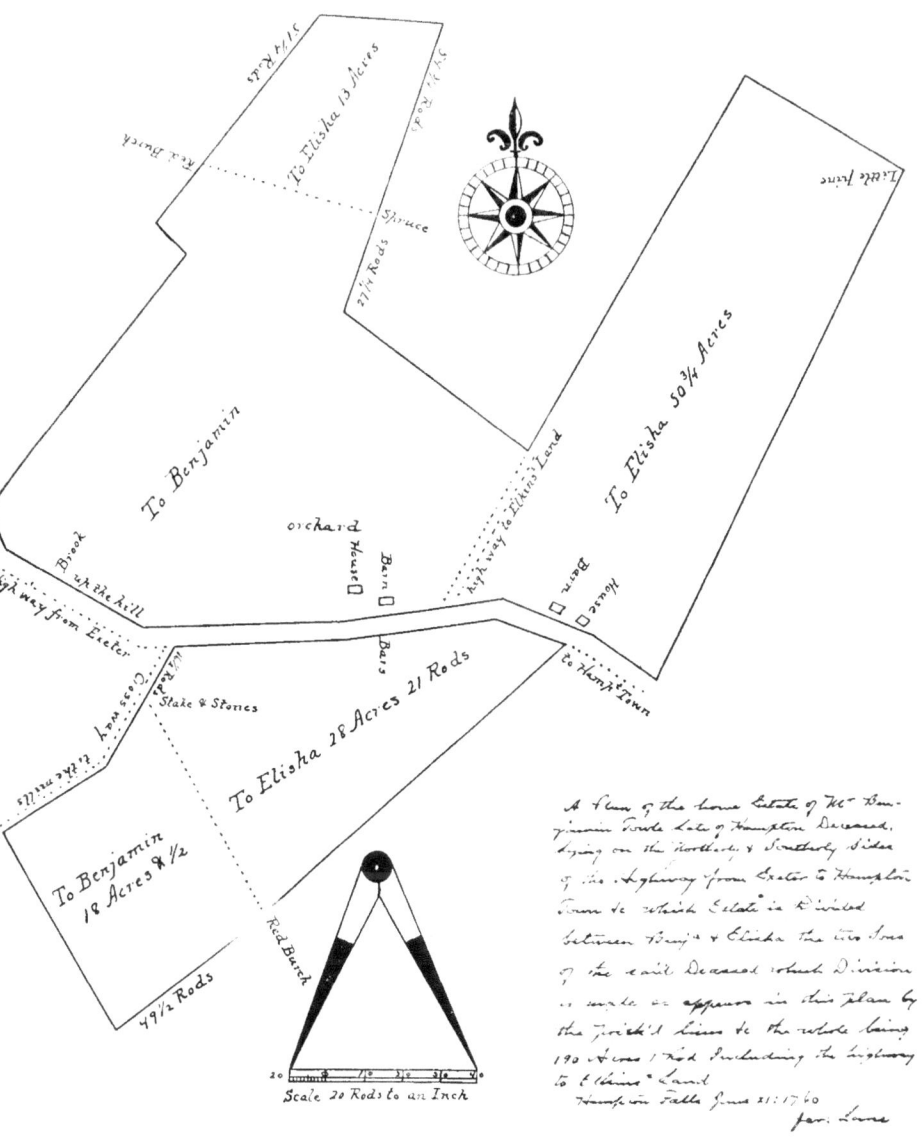

Scale 20 Rods to an Inch

A Plan of the home Estate of Mr Benjamin Towle late of Hampton Deceased, lying on the Northerly & Southerly Sides of the Highway from Exeter to Hampton Town &c which Estate is Divided between Benja & Elisha the two Sons of the said Deceased which Division is made as appears in this Plan by the prick'd lines &c the whole being 190 Acres 1 Rod Including the highway to Elkins Land
Hampton Falls June 21: 1760
       per. Lowe

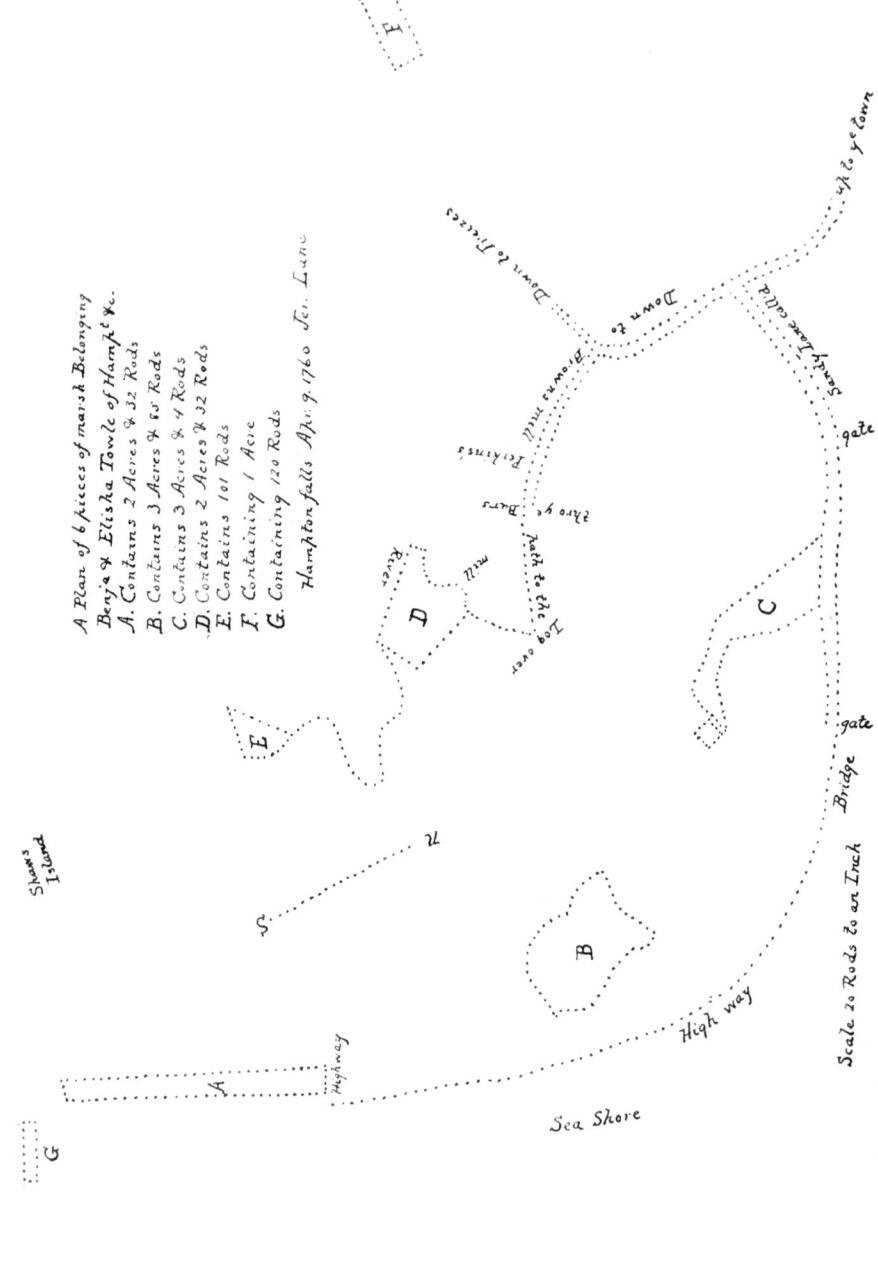

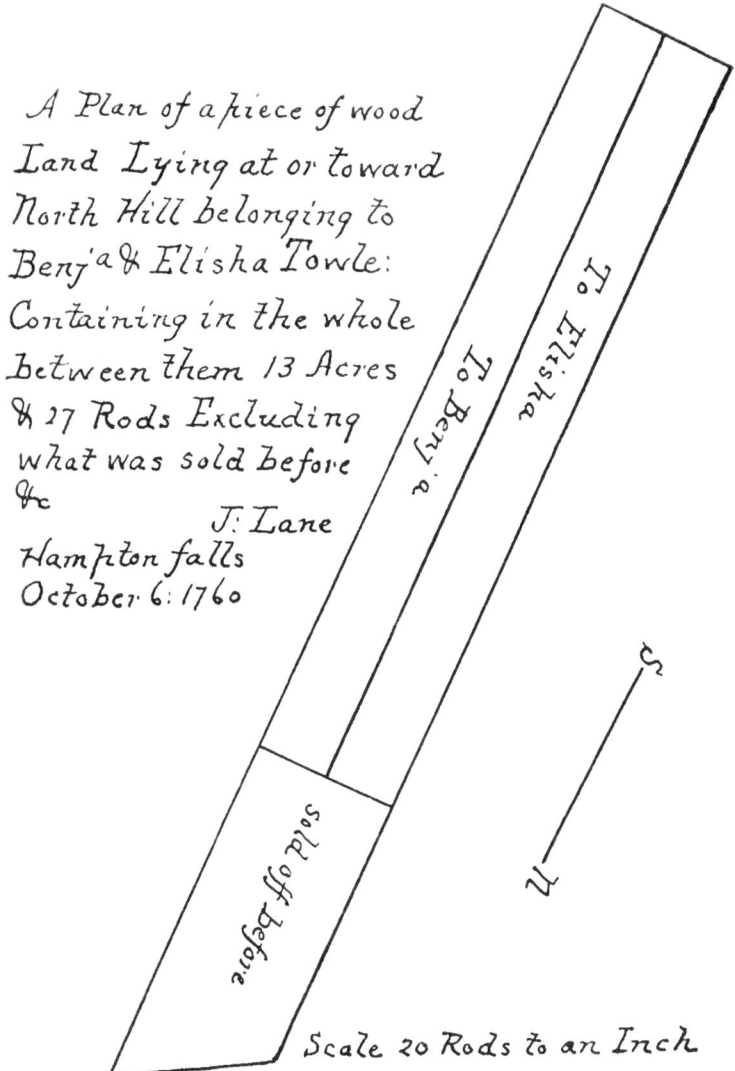

DANIEL DOW 1758 SALEM

[Administration on the estate of Daniel Dow of Salem, yeoman, granted to Nathaniel Dow of Salem, yeoman, Feb. 14, 1758.]

[Probate Records, vol. 20, p. 506.]

[Bond of Nathaniel Dow, with Andrew Balch, gentleman, and Peter Merrill, blacksmith, as sureties, all of Salem, in the sum of £2000, Feb. 14, 1758, for the administration of the estate; witnesses, Joshua Thorndike, Ephraim Woodbury.]

[Warrant, Feb. 14, 1758, authorizing John Hall, Jr., yeoman, and Daniel Massey, both of Salem, to appraise the estate.]

[Inventory, March 9, 1758; amount, £1586. 15. 0; signed by John Hall, Jr., and Daniel Massey.]

SAMUEL STACKPOLE 1758 SOMERSWORTH

[Administration on the estate of Samuel Stackpole of Somersworth granted to Philip Stackpole of Somersworth, yeoman, Feb. 22, 1758.]

[Probate Records, vol. 20, p. 435.]

[Bond of Philip Stackpole, with John Hall of Somersworth, yeoman, and Samuel Hall of Portsmouth, tanner, as sureties, in the sum of £500, Feb. 22, 1758, for the administration of the estate; witnesses, William Parker, Sargent Currier.]

[Warrant, Feb. 22, 1758, authorizing James Hobbs, gentleman, and Daniel Goodwin, yeoman, both of Somersworth, to appraise the estate.]

[Inventory, attested April 25, 1758; amount, £2693. 7. 0; signed by James Hobbs and Daniel Goodwin.]

TIMOTHY DAVIS   1758   PORTSMOUTH

The Deposition of Joseph Moulton Aged Seventy two & of Abigail his wife Aged Seventy Years & of Jeremiah Libbey Aged Sixty Nine Years all of Portsmouth in the Province of New Hampshire in New England these Deponents Testifie that they knew & are well Acquainted with Timothy Davis of Berwick in the County of York in the Province of the Massachusetts Bay who is the Reputed son of Timothy Davis Late of Portsmouth aforesaid Deceased who was the Reputed son of Timothy Davis formerly of said Portsmouth who died near about Forty Years ago That the said Timothy first named was the Eldest son of the said Timothy his father born in s^d Portsm^o as was also his father & was the Eldest son of his Father That the said Persons were Born in said Portsm^o as aforesaid were brought up there & lived in the Neighbourhood of these Deponents That the Said Timothy Davis the Eldest who Deceased so long ago lived in Portsmouth aforesaid but was Reputed to have been Born in Wales being Commonly Called a Welsh Man & it was Commonly said in his time that he had an Estate in some part of Wales That he Died in said Portsmouth Leaving Several Children with whom these Deponents were well Acquainted of Which the Second Timothy above named was the Eldest That all the s^d Timothys followed the Trade of a Joiner & farther say not

                                         Joseph Moulton
                                         Abigail Moulton
                                         Jeremiah Libbey

[Attested March 1, 1758.]

[Province Deeds, vol. 55, p. 308.]

[See estate of Timothy Davis, 1736, vol. 2, this series, p. 609.]

PHILIP FLANDERS   1758   CHESTER

[Hannah Flanders renounces administration on the estate of her husband, Philip Flanders of Chester, March 2, 1758, in favor of Lieut. Samuel Roby of Chester, she having no children of age; witnesses, Samuel Emerson, Nathaniel Emerson.]

[Administration granted to Samuel Roby of Hampton Falls, gentleman, March 21, 1758.]

[Probate Records, vol. 20, p. 453.]

[Bond of Samuel Roby, with Samuel Emerson of Chester and Josiah Batchelder of Hampton Falls, yeoman, as sureties, in the sum of £500, March 21, 1758, for the administration of the estate; witnesses, William Parker, David Sewall.]

[Warrant, March 21, 1758, authorizing Andrew Craige and John Webster, both of Chester, yeomen, to appraise the estate.]

[Inventory, May 19, 1758; amount, £794. 0. 0; signed by Andrew Craige and John Webster.]

[Commission, June 28, 1758, to Samuel Emerson and John Webster, innholder, both of Chester, to receive claims against the estate.]

[List of claims, March 26, 1759; amount, £467. 5. 4; signed by Samuel Emerson and John Webster.]

[Account of the administrator; receipts, £764. 0. 0; expenditures, £484. 2. 8; allowed April 25, 1759.]

[Settlement of claims; amount of claims, £634. 11. 2; amount distributed, £279. 17. 4; allowed May 5, 1759.]

JOEL JUDKINS 1758 BRENTWOOD

In The Name of God Amen This Eleventh Day of March one Thousand Seven hundred and fifty Eight I Joel Judkins of Brintwood in our Province of New Hamp^r In New England Yeoman Being Sick of Body * * *

Imprimas I give and bequeath To my Son Joseph Judkins The one half of all my Real Estate that I have not allredy Disposed of in Brintwood or Else where Except The Lott before my Dwelling house on y[e] South westerly Side of the High way that Leads to Crawles falls adjoyning on Thomas Chritchets Land; and The Little Lott by the Pond on the northeasterly Side of said high Way and the orchard on the northerly Side of the high way aforsd — att the Southeasterly End of the house Containing aboute Two acers The three peaces afors[d] Joseph is to have no parte of and all three Peaces Contain aboute five acers and an half Takeing in y[e] Barn House and Well — which Samuel is to have with y[e] other half of all

Item I Give and bequeath To my Son Samuel Judkins the House Barn well and Three Peaces of Land Last mentioned over and above the one half of my Estate afors[d] and the one Half of the Remaining Parte of my Estate To be Equally Divided Between him & his Brother Joseph Provided and upon Conditions that they and Each of Them Submitt to the primises And Preform the duties hereafter Injoyned them and my will is that Joseph & Samuel Shall have the Stears Equally Betwen them and that the old farrow Cow to be fated att Samuels Cost for Beaf for the famely this fall & to be killd & Equally Divided Betwen His mother my wife and his Sister Sarrah my Daughter & him and my will is that Joseph Shall have all my wareing apparel

Item I give and bequeth to my Wellbeloved wife Anna Judkins The Privelidge of Living in my house with Samuel my Son and Daughter Sarah as Long as She Remains my widow and my will is that If Samuel Sees good to pull Down the house it being old and Sett up an other in y[e] place for y[e] use of his mother & Sarah as aforsd he may Do it allso I give to my wife one Cow to be kept winter and Summer for her use as Long as She Remains my widow by Joseph & Samuel

Allso I Give to my wife my best fether Bed and Beding Belonging Thereto as Long as She Remains my widow and the one half of all my movebales within Doors which half y[e] Bed afors[d] is parte of to be for her use as Long as She Remains my widow as aforsᵈ after that to Returne to my Daughters Mary Bean abigail Gorden & Rebeca Lord

Allso I Give To my Daughter Sarah Judkins The use of the other half of my moveabls within Doors for Ever If She Should marey If not no Longer then her Life time & allso one Cow and Two Sheep To be kept Intirely for her use as Long as She Liveth and on married as aforsᵈ winter & Summer By my Two Sons as aforsᵈ they to be at Equall Cost therein and If She marries to be hers for Ever and allso a privelige of Liveing In the house on the Same Terms of her mother: and in Case She Should not marey the Cow & Sheep to Returne To Joseph and Samuel att her Decase and the movebals aforsᵈ to Returne To my three Daughters To witt Mary Bean abigail Gorden & Rebeca Lord or their hairs

Item I Give and bequeth To my Daughter Mary Bean one hundred Pounds old Tenor to be paid by my Son Joseph Judkins in Two Years after my Decase or her hairs If She Should not Live to yᵗ time

Item I Give To my Daughter abigail Gorden one Hundred Pounds old tenor to be paid By Samuel my Son in Two Years after my Decase: N: B: I Give and bequeth to my wife all That is before or after mentiond in this will Provided and on Conditions She aquits her Thirds of my Estate and not Else

Item I Give to my Daughter Rebeca Lord one Hundred Pounds old Tenor to be paid By Samuel my Son in Two years and an half after my Decase: and my Son Samuel to pay Sarah one Hundred pounds old Tenor att marige Day over & above her maintainenc aforsᵈ

Item I Give to Jonathan Judkins my Grand Son the Son of Zecheriah Judkins my Son Decasᵈ Sixty pounds old Tenor to be paid when he is Twenty one years of age If he Lives To it In Lue of his fathers Portion his father haveing had his Portion allredy By Joseph & Samuel Equally

Item I give to my Grand Daughter Rebecca Judkins Daughter To my Son Zecceriah Judkins aforsᵈ Decsᵈ Ten pounds old tenor

To be paid when She arives to ye age of Eighteen years by my Sons afors^d

Item I give to abigaill Hutchenson Daughter of John Huchenson of Iping Ten pounds old tenor to be paid when She arives to the age of Eighteen years By my Sons afors^d allso my will is that my wife and Sarah my Daughter Shall Have an Honourable maintainance out of my Estate and that my Two Sons Joseph and S^{11} Aforesaid Shall find and Suply Them with all Things Comfortable and Nessessary for their Suport Dureing the time thay Remain unmaried and to keep my wife Two good Sheep for her use & profits winter and Sumer for The Term afors^d and that my wife an Daughter aforsd Shall Have Two thirds of the appels that Grow in the orchards that is one third a pace During ye Term afors^d and the Privilige of Some good Spots of Land If thay See fitt to Improve it for Sowing of flax and good Garden or Gardens where thay Chuse it Dureing S^d Term and allso the mare To be for all their use as they Shall have ocation and allso that my wife Shall have the privelige to keep a Swine She now hath of her own Dureing S^d Term and my will Is that all my Just Debts and funerall Charges Shall Be Paid oute of my Estate By my Two Sons Joseph and Samuel Equally and the Estate beformentioned that is ye Lands To be Equally Divided betwen my Two Sons afors^d Except The three Small peaces before Excepted which are my Son Samuels as afors^d and they the Said Joseph and Samuel To hold S^d Lands to them and their hairs for Ever and I Do Hereby make ordain and Appoint my well Beloved and Trusty friend James Bean of Brintwood and Provence aforesaid yeoman Sole Executor * * *

Joel Judkins

[Witnesses] Thomas Critchet, Anne Critchet, John Sleeper. [Proved May 31, 1758.]

[Warrant, May 31, 1758, authorizing John Sleeper and James Dudley, both of Brentwood, yeomen, to appraise the estate.]

[Inventory, June 28, 1758; amount, £4061. o. 6; signed by John Sleeper and James Dudley.]

[Account of the executor; receipts, £1811. o. 6, personal estate; expenditures, £572. 4. 6; allowed Aug. 29, 1759.]

[Guardianship of Jonathan Judkins, minor, aged more than 14 years, son of Zachariah Judkins of Brentwood, yeoman, granted to Jonathan Smith of Brentwood, cordwainer, March 27, 1759.]
[Probate Records, vol. 21, p. 203.]

[Bond of Jonathan Smith, with James Proctor of Kingston, blacksmith, and John Sleeper of Brentwood, trader, as sureties, in the sum of £500, March 27, 1759, for the guardianship of Jonathan Judkins; witnesses, William Parker, David Sewall.]

JOHN BRACKETT   1758   GREENLAND

In the Name of God amen, the Seventeenth Day of March in the year of our Lord one Thousand Seven hundred and fifty Eight I John Bracket of Greenland in the province of Newhampshire in Newengland Gentlman Being very week in Body * * *

Item I Give and Bequeath unto my Granddaughter Mary Bracket the Daughter of my Son Thomas Bracket Late of Greenland afore Said Deceased a peace of Land Laying in Greenland aforesaid Between the Road that Leads to hampton and the Road that that Leads to Stratham which peace of Land Contains about a quarter of an acre be the Same more or Less it being one half within Said Bounds the other half thereof is owned by my Brother James Bracket and if my Said Granchild Should Dye without Lawfull Issue the Said premesses Shall Return to my Son Joshua Bracket I haveing alrady Given to my Said Son Thomas Bracket Deceas^d his portion of my Estate by a Deed of Gift

Item I Give and Bequeath unto my well Beloved wife Elisabeth Bracket my negro named pay and my horse and Rideing Chair and one third of my Estate Dureing her Nauteral Life

Item I Give and Bequeath unto my Son George Bracket his heirs and assigns for Ever all the Land madow ground Thatch Ground and flats that I have in Greenland afore s^d and in Stratham in Said province with all Buildings privelages and appurtinances Standing and Being thereon Exepting the Land Marsh and flats I Bought of Coffin —

I also Give unto my Said Son George Bracket his heirs and assigns the one half of my part of the Sawmill Standing at a place Called wadleghs falls in Durham in Said province with all the priveladges and appurtinances there unto Belonging and also one half of my Land in Nottingham in Said province that I have in partnership with Samuel Bracket James Bracket and Issa foss also all my Stock of Cattle Sheep horses Swine Exepting one horse alrady Given to my wife and all my Utancials for husbandarey and all my wareing Cloaths and my Clock and if my Said Son Should Dye without Lawfull Issue then the Said premesses Shall Return To my Surviveing Childred Equally to be Devided among them

Item I Give and Bequeath unto my Son Benning Bracket his heirs and assigns for Ever and my Land marsh and flats I have in Stratham afore Said that I Bought of peter Coffin and also Seventy acers of Land in Newmarket in Said province that I Bought of Joseph Smart be the Same more or Less also the other half of my part of the Sawmill Standing on wadleighs falls So Called in Derham afore Said with all priveladges and appurtinances thereunto Belonging and all the Land I have in Durham and Newmarket afore Said in a Grant of Land Called Simonses Grant and also that Twenty acres of Land in Durham afore Said that Abner Coffin is Now in possession of or the Money Said Coffin Shall pay for the Redemcion thereof and the other half of My Land in Nottingham afore Said that I have in pertnership with Samuel Bracket James Bracket and Isaac foss — I also Give unto my Said Son Benning Bracket one yoak of oxen Two

Cows Eight Sheep and one horse to be paid and Delivered unto him by my Son George Bracket when my Said Sun Benning arives to the age of Twenty one years and Two Chains one Ring and Staple and a New plow and plow iorns if he Dyes without Lawful Issue Said premesses to Return to my Surviveing Children

Item I Give unto my Son Joshua Bracket Two Thousand pounds money Equal to the present Currincy of old Tenor at this Time to be paid unto him by my Son George Bracket within Six months after my Decease and also Mr Henrys works upon the Bible in five voloms — and a mare that he Calls his and one Cow and my Long Gun that was my fathers

Item I Give unto My Son John Bracket Sixty pounds Money Equal to the Currincy of old Tenor at this Time yearly to be paid him by my Son George Bracket Dureing the Time of my Said Son Johns Nauteral Life

Item I Give unto my four Sons Joshua John George and Benning Brackets Each of them a Bad and Bading

Item I Give unto My Daughter Mary Bracket Six hundred pounds money Equal to the Currincy of old Tenor at this Time To be paid unto her by my Son George Bracket within Twelve months next after my Decease and one half of all my Indore household Goods not alrady Desposed of to be Delivered to her at my wifes Decease

Item I Give unto my Daughter Elisabeth Bracket Six hundred pounds Equal to the Currincy of old tenor at This Time to be paid to her by my Son George Bracket within Twelve months next after my Decease and one half of all my Indore house hold Goods Not alrady is not Desposed of to be Delivered unto her at my wifes Decease

Item I Give and bequeath unto My four Sons and Two Daughters viz Joshua John George Benning Mary and Elisabeth Brackets theire heirs and assigns all my out Lands not alrady Desposed of Laying in Nottingham Ipsom and Bow all within Said province To be Equley Devided Between them

Item I Give unto My Son George Bracket all my money bonds Notes and Debts and all my Trooping furnitior —

Item I Do hereby apoynt and or Dain my well Beloved wife Elisabeth Bracket and My Trusty Son George Bracket My Sole Executors * * *

John Brackett

[Witnesses] James Brackett, nathanil watson, waldron kinnison. [Proved Feb. 28, 1759.]

[Bond of Elizabeth Brackett, widow, and George Brackett, yeoman, with William Weeks, gentleman, and James Brackett, yeoman, as sureties, all of Greenland, in the sum of £1000, Feb. 28, 1759, for the execution of the will; witnesses, William Parker, John Dennett.]

JEREMIAH BROWN   1758   HAMPTON FALLS

In the Name of God Amen this twentieth Day of March In the year of Our Lord Christ Seventeen hundred and fifty Eight, I Jeremiah Brown of Hampton-falls in the Province of New Hampshire in New England Yeoman * * *

Item I Give and Bequeath to my wellbeloved Wife Mary The Use Income and Improvement of One half of my Dwelling House and one half of my Barn And One half of my Place where I now live vizt of the Mowing, Orchard, Pasture, & Planting Land Also the Use of my Horse, And two Cows and four Sheep to be Provided Out of my Stock of Creatures, All the foregoing she is to have the Use And Improvement of During the time she shall Remain my Widow And no Longer I Also Give her All my Household Goods to Dispose of As she Pleases

Item I Give And Bequeath to my Son Jedediah Brown his heirs and Assigns a Lott of Land which I Purchased of Daniel Gale lying in the Township of Chester in the Province aforesaid Containing by Estimation One hundred Acres, Also the use benefit And Improvement of a Part of my Orchard by the falls River so Called which I Purchased of Jonathan Longfellow; Namely my said Son Jedediah and my Son Elisha Brown are to have the Improvement Equally between them of One half of said Orchard Until five years after my Son Jonathan Brown shall Come to the Age of twenty one years And no longer —

Also five Acres of Marsh by Blackwater River so Called which I Purchased of my Brother Thomas Brown Also One half my Husbandry Tools And two oxen And One Cow to be Deliverd to my said Son Jedediah when he shall Come to the Age of twenty One years by my Executor

Item I Give and Bequeath to my Son Jonathan Brown his heirs and Assigns to Come into Possession when he shall Arrive at the Age of twenty One Years A Piece of Land Situate in Hampton falls aforesaid which I Purchased of Jonathan Longfellow Containing About twenty Acres lying by the falls River so Called, Also A Piece of Land lying by Little hill so Called Containing About twelve Acres, Also five Acres of Marsh which I Purchased of David Swett Also two Cows to be Deliverd him when he arrives at the Age of twenty one years by my Executor my said Son Jonathan having now a yoke of Steers which I allow to be his own And he is to have the Liberty of Keeping them or Another yoke in their Room Upon my Place untill he shall arrive at the Age of twenty One Years and then to take them to his own use And further my will is that my Said Son Jonathan shall Live And Carry on with his Brother Elisha And have his Support out of the Place untill he is twenty one years of Age

Item I Give and Bequeath to my Son Elisha Brown his heirs and assigns all my Estate both Real And Personal not Otherwise Disposed of And I Order him to Pay all Such Debts as I owe and to Receive such As are Due to me And further My will is that my Sons Elisha & Jonathan shall Assist their Brother Jedediah about Building a House on his Land at Chester by Labouring with him to get up the frame and board the Same

Lastly I do Constitute and Appoint my Son Elisha Brown Sole Executor of this my will * * *

his
Jeremiah + Brown
mark

[Witnesses] Joseph Pearkins, Daniel Chase Green, Paul Greenleaf.

I Jeremiah Brown abovenamed being thro' the Goodness of God Yet in the Land of the living and of a Sound Disposing mind and Memory this Eighth Day of June Anno Domini 1758 Do hereby add to my foregoing Will this which follows being Desirous to Prevent All Disputes among my Children after my Decease Namely my will is and I do hereby Order That in Case any thing shall be Recoverd Against my Estate by Any Person to whom I have Sold Lands with Warranty on account of the failure of my title thereto, that then whatsoever shall be so Recoverd shall be Paid and born Equally Among my three Sons beforementioned Elisha Jedediah and Jonathan, I having Disposed of my Estate Among them in such a manner as Renders this to be Just and Equal * * *

The mark of
Jeremiah + Brown

[Witnesses] Meshech Weare, Joseph Pearkins, Paul Greenleaf. [Proved June 28, 1758.]

[Mary Brown, widow, accepts the terms of the will and waives inventory June 26, 1758.]

[Bond of Elisha Brown, yeoman, with Meshech Weare and Joseph Perkins, yeoman, as sureties, all of Hampton Falls, in the sum of £1000, June 28, 1758, for the execution of the will; witnesses, William Parker, Josiah Hilton.]

CHARLES ROWE   1758   HAMPTON FALLS

[Judith Rowe renounces administration on the estate of her husband, Charles Rowe of Hampton Falls, March 22, 1758, in favor of Nathan Rowe of Hampton Falls; witness, Benjamin Rowe.]

[Administration on the estate of Charles Rowe, blacksmith, granted to Nathan Rowe, yeoman, March 24, 1758.]

[Probate Records, vol. 20, p. 454.]

[Bond of Nathan Rowe, with Meshech Weare of Hampton Falls and Noah Emery of Exeter, gentleman, as sureties, in the sum of £500, March 24, 1758, for the administration of the estate; witnesses, John Goffe, Moses Blaisdell.]

[Warrant, June 28, 1758, authorizing Richard Nason, gentleman, and Elisha Prescott, yeoman, both of Hampton Falls, to appraise the estate.]

[Inventory, Sept. 18, 1758; amount, £263. 18. 0, personal estate; signed by Richard Nason and Elisha Prescott.]

[Additional inventory, Nov. 25, 1759; amount, £105. 0. 0; signed as above.]

[List of claims against the estate; amount, £226. 15. 8; signed by Richard Nason and Caleb Sanborn; attested Jan. 1, 1760.]

[Account of the administrator; receipts, £370. 8. 0, persona estate; expenditures, £196. 2. 0; allowed Sept. 10, 1760.]

[Settlement of claims; amount of claims, £226. 15. 0; amount distributed, £174. 6. 0; allowed Sept. 16, 1760.]

SAMUEL HUNTRESS   1758   NEWINGTON

In the Name of God, Amen the Twenty Ninth Day of March in the Thirty first Year of his Maj^{tes} Reign Anno Domini 1758,

I Samuel Huntriss of Newington in the province of Newhamp^r in New England Yeoman knowing my Mortalitie * * *

I give and bequeath to my beloved wife Mary over and above her Dower five Shillings

Item I give unto my ffive Chilldren Viz^t William Solomon Joseph Abigail Wife of Phinehas Coalman and Eliz^a the wife of Samuel Fabyan ffive Shillings Each —

Item I give unto my s^d Son William Huntriss two thirds of all the land I own in Newington aforesaid where I now Dwell be the whole Tract fforty Acers More or less, and all my Oxen Cows Horses or Horse kind Sheep Swine that is to Say all my Cattle of all kinds Except what I Shall hereafter give by this my last will to my Said Son Joseph, Togeather with my Dwelling house Barn out houses, orchards, gardens &c with all the Privelidges thereof What Soever within Doors and without Except before Excepted to him the s^d William Huntriss his heirs and assigns for Ever in Fee Simple

Item I give unto the Chillderin of my Son George Huntriss and my Said Son Solomon Huntriss all my Right title Intrest Estate and Demand which I have to any lands in the Town Ship of Barnstead in the Province aforesaid to be Equally devided between them the Said Chillderin of my Said Son George Huntriss Deceased and my Son Solomon aforesaid to them the S^d Childeren of the Said George and the s^d Solomon in Severalty and to there Several and Respective Heirs and assigns in Fee Simple for ever Except it shall so happen that the s^d Chillderen Shall Die before they arive to ffull age in the law or the Said Solomon Shall happen to Die with out lawfull Issue of his Body then the S^d Device or Devices part or parts of S^d Lands Shall revert to the s^d William and Jos: in the ffollowing Proportion to be justly divided between them according to Quantity and quality vizt two thirds thereof to the s^d William Huntriss and one third thereof to the Said Joseph Huntriss

Item I give unto my Said Son Joseph Huntriss the one third part of the Said land whereon I now Dwell the whol being fforty

Acers more or less the Other two thirds of said fforty Acers I haveing before in this my last will given to my said Son William I also give my said son Joseph one half of that Dwelling house wherein my Brother John Huntriss Deceased used to live which half was given me by my honoured ffather I also give to my s^d Son Joseph one good Cow and four Sheep one Dozen of my Peauter Plates and two peater Dishes one of the leargest Size the Other of the lesser Size

Item I give unto my two gransons the Sons of my Son Samuel Huntriss Deceased ffive pounds old Tenor money Each if they Shall arive to the age of Twenty one years.

All the Rest and Residue of my Estate wheither real or personal I give and bequeath to my aforesaid Willm Huntriss and I doe hereby Constitute and Appoint him my said Son William Huntriss Executor * * *

          his
       Sam^{ll} + Huntriss
          Mark

[Witnesses] Geo Walton, Josiah Downing J^r, Noah Rawllings. [Proved May 20, 1758.]

[Mary Huntress, widow, acknowledges receipt of one third of the personal estate and waives inventory May 22, 1758; witnesses, James Pattinson, Valentine Mathes.]

JOSEPH KIMBALL   1758   HAMPSTEAD

[Administration on the estate of Joseph Kimball of Hampstead, yeoman, granted to his widow, Sarah Kimball, March 30, 1758.]

[Probate Records, vol. 21, p. 35.]

[Bond of Sarah Kimball, with John Kent of Hampstead and John Dustin of Plaistow, yeomen, as sureties, in the sum of £2000, March 30, 1758, for the administration of the estate; witnesses, Ebenezer Kimball, Daniel Little.]

[Inventory, April 22, 1758; amount, £4831. 18. 0; signed by Daniel Little and John Kent.]

[Commission, March 28, 1764, to Thomas Little, John Ingalls, and Willett Peters, all of Plaistow, yeomen, to set off the widow's dower.]

Province of } In obedience to a Warrant to us Directed Newhampshear } from the Honor[ble] Richard Wibird Esqr Judge of the Probate of Wills &c for said Province

We Have set of to the Widow sarah Kimball for her Dower out of the Reall Estate of her Late Husband Joseph Kimball Late of Hampstead yeoman Deceas[d] aboute twenty acres of Land where the house stands and is bounded at the northeast Corner with a stake and stons also a bound of John Kents Land thence westerly by his Land aboute forty one Rods to a White oake tree marked thence southerly partly by s[d] Kents Land and Partly by John Ingalls Land and partly by Jonathan Nelsons Land to a Red oake stump by the Roade being aboute seventy four Rods thence Easterly and Northerly Round by the Roade to the first Bounds and also the House on the same and one third of the Barn the East End thereof with a Convenient way to the barn and a Convenient barn yard

Dated Hampstead April y[e] 19: 1764   John Ingalls
                                       Thomas Little

[Account of the administratrix; receipts, £2240. 18. 0; expenditures, £2290. 11. 4; allowed Oct. 31, 1764.]

[Guardianship of Patty Kimball, minor, aged more than 14 years, daughter of Joseph Kimball of Hampstead, granted to Sarah Kimball Oct. 31, 1764.]

[Probate Records, vol. 23, p. 322.]

[Bond of Sarah Kimball, widow, with Samuel Brown, yeoman, as surety, both of Hampstead, in the sum of £500, Oct. 31, 1764, for the guardianship of Patty Kimball; witnesses, William Parker, William Vaughan.]

[Additional account; receipts, £67. 13. 0; expenditures, £27. 2. 2; mentions "bringing up the Children"; allowed Oct. 26, 1768.]

[Administratrix's account of the settlement of the estate; receipts, £2240. 18. 0; expenditures, £3438. 10. 6; allowed Jan. 26, 1769.]

[Probate Records, vol. 25, p. 332.]

JOHN MERRILL, JR.   1758   BOW

Portsmouth March 30th 1758 —
To the Honble Richard Wibird Esqr Judge of Probate for the province of New Hampshire.

The Humble Request of Timothy Walker of pennicook In said province, for & In Behalf of the Heirs if Such there are of John Merrill of said Pennicook, & for & In Behalf of the Father of said Merrill by his Desire, Shews —

That the said Merrill Was Out in the Army the Last Year, & is missing, Whether Dead or alive no one Can tell, & the Wife of the said John, your Requester, as well his Father is Informed, Calls her self a widow, & has applyed, or will Soon for a Letter of Administration on ye Estate of her Husband Jno Merrill as tho Dead, & now Just on the point of Marriage, Wherefore Your Informer for & in Behalf of the Heirs, Altho by No Legal authority, & for & in Behalf of his Fathar, by his Desire, prays that your Honour will not Grant Any Letter of Administration to the wife of the said John Merrill; Untill hes Dead by Law, or otherways, Your honour may have farther Intelligence of the facts, or as In your wisdom Shall think proper to Act. —

Timothy walker

[Administration on the estate of John Merrill of Bow, yeoman, granted to his father, John Merrill of Bow, yeoman, Aug. 27, 1760.]

[Probate Records, vol. 21, p. 480.]

[Bond of John Merrill, with Timothy Walker and John Webster as sureties, all of Bow, in the sum of £500, Aug. 27, 1760, for the administration of the estate; witnesses, William Parker, Solomon Loud, Jr.]

[Inventory, Nov. 21, 1760; amount, £1829. 8. 0; signed by Richard Eastman and Ezra Carter.]

[Account of the administrator; receipts, £99. 4. 10½; expenditures, £128. 18. 4; mentions "Paid the Doctors for Attendance on two the Deceased children which died"; allowed May 31, 1768.]

RUTH CHASE 1758 LONDONDERRY

[Bond of Stephen Spaulding of Londonderry, yeoman, with Nathan Cross, yeoman, and Samuel Greeley, gentleman, both of Nottingham West, as sureties, in the sum of £1000, March 31, 1758, for the administration of the estate of Ruth Chase of Londonderry, widow; witnesses, William Richardson, Daniel Marshall.]

[Warrant, March 31, 1758, authorizing William Richardson of Pelham and Samuel Greeley of Nottingham West, gentlemen, to appraise the estate.]

[Inventory, April 13, 1758; amount, £1800. 0. 0; signed by William Richardson and Samuel Greeley, Jr.]

[Commission, Dec. 12, 1759, to Samuel Greeley, Daniel Marshall, Reuben Spaulding, Samuel Hill, and Roger Chase, all of Nottingham West, to divide the real estate into five shares, a double share for the oldest son. On the reverse are the names "Abig^l Chase Ruth Kelly Mary Kelly Eliz^a mar^{d}sis Dec^d (Dorothy Beetle Abiel Beetle) Joseph Kelly Eldest Son of London^d Oliver Saunders of New Salem Roger Chase of Nottingham West."]

[Bond of Joseph Kelly of Londonderry, yeoman, with Roger Chase of Nottingham West and Oliver Saunders of Salem, yeomen, as sureties, in the sum of £500, Feb. 14, 1760, to pay the other children their shares of the estate of his mother, Ruth Chase, as follows: to Abigail Chase, Ruth Kelly, and Mary Kelly £62. 10. 0 each, and to Dorothy Beetle and Abiel Beetle, children of Elizabeth Beetle, deceased, who was a daughter of the intestate, the share of the said Elizabeth, £62. 10. 0, to Dorothy when 18 years of age, and to Abiel when 21; witnesses, William Parker, William Parker, Jr.]

JOSEPH BLANCHARD   1758   NASHUA

In the name of God Amen I Joseph Blanchard of Dunstable in the Province of New Hampshire * * *

Item that all my Children under Twenty one Years be Brought up taken care of & Educated by & at the Discretion of my Ex^{or} hereafter named, the Expence to be paid out of my real Estate Untill Each of them Severally Come to the age of Twenty one years & not to be any part of their portion & in as much as my Son Joseph Blanchard, in Lands & otherwise hath had advance what I Esteem to be Equal to five thousand pound at 3 pound ten pr Dollar old Tenor, that there be no further advance for his portion untill Each of his Brothers & Sisters has had of Equal value —

And that my Daughter Rebecca the wife of Mr James Minot has had by Deed to her Husband and other ways what I esteem to be Equal to four Thousand pounds old Tenor all in Bill of New Hampshire the Value Determin'd at three Pound ten Per Dollar.

& that my S^d Executr^x Divide & Sett off to the remander of my Children (viz) Katharine Jon^a Sarah James Jotham augustus, & Hannah so much of my real Estate as She Shall at any time think fit always to observe that they all Who have not as yet marryed have in Equal proportions untill they have four thousand pounds old Tenor Each at three pound ten Per Dollar & Each Son when he Comes to Lawful age Shall have his Choice as to Scituation & that the remander of my Estate real & personal, (Except what I hereafter give to my wife) be Divided in Equal Shars Amoung all my Children married & unmarried, reserving to my Ex^{ix} full power, in this Last Division to give more or less to any Child as they are more or less Dutyful

Item I give & Bequeath to my Weell Beloved Wife Rebecca The Dwelling House I now live in with all the Furniture there unto appertaining, The Farm I now live on, Improv'd & Unimproved with all the Building Stock & Tools of Husbandry of every Kind there unto Belonging, Likewise my Negro Man servant Called Cesar, free from all Incumbrances, to be Solely at Her disposal her Heirs & Assigns forever, Like wise my part in the Social Library at Portsmouth, All my fire Arms Swords Watch & Wearing apparrell & all my Provision of every kind

Notwithstanding anything before Written I give & bequeath unto Elizabeth Parker the Daughter of the Revd Mr Tho: Parker of Dracut Two hundred Pound old Tenor at the value of the Money the 29 of June Seventeen Hundred fifty five, to be paid a year after my Decease

and my said wife Rebecca Blanchard Depending on her tender Care & Equal Affection to all my Children who with tender Kindness & reverend Respectful behaviour Carry towards her do Committ the aforesaid trust to her & Constitute Ordain & appoint her Sole Executrix of this my Last will & Testament: Dated April 6th in The Thirty first year of his Majestys Reign A D 1758

Joseph Blanchard

[Witnesses] Zacheus Lovewell, Mathew Thornton, Elias Smith. [Proved May 3, 1758.]

[Bond of Rebecca Blanchard of Dunstable, widow, with James Minot, gentleman, and Joseph Blanchard, both of Merrimack, as sureties, in the sum of £5000, May 3, 1758, for the execution of the will; witnesses, Katharine Blanchard, Jonathan Blanchard.]

[Bond of Jonathan Blanchard of Merrimack, with James Blanchard of Dunstable and Oliver Parker of Monadnock No. 7, yeomen, as sureties, in the sum of £1000, Nov. 2, 1774, for the administration, with will annexed, of the estate; witnesses, Samuel Hale, Jr., William Chadbourne.]

[Inventory, June 15, 1776; lands in Dublin, Stoddard, and Fitzwilliam, £185. 0. 0; signed by Enoch Hale and Samuel Moore.]

THOMAS CANNEY   1758   DOVER

In the Name of God Amen the tenth Day of April in the year of our Lord Christ Seventeen hundred and fifty Eight I Thomas Canne of Dover in the Province of New Hampshire in New England yeoman being Something Aged & Infirm in body * * * (2ly) I Give & Bequeath to My Eldest Son Thomas Canne ten acres of Land more or less where he now Dwells also one hundred pounds old tenor at my Decease to be paid him by my Said Execu^r which with three hundred pounds old Tenor more I paid him my Self heretofore which Sums together with what I have already Given him is in full of his Portion out of my Estate. Item I Give to my Daughter Susanna Hanson one hundred pounds old Tenor to be paid her by my Execu^r in three years after my Decease. Item I Give to my Daughter Martha Meder one hundred pounds old Tenor to be paid her in three years after my Decease in Manner aforesaid. Item I Give to my Son Benjamin Canne one hundred pounds old tenor to be paid him in manner & term afore S^d which Sum together with what I have already Given him Compleats his Portion. Item I Give to my Daughter Rose Canne one hundred pounds old tenor to be paid her by my Execu^r also, one Fether Bed and furniture for the

Same also one Iron Pot one Iron Skilott one frying pan & one Pewter Platter, together with free & full Liberty of one Room in my house to Dwell in and also to have an equal Share or Comfortable Support out of my Real & Personal Estate So long as She Shall remain Single & unmarried. Item I Give to my Son William Canne one hundred pounds old tenor to be paid him by My Said Execu^r in manner & term aforesaid which with what I have already Given him Compleats his Portion. Item I Give to my Son John Canne all my homsted farm where I now Dwell except a small orchard with the Land whereon it Stands Joyning to Ephraim Tibbets's Land &c I likewise give to my Said Son John Canne all the Edifices buildings & other orchards thereon together with all that tract or tracts of Land of mine on the westerly Side of the back River also one Right in the ox Pasture So Call'd together with one piece of thatch Bed at or near patridge point also one fether bed & furniture for the Same together with all my farming Utencels (Viz^t) Plows harrows Cart & wheels Sleds Yoaks Chains axes &c with all the Iron work in or about my house except what I have already Given to my Daughter Rose Canne to be to him the S^d John Canne his heirs & assigns forever he & they Carefully Complying with & paying out the above Metioned Debts and Legacies. Item I Give to my Grand Son Joseph Canne the within mentioned Small orchard with the Land whereon it Stands Joying to Land which formerly belonged to Joseph Hall Deceased also to the Land of Eph^r Tibbets aforesaid and I Desire that my Son Benj^a Canne may have the Care and management of the Same for my S^d Grand Son untill he is Twenty one years of age. Item I Constitute & appoint My Son John Canne Sole Executor * * *

his
Thomas + Canne
Mark

[Witnesses] Elijah Tuttel, Nathaniel Austin, Alex^r Caldwell.
April 10th 1760
P: S; Mem^o I Give & Bequeath unto my Daughter Rose Canne

over & above what is mention'd in the foregoeing Will (vizt) one Fire Shovel on p^r of Tonges and one Tramel. And all the Rest & Residue of my Estate Real & personal or of whatever name Nature or kind or where Soever the Same is or Shall be found I Give & Bequeath to be Divided in equal Shares or proportions amongest all my Children * * *

his
Thomas + Canne
Mark

[Witnesses] Elijah Tuttel, Nathaniel Austin, Alex^r Caldwell. [Proved June 30, 1762.]

[Inventory, attested July 27, 1763; amount, £11,518. o. 3; signed by Joseph Hanson and Thomas Tuttle.]

SAMUEL DUDLEY   1758   EXETER

In the Name of God amen. the Thirteenth day of april annoque Domini one Thousand Seven hundred and fifty Eight I Samuel Dudley of Exeter in the Province of Newhampshire in New England yeoman being week in body * * *

Item I Give and bequeath to my Sister Mary Watson one hundred Pounds Equal to old tenor bills of Publick Credit to be Paid by my Executor out of my Estate.

Item I Give and bequeath to my Sister Elizabeth Dudley one hundred Pounds Equal to old tenor bills of Publick Credit to be Paid by my Executor out of my Estate.

Item I Give and Bequeath to my Sister Sarah Leavit one hundred Pounds Equal to old tenor bills of Publick Credit to be Paid by my Executor out of my Estate.

Item I Give and bequeath to my Sister Marcy Thing one hundred Pounds Equal to old tenor bills of Publick Credit to be Paid by my Executor out of my Estate.

Item I Give and bequeath to my Brother Jonathan Dudley of Brintwood alias Keenborough in the Province aforesaid all my land and orchard lying in Exeter aforesaid, and all my other Estate Real and Personal whare Ever it may be found to be his his heirs and assigns forever he or they Paying out as above mentioned.

Finally I do hereby Constitute appoint make and ordain my brother Jonathan dudley aforesaid my Sole Executor * * *

his
Samuel + dudley
Mark

[Witnesses] Samuel Blake, Jeremiah Ellsworth, John Purmort. [Proved Feb. 28, 1759.]

[Bond of Jonathan Dudley, with Jeremiah Ellsworth as surety, both of Brentwood, in the sum of £500, Feb. 28, 1759, for the execution of the will; witnesses, Joseph Newmarch, William Parker.]

JOHN CURRIER 1758 PLAISTOW

In The Name of God Aman The Last will and Testament of John Currier of Plastow In the Provence of New hamsher in New england yeaman — Being Very sick and weak in Body * * *

Imprimes I Give unto my son John Twenty acors of Land he paying to my Executors one Hundred pounds of silver money of the old taner that is to say in Dolers at forty and five shillings per Doler also I order my son John to pay to my Executors one Hundred pounds of Hamsher money of the old taner that is to say to be in Vallew as good as one Hundred pounds old taner is at this day and the said Land that I Give to my son John is part of the Land that I Now live one and the west End of my Land and is bounded as followeth — Begining at the southwest angel or Corner with a stake and stones it also being Daniel whittickers Nortwest corner Bounds of his Land thence a way Easterdly By Whittickers Land about Eighty and five Rhods and a haf to a walnut tree marked standing Near the Line of whitickers Land Thence a way Northerdly about Thirty seven Rhods and a haf to a walnut tree marked Near the Line of Theoder Adkissons Esqr Land thence a way westerdly By adkissons Land a Bout Eighty five Rhods and a haf to a stake and stones Thence a way Southerdly about Thirty seven Rhods and a haf to the furst Bounds mentioned; the southwest corner Bounds of this Land was Daniel Whittickers origenal Bounds Now Bounds of Timothy Lads Land which Land when the money a Bove said is paid is the full of his portion as I say out of my Estate Both Rael and Personal —

Item I Give unto my daughter sarah fifty pounds old taner of Hampsher money to Be paid to her by my Executors when she is Eighteen years of age and the money when paid is to be made as good in Vallew as it is at this day: when paid which is as I Say her full part out of my Estate Both Rael and personal

Itam I Give unto my Daughter Rachel fifty pounds old taner of New hamsher money or Bills of Creddet to be paid to Her by my Executors when she arive to the age of Eighteen and the money when paid is to be made as good in vallew as fifty pounds old taner is at this day which is as I say her full part out of my Estate Both Rael and Personal —

Itam I Give unto my Daughter mary fifty pounds of Hamsher money of the old taner to Be paid to her By my Executors to her when she coms to the age of Eighteen and the money when paid is to be made as good to her By my Executors as fifty pounds old taner is at this day of the date hereof which is as I say her full part out of my Estate Both Rael and personal —

Itam I Give unto my Grand Daughter anne Marbel five pounds old taner of Hamsher money to be paid by my Executors when she a Rive to the age of Eighteen and the money when paid to be made as good as it is at this day which money with what I have given her mother here to fore is her full part out of my Estate Both rael and personal as I Say

Itam I give unto my son Daved all my Rael and personal

Estate which I have not Expresly Disposed of in this my Last will and testament with paying all my just debts —

Finally I do hereby Nominate and apoint my son Daved and Mr Timothy Lad of Plastow to Be my Sole Executors * * *

In Testimony I do Hereunto set my hand and affix my seal the fourteenth day of aprel in the year of our Lord one thousand seven Hundred and fifty Eight and in the Thirty furst year of his majesties Raign —

his
John + Currier
Mark

[Witnesses] Moses Page, John Webster junr, Daniel Poor.
[Proved May 31, 1758.]

[Warrant, May 31, 1758, authorizing Tristram Knight and Jonathan Page, both of Plaistow, gentlemen, to appraise the estate.]

[Inventory, June 6, 1758; amount, £4743. 1. 0; signed by Tristram Knight and Jonathan Page.]

WALTER WEEKS, JR.   1758   GREENLAND

[Administration on the estate of Walter Weeks, Jr., of Greenland granted to Mary Weeks, widow, April 18, 1758.]

[Probate Records, vol. 20, p. 473.]

[Bond of Mary Weeks, with Walter Weeks and Abraham Dearborn, yeomen, as sureties, all of Greenland, in the sum of £1000, April 18, 1758, for the administration of the estate; witnesses, William Parker, David Sewall.]

[Warrant, April 18, 1758, authorizing Enoch Clark, innholder, and James Brackett, yeoman, both of Greenland, to appraise the estate.]

[Inventory, May 9, 1758; amount, £3050. 4. 0; signed by Enoch Clark and James Brackett.]

[Account of the administratrix; receipts, £2007. 11. 4, personal estate; expenditures, £554. 19. 0; mentions "bringing up Walter Weeks a minor under seven years of age till this Day"; allowed Sept. 26, 1759.]

[Additional account of Andrew Wiggin, 3d, and Mary, his wife, formerly Mary Weeks, administratrix; receipts, £1759. 3. 0; expenditures, £587. 10. 0; mentions "Maintenance of Walter Weeks a Minor from 26 Septr 1759 till he was 7 years old being 228 Weeks"; allowed June 24, 1772.]

JOHN BUTTERFIELD   1758   NASHUA

[Mary Butterfield renounces administration on the estate of her husband, John Butterfield, April 22, 1758, in favor of her son, Thomas Butterfield; witness, Jonathan Blanchard.]

[Administration on the estate of John Butterfield of Dunstable, yeoman, granted to Thomas Butterfield of Dunstable, yeoman, June 13, 1758.]

[Probate Records, vol. 21, p. 11.]

[Bond of Thomas Butterfield, with Ebenezer Harris and Thomas Lund, yeomen, as sureties, all of Dunstable, in the sum of £500, June 13, 1758, for the administration of the estate; witnesses, Hannah Dow, Jonathan Lovewell.]

[Warrant, June 13, 1758, authorizing Jonathan Lund and Elnathan Blood, both of Dunstable, yeomen, to appraise the estate.]

[Inventory, attested Aug. 9, 1758; amount, £4060. 16. 0; signed by Jonathan Lund and Elnathan Blood.]

[Return of claims against the estate, Dec. 1, 1769, one, only, being allowed, that of Thomas Butterfield for £3266. 13. 6, or in lawful money, £163. 6. 8; signed by Jonathan Lovewell and Samuel Roby.]

[Account of the administrator; receipts, £181. 2. 0, personal estate; expenditures, £35. 13. 9; allowed Feb. 7, 1772.]

[Settlement of the balance of the estate on Thomas Butterfield, sole creditor, Feb. 7, 1772.]

PELATIAH RUSSELL 1758 LITCHFIELD

[Administration on the estate of Pelatiah Russell of Litchfield, yeoman, granted to Olive Russell, widow, April 22, 1758.]

[Probate Records, vol. 20, p. 531.]

[Bond of Olive Russell of Litchfield, with Samuel Moore of Litchfield, gentleman, and John Goffe of Derryfield as sureties, in the sum of £500, April 22, 1758, for the administration of the estate; witnesses, Margaret Moore, Sarah Goffe.]

[Bond of Timothy Underwood, yeoman, with James Pollard, gentleman, as surety, both of Westford, Mass., in the sum of £500, Dec. 10, 1760, for the guardianship of Pelatiah Russell, in his ninth year, son of Pelatiah Russell; witnesses, Gershom Fletcher and Andrew Bordman.]

[Middlesex Co., Mass., Probate Files.]

GEORGE LITTLE 1758 PLAISTOW

The last will and testament of George Little of the town of Plastow in the Province of new hamshire in new england yeoman
* * *

Imp^r whereas my son Thomas Little have received his whole portion by deeds of gift I give him five shillings in lawful mony of new England

Item whereas my Son George Little have received his whole portion in land and other Species I give him five Shillings in lawful money of new England

Item whereas my Son Ezekil Little have received his whole portion in land and other species I give him five shillings in lawful mony of New England

Item I give to my Daughter Edna Ela all my household goods that is in my possesion

Item I give to my son Joseph Little whom I constitute make and ordain my whole and sole executor of this my last will and testament my dwelling house and all the land and orchard adjoyning to the house being about five acers and all my land on the west sid of the road that I have not givend to my son Ezekiel bounded as followeth begining at the road at a stake with stones about it which is Ezekiel northerly bounds and the runing westerly about seventy rods to a stake with stones about it and then norwesterly to a stake with stones about it at the corner of the rye feild and then notherly to a red oak tree near the brook and then runing easterly by the parsonage medow about one hundred and sixty rod to the land of Caleb Emersons land and then southerly and easterly by said Emersons land to the road and then southerly by the road to the bounds first mentioned it being about ninty acers and I give to my son Joseph all my estate real and parsonal that is not above given away in this my last will and testament: and to receive all the detes that are due to me and to pay all the detes that I do owe and legecies and also my funeral charges: and this is my last will and testement haveing my perfect memory and understanding as witness my hand and seal this twenty fourth day of April annoque domini one thousand seven hundred and fifty eight

George Little

[Witnesses] Eldad Ingalls, Stephen Dole, John Ingalls.
[Proved July 30, 1760.]

[Bond of Joseph Little, with Eldad Ingalls and Stephen Dole as sureties, all of Plaistow, in the sum of £500, July 30, 1760, for the execution of the will; witnesses, none.]

JAMES BERRY   1758   GREENLAND

[Administration on the estate of James Berry of Greenland, yeoman, granted to James Berry of York, Me., and Francis Berry of Greenland April 26, 1758.]

[Probate Records, vol. 21, p. 4.]

[Bond of James Berry of York, Me., and Francis Berry of Greenland, yeoman, with Abner Fogg of North Hampton and Paul March of Portsmouth, gentlemen, as sureties, in the sum of £1000, April 26, 1758, for the administration of the estate; witnesses, William Parker, David Sewall.]

[Warrant, April 26, 1758, authorizing William Haines, Jr., Simeon Dearborn, yeoman, and Enoch Clark, innholder, all of Greenland, to appraise the estate; mentions the administrators as sons of the deceased.]

[Inventory, June 6, 1758; amount, £6953. 6. 0; signed by Simeon Dearborn, Enoch Clark, and William Haines, Jr.]

[Account of the administrators; receipts, £682. 6. 0, personal estate; expenditures, £545. 15. 0; allowed Sept. 27, 1759.]

[Agreement of the heirs, June 25, 1760, to submit all differences to Samuel Veasey of Stratham, yeoman, Ebenezer Sanborn of North Hampton, gentleman, and Samuel Fabyan of Newington, yeoman, for decision; signed by James Berry, Francis Berry, Richard Berry, Robert Tufton Philbrook, and Henry Dow in behalf of his mother, Charity Dow.]

[Warrant, Feb. 17, 1761, authorizing Richard Jenness, 3d, of Rye, Ebenezer Johnson, William Haines, William Berry, yeomen, and John Folsom, innholder, all of Greenland, to set off the widow's dower.]

Province of } By order from the Honb{le} Richd Wibird
New Hampshire } Judge of the Probate of wills for Said Province &{c}

we the Subscribers have Set off to Eleanor Berry of Greenland Wedow her Part of the Estate of her Late Husband James Berry Dec{d} viz

the Land on the west Side of the high way from the house begening at Chapmans Land & runing by Said high way twenty Rods to a noch in the fence and at the West end of Said Land twenty Rods from Land of Joseph Heans Deceased to a white Borch tree marked —

the Land where the house Stands the full one third on the North Side twenty five Rods from Chapmans Land by Said high way to a noch in ye fence & twenty five Rods at the East End by Land of w{m} wallas to Bounds in ye fence

the one halfe of ten acres by John Heans Land next to Said Heans Eight Rods in weadth as the Bounds Stand in the fence

the north End of the house Lower Room & Chamber with ye Small Celer under said house

also the west End of the Barn ten feet in Length with a privaladge of the Barn flooer for thrashing

the Pear tree & Six apple trees in the Grate orchard that is marked

Greenland January 24th 1761   Ebenezer Johnson
                                    Richd Jenness 3d
                                    William Berray

[Commission, March 31, 1761, to Richard Jenness, 3d, of Rye, Ebenezer Johnson, William Berry, yeomen, William Weeks, gentleman, and John Folsom, innholder, all of Greenland, to divide the real estate. The committee report against the division, and appraise the real estate at £6276. 13. 0; signed by Ebenezer Johnson, Richard Jenness, 3d, and William Berry.]

[Additional account of the administrators; receipts, £1646. 17. 0; expenditures, £1514. 4. 4; allowed March 31, 1761.]

[Warrant, April 6, 1765, authorizing Richard Jenness, 3d, and Joseph Brown, yeomen, both of Rye, Levi Dearborn of North Hampton, physician, John Folsom, and Enoch Clark, both of Greenland, innholders, to divide the real estate.]

[Probate Records, vol. 23, p. 408.]

Province of } Pursuant to a Warrant Directed to us the
New Hampsh^r } Subscribers from the Honble Richard Wibird Esqr Judge of the Probate of Wills &c for Said Province to Divide the Real Estate of James Berry late of Greenland Deceasd Intestate among the Children of Said Deceased

1st To the heirs of William Berry Eldest Son of the aforesaid James Berry Deceased two Shares of Land Bounded as follows Viz on the West Side of the Highway with Land of the Widow Chapman & Land of the Heires of Joseph Haines on the North Land of Francis Berry & Joseph Berry on the South & Land of Robert Tuftin Philbrick on the West Containing Twenty one Acres and a Half as it is Laid out & Bounded also the Barn as it Stands on the East Side of the Highway to the aforesaid Heirs of William Berry Deceased for their Two Shares —

2^ly Laid out to Francis Berry his Share or part of Land on the East Side of the Highway where the House Stands Containing ten Acres with Land of the Widow Chapman on the North begining at the Widow Chapman Land & Runing by the Highway thirteen Rods to a Stake in the Ground & Carrying that Bredth of thirteen Rods to William Wallases Land as the Bounds now Stands Also the Sixth part of the House as it is Divided —

3^ly Laid out to Priscilla Philbrick her Share or part of Land lying on the East Side of the Highway Containing Twenty Acres Bounding Northerly on Land of Francis Berry aforesaid & from Said Francis Berrys Land by the Highway Seventeen Rods & 2 feet to a Stake in the Ground Carrying that Bredth of Seventeen Rods & two feet to Land of William Wallaces as the

Bounds Now Stands Also the Sixth part of the house as it is Divided —

4^{ly} Laid out to James Berry his Share or part of Land Containing Eleven Acres on the East Side of the Highway Bounding with Land of Priscilla Philbrick on the North & Runing from her Land Southerly by the highway Seventeen rods & fourteen feet to a Stake in the Ground And Carrying that Bredth of Seventeen rods & fourteen feet to Land of William Wallice as the Bounds now Stands also the one Sixth part of the House as it is Divided —

5^{ly} Laid out to Richard Berry his part or Share of Land Containing twelve acres on the East Side of the Highway Bounding with Land of James Berry on the North & Runing from Said James Berry's Land Southerly by the Highway Twenty two rods & three feet to a Stake in the Ground and Carrying that Bredth of 22 rods & 3 feet to William Wallases Land, Also the one Sixth part of the House as it is Divided —

6^{ly} Laid out to Joseph Berry his Share or part of Land Containing twelve Acres and one half be the Same more or Less Bounding Westerly on the above Said Highway Southerly on the Highway that Leads to Rye & Easterly on land of William Wallice as the Stake Drove in the Ground now Stands, Also four acres one Hundred & Twenty rods more or Less on the West Side of the Highway Bounding Easterly on Land of Francis Berry Northerly on Land Laid out to the Heirs of William Berry Dec^d Westerly on Land of Robt Tuftain Philbrick & Southerly on the one Acre Laid out to Charity Dow as the Bounds now Stands Also the one Sixth part of the House as it is Divided —

7^{ly} Laid out to Charity Dow her Share or part of Land Containing ten acres Bounding Northerly on Land of John Haines Easterly on the Highway & Southerly on land of William Wallaces as Said Ten Acres is laid out & Bounded also one Acre of Land on the West Side of the Highway with Land of Francis Berry on the East Land laid out to Joseph Berry on the North &

Land of John Haines on the South — All the aforesaid Pieces of Land lying & being in Greenland aforesaid and was the Estate of James Berry Late of Greenland Deceased Survayed & Divided by us this 23^d Day of April 1765

          Richd Jennes 3^d
          Enoch Clark
          John Folsom
          Joseph Brown

[Probate Records, vol. 23, p. 408.]

SAMUEL JACKSON   1758   PORTSMOUTH

In the Name of God Amen The Last will and Testament of Samuel Jackson I Samuel Jackson of Portsmouth in the Province of New Hampshire Joyner being Week in body   *   *   *

Item I give unto my well beloved wife all that my house and Lands where I now Live, and all the Lands I purchased from her Father Moore during her Natural Life, and all the Land that was my Fathers on the north side the fresh Marsh Creek that I am now possed off, I give to her to be Improved by her towards the Support of her Children untill the Youngest of them Shall arive to the age of Eighteen Years, and all my household goods (Except one bed & beding therefor) with my Two Cows & one heifer, to be at her own disposall.

Item I give unto my Sons Joseph Nathaniel Samuel Thomas & Richard and to my Daughter Mary (they being Children I had by my first wife) all my Land in Kittery in the County of York that was part of the Estate of their Grandfather Hill to be divided in Equal Shares to be to them their heirs and assigns and my will is that if any one or more of my said Children should die Intestate under the age of Twenty one Years And his or her part not disposed off (if more than Twenty one Years old) his her or their part shall be divided to and among the Survivors or Survivor of them in Equal Shares.

Item I Give unto my Son Jonathan my Daughters Elizabeth Margaret and Sarah after the decease of my wife, all that my house and Land where I now live, and all the Land I purchased from their Grandfather moore in Equal Shares only the peice of flats Grounds to be to Jonathan more than his Share of the whole, to be to them their heirs and assigns and if any or either of four Last mentioned Children shall die under the age of Twenty one Years, or if more than Twenty one Years old Intestate and his part not disposed of It shall be Equally divided among the Survivors or Survivor of them

Item I give unto my Son Samuel my Gun that was my Brother Joshua's —

Item I give unto my Son Richard all my working tools —

Item I give unto my Daughter Mary one bed & beding, it being the Same that was her mothers, and all her mothers wearing apparrell

And after my youngest Child is arived to the age of Eighteen Years, then it is my will that the Land Lying on the north side the fresh marsh Creek in Said Portsmouth, and that I gave my wife the Improvement of untill that time, shall be sold by my Executor and the money Raised by the Sale thereof shall be Equally divided among my Children I had by my first wife or in Case of the death of any to be to the Survivor as I mentioned by the Lands herein given them and my Executor I impower to Sell the Same —

Item After the Settlement of my Estate by my Executor, what of Cash shall Remain in the hands of my Executor I Give one third part thereof unto my Beloved wife to be paid her by my Executor. I also Give her my Canoe —

Item The other Two thirds parts of the aforesaid Cash I give in Equal Shares to and among my Children I had by my first wife, to be paid to the Boyes when, and as they arive to the age of Twenty one Years, and to the Girl when and as She arives to the age of Eighteen, and I desire my Executor to take Each Childs Share that is under age as aforesaid & put it out to Interist untill they Severally arive to age as aforesaid, and if any or either of my Children shall die under the age aforesaid then his her or their part of the Said money shall be equally divided among the Survivors of them

Item All the Rest Residue and Remainder of my Estate if any their be I give to be divided among my Children I had by my first wife — And I Constitute and Appoint my brother Nathaniel Jackson Sole Executor * * * and In Testimony whereof I the Said Samuel Jackson have hereunto Set my hand and Seal this Twenty Sixth day of April in the thirty first Year of his majestys Reign annoque Domini one thousand Seven hundred and fifty Eight 1758

Samuel Jackson

[Witnesses] George Marshall, Joseph Davis, Cutts Shannon. [Proved May 31, 1758.]

[Warrant, May 31, 1758, authorizing Samuel Waters and Samuel Penhallow, shopkeeper, both of Portsmouth, to appraise the estate.]

[Inventory, June 23, 1758; amount, £6104. 15. 5; signed by Samuel Waters and Samuel Penhallow.]

[Richard Jackson, minor, aged more than 16 years, son of Samuel Jackson, makes choice of Nathaniel Jackson of Portsmouth, cordwainer, as his guardian Sept. 19, 1758; witnesses, William Parker, David Sewall.]

[Guardianship of Richard Jackson granted to Nathaniel Jackson Sept. 19, 1758.]

[Probate Records, vol. 21, p. 57.]

[Bond of Nathaniel Jackson, with Michael Whidden, Jr., joiner, as surety, both of Portsmouth, in the sum of £500, Sept. 19, 1758, for the guardianship of Richard Jackson; witnesses, William Parker, David Sewall.]

[Account of the administrator; receipts, £2642. 14. 1, personal estate; expenditures, £2590. 14. 1; allowed March 25, 1761.]

ISRAEL SANBORN   1758   NEWMARKET

In the Name of God Amen the twenty ninth Day of April 1758 I Israel Samborn of Newmarket in the Province of Newhampshire Black Smith Being listed in the Kings Service and going into the Armie Uncertain where I shall Ever Return or Not * * * first I Give all my land and mobibles to my Brother Benjamin and Joseph to be Divided Equal Between them I Give to my Honoured Mother Elizabeth folsom one hundred and forty pounds acording to Dollars Six pound per dollar to Come out of my brother Josephs part that I Give him as fast as the Land produces it. I Give to my Sister mary fox twenty pounds Equal to Dollars Six pound per Dollar to Be paid out of my brother Benjamins part —

If my Brother John Comes home and I Dont I Give him all that was willed to me by our honoured father But If not I Give it all to my honoured mother * * *

In witness whereof I have hereunto Set my hand and Seal this twenty Eighteth Day of April one thousand Seven hundred and fifty Eight and In the 31 year of his majesties Reign
                                               Israel Sanborn

[Witnesses] Moses Coffin, John Samborn, Mary pike.
[Proved Nov. 28, 1759.]

[Bond of Benjamin Sanborn of Newmarket, cordwainer, with Moses Coffin of Epping and John Sanborn of Newmarket, yeomen, as sureties, in the sum of £800, Nov. 28, 1759, for the administration of the estate, with will annexed; witnesses, Shadrach Bell, David Sewall.]

JAMES GILMORE   1758   WINDHAM

In ye Name of god amen I James Gillmoor of the parish of Windham within the province of Newhampshire in New England Gentleman: Being Sick and Indisposed in Body * * *

Item my Will is that my Dearly Beloved Wife Margrat Gillmoor Shal Be paid By my Exa^tors the Sum of thirty Eight Dollars which is now Due to me upon notes of hand; and Like wise all my houshould furniture for her use and Benefict Dureing her Naturall Life

Item my Will is that my Wife Shall have my Mear Saddle and Bridle and her Choice of two of my Cows given her By my Exa^tors

Item my Will is y^t my wife Shall have given her By my Son in Law Gann Armour he In joying my Real Estate twenty Six Bushalls of Indean Corn and four Bushalls of Riey and four Barralls of Syder and Cute her wood and Bring it hom to her what is Necesary for her fire; and the afore said Mear and Cows to be keept for her Bouth Sumer and Winter all these articles afores^d to Be performed By the S^d Gann Armour Yearly and Every year Dureing her Naturall Life —

Item my Will is that my Beloved Son Gann Armour and Jenet Armour his Wife Shall have and In joy all my Real Estate and all the money that is Due to me upon notes or Bounds Exclusife of the afore mentioned Dollars: and Likewise all my Stock of Chattle Exclusife of the afores^d Mear and Cows: and also all my farming utentils for their use and Benefite: he paying the Sums here after mentioned to my other Children and to other hereafter mentioned: Said Sums is as followeth and Days of payment the first payment of the one half is at the End of two years after my Decease and the other half at the End of four years

Item my Will is that my Son Gann Armour pay out of my Estate to my Son in Law Samuell m^caddams and Mary m^caddams his wife the Sume of five hundred pound old tenor and also to Each of their Children: that is Janet — John — Margrat —

and James m^{c}addams the Sum of one hundred pound old tenor — Likwise to my Son in Law John Stuart and Margrat Stuart his Wife the Sum of one hundred and fifty pounds old tenor and to Each of thire three Childern he hath By my Doughter Margrat Stuart that is Sarah and John Stuart and the youngest which is not yet Baptizt the Sum of one hundred and fifty pound old tenor — and Likewise to my Son in Law James Gillmoor and Augness Gillmoor his Wife the Sum of three hundred pounds old tenor — and also to James Gillmoor a Child Son to the afores^d James Gillmoor and Augness Gillmoor the Sum of four hundred pound old tenor and Likwise to jean Armour and Mary Armour Children to the afores^d Gann Armour and Janet Armour his Wife to Each of them the Sum of three hundred and fifty pound old tenor — But if Dollars Should Be Com Less then Six pound pr Dollar; then these afores^d Sums to Be Less accordingly —

Item my Will is that David Gillmoor the Boy that Lives with me have one hundred pound old tenor paid him By my Son in Law Gann Armour out of my Estate at the End of four years after my Deceass

Item my will is that Anthony Eady that is Bound to Serve me Shal have fifty pound old tenor paid to him By the afore S^d Gann Armour out of my Estate at the End of the time he is Bound provided he serves out his time honestly and is obedient to my wife Margrat Gillmoor his Mistress But if not I allow him Nothing —

Item my Will is y^t my Son Gann Armour pay out of my Estate to the first Minister in this parish of Windham as Soon as Settled the Sum of fifty pounds old tenor; — and Likwise fifty pound old tenor to the Bulding of a pulpet in the Meetting hous of S^d Windham as Son as the work is Don —

and I Do here By Constitute nominate and appoint my Beloved Son in Law Gann armour afore mentioned and Samuel Morison of Windham a fore S^d Gentleman — my Exacutors * * * in Witness whereof I have here unto Sett my hand

and Seal this Ninteenth Day of May and in the thirty first year of his Majesties Reigne anno Domi 1758

his
James + Gillmoor
Mark

[Witnesses] William Thom, John Thom, William Thom Junr. [Proved June 28, 1758.]

[Inventory, Aug. 29, 1758; amount, £5550. 10. 0; signed by John Cochran and William Thom.]

[Guardianship of James Gilmore granted to his father, James Gilmore, June 28, 1758.]

[Probate Records, vol. 21 p. 8.]

[Bond of James Gilmore, with Gain Armour and William Thom as sureties, all of Windham, in the sum of £1000, June 28, 1758, for the guardianship of James Gilmore; witnesses, William Parker, Nathan Rowe.]

[Guardianship of Sarah Stewart and John Stewart granted to their father, John Stewart, April 30, 1766.]

[Probate Records, vol. 24, p. 249.]

[Bond of John Stewart of Haverhill, Mass., with Nathaniel Woodman and William Wheeler, both of Salem, as sureties, in the sum of £500, April 30, 1766, for the guardianship of his children, Sarah Stewart and John Stewart, for the estate given them by their grandfather; witnesses, William Vaughan, William Parker.]

ARTHUR NESMITH　　　1758　　　　LONDONDERRY

[Administration on the estate of Arthur Nesmith of Londonderry granted to Margaret Nesmith of Londonderry, widow, May 24, 1758.]

[Probate Records, vol. 21, p. 76.]

[Bond of Margaret Nesmith, with John Hopkins and James Wilson, yeomen, as sureties, all of Londonderry, in the sum of £1000, May 24, 1758, for the administration of the estate of Arthur Nesmith, cooper; witnesses, John Hopkins, Samuel Barr.]

[Warrant, May 24, 1758, authorizing John Barnett and George Duncan, both of Londonderry, yeomen, to appraise the estate.]

[Inventory, attested March 22, 1759; amount, £3382. 16. 0; signed by John Barnett and George Duncan.]

JOSEPH REDMAN   1758   HAMPTON

In the Name of God amen this twenty forth Day of May Anno Domini 1758 In the thirty first year of his majestys Reign I Joseph Redman of Hampton in the province of Newhampshire in New England yeoman being Sick and weeak In Body   *   *   *

First I give and bequeath to my Son John Redman all my land Laying in my home place and adjoyning to Itt Excepting Six acres in the first range Joyning upon Little river marsh Southerly and wersterly upon william Masting which I bequeath to my Son David Redman

2dly I gve unto My Son John Redman all my buildings Dweling House Barn on itt with all my lands in the first Division of the five Devisions in hampton both on the northerly and Southerly Side of little River with my land in The East field So Called and my Spring Marsh So Called And my Boares marsh bought of Daniel Moulton With my marsh on the Northerly Side of the beach Casway Joyning Southerly to palmers marsh Excepting the above mentioned Six acres

3dly I Give and bequeath to my Son trustrim Redman my Share of land att north hill in the Second North Devision In s^d Hampton with my Share of Marsh and a Share of thatch Ground both laying on the ox Common and my Share of upland on S^d

ox Common with my Share of hucklebury Marsh So Called and a little Share of marsh in little marsh partly Covered with Sand

4^{ly} I Give and bequeath to my son David Redman One hundred pounds in money old tenor sixty pounds of to be paid by my Son John Redman and Forty pounds to be paid by my Son trustrim in one year after my Decease

5^{ly} Itt is my will that my S^d Sons John Readman Trustrim Redman and David Redman Shall have all my right and land Laying in Chichester in S^d Province and Devided Eaqueally between them with my apparall and my Movables in the house I also Give to my s^d three Sons Equally between them

6^{ly} I give to My S^d two Sons John and trustrim all my Stock of Cattle and husbandry Emplements Eaqualy Between them

7^{ly} I Give and bequeath to my Daughter hannah Godfree Wife to Nathan Godfree five pounds old tenor to be paid By my S^d Son John

8^{ly} I Give and bequeath to my Daughter patience Newman wife to Benjamin Newman five pounds old tenor to be Paid by my Son trustrim

I Doe likewise apoint and ordain my S^d Sons John Redman and Trustrim Redman to be Executors * * *

Joseph Redman

[Witnesses] John Lester, mary Peacock, Samuel Greenfield.
[Proved June 28, 1758.]

DANIEL CLEMENT   1758   SANDOWN

[Administration on the estate of Daniel Clement of Sandown, yeoman, granted to Sarah Clement of Hampstead, widow, May 29, 1758.]

[Probate Records, vol. 21, p. 4.]

[Bond of Sarah Clement, with Theophilus Eaton, yeoman, and William Marshall as sureties, all of Hampstead, in the sum of £500, May 29, 1758, for the administration of the estate; witnesses, William Parker, William Weeks.]

[Inventory, June 27, 1758; amount, £3022. 0. 0; signed by Theophilus Eaton and William Marshall.]

PATRICK MELVIN   1758   CHESTER

In the Name of God Amen I Patrick melven of Chester in the Province of New hamp^r in Newengland Weaver Being Very weak in Body * * *

Imprimes I Give to mary my Well Beloved wife the whole of my Personell Estate for her to use Improve and Dispose of as She Sees cause, and also the Improvement of one third of my Reall Estate During Life

Item I Give to my Son Benjamin Melven my homesteed place where on I Dwell Containing twenty acres more or Less and also all my Lands that I Purchesed from adam Smith as by his Deed to me may fully appear be it more or Less: and also the Improvement of two thirds of my five acres that I Purchesed from Jonas Clay till my two Children shall Come of Lawfull age to whome I shall Give the same; he paying and Performing as I shall here after order

Item I Give to my son Abreham Melven the Sum of Two Hundred Pounds old tenor to be Paid to him by my son Benjamin when he shall arive to the age of twenty years old

Item I Give to my Daughter Elisebath melven the Sum of two Hundred Pounds old tenor to be Paid to her when she shall arive to the age of twenty one years old or marriage Day; to be Paid to her by my son Benjamin melven

Item I Give to my Daughter mary melven the sum of two Hundred Pounds old tenor to be Paid to her out of my Estate by my son Benjamin Melven when she shall arive to the age of twenty one years old or Day of marriage

Item I Give to my Daughter Sarah melven the sum of two Hundred Pounds old tenor to be Paid to her out of my Estate by my son Benjamin melven when she shall Arive to the age of twenty one years old or Day of marriage

Item I Give to my son John melven the sum of Two Hundred Pounds old tenor to be Paid to him out of my Estate by my son Benjamin melven when he shall arive to the age of twenty one years old; and I also Give him the one Half of my five acres of Land that I Purchesed from Jonas Clay as by Deed may appear

Item I Give to my Daughter Lydia melven the sum of two Hundred Pounds old tenor to be Paid to her out of my Estate by my son Benjamin melven when she shall arive to the age of twenty one years old or Day of mariage; and I also Give to her the one Half of my five acres of Land that I Purchesed from Jonas Clay as by Deed may appear

Item I Give to my Daughter Jean melven the sum of two Hundred Pounds old tenor to be Paid to her out of my Estate by my son Benjamin melven when she shall arive to the age of twenty one years old or Day of marriage

Item It is my will that my funurell Charges shall be Paid in Equell Proportion out of Each ones proportion as I have Given to them: and I Do appoynt my well Beloved wife mary and my son Benjamin melven to be my Executros * * * In witness to all above written I Have here unto set my hand and affixed my seal the 29th Day of may annodomini 1758 first above written

his
Patrick + melven
mark

[Witnesses] thomas Willson, David Nutt, Sam[ll] Emerson.
[Proved April 25, 1759.]

[Bond of Benjamin Melvin, yeoman, with Samuel Emerson as surety, both of Chester, in the sum of £500, April 25, 1759, for the execution of the will; witnesses, Zaccheus Clough, William Parker.]

[Receipt of Mary Melvin, April 24, 1759, for the personal estate bequeathed to her in the will; witnesses, Samuel Roby, Samuel Emerson.]

MOSES LEAVITT   1758   HAMPTON

[Additional account of the administratrix, Sarah Dearborn, wife of Jonathan Dearborn, formerly widow of Moses Leavitt; mentions support of a child under seven years of age one year after former account; allowed May 31, 1758.]

[Guardianship of Mary Leavitt, minor, aged more than 14 years, daughter of Moses Leavitt of North Hampton, granted to John Weeks of Hampton Dec. 8, 1758.]

[Probate Records, vol. 21, p. 125.]

[Bond of John Weeks, with Benjamin Prescott and Stephen Haley, husbandmen, as sureties, in the sum of £1000, Dec. 8, 1758, for the guardianship of Mary Leavitt, minor, daughter of Moses Leavitt of North Hampton; witnesses, William Parker and D. Sewall.]

[See estate of Moses Leavitt, 1745.]

DAVID ROBERTS   1758   PLAISTOW

[Administration on the estate of David Roberts of Plaistow, yeoman, granted to Joanna Roberts, widow, May 31, 1758.]

[Probate Records, vol. 20, p. 506.]

[Bond of Joanna Roberts of Plaistow, with Thomas Johnson of Plaistow and Nathaniel Dow of Salem, yeomen, as sureties, in the sum of £500, May 31, 1758, for the administration of the estate; witnesses, William Parker, James Stoodley, Jr.]

[Warrant, May 31, 1758, authorizing Thomas Johnson and Moses Stevens, both of Plaistow, yeomen, to appraise the estate.]

[Inventory, Aug. 28, 1758; amount, £1557. 4. 0; signed by Moses Stevens and Thomas Johnson.]

[Warrant, April 25, 1759, authorizing Thomas Johnson, yeoman, Jonathan Carleton, gentleman, Moses Stevens, John Knight, and Bartholomew Heath, yeomen, all of Plaistow, to set off the widow's dower.]

Province of New-Hampshire } we the Subscriber being appointed a Comitte to set off to Joanna Roberds widow Relict of David Roberds late of Plastow Decased her Dower of thirds of the Real Estate of her late Husband aforesaid as is hereafter mentioned about nine acres & one quarter of Land with the House & Barn standing on the Same Excluding the shop said Land is Bounded as followeth (viz) begining at a stake & stones by a Road thence Runing westerly by land of Henry Heseltine about twenty Eight Rods to a stake & stones thence by land of s^d Estate about forty five Rods southerly to two white oak trees by Land of Bartholomew Heath thence by s^d Heath about Eleven Rods & one half to a stake & stones thence Northeasterly by Land of s^d Estate about Sixty Rods to a stake & stones by s^d Road thence Northwesterly by s^d Road about twenty one Rods to the Bound first mentioned
In Witness whereof we have set to our Hands
Plastow May 28th 1759   Thomas Johnson
                                   Bartholomew heath
                                   John Knight

[Account of the administratrix; receipts, £1789. 10. 6; expenditures, the same; mentions "maintaining 2 of the dec^{ds} Children from Feby 17, 1757, to Octr 29, 1760, being both now under Seven Years of age"; allowed Oct. 29, 1760.]

JACOB MORSE   1758   KINGSTON

[Administration on the estate of Jacob Morse of Kingston, yeoman, granted to his widow, Abigail Morse, May 31, 1758.]
[Probate Records, vol. 21, p. 11.]

[Bond of Abigail Morse, widow, with Orlando Bagley, gentleman, and Ralph Blaisdell, yeoman, as sureties, all of Kingston, in the sum of £1000, May 31, 1758, for the administration of the estate; witnesses, Jeremy Webster, Jonathan Blaisdell.]

[Warrant, May 31, 1758, authorizing Jeremy Webster and Jonathan Blaisdell, yeoman, both of Kingston, to appraise the estate.]

[Inventory, June 16, 1758; amount, £3356. 1. 0; signed by Jeremy Webster and Jonathan Blaisdell.]

[Account of the administratrix; receipts, personal estate as inventoried and £7. 8. 0; expenditures, £392. 16. 0; mentions two children under 7 years of age; allowed Sept. 30, 1761.]

[Guardianship of Mary Morse and Sarah Morse, minors, aged more than 14 years, and of Abigail Morse and Ruth Morse, minors, aged less than 14 years, daughters of Jacob Morse, granted to Moses Cooper of Newbury, Mass., March 5, 1764.]
[Essex County, Mass., Probate Records, vol. 341, p. 133.]

[Bonds, one for each ward, of Moses Cooper, yeoman, with Nathan Chase of Newbury, Mass., yeoman, and Abner Morse of Kingston as sureties, in the sum of £1000 on each bond, March 5, 1764; witnesses, Samuel Rogers and Samuel Rogers, Jr.]
[Essex County, Mass., Probate Files.]

JOHN MORRISON   1758   EPPING

[Administration on the estate of John Morrison of Epping granted to Mary Morrison of Epping May 31, 1758.]
[Probate Records, vol. 20, p. 533.]

[Bond of Mary Morrison, widow, with Ebenezer Morrison and Ezekiel Brown, husbandman, as sureties, all of Epping, in the sum of £1000, May 31, 1758, for the administration of the estate; witnesses, William Parker, Cutts Shannon.]

[Inventory, attested Aug. 29, 1758; amount, £7578. 10. 5; signed by Jonathan Rundlett and Jacob Freese.]

[Account of John Perkins of Epping and Mary, his late wife, administratrix; receipts, £4940. 14. 1, personal estate; expenditures, £3367. 10. 3; allowed Aug. 29, 1764.]

[Guardianship of Mary Morrison, John Morrison, and David Morrison, children of John Morrison, granted to Moses Baker Aug. 29, 1764.]

[Probate Records, vol. 23, p. 290.]

[Bond of Moses Baker of Candia, yeoman, with John Perkins of Epping, yeoman, as surety, in the sum of £500, Aug. 29, 1764, for the guardianship of Mary Morrison, John Morrison, and David Morrison, aged less than 14 years, children of John Morrison; witness, William Vaughan.]

[Bond of Moses Baker of Candia, with Ezekiel Brown, gentleman, and Thomas Dearborn, yeoman, both of Epping, as sureties, in the sum of £200, Feb. 8, 1771, for the guardianship of John Morrison, minor, aged more than 14 years, son of John Morrison; witnesses, Elizabeth Parker, William Parker, Jr.]

ABNER WHEELER   1758   SALEM

In the Name of God Amen the Last Will & Testament of Abner wheeler of Salem in the Province of New Hampshire in New England Yeoman * * *

Imprimis I give & bequeath to my Brother Jonathan Wheeler jun^r all & Singular of my Lands he paying to my Brother William Wheeler Fifty Spanish Milled Dollars within the Term of One Year after my Decease.

Item I give & bequeath unto my Brother William Wheeler whom I do hereby constitute & appoint my Sole Executor of this my last will all those Debts by Bonds Notes of Hand or otherwise that are due to me as likewise all my Stock Moveables Household stuff & Cloathing. I likewise give him Fifty Spanish Milled Dollars to be paid him by my Brother Jonathan Wheeler jun[r] as above mentioned I give him these things he paying all my just Debts executing this my will & paying my funeral Charges, & I do hereby publish & declare this to be my Last will & Testament This Second Day of June Anno Domini One Thousand Seven Hundred Fifty & Eight & in the Thirty First Year of the Reign of our Sovereign Lord George the Second of Great Brittain France & Ireland King Defender of the Faith &c

his
Abner + Wheeler
Mark

[Witnesses] Abner Bayley, Mary Bayley, Hannah Patee. [Proved Nov. 15, 1758.]

[Bond of William Wheeler of Salem, yeoman, with John Webster of Plaistow, gentleman, as surety, in the sum of £4000, Nov. 15, 1758, for the execution of the will; witnesses, William Parker, Samuel Parker.]

WILLOUGHBY TAYLOR 1758   EXETER

In The name of God amen This Third Day of June anno Domini 1758 I Willibey Tayler of Exeter in the Province of Newhamp[r] Cordwiner being in helth of body and of a Sound and Perfect mind & memory Thankes be to allmighty God for the Same; but am Desined to go into The Desined Expedition now forming against his majesties Enemies   *   *   *

First I Give and bequeave unto my brother William Tayler and to his heirs and assing for Ever all my Real and Personall Estate, Lying and being in Exeter or Else where my Said Brother William to Come into Porsission Emeaditaly after my Decease viz all that acre of Land which I Purchesed of Caleb Gilman where I have Erected 1 new House and all The Land and other Estate which falls to me as an heir to my Hone^d Father Joseph Tayler Late of Exeter Deceased, and I hereby appoint my beloved brother William Tayler of The Same town & Province afore Said to be Sole Excu^r * * *

Willoughby Taler

[Witnesses] Caleb Gilman, Robart Kimball, Theo: Smith. [Proved Aug. 30, 1758.]

Fort Edward July ye 24th 1758

My Dear I can send you but a few lines to let you know Yesterday as a Number of Carts with a Gaurd went from this place towards Lake George were Attackt By the Indians who made a great Slaughter upon them wee heard the Guns and turn out and pursued the enemy with all Speed the mischief being done about 4 miles of wee came upon some of them, when they took into the woods & wee followed them; when they halted; and a fire begun upon both Sides, there was one man shot through the Shoulder within 10 foot of me, they kil^d but one of Capt Gilmans men his name was Willoughby Tayler —

Wee were engaged with them near two hours att length they went of but the Slaughter they made upon the Gaurds and upon the Oxen was very Shocking wee buried twenty five two of them were women, and they kiled 100 & Odd Cattle and destroy^d a Great Quantity of Liquors & Provisions —

being in hast I must Conclude with very kind love to you and our dear Children which is all att Present from your Loving husband till Death

William Harris

[Addressed] To Mr William Harris Att Exeter In New Hampshire

[Bond of William Taylor, with Caleb Gilman and Robert Kimball as sureties, all of Exeter, in the sum of £500, Aug. 30, 1758, for the execution of the will; witnesses, William Parker, James Stoodley, Jr.]

SAMUEL PRESCOTT   1758   HAMPTON FALLS

In the Name of God amen this third Day of June In the year of Our Lord Christ One thousand Seven hundred and fifty Eight. I Samuel Prescutt of Hampton falls in the Province of New Hampshire Esqr   *   *   *

Item I Give and Bequeath to my Son Jeremiah Prescutt to him his heirs and Assigns forever All the Land I have in the Parish of Eping in the Province aforesaid lying on the Southerly Side of Lampereel River so Called, I having already Given him a Deed of ten acres on the Notherly Side of said River. And further I Give to my said Son his heirs and assigns the One half of a Last hundred Acre Lott so Called in the Township of Chester in the Province aforesaid which Lott is Number 34, to be Equally Divided as to Quantity & Quality I Also Give him One third part of a Piece of Salt Marsh Containing About five Acres Lying near the falls River so Called in Hampton falls aforesaid; Also two hundred Pounds old Tenor to be Paid him by my son William Prescutt, Also my Sword, Walking Cane, And Great Bible

Item I Give And Bequeath to my Son Samuel Prescutt to him his heirs and assigns forever twenty Acres of Land in Hampton falls aforesaid where his Dwelling House now is Bounding Easterly on Exeter Road And so to go Westerly Carrying the whole Wedth of my Land 'till twenty Acres are Compleated. Also a Piece of Land in Hampton falls aforesaid by the Crankway so Called Containing about twenty one Acres, Also a Piece of

Land in Hampton falls aforesaid on the Easterly Side Taylors River so Called Containing About twenty Acres And is part of the Land I Bought of John Swain & Nathanael Prescutt Bounding by said Taylors River Westerly, by land of Joseph Sanborn Southerly, by land left for a way Easterly, And by land belonging to the heirs of Joseph Garland Deceasd Northerly Also one Acre of Marsh on the Southerly Side of my Marsh by Swains Creek so Called. Also One half that hundred Acre Lott in Chester aforesaid of which I have given the Other half to my son Jeremiah Also One feather Bed and Beding. And I Order him my said Son Samuel to Pay One hundred Pounds old Tenor to my Son John Prescutt and One hundred Pounds old Tenor to my Son Joseph Prescutt One half to be paid within One year after my Decease, and the Other half within two years after my Decease

Item I Give and Bequeath to my Son John Prescutt his heirs and assigns a Piece of Land lying in the Parish of Eping in the Province aforesaid where he now lives Containing About fifty four Acres Bounding Southerly partly on land I gave to my Son Joseph And partly on land my said Son John Bought of his Brother Jeremiah, Notherly on Land belonging to the heirs of Jonathan Prescutt Deceas'd, Also one half of a first hundred Acre Lott so Called in Chester aforesaid Number 83. Also one third part of a Piece of Marsh of About five acres lying near the falls River so Called in Hampton falls aforesaid. Also one feather Bed And Beding. Also One hundred Pounds old Tenor to be Paid him by my Son Samuel Prescutt.

Item I Give and Bequeath to my Son Joseph Prescutt to him his heirs And Assigns A Piece of Land lying in Eping aforesaid where he now lives Containing About forty four acres. Also nine acres of Land on the Notherly Side of Lampereel River so Called Bounding Southerly by said River, Notherly by land of my Son John. Also one half of that hundred Acre Lott in Chester aforesaid of which my Son John has the Other half. Also one third part of a Piece of Marsh of About five acres lying near the falls River so Called in Hampton falls aforesaid. Also one hundred Pounds old Tenor to be Paid him by my Son Samuel.

Item I Give and Bequeath to my Son William Prescutt to him his heirs and assigns All my Home Place Land and Buildings Except what I have Already Given to my Son Samuel Containing About fifty two Acres where my House and Barn Stand. Also a Piece of Land I Bought of Caleb Swain Containing About twenty Acres. Also a Piece of Land which I Purchased of Robert Row and Nathanael Prescutt on the Westerly Side of Taylors River. Also a Piece of Land in Hampton falls aforesaid which I Lately Purchased of Reuben Sanborn Containing About thirty Acres. Also About three Acres of Salt Marsh by Swains Creek so Called being the Remainder of what marsh I have at that Place not given to my Son Samuel. Also all the Land which belongs to me in the Township of Chester aforesaid not before Disposed of in this my will. I Also Give him my Clock, And one feather bed and beding And all my Husbandry and Carpentry Tools, And my Gun And Desk, And I Order my said Son William to pay to my Son Jeremiah two hundred Pounds old Tenor one half within One Year after my Decease And the Remainder within two years after my Decease. I Also Order my Said Son William to Pay the Sum of four hundred and Ninety Pounds old Tenor Equally between my four Sons Jeremiah, Samuel, John, and Joseph within one year after my Decease

Item I Give and Bequeath to my Grandson Samuel Prescutt Son of Jeremiah, twenty Pounds old Tenor to be paid him when he arrives at the age of twenty one years by my Executor

Item I further Give to my Sons Samuel and William Equally Between them my Part of the old Sawmill so Called in Hampton falls aforesaid And Priviledges thereto belonging

Item My will is And I do hereby Order that after my Debts And funeral Charges shall be Paid, My Stock of Creatures Wearing Apparell, Moveables within Doors, Not before Disposed of in this my will, And my Bonds, Notes, and Money As also what Lands I own in a tract of land Granted to Ichabod Robie Esq[r] and Others, shall be all Equally Divided Among my five Sons beforementioned And further my will is and I do hereby Order that if anything shall be Recover'd Against my Estate on account of a Piece of Land which I have Sold lying in Kensington in the Quarter of Mile so Called which is now in Controversy in the Law, That my Son William shall Pay the Same 'till it Amounts to the Sum of three hundred Pounds old Tenor, and if Any thing more than that Sum shall be Recoverd that the Remainder shall be paid and Satisfied Equally by my Sons Jeremiah, Samuel, John, Joseph, & William

Lastly I do by these presents Constitute and Appoint my Son William Prescutt Sole Executor   *   *   *

Sam[ll] Prescut

[Witnesses] Meshech Weare, Elisha Prescut, Malachi Shaw.
[Proved June 28, 1758.]

[Jeremiah Prescott, Samuel Prescott, John Prescott, and Joseph Prescott, sons of Samuel Prescott, accept the provisions of the will and waive inventory of the personal estate June 20, 1758.]

[Bond of William Prescott, yeoman, with Meshech Weare and Elisha Prescott, yeoman, as sureties, all of Hampton Falls, in the sum of £1000, June 28, 1758, for the execution of the will; witnesses, William Parker, Josiah Hilton.]

BENJAMIN ROWE   1758   NEWINGTON

In the Name of God Amen I Benjamin Row of Newington In the Province of New-hampshire in New-England, being about to Goe Into the War   *   *   *   Imprimis I Give And bequeeth to My Mother Rachel Row Widdow fifty Pounds old Tenor To be paid Unto her by my Executor who Is hereafter to be Mentioned And the Rest to be Equally Divided Among My Sisters that Shall Survive Me: And All to be paid to them by the Executor of this My Last will And Testament and to be paid with In Six Months After they Receive a Certain Account of My Decease In Case God should so order It in his Providence that I should not Return to my friends Again. And I Doe with All Constitute And Appoint my frind & Cozen Jonathan Quint to be the Sole Executor of This My Last Will And Testament. In Witness Whereof I have To These presents set my hand And Seal This Third Day of June In The Thirty first Year of the Reigne of our Sovereigne Lord George The 2^d of Great Brittaine &c King Defender of the faith And In the Year of our Lord God 1758.

Benjamin Row

[Witnesses] Joseph Adams, Benj: Adams, John + Brown.
his
marke

[Proved Nov. 29, 1758.]

[Bond of Jonathan Quint, yeoman, with Benjamin Adams, gentleman, as surety, both of Newington, in the sum of £1000, Nov. 29, 1758, for the administration of the estate; witnesses, William Parker, Moses Barnett.]

JOSEPH BARNES　　　1758　　　PORTSMOUTH

[Guardianship of Joseph Barnes, minor, aged more than 14 years, son of Joseph Barnes of Portsmouth, potter, granted to Mark Langdon of Portsmouth, gentleman, June 3, 1758.]

[Probate Records, vol. 20, p. 533.]

[Bond of Mark Langdon, with Thomas Pattinson and James Hewitt, mariners, as sureties, all of Portsmouth, in the sum of £500, June 3, 1758, for the guardianship of Joseph Barnes, son of Joseph Barnes, deceased; witnesses, William Parker, David Sewall.]

MOSES CAVERLY   1758   BARRINGTON

In The name of God Amen. The Last will and Testament of Moses Caverly of Barrington in the Province of New Hampshire Bricklayer * * *

Item I Give and Bequeath unto my Dearly beloved wife Margaret Caverly all my Real Estate in Barrington aforesaid during her Natural Life and the Improvement of all my houshold furniture so long as she shall live

Item. To my Two Sons Moses and Thomas Caverly I give (after the decease of my said wife) all my Real Estate in said Barrington aforesaid to them their heirs and assigns to be Divided in Equal Shares between them, and also my Stock of Cattle and Utensels to be divided as aforesaid —

Item. To my Two Sons William and Nathaniel Caverly I give five Shillings new Tenor Each, they having had a house and Land at Islington by Deed

Item. To my Daughter Mary Nelson I give Twenty pounds old Tenor to be paid by my Two Sons Moses and Thomas viz Ten pounds to be paid to her by Each of them —

Item. To my Two Daughters Sarah and Hannah Caverly. I give (after the decease of my wife) all my household furniture to be Equally divided Between them —

Item. My Brick Yard in the Rock field so Called in Portsmouth in the Province aforesaid and the way leading from the Road thereto I order to be Sold by my Executor and the money Raised thereby to be applyed to the payment of my Debts and funeral Expences, and after the payment of the Same, the Residue if any there by shall be divided Equally between all my Daughters —

Item. all the Rest Residue and Remainder of my Estate after the payment of the Legacy given to my Daughter Mary I give unto my aforesaid Two Sons Moses and Thomas Caverly their heirs and assigns —

And I Do appoint my said Son Moses Caverly to be Sole

Executor of this my last will and Testament, hereby Revoking & making Void all Wills & Testaments by me heretofore made, Ratifying & Confirming this & no other to be my last will and Testament. In Testimony whereof I the said Moses Caverly have hereunto Set my hand and Seal the Twelfth day of June in the thirty first Year of his Majestys Reign annoque Domini One thousand Seven hundred & fifty Eight

Moses Caverly

[Witnesses] Jacob Treadwell, Nathanael Jackson, Cutts Shannon.

[Proved April 17, 1765.]

[Bond of Moses Caverly of Barrington, yeoman, with William Earl Treadwell of Portsmouth, merchant, as surety, in the sum of £500, April 16, 1765, for the execution of the will; witness, William Parker.]

ARCHIBALD STARK   1758   MANCHESTER

In the Name of God Amen June 22^d Annoque: Dom. 1758 I Archibald Stark of Derryfield & Province of New Hampshire Yeoman, Being weak in Body * * * I Bequeath to my well-beloved wife Elinor Stark one third part of the Income of my Estate, During her Life. Item I Bequeth my whole Estate Real & Personal to my Children William Stark, John Stark Archibald Stark Samuel Stark, Henry Stark, Isabel Stirling & Jean Stinson To be Divided in Equal Shars amongest them, after they have Performed as above & given to every one of my Grand-Children a Cow or the Value thereof in Money.

Finally I Ordain & Appoint my Two Sons William Stark & John Stark Executors * * *

Archebld Stark

[Witnesses] Caleb Towle, Benjamin Sleeper, Caleb towl jun^r.
[Proved Aug. 4, 1758.]

[Inventory, attested Jan. 29, 1759; amount, £9618. 12. 0; signed by Matthew Patten and Thomas Hall.]

[List of claims against the estate; amount, £4161. 3. 8; signed by Matthew Patten and Alexander McMurphy; attested June 12, 1760.]

[Account of the executor; receipts, £1618. 12. 0, personal estate; expenditures, £4624. 17. 2; allowed Oct. 31, 1765.]

RICHARD HEATH 1758 PLAISTOW

[Miriam Heath of Plaistow renounces administration on the estate of her husband, Richard Heath of Plaistow, yeoman, in favor of Lieut. Thomas Hale and Ensign Benjamin Richards, both of Plaistow, June 24, 1758; witnesses, Thomas Little, Mary Little.]

[Administration granted to Thomas Hale and Benjamin Richards Nov. 29, 1758.]

[Probate Records, vol. 21, p. 110.]

[Bond of Thomas Hale, gentleman, and Benjamin Richards, yeoman, with John Wentworth of Somersworth and Andrew Craige of Chester, gentlemen, as sureties, in the sum of £500, Nov. 29, 1758, for the administration of the estate; witnesses, Cutts Shannon, William Parker.]

[Warrant, Nov. 29, 1758, authorizing Thomas Little, yeoman, and Tristram Knight, gentleman, both of Plaistow, to appraise the estate.]

[Inventory, attested Feb. 23, 1759; amount, £1387. 11. 0; signed by Tristram Knight and Thomas Little.]

[Commission, Feb. 28, 1759, to Thomas Little and Tristram Knight to receive claims against the estate.]

[List of claims, Sept. 25, 1759; amount, £1327. 1. 10; signed by Tristram Knight and Thomas Little.]

[Settlement of claims; amount of claims, £1327. 1. 10; amount distributed, £445. 2. 3; allowed Nov. 30, 1759.]

[Account of Benjamin Richards, surviving administrator; receipts, £1460. 0. 0; expenditures, £569. 15. 6; mentions "allowed the Widow out of the Inventory for her Support and maintaining a Child . . . . paid for the funeral of a Child under age"; allowed Jan. 12, 1760.]

STEPHEN GILMAN   1758   KINGSTON

[Administration on the estate of Stephen Gilman of Kingston, yeoman, granted to his widow, Mary Gilman, June 28, 1758.]
[Probate Records, vol. 21, p. 11.]

[Bond of Mary Gilman, with Daniel Gilman and Nathaniel French, gentlemen, as sureties, all of Kingston, in the sum of £500, June 28, 1758, for the administration of the estate; witnesses, Ruth Brown, Josiah Bartlett.]

[Inventory, attested Aug. 29, 1758; amount, £2212. 13. 0; signed by Samuel Winsley and Josiah Bartlett.]

[Account of the administratrix; receipts, £1391. 0. 0; expenditures, £1995. 6. 0; mentions "Bringing up 2 Children under seven years old 364 weeks. . . . Extra Costs in nursing & Providing for the youngest Child being a Cripple nine years": allowed Oct. 26, 1768.]

Province of } We the Subscribers being appointed a Committee to Set off to Mary Gilman Widow &
New Hamps^r Relict of Stephen Gilman late of Kingston yeoman Deceased her Dower which happens to her of the real Estate of which he died Seized — Have proceeded & set off to her twelve Acres more or less of Land with the buildings thereon bounded as follows vizt

beginning at a White oak Stake marked & Standing (near the fence at the Country Road) twenty Rods South of the Northwest Corner of the late homestead of said Deceased thence running Southerly by said Road about twenty Rods to the highway leading to the Spring (so called) then running Easterly partly by said high way & partly by Land of John Fifield to land said Mary heretofore sold to Dr Josiah Bartlett, then running northerly by said Bartlets Land Twenty Rods, then Running westerly to the said White oak Stake — November 28th 1768

      Eben^r Stevens ⎫
      Wm Parker jr ⎬ Committee
      Josiah Bartlett ⎭

JOB ROWELL   1758   SALISBURY, MASS.

[Administration de bonis non on the estate of Job Rowell of Salisbury, Mass., granted to Sarah Rowell June 28, 1758.]

[Probate Records, vol. 20, p. 518.]

[Bond of Sarah Rowell, widow, with Samuel Bernard, gentleman, and Eliphalet Merrill, yeoman, as sureties, all of South Hampton, in the sum of £1000, June 28, 1758, for the administration of the estate, the executor being deceased; witnesses, William Parker, James Stoodley, Jr.]

JEREMIAH LEAVITT   1758   EXETER

[Administration on the estate of Jeremiah Leavitt of Exeter, gentleman, granted to his widow, Mary Leavitt, June 28, 1758.]

[Probate Records, vol. 21, p. 5.]

[Bond of Mary Leavitt, with Samuel Fogg, yeoman, and Ephraim Robinson, trader, as sureties, all of Exeter, in the sum of £1000, June 28, 1758, for the administration of the estate; witnesses, William Parker, Abel Brown.]

[Warrant, June 28, 1758, authorizing Ephraim Robinson and John Purmort, both of Exeter, to appraise the estate.]

[Inventory, July 25, 1758; amount, £2526. 7. 0; signed by Ephraim Robinson and John Purmort.]

[Commission, April 24, 1759, to Ephraim Robinson and Noah Emery, both of Exeter, gentlemen, to receive claims against the estate.]

[List of claims, April 25, 1760; amount, £3742. 9. 5; signed by Ephraim Robinson and Noah Emery.]

[Account of Benjamin Connor and his wife Mary Connor, administratrix; receipts, £4109. 8. 0; expenditures, £1551. 5. 4; mentions "Support of 2 Children under Seven Years of Age 2 Years & Six months Each"; allowed Oct. 10, 1760.]

[Settlement of claims; amount of claims, £3742. 9. 5; amount distributed, £2558. 2. 8; allowed Nov. 18, 1760.]

SAMUEL WENTWORTH 1758   SOMERSWORTH

[Administration on the estate of Samuel Wentworth of Somersworth, yeoman, granted to Sarah Wentworth of Somersworth, widow, June 28, 1758.]

[Probate Records, vol. 21, p. 12.]

[Bond of Sarah Wentworth, with Otis Baker, merchant, and Isaac Horne, husbandman, both of Dover, as sureties, in the sum of £1000, June 28, 1758, for the administration of the estate; witnesses, William Parker, James Stoodley, Jr.]

[Warrant, June 28, 1758, authorizing Moses Carr, physician, and Ezekiel Wentworth, yeoman, both of Somersworth, to appraise the estate.]

[Inventory, Sept. 19, 1758; amount, £6865. 0. 6; signed by Moses Carr and Ezekiel Wentworth.]

WARD LOCKE   1758   KENSINGTON

[Margaret Locke of Kingston renounces administration on the estate of her son, Ward Locke of Kensington, housewright, June 30, 1758, in favor of Moses Shaw of Kensington; witnesses, William Parker, Jr., Joseph Greeley, Jr.]

[Administration granted to Moses Shaw July 26, 1758.]
[Probate Records, vol. 21, p. 24.]

[Bond of Moses Shaw, housewright, with William Parker of Kingston and Joseph Cilley of Nottingham, gentleman, as sureties, in the sum of £400, July 26, 1758, for the administration of the estate; witnesses, William Parker, John Hall.]

[Inventory, Oct. 8, 1759; amount, £707. 15. 0; signed by William Parker and Jonathan Perkins.]

———— STEVENS   1758

Honrabil Sir I Recived a sititation from your Hon[r] Last wiek bearing Date 24 of January Kept up one purpos I supose to non pluses me and was Likewise suprayising to me for mr John Hoog told me he had settled the afear but sir when my husband Dayed July Last was twelve months I was then the Likelest to a dayed and Lay two month after he Dayed with 4 small Childring about me in the woods destitute almost of either brede or meate but was suplayd by the Charety of Christian pepoal; and had but a smal stock only 3 Cows 2 heffers and a hors and having no hay to Keepe them Got them praysed and payd deets with the price of them which I Cann Shew: but Sir I Cann not Com this Sesean of the year having no hors and not abel to hayer one and Likwise the warning so short that itt is Imposable for me to attend the Last wedensday of february Covant but as sown as it is posabel for me to traviel I will Com and setle Evirey thing in that Regard in a klear Light and prays that adiminestration may not be

Granted for thes Resons and many others untill I Com which is sir from a destitute widow

Londonderry february ye 23: 1759

her
Sarah × Stevens
mark

JOHN DINSMOOR   1758   NEW IPSWICH

[Hannah Dinsmoor renounces administration on the estates of her sons, John Dinsmoor and Asa Dinsmoor, July 4, 1758, in favor of her son, Abraham Dinsmoor; witnesses, Benjamin Wright, Gershom Drury.]

[Administration on the estate of John Dinsmoor of New Ipswich granted to Abraham Dinsmoor of Hollis, yeoman, July 6, 1758.]

[Probate Records, vol. 21, p. 19.]

[Bond of Abraham Dinsmoor, with Samuel Thurston of Epping and Abner Thurston of Stratham, yeomen, as sureties, in the sum of £500, July 6, 1758, for the administration of the estate; witnesses, William Parker, Moses Thurston.]

[Warrant, July 6, 1758, authorizing Samuel Cummings, gentleman, and Stephen Ames, yeoman, both of Hollis, to appraise the estate.]

[Inventory, Oct. 23, 1758; amount, £1385. 18. 0; signed by Samuel Cummings and Stephen Ames.]

JOHN HOLLAND, JR.   1758   EXETER

[Administration on the estate of John Holland, Jr., of Exeter, laborer, granted to John Odlin of Exeter July 6, 1758.]

[Probate Records, vol. 21, p. 29.]

[Bond of John Odlin, with James Leavitt and Noah Emery,

both of Exeter, gentlemen, as sureties, in the sum of £500, July 6, 1758, for the administration of the estate; witnesses, Theophilus Smith, Jonathan Loud.]

[Warrant, July 6, 1758, authorizing Noah Emery and James Leavitt to appraise the estate.]

[Inventory, July 8, 1758; amount, £782. 10. 3; signed by James Leavitt and Noah Emery.]

[Account of the administrator; receipts, £782. 10. 8, personal estate; expenditures, £77. 14. 8; allowed March 31, 1762.]

ASA DINSMOOR   1758   HOLLIS

[Administration on the estate of Asa Dinsmoor granted to Abraham Dinsmoor of Hollis, yeoman, July 6, 1758.]
[Probate Records, vol. 21, p. 19.]

[Bond of Abraham Dinsmoor, with Samuel Thurston of Epping and Abner Thurston of Stratham, yeomen, as sureties, in the sum of £500, July 6, 1758, for the administration of the estate of Asa Dinsmoor of Hollis, yeoman; witnesses, William Parker, Moses Thurston.]

[Warrant, July 6, 1758, authorizing Samuel Cummings, gentleman, and Stephen Ames, yeoman, both of Hollis, to appraise the estate.]

[Inventory, Oct. 23, 1758; amount, £400. 0. 0; signed by Samuel Cummings and Stephen Ames.]

WILLIAM CHADDOCK   1758   SOMERSWORTH

[Administration on the estate of William Chaddock of Somersworth, mariner, granted to Abra Chaddock of Somersworth, widow, July 26, 1758.]
[Probate Records, vol. 21, p. 23.]

[Bond of Abra Chaddock, with William Wentworth, gentleman, and William Stackpole, yeoman, as sureties, in the sum of £1000, July 26, 1758, for the administration of the estate; witnesses, William Parker, James Hobbs.]

[Inventory, Aug. 30, 1758; amount, £3559. 10. 0; signed by Moses Carr and James Hobbs.]

JOSEPH COCHRAN   1758   BEDFORD

[Administration on the estate of Joseph Cochran of Bedford, yeoman, granted to Margaret Cochran of Bedford, widow, and Samuel Cochran of Litchfield, yeoman, July 26, 1758.]

[Probate Records, vol. 21, p. 30.]

[Bond of Margaret Cochran and Samuel Cochran with Samuel Patten and Robert Walker, both of Bedford, yeomen, as sureties, in the sum of £900, July 26, 1758, for the administration of the estate; witnesses, Matthew Patten, Elizabeth Patten.]

[Warrant, July 26, 1758, authorizing Samuel Patten and Robert Walker, both of Bedford, yeomen, to appraise the estate.]

[Inventory, Sept. 22, 1758; amount, £5097. 10. 9; signed by Samuel Patten and Robert Walker.]

[Account of the administrators; receipts, £2850. 9. 6, personal estate; expenditures, £652. 15. 2; mentions "maintaining two Children of said Intestate 64 Weeks Each . . . . To a Negro Infant appraised at £40 allow^d the accountant for its maintenance"; allowed Sept. 26, 1759.]

[Additional account of the administrators; receipts, £109. 17. 8½; expenditures, £71. 5. 10; mentions "Boarding Victualling &c Agnes Cochran Daughter of the Deceasd Six years & Eight Months . . . . Boarding victualling &c Mary Cochran Daughter to the Deceased Six years & Eight Months"; allowed Oct. 30, 1765.]

[Petition of James Steele of Bedford, yeoman, Nov. 9, 1774, who married Margaret, widow of Joseph Cochran, for the setting off of the widow's dower.]

[Commission, Nov. 9, 1774, to Robert Walker, gentleman, Thomas Boyes, James Aiken, John Moore, yeomen, all of Bedford, and Alexander Gilchrist of Goffstown, yeoman, to set off the widow's dower.]

To the Honourable John Sherburne Esqr Judge of the probate of Wills for the County of Rockingham

Honrd Sir, Pursuant to your order to us to Divide the Estate of Joseph Cochran Late of Bedford Deceased, and set off the Dowrey that happens to Margret Steel Widow of the said Joseph Cochran now the wife of James Steel. Agreeable therto we have made the following Division (Viz) Begining at a white pine Stump at the west End of said farm thirty three Rods from the south west Corner bound thereof, to Run East from said stump, till it come to the East Line of the farm, and North from the formentioned stump thirty two Rods to a stake and Stones that is in the West Line of said farm, thence East Parralill to the first Mentioned Line till it come to the East End of said farm, Reserving the orchard that is about the Midle of said farm which happens to be in that Part set off to Steel and his wife, for the use of the Heirs, Excepting three Rows of Apple trees on the south side of the orchard from the West to the East End thereof, which three Rows the said Steel and his Wife is to have for their use and Improvement, Said Steel and his wife is to have the house and ten feet of the East End of the Barn that is on said farm, Reserving a lane two Rods wide from the high Way that is at the West End of said farm in to the barn and the floorway of the barn for a Priviledge for all the Parties that Improve any Part of said farm to Enjoy in common, Likewise said Steel and his wife is to have the Improvement of a Lot of

Medow in Crosbys medow (So Called) that belonged to said farm Excepting two acres on the south Side of said Lot of medow, which two acres is Reserved for the use of the Heirs

Bedford March 29: 1775

Robert Walker
John Moor Junr
Alex^r Gilcrist
James Aikin
Thomas Boies

STEPHEN ROBERTS   1758   DOVER

[Administration on the estate of Stephen Roberts of Dover, tanner, granted to Keziah Roberts of Dover, widow, July 26, 1758.]

[Probate Records, vol. 21, p. 24.]

[Bond of Keziah Roberts, with Joseph Bickford and Timothy Roberts, yeomen, as sureties, all of Dover, in the sum of £500, July 26, 1758, for the administration of the estate; witnesses, William Parker, Ebenezer Long.]

[Warrant, July 26, 1758, authorizing Timothy Robinson and Alexander Caldwell, both of Dover, yeomen, to appraise the estate.]

[Inventory, Nov. 28, 1758; amount, £8029. 6. 0; signed by Timothy Robinson and Alexander Caldwell.]

GERSHOM WENTWORTH 1758   SOMERSWORTH

In the Name of God Amen, The Second Day of August in the Year of our Lord one Thousand Seven Hundred & fifty Eight, I Garshom Wentworth of the Town of Somersworth in the Province of New Hampshire in New England Gentleman * * *

Imprimis I give and bequeath to My dearly beloved Wife Sarah ye Improvement of the one half of my Estate both real & personal during her widowhood and if She marries again then the one third of My real & personal Estate during her natural life.

Item I give and bequeath to My beloved Sons Gershom Wentworth & Benjamin Wentworth all my lands in Somersworth, in Rochester, in the New Township at the Head of Berwick commonly known by ye Name of Towwow, & else where, with all ye buildings thereon standing (excepting ye lands hereafter to be Mentioned) together with all ye appurtenences priviledges & commodities to the same belonging, equelly to be divided between them, to them their Heirs & assigns for ever, except ye Improvement of part thereof as afore said.

Item I give and bequeath to My two Said Sons Gershom & Benjamin all My Interest in Saw Mills in S^d Somersworth, together with all the appurtenances & priviledges to the same belonging to be equally divided between them, to them their Heirs and assigns for ever excepting the Improvement of part thereof as af^{rs}^{d}.

Item I Give to my two S^d Sons Gershom & Benjamin, to each of them one feather bed.

Item I give & bequeath to My S^d beloved Son Gershom My Silver Tankard, to him his Heirs & assigns after the decease of my S^d wife Sarah.

Item I give & bequeath to my S^d beloved Son Benjamin My Silver Kan & all My Silver spoons to him his Heirs & assigns after ye decease of My Said Wife Sarah.

Item I give and bequeath to My beloved Grand Daughter Sarah Baker ye Child of My beloved Daughter Lydia deceasd all my Interest in lands in Canterbury together with all ye appurtenances & priviledges to ye same belonging to her her Heirs & assigns for ever.

Item I give & bequeath to my Said beloved Grand Daughter Sarah, the one half of my Second Division Lot in Rochester which my beloved Brother Paul Wentworth gave me in His last will & Testament and also all my lands in the Third Division of lands in S^d Rochester together with all the appurtenences & priviledges to ye same belonging, to her her Heirs & assigns for ever.

Item I give & bequeath to the present Church of Christ in Somersworth two Hundred Pounds old Tennor ye use or Interest of S^d Sum to be Improvd by S^d Church for ye use & benefit of S^d Church, as Said Church shall think or Judge for ye best, the S^d two Hundred pounds to be paid equally by my two S^d Sons Gershom & Benjamin within one year after my decease.

Item I give and bequeath to my two S^d Sons Gershom & Benjamin the one half of my Stock of Creatures, & the other half also & all the rest of my Household Goods after my S^d wife Sarahs Decease.

Item Its My will that My two S^d Sons Gershom & Benjamin pay equally between them all my lawfull Debts, and all My funeral Charges.

Item all ye rest of My Estate both real & personal I give & bequeath to my two S^d Sons Gershom & Benjamin, to be equally divided between them, to them their Heirs & assigns for ever.

Item I do hereby Constitute make & ordain My S^d Beloved Wife Sarah and my Said beloved Son Gershom my Sole Executors * * *

                                              Ger: Wentworth

                his
[Witnesses] John + James, Ebenezer Ricker, Thomas Wentworth.   Mark

[Proved June 27, 1759.]

[Sarah Wentworth declines to act as executor of the will of her husband, Gershom Wentworth, June 25, 1759; witnesses, Ezekiel Wentworth, Mercy Ricker.]

[Bond of Gershom Wentworth, with Benjamin Wentworth and John James as sureties, all of Somersworth, yeomen, in the sum of £1000, June 27, 1759, for the execution of the will; witnesses, William Parker, Benjamin Prescott.]

JESSE WORCESTER 1758 NEWBURY, MASS.

[Administration on the estate of Jesse Worcester of Newbury, Mass., yeoman, granted to Francis Worcester of Hollis, yeoman, Aug. 19, 1758.]

[Probate Records, vol. 21, p. 42.]

[Bond of Francis Worcester, with Joseph Knight, saddler, and James Thurston, blacksmith, both of Exeter, as sureties, in the sum of £1000, Aug. 19, 1758, for the administration of the estate of his brother, Jesse Worcester; witnesses, Abner Thurston, Theophilus Smith.]

[Inventory of the estate in New Hampshire, Aug. 19, 1758, 30 acres of land in Brentwood, £600. 0. 0; signed by Theophilus Smith and Abner Thurston.]

[Account of the administrator; receipts, £360. 0. 0; expenditures, £727. 12. 0; allowed Nov. 12, 1761.]

NATHANIEL MESERVE 1758 PORTSMOUTH

[Bond of George Meserve, merchant, with William Earl Treadwell, merchant, and Paul March, gentleman, as sureties, all of Portsmouth, in the sum of £5000, Aug. 18, 1758, for the administration of the estate of Nathaniel Meserve of Portsmouth; witnesses, William Parker, David Sewall.]

[Warrant, Aug. 19, 1758, authorizing John Moffatt, Jacob Sheafe, and Samuel Penhallow, merchants, all of Portsmouth, to appraise the estate of Nathaniel Meserve, administration, with will annexed, being granted to his son, George Meserve.]

BENJAMIN SMITH   1758   HAVERHILL, MASS.

[Certificate of Sargent Smith, Aug. 21, 1758, that he is administrator of the estate of Benjamin Smith of Haverhill, Mass., and that he has settled his accounts in Essex County, Mass.; witness, Nathaniel Peaslee Sargent.]

We the Subscribers are well knowing that Benj^a Smith late of Haverhill in ye County of Essex deceas'd Intestate who died about Sixteen Years ago, left but four Children & Heirs ye Eldest named Benjamin, ye Second named Ballard & ye third named Abigail, & the last named Dorothy & that Dorothy the Widdow of ye s^d Benj^a is now married to Obadiah Johnson & in full Life as we are Informed —

Dated Haverhill Augt 21st 1758

                                        Thomas Abbot
                                        Sargent Smith

[Administration on the estate of Benjamin Smith, joiner, granted to Sargent Smith of Newbury, Mass., yeoman, Oct. 3, 1758.]

[Probate Records, vol. 21, p. 83.]

[Bond of Sargent Smith of Newbury, Mass., yeoman, with John Webster, gentleman, and Daniel Poor, yeoman, both of Plaistow, as sureties, in the sum of £2000, Oct. 3, 1758, for the administration of the estate; witnesses, John Green, Nathaniel Peaslee Sargent.]

[Inventory of estate in New Hampshire, Oct. 5, 1758; land in Plaistow, £480. 0. 0; signed by John Webster, Timothy Ladd, and Daniel Poor.]

[Warrant, Oct. 13, 1758, authorizing Col. James White, Tristram Knight, John Webster, gentlemen, Timothy Ladd, and Daniel Poor, yeomen, all of Plaistow, to appraise the estate in New Hampshire for settlement on the oldest son; return of 43 acres of land in Plaistow at £537. 10. 0; signed by James White, Tristram Knight, John Webster, and Timothy Ladd.]

[Order of court, Dec. 18, 1758, settling the real estate on Benjamin Smith, oldest son, he to pay the others their shares.]

[Bond of Thomas Abbott of Andover, Mass., yeomen, in behalf of Benjamin Smith of Andover, Mass., blacksmith, with Daniel Poor and Samuel Kimball, both of Plaistow, yeomen, as sureties, in the sum of £1000, Dec. 18, 1758, for the payment to the other heirs of their shares; witnesses, Joshua Emery, Nathaniel Peaslee Sargent.]

[Account of the administrator against the estate; amount, £118. 0. 0; allowed Dec. 18, 1758.].

BETTY MACE   1758   DOVER

In The Name of God Amen the twenty third Day of August 1758 I Betty Mace of Dover In the Province of New Hamp^r Being Sick & weak in Body * * *

Item I Give & bequeath to my Hon^d Mother Eliz^a Harford my black Gound & Riding-Hood

Item I give & bequeath to my Sisters Patience Ham & Ann Evers all my wearing apparrel not before mentioned to be Equally Divided between them

Item I Give & bequeath to my Couzin Elizabeth Nethersell Daughter of my brother Joseph Harford & to her Heirs forever all my real & personal Estate Debts & moveable Effects whatsoever

Item I Constitute ordain & appoint my friend Thomas Westbrook Waldron sole Executor * * *

Betty Mace

[Witnesses] Silvanus Hussey, Zaccheus Purintun, William Wentworth.

[Proved Sept. 27, 1758.]

Whereas Betty Mace Late of Dover in the Province of New Hampshire Widow Deceasd Appointed me Sole Executor of her Last Will & Testament but In Consideration that the Residuary Legatee who was when Said Will was made a Singlewoman Inncapable of the Executorship thereof is now married & her Husband Desiring to have the management thereof in his own hands I hereby Renounce & Relinquish the Said Trust and Submit the Same to the Disposition of the Law Witness my hand the 15th day of March 1759

Thos W^k Waldron

[Bond of Samuel Heard, Jr., yeoman, with Thomas Westbrook Waldron, gentleman, as surety, both of Dover, in the sum of £1000, March 15, 1759, for the administration, with will annexed, of the estate; witnesses, William Parker, David Sewall.]

JOHN PAINE   1758   PORTSMOUTH

To the Honble Richard Wibird Esqr Judge of the Probate of Wills and Granting administration on the Estates of Persons deceased within the Province of New Hampshire.

Whereas John Pain Late of Portsmouth within the Province of New Hampshire Joyner deceasd died Intestate Leaving neither widow nor Children, and no Relation nigher than an Aunt, and I am that Person & as adm^n of said Estate by Law is my Right, I pray that Your Hon^r will Grant administration of said Estate to my Two Children viz Joseph Buss and Hannah Horney Jointly, and after the payment of Debts due from said Estate & the Same is Settled if no other distribution should be made, I desire the Same may be divided Equally Between my said Children — & desire that one half of the movables may be deliverd to my said Daughter, she giving Security to pay half the debts due from said Estate

Portsmouth, August 24, 1758   her
Witness, Nathl Fellows   Lydia ✕ Buss
                                                   Mark

[Administration granted to Joseph Buss, joiner, and Hannah Horney, widow, both of Portsmouth, Aug. 30, 1758.]

[Probate Records, vol. 21, p. 52.]

[Bond of Joseph Buss and Hannah Horney, with John Shackford and William Pearson, shopkeeper, as sureties, all of Portsmouth, in the sum of £500, Aug. 30, 1758, for the administration of the estate; witnesses, William Parker, Samuel Hart.]

[Warrant, Aug. 23, 1758, authorizing Hunking Wentworth and Samuel Penhallow, merchant, both of Portsmouth, to appraise the estate.]

[Inventory, Aug. 30, 1758; amount, £1988. 16. 6; signed by Hunking Wentworth and Samuel Penhallow.]

[Account of the administrators; receipts, £1701. 8. 9; expenditures, £2276. 4. 11; mentions "Sundrys Supply the dec[d] for mourning on His mothers death. . . . paid for the dec[ds] Funeral in Jamaca"; allowed July 29, 1761.]

[Caveat, Jan. 27, 1762, by Joseph Sherburne of Boston, Mass., representing John Paine, father of the deceased, against the allowance of the accounts of the administrators.]

[Additional account of Hannah Horney, surviving administrator; receipts, £622. 16. 2; expenditures the same; allowed April 29, 1762.]

LYDIA BUSS   1758   PORTSMOUTH

In the Name of God Amen. The Last will and Testament of Lydia Buss. I Elizabeth Buss of Portsmouth in the Province of New Hampshire Widow being aged and Infirm * * *

Item unto my Son Joseph Buss I give Twenty Shillings old Tenor

Item unto my Daughter Hannah Horney & her heirs and assigns I give the one quarter part of the Real Estate that was my

Late husbands and after his decease was the Share of Mary Buss late of Portsmouth Single woman deceased (my daughter), and on her decease decended to me as next of Kin, which is the Share I hereby dispose of, and I also give unto my said Daughter all the Personal Estate that was my said Daughter Marys as well what was her Share in her fathers Estate as otherwise, also the One half of the Estate that fell to me by the Death of my Nephew John Pain Late of said Portsmouth Joyner deceasd, be the Same Real or parsonall. And as to the Thirds of the movable Estate that was my said Husbands and fell to me at the time of his death, I will that the Same shall Be disposed off so far as to defray and pay of all Debts Due from me, and my funeral Expences and if after the payment thereof any thing shall Remain I will that the Same shall be Equally divided Between my Son Joseph and Daughter Hannah —

Item. To my Son Joseph I Give the one half of the aforesaid Estate that fell to me by the Death of my said Nephew and all other of my Estate if any there be shall be Equally divided between my said Children. And I appoint my said Son Joseph and Daughter Hannah to be Executors of this my last will and Testament and hereby Revoke all other wills and Testaments by me formerly made Ratifying and Confirming this and no other to be my last will and Testament In Testimony whereof I have hereunto Set my hand & seal this Twenty Six day of August anno Domini 1758

her
Lydia + Buss
mark

[Witnesses] Nath[l] Fellows, James Thompson, Rich[d] Greley, Cutts Shannon.

[Proved Jan. 31, 1759.]

[Caveat of Joseph Buss of Portsmouth, Oct. 25, 1758, against the probate of his mother's will on the grounds of mental incompetency.]

[Summons, Nov. 28, 1758, to Clement Jackson, Hannah Hale, Ann Yeaton, and Priscilla Downs, single women, all of Portsmouth, to appear and testify as to the testator's sanity.]

[John Nelson states that he was prevented from appearing in court by the death of one of his children and the sickness of his wife and two other children; dated Exeter, Nov. 28, 1758.]

The deposition of Priscilla Down of Lawfull age testifieth & saith that she was well acquainted with Miss Lydia Buss for nine or ten months before her Death & that she the said Lydia was very Childish & forgetfull for all that time often forgetting & denying that she had eat her meals when I well rembered she had eat them, and mistaking the evening for the morning, & neglecting to warm her bed in the Coldest night in winter she would warm it in the hottest night in Summer — And in her last Sickness when she was at her Daugher Hornys She w^d Say she was at Mr Mark Wentworth's house & that she wanted to get home, & when she was told that she was at her Daughter Hornys she w^d say her Son Horny was angry with her for Staying there & Complained that he did not Come up to see her and many Such like Childish actions & word too many to enumerate which shew the want of reason & understanding

her
Priscilla X Down
mark

Sworn in Court Novr 30th 1758
    attest Wm Parker Reg^r

The Deposition of George Gains of Lawful age Who testifieth & saith that he was well acquainted with Miss Lydia Buss late of Portsmouth widow deceased & that he knew her well for Six years before her death, All which time this deponent says She was very Childish and weak in her understanding being very old & subject to fits, & as this deponent veryly thinks not of disposing mind & memory fit to make a will. And that she was full of

Childish actions Such as denoted want of reason & understanding. That one day last June this deponent was papering a room for Mr Joseph Buss where the said Lydia Buss came & picked up the strips of paper & had them put on her head as Ribbands & wore them as Such & seem'd greatly pleased with them as a Child w^d with any Toys & would have wore them to her Daughter Horneys unless she had been hindred by her Said son Joseph Buss. And that Sometime in February last her Nephew John Paine being gone a voyage to Jamaica & having Saild in January last & being looked for in may or June folloing she the said Lydia in the Said month of February last laid by for her Said Nephew a piece of roasted pork & kept it till it stunk Saying the said John Paine was very fond of roast Pork, & that in the month of march last she would very often enquire once or twice a week whether the Brig (in which her nephey Saild) was expected Soon altho she was always informed it would not arrive before may or June — And after the news came that her said nephew was dead in Jamaica she would often Say she wished the Brig w^d arrive that she might see her Said nephew, and that in winter time after the said Brig was Saild & might probably have got to Jamaica She the said Lydia w^d often in a great Storm inquire whether it did not endanger the Brig & seemed very anxious about the poor boy as she Calld the said John Pain. And that she was full of such like Childish Talk and actions.

Sworn in Court Novr 30th 1758 attest   George Gains
    Wm Parker Reg^r

[Bond of Joseph Buss of Portsmouth, joiner, with Joseph Alcock of Portsmouth, shopkeeper, as surety, in the sum of £100, Jan. 31, 1759, to prosecute his appeal against the probate of the will, contested between himself and his sister, Hannah Horney of Portsmouth, widow, and allowed by the Judge of Probate; witnesses, Hunking Wentworth, Thomas Palmer.]

BENJAMIN CHOATE   1758   KINGSTON

[Bond of Ruth Choate, widow, with William Calfe, cordwainer, and Benjamin Swett, yeoman, as sureties, all of Kingston, in the sum of £2000, Aug. 28, 1758, for the administration of the estate of Benjamin Choate of Kingston, yeoman; witnesses, Jeremy Webster, Simeon Brown.]

[Warrant, Aug. 18, 1758, authorizing Jeremy Webster and William Calfe, both of Kingston, to appraise the estate.]

[Inventory, Aug. 28, 1758; amount, £3575. 5. 0; signed by Jeremy Webster and William Calfe.]

[Account of the administratrix; receipts, £911. 5. 0, personal estate; expenditures, £660. 13. 0; mentions "Supporting one Child from four years old to seven"; allowed Sept. 30, 1761.]

[Commission to Jeremy Webster, Josiah Bartlett, John Calfe, gentleman, Solomon Wheeler, and Simmons Secomb, yeomen, all of Kingston, to divide the real estate.]

Province of New Hamps: Rockingham:
Pursuant to Warrant from the Honb^{le} John Wentworth Esqr Judge of the Probate of Wills &c for the County of Rockingham in the Province afores^d to us the subscribers directed appointing us a Com^{tee} to Divide the real estate of Benjamin Choate late of Kingstown in the County afores^d deceas'd to & among the widow & Children of the deceas'd: We have proceeded & have divided & set off the s^d estate as followeth viz:

1st To Ruth widow of the deceasd (now wife of William Sleeper) for her right of dower (or thirds) in s^d estate as followeth

1st In the Home place: beginning at the High way going through s^d Kingstown, at the southwesterly Corner of the premisses & from thence running Northerly by s^d High way to the North westerly Corner of the Barn and so on by the s^d High way to a stake about one rod Northerly from the North westerly Corner of the dwelling House, then easterly four rods to a stake;

then southerly about twelve rods to a stake, then Easterly to the south westerly Corner of Solomon Wheelers land then still easterly by s^d Wheelers land till it comes to Joshua Bartlets Junr land on which he now lives, then south crossing the premisses, to the Southerly Line of the premisses, then westerly to the forementioned Highway to the place where it first began Nine acres more or less; with the fore room in the Dwelling House & the chamber & garret over it & one Half of the cellar under it & one third of the Barn viz: the easterly end thereof; But it is to be understood here and our true Intent & meaning is that there be a priviledge from the High way to the House & also the Barn and about each of them for the children to go to, & from, the s^d Buildings to use & Improve their respective parts of, & Interest in them as Convenient as may be

2^{ly} In the woodland as followeth viz: four acres more or less Scituate in s^d Kingstown being laid out to the right of Benjamin Choate father of the forementioned Benjamin Choate, & is Bounded as may appear on s^d Kingstown Book of records; and eight acres Joyning to the s^d four acres which is part of Nine acres purchas'd of Dr Simeon Brown s^d eight acres Bounded as followeth viz: beginning at the Northerly End or side of the s^d Nine acres & takeing the whole width thereof to Extend southerly as the land lays, so far as to leave one acre on the southerly side or end thereof, which s^d acre is set off to one of the children as shall be hereafter mentioned

2^{ly} To Ruth daughter of the deceasd, now the wife of Benjamin Judkins for her share in the premisses seven acres more or less Beginning at the North Easterly Corner Bounds of the whole tract on the High way going to Trickleing falls (so called) & Joyning land of Joshua Woodman jun^r and from thence to run southerly by s^d High way about thirty rods to a stake & stones, then westerly about forty rods to a Black Oak Tree marked, then Northerly to a stake & stones at the south westerly corner of s^d Woodmans land then easterly by s^d Woodmans land to the place where it first began with one fifth part of the dwelling

House & Barn exclusive of the widows thirds & prividge to go to them to use & Improve them

2 3 The Second & Third shares to Ammi Choate the eldest son of the deceasd Bounded as followeth viz: Beginning at the s^d High way going to the Trickleing falls (so called) at the stake & stones the Bounds of the first share & from thence running westerly by the s^d first share to a Black Oak Tree the Bounds thereof, then southerly to a Pitch Pine Tree & so on the same Course to Land belonging to the Hiers of Mr Benjamin Choate father to the forementioned Benjamin Choate deceasd then easterly by the last mentioned land, to ten acres of land which is part of the premisses hereby divideing then southerly as the s^d ten acres lays to the south westerly corner thereof, then Easterly to the south Easterly Corner Bounds of the whole tract then Northerly about sixty rods to the stake & stones first mentioned, and two fifths of the remaining part of the Dwelling House & two fifths of the remaining part of the Barn exclusive of the widows thirds, with convenient priviledge of land from the High way to the s^d House & Barn & about them both to use & Improve the same

4^{ly} The fourth share to Simeon Choate Bounded as followeth viz Beginning at a stake & stones the North westerly corner Bounds of the first share also the south westerly corner Bounds of the forementioned Joshua Woodman jun^r land & from thence running southerly by the first, & part of the second & third shares to the souther: Line of the premises hereby divided, then westerly on the s^d Line to the widows thirds then North by the s^d thirds to the south westerly corner Bounds of Joshua Bartlets Junr land, then Easterly by s^d Bartlets land to the place where it first began Eleven acres more or less and one fifth of the remaining part of the Dwelling House & Barn Exclusive of the widows thirds with a Convenient priviledge of land to go from the High way to them & about them to use & Improve them

5^{ly} The fifth & last share to Benjamin Choate Bounded as followeth viz: Beginning at the North westerly Corner Bounds of the forementioned Solomon Wheelers land by the High way called Scotland rode & from thence running westerly by s^d rode or way to the main rode going thro' s^d Kingstown then southerly by the last mentioned rode or High way Eight rods to a stake which is a Bounds of the widows thirds then Easterly by the s^d thirds four rods to a stake another Bounds of the s^d thirds then southerly still by the s^d thirds Twelve rods to a stake which is also another Bounds of the s^d thirds then Easterly by the s^d thirds to Solomon Wheelers land fore mentioned, then Northerly by s^d Wheelers Land to the first mentioned High way three acres & an Half more or less, and one acre in the forementioned wood land it being part of Nine acres forementioned in setting off the widows thirds; & is part of the s^d nine acres, & lays on the southerly side thereof to run the whole length thereof from east to west & to be of an Equal Breadth in all places & is Bounded Northerly on part of the s^d thirds, also we set off to the s^d Benjamin one fifth of the remaining part of the dwelling House & Barn with Convenient priviledge to go from the s^d High way to them & about them as there shall be Occasion in their useing & Improveing of them

In witness whereof we have hereunto set our hands this Seventeenth Day of april in the 12th year of his majestys Reign annoq: Domini 1772

         Jeremy Webster
         Josiah Bartlett
         John Calef
         Solomon Wheeler
         Simmons Seccomb

[Additional account by William Sleeper and Ruth Sleeper, formerly Ruth Choate, administratrix; receipts, £16. 10. 7½; expenditures, £8. 1. 0; allowed April 29, 1772.]

ANN CLOUGH   1758   BRENTWOOD

[Administration on the estate of Ann Clough of Brentwood granted to Jacob French of South Hampton, yeoman, Aug. 28, 1758.]

[Probate Records, vol. 21, p. 42.]

[Bond of Jacob French, with Samuel French of South Hampton, gentleman, and Reuben Sanborn of Hampton Falls, yeoman, as sureties, in the sum of £500, Aug. 28, 1758, for the administration of the estate of his mother, Ann Clough; witnesses, William Parker, Samuel Slade.]

[Agreement, Jan. 2, 1759, of Jacob French, William French of Hampton Falls, Samuel Winslow and wife Jane, formerly Jane French, Nathan Sanborn and wife Jemima, formerly Jemima French, all of Epping, Daniel Roby of Chester and wife Anna, formerly Anna French, Winthrop Clough of Kensington and wife Rachel, formerly Rachel French, Anthony Peavey and wife Mary, formerly Mary French, children of Ann Clough, formerly Ann French, widow of Jacob French of Hampton Falls, joiner, as to the division of her personal estate; witnesses, Elijah Cram, James Russell.]

JONATHAN HILLIARD   1758   HAMPTON FALLS

In the Name of God Amen this twenty Ninth Day of August Anno Domini 1758 In the thirty Second Year of his Majestys Reign I Jonathan Hilyard of Hampton falls in the Province of New Hampshire in New England Yeoman * * *

Item my Will is as to my well beloved wife Mary that she have the same part and Share of my Estate Real and Personal As the Law allows

Item I Give and Bequeath to my Son Joseph Hilyard his heirs and assigns Six Acres of Land at the Southwesterly Corner of my Land where I Live Bounding Southerly by the Way which goes by my House to Hogpen so Called to be twenty Rods in wedth upon said way, and so to Run back from said way Carrying the same wedth by the Side of Capt Nason's land untill Six acres are Compleated, I also give to my said Son two acres of Marsh which I Bought of Abner Sanborn

Item I Give and Bequeath to my Son Benjamin Hilyard his heirs and Assigns All the Remainder of my Land in Hampton be the Same more or Less With my Dwelling House and Barn and all my Buildings And all Appurtenances to said Land and Buildings belonging or Appertaining And in Consideration hereof I Order him my said Son Benjamin to Purchase forty acres of Good Land Suitable for to Settle upon in the Township of Chester or Nottingham or in Some other Town as Convenient for to Settle in as said Towns are And to Convey said forty acres of Land to my Son Jonathan Hilyard when he said Jonathan shall Arrive at the age of twenty one years so that he my said Son Jonathan may have & injoy the Same to him his heirs and assigns which is part of the Settlement I Design for my said Son Jonathan I Also Order my said Son Benjamin to pay to his Sisters as hereafter mentioned

Item I Give And Bequeath to my Son Jonathan Hilyard his heirs and assigns my Right in the tract of Land Granted to Ichabod Robie Esqr And Others by the Purchasers of the Right of John Tufton Mason Esqr, Also the forty acres of Land my Son Benjamin is to purchase for him As Above Ordered, And further I Order my said Son Benjamin to pay what shall from time to time be Due upon the above mentioned Right that so the Same may not be forfeited

Item I Give and Bequeath to my Daughter Rachel Sanborn Six sheep to be Deliverd her by my Executor.

Item I Give and Bequeath to my Daughters Hannah, Elizabeth, Nanne, Mary and Marcy Each of them fifty Pounds New Tenor to be paid to Each of them As they Respectively Arrive to the age of twenty one years by my Executor hereinafternamed

Item I Give And Bequeath to Marcy Taylor who formerly lived with me twenty five Pounds New Tenor to be paid her by my Executor within four years after my Decease or at the time of her being married which shall first happen

Item I Order that my Husbandry Tools shall be kept for managing my Place my wife Mary to have the use of them with my said Son Benjamin And as to my Stock of Creatures after my Debts and funeral Charges shall be paid the Remainder to my Son Benjamin

Lastly I Do by these presents Constitute & Appoint my Son Benjamin Hilyard Sole Executor * * *

Jonathan Hilyard

[Witnesses] Meshech Weare, Joseph Chase hilyard, Joseph Pearkins.

[Proved Nov. 30, 1758.]

[Warrant, Nov. 30, 1758, authorizing Meshech Weare and Deacon Josiah Batchelder, both of Hampton Falls, to appraise the estate.]

[Inventory, Jan. 10, 1759; amount, £10,186. 16. 0; signed by Meshech Weare and Josiah Batchelder.]

[Guardianship of Mercy Hilliard, minor, daughter of Jonathan Hilliard, granted to Joseph Chase Hilliard of Kensington, yeoman, June 27, 1770.]

[Probate Records, vol. 26, p. 256.]

[Bond of Joseph Chase Hilliard, with Richard Nason of Hampton Falls and Stephen Prescott of Kingston, yeoman, as sureties, in the sum of £500, June 27, 1770, for the guardianship of Mercy Hilliard, aged less than 14 years, daughter of Jonathan Hilliard; witnesses, John Wentworth, Nathan Green.]

[Guardianship of Mary Hilliard, minor, aged more than 14 years, granted to Joseph Chase Hilliard of Kensington, yeoman, July 12, 1770.]

[Probate Records, vol. 26, p. 457.]

[Bond of Joseph Chase Hilliard, with Caleb Shaw of Kensington, gentleman, as surety, in the sum of £200, July 12, 1770, for the guardianship of Mary Hilliard, daughter of Jonathan Hilliard; witnesses, John Shaw, William Parker, Jr.]

ISAAC HANSON   1758   DOVER

[Administration on the estate of Isaac Hanson of Dover, yeoman, granted to Susanna Hanson of Dover, widow, Aug. 30, 1758.]

[Probate Records, vol. 21, p. 43.]

[Bond of Susanna Hanson, with Ichabod Canney of Dover and Benjamin Canney of Somersworth, yeomen, as sureties, in the sum of £1000, Aug. 30, 1758, for the administration of the estate; witnesses, William Parker, Thomas Hart.]

[Warrant, Aug. 30, 1758, authorizing Joseph Austin and Joseph Hanson, Jr., both of Dover, yeomen, to appraise the estate.]

[Inventory, Oct. 9, 1758; amount, £7929. 4. 0; signed by Joseph Austin and Joseph Hanson.]

[Administration de bonis non granted to Ichabod Canney of Dover, yeoman, Sept. 23, 1760.]

[Probate Records, vol. 21, p. 500.]

[Bond of Ichabod Canney, with Benjamin Canney of Dover and John Plummer of Rochester, yeomen, as sureties, in the sum of £500, Sept. 23, 1760, for the administration de bonis non of the estate; witnesses, Cutts Shannon, John Hogg.]

Province of } We the Subscribers being apointed with others
New Hams[r] } by the Hon[ble] John wentworth Esq[r] Judge of Probate of wills for said Province as ℔ Warrant to us directed To Devide the Rale Estete of Isaac Hanson Late of Dover Decs[d] among his Childrin by the Request of the oldest Son, we have

divided the Estate as hereafter to them as it appeared to us it might be done

first — To Tobias Hanson the oldest Son Two Shires the Dweeling House and Part of the homestead Land bounding as followeth viz Begining by the main Road that Leeds through Cochecho South 12^d west Eighteen Rods from the west Cornor of the afores^d Land Runing Noth 80^d East Eight Rods then South 10^d east five Rods then noth 80^d East Seventy four Rods to Sheffelds Land So Call^d then by Sheffelds Land south 45^d east Eleven Rods to George Hansons Land then by s^d Georges Land South 31^d west Sixty Two Rods then noth fifty eight Degrees west fifty Seven Rods then south 89^d west Sixteen Rods to the Road then by s^d Road to the first bound Containing nineteen acres more or less all within these afores^d bound we set of to the afores^d Tobias Hanson for his Two Shers in the afores^d Estate Together with the barn now standing on his sisters Hannah Right or Loot of Land in the afores^d Estate we alowing the afores^d Tobias Hanson six months from the Date hearof to take of the afores^d barn. If s^d barn is not Remov^d with in the afores^d time alow^d then his afores^d sister Hannah Hanson to keep the afores^d barn —

2ly — To Lydia watson part of the home Stead Land begining noth 69^d East Seven Rods and a half from the west Cornor of saide Land Runing South 18^d East fifteen Rods then noth 76^d East Twenty Two Rods then Runing noth 18^d west Twelve Rods then South 76^d west eleven Rods then noth 29^d west three Rods then to the first bounds Containing one acre and Three Quarters, more Land eight acres and half Lying on the south Sid of the Road that Leeds from Cochecho to Jon^a Bickford in Dover bounding Notherly by the way and Southerly by Elijah Tuttels Land and Westerly Partly by Moses and Aron Wingate and Partly by Caleb Hodgdon there Land all within these afores^d Lydia bounds more or less we set of to the afores^d Lydia Watson for her Right in the fores^d Estate

3^{ly} — To Hannah Hanson Part of the home Stead begining by the main Road that Leeds through Cochecho att Benj^a Hanson Land Runing noth 12^d east eight Rods then noth eighty nine Degrees east Sixteen Rods then South 58^d east fifty seven Rods to George Hanson Land then by s^d Georges Land South 31^d west thirty eight Rods then noth 82^d west Twenty nine Rods then noth 37^d west Teen Rods and a half to Enock Hoige Land then by s^d Hoiges Land noth 16^d east twenty Rods then noth Two Degrees east Twenty four Rods by the wi^d Sarah Hanson Land then noth 58^d west Partly by the wi^d Sarah and Partly by Benj^a Hanson their Land to the first bounds Containing Thirteen acres all within these afores^d Hannah bounds more or Less we set of to the afores^d Hannah Hanson for her Right in the afores^d estate excepting the barn Standing on the afores^d Hannah Land low^d to her brother Tobias If the afores^d Tobias Hanson moves it of from the afores^d Hannah Land within the time we alow^d him If not Removd within the Time alowed then the afores^d Hannah Hanson to have the afores^d barn for her own —

4^{ly} — To Isaac Hanson Part of the homestead Land begining att the west Cornor of s^d Land by the Road Runing South 12^d west Eighteen Rods by s^d Road then noth 80^d East eight Rods then South 10^d East five Rods then noth 80^d east Seventy four Rods to Sheffelds Land so Cal^d then noth 45^d west Twenty eight Rods by Sheffeld then noth 67^d west six Rod then South 67^d west twenty seven Rods by Humphry Hansons Land Late of Dover Deces^d then South 18^d east twelve Rods then South Seventy six Degres west Twenty Two Rods then noth 18^d west fiften Rods then a Strate Corse to the first bounds Containing nine acres more or Less all with in these afores^d Isaac bounds we set of to the afores^d Isaac Hanson for his Right in the afores^d Estate —

5^{ly} To Susannah Hanson and Rose Hanson the out Land Lying on the west side of the mane Road that Leeds from Cochecho to Rochester att black water So Cal^d and Lying Partly in the Town of Summerworth and Partly in Dover afores^d Containing Eighty acres to be Equelly Divided between the afores^d Susannah and

Rose acording to Quonitty and Quolity for there Part of the aforesaid Estate

All which is Humbly Submitted by us acording to the best of our Judgment. Dover april 6th 1771 —

       Joshua Wingate }
       Joseph Roberts } Committee
       Elijah Estes }

[Account of the administrator; receipts, £75. 18. 0; expenditures, £76. 12. 9; allowed May 22, 1771.]

FRANCIS ROBERTS   1758   SOMERSWORTH

[Administration on the estate of Francis Roberts of Somersworth, yeoman, granted to Moses Carr of Somersworth, physician, Aug. 30, 1758.]

[Probate Records, vol. 21, p. 47.]

[Bond of Moses Carr, with James Philpot of Somersworth, mariner, and James Kielle of Dover, tailor, as sureties, in the sum of £500, Aug. 30, 1758, for the administration of the estate; witnesses, William Parker, Thomas Hart.]

[Warrant, Aug. 30, 1758, authorizing John Wentworth, gentleman, and Moses Stevens, tanner, both of Somersworth, to appraise the estate.]

[Inventory, attested Dec. 28, 1758; amount, £5090. 15. 0; signed by John Wentworth and Moses Stevens.]

[Account of the administrator; receipts, £2167. 14. 0; expenditures, £2191. 12. 3; allowed June 30, 1762.]

[Additional account; receipts, £3616. 0. 8; expenditures, £3481. 17. 3; allowed April 29, 1772.]

Rockingham ss

To the Honble John Wentworth Esqr Judge of the probate of wills &c for the County of Rockingham

Humbly shews Love Roberts of Somersworth in the County of Rockingham yeoman that your Petitioner owns one Half of one Hundred Acres of Land with the Buildings on the Same in Somersworth afores[d] which descended & Came unto your Petitioner & Francis Roberts late of said Somersworth dec[d] from their Father Love Roberts late of Somersworth afores[d] Gent[m] dec[d] which said Estate your Petitioner and the s[d] Francis held in Common & undivided with Francis till his Death & Now is held in Common and undivided by your Petitioner to whom one Moiety belongs & the other moiety to Betty, Sarah, Francis, John & Molly Children & Heirs to the said Francis wherefore your Petitioner prays your Honor to Issue your Warrant to Five sufficient Freeholders to divide the premises afores[d] into two equal parts the one Moiety to hold to your Petitioner in severalty & the other to the Heirs of said Francis & set them off by good & sufficient metes & Bounds

Portsm[o] April 29th 1772   Love Roberts

[The court ordered notice to be served on Charles Baker, guardian of Molly, Francis, and John Roberts, John Ham and his wife Betty, daughter of Francis Roberts, and Sarah Roberts.]

[Warrant, May 4, 1772, authorizing Ichabod Rollins, James Garvin, gentlemen, Francis Yeaton, Jonathan Wentworth, and John Pike, husbandmen, to divide the estate held in common.]

Pursuant To a Warrant To us directed By the Hon[e] John Wentworth Esq[r] Judge of Probate for the County of Rockingham, To divide the Real Estate of Love Roberts, late of Somersworth in said County dec[d] between Love Roberts Son to the said deceased and the Heirs of Francis Roberts late of Somersworth afores[d] deceased, We have divided the same in the Following Manner —

To the Heirs of said Francis, the western End of the Homestead Scituate on the South side of the road that leads from Salmon falls to the Meeting House in said Town, Begining at the

N: W: Corner of s^d Land then So: 24° East Six Chains Then So: 11° 30. E. Nine Chains, So: 50° E: Nine Chains Sixty links — North seventy five degrees E: Thirteen Chains Twenty links — No: 39° E: Twelve Chains fifty links — North 13° W: Nine Chains fifty Links — So: 87° 30 W: Twelve Chains No: 15° W: Eight Chains — So: 62° W: Three Chains — So: 68° W: Seven Chains — Then on a strait Course to The first Bounds, Containing Fifty four Acres — also a Tract of Land at Black-Water (so Called) in s^d Town — Begining at the N E Corner of the Parsonage in s^d Town, Then No: 6° W: Thirteen Chains — So: 84° W: Fifteen Chains Fifty links — So: 6° E: Thirteen Chains So: 84° W: Eleven Chains fifty links — So: 6° E: 7:50 No: 84° E Thirteen Chains 50 L to the Parsonage afores^d — No: 6° West 7:50 — No: 84° E Thirteen Chains Sixty links to the first Bound Containing Thirty Six Acres also half a Right in the Town of Canterbury in the County of ———

To the s^d Love the Eastern End of s^d Homes^d Begining at the N: E: Corner of the Heirs of s^d Francis then So: 13° E Nine Chains fifty Links — So: 39° W: Twelve Chains Fifty Links — So: 75° W: Thirteen Chains Thirty Links — So: 50° E Eight Chains Forty Links — No: 87° E: Six Chains fifty Links No: Fifty five degrees E: Seventy five Links — No: 86° E Four Chains So: 84° E Three Chains No 15° E Nine Chains No: 46° E: 5 Chains — No: 66° 30^m E. seven chains — No: 41° E: 2½ Chains No: 6° E: Three Chains 75 links — No 15° W: Six Chains fifty links — No: 29° 30^m W: Five Chains Fifty Links — So: 79° W: Three Chains — West One Chain fifty links So: 87° W: Nine Chains Eighty Eight Links — Then on a strait Course to the first Bound, Containing Forty four Acres — Also to the s^d Love or his Assigns, the remainder of the Tract of Land at black Water afores^d Beginning at the S: E: Corner of the Parsonage afores^d Then runing S: 84° W Thirteen Chains Sixty links No: 6° W Three Chains — So: 84° W: Thirteen Chains 50 Lk — So: 6° E Three Chains No: 84° E: Three Chains forty seven links — So: 10° E. Twelve Chains — No: 80° E: Twenty Three Chains

Fifty links — Then on a Strait Course to the first Bound Containing Thirty Acres — also the remaining half of the right afores[d] in the Town of Canterbury — Dated at Somersworth the 26 day of May, 1772

Icha[d] Rollins
James Garvin
Jon[a] Wentworth } Committee
Francis yeaton
John Pike

[Warrant, Dec. 25, 1772, authorizing Ichabod Rollins, James Garvin, Francis Yeaton, Jonathan Wentworth, and John Pike to divide the real estate.]

Pursuant to a Warrant To us directed By the Hon[e] John Wentworth Esq[r] Judge of Probate for the County of Rockingham To divide the Real Estate of Francis Roberts late of Somersworth in s[d] County dec[d] Between the Wid[w] of s[d] Francis and his heirs, We have divided the Same in the Following Manner —

To the Wid[w] of s[d] Francis the Eastern End of the homes[d] Begining at the N: E: Corner of s[d] Land by the Road that leads from Salmon-falls to the Meeting-house in s[d] Town Then Runing So: 15° E 8 Chains — No: 87° 38 E 12 Chains So 13° E 9 Chs 50 Ls — So: 39° W: 12 Chs 50 Ls No: 22° W: 25 Chs 40 Ls to the Road afores[d] Then on a Strait Course to the First Bound — Containing 19 Acres & half — To Francis Roberts Son to s[d] Francis dec[d] Sixteen Acres and one Quarter Begining at the N W Corner of the Wid[ws] Thirds By the Road afores[d] then Runing So 22° E 25 Chs 40 Ls — So: 75° W: 7 Chs — No: 21° W: 24 Chs 20 Ls to the Road afores[d] Then on a strait Course to the First Bound — To John Carr Roberts Son to the s[d] Francis dec[d] Nine Acres and 20 Poles Begining at the N: W: Corner of s[d] Francis Then runing So: 21° E 24 Chs 20 Links — So: 75° W: 4 Chains 90 links — No: 19° W: 24 Chains to the road afores[d] then on a Strait Course to the First Bound — To Molly Roberts daughter to the s[d] Francis dec[d] Nine Acres and 20 Poles Begining at the N: W: Corner of s^d John, Then Runing So: 19° E 24 Chs So: 75° W: one Chain Forty Links No: 50° W: 9 Chs 60 Links No 11° W 9 Chains — No: 24° W: 6 Chains to the road afores^d Then on a Strait Course to the First Bound — To Betty Ham daughter to the s^d Francis dec^d Six Acres at Black Water in s^d Town, Begining Three Chains To the No^d of the S: W: Corner of the Parsonage in s^d Town, runing W: 6° S 13 Chs 50 Links — No: 6° W: 4 Chs 40 L East 6° No: 13 Chains 50 L to the Parsonage afores^d — So: 6° E 4 Chs 40 Ls To the First Bound — Also half a Right in the Town of Canterbury in County of ——— To Sarah Roberts Daughter to the s^d Francis Dec^d Thirty Acres at Black Water afores^d Begining at the N: E: Corner of the Parsonage afores^d Runing W: 6° S 13 Chains and Half — So: 6° E. 7 Chains and half — W: 6° S 13 Chs 50 L — No: 6° W 7 Chains & Half — E: 6° No: 11 Chs 50 Links N: 6° W: 13 Chs — E: 6° No: 15 Ch 50 Ls Then So: 6° E 13 Chains To the First Bound — Dated at Somersworth December 21st 1772

Icha^d Rollins
James Garvin
Jon^a Wentworth } Committee
Francis Yeaton
John Pike

[Additional account of the administrator; receipts, £3616. 0. 8; expenditures, £3626. 13. 11; mentions "half of a Negro man"; allowed Aug. 31, 1774.]

NATHANIEL TUCKERMAN   1758   PORTSMOUTH

[Administration on the estate of Nathaniel Tuckerman of Portsmouth, mariner, granted to John Tuckerman of Newcastle, fisherman, Aug. 31, 1758.]

[Probate Records, vol. 21, p. 55.]

[Bond of John Tuckerman, with Joseph Brewster, shopkeeper, and George Boyd, rope-maker, both of Portsmouth, as sureties, in the sum of £1000, Aug. 31, 1758, for the administration of the estate; witnesses, William Parker, David Sewall.]

BENJAMIN THOMAS   1758   NORTH HAMPTON

In the Name of God Amen I Benjamin Thomas of North Hampton in the Province of New Hampshire Gent. being aged * * *

Item I give to Abigail my beloved wife the use & Improvement of my Part of the Dwelling House wherein I live with Liberty of the use of the Well Cellar & Dairy Room thereto belonging with liberty of taking as many Apples as She Shall have Occasion to use for her Self out of my Orchard & Land Sufficient for a Garden as She Shall judge Convenient and besides this I give her one hundred Pounds of Pork & One hundred Pounds of Beef and the use of two good milch Cows maintain'd Winter & Summer with Sufficient fire wood to be hal'd & Cut at her Door with Ten Bushels of Indian Corn & two Bushels of English two Bushels of Malt & three Barrels of Cyder when my Orchard produces fruit Sufficient for it with Twelve pounds of Flax from the Swingle with three pounds of Sheeps wool all these Particulars to be provided for her yearly by my Executor during the time she shall Remain my Widow I also give her all the Goods & Estate She bro't to me at her marriage with me and that house hold Furniture which has been made or Purchased Since we have lived together by us and also a Decent Suit of Mourning — and in Default of my Said Execut^{rs} finding and Providing for my Said wife the Particulars above mentiond yearly I hereby give her Power to Dispose of any part of my Personal Estate or to Enter & take the Profits of any Part of my Real Estate Equal in Value to what Shall be wanting and in Arrearage of the Said paym^{ts} or Provision aforesaid Yearly — this is to be in Lieu of her Dower —

Item I give to my Son Jonathan my Great Coat and to my Son Benjamin Thomas twenty Shillings old Tenor I having given them their part & Portion of my Estate and as much as I can afford them —

Item I give to my Grandsons Elisha & William the Sons of my Son James Deceased all my wearing Apparel Except what is otherways herein Particularly Dispos'd of — to be Equally Divided between Them — Item I give to my Grand Daughter Abigail Nudd all my Household Furniture within doors not herein before given to my wife Provided the Said Abigail Shall live to the Age of Eighteen years but if she Shall Die before she arrives at that age then the Said Goods are to be for her Sister Martha these being the Daughters of my Daughter Abigail Deceas'd. I also give to Each of my Grand Children not herein Named and who are Children of my Said Daughter Deceased and the Children of my Son James Deceasd who are not before herein named five Shillings old Tenor Each —

Item I give to my Son Elisha my best Strait Bodied Coat and all my other Personal Estate not herein before Disposed of to Enable him to pay all my Debts & Legacies and to give & Provide for me a Decent Funeral & make the Yearly Payments aforesaid to my wife I also give & Devise to my Son Elisha all my Real Estate to him his Heirs & assigns forever upon Condition of his making Said Yearly payments to my Said Wife as above mentioned & permitting her to use & Improve that part of the Same herein before given to her use according to the Limitation aforesaid Quietly & Peaceably and after her Interest & use therein shall be Determined either by her Death or marriage then my Said Son to have & hold the whole as aforesaid but if he Should Sell the Same before my wifes term therein as afores[d] Shall be Ended I hereby Subject the whole of my Said Real Estate to answer for the bequests made to her as above mentioned & give her by these Presents full Power to Enter into the Same for that End — in whose hands Soever it shall be

Lastly I hereby appoint my Son Elisha to be Sole Execut[r] of this my last Will & Testament and hereby Revoke all other wills by me heretofore made In Witness whereof I have hereunto Set my hand & Seal the 12th Day of Septembr Anno Domini 1758

Benj[a] Thomas

[Witnesses] Daniel Samborn, Reuben Gove Dearborn, Charles Crymbel, William Parker.

In the Name of God Amen I Benjamin Thomas within Named having Considered my foregoing Will & there being Some alteration in my Circumstances Since I made the said Will as some other Reason for making an Alteration I Judge it proper to make this as a Codicel to my Said Will & Testament In the first place I give to my Said Wife my horse which I now Own or if I shall Change him for any other that which I shall own at my Decease to be at her own Disposal — To my Grand Daughters Abigail Nudd & Martha Nudd I give all my household furniture within Doors which in my Said Will is given only to Abigail I now give the Same to them both Equally Divided and if one of them Dies before marriage the Survivor to have the whole — And as to the Devise in my Said Will which I have in my Said Will made to my Son Elisha Considering that he does not manage his Affairs with Prudence & good Husbandry I Revoke every article thereof & give him only a Strait Bodied Homespun Coat of my wearing Apparel & twenty Shillings old Tenor besides what he has already had of my Estate And all & Every matter article & thing which in my said Will is given & Devised to my Said Son Elisha I hereby give & Devise the Same to my Grand Son James Nudd to hold to him his heirs & assigns he & they doing & Performing for my said Wife what my Said Son Elisha is orderd to do In my Said will and to hold to him the said James under the Same Conditions & Limitations as fully & Effectually as if the same Estate had been at first Devised & given to him the Said James In all other Respects I confirm my Said Will and order & Ordain this Codicil to be Considered as part of my last Will & Testament In Witness whereof I have hereunto Set my hand & Seal the 15th Day of May Anno Domini 1760

Benj Thomas

[Witnesses] Abigail Parker, Samuel Parker, Sol° Lowd, Wm Parker.
[Proved Nov. 26, 1766.]

JOSEPH HANSON   1758   DOVER

[Administration on the estate of Joseph Hanson of Dover granted to his son, Ephraim Hanson of Dover, innholder, Sept. 12, 1758.]

[Probate Records, vol. 21, p. 57.]

[Bond of Ephraim Hanson, with Dependence Bickford, yeoman, and James Kielle, tailor, as sureties, all of Dover, in the sum of £2000, Sept. 12, 1758, for the administration of the estate; witnesses, William Parker, Thomas Wendell.]

[Warrant, Sept. 13, 1758, authorizing William Shackford and Thomas Westbrook Waldron, both of Dover, gentlemen, to appraise the estate.]

[Inventory, Nov. 4, 1758; amount, £25,266. 14. 11; signed by William Shackford and Thomas Westbrook Waldron.]

[Guardianship of John Burnham Hanson, minor, aged more than 14 years, son of Joseph Hanson, granted to Valentine Mathes Jan. 22, 1759.]

[Probate Records, vol. 21, p. 145.]

[Bond of Valentine Mathes of Durham, yeoman, with Winthrop Burnham of Durham, tanner, and Nathaniel Adams of Portsmouth, merchant, as sureties, in the sum of £500, Jan. 22, 1759, for the guardianship of John Burnham Hanson; witnesses, Winborn Adams, Meriel Burnham.]

JAMES CLEMENTS   1758   SOMERSWORTH

In the Name of God Amen. The Twentieth day of Sepr in ye year of Our Lord One Thousand Seven Hundred & fifty Eight I

James Clements of The Town of Somersworth in the province of New: Hampshire in New England, Husbandman * * *

Imprimis I give & bequeath to my dearly beloved Wife Sarah, the one quarter of the Income of my Homestead Yearly, During her widowhood, & if she marries again, then ye Improvement of one Third of My Homestead, during her natural life

Item I Give & bequeath to my said Wife Sarah all my personal Estate as Household Goods Stock of Creatures &c excepting my Gun

Item I give & bequeath to my S^d wife Sarah the use of My House during her widowhood & if she marries again, then the use of one half of My House during her natural life

Item I give & bequeath To My beloved Son Job the one half of all My lands in Somersworth, Rochester, Dover & elsewhere to him his Heirs & assigns for ever.

Item I give & bequeath to My belved Son Abner, the other half of all My lands in Somersworth, Rochester, Dover & elsewhere, to him his Heirs & assigns for ever.

Item Its my will that my Said Sons Job & Abner cut & hall equally between them so Much firewood for My s^d wife Sarah, as she shall have occasion to burn during her widowhood.

Item I give and bequeath to My beloved Daughter Abigail fifty pounds old Ten^r after the rate of Dollers at Six pounds old Tennor to be paid equally by My two Said Sons Job & Abner within Seven years after My decease

Item I give & bequeath to my beloved Daughter Shuah fifty pounds old Ten^r after ye rate of Dollers at Six pounds old Tennor to be paid equally by my two Said Sons Job & Abner within Seven years after my decease.

Item I give & bequeath to My beloved Daughter Sarah fifty pounds old Tennor after ye rate of Dollers at Six pounds old Ten^r to be paid equally by My two s^d Sons Job & Abner within Seven years after My decease.

Item I give and bequeath to my beloved Son Abner My dwelling House after My wife has done with it, He helping My Son

Job to build another End to the house he lives in, that is being at half the Cost.

Item I give and bequeath to my beloved Grandaughter, Sarah, ye daughter of my beloved Son John deceasd Two Hundred pounds old Ten^r after ye rate of Dollers at Six pounds — to be paid equally by My s^d Sons Job & Abner, when she arrives at ye age of Eighteen Years, but if she dies before she arrives at S^d age, they are to keep Said Soms to themselves

Item I give & bequeath to My S^d Grandaughter Sarah Eight good sheep to be paid her equally by My two Sons Job & Abner

Item Its My will that My S^d Sons Job & Abner give each of them a Cow, to my s^d Grandaughter Sarah, when she arrives at ye aforesaid age. If she Marries befor said age, she is to be paid when she marries

Item I give & bequeath to My Grandson James, ye Son of My S^d Son Abner My Gun.

Item I will that My s^d Sons Job & Abner pay My funeral Charges & all My Lawfull Debts,

Item I do hereby Constitute Make and ordain My S^d Sons Job & Abner My Sole Executors * * *

James Clements

[Witnesses] Samuel Russell, Samuel Rendel Juner, Daniel Pike.

[Proved Oct. 31, 1764.]

[Sarah Clements, widow, accepts the terms of the will and waives inventory Oct. 31, 1764; witnesses, James Pike, Moses Stevens.]

[Bond of Job Clements and Abner Clements, with Samuel Randall, gentleman, as surety, all of Somersworth, in the sum of £10,000, Oct. 31, 1764, for the execution of the will; witnesses, John Sullivan, William Vaughan.]

JOHN YOUNG   1758   KINGSTON

[Administration on the estate of John Young of Kingston, wheelwright, granted to Dorothy Young of Kingston, widow, Sept. 27, 1758.]

[Probate Records, vol. 21, p. 58.]

[Bond of Dorothy Young, with Benjamin Cilley, yeoman, and Aaron Young, millwright, as sureties, all of Kingston, in the sum of £2000, Sept. 27, 1758, for the administration of the estate; witnesses, David Sewall, Jonathan Sanborn.]

[Inventory, Jan. 30, 1759; amount, £4037. 6. 0; signed by Thomas Eakens and James Proctor.]

[Moses Young, aged about 19 years, makes choice of his uncle, Jonathan Young of Kingston, gentleman, as his guardian Feb. 5, 1759; witnesses, John Sleeper, Edward Sargent, Nathaniel Etheridge.]

[Guardianship of Moses Young, minor, aged more than 14 years, son of John Young, granted to Jonathan Young of Kingston, gentleman, Feb. 6, 1759.]

[Probate Records, vol. 21, p. 192.]

[Bond of Jonathan Young, with Aaron Young and Benjamin Sanborn as sureties, all of Kingston, in the sum of £500, Feb. 6, 1759, for the guardianship of Moses Young, son of John Young of Kingston, yeoman, deceased; witnesses, Nathaniel Huntoon, Jacob Garland.]

[List of claims against the estate, June 10, 1760; amount, £1237. 8. 7; signed by Jeremy Webster and William Parker.]

[Warrant, Feb. 14, 1760, authorizing Jeremy Webster, Jonathan Greeley, Josiah Bartlett, physician, William Parker, gentleman, and Thomas Batchelder, joiner, all of Kingston, to set off the widow's dower.]

Province of New Hamps^r

Pursuant to Warrant from the Honb^{le} Court of Probate of Wills &c for s^d Province We the subscribers have proceeded & set off to Dorothy Tompson now the wife of Thomas Thompson formerly Widow & Relict of John Young Late of Kingstown in s^d Province deceasd her Dower (or Thirds) in the Estate of her former Husband the s^d John Young described & Bounded as followeth viz: all the Land belonging to the deceas'd in his Life time that Lays on the Easterly side of the High way going by Alder Meadow Mill (so Called) to the North Rode (so Called) and on the Easterly side of the Brook that runs from the s^d mill till it Comes into Lieu^t Samuel Colcords Land as it lays & is Bounded; seven acres be it more or Less; as witness our hands the 3^d day of March Anno: dom: 1760

        Jeremy Webster
        Wm Parker
        Thomas Bachelder

[Account of Thomas Thompson and his wife Dorothy, administratrix; receipts, £3661. 3. 0; expenditures, £1838. 7. 2; mentions "Sundries in Inventory by mistake which were given by said Deceased in his life time to one of his Sons for house keeping .... maintenance of a Child under 7 years 2 years 3 Months"; allowed Nov. 14, 1760.]

WILLIAM MORRISON 1758   NOTTINGHAM

[Administration on the estate of William Morrison of Nottingham, yeoman, granted to James Morrison of Nottingham Sept. 27, 1758.]

[Probate Records, vol. 21, p. 65.]

[Bond of James Morrison, with Thomas Simpson and James Kelsey as sureties, all of Nottingham, yeomen, in the sum of

£2000, Sept. 27, 1758, for the administration of the estate; witnesses, William Parker, David Sewall.]

THEOPHILUS COLBY   1758   SANDOWN

[Administration on the estate of Theophilus Colby of Sandown, yeoman, granted to Priscilla Colby, widow, Sept. 27, 1758.]

[Probate Records, vol. 21, p. 76.]

[Bond of Priscilla Colby, with Benjamin Tucker of Sandown, yeoman, and John Woodman of Hampstead, cooper, as sureties, in the sum of £2000, Sept. 27, 1758, for the administration of the estate; witnesses, John Muzzey, John Hogg.]

[Warrant, Sept. 27, 1758, authorizing John Hogg, gentleman, and John Muzzey, yeoman, both of Hampstead, to appraise the estate.]

[Inventory, attested Oct. 2, 1758; amount, £846. 5. 0; signed by John Hogg and John Muzzey.]

[Account of the administratrix; receipts, £891. 15. 0; expenditures, £595. 8. 6; mentions "maintaining 1 of the Deceas'd Children 3½ years She being 7 years old in May 1759 . . . . Ditto another Child 4¾ Years She being now of that Age"; allowed Nov. 26, 1761.]

SAMUEL FLANDERS   1758   BRENTWOOD

[Administration on the estate of Samuel Flanders of Brentwood, yeoman, granted to Mary Flanders, widow, Sept. 27, 1758.]

[Probate Records, vol. 21, p. 76.]

[Bond of Mary Flanders, with Orlando Weed of Brentwood and Benjamin Cilley of Kingston as sureties, in the sum of £500,

Sept. 27, 1758, for the administration of the estate; witnesses, William Parker, David Sewall.]

[Warrant, Sept. 27, 1758, authorizing Orlando Weed and Joseph Godfrey, both of Brentwood, yeomen, to appraise the estate.]

[Inventory, Oct. 19, 1758; amount, £4010. 6. 0; signed by Orlando Weed and Joseph Godfrey.]

[Account of the administratrix; receipts, £1542. 6. 0, personal estate; expenditures, £767. 18. 6; allowed Oct. 31, 1759.]

[Warrant, Nov. 1, 1759, authorizing Daniel Beede, Joseph Godfrey, Ebenezer Sleeper, Jonathan Cram, and Leander Weed, all of Brentwood, to set off the widow's dower.]

[Warrant, March 25, 1761, to the same parties to divide the real estate.]

[Additional account of expenditures by the administratrix; amount, £74. 0. 0; Onesiphorus Flanders, Samuel Flanders, and Mehitabel Flanders certify, May 27, 1761, that their mother has done the work on the cellar as charged; Daniel Beede and Edward Locke certify to the same; allowed May 27, 1761.]

Province of } To the Hon[ble] Richard Wibird Esq[r] Judge of
New Hamp[r] } the Probate of wills &c for said Province

Whereas by your Hon[rs] warrant we y[e] subscribers ware appointed a Committee to divide the Real Estate of Samuel Flanders Late of Brintwood in said Province deceas[d] Intestate to & amonge the widow and Childran of the said deceas[d] agreeable to Law Accordingly we have mett view[d] valued Divided & set off thee said Estate In shares as followeth viz

1st To Mary Flanders y[e] widow of y[e] s[d] Deceas[d] her Dower or third part as follows Begining on Lyfords Land Runing westerly Carrying the whole Bredth of y[e] s[d] Deces[ds] till it Comes to y[e] high that Leads by the said deces[d] house & binding on Every part of y[e] East side of s[d] way & on the west side of Said way

Begining at Eph^m Morrills Land Runing northerly on said way Twelve rods to a stump than west & by North 140^ty Rods to the head of ye Lott than Southerly Twelve Rods to s^d morrills Northwest Corner than Easterly on morril to the afore said way Seventeen acers more or Less & ye fore Room in the house with ye one half ye Celler & the one half of the Chamber &c —

The other Two thirds we have Divided & set off to and amonge ye children of said Deceas^d as followeth viz To Rhoda the 1st Share Begining at a stump Mention^d for a bounds of the widows 3^d from said stump Runs northerly on Said way Thirteen Rods & one half than to Run west & by North Carrying the Bredth of s^d 13½ Rods sixty Rods five acers more or Less and ye one Twelfth part of the Said dwelling house To Samuel the 2 & 3^d Shares Begining at a stake Being the South west Corner of Rhoades from thence Runs North 27 degrees East Twenty Rods & one half to a stake than runs west & by north Carrying ye Bredth of ye 20 & ½ Rods 80^ty Rods to the way at the head of ye Lott Ten acers more or Less & ye Sixth part of s^d House To Abigail the 4th Share begins at ye north East Corner of Sam^lls Being a stake than Runs north 27 Degrees East Ten rods & one quarter to a stake than west & by North Carrying the Bredth of 10 & ¼ Rods to the afore said way five acers more or Less & the one Twelfth part of the said house To Mary ye 5th Share Begining at a stake Being the north East Corner of Abigails from thence Runs north 27 Degrees East Ten Rods & one quarter to David Weeds Land than Runing westerly Binding northerly on weed & southerly on Abigail to ye afore said way five acers more or Less & ye Twelfth part of s^d house To Oniciphoras the 6th share Begins at a stake Being ye north East Corner of Rho^ds Share Runs northerly binding on said way Thirteen Rods & one half to a stake than west & by north Carrying ye same Bredth of 13 & ½ Rods to Sam^lls & Abigails shares five acers more or Less & ye Twelfth part of the Said House Mehetabels the 7th share Begins at the stake Last mention^d & Runs northerly binding on said way thirteen Rods & two thirds to David Weeds Land than west & by north Carrying the Bredth of thirteen Rods & two thirds of a rod to Marys Share five acers more or Less & ye twelfth part of the said house

The above Division was made by us the subscribers this 30th day of march Anno Dom 1761 According to the Best of our Judgment & Discretion

>Ebenezer Sleeper
>Joseph Godfry
>Daniel Beede
>Committee

JOSIAH HUNTOON 1758 NEWMARKET

[Administration on the estate of Josiah Huntoon of Newmarket, cordwainer, granted to Joanna Huntoon of Newmarket, widow, Sept. 27, 1758.]

[Probate Records, vol. 21, p. 91.]

[Bond of Joanna Huntoon, with Edward Hilton and Thomas French, yeomen, as sureties, all of Newmarket, in the sum of £500, Sept. 27, 1758, for the administration of the estate; witnesses, Daniel Huntoon, Mary Hilton.]

[Warrant, Sept. 27, 1758, authorizing Charles Rundlett and Josiah Hilton, both of Newmarket, yeomen, to appraise the estate.]

[Inventory, attested Nov. 29, 1758; amount, £1136. 0. 0; signed by Josiah Hilton and Charles Rundlett.]

PETER COCHRAN 1758 AMHERST

[Administration on the estate of Peter Cochran of Souhegan West, yeoman, granted to Jane Moore of Londonderry, widow, Sept. 28, 1758.]

[Probate Records, vol. 21, p. 163.]

[Bond of Jane Moore, with Samuel Moore and Robert Moore, yeomen, as sureties, all of Londonderry, in the sum of £500, Sept. 28, 1758, for the administration of the estate; witnesses, Agnes Moore, Mary Moore.]

[Warrant, Sept. 28, 1758, authorizing Robert Clark and John Wallace, both of Londonderry, yeomen, to appraise the estate; mentions Jane Moore as sister of the deceased.]

[Inventory, attested Dec. 12, 1758; amount, £1306. 5. 0; signed by John Wallace and Robert Clark.]

[Additional inventory, Sept. 22, 1760; amount, £92. 15. 0; signed as above.]

[Account of the administratrix; receipts, £1128. 15. 0; personal estate; expenditures, £442. 4. 0; allowed Sept. 23, 1760.]

JOHN HAZELTON   1758   CHESTER

[Administration on the estate of John Hazelton of Chester, yeoman, granted to Mary Hazelton of Chester, widow, Sept. 27, 1758.]

[Probate Records, vol. 21, p. 97.]

[Bond of Mary Hazelton, with Samuel Emerson and Daniel Webster, yeoman, as sureties, all of Chester, in the sum of £500, Sept. 27, 1758, for the administration of the estate; witnesses, Thomas Wells, Nathaniel Emerson.]

[Inventory, Oct. 9, 1758; amount, £7135. 13. 0; signed by Thomas Wells and Daniel Webster.]

[Account of the administratrix; receipts, £2715. 13. 0; expenditures, £237. 12. 0; mentions two children under 7 years of age; allowed Sept. 26, 1759.]

[Warrant, May 30, 1766, authorizing Samuel Emerson, Thomas Wells, gentleman, Ephraim Hazelton, Thomas Hazelton, yeomen, and Thomas Wells, Jr., husbandman, all of Chester, to divide the real estate.]

[Probate Records, vol. 24, p. 410.]

Province of } We the Subscribers being appointed by the Newhampshire } Honorabl Judge of Probat for Said Province to Set of and Divide the Real Estate of John Hasseltine of Chester Decased agreable to a warrant sent to us have Don it as followeth —

first we have set of to mary Hall Late wife of the Said Deceased ten acrs of Land for hir thirds in the homstead Laying on the Southerly Side bounded first at the Southeasterly Corner at a Stake and Stons then Runing westerly by Deacon Hasseltine Land one Hundred Rods to a Stake and stons by Jeams Akins Land then abouth north East by s^d aikins Land Seventeen Rods to a Stake and Stons then Runing about South East to a stake and stons by the High way then by s^d High way fifteen Rods to the first bounds mentioned allowing hir one third of the house on the Same but Reserving Liberty and a Priveledg for Sam^{ll} Hasseltine to Improve the other parte of s^d house as he sees Cause

2^{ly} we have set of to Sam^{ll} Hasseltine Elder Son of the Deceased a Duble Shear Containing twenty acrs of Land more or Les Laying on the homstead Laying on both sids of the high way the first peace Laying on the west side and is bounded Eastly on s^d High way Southerly on what Land we set of for thirds and Northwesterly on Land Now in poseson of Jeams and John Akens the other peace about six Acrs Laying on the East Side of the high way boundering on s^d high way Southerly on the High way Leading to the Saw mill Easterly on majer tolfords Land and Northerly on Land in Poseson of John Akens —

3^{ly} we have set of one single Shear to Jeams Hasseltine ten Acers of Land more or Les Laying in Sandown bounding westerly on the High way Leading from Chester toward Haverhill Norther on Aron Rowell Land Easterly on a High way and Southerly on williams Follinsbees Land with about one Acer

Laying on the westerly side of s^d High way Leading towards Havehrill Northerly on s^d Rowell Land westerly on Londonderry Line and southerly on s^d Follinsbees Land together with fifty Acrs more or Les Laying in Chester in the second part of the Second Division that is Number fifty five Laying on the southerly side of Said Lot Boundind Southerly on Dearbons Land Easterly and westerly on Land Left for High way so taking Exactly half the wedth of Said Lot to stakes and stons at Each Ende

4^ly we have set of to Belle Hasseltine one single share Containing about seventy Acrs more or Les Laying in three peaces the first in Sandown in . . . . wests Division Next Chester Containing about 20 Acrs more or Les Bounding on the north side upon Land of Sam^ll Keens Land Southerly on Capt thomus wills Land Laying about Eight Score Rods in Length the second peace Lays by Akens mill So Called in Chester and Containing ten acres and is Bounded on Northeasterly on Jacob Hills Land Norwesterly on williams Craffords Land Southwesterly and South Easterly on Land Left for High ways the third peace Ly in Chester and Contains fifty acers more or Les Laying on the Northerly sid of that Hundred Acer Lot in the Second part of the Second Division that is Nomber fifty five and is Bounded as foleth Northerly on Land of Col^o Jonathan moultons Easterly and westerly on Land Left for High ways and Southerly on the Land we have set of to Jeams Hasseltine

5^ly we have set of to John Hasseltine one single share Containing about one Hundred and fifty Acers more or Les Laying in three peaces Laying in the township of Chester the first peace Contains the whole of that Eight acer Lot in the third Division that Number 20 as s^d Lot is Layd out and bounded as by the Records of Chester as the Same may more fuly appear the second peace Contains forty acers more or Les being one Half of that 80 Acre Lot in the s^d third Division that is Number twenty one and is not Divided the third peace Contains about thirty Acres more or Les in the forth Division it being full Half of that Sixty Acre

Lot that is Number 92 Laying near tower Hell pond not Divided
Chester march 20th 1767   Sam^{ll} Emerson
                                             Ephraim Hasseltine
                                             Thomas Hasseltine

---

SIMON GODFREY   1758   NORTH HAMPTON

[Administration on the estate of Simon Godfrey of North Hampton, cordwainer, granted to Abigail Godfrey, widow, Sept. 29, 1758.]

[Probate Records, vol. 21, p. 80.]

[Bond of Abigail Godfrey, with John Allen, yeoman, and Timothy Jones, innholder, as sureties, all of Greenland, in the sum of £500, Sept. 29, 1758, for the administration of the estate; witnesses, William Parker, David Sewall.]

[Inventory, attested Dec. 27, 1758; amount, £452. 16. 5; signed by Joseph Clark and Timothy Jones.]

[Account of the administratrix; receipts, £941. 11. 5, personal estate; expenditures, £934. 12. 6; mentions "230 Weeks maintaining One of the dec^d Children yet under 7 years old"; allowed Dec. 29, 1762.]

JOSEPH HADLEY   1758   HAMPSTEAD

The Last Will and Testament of Joseph Hadly of Hampstead in the Province of New Hampshire Yeoman * * *

first I Give and Bequeath to Annah my Dearly Beloved wife All my Household Stuf to be by her freely Posess^d and Enjoy^d and allso the Improvement of my Stock So Long as She Remains my widow (Excepting only one Cow which my Daughter Hannah is to have at my Deceese —

Secondly I Give and Bequeath to my Beloved Son Joseph the Sum of ten Pounds old tenor —

thirdly I Give and Bequeath to my Beloved Daughter Easther the Sum of ten Pounds old tenor

forthly I Give and Bequeath to my Beloved Daughter Elisabeth the Sum of ten Pounds old tenor

fifthly I Give and Bequeath to my Beloved Daughter Hannah the Sum of ten Pounds old tenor; and allso one Cow at my Deceese

Sixthly I Give and Bequeath to my Beloved Daughter Mary the Sum of ten Pounds old tenor

Seventhly I Give and Bequeath to my Belov^d Daughter Susanna the Sum of ten Pounds old tenor

Lastely I Give and Bequeath to my two Belov^d Youngest sons namely David and Daniel; whom I Likewise Constitute and Appoint the Sole Executors of this my Last Will and testament Equaly alike (and as tennants in Common and of Equal Propriatey) All and Singaler the whole of my Real and Personall Estate which I have not Disposd of above in this my Last will and testament * * * In Testimony whareof I have hereunto Sett my hand & Seal this fourth Day of occt^r Anno Domi 1758

his
Joseph + Hadly
mark

[Witnesses] Samuel +^{his} Hadly, Nicodenes Watson, John Johnson.   mark

[Proved Oct. 25, 1758.]

[Inventory, attested Feb. 24, 1759; amount, £3228. 10. 0; signed by John Johnson and Nicodemus Watson.]

JOHN OBER, JR.   1758   SALEM

[Administration on the estate of John Ober, Jr., of Salem, yeoman, granted to Anna Ober of Salem, widow, Oct. 4, 1758.]

[Probate Records, vol. 21, p. 95.]

[Bond of Anna Ober, with John Ober and Ebenezer Woodbury, yeoman, as sureties, all of Salem, in the sum of £2000, Oct. 4, 1758, for the administration of the estate; witnesses, John Dinsmoor, Andard Armour.]

[Inventory, Oct. 16, 1758; amount, £1882. 10. 0; signed by Andrew Balch and John Hall.]

ELLIOT VAUGHAN   1758   PORTSMOUTH

[Administration on the estate of Elliot Vaughan of Portsmouth granted to Anna Vaughan of Portsmouth, widow, Oct. 11, 1758.]
[Probate Records, vol. 21, p. 84.]

[Bond of Anna Vaughan, with William Bennett, gentleman, and Daniel Peirce as sureties, all of Portsmouth, in the sum of £1000, Oct. 11, 1758, for the administration of the estate; witnesses, William Parker, David Sewall.]

[Warrant, Oct. 11, 1758, authorizing Eleazer Russell and Samuel Penhallow, merchant, both of Portsmouth, to appraise the estate.]

[Inventory, Oct. 18, 1758; amount, £42,955. 14. 6; signed by Eleazer Russell and Samuel Penhallow.]

[License to the administratrix, Dec. 1, 1760, to sell "a Certain Island in Portsmouth aforesaid situate in the Northerly part of said Town near the Ferry Place to Kittery with a Ware house thereon standing".]

[Administration on the estate of Elliot Vaughan of Portsmouth granted to James Noble of Boston, Mass., Aug. 15, 1758.]
[York County, Me., Probate Records, vol. 10, p. 45.]

[Inventory of the estate in York county, Me., Nov. 9, 1758; amount, £1830. 15. 0; lands in Scarborough, Me.]
[York County, Me., Probate Records, vol. 10, p. 92.]

[Administrator's account against the estate; amount, £12. 8. 0; claims against the estate, £735. 11. 0; allowed June 21, 1759.]

[York County, Me., Probate Records, vol. 10, p. 92.]

PARKER DOLE   1758   PLAISTOW

[Administration on the estate of Parker Dole of Plaistow, cordwainer, granted to Hannah Dole of Plaistow, widow, Oct. 13, 1758.]

[Probate Records, vol. 21, p. 85.]

[Bond of Hannah Dole, with Tristram Knight, gentleman, and Timothy Ladd, yeoman, as sureties, all of Plaistow, in the sum of £1000, Oct. 13, 1758, for the administration of the estate; witnesses, Daniel Little, Joseph Little.]

[Warrant, Oct. 13, 1758, authorizing Tristram Knight and Timothy Ladd to appraise the estate.]

[Inventory, attested Oct. 16, 1758; amount, £3761. 6. 6; signed by Tristram Knight and Timothy Ladd.]

PETER ARCHDEACON   1758   PORTSMOUTH

[Administration on the estate of Peter Archdeacon of Portsmouth, mariner, granted to Andrew Clarkson of Portsmouth, merchant, Oct. 17, 1758.]

[Probate Records, vol.. 21, p. 85.]

[Bond of Andrew Clarkson, with Thomas Hart, merchant, and George Libby, mariner, as sureties, all of Portsmouth, in the sum of £500, Oct. 17, 1758, for the administration of the estate; witnesses, William Parker, David Sewall.]

[Inventory, Nov. 27, 1759; amount, £95. 5. 0; signed by Eleazer Russell and Samuel Penhallow.]

DOROTHY JACKSON   1758   PORTSMOUTH

In the Name of God amen the Nineteenth day of October in the Year of our Lord 1758, I Dorothy Jackson of Portsmouth in the Province of New Hampshire Innholder, Widow of Ephraim Jackson late of Portsmouth aforesaid Cooper Deceased being Aged and weak in body * * *

Item I Give unto My Son in law * Johnson Jackson the Sum of ten Shillings

Item; I Give unto My Son in Law Jeffry Jackson the Sum of ten Shillings —

Item, I Give unto My Son in law Joseph Jackson the Sum of ten shillings also one Carved Casse of Draws, and a Suit of White Curtains & vallins for a Bed

Item I Give unto My Son William Jackson the Sum of ten Shillings

Item I Give unto each of the Children of My Son-in-law Ephraim Jackson Deceased the Sum of five Shillings —

Item, I Give unto My Son in law John Murphy the Sum of ten Shillings

Item I Give unto My Daughter-in-law Elizabeth Churchill the Sum of Ten Shillings —

Item. I Give unto My Daughter-in-law Mary Monson the Sum of ten Shillings —

Item I Give unto My Daughter Dorothy Whipple the Sum of ten Shillings —

Item I Give unto My Daughter in law Hannah Bestow the Sum of ten Shillings —

And as to the rest and residue of My Estate both real and personal that I leave at the time of My Decease after My just Debts And funeral Charges are paid out of the Same, I Give and bequeathe the Same to and among all the before Named Children of My late Husband Ephraim Jackson Deceased Males and females viz. to Johnson Jackson, Jeffry Jackson, Joseph Jackson,

* Stepson.

William Jackson, the Children of Ephraim Jackson jun[r] Deceased, Elizabeth Churchill Mary Monson and Hannah Bestow, and to their heirs and Assigns forever to be Divided equally among the Said Children and the Children of My Said Son-in-law Ephraim that is for both the Children of My Said Son-in-law Ephraim to have one Shear, or an equal part with one of the Children of My Said Husband, equally between them both

And I the Said Dorothy Jackson Do hereby Constitute Make and Ordain Thomas Bickford of Portsmouth in New Hampshire aforesaid Schoolmaster and John Marshall of Portsmouth aforesaid Boat builder Executors * * *

Dorothy Jackson

[Witnesses] W[m] Hooker, the Mark of Mary + Stoneman, alec stonman.

[Proved Jan. 31, 1759.]

[Administration with will annexed granted to John Murphy Nov. 25, 1761.]

[Probate Records, vol. 22, p. 279.]

[Bond of John Murphy, mariner, with John Churchill, yeoman, and Nathaniel Furber, boat-builder, as sureties, all of Portsmouth, in the sum of £500, Nov. 25, 1761, for the administration, with will annexed, of the estate; witness, William Parker.]

[Warrant, Jan. 26, 1763, authorizing Eleazer Russell and Samuel Penhallow, merchant, both of Portsmouth, to receive claims against the estate.]

[List of claims, Nov. 17, 1763; amount, £1541. 11. 2; signed by Eleazer Russell and Samuel Penhallow.]

[Account of the administrator; receipts, £1528. 15. 8; expenditures, £618. 15. 8; allowed March 10, 1764.]

[Settlement of claims; amount of claims, £1541. 11. 2; amount distributed, £910. 0. 0; allowed March 21, 1764.]

LEONARD CUMMINGS 1758 LONDONDERRY

[Administration on the estate of Leonard Cummings of Londonderry, yeoman, granted to Jane Cummings of Londonderry, widow, Oct. 25, 1758.]

[Probate Records, vol. 21, p. 91.]

[Bond of Jane Cummings, widow, with John Senter and Samuel Senter, husbandmen, as sureties, all of Londonderry, in the sum of £1000, Oct. 25, 1758, for the administration of the estate; witnesses, John Lovewell, Jonathan Lovewell.]

[Warrant, Oct. 25, 1758, authorizing William Butterfield and Samuel Senter, both of Londonderry, yeomen, to appraise the estate.]

[Inventory, Nov. 25, 1758; amount, £3182. 19. 0; signed by William Butterfield and Samuel Senter.]

[Guardianship of Jerathmeel Cummings and Rachel Cummings, minors, aged more than 14 years, and Silas Cummings, aged less than 14 years, children of Leonard Cummings, granted to Joel Parkhurst of Dunstable, Mass., yeoman, Feb. 21, 1766.]

[Probate Records, vol. 24, p. 172.]

[Bond of Joel Parkhurst of Dunstable, Mass., yeoman, with Noah Tarbox of Londonderry and John Fletcher of Dunstable as sureties, in the sum of £5,000, Feb. 21, 1766, for the guardianship of Jerathmeel Cummings and Rachel Cummings, aged more than 14 years, and Silas Cummings, aged less than 14 years; witnesses, Leod Tarbox, John Clark, Eleazer Farwell, James Whitney.]

[Bond of Joel Parkhurst, husbandman, with Joseph Spaulding, husbandman, as surety, both of Dunstable, Mass., in the sum of £500, Sept. 14, 1769, for the guardianship of Silas Cummings, minor, in his fifteenth year, son of Leonard Cummings; witnesses, Joseph Lee and Nathan Barrett.]

[Middlesex Co., Mass., Probate Files.]

BENJAMIN DAVIS   1758   PLAISTOW

[Administration on the estate of Benjamin Davis of Plaistow, yeoman, granted to Ruth Davis of Plaistow, widow, Oct. 25, 1758.]

[Probate Records, vol. 21, p. 86.]

[Bond of Ruth Davis, with James Pike of Plaistow, yeoman, and John Johnson of Hampstead as sureties, in the sum of £1000, Oct. 25, 1758, for the administration of the estate; witnesses, William Parker, William Gilchrist.]

[Warrant, Oct. 25, 1758, authorizing James Pike and Moses Stevens, both of Plaistow, yeomen, to appraise the estate.]

[Inventory, Jan. 26, 1759; amount, £3804. 7. 8; signed by James Pike and Moses Stevens.]

[Account of the administratrix; receipts, £1162. 5. 2, personal estate; expenditures, £348. 8. 4; mentions "maintaing 3 of the dec^{ds} Children Under Seven years old Since his decease viz Ruth from Septr 16, 1758 to June 19th 1759, is 39 weeks (then Seven years old) Moses from D^o to Octr 31 1759, (said Child born Jany 27, 1755) 57 weeks Amos from D^o to D^o (born May 8, 1757) 57 weeks"; allowed Oct. 31, 1759.]

DANIEL LADD   1758   EPPING

[Administration on the estate of Daniel Ladd of Epping, yeoman, granted to Alice Ladd of Epping, widow, Oct. 25, 1758.]

[Probate Records, vol. 21, p. 91.]

[Bond of Alice Ladd, with Philip Wadleigh of Exeter and Joseph Wadleigh of Brentwood, yeomen, as sureties, in the sum of £500, Oct. 25, 1758, for the administration of the estate; witnesses, James Stoodley, Jr., William Parker.]

[Warrant, Oct. 25, 1758, authorizing Ezekiel Brown and Abraham Brown, both of Epping, yeomen, to appraise the estate.]

[Inventory, attested Dec. 26, 1758; amount, £1785. 11. 0; signed by Ezekiel Brown and Abraham Brown.]

[Guardianship of Nathaniel Ladd, minor, aged more than 14 years, son of Daniel Ladd, granted to John Dow of Epping Jan. 30, 1760.]

[Probate Records, vol. 21, p. 384.]

[Bond of John Dow, yeoman, with Daniel Tilton of Exeter, trader, and Richard Hoyt of Epping, yeoman, as sureties, in the sum of £500, Jan. 30, 1760, for the guardianship of Nathaniel Ladd; witnesses, William Parker, John Langdon, Jr.]

JOHN PURMORT   1758   EXETER

[Administration on the estate of John Purmort of Exeter, joiner, granted to Hannah Purmort Oct. 25, 1758.]

[Probate Records, vol. 21, p. 213.]

[Bond of Hannah Purmort, widow, with Ephraim Robinson, gentleman, and Daniel Grant, cabinet-maker, as sureties, all of Exeter, in the sum of £1000, Oct. 25, 1758, for the administration of the estate; witnesses, Benjamin Dow, Noah Emery.]

[Warrant, Oct. 25, 1758, authorizing John Gilman and Ephraim Robinson, shopkeeper, both of Exeter, to appraise the estate.]

[Inventory, Jan. 1, 1759; amount, £9206. 8. 6; signed by John Gilman, Jr., and Ephraim Robinson.]

[List of claims against the estate, Sept. 20, 1760; amount, £6914. 3. 5; signed by John Gilman, Jr., and Ephraim Robinson.]

WILLIAM CUMMINGS   1758   NASHUA

[Administration on the estate of William Cummings of Dunstable, yeoman, granted to Lucy Cummings of Dunstable, widow, Oct. 25, 1758.]

[Probate Records, vol. 21, p. 91.]

[Bond of Lucy Cummings, with Zaccheus Lovewell and Noah Johnson, husbandman, as sureties, all of Dunstable, in the sum of £500, Oct. 25, 1758, for the administration of the estate; witnesses, Samuel Cummings, Jonathan Lovewell.]

[Inventory, Nov. 20, 1758; amount, £8210. 3. 4; signed by Samuel Cummings and Francis Worcester, Jr.]

[Petition of the widow for an allowance from the estate, no date, "having a great fammily and Divers Small Children and one but about a month old."; witness, Whitcomb Powers.]

[Account of the settlement of the estate; receipts, £2983. 9. 8; expenditures, £3160. 1. 3; allowed June 24, 1761.]

[Caveat of Stephen Powers of Hollis in his own behalf, and as an heir to the estate, Jan. 30, 1762, against the allowance of the account of Lucy Cummings, administratrix, without notice.]

[Warrant, Oct. 27, 1763, authorizing Samuel Cummings, Francis Worcester, Jr., and Benjamin Blanchard, Jr., all of Hollis, to set off the widow's dower to Lucy Kendall, wife of Ebenezer Kendall of Dunstable, Mass., yeoman.]

Province of New Hamp^r } Pursuant to a Warrant to us from the Hono^{ble} Richard Wibord Esqr Judge of Probats of Wills for the Province of New Hampsheir To seat of to Lucy Kendall late widow of Deacon William Cumings late of Dunstable Deceased her Part or Dower of thirds in the Deceseds Estate During her life—we have Seat of to the said Lucy Kendall about 40: acres on the westerly side the Homsted as is Discribed in the Plan which we have taken of the same the Dwelling House stands on the Land set of to the s^d Lucy and she is to have the west End of the House the lowar rom Chamber and garat and one half of the sellor with one half of the liberty of the Enterry and stears in to the Chamber and garrat with liberty of Baken in the oven in the East rom and the said Lucy is to have one half of the Barn with Sutable yard rom and liberty of passing

and repassing to and from the Barn and the Children of this
. . . . to have the East End of the Dwelling House from the
garret to the bottom with half the sollor and Enterry and stears
and sutable yeard rom for laying wood and the s^d Children is to
have the benifit of the old House that stands on the Said Lucys
thirds

Holles March the 6th 1764   Francis Worcester
                                           Benjamin Blanchard
                                           Saml Cumings

[Additional account of the settlement of the estate; receipts, £2237. 11. 8; expenditures, £3030. 9. 9; mentions "Boarding Clothing & Maintaining Three children under seven years of age (viz) Caleb Cumings from Septem^r 1, 1759 till January 1st 1762, at which time he arived to Seven years. . . . Joshua Cumings from Septem^r 1st 1759 till Feb. 1st 1764 at which time he was seven years of age . . . . Larnard Cumings from January 31 1759, till this day, or untill he shall be seven years of age"; allowed March 27, 1764.]

[Guardianship of Caleb Cummings, Joshua Cummings, and Larned Cummings, aged less than 14 years, children of William Cummings, granted to Samuel Hobart April 11, 1764.]

[Probate Records, vol. 23, p. 214.]

[Bond of Samuel Hobart, with John Hale and John Atwell, joiner, as sureties, all of Hollis, in the sum of £100, April 11, 1764, for the guardianship of Caleb Cummings, Joshua Cummings, and Larned Cummings; witnesses, Jonathan Johnson, John Williams.]

[Guardianship of Philip Cummings, minor, aged more than 14 years, son of William Cummings, granted to William Cummings April 23, 1764.]

[Probate Records, vol. 23, p. 218.]

[Bond of William Cummings of Dunstable, yeoman, with Stephen Powers and John Atwell, yeoman, both of Hollis, as sureties, in the sum of £3000, April 23, 1764, for the guardianship of Philip Cummings; witnesses, Samuel Hobart, Joshua Boynton.]

[Warrant, April 27, 1764, authorizing Samuel Cummings, John Hale, Francis Worcester, Jr., yeoman, Benjamin Blanchard, Jr., and David Hobart, gentleman, to appraise the remainder of the real estate for settlement upon the oldest son. Return of appraisal at £1866. o. o, April 30, 1764, signed by Samuel Cummings, Francis Worcester, John Hale, and Benjamin Blanchard.

A note adds "Childrens Names, William Philip, Lucy, Bridgett Elisabeth Rebecca Caleb: Joshua Larnard but Ebenezer has got a deed of gift of 100 acres of Land which was apprisd at £800 which is more than his Equal, or Double Share."]

[Appraisal of the two thirds of the real estate at £70. o. o sterling, attested July 3, 1765; signed by Samuel Cummings, Francis Worcester, and Benjamin Blanchard; order of court settling the estate upon William Cummings, second son, the oldest son, Ebenezer, having received his share.]

[Guardianship of Caleb Cummings, minor, aged more than 14 years, son of William Cummings, granted to Samuel Tarbell June 14, 1770.]

[Probate Records, vol. 5, p. 232.]

[Bond of Samuel Tarbell of Mason, with Stephen Powers and John Atwell of Hollis as sureties, in the sum of £500, June 14, 1770, for the guardianship of Caleb Cummings; witnesses, Samuel French, Ephraim Lund.]

[Bond of Samuel Tarbell, with Nathan Coburn and David Sloane as sureties, all of Mason, in the sum of £500, March 13, 1771, for the guardianship of Caleb Cummings; witnesses, David Farnsworth, Richard Lawrence.]

DANIEL TITCOMB   1758   DOVER

In the Name of God Amen, I Daniel Titcomb of Dover in ye Province of New Hamps^r in New-England Blacksmith; Being Exercised with great Bodily Infirmities * * *

Imprimis. I Give to my Beloved Wife Anne Titcomb the free & full use & Improvement of ye Westerly lower Room in My Dwelling House, & Such a Priviledge in ye Celler under it as She Shall have Occation of for her own use; And also the use and Improvement of ye one half Part of my Barn, During ye Term of her Continuing my widow; I also Give unto my S^d wife ye one half Part of the Produce of my Homestead Land of every kind, & my will is that ye one half Part of ye Hay Produced by my Mowing Land, & one half Part of ye Crops of every kind, Produced by my Tillage Land, Shall be well & Seasonably Secured & Housed, by my Son Daniel Titcomb, or at his Cost & Charg, for ye Use of my S^d wife, Yearly & every Year, During ye afores'd Term of her Continuing my widow; But in Case She Shall Marry, then my Will is that She Shall have her Proper Dowry out of my Estate, as by Law Established. My will also further is that my S^d Wife Shall have ye free liberty of using So much of ye fire-Wood Standing & Being upon my Said Land as She Shall have occation of to Support one Comfortable fire During ye afores'd Term of her Continuing my widow. I also Give unto my S^d Wife all my Household Goods, Beds Beding & furniture belonging unto them, & also all my Live Stock of Cattle Sheep & Swine to her own Disposal.

Item I Give unto my Son John Titcomb fifty Pounds, old Tenor, to be Paid him by my S^d Son Daniel Titcomb, within ye Term of Six Months, after my Decease, & ye Decease of my S^d Wife.

Item, I Give unto my S^d Son Daniel Titcomb, & to his Heirs & Assigns for ever, all my S^d Homestead Land, together with my Dwelling House, Barn, Smiths Shop, & all other Buildings Standing & Being upon S^d Land, Excepting ye Use & Improvement of Such a Part of yᵉ Sᵈ Dwelling House & Barn, & Such a Part of yᵉ Produce of Sᵈ Land as I have in & by this Will, allow'd & Given to my Sᵈ wife, During yᵉ Term of her Continuing my widow, and Such a Part as is Allowed her by Law During yᵉ Term of her natural life. I also Give to my Sᵈ Son Daniel all my Smiths Tools & Utensils.

Item. I Give unto my Son David Titcomb fifty Pounds, old Tenor, to be Paid him by my Sᵈ Son Daniel Titcomb, within yᵉ Term of one Year after my Decease, & yᵉ Decease of my Sᵈ Wife.

Item. I Give unto my Son Enoch Titcom Two Hundred Pounds, old Tenor, to be Paid him, by my Sᵈ Son Daniel Titcomb, within yᵉ Term of Two Years after my Decease & yᵉ Decease of my Sᵈ wife.

Item. I Give unto my Son Benjamin Titcomb & to his Heirs & Assigns for ever, all my Land in Rochester being yᵉ one moiety or half Part of a Tract of Land which I together with John Plumer of Sᵈ Rochester lately Purchased of Joseph Watson of Dover afores'd & which Tract is now Posses'd by my Self & Sᵈ Plumer as Tenents in Common.

Item, I Give unto my Daughter, Sarah Winget one Hundred Pounds, old Tenor, to be Paid her by my Sᵈ Son Daniel Titcomb, within yᵉ Term of one Year after my Decease & yᵉ Decease of my Sᵈ Wife.

Item I Give unto my Daughter Mary Titcomb Two Hundred Pounds, old Tenor, to be Paid her by my Sᵈ Son Daniel Titcomb within yᵉ Term of Two Years after my Decease, & yᵉ Decease of my sᵈ wife. And my Will also is that my Sᵈ Daughter Mary Shall have yᵉ liberty of living in that Part of my Dwelling House which I have herein Allotted & Asign'd unto my wife to live in, So long as my Sᵈ Daughter Shall live unmarried.

Item, I Give unto my Daughter Elisabeth Plumer fifty Pounds, old Tenor, to be Paid her by my Sᵈ Son Dan[ll] Titcomb within yᵉ Term of Two Years after my Decease, & yᵉ Decease of my Sᵈ Wife.

Item I Give unto my Daughter Abigail Libbe fifty Pounds, old

Tenor, to be Paid her by my S^d Son Dan^ll Titcomb within ye Term of Two Years after my Decease & ye Decease of my S^d Wife.

And I do hereby Constitute make & Ordain my S^d Wife Anne Titcomb my Sole Executrix * * * In Witness whereof I do hereunto Set my hand & Seal this Twenty Seventh Day of October Anno Domini one Thousand Seven Hundred & fifty Eight, & in ye Thirty Second Year of ye Reign of his Majesty King George ye Second.

Daniel Titcomb

[Witnesses] William Shackford, Benj^a Lebby, Peter Tibbets.
[Proved March 28, 1759.]

[Bond of Ann Titcomb, widow, with Daniel Titcomb, yeoman, James Kielle, tailor, and John Titcomb as sureties, all of Dover, in the sum of £6000, March 28, 1759, for the execution of the will; witnesses, John Clark, William Shackford, and D. Sewall.]

NATHAN MANN   1758   WINDHAM

[Mary Mann of Windham, being, "Infirm of bodey," renounces administration on the estate of her husband, Nathan Mann, in favor of James Wilson, chief creditor; dated at Londonderry, Oct. 30, 1758; witnesses, Samuel Barr, John Barr.]

[Administration on the estate of Nathan Mann of Windham, husbandman, granted to James Wilson of Londonderry, yeoman, Nov. 21, 1758.]

[Probate Records, vol. 21, p. 102.]

[Bond of James Wilson, yeoman, with William Crawford of Chester and Gain Armour of Windham, yeomen, as sureties, in the sum of £2000, Nov. 21, 1758, for the administration of the estate; witnesses, Samuel Barr, John Wilson.]

[Inventory, Nov. 25, 1758; amount, £2426. 8. 0; signed by Samuel Barr and James Dunlop.]

[Account of the administrator; receipts, £948. 8. 0, personal estate; expenditures, £777. 14. 2; allowed Sept. 27, 1759.]

ANN CREIGHTON 1758 EXETER

[Administration on the estate of Ann Creighton of Exeter, widow, granted to Thomas Creighton of Exeter, shipwright, Nov. 14, 1758.]

[Probate Records, vol. 21, p. 95.]

[Bond of Thomas Creighton, with Nathaniel Folsom, gentleman, and Jonathan Lord, tailor, as sureties, all of Exeter, in the sum of £1000, Nov. 14, 1758, for the administration of the estate; witnesses, William Parker, Mary Parker.]

[Warrant, May 28, 1764, authorizing Samuel Gilman, Jr., Nathaniel Folsom, Noah Emery, gentlemen, Daniel Tilton, and Theophilus Gilman, traders, all of Exeter, to divide lands held in common by Martha Pearson of Portsmouth, widow, and the heirs of Ann Creighton.]

[Probate Records, vol. 23, p. 350.]

Province of { Pursuant to a Warrant from the Hon[ble] New Hampshire Richard Wibird Esq[r] Judge of the Probate of Wills &c for Said Province, Appointing us the Subscribers a Committee to make Partition & Division of Lands held in Common & undivided by Martha Pearson of Portsmouth in Said Province Widow, and the Heirs of Ann Creighton Deceas'd (Agreeable to a Special Act or Law of Said Province Authorizing the Judge of Probate for Said Province for the time being to make Partition & Division of Said Lands as he is by Law Enabled to do of the Estates of Persons dying Intestate) and to

Set forth Each part by metes & bounds To Hold to the respective parties in Severalty —

We have Accordingly made Partition & Division of Said Lands in manner Following — Namely We have Proportioned & Set off to the Heirs of the Said Ann Creighton Forty rods of Land in Exeter in Said Province Adjoyning to Lands heretofore Jabez Smith's Deceas'd & Lying on the Northerly Side of the road leading from the Great Bridge in Exeter towards Stratham & begins at the road aforesaid About two feet Eastward of the South Easterly Corner of a Shop or Storehouse lately belonging to & occupied by the said Jabez Smith Deceas'd, and from thence to run South Seventy five Degrees East Sixty feet by Said road to a Stake & Stones, & from thence to run North Four Degrees West Eleven rods Seven feet & three Inches to a Stake, and thence North Seventy five Degrees West Sixty feet to a Stake and from thence South four Degrees East Eleven rods Seven feet and three Inches partly by Lands of Joshua Wilson & partly by Lands lately the Said Jabez Smith's, now in Possession of James Thurstin to a Stake and Stones where it begins. And also about an Acre & a half and thirty three rods of Land in Said Exeter bounded as follows viz beginning at the Westerly Corner of Eight acres of Land held in Common by the Said Parties at a Stake Standing where Hampton road & Stratham road meet Exeter road And from thence to run South fifty Eight Degrees East by Hampton road aforesaid Eighteen rods, thence South Seventy Degrees East Ten rods, Thence South Eighty Degrees East Six rods by Said road, Thence North Ten Degrees East Six rods to a Stake, Thence about North Fifty Six Degrees West Twenty Seven rods and one foot to Stratham road aforesaid and from thence by Said Stratham road Twelve rods to the Corner of the Eight acres aforesaid begun at. And also Two Acres & Seventy rods of Land in Exeter aforesaid bounded as Follows viz Begining at the North Easterly Corner of the Land Lately Called & known by the name of Joshua Wilson's Field, Adjoining to Theophilus Smith Esq^{rs} Land at Stratham road aforesaid & from thence to run South thirty Degrees West Twenty five rods by Said road to a Stake and Stones, And then to begin again at the aforesaid North Easterly Corner and to run North forty five Degrees West Five rods & an half by Said Smith's land, and thence West Twenty five rods, Thence South about Thirty two Degrees East by Joshua Wilson's land to the Southerly End of the Twenty five rods line aforesaid at Said Stratham Road, All which Pieces of Land as before Described we have Sett off to the Said Heirs of the Said Ann Creighton Deceas'd To Hold to them in Severalty —

And to the Said Martha Pearson We have Proportioned and Set off Forty rods of Land in Exeter aforesaid on the Northerly Side of the road Leading from Exeter Great Bridge towards Stratham and bounded as Follows viz begining at a Stake Standing by Said Road at the South Easterly Corner of the aforementioned Forty rods of Land herein before Set off to the Said Heirs of Ann Creighton Deceas'd and from thence to run by the Same Forty rods of Land North four Degrees West Eleven rods Seven feet & three Inches, thence South Seventy five Degrees East by Joshua Wilson's land Sixty feet, Thence South four Degrees East by Said Wilson's land Eleven rods Seven feet & three Inches to the road aforesaid Leading towards Stratham, to a Stake & Stones Thence North Seventy five Degrees West by the road aforesaid Sixty feet to the Stake begun at — And also about Six Acres and Forty Seven rods of Land in Said Exeter lying South Eastwardly of the aforesaid Stratham road & Northerly of the Said Hampton road and Bounded as Follows viz Begining at Stratham road aforesaid At a Stake Standing at the North westerly Corner of the aforesaid one acre & a half & thirty three rods of land before Set off to the Said Heirs of Ann Creighton Deceas'd, and from thence to run about South Fifty Six Degrees East Twenty Seven rods & one foot to a Stake, Thence South Ten Degrees West Six rods to Hampton road aforesaid, Thence by Said road South Eighty Degrees East two rods, Thence South Eighty five Degrees East Twenty four rods & an half by the Said Hampton road, Thence North Twenty three Degrees West about Forty Eight rods to Stratham road aforesaid, Thence South about Forty Eight Degrees West about

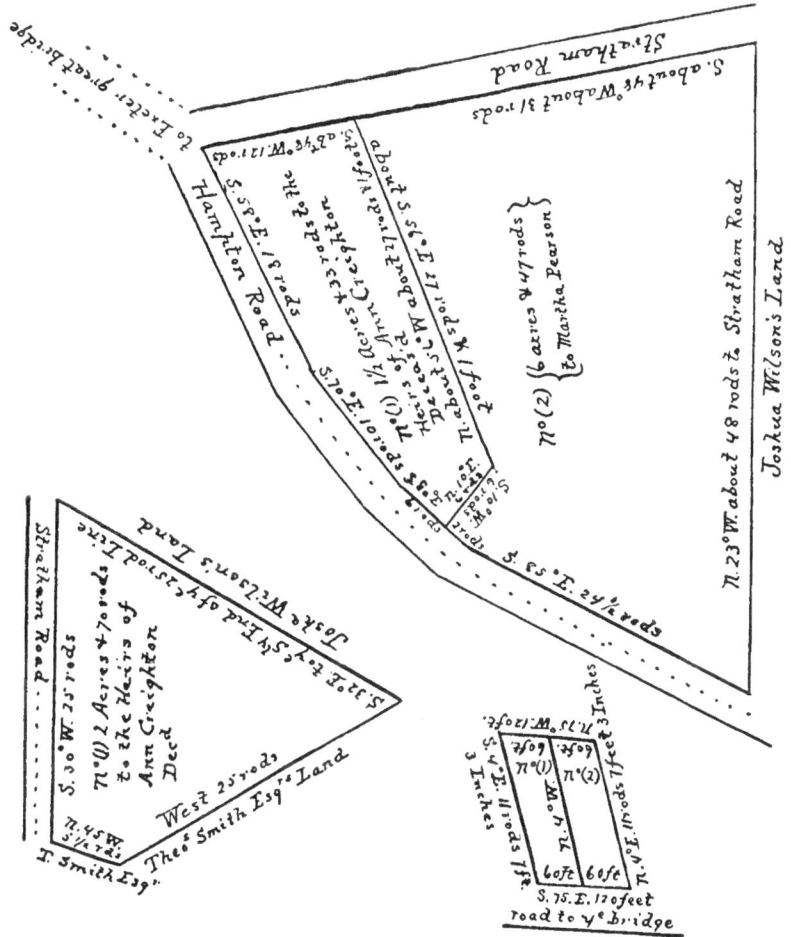

thirty one rods by Said Stratham Road to the Corner begun at — Which Two pieces of Land last bounded & Described we have Sett off to the Said Martha Pearson To Hold to her in Severalty

— Done at Exeter this Twenty Eighth day of July Anno Domini 1764.

Sam¹ Gilman j^r
Noah Emery
Nath¹¹ Folsom
Theo^s Gilman
} Com'ittee

SAMUEL MERRILL, JR. 1758   HUDSON

[Administration on the estate of Samuel Merrill of Nottingham West, husbandman, granted to Rebecca Merrill of Nottingham West, widow, Nov. 17, 1758.]

[Probate Records, vol. 21, p. 171.]

[Bond of Rebecca Merrill, with Ebenezer Blodgett and Jeremiah Blodgett, housewrights, as sureties, all of Nottingham West, in the sum of £2000, Nov. 17, 1758, for the administration of the estate; witnesses, Thomas Colburn, Jonathan Lovewell.]

[Inventory, Dec. 4, 1758; amount, £471. 3. 6; signed by Thomas Colburn and George Burns.]

[Account of the administratrix; receipts. £963. 17. 4, personal estate; expenditures, £709. 11. 0; mentions "maintenance of 2 children of the said Deceased under the age of seven years from the last of September 1758 to this day"; allowed May 8, 1760.]

[Bond of Samuel Merrill of Nottingham West, with Ezekiel Chase of Nottingham West and Joseph Butler of Pelham as sureties, in the sum of £1000, May 16, 1760, for the guardianship of Abel Merrill and Rachel Merrill, aged less than 14 years, children of Samuel Merrill, Jr.; witnesses, Eleazer Whiting, Hugh Tallant.]

[Guardianship of Abel Merrill, minor, aged more than 14 years, son of Samuel Merrill, Jr., granted to Daniel Merrill April 14, 1763.]

[Probate Records, vol. 22, p. 544.]

[Bond of Daniel Merrill, yeoman, with Nathaniel Merrill, clerk, and James Sherburne, yeoman, as sureties, all of Pelham, in the sum of £500, April 14, 1763, for the guardianship of Abel Merrill; witnesses, Catherine Parker, William Parker.]

[Bond of John Hamblett, cooper, with Amos Richardson and Josiah Hamblett, yeomen, as sureties, all of Pelham, in the sum of £10,000, March 28, 1764, for the guardianship of Isaac Merrill, aged less than 14 years, son of Samuel Merrill of Nottingham West, yeoman, deceased; witnesses, John Kimball, Samuel Davis.]

Pursuant to the order of the Judge of Probate of Wills &c for the Province of New Hampshire we the subscribers have viewed the Real Estate of Samuel Merril Ju^r Late of Nottingham west yeoman Deceased Intestate which said Estate is in Nottingham west in said Province and contains abote Forty acres bounded Northerly and Easterly by Daniel merrils Land southerly & westerly by Tyngs land and have set off to Rebecca Merrill the Widow of said Interstate her Dower being one third of the same bounded as followeth begining at the Northeast corner from thence runing westerly by Daniel Merrils land Eighty Three Rods from thence runing southerly Twenty three rods to a stake and stons from thence Runing Easterly Seventy one Rods to a stake and stons by the Town Rode thence Northerly by said roade Twenty three Rods to the Bounds first mentioned where we began —

and the Remaining two thirds of said Real Estate we Judge can not be divided amoungst the Children without Prejudice and Spoiling the whole for a settlement and we have appraised the said two thirds and Judge the present Value of it to be Twenty five Pounds five shillings & four pence Lawfull Sterling money of Great Britan Nottingham west May y[e] 4th 1769 —

George Burns
Sam[ll] moor
Henry Chase
Nehemiah Hadley
} Committee

CHRISTOPHER PRITCHARD   1758   NEWCASTLE

[Administration on the estate of Christopher Pritchard of Newcastle granted to Shadrach Bell of Newcastle Nov. 20, 1758.]

[Probate Records, vol. 21, p. 101.]

[Bond of Shadrach Bell, innholder, with Joseph Newmarch and Thomas Bell as sureties, all of Newcastle, in the sum of £500, Nov. 20, 1758, for the administration of the estate of Christopher Pritchard, mariner; witnesses, Nathaniel Sargent, Benjamin Randall.]

[Warrant, Nov. 20, 1758, authorizing Nathaniel Sargent, physician, and Benjamin Randall, mariner, both of Newcastle, to appraise the estate.]

[Inventory, Jan. 3, 1759; amount, £410. 12. 6; signed by Nathaniel Sargent and Benjamin Randall.]

[Account of the administrator; receipts, £438. 17. 0; expenditures, £228. 6. 11; allowed Nov. 23, 1759.]

WILLIAM MILLS   1758   CHESTER

[Administration on the estate of William Mills of Chester, husbandman, granted to John Mills of Chester, yeoman, Nov. 29, 1758.]

[Probate Records, vol. 21, p. 103.]

[Bond of John Mills, with Andrew Craige and John Underhill as sureties, all of Chester, yeomen, in the sum of £500, Nov. 29, 1758, for the administration of the estate; witnesses, William Parker, Benjamin Adams.]

[Inventory, Feb. 22, 1759; amount, £2363. 0. 0; signed by William Litch and James Crossett.]

THOMAS WENTWORTH 1758   SOMERSWORTH

[Administration on the estate of Thomas Wentworth of Somersworth granted to Mary Wentworth of Somersworth, widow, Nov. 29, 1758.]

[Probate Records, vol. 21, p. 107.]

[Bond of Mary Wentworth, with John Wentworth of Somersworth and Thomas Hale of Plaistow, gentlemen, as sureties, in the sum of £500, Nov. 29, 1758, for the administration of the estate; witnesses, William Parker, Cutts Shannon.]

[Warrant, Nov. 29, 1758, authorizing Moses Stevens and Benjamin Warren, both of Somersworth, tanners, to appraise the estate.]

[Inventory, Dec. 25, 1758; amount, £1925. 0. 0; signed by Moses Stevens and Benjamin Warren.]

[Account of the administratrix; receipts, £1705. 10. 0; expenditures, £1856. 18. 0; mentions "Bringing up 4 Children 500 weeks all added together"; allowed June 28, 1769.]

JOHN REDMAN   1758   NOTTINGHAM

[Administration on the estate of John Redman of Nottingham, yeoman, granted to Nicholas Smith of Brentwood, yeoman, Nov. 29, 1758.]

[Probate Records, vol. 21, p. 276.]

[Bond of Nicholas Smith, with Jeremiah Bean of Brentwood, yeoman, and Theophilus Gilman of Exeter, blacksmith, as sureties, in the sum of £1000, Nov. 29, 1758, for the administration of the estate; witnesses, Theophilus Smith, John Gilman, Jr.]

[Warrant, Nov. 29, 1758, authorizing Theophilus Smith and John Gilman, Jr., both of Exeter, to appraise the estate.]

[Inventory, Nov. 22, 1758; amount, £7286. 2. 6; signed by Theophilus Smith and John Gilman, Jr.]

[Commission, June 9, 1759, to Noah Emery and Nicholas Gilman, both of Exeter, gentlemen, to receive claims against the estate.]

[Warrant, May 14, 1760, authorizing Theophilus Smith, John Gilman, both of Exeter, Benjamin Shepard, Joseph Morrill, and Robert Kelsey, all of Nottingham, to set off the widow's dower.]

[Additional inventory, filed Feb. 12, 1761; amount, £520. 10. 0; signed by Theophilus Smith and John Gilman, Jr.]

Province of New Hampshire } Pursuant to a Warrant to us Directed by the Hon[ble] the Judge of Probate for Said Province Appointing us a Committee to Sett off to Sarah Redman of Nottingham in said Province widow Relict of John Redman late of Said Nottingham Yeoman Deceas'd, her Dower of the Estate of which he Died Seiz'd In Said Province & to Sett forth the Same by Metes & bounds to hold to her in Severalty We have Accordingly Sett off to the Said Sarah Redman for her Dower of the Said Estate a Certain Piece of Land in Said Nottingham Containing about Forty three acres & an half of Land more or Less bounded as follows viz begining at the Northerly Corner of the Lott Numbered Seventeen in Bow Street & on the North Easterly Side of Said Street — & from thence to run North forty three Degrees East Seventy three rods to the North East Side of Said Redman's land, Thence South forty three Degrees East Ninety one rods to the Corner of Said Land Thence South forty three Degrees West Sixty one rods to another Corner of Said Land Thence South forty three Degrees East twenty one rods, Thence South fifty five Degrees West, Twelve rods, Thence North fifty three Degrees West one hundred & twelve rods to the bounds begun at — Which Premisses we have Sett off to the Said Sarah Redman for her Dower (which happens to her of the Said Estate of which the Said John Redman Dyed Seiz'd) in Severalty During the Term of her Natural Life, as Witness our hands the third day of February Annoque Domini 1761. —

John Gilman Jr
Benj^a Shepard
Joseph morrill
Robert Kellse

[List of claims against the estate; amount, £5240. 12. 5; signed by Noah Emery and Nicholas Gilman; attested June 23, 1761.]

[Account of the administrator; receipts, £7925. 15. 6; expenditures, £2963. 15. 6; allowed Oct. 12, 1761.]

[Settlement of claims; amount of claims, £5240. 12. 5; amount distributed, £4962. 0. 0; allowed Nov. 23, 1761.]

JOSHUA BABB   1758   PORTSMOUTH

[Administration on the estate of Joshua Babb of Portsmouth granted to Philip Babb of Portsmouth, husbandman, Nov. 29, 1758.]

[Probate Records, vol. 21, p. 114.]

[Bond of Philip Babb, with George Waldron and Nathaniel Muchmore, yeomen, as sureties, all of Portsmouth, in the sum of £1000, Nov. 29, 1758, for the administration of the estate of Joshua Babb, glazier; witnesses, David Sewall, William Parker.

[Warrant, Nov. 29, 1758, authorizing Cutts Shannon and John Elliot, both of Portsmouth, gentlemen, to appraise the estate.]

[Inventory, attested Jan. 31, 1759; amount, £928. 15. 0; signed by Cutts Shannon and John Elliot.]

[Commission to Eleazer Russell and Samuel Penhallow, merchant, both of Portsmouth, to receive claims against the estate.]

[List of claims, April 30, 1760; amount, £590. 16. 0; signed by Eleazer Russell and Samuel Penhallow.]

[Account of the administrator; receipts, £1300. 0. 0; expenditures, £310. 11. 6; allowed April 30, 1760.]

JONATHAN CROCKETT 1758   PORTSMOUTH

In the Name of God Amen, The first Day of December Seventeen Hundred & fifty Eight — I Jonathan Crocket of Portsmouth in the Prov^e of New Hampsh^e Mariner being now of a sound & disposing mind & memory tho weak of Body * * *

Item I give unto my only Daughter Elizabeth Crocket five Pounds old Tenor to be pd by my Executrix when my S^d Daughter Shall arrive at ye age of Eighteen years —

The Residue of my Estate real & personal wheresoever & whatsoever I give & bequeath unto my Beloved Wife Elizabeth Crocket To Have & To Hold to her & her Heirs & assigns forever

and I do hereby constitute & appoint my Said Wife Elizabeth Crocket Executrix * * *

                         his
               Jonath X Crocket
                     mark

[Witnesses] D Peirce, Hannah Dame, Hannah Chadbourne.
[Proved Jan. 31, 1759.]

BENONI FORBUSH 1758 AMHERST

[Administration on the estates of Benoni Forbush of Souhegan West, yeoman, and Mary Forbush, his widow, granted to John Shepard of Souhegan West, gentleman, Dec. 5, 1758.]

[Probate Records, vol. 21, p. 122.]

[Bond of John Shepard, with Thomas Parker of Litchfield and James Kielle of Dover, yeomen, as sureties, in the sum of £2000, Dec. 5, 1758, for the administration of the estate; witnesses, John Hart, Thomas Westbrook Waldron.]

[Warrant, Dec. 5, 1758, authorizing Robert Reed and Samuel Gray, both of Souhegan West, yeomen, to appraise the estate.]

[Inventory, attested Feb. 19, 1759; amount, £110. 0. 0, real estate; signed by Robert Reed and Samuel Gray.]

[Commission, March 28, 1759, to Joseph Blanchard of Merrimack and Samuel Patten of Bedford, yeoman, to receive claims against the estate.]

[List of claims, Sept. 28, 1759; amount, £503. 2. 11; signed by Joseph Blanchard and Samuel Patten.]

[Account of the administrator; receipts, £782. 0. 0; expenditures, £403. 18. 0; allowed April 25, 1760.]

[Settlement of claims; amount of claims, £465. 2. 11; amount distributed, £378. 2. 0; allowed April 26, 1760.]

MOSES STICKNEY 1758 HAMPTON FALLS

[Administration on the estate of Moses Stickney of Hampton Falls, husbandman, granted to Nathaniel Gove of Hampton Falls, husbandman, Dec. 6, 1758.]

[Probate Records, vol. 21, p. 125.]

[Bond of Nathaniel Gove, with Reuben Sanborn, yeoman, and Wade Stickney, husbandman, as sureties, all of Hampton

Falls, in the sum of £1000, Dec. 6, 1758, for the administration of the estate; witnesses, Wyseman Clagget, Cutts Shannon.]

[Warrant, Dec. 6, 1758, authorizing Jonathan Gove and Abner Philbrick, both of Hampton Falls, yeomen, to appraise the estate.]

[Inventory, attested Feb. 19, 1759; amount, £2922. 10. 0; signed by Jonathan Gove and Abner Philbrick.]

ONESIPHOROUS PAGE   1758   KINGSTON

[Administration on the estate of Onesiphorous Page of Kingston, husbandman, granted to Ebenezer Batchelder of Kingston, yeoman, Dec. 9, 1758.]

[Probate Records, vol. 21, p. 126.]

[Bond of Ebenezer Batchelder, yeoman, with John Darling, yeoman, and Thomas Batchelder, joiner, as sureties, all of Kingston, in the sum of £300, Dec. 9, 1758, for the administration of the estate; witnesses, John Sanborn, William Parker, Jr.]

[Warrant, Dec. 9, 1758, authorizing Edward Fifield and William Parker, Jr., both of Kingston, gentlemen, to appraise the estate.]

[Inventory, Dec. 19, 1758; amount, £250. 6. 0; signed by Edward Fifield and William Parker, Jr.]

[Account of the administrator; receipts, £459. 16. 6; expenditures, £399. 2. 4; mentions "Deceased wages receivd out of the Province Treasury. . . . p^d Joseph Eastman for keeping David Page a son of said Deceased under Seven Years of Age, from the 19th of feb^y 1759"; allowed Jan. 28, 1761.]

[Additional account; receipts, £60. 13. 8; expenditures, £34. 15. 0; filed Sept. 2, 1761.]

DANIEL BATCHELDER 1758   KENSINGTON

[Administration on the estate of Daniel Batchelder of Kensington, joiner, granted to Mary Batchelder of Kensington, widow, Dec. 15, 1758.]

[Probate Records, vol. 21, p. 249.]

[Bond of Mary Batchelder, with Jeremiah Fogg, clerk, and James Fogg, yeoman, as sureties, all of Kensington, in the sum of £1000, Dec. 15, 1758, for the administration of the estate; witnesses, William Parker, Jr., Sarah Fogg.]

[Warrant, Dec. 15, 1758, authorizing William Parker of Kingston, gentleman, and John Sherburne of Kensington, joiner, to appraise the estate.]

[Inventory, Dec. 15, 1758; amount, £3250. 13. 6; signed by William Parker, Jr., and John Sherburne.]

[Account of the administratrix; receipts, £1443. 13. 6, personal estate; expenditures, £2387. 5. 10; mentions "By Maintenance of 3 Children under Seven Years of Age the first 156 weeks the Second 234 weeks the third 253 weeks"; allowed Oct. 10, 1763.]

[Guardianship of Elizabeth Batchelder, Abigail Batchelder, and Hannah Batchelder, aged less than 14 years, children of Daniel Batchelder, granted to Joseph Wadleigh, Jr., Oct. 10, 1763.]

[Probate Records, vol. 23, p. 120.]

[Bond of Joseph Wadleigh, Jr., with Joseph Wadleigh as surety, both of Kensington, in the sum of £500, Oct. 10, 1763, for the guardianship of Elizabeth, Abigail, and Hannah Batchelder; witnesses, William Parker, Jr., Michael Brown.]

ELISHA LEAVITT   1758   STRATHAM

[Administration on the estate of Elisha Leavitt of Stratham, cordwainer, granted to Elizabeth Leavitt of Stratham, widow, Dec. 27, 1758.]

[Probate Records, vol. 21, p. 136.]

[Bond of Elizabeth Leavitt, with James Merrill, Jr., of Stratham and Timothy Jones of Greenland, joiners, as sureties, in the sum of £500, Dec. 27, 1758, for the administration of the estate; witnesses, none.]

[Warrant, Dec. 27, 1758, authorizing Joshua Neal, housewright, and Satchell Clark, cooper, both of Stratham, to appraise the estate.]

[Inventory, Jan. 2, 1759; amount, £394. 15. 0; signed by Joshua Neal and Satchell Clark.]

[Commission, March 28, 1759, to Theophilus Smith of Exeter and Joshua Neal of Stratham, gentleman, to receive claims against the estate.]

[List of claims, Oct. 10, 1759; amount, £269. 1. 10; signed by Theophilus Smith and Joshua Neal.]

[Account of the administratrix; receipts £421. 11. 8; expenditures, £336. 11. 6; mentions "By charges in the Sickness & funeral of a Child which Died und^r Seven Years of age"; allowed Jan. 30, 1760.]

[Settlement of claims; amount of claims, £269. 1. 10; amount distributed, £85. 0. 0; allowed March 21, 1760.]

RUTH BEAN   1758   EXETER

[Administration on the estate of Ruth Bean of Exeter, widow, granted to James Bean of Brentwood Dec. 27, 1758.]

[Probate Records, vol. 21, p. 136.]

[Bond of James Bean, with Timothy Jones of Greenland, joiner, and John Bergin of Newmarket as sureties, in the sum of £1000, Dec. 27, 1758, for the administration of the estate; witnesses, William Parker, James Graves.]

[Warrant, Dec. 27, 1758, authorizing John Odlin and Samuel Gilman, both of Exeter, gentlemen, to appraise the estate.]

[Inventory, April 10, 1759; amount, £3584. 15. 0; signed by John Odlin and Samuel Gilman, Jr.; attested by James Bean, Quaker.]

SAMUEL HAMILTON   1758   NEWMARKET

[Administration on the estate of Samuel Hamilton of Newmarket granted to John Bergin of Newmarket Dec. 27, 1758.]
[Probate Records, vol. 21, p. 134.]

[Bond of John Bergin, glazier, with Samuel Hart, joiner, and William Kennedy, laborer, both of Portsmouth, as sureties, in the sum of £1000, Dec. 27, 1758, for the administration of the estate of Samuel Hamilton, schoolmaster; witnesses, Cutts Shannon, William Parker.]

[Warrant, Dec. 27, 1758, authorizing Joseph Smith and Joseph Judkins, yeoman, both of Newmarket, to appraise the estate.]

[Inventory, March 27, 1759; amount, £28. 15. 0; signed by Joseph Smith and Joseph Judkins.]

NATHANIEL WEARE   1758   HAMPTON FALLS

[Administration on the estate of Nathaniel Weare of Hampton Falls, yeoman, granted to Mehitabel Weare of Hampton Falls, widow, Dec. 29, 1758.]
[Probate Records, vol. 21, p. 213.]

[Bond of Mehitabel Weare, with Meshech Weare and Andrew Webster, shipwright, as sureties, all of Hampton Falls, in the sum of £500, Dec. 29, 1758, for the administration of the estate; witnesses, Caleb Sanborn, Jeremiah Lane.]

[Warrant, Dec. 29, 1759, authorizing Jonathan Swett and Caleb Sanborn, both of Hampton Falls, gentlemen, to appraise the estate.]

[Inventory, Jan. 4, 1759; amount, £557. 0. 0; signed by Caleb Sanborn and Jonathan Swett.]

[Warrant, June 26, 1759, authorizing Meshech Weare and Caleb Sanborn, innholder, both of Hampton Falls, to receive claims against the estate.]

[List of claims, Dec. 26, 1759; amount, £2146. 19. 0; signed by Meshech Weare and Caleb Sanborn.]

[Account of Mehitabel Shaw, administratrix; receipts, £557. 0. 0, personal estate; expenditures, £560. 12. 0; mentions "For a Nurse and Necessaries in my Lying in with a Child After the father went in the Army. . . . For Expences for bringing up of three Children from the time of the Death of their Father on the 25th of Novr 1758 being one year and Nine months, the Eldest of them being not yet Six years old"; allowed Aug. 27, 1760.]

[Guardianship of Mary Weare, Elizabeth Weare, and Mehitabel Weare, aged less than 14 years, daughters of Nathaniel Weare, granted to Jonathan Moulton Feb. 24, 1763.]

[Probate Records, vol. 22, p. 541.]

[Bond of Jonathan Moulton of Hampton, with Hunking Wentworth and Cutts Shannon, gentleman, both of Portsmouth, as sureties, in the sum of £1000, Feb. 24, 1763, for the guardianship of Mary, Elizabeth, and Mehitabel Weare; witnesses, William Vaughan, George Libby.]

JOSEPH PERKINS   1759   DURHAM

[Administration on the estate of Joseph Perkins of Durham, husbandman, granted to Joseph Hicks of Dover, gentleman, Jan. 12, 1759.]

[Probate Records, vol. 21, p. 140.]

[Bond of Joseph Hicks, with Samuel Hale of Portsmouth and Thomas Westbrook Waldron of Dover, gentlemen, as sureties, in the sum of £500, Jan. 12, 1759, for the administration of the estate; witnesses, Thomas Parker, Jr., Jonathan Blanchard.]

[Warrant, Jan. 12, 1759, authorizing Hubbard Stevens, tanner, and Miles Randall, yeoman, both of Durham, to appraise the estate.]

[Inventory, attested May 30, 1759; amount, £292. 8. 0; signed by Hubbard Stevens and Miles Randall.]

[Commission, Nov. 13, 1759, to Benjamin Mathes, gentleman, and Jonathan Chesley, husbandman, both of Durham, to receive claims against the estate.]

[List of claims, April 10, 1760; amount, £728. 2. 0; signed by Benjamin Mathes and Jonathan Chesley.]

[Account of the administrator; receipts, £703. 8. 0, personal estate; expenditures, £337. 8. 0; allowed March 26, 1761.]

[Settlement of claims; amount of claims, £728. 2. 0; amount distributed, £366. 0. 0; allowed April 22, 1761.]

TIMOTHY GILMAN   1759   NEWMARKET

[Administration on the estate of Timothy Gilman of Newmarket granted to Deborah Gilman of Newmarket, widow, Jan. 12, 1759.]

[Probate Records, vol. 21, p. 140.]

[Bond of Deborah Gilman, with John Bergin of Newmarket, glazier, and Zebulon Giddings of Exeter, trader, as sureties, in the sum of £500, Jan. 12, 1759, for the administration of the estate; witnesses, William Parker, James Gilman.]

[Warrant, Jan. 12, 1759, authorizing Winthrop Hilton, gentleman, and Peter Folsom, yeoman, both of Newmarket, to appraise the estate.]

[Inventory, Jan. 16, 1759; amount, £3618. 6. 0.]

―――― WILSON 1759 LONDONDERRY

Londonderry January ye 20 1759

Sir after Duerespects thes Coms to Inform you that Benjamin Willson of this town is Coming Down to Portsmouth to Adminester on his fathers Estat who is Leatly Deceased and the Widow and his oldest son is both Alive and the widow Praid me to writ to you that he May be stopt till the Wether be a litell modrat that she Can Com Down or that she may have time to appoint Some Proper Person to Adminester on said Estat there is nothing to Adminester on but a small Mater of Personall estat which will hardly Clear the Charges this is all that is Nidfull at Present from sir your humbel ser^t

Robt Wallace

ENOCH CLARK 1759 GREENLAND

In the Name of God Amen, The twenty third day of January 1759. I Enoch Clark of Greenland, in the Province of New Hampshire, Inholder, being under bodily Indisposition * * *

Imprimis I give & bequeath to Mary my beloved wife, the third Part of all my real Estate in Greenland to be under her Improvement or for her use & benefit, during her natural life, according to The direction of the Law in such Case; also I give her sixteen Pounds lawful money of Great Britain, or equal thereto, in whatsoever may be the lawful Currency of the Province aforesaid, to be Paid by my Executor, also one good Cow, six Sheep, my riding Chair The third part of all my household Furniture, excepting a Clock & Desk, & the third part of all the Eatables such as Grain, Meat & Sauce, which may be in my house at the time of my Decease; also Six Cord of good fire wood annually, during her widow-hood to be cut & Haled to her Door, one half of it by my Son Joseph & the other Half by my Son Enoch, or by their Heirs or assigns; also my large Bible during her natural life, & after her Decease to Mary Clark, the Second Daughter of my Son Joseph, & in case of her Decease, before Then, it shall return to my Son Enoch, or his Heirs —

Item I give & bequeath to my Son Joseph the house where he Now lives, in Greenland, with all the Land adjoining thereto, which belongs to me, and all the Buildings thereon, & appurtenances thereunto Belonging, excepting eight acres adjoining to Land of Lieut. Nathan Johnson's; also I give him all the Implements of Husbandry on said Farm, which belong to me, that is to say a Cart, Ploughs, iron Chains one iron bar & all the Moveables belonging to me within said house; And the Mare which is now on said farm & a Steer coming in three, also one Half of a Pew in the meeting house in Greenland adjoining to the Pew which belongs to Mr Tufton Philbrook —

Item I give & bequeath to my Son Greenleaf one Acre of Land in said Greenland, adjoining on the easterly part to a Lot of Land which I Sold to Mr Thomas Odiorne, & running back to the Ditch in the bog & By said Ditch, & fronting on the Country road leading to Exeter, so Far West as to make one Acre; also I give him one half of the above mentioned eight Acres of Land reserved out of the farm which I have given to my Son Joseph & adjoining to Land of Lieut. Nathan Johnson's aforesaid; also I give him a mortgage Deed of twenty five acres of Land in Exeter, which I have from Constantine Gilman, the bounderies of which are specified in said Deed bearing Date the twenty second day of October, Anno Domini 1754; also a quantity of house Timber hewed, lying near my Barn, & about twelve hun[d] feet of pine boards sixteen pounds lawful Money of Great Britain, or equal thereto in whatever may be The lawful Currency of the aforesaid Province, to be paid by my Executor, also one Cow, one of the middling sort of my Feather Beds One Coverlaid, one pair of tow & linnen Sheets, one of my pewter Dishes of the middling Size, and six plates of the smallest Size; also Half of a Pew in the meeting house aforesaid, on the left hand of The Pulpit adjoining to a Pew of the late Cap[t] Jn[o] Bracketts, & a whip Saw —

Item I give & bequeath to my Son Ebenezer two fifty Acre Lots of Land lying in Notingham East in the aforesaid Province, which I bought of Tho[s] Burleigh, with the house & barn thereon & all the Appurtenances thereunto belonging, & five pounds lawful money of Great Britain, or equal thereto in whatsoever may be the lawful Currency of said Province & my beaver Hat; also one of the middling Sort of my beds, one Coverlaid, one pair of tow & linnen Sheets, one Cow, one Pewter Dish of the middling size; & six plates of the smallest, a cros-cut Saw, the shortest of my Guns, & half of the Forementioned Pew adjoining to M[r] Tufton Philbrook's Pew —

Item I give & bequeath to my Son Daniel twelve acres of Land which I bought of Tho[s] Burleigh, lying in Notingham aforesaid & all the Land that I have in Ipsum & the Sum of Forty pounds lawful money of Great Britain to be paid to Him at the Age of twenty two Years, if he shall arrive to that Age; thirty two pounds of said sum to be paid by my Executor, & eight pounds by my Son Joseph, or by their Heirs or assigns; also I give him one of the middling Sort of my feather Beds, one Coverlaid two tow & linnen Sheets, one pewter Dish, middling size, six plates of the middling Size, one of the best of my large silver Spoons, half of a Pew in the Gallery & six Sheep —

Item I give & bequeath to Rev[d] Sam[l] Macclintock forty Shillings lawful money of Great Britain, or equal thereto in whatsoever may be the lawful Currency of said Province to be paid By my Executor —

Item I give & bequeath to the Parish of Greenland forty Shillings lawful money of Great Britain, or equal thereto in whatsoever may be the lawful Currency of the Province aforesaid, towards purchasing a Bell for the Meetinghouse in said Greenland, to be paid to the Parish by my Executor, when said Parish shall buy or send for a Bell; on condition that he shall be truly paid by said Parish, agreeable to their Vote, the ballance of the account of building the Meetinghouse which is due to me —

Item I give & bequeath to my four youngest Sons, viz. Enoch Greenleaf, Ebenezer & Daniel, all my wearing apparrell, to be equally divided between them —

Item I give to my Negro Woman Phillis her Freedom after serving Fifteen Years from the date hereof; me, during my life (& in case of My Decease before the Expiration of said Term) my Son Enoch or His Heirs or assigns the remaining Part of said Term —

Item I give & bequeath to my Son Enoch whom, I constitute & appoint sole Executor of this my Last will & Testament the dwelling House where I now live with all the Land adjoining thereto (except The abovementioned acre given to my Son Greenleaf) and all the Buildings thereon & appurtenances thereunto belonging, also four acres of the aforesaid eight Acres of Land, adjoining to Land of Lieut. Nathan Johnson's aforesaid; also a Lot in the cedar Swamp in Greenland which I bought of one Sherburne; also half of the aforesaid Pew on the left hand of the Pulpit adjoining to a Pew of the Late Capt. Jn° Brackett's reserving the Privilege to my wife of sitting in said Pew during her Life; also all my Money, Bills, Bonds, & Debts, all my store of spirituous Liquors, all my live Stock, All my Casks, my Clock Desk & all my other houshold Furniture Except what is given away already & mentioned under the above Articles, and all & every other Part or Parcel of my Estate, whether Real or personal which I have not given away already in this My Last will & Testament, or which may not be given away Before my Decease, and I appoint him his Heirs Executors or assigns to see that all the abovementioned Articles of this my last will And Testament be faithfully fulfill'd according to my Intention Therein express'd, & to pay all my just Debts & funeral Charges, out of his Legacy * * *

Enoch Clark

[Witnesses] Joseph Moultin jun^r, John Folsom, Joshua Pickerin Ju^r.

[Proved Feb. 28, 1759.]

Mary Clark signified & declared Her Consent to this last will & Testament of her Husband lately Deceas'd in presence of us

John Folsom
Joshua Pickerin Ju^r

[Bond of Enoch Clark, innholder, with John Folsom and Joshua Pickering, Jr., as sureties, all of Greenland, in the sum of £1000, Feb. 28, 1759, for the execution of the will; witnesses, William Parker, John Dennett.]

[Daniel Clark of Greenland, minor, aged more than 14 years, son of Enoch Clark, makes choice of his brother, Joseph Clark of Greenland, cooper, as his guardian, March 22, 1759; witnesses, Enoch Clark, Robert Bryent.]

[Guardianship of Daniel Clark granted to Joseph Clark April 25, 1759.]

[Probate Records, vol. 21, p. 219.]

[Bond of Joseph Clark, with Enoch Clark and William Johnson, yeoman, as sureties, all of Greenland, in the sum of £1000, April 25, 1759, for the guardianship of Daniel Clark; witnesses, William Parker, Moses Stevens.]

[Warrant, Feb. 18, 1761, authorizing Richard Jenness, 3d, of Rye, Levi Dearborn of North Hampton, physician, Joseph Brown of Rye, yeoman, James Brackett, and Thomas Odiorne to set off the widow's dower.]

Prov[e] of } Memorandum of one third part of the Real
New Hamp[r] } Estate of M[r] Enoch Clark Late of Greenland
Deceas'd sett of to his widow Mary Clark by us the Subscribers
Appointed for that end by the Hon[ble] Rich[d] Wibird Esq[r] Judge
of Probate of Wills &c this 27 Day of Feb[ry] 1761 — viz[t] —

The Westerly end of the Barn belonging to the whomstead
ten foot from the west end up & down with the privilege of
using the Barn floor & keeping her riding Chair therein

The working Shop begining at one third of the Chimney &
runing South to the beem then east to the side as mark'd out —

One third of the acre given to Greenleaf Clark four rods & a
half fronting the road & running that breadth the whole Depth
back — the westerly part of s[d] acre —

The whole westerly end of the Land of s[d] Deceas'd beginning
at Greenleaf Clarks fence & running westerly to the corner by
the schoolhouse about fourteen rod then running Southerly
twenty six rod then easterly twenty two rods then Northerly to a
fence in the bog running to Greenleafs acre then by his fence to
the Road.

The Garden one rod the south side of the Garden the whole
depth —

The orchard beginning at the North west corner of the milk
house & running Westerly four rods & half, then Southerly two
rods & Quarter then Easterly five rod & half to the house with
liberty to pass round the House —

Cedar Swamp beginning at the North West corner & running
Southerly Sixteen rods then easterly six rods to a mark'd tree
then runs Northerly sixteen rods then Westerly to the first
mentioned bounds

Joseph Clarks House the east end of the Chamber as the Petition now stands & the North or kitchin Room below, & the east
end of the Cellar one third

The East end of Jos Clarks Barn as far North as the main post
or fence, & one third of Barn floor —

The Northerly end of the Pasture the easterly side of the road as is parted by a stone wall, likewise the North end of the orchard & all the field above the orchard beginning one rod above a pair of Barrs which Barrs are about six rods above Jos Clarks House so as to take in three rows of apple trees to the North.

The Pasture Joyning Lt Nathan Johnson beginning Eleven rods from the fence & running Westerly by the Road thirteen Rods then running back to the other fence so as to make two acres & two thirds —

The outer Cellar Six foot & half from the South end across.

The Inner Cellar three foot & Eight Inches from the West side, the whole length

The Kitchin part of the mansion House & the bedroom next to it & the garret over the west end with liberty of a passage to the garret & Cellar & Well also liberty of the back yard by the Well —

Five rod of Land Deep Next to Thos Odiornes & Eight rod in length by the road running from s^d Odiornes Land easterly towards the meetinghouse

Liberty of setting a pig pen at the South end of the Kitchen^r & a passage round the House & liberty of the fore yard to pass & repass

       Richd Jenness 3^d
       Levi Dearborn
       Thos Odiorne
       Joseph Brown
       James Brackett

AVERY SANDERS   1759   HAVERHILL, MASS.

[Administration on the estate of Avery Sanders of Haverhill, Mass., joiner, granted to Joseph Clark of Methuen, Mass., yeoman, Jan. 24, 1759.]

[Probate Records, vol. 21, p. 145.]

[Bond of Joseph Clark, with Peter Merrill and Richard Dow, both of Salem, yeomen, as sureties, in the sum of £2000, Jan. 24, 1759, for the administration of the estate; witnesses, David Sewall, John Langdon.]

JONATHAN PRESCOTT   1759   HAMPTON FALLS

[Abigail Whidden, late of Hampton Falls, renounces administration on the estate of her son, Jonathan Prescott of Hampton Falls, Jan. 30, 1759, in favor of her husband, James Whidden of Nottingham; witnesses, Joseph Cilley, Robert Harvey.]

[Administration granted to James Whidden, yeoman, Jan. 31, 1759.]

[Probate Records, vol. 21, p. 146.]

[Bond of James Whidden, with Joseph Cilley and Robert Harvey, both of Nottingham, gentlemen, as sureties, in the sum of £1000, Jan. 31, 1759, for the administration of the estate; witnesses, John Shackford, William Parker.]

[Warrant, Jan. 31, 1759, authorizing Thomas Simpson and John McCrillis, Jr., both of Nottingham, yeomen, to appraise the estate.]

[Inventory, attested June 25, 1759; amount, £482. o. o; signed by John McCrillis and Thomas Simpson.]

GEORGE SEWARD   1759   PORTSMOUTH

[Administration on the estate of George Seward of Portsmouth, cordwainer, granted to his son, George Seward of Portsmouth, boat-builder, Jan. 31, 1759.]

[Probate Records, vol. 21, p. 146.]

[Bond of George Seward, with John Shackford and Joseph Cotton, boat-builder, as sureties, all of Portsmouth, in the sum of £1000, Jan. 31, 1759, for the administration of the estate; witness, Daniel Gilman.]

[Inventory, Feb. 28, 1759; amount, £2065. 7. 0; signed by Daniel Jackson and Samuel Waters.]

[Administrator's account of the settlement of the estate; receipts, £1025. 7. 0; expenditures, £491. 19. 10; allowed May 28, 1760; mentions "my Mothers Funeral."]

[Probate Records, vol. 21, p. 449.]

WILLIAM BRUCE   1759   DURHAM

[Administration on the estate of William Bruce of Durham, trader, granted to Elizabeth Bruce of Durham, single woman, Jan. 31, 1759.]

[Probate Records, vol. 21, p. 150.]

[Bond of Elizabeth Bruce, with Joseph Atkinson, physician, and Hercules Mooney, schoolmaster, as sureties, all of Durham, in the sum of £1000, Jan. 31, 1759, for the administration of the estate; witnesses, S. Livermore, Cutts Shannon.]

[Inventory, attested May 30, 1759; amount, £4100. 8. 6; signed by Jonathan Woodman and Miles Randall.]

[Account of the settlement of the estate by John Lane and wife Elizabeth Lane, administratrix; receipts, £3153. 13. 6, personal estate; expenditures, £3587. 15. 3; allowed Nov. 24, 1762.]

BENJAMIN KIDDER   1759   BEDFORD

[Administration on the estate of Benjamin Kidder granted to his brother, John Kidder of Derryfield, Feb. 8, 1759.]

[Probate Records, vol. 21, p. 171.]

[Bond of John Kidder, yeoman, with John Goffe and John Moore, gentleman, as sureties, all of Derryfield, in the sum of £500, Feb. 8, 1759, for the administration of the estate of Benjamin Kidder of Souhegan East, yeoman; witnesses, Benjamin Smith, Matthew Patten.]

[Warrant, Feb. 9, 1759, authorizing Moses Barron of Bedford and John Moore of Derryfield, gentlemen, to appraise the estate of Benjamin Kidder, Jr.]

[Inventory, May 30, 1760; amount, £153. 4. 5½; signed by Moses Barron and John Moore; mentions "his wages in his majesties Service 1757 £51. 5. 4."]

ENOCH CHALLIS   1759   SOUTH HAMPTON

[Dorothy Challis renounces administration on the estate of her husband, Enoch Challis of South Hampton, in favor of her brother, Peleg Challis, Feb. 12, 1759.]

[Administration granted to Peleg Challis of Amesbury, Mass., yeoman, Feb. 28, 1759.]

[Probate Records, vol. 21, p. 181.]

[Bond of Peleg Challis, with David Bagley of Newton and Benjamin Batchelder of Chester, yeomen, as sureties, in the sum of £1000, Feb. 28, 1759, for the administration of the estate; witnesses, William Parker, John Dennett.]

[Warrant, Feb. 28, 1759, authorizing Daniel Goodwin and John Elliot, both of South Hampton, yeomen, to appraise the estate.]

[Inventory, March 27, 1759; amount, £7735. 6. 4; signed by John Elliot and Daniel Goodwin.]

[Warrant, May 22, 1759, authorizing Jeremy Webster, Joseph Bean, innholder, Nathan Ordway, yeoman, all of Kingston,

Jonathan Kimball, and Daniel Goodwin, both of South Hampton, yeomen, to set off the widow's dower.]

Province of } To the Honb^{le} Richard Wibird Esqr Judge
New Hamps: } of the Probate of Wills &c for the Province afores^d

Pursuant to your Hon^{rs} Warrant to us directed appointing us a Com^{tee} to set off to Dorothy Challis of South Hampton widow her dower which happeneth to her of the Real Estate of her Late Husband Enoch Challis of South Hampton aboves^d deceas^d &c — We haveing met at the place & viewed the premises &c & maturely Considered the Case & Circumstances have set off to the s^d widow the s^d Dorothy for her thirds or Dower in s^d Estate as followeth viz: Beginning at the south westerly Corner of the deceas'ds Lands or Estate & running North Easterly on the High way fifty & Nine Rods to a stake by the fence: then North westerly to a Poplar Tree standing at the Northwestermost part of the s^d Lands s^d tree is marked on four sides: and in Case the s^d Poplar tree should not stand exactly in the Line of the s^d land; our meaning is that this Line shall run that Course thro' the s^d Estate to the Northwestermost part thereof: then south westerly as the deceas^d Land Lays to the North westerly corner thereof being about fifty six Rods then South Easterly on that line of the whole tract to the place where it first began: thirty three acres more or less: also the New Dwelling House being on the s^d thirds: with the one Half of the Barn viz: the westerly End thereof: with full liberty & priviledge to use & Improve her s^d part of the s^d Barn in summer & in winter as Occasion may serve: the s^d premises with the Appurtenances as above mentioned & described: we set off to the s^d widow for her Dower of the Real Estate of her s^d Late Husband: — as witness our hands the 31st day of May Anno: Domini 1759

Jeremy Webster }
Joseph Bean }
Jonathan Kimball } Com^{tee}
Nathan Ordway }
Daniel Goodwin }

[Guardianship of Lydia Challis, Sarah Challis, and Thomas Challis, aged less than 14 years, children of Enoch Challis, granted to Micah Hoyt of Newton March 1, 1760.]

[Probate Records, vol. 21, p. 395.]

[Bond of Micah Hoyt, yeoman, with William Smith and Samuel Brown, both of Kingston, yeomen, as sureties, in the sum of £1000, March 1, 1760, for the guardianship of Lydia Challis, Sarah Challis, and Thomas Challis; witnesses, William Parker, Jr., Eliphalet Coffin.]

[Account of the administrator; receipts, £1847. 18. 0, personal estate; expenditures, £1862. 7. 8; mentions "bringing up the Young Children"; allowed May 28, 1760.]

Province of New Hampshire
To the Honourable John Sherburn Esqr Judge of probates of Wills for the County of Rockingham

The petetion of Lydia Varnum widow to Peter Varnum Deceas^d and Daughter of Enoch Challis of Newtown in said province Deceased Humbly Sheweth that whereas my uncle Peleg Challis who administred on the estate of my said Father Deceased Lives in Amesbury in the province of the massachusetts Bay; and my said Father Left three children Liveing: and my grand father Micah Hoit of s^d newtown was Guardian for all of the three my Father Died Seized of an estate of an Hundred acres of Land in said Newtown and my uncle who was the administrator Sold aboute twenty acres to pay my Fathers Debts and Since my Grandfather is Deceased and there have been no Settlement and your petetioner is a poor widow Left with won child and wants to have my part of my Fathers Estate to Improve towards Supporting my Self and child of aboute 18 months old: I am the Eldest of my Fathers children there is a Sister aboute twenty years old and a Brother aboute Eighteen or Nineteen and the Estate is now Improved by my uncles Benjamin and Samuel Hoits Sons to my said Grandfather Micah Hoit Deceas^d & we did not Chuse Guardians for our Selves as we might have don your petetioner prays your Hon^r to appoint a Committee to Divide said Estate So that your petetioner may have some Encum and that it be don as soon as may be and your petetioner who as in Duty bound Shall Ever pray

 Newtown 11th April: 1775

her
Lydia × Varnum
mark

 Test Caleb Pilsberry

[Additional account of the administrator; receipts, £2. 4. 10; expenditures, £11. 14. 0; attested May 31, 1775.]

DAVID BLAIR   1759   LONDONDERRY

 In the Name of God amen the Sixteen Day of Feb^r one thousand Seven hundred and fifty nine I David Blair of Londonderry within his Maj^{tis} provance of Newhamps. in Newingland yeman being in helth and Steringh * * *

 Imprimesses I Give and bequeath unto My wellbeloved Brother William Blair all my Reale and personall Estate that I am possesed of or hes a right unto after My Debts and funerall Charges is pay^d and the legecies hereafter mentioned

 Etam I allow to be pay^d out of my Estat to my Sister ann Cliningens ten Shillings Starling —

 Itam I allow to be pay^d out of my Estat to my Sister Elesebeth Blair twinty pounds Starling —

 Itam I allow to be pay^d out of my Estat to my Brother will^m Blairs Son william ten Shillings Starling —

 Itam I allow to be pay^d out of my Estat to my Brother will^m Blairs Daughter Jean Blair twinty pounds Starling —

 Itam I allow to be pay^d out of my Estat to my Brother will^m Blairs Daughter Frances Blair ten Shillings Starling and Likewise I Constitute make and ordain my Brother william Blaire and Moses Barnett to be my Sole Executors * * *

David Blair

[Witnesses] Robᵗ Clindinin, William Vance, Samuel Barr.
[Proved Aug. 28, 1765.]

[Bond of William Blair, husbandman, with Robert Clendenin, husbandman, and Samuel Livermore as sureties, all of Londonderry, in the sum of £200, Oct. 2, 1765, for the execution of the will; witnesses, Peter Green, Samuel Eaton.]

SAMUEL WEYMOUTH   1759   SOMERSWORTH

[Administration on the estate of Samuel Weymouth of Somersworth, yeoman, granted to John Mason of Somersworth, husbandman, Feb. 22, 1759.]

[Probate Records, vol. 21, p. 163.]

[Bond of John Mason, with Jacob Lavers of Portsmouth, joiner, and George Horne of Dover, yeoman, as sureties, in the sum of £2000, Feb. 27, 1759, for the administration of the estate; witnesses, William Parker, David Sewall.]

[Esther Mason, wife of John Mason, authorizes her husband to receive what is due her from the estate of her brother, Samuel Weymouth, 1759; witnesses, William Perkins, Joseph Tate.]

NEHEMIAH GOULD   1759   MASON

[Bond of Esther Gould, widow, with Phineas Waite and William Parker, yeomen, as sureties, all of Groton, Mass., in the sum of £100, Feb. 25, 1759, for the administration of the estate of her husband, Nehemiah Gould of No. 1; witnesses, James Reynolds and William Lawrence.]

[Middlesex Co., Mass., Probate Files.]

[Account of the settlement of the estate; mentions "Bringing up her Posthumes Child to this time being four Years And nine months . . . . Supporting three other of the deceased Children all under seven years of age Two of which were Supported by her more then Two years Each & the other nine months"; allowed June 25, 1764.]

[Middlesex Co., Mass., Probate Files.]

BENJAMIN THOMPSON 1759   LONDONDERRY

[Administration on the estate of Benjamin Thompson of Londonderry, yeoman, granted to Janet Thompson of Londonderry Feb. 27, 1759.]

[Probate Records, vol. 21, p. 213.]

[Bond of Janet Thompson, widow, with John Crombie and John Crombie, Jr., yeomen, as sureties, all of Londonderry, in the sum of £1000, Feb. 27, 1759, for the administration of the estate; witnesses, William Blair, Moses Barnett.]

[Warrant, Feb. 27, 1759, authorizing Samuel Barr, Moses Barnett, gentleman, and William Blair, 3d, all of Londonderry; to appraise the estate.]

[Barbara Thompson, aged more than 14 years, and James Thompson, aged about 12 years, children of Benjamin Thompson, make choice of James Carr of Goffstown as their guardian April 23, 1759; witnesses, Moses Barnett, Samuel Barr.]

[Guardianship of Barbara Thompson, minor, aged more than 14 years, and of James Thompson, aged less than 14 years, children of Benjamin Thompson, granted to James Carr of Goffstown April 25, 1759.]

[Probate Records, vol. 21, p. 220.]

[Bond of James Carr, with John Goffe of Derryfield and Samuel Moore of Litchfield, gentleman, as sureties, in the sum of £1000, April 25, 1759, for the guardianship of Barbara and James Thompson; witnesses, William Parker, Timothy Walker, Jr.]

[Inventory, attested July 23, 1759; amount, £6343. 16. 11; signed by Samuel Barr and Moses Barnett.]

[Account of the administratrix; receipts, £1943. 16. 11, personal estate; expenditures, £2032. 3. 3; mentions "maintainance of a Child under Seven 2 Years to January 24, 1761"; allowed Nov. 26, 1760.]

[Additional account of the administratrix; receipts, £500. 0. 0; expenditures, £1246. 8. 8; mentions "maintaining of a Child under Seven years of age 2 years & Eight Months . . . . Necessaries for Schooling the Children"; allowed Nov. 30, 1763.]

[Guardianship of James Thompson minor, aged more than 14 years, son of Benjamin Thompson, granted to Robert Clark Nov. 30, 1763.]

[Probate Records, vol. 23, p. 121.]

[Bond of Robert Clark of Londonderry, yeoman, with James Caldwell of Bedford, yeoman, and Samuel Emerson of Chester as sureties, in the sum of £500, Nov. 30, 1763, for the guardianship of James Thompson; witnesses, William Parker, Jr., William Vaughan.]

JONATHAN STOODLEY 1759 PORTSMOUTH

[Administration on the estate of Jonathan Stoodley of Portsmouth, mariner, granted to Mary Stoodley of Portsmouth, widow, Feb. 28, 1759.]

[Probate Records, vol. 21, p. 167.]

[Bond of Mary Stoodley, with John Shackford and John Dennett, gentleman, as sureties, all of Portsmouth, in the sum of £500, Feb. 28, 1759, for the administration of the estate; witnesses, William Parker, George Seward.]

[Warrant, Feb. 28, 1759, authorizing Hunking Wentworth

and Samuel Penhallow, merchant, both of Portsmouth, to appraise the estate.]

[Inventory, Oct. 4, 1759; amount, £6114. 11. 0; signed by Hunting Wentworth and Samuel Penhallow.]

[John Stoodley, minor, aged more than 14 years, son of Jonathan Stoodley, makes choice of Samuel Treadwell of Portsmouth, boat-builder, as his guardian June 18, 1768; witnesses, Samuel Parker, Joseph Moulton.]

[Bond of Samuel Treadwell, with Nathaniel Treadwell of Portsmouth, tanner, as surety, in the sum of £500, June 18, 1768, for the guardianship of John Stoodley; witnesses, Joseph Moulton, Samuel Parker.]

[Citation to Mary Furber, administratrix, Oct. 20, 1790, to render an account of the estate.]

[Account of the administratrix; receipts, £130. 14. 6½; expenditures, £107. 10. 10; mentions "maintainance of John before he arrived to seven years of age being in the whole 38 weeks. . . . maintainance of Elizabeth before she arrived to seven years of Age five Years & eight months"; allowed Feb. 16, 1791.]

Rockingham ss To the honorable Oliver Peabody Esq[r] Judge of the Probate of wills &c within & for the County of Rockingham

Humbly shew the subscribers that they are tenants in Common of a messuage and lot of Land situate in Portsmouth in said County being two thirds of the real estate of which Jonathan Stoodley late of Portsmouth aforesaid dec[d] died seized they therefore pray your honor to order partition of said estate between them agreeable to their respective claims viz to Nath[l] Folsom two sixth being the double share that belonged to James Stoodley son of said dec[d] and to Mary Furber one sixth as heir of her son John Stoodley, to Robert Ham one sixth which belonged to Mary Treadwell dec[d] to Catherine Treadwell one sixth & to Elizabeth Gookin one sixth — and as in duty bound will pray

Portsmouth Feb[y] 16th 1791

        Nath[l] Folsom for James
        Stoodly 2 shares
        Robert Ham
        Mary Furber
        Nath[l] Treadwell j[r]
        Na[l] Gookin

[Warrant, Feb. 16, 1791, authorizing John Fernald, Daniel Hart, Jacob Walden, Thomas Sheafe, and Thomas Chadbourne, all of Portsmouth, to divide the real estate.]

State of New Hampshire } Pursuant to the Warrant to us
 Rockingham ss   directed by the Hon[ble] Oliver Peabody Esquire Judge of the Probate of Wills &c for the said County We have made a Division of the Estate of Jonathan Stoodly late of Portsmouth deceased as mentioned in said Warrant to us directed as follows Viz[t]

Mary Furber widow for her Dower to have the Eastern Front Room Closet Bed Room Store Room over the Shop and Shop Cellar under the Bed Room with all the Avenues leading to them, with the priviledge of the front Entry and a passage way to hir Cellar from the front Cellar door near the Shop and of the Yard at the West End of the house which is to be in Common Amongst the heirs —

Mary Furber and Nath[l] Folsom to have the large front Chamber and the two Small Chambers at the Eastern End of it Adjoining thereto and the south half of the Eastern Garrett and one Cellar at the left hand as you pass down the Cellar stairs Eight feet by six feet the Other Cellar is Eight feet Square south of the south East Chimney — with all the avenues leading to them and the priviledge of the front Cellar door and front Entry and the Western Yard which is to be in Common as before described

378   NEW HAMPSHIRE WILLS

40 feet Western End

Nath⁷ Folsom — N° 1, 8½ feet on front	This Plan sheweth the Number of feet of Land by Division and set off to Each Respective Right or Share together with the Widows Dower, which is to take Place at the demolishing the House —
Nath⁷ Folsom — N° 2, 8½ feet on front	
Nath⁷ Treadwell — N° 3, 8½ feet on front	
Mary Furber — N° 4, 8½ feet on front	
Nath⁷ Gooking — N° 5, 8½ feet on front	
Robert Ham — N° 6, 8½ feet on front	
Widows part of Dower of the Land — 16 feet on front	

67 feet on this Line which we have Call'd Deer Street

67 feet on this Line westerly

40 feet on this Line on Fore Street

NEW HAMPSHIRE WILLS 379

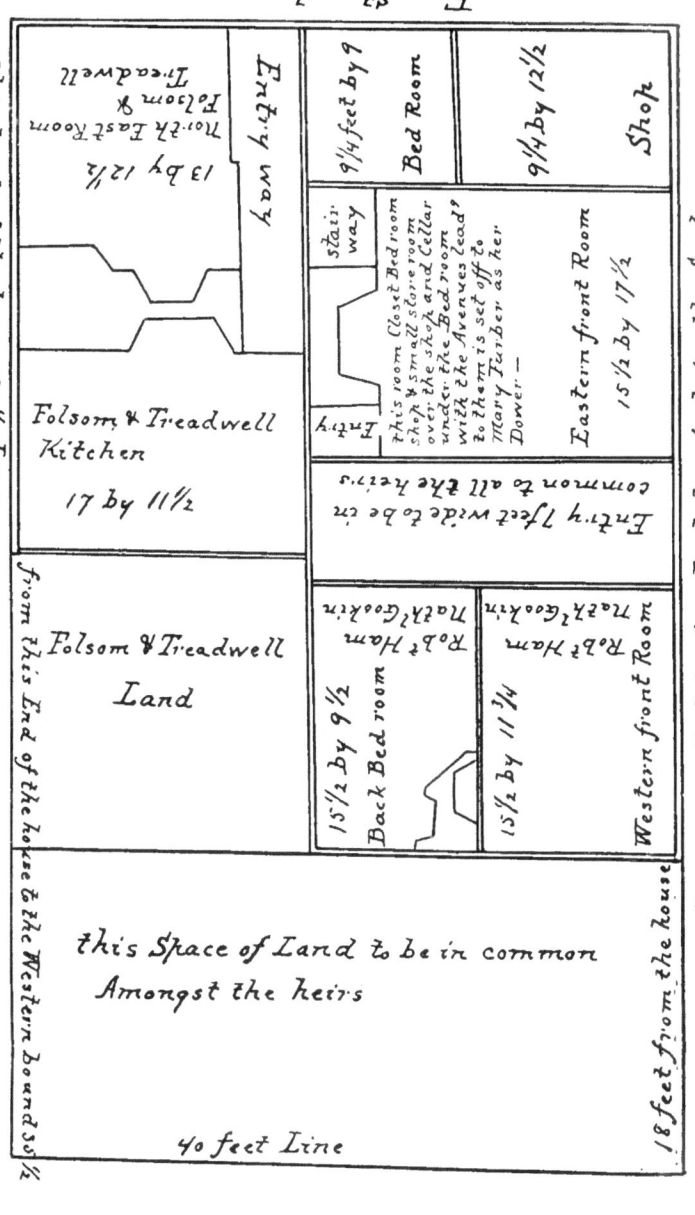

Nath¹ Gookin and Robert Ham to have the two Western Lower Rooms and the Cellar under them and the North half of the Eastern Garrett with the priviledges of the Yard Cellar door and Entry as described above

Nath¹ Treadwell & Nath¹ Folsom to have the whole north East part of the House fronting Fore Street and Cellar under it, the whole of the Land untill it comes squair with the western End of the Great House and the priviledge of the front Entry and Western Yard in Common with the rest of the heirs as above discribed

And when the House shall be down then Each respective heir to have the Number feet of Land as by Division is set of to them in the Plan hereto Anexed Reference there to being had as may more fully appear

Portsmouth 7th March 1791 Witness our hands

David Hart
Jacob Walden
Thomas Chadbourn

ANDREW WATKINS   1759   NEWCASTLE

[Administration on the estate of Andrew Watkins of Newcastle, gentleman, granted to Jane Watkins, widow, Feb. 28, 1759.]

[Probate Records, vol. 21, p. 199.]

[Bond of Jane Watkins, with Joseph Newmarch and George Frost, mariner, as sureties, all of Newcastle, in the sum of £500, Feb. 28, 1759, for the administration of the estate; witnesses, William Parker, John Folsom.]

[Warrant, Feb. 28, 1759, authorizing Nathaniel Sargent, physician, and John Simpson, mariner, both of Newcastle, to appraise the estate.]

[Inventory, May 29, 1759; amount, £1898. 12. 0; signed by Nathaniel Sargent and John Simpson.]

SAMUEL HARDY 1759 STRATHAM

[Administration on the estate of Samuel Hardy of Stratham, cordwainer, granted to Sarah Hardy of Stratham, widow, Feb. 28, 1759.]

[Probate Records, vol. 21, p. 183.]

[Bond of Sarah Hardy, with David Burleigh of Stratham, yeoman, and John Nelson of Exeter, shipwright, as sureties, in the sum of £1000, Feb. 28, 1759, for the administration of the estate; witnesses, William Parker, John Dennett.]

[Warrant, Feb. 28, 1759, authorizing David Stevens and Jacob Lowe, both of Stratham, husbandmen, to appraise the estate.]

[Inventory, attested June 27, 1759; amount, £227. 15. 0, personal estate; signed by Jacob Lowe and David Stevens.]

DANIEL DAVIS 1759 DURHAM

[Administration on the estate of Daniel Davis of Durham, yeoman, granted to Elizabeth Davis of Durham, widow, Feb. 28, 1759.]

[Probate Records, vol. 21, p. 192.]

[Bond of Elizabeth Davis, with Ephraim Davis and Valentine Mathes, yeomen, as sureties, all of Durham, in the sum of £1000, Feb. 23, 1759, for the administration of the estate; witnesses, John Burnham Hanson, Jonathan Drown.]

[Warrant, Feb. 23, 1759, authorizing Joseph Smith and Joseph Sias, trader, both of Durham, to appraise the estate.]

[Inventory, Aug. 27, 1759; amount, £11,975. 15. 0; signed by Joseph Sias and Joseph Smith.]

[Warrant, April 13, 1764, authorizing Joseph Smith, Ebenezer Thompson, physician, Jeremiah Burnham, Miles Randall, and

Jonathan Woodman, yeomen, all of Durham, to divide the real estate.]

[Probate Records, vol. 23, p. 310.]

Pursuant to a warrant from the hon[le] Richard Wibird Esq[r] Judge of the Probate of wills &[c] for the province of Newhampshire Appointing us the Subscribers a Committee to Divide the Real Estate of Daniel Davis Late of Durham in Said province yeoman Deceased intestate among the wife and Children of Said intestate — accordingly we have made a Division of said Estate in manner Following viz —

1st To Elizabeth Davis widow & Relict of Said intestate for her thirds in Said Estate part of the homestead Farm viz. Sixteen acres of up Land, Together with the Flatts adjoining, Butted & Bounded as followeth Beginning by the highway adjoining to Land Belonging to the heirs of Francis Footman Deceased & Running by Said highway North 54° west 32 Rods to a heap of Stones & then North 40° East 132 Rods to a Stake by the Salt marsh & So the Same point of Compass to the Channel of the Creek the Line between Said Estate and Abraham Stevensons land & then by Said Channel to the afores[d] Footmans Land & by Footmans Land to the first bounds — also Twenty one acres of Land on the opposite side of the highway aforsaid Beginning By Said highway at a heap of Stones adjoining Land Sat of to thomas one of the heirs and Running By the highway South 54° East 22 Rods to Land Sat of to Sarah one of the heirs & then South 32° west 59 rods then South 78° East 7 rods then South 53° west 24 rods — then north 58° west 39 rods and then North East to the first Bounds, also one half of the Dwelling house on Said Farm being the East End & one half the Barn with Liberty to Pass and Repass from the highway to Each & the priviledge of Laying wood &[c] by the Door of said house —

2[dly] To Obadiah Davis Eldest Son of Said intestate for his Double Share in Said Estate the following peices of Land all in the town of Durham afors[d] viz. 12 acres of Land at a place Called the hook being Said intestates share or Lot in the Second

Division of Common Lands in Said town also five acres of Land at North River being said intestates share in the third Division of Common Lands in Said town also 24 acres of Land Laid out to Said Intestate on the South Side of Little River for Butts & Bounds thereof Reference Being had to the Return on said town records also 17 acres of Land Laid out to Said intestate at a place Called the hornswoods for Butts & Bounds thereof Referance being had to the return under the lottlayers hands on said town Records —

3dly To Thomas Davis Second Son of Said intestate for his Share in Said Estate part of the homestead viz about fourteen acres & 3 quarters of an acre of Land, Six acres and 3 quarters is butted and bounded as followeth beginning by the highway adjoining to Land Sat of to the widow at a heap of Stones and Running North 40° East 132 Rods to the flatts & then about N W. 6 Rods & ½ to a stake & then South 41° 30¹ to the aforsaid highway & by that to the first bounds including the flatts that fronts against it also about 8 acres on the opposite of the highway Beginning at a heap of Stones by the widows thirds & Running South west 108 Rods to a heap of stones & then N. 58° west 12 Rods & then to a heap of stones and then N E 108 Rods to the highway & By that to the first bounds also the Lower Room in the west End of the house & ½ the barn with Liberty to pass & Repass from the highway to Each —

4^{thly} To francis Davis third Son of Said intestate for his Share the following Lands viz. one whole Share or Right of land in the town of Canterbury originally granted to Said intestate also 37½ acres of Land in the town of nottingham being the Eastern Part of the Lot N° 45 in the Second Division in winter Street & was originally granted unto one David Chaffins also 8 acres of Common Grant in Said Town of Durham not Laid out & was part of said intestates share in the first Division of Common Lands in s^{d} Town —

5^{thly} To Elizabeth Cromett Eldest Daughter of Said intestate for her share Part of the homestead viz about 18 acres & 3 quarters of an acre of Land 8 acres & 3 quarters is Butted & bounded as followeth Beginning by the highway adjoining to Zurviahs share one of the heirs at a heap of Stones and Running North forty five Degrees East 132 Rods to the flatts & then N. W one rod & then S W 21 Rods & then South 81° West 15 Rods & then S W to the highway & by that to the first bounds Together with all the thatch bed & Saltmarsh fronting or that was improved by the Intestate to the westard thereof also about 10 acres on the opposite Side of the highway Beginning by Zurviah Share at a heap of Stones & Running S W 108 rods to a heap of stones & then N 58° west to the parsonage or Town lot & by that to the highway & so by that to the first bounds also the west Chamber in the house —

6thly To Sarah Davis Daughter of Said intestate for her Share in Said Estate 4 acres & ½ an acre in the homestead Butted & Bounded as followeth viz Beginning by the highway adjoining the widows thirds & Running South 32° west 59 Rods and then South 78° East Nineteen Rods then N 36° East 30 rods & then N 32° west 17 Rods & then north 32° E 17 Rods to the road & then to where it Began being four Rods — also the 5th Part of the Second Third & fourth Divisions of Lands in the Town of Rochester that Belongs to the Original Right of Col¹ James Davis Late of said Durham Deceased also 18 acres of the Common or undivided Lands in said Town of Durham & is Part of the Original Right of said Intestate in the first Division of Common Lands in said Town —

7thly To Phebe Davis Daughter of Said intestate for her Share in Said Estate part of the homestead viz about 13 acres and 3 Quarters of an acre Six acres and three Quarters is Butted & Bounded as followeth beginning by the highway adjoining to Thomas⁵ Share at a heap of Stones & Running North 41° 30¹ East 132 rods to the flatts & then Northwest 6 rods ½ to a Stake & then South 43° west to the highway to a heap of Stones & then by the highway to the first bounds with the thatch bed that fronts it. Also Seven acres of Land on the opposite Side of the highway beginning at a heap of Stones by thomas Share & Running S W 108 rods to a heap of Stones & then N 58° west 10 Rods & ½ Rod to a heap of stones & then N E 108 Rods to the highway & by that to the first bounds —

8^thly To Zurviah Davis Daughter of Said intestate for her Share in Said Estate part of the homestead viz about fourteen acres. Six acres is Butted & Bounded as followeth Beginning by the highway adjoining to Phebes Share at a heap of Stones & Running N 43° East 132 Rods to the flatts to a Stake & then N W 6 rods & ½ rod to a Stake & then South 45° west 132 Rods to the highway to a heap of Stones & By that to the first bounds with the thatch bed that fronts &c also about 8 acres on the opposite Side of the highway beginning by Phebes Share & Running S W 108 Rods to a heap of Stones & then N 58° west 12 Rods & then North East to the highway & by that to the first bounds Excepting out of it the house & Barn Sat of to other heirs & Liberty to Pass & Repass — witness our hands at Durham the 25th Day of September in the fourth year of his majesties Reign A D 1764.

Joseph Smith
Ebenezer Thompson } Committee
Jerem^h Burnum Jun

[Account of the administratrix; receipts, £2582. 0. 6, personal estate; expenditures, £1327. 17. 0; mentions "maintaining one Child 9 months"; allowed Nov. 8, 1764.]

[Guardianship of Francis Davis minor, aged more than 14 years, son of Daniel Davis, granted to Ebenezer Thompson Oct. 31, 1764.]

[Probate Records, vol. 23, p. 323.]

[Guardianship of Thomas Davis, minor, aged more than 14 years, son of Daniel Davis, granted to Ephraim Davis Oct. 31, 1764.]

[Probate Records, vol. 23, p. 322.]

[Bond of Ebenezer Thompson, physician, with Joseph Smith and Ephraim Davis, yeoman, as sureties, all of Durham, in the sum of £500, Oct. 31, 1764, for the guardianship of Francis Davis; witnesses, Wyseman Claggett, John Sullivan.]

[Bond of Ephraim Davis, yeoman, with Joseph Smith and Ebenezer Thompson, physician, as sureties, all of Durham, in the sum of £500, Oct. 31, 1764, for the guardianship of Thomas Davis; witnesses, Wyseman Claggett, John Sullivan.]

JAMES NELSON   1759   PORTSMOUTH

[Guardianship of the children of James Nelson of Portsmouth granted to Samuel Sherburne of Portsmouth, husbandman, March 1, 1759.]

[Probate Records, vol. 21, p. 201.]

[Bond of Samuel Sherburne, with John Nelson, shipwright, and Thomas Flanders, joiner, both of Exeter, as sureties, in the sum of £500, March 1, 1759, for the guardianship of the children of James Nelson, deceased; witnesses, David Sewall, John Langdon.]

NATHANIEL MESERVE   1759   PORTSMOUTH

[Administration on the estate of Nathaniel Meserve, Jr., of Portsmouth, shipwright, granted to Sarah Meserve March 2, 1759.]

[Probate Records, vol. 21, p. 249.]

[Bond of Sarah Meserve, widow, with Mark Hunking, mariner, and George Meserve, merchant, as sureties, all of Portsmouth, in the sum of £1000, March 2, 1759, for the administration of the estate; witnesses, Michael Whidden, James Whidden.]

[Inventory, June 20, 1759; amount, £7296. 3. 7; signed by John Shackford and Jacob Sheafe.]

[Commission, May 4, 1771, to Samuel Penhallow, Samuel Hale, William Torrey, —— Whipple, and John Parker, all of Portsmouth, to divide the real estate.]

Province of } Pursuant to a Warrant from the Honble John New Hamp^s } Wentworth Esqr Judge of the Probate of Wills &c for said Province directed to us to divide the Real Estate of Nathl Meserve late of Portsmouth in said province Shipwright dec^d Intestate — we have done the same in the following manner — vizt

We have set off to Sarah the Wife of Nehemiah Wheeler who was Wife of said Intestate a part of the Mansion House belonging to the Estate of said deceased scituated in Portsmouth aforesaid vizt the Southwest Room in s^d House with the Chambers over it & the Cellar under it and a piece of Land adjoining bounded as follows Southerly by Land belonging to the Heirs of George Meserve dec^d Fifty one feet, Westerly by Land of John Hart & the Heirs of Jonathan Odiorne dec^d Twenty five feet, Northerly by Land hereafter set off to Jane Meserve one & fifty feet, Easterly by the yard adjoining s^d House twenty five feet. —

To Henry Meserve the Son of said Intestate we have set off a certain Tract of Land in Portsm^o aforesaid containing three acres bounded as follows viz Northerly by a Road that leads to Newington Easterly by Land of John Martin & Hunking Wentworth Esqr Southerly by Land of John Penhallow & Eleazer Russell, & Westerly by Land of John Hart Esqr also another piece of Land, adjoining to the Mansion House of said deceased bounded Easterly by a Street thirty feet, Southerly by said House, & Land hereafter set off to Sarah Meserve Eighty Seven feet, Westerly by Land of John Hart j^r thirty feet, & Northerly by said Harts Rope walk Eighty Seven feet —

To Sarah Meserve Daughter of said Intestate we have set off the Kitchen in said Mansion House & the Northwest Chamber over it & the Cellar under it, with a piece of Land adjoining bounded Northerly by Land set off above to Henry Meserve one & fifty feet, Easterly by a yard on the West End of said House

Eight feet, Southerly by Land hereafter set off to Mary Meserve one & fifty feet, Westerly by Land of John Hart Eight feet.

To Mary Meserve Daughter of said Intestate we have set off the North East Room in said Mansion House with the Chamber over it & the Cellar under it, and a piece of Land Sixteen feet wide & one & fifty feet long adjoining to the last mentioned piece sat off to the said Sarah. —

To Jane Meserve Daughter of said Intestate we have set off the South East Room in the said Mansion House with the Chamber over it & the Cellar under it & a piece of Land adjoining to the last mention'd piece sat off to Mary Meserve above, being Eight feet wide & one & fifty feet long. — The Yards on the South Side & the west End of said House, & the Entries in s^d House & the Well to be in Common among the Parties. —

Portsmouth May 10th 1771　　　　Saml Penhallow
　　　　　　　　　　　　　　　　　Willm Torrey
　　　　　　　　　　　　　　　　　Jno Parker

——— POMEROY　　　　1759　　　　GOFFSTOWN

[Mehitabel Pomeroy of Goffstown makes choice of Capt. Moses Barron of Bedford, gentleman, as her guardian, March 3, 1759; witnesses, John Goffe, William S. Harvey.]

BENJAMIN GARFIELD　1759　　　　HINSDALE

[Bond of Eunice Garfield of Hinsdale, widow, with Benjamin Bellows of Walpole and Oliver Willard of Brattleborough, Vt., gentleman, as sureties, in the sum of £1000, March 8, 1759, for the administration of the estate of Benjamin Garfield of Hinsdale, yeoman; not signed or witnessed.]

JOHN HOUSTON   1759   NASHUA

[Administration on the estate of John Houston of Dunstable, carpenter, granted to Hannah Houston of Dunstable, widow, March 8, 1759.]

[Probate Records, vol. 21, p. 213.]

[Bond of Hannah Houston, with Nehemiah Lovewell of Dunstable, gentleman, and Timothy Taylor of Merrimack, husbandman, as sureties, in the sum of £2000, March 8, 1759, for the administration of the estate; witnesses, Noah Johnson, Jonathan Lovewell.]

[Warrant, March 8, 1759, authorizing Noah Johnson and Nehemiah Lovewell, both of Dunstable, husbandmen, to appraise the estate.]

[Inventory, March 12, 1759; amount, £293. 5. 6; signed by Noah Johnson and Nehemiah Lovewell.]

[Account of the administratrix; receipts, £1079. 2. 0, personal estate; expenditures, £1091. 11. 6; mentions "maintance of Noah a child of the Intestate under ye age of 7 years 205 weeks. . . . Nursing & Vittilling 4 children of the Intestate 20 weeks each at 40/ p^r week being all sick togather. . . . Nursing Hannah a daughter of the Intestate 6 years & 3 months being sick"; allowed Oct. 31, 1765.]

ARTHUR GRAHAM   1759   LONDONDERRY

[Administration on the estate of Arthur Graham of Londonderry, yeoman, granted to Eleanor Graham of Londonderry, widow, March 10, 1759.]

[Probate Records, vol. 21, p. 276.]

[Bond of Eleanor Graham, with Samuel McKeen and Samuel Smith as sureties, all of Londonderry, in the sum of £500, March

10, 1759, for the administration of the estate; witnesses, Joseph Butler, David Campbell.]

[Warrant, March 10, 1759, authorizing Samuel Anderson and Hugh Graham, both of Londonderry, yeomen, to appraise the estate.]

[Inventory, attested April 16, 1759; amount, £2905. 10. 0; signed by Hugh Graham and Samuel Anderson.]

JOSEPH PALMER 1759 PEMBROKE

In the Name of God Amen this Fifteenth Day of March Annoq. domini Seventeen Hundred Fifty & Nine, I Joseph Palmer late of Stratham in the Province of New-Hampshire in New-England yeoman, now residing at a Place Called Buckstreet in said Province being now very Weak and Infirm in Body * * *

Imprimis I give & bequeath unto Sarah my beloved wife (whom I do hereby constitute & ordain my sole Executrix of this my last well & Testament) all the money due to me from all Persons whomsoever & all my cattle, and Houshold Goods & Even all my moveable Estate whatsoever or wheresoever

Item My will is that my said Executrix (at my Decease) pay unto my beloved Daughter Elizabeth (the now Married Wife of Stephen Thirston of said Stratham) Forty Shillings in Bills of the old tenor which with what I have already given Her I judge to be her Equall part of my Estate

Item My will is that my said Executrix pay all My Debts Funerall Charges & the cost of Proving this my last will &c

Item I give and bequeath unto my beloved Son Daniel Palmer and to his Heirs & Assigns forever about seventy acres of Land Situate Lying & Being in the Town of Bow in said Province viz one quarter part of the first Division Lot of that Right in said Bow that origionally belonged unto cap^t John Gilmon; said

Division is N° twenty and lies in the Fourth Rang of the first Division Lots in said Bow; — and also the first Division Lot of that Right in S^d Bow that origionally belonged to Chase Wiggin said Lot is No Nineteen & lyes in said Range, Together also with one Moity or half part of the first Division Lot of that Right in said Bow that origionally belonged unto Ens^n Joseph Merril said division is N° Eighteen & lyeth in said Range: the said half part is to lye Adjoying to the aforementioned Lot N° Nineteen

Item I give and Bequeath unto my beloved son John Palmer and to his Heirs & assigns forever about sixty acres of land situate Lying & Being in the aforesd Town of Bow; viz the other Moiety or half part of the aforementioned Lot N° Eighteen together also with the first Division Lot of that Right in said Bow that origionally belonged to John Satchel said Lot is No seventeen and lyeth in the aforementioned Range —

Item My will is that my afore mention Son Daniel when he shall arive at the age of Twenty Three years shall pay Unto My Beloved Daughter Mehetable Palmer twenty Five Spanish mill'd Dollars of full weight or so much in any lawful money that shall then be passing in said Province as shall be Equall in vallue thereto

Item My will is that my aforementioned son John when he Shall arive at the age of twenty three years shall pay unto My beloved Daughter Hannah Palmer twenty Five Spanish Mill'd Dollars of full Weight or so much in any lawfull money that shall then be passing in said Province as shall be Equall in Vallue thereto * * *

Joseph palmer

[Witnesses] David Connor, Samuel Innes, Samuel Connor.
[Proved May 30, 1759.]

[Bond of Sarah Palmer of Bow, with Jonathan Robinson of Stratham and David Connor of Buckstreet, yeomen, as sureties, in the sum of £500, May 30, 1759, for the execution of the will; witnesses, William Parker, John Wingate.]

RUTH LANG　　　　1759　　　　GREENLAND

In the Name of God Amen —

I Ruth Lang of Greenland in the Province of New Hampshire in New England widdow * * *

Imprimes I Give Unto my son Nathaniel Shearburn of Portsm° five shilling New Tenor to be paid by my Executor within one Year after my Deceas.

Item I Give Unto my Daughter Mary Philbrock wife of Caleb Philbrock five shillings New Tenor to be paid by my Executor within one Year after my Deceas.

Item I Give Unto my Son John Shearburn of Kensington five shillings New Tenor to be paid by my Executor within one Year after my Deceas.

Item I Give unto my Daughter Ruth Row of Kensington five shillings New Tenor to be paid by my Exect^r within one Year after my Deceas.

Item I Give unto my Daughter Pressilla Sandborn five shilling New Tenor to be paid by my Executor within one Year after my Decease

Item All The Rest and residue of my Estate Real and Personel of what Nature or kind soever wheresoever the same may be found I Give and Bequeath unto my Son in Law Matthias Hains of Greenland

Lastly I Appoint and Ordain Matthias Hains aforesaid to be my sole Executor to this my Last will and Testamen ordering him to pay the Legassies as abovsaid. —

In Witness whereof I have hereunto set my Hand and Seal this 19th Day of March Anno Domini 1759 and in the 32^d Year of the Reign of George the Second King &c

　　　　　　　　　　　　　　　　　her
　　　　　　　　　　　　　　Ruth + Lang
　　　　　　　　　　　　　　　　Mark

[Witnesses] William Haines, William Blazer, Levi Dearborn.
[Proved Feb. 10, 1761.]

[Bond of Matthias Haines, gentleman, with William Haines, yeoman, as surety, both of Greenland, in the sum of £500, Feb. 10, 1761, for the execution of the will; witnesses, Solomon Loud, Jr., William Parker.]

MATTHEW GAULT   1759   CHESTER

In the Name of God, Amen this nineteenth Day of March Annoq. Domini one thousand seven Hundred fifty & nine I Matthew Gaalt of Chester in the province of New-Hampshire in New-England, Husbandman * * * And as touching my woldly Estate wherewith it has pleased God to bless me in this life I give and Bequeath the whole of it unto Elizabeth my now Married & well beloved wife (whom I do hereby constitute & ordain my Sole Executrix of this my last will & Testament) and to her Heirs and Assigns for Ever, that is to say I give to my said wife and to her Heirs & Assigns for ever — the whole of all & Each of those Lots of Lands that were given unto me &c by my Honoured father Samuel Gaalt of said chester in said Province in and by his deed to me under his hand & seal Bearing Date the twenty ninth Day of January annoq. Domini seventeen Hundred fifty & nine together with all the money due to me from any person or persons whatsoever and all my cattle Hous Hold goods or moveable Estate whatsoever and Even the whole of My worldly Estate & Interest Either in possession or Reversion

and furthermore My will is that My funerall charges and all the debts lawfully due from me to any person or persons whatsoever be paid out of my Estate by My Said Executrix * * *

                                                  Matthew Galt

[Witnesses] John Noyes, Asa foster, Abigail whittemore.
[Proved Aug. 29, 1759.]

JAMES LIGGETT   1759   LONDONDERRY

In the Name of God Amen I James Ligget of Londonderry within the province of New hampshire In New england yeoman * * *

Itim my Will is that my Beloved Brothers John Ligget and Samuel Ligget now Living in the Kingdom of Ireland Shall Posses all my Reall Estate in the Peack (so caled) which is the Place I Bult and improved upon In Equall Shairs to them their Heairs and assighns for Ever: they the afore Said John and Samuell paing in Equall Shairs to my beloved Sisters Effey Ligget who was maried to John Smith to hir or hir Heairs or asigns the Sum of two Hundred Pounds old tenor and to my Sister Kathrin Ligget who was married to Archibald macKonechey the sum of two Hundred Pounds old tenor, to Hir or hir heairs or assighns —

Itim my Will is that my third Devision and mendiment Land and Likewise my Half of the fourth Devision and a peace of midow Laying in hittitite (so caled) Shall be sold by my Exactor —

Itim my Will is that Robert macmurphy Shall have the Income of my Home Place untill the Heairs Comes hear to Receve Said Place free of Rent

Itim my Will is that Jane macmurphy Shall have two Hundred Pounds old tenor out of the money of which above mencioned lands shall be Sold for

Itim my Will is that Robert macmurphy Shall Have all my Personal Estate —

And I do Hearby Nominate Constitute and apointe my well beloved freand Robert macmurphy of Londonderry afore Said yeoman Exacitor of this my Last Will and testament and I Do Hearby utterly disalowe Revocke and Disanull all and Every other testament Will and Legaceis by me Done or Bequeathed In wittnes whereof I have heare unto Set my hand and Seall this twenty first Day of march and in the thirtey Second year of his Majesties Reign anno: Domo: 1759

James Ligget

[Witnesses] Sam'l Houston, Alex' Houston, John + mils his mark

[Proved Feb. 18, 1760.]

[Warrant, Feb. 19, 1760, authorizing Samuel Houston and Alexander McMurphy, both of Londonderry, yeomen, to appraise the estate.]

[Inventory, attested June 18, 1760; amount, £2634. 12. 0; signed by Samuel Houston and Alexander McMurphy; mentions real estate in The Pike, so called, in Londonderry.]

GEORGE CLARK   1759   PORTSMOUTH

[Administration on the estate of George Clark of Portsmouth, mariner, granted to John Long, commander of the ship Winchelsea, April 4, 1759.]

[Probate Records, vol. 21, p. 213.]

[Bond of John Long "now resident in Portsmouth Commander of the Ship Winchelsea", with Mark Hunking Wentworth and Wyseman Claggett, both of Portsmouth, as sureties, in the sum of £2000, April 4, 1759, for the administration of the estate; witnesses, John Knight, Jr., Henry Apthorp.]

[Account of the administrator; receipts, £49. 9. 0; expenditures, £27. 14. 10; allowed May 23, 1759.]

WILLIAM LANG   1759   PORTSMOUTH

In the Name of God amen the fifth day of april one thousand Seven hundred and fifty nine I William Lang of Portsmoth in the Province of New Hampshire Husbandman Being Very Sick & Week in Body * * *

Imprimis I Give to my well beloved Wife Susanna Lang the one half of My Reale Estate also the one halfe of my House hold

Goods for and during her widowhood & if She Marrays to Dispose of amongst my Children as She Shall here after think most Proper —

Itam I Give to my Well beloved Son Willim Lang and to his Heirs and assigns for Ever the one halfe of a forty acre Lot of Land in the town Ship of Chester that I Bought of Simon Barry

Itom I Give to my well beloved Son John Lang Nine Dollers or that Value to be paid him in Paper Bill by my Executors with in one Month after my Decease

Itom I Give to my Son Benjamin Lang and to his Heirs and assigns for Ever the one halfe of a thirty acre Lot of Land in the township of Chester it being Land I Bought of Simon Bary of Rye

Item I Give to my well beloved son thomas Lang and to his Heirs and assigns for Ever the one half of one Eighty acre Lot of Land in the town Ship of Chester it being Land I Bought of Simon Bary

Item I Give to my well beloved Son Mark Lang the Halfe of all my Real Estate not before Disposed of in this my Last will also halfe of my Parsnel Estate

Item I Give to my wellbeloved Daughter Susanna Yeaten one Doller to be paid her by My Executors within one month after my Decease

Item I Give to my Well Beloved Daughter Molly Lang Seventeen Dollers or that Value in Bills of Creadit to be paid her by my Executors within one month after my Decease

Item I Give to my Grand Child John Rand ten Pounds old tenor Bills or that Value to be Paid him with intrest at fifteen pr Cent if he Shall Live to the age of twenty one years old to be paid by my Executors

Item I Give to my Grand Child Rachel Rand ten Pounds old tenor Bills or that Value to be paid her by my Executors with intrest at fifteen pr Cent if She Shall Live to the Age of Eighteen years old

Item I Give to my Grand Child Lucia Rand ten Pounds old

tenor Bills or that Value to be Paid her by my Executors with intrest at fifteen pr Cent if She Shall Live to the age of Eighteen years old

I Likewise Constitute make & ordane my wellbeloved wife Susanna & my well beloved Son Mark Lang to be Sole Executors * * *

his
Willim + Lang
Mark

[Witnesses] John Norton, Jonathan Norton, Richd Jenness 3^d. [Proved Aug. 29, 1759.]

[Bond of Susanna Lang, with Richard Jenness, 3d, gentleman, and Walter Weeks, yeoman, both of Greenland, as sureties, in the sum of £2000, Aug. 29, 1759, for the execution of the will; witnesses, David Sewall, Jonathan Jewett.]

JAMES AYERS   1759   LONDONDERRY

In The Name of God Amen I James Eyers of Londonderry Yeman & Treader in ye Provance of New-Hampshire in New England, Being Sick and full of pain * * *

Imprimes Unto my well Beloved wife the one third of all my Reall and personall Estate Durin her life and then to Devolve to my Children in proportion as my Other Esteate —

Item I Bequeth to my Sons will^m and Sam^{ll} my Home lott will^m To have the South and Sam^{ll} the North side of said lott and it is my will thatt the Exec^r of this my last will and Testment may sell to the Best Advantage thatt lott or percell of land I Bought of John and David McAlester and after the Debts of s^d Place are paid it is my will thatt my four Doughters have there Equell part with my two Sons of w^t Remains of S^d lott of land —

My Personall Estate Exceep whatt is Bequethed to my wife is to Divoulve to my two Sons —

And of this my Last will and Testment I Do nominate and Appoint my Natrull Son Wm Eyars & and my Trusty freind Edward Aken son to Nath[ll] Aken To be wholl and Sole Ex[rs] to this my last will & Testment

James Eayers

[Witnesses] Elizabath + Elison, Anna + Boyd, Sam[ll] Cochran.
           her   her
           mark   mark

[Proved at Boston, Mass., May 4, 1759.]

[William Ayers of Londonderry declines executorship of his father's will June 26, 1759; witnesses, Thomas Wallace, Robert Wallace.]

[Warrant, June 1, 1759, authorizing Samuel Fisher and Thomas Wallace, both of Londonderry, yeomen, to appraise the estate.]

[Inventory, June 20, 1759; amount, £3456. 11. 6; signed by Samuel Fisher and Thomas Wallace.]

[Account of Edward Aiken, executor, receipts, £4231. 3. 11; expenditures, £4253. 9. 6; filed Sept., 1763.]

EBENEZER WESTON   1759   AMHERST

In the Name of God Amen — this Twenth fourth Day of April A D 1759 I Eben[r] Weston of a place Called Souhegan west (N B) in the Province of NewHamp[e] Yeoman   * * *

Imprimis I give to my well beloved Wife Ruth Weston Six Bushels of Endian Corn four Bushels of Rye one Bushel of Wheet Yearly but if the s[d] Bushel of Wheet should not be produced on my place then an Equivalant In Rye & one Bushel of malt yearly & Ninety pounds of Poark Forty pounds of Beaff Annually with three peck[s] of Beans one Bushel & an half of Turnups & Ten pounds of Flax & one Bushel And an half of Petatoes yearly

And a good Cow keept well for her from year to year so long as Shee shall remain my widdow and to have a Horse found her when & where shee shall have occation so long as Shee Shall remain my widdow & half ye Ground that is now fenced in for a garding ye same to be Well fenced & Well Dunged so long as Shee Remains my Widdow with nine Shillings Sterling Money of great Britain Annually so Long as Shee remains my Widdow with the Full Privilidge of my house of every part thereof During the aforesd period With the house Hold Moveable Effects which Shee Brought me to her Self for her own use & Benefit for ever & as much wood Brought to the Door & cut fit for ye fire so Long as Shee Shall Remain my Widdow And if my Wife should marry again then my will is that Shee Quit the Legacies only those Effects shee Brought —

Item I Give to my Sons Eben^r Weston Ju^r & Dan^ll Weston their Heirs and assigns for ever All my Real Estate or Estate in Lands As shall Appear by Deed or Deeds viz to Eben^r Weston afores^d Thirty five acres on the Easterly Side of ye farm I now live on Adjacent to the Tract my son Eben^r Afores^d purchased of me with one moiety of ye Intervail belonging To that Tract of Land I Bought of Co^ll Eben^r Nichols Including the Intervail that is Included in ye Deed the s^d Eben^r hath of the Land he bought of me — & After my Wifes Decease the house I give To Dan^ll Aforesd or if my wife should Contract Matrimony then s^d House to be Da^lls As afores^d & my Barn to be Divided Equally between Eben^r & Dan^ll as afores^d & my Stock to be Equaly Divided between Eben^r & Dan^ll I Likewise Constitute & ordain the s^d Eben^r Ju^r my sole Executor of this my Last Will & Testament And the s^d Eben^r To Levy & Rais out of ye premises money to pay my Debts & Funeral Charges & s^d Eben^r & Dan^ll to pay the Legacies herein before & hereafter mentioned by Parts as here Destin^d Eben^r Weston to provide one third of my wife^s maintainance As Allowed herein & Danil ye other Two thirds & my Wifes Funeral Charges my Executor to Levi out of my Estate —

Item it is my Will that the S^d Ebener Ju^r Should pay my Daughter Mehetibel Nichols one pound Sterling money As a Legacey out of my Estate & to Elezebeth Larrabee my Daughter one pound Sterling money in Two years after my Decease

Item it is my will that Daniell aforesd should have all my Real Estate which I have not given to Eben^r afores^d on his Paying the Legacies mentioned herein To Hepzibah Weston my Daughter Six pounds Sterling money to be paid In Two months After my Decease, And the s^d Dan^{ll} to pay my son Thos Weston Six pounds as Aforesd viz Sterling money in Two months after my Decease Likewise to pay to Isaac my son the same sum at the same time as to ye other Children viz Hepzibeth & Thomas Allso it is my Will that Eben^r Juner as aforesd should pay To my Daughters Tabatha & Son Southrick Six pounds Sterling money to Each of them In Two months After my Decease

Item it is Will that Hepzibah & Tabatha should have all my house hold goods Excepting what I Disposed of In this Testament heretofore which shall be Estimated as part of their portion before bequathed & what ye Effects are valued at Shall be Equaly Divided among my Children which have none of my real Estate That is Excluding Mehitabel & Elezebeth before mentioned * * *

Ebenezer Weston

[Witnesses] Semeel Lamsen, William odell, John Shepard Junr.

[Proved May 26, 1761.]

[Warrant, Feb. 5, 1761, authorizing Samuel Lamson and John Shepard, Jr., both of Amherst, to appraise the estate.]

[Inventory, May 25, 1761; amount, £7140. 15. 8; signed by Samuel Lamson and John Shepard, Jr.]

[Bond of John Shepard, Jr., of Amherst, with Samuel Lamson of Amherst and Nathaniel Bartlett of Plaistow as sureties, in the sum of £500, May 27, 1761, for the guardianship of Thomas and

Isaac Weston, minors, aged more than 14 years, children of Ebenezer Weston; witnesses, William Parker, Samuel Little, Jr.]

JONATHAN JONES   1759   AMESBURY, MASS.

[Mehitabel Jones renounces administration on the estate of her husband, Jonathan Jones of Amesbury, Mass., April 24, 1759, in favor of her oldest son, Daniel Jones of South Hampton; witnesses, Barnes Jewell, Dorothy Jewell.]

[Warrant, April 25, 1759, authorizing Abner Morrill and Eliphalet Merrill, both of South Hampton, yeomen, to appraise the estate, administration of which is granted to Daniel Jones.]

[Inventory, May 3, 1759; amount, £6195. 15. 0; signed by Abner Morrill and Eliphalet Merrill.]

[Petition of the widow, of Amesbury, Mass., for the setting off of her dower, and suggesting Joseph Jewell, Reuben Dimond, Benjamin Brown, Richard Collins, and Deacon John Ordway as a committee.]

[Petition of the widow, May 20, 1760, for the setting off of her dower, and suggesting Deacon Joseph French, Reuben Dimond, Deacon Samuel Currier, Richard Collins, all of South Hampton, and Jeremy Webster of Kingston as a committee.]

[Warrant, May 28, 1760, authorizing Jeremy Webster of Kingston, Joseph French, Reuben Dimond, Samuel Currier, and Richard Collins, all of South Hampton, to set off the widow's dower.]

Province of New Hampshir } Whereas we the Subscribers Were Appinted by the Honourable Richard Wibird Esqr Judge of the probate of wills &c within and for said province and authorized and Impowered to sett off to Mehitable Jones of Almsbery in the county of Esex and province of the Massatusetts bay widow her dower which hapneth to her of the Real Estate of Jonathan Jones of said Almsbury Deceased lying in South Hampton in the province of New Hampshir aforesd and accordingly We have Set off to the widow of the Deceased for her third part of six acers and thirty three Rods of land belonging to the home stead bounded as fowlleth Begining at ye River next to Joseph Jewels land thence Runing by ye River Northly the whole width of the land till it comes to the land set off to Abigal pike formerly the widow of Joseph Gould Deceased thence Runing from sd River by the line of ye sd pikes land fifty six Rods westerly to a stake and stones and then Runing five Rods and one foot southerly to a stake and stones and then Runing Eaighteen Rods westerly to a stake and stones thence Runing sixteen Rods to the west side the back Door of the Dweeling house thence to follow ye province line Easterly till it meets Joseph Jewels land and then to follow the Line by said Jewels land Down to the River the bound first Mentioned and also the west bay and half the Barn floor Bay in the Barn Reserving a conveniant privilege for ye use of the other part of the Barn.

then we set off to the Widow one third part of the orchard Begining at Cristopher Goulds corner bound from thence Runing Eaight Rods by the line of the said Gould land northerly to a stake and stones and then Runing westerly across the orchard to a stake and stones standing nere the River and then Runing southerly by the River to the original bound of said land then Runing Easterly to the Bound first Mentioned Reserving a conveniant passing way to pass and Repass to the other part of the orchard through ye said third part then we set off six acers and Sixty four Rods of Land Lying on the Northerly side powes River Begining at Sam[ll] Jones north westerly Corner bound Next to Capt John Currier land thence Runing by ye line of the said Curriers land in part and by ye land of sam[ll] straw in part till it Comes to a stak and stones standing in the line next to the said Straws land then Runing by the line of Jacob Jones land fourteen Rods Easterly then Runing southerly fourteen Rods in

Width till it Comes to the said Sam^ll Jones land first mentioned Reserving a Convenient passing way to pass and Repass from the widows land through the other part of the Estated of ye sd Jonathan Jones Deceased out to ye high way which we Judge to be her full third part of the Real Estated of ye sd Deceased this is our Return as Witness our hands this tenth Day of july ano Dom^ni 1760

        Reuben Dimond
        Joseph french
        Samuel Currier

[Account of the administrator; receipts, £3085. 5. 0; expenditures, £2089. 19. 3; allowed Dec. 31, 1760; additional account; receipts, £995. 5. 9; expenditures, £772. 11. 7; allowed Dec. 1, 1763; another of expenditures of £460. 0. 0, allowed Sept. 30, 1772; another of expenditures of £26. 18. 9, allowed Oct. 25, 1788.]

MOSES VARNEY   1759   DOVER

[Administration on the estate of Moses Varney of Dover, yeoman, granted to Phoebe Varney, widow, and James Varney, yeoman, both of Dover, April 25, 1759.]

[Probate Records, vol. 21, p. 222.]

[Bond of Phoebe Varney and James Varney, with Nathaniel Austin and Elijah Tuttle, yeomen, as sureties, all of Dover, in the sum of £1000, April 25, 1759, for the administration of the estate; witnesses, William Parker, W. Claggett.]

[Warrant, April 25, 1759, authorizing Joseph Austin and Joseph Hanson, both of Dover, yeomen, to appraise the estate.]

[Inventory, Oct. 8, 1759; amount, £10,718. 18. 0; signed by Joseph Austin and Joseph Hanson.]

[Account of the administratrix; receipts, £1930. 2. 2, personal estate; expenditures, £2031. 4. 2; allowed April 23, 1764.]

[Warrant, April 29, 1765, authorizing Thomas Westbrook Waldron, Joshua Wingate, gentlemen, Alexander Caldwell, yeoman, Ephraim Hanson, innholder, and Joseph Hanson, yeoman, all of Dover, to divide the real estate.]

Province of   } Pursuant to a Warrant from the Hono^{ble} the
New Hamp^r } Judge of Probate of Wills & for Granting Letters of Administration for the Province aforesaid — Wee the Subscribers have Divided the Estate of Moses Varney Late of Said Dover Dec^d according to the Annex^d Plan — vizt —

To His Widow Phebe Varney her thirds N° 3: 4 & 6 in the homested & Eight acres N° 7, in the home Lot at Rochester with a Priviledge of Passing & repassing to & from any of her Said thirds through any of the heirs parts where it may adjoyn thereto & most Conveniently Suit unto the road or roads as also the room in the west End of the Dwelling house —

To James Varney the Eldest Son N° 1: & 2 In the homested & also thirty acres in a third Division Lot N° 49: in the Town of Rochester aforesaid within which is Comprehended the shares of Sarah the wife of Solomon Leighton & Lydia the wife of Solomon Varney which he Purchased of them by Deeds Duly Authenticated —

To Elijah Varney his share N° 5: in the homested & also Eight acres N° 8: in the s^d home Lot at Rochester within which is Comprehended the Share of Humphry Varney which he Purchased of him by a Deed Duly Authenticated therefor —

To Peter Benjamin & Elizabeth Varney the whole Second Division right in the Town of Rochester aforesaid N° 101 also the fourth Division belonging to said right & also three Eighths of one third of another fourth Division in Said Rochester Equally Divided Between them

To Mordeca Varney his Share thirty acres in a Second Division in Said Rochester N° 79: & also Eighteen acres in a third Division Lot in said Rochester N° 5 Both pieces In Comon with the other owners of Said Lots it being the Deceas^{ds} right therein

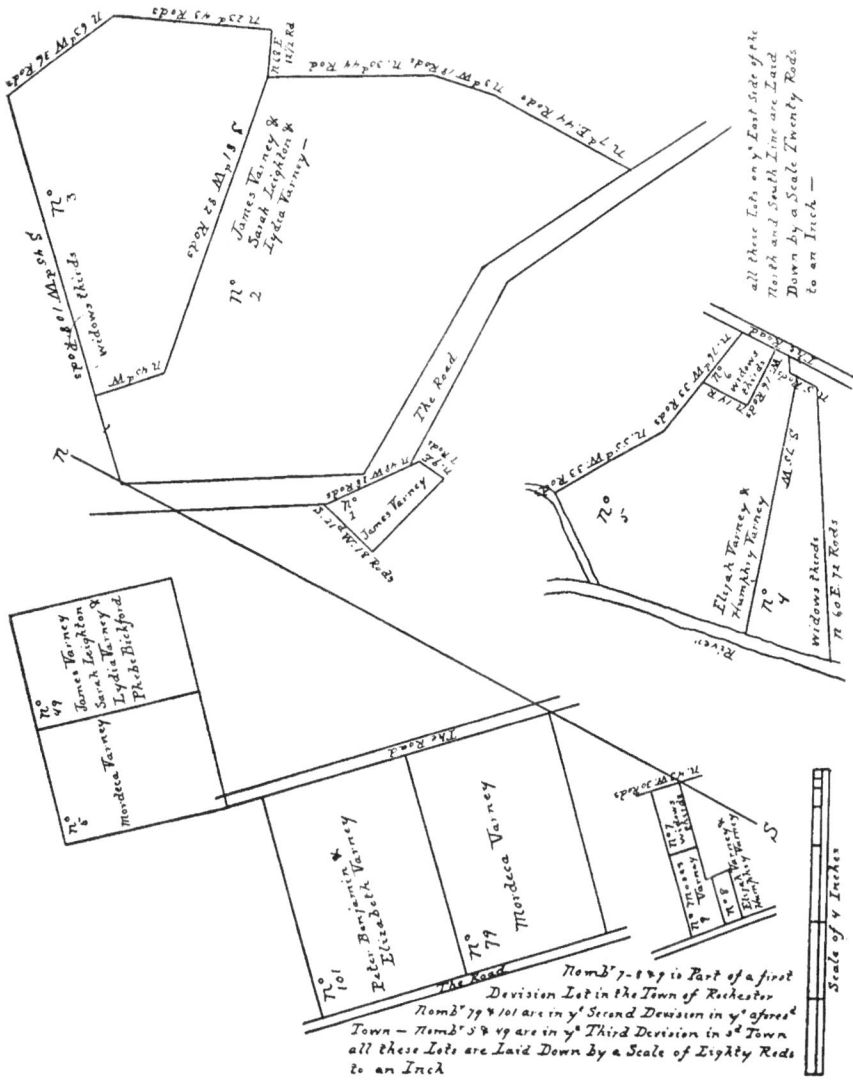

To Moses Varney twenty four acres in the said home Lot at Rochester N° 9

To Phebe the wife of Joseph Bickford jun^r one hundred & ten acres in the third Division in Said Rochester N° 49

All which Contains the whole of the Estate Shewn us to Divide & is Humbly Submitted By us the Subscribers — Dover July 26th 1765 —

Joshua Wingate
Alex^r Caldwell
Jos: Hanson
Eph^m Hanson

JONATHAN JONES   1759   SOUTH HAMPTON

[Administration on the estate of Jonathan Jones of South Hampton granted to Daniel Jones of South Hampton April 25, 1759.]

[Probate Records, vol. 21, p. 219.]

[Bond of Daniel Jones, with Abner Morrill and Eliphalet Merrill as sureties, all of South Hampton, in the sum of £1000, April 25, 1759, for the administration of the estate; witnesses, William Parker, Timothy Walker, Jr.]

[Caveat of William Parker, Jr., May 15, 1760, in behalf of the heirs, against the allowance of the administrator's account without their appearance.]

[Warrant, June 12, 1761, authorizing Jeremy Webster of Kingston, William Rowell of Newton, Richard Collins, Joseph Jewell, and Joseph Collins, yeomen, all of South Hampton, to divide the estate.]

Province of } Pursuant to a Warrant from the Honb^{le} New Hamps: } Richard Wibird Esqr Judge of the Probate of Wills &c for said Province appointing us the subscribers a Com^{tee} to divide the real Estate of Jonathan Jones Late of South Hampton Deceas'd Intestate to & among the Children of s[d] Deceas'd &c —

We have proceeded & divided the s[d] estate as followeth: makeing two divisions thereof: The first in the Home place: and have set of to Moses Jones the first share in the s[d] first Division Bounded as followeth viz: beginning at the Province Line and on a High way going by s[d] estate where it is Bounded with a stake & stones; from thence running easterly to Land set off to the widow of the deceas'd for her thirds or right of dower, in the s[d] estate where it is Bounded with a stake near the Back door of the Dwelling House of the deceas'd: then Northerly on the s[d] thirds about six rods to a stake: then westerly to the s[d] Highway to a stake by the fence: then southerly on s[d] way about six rods to the place where it first began: one Quarter of an acre more or Less —

2[ly] The second share to Samuel Jones Beginning at a stake by the s[d] way the Bounds of the first share: from thence running easterly by s[d] first share to the s[d] thirds where it is Bounded with a stake, which is the Bounds of the s[d] first share: then Northerly on s[d] thirds about five rods to a stake: then westerly to the s[d] way to a stake, then southerly on the s[d] way about five rods to the place where it first began, one Quarter of an acre more or Less —

3[ly] The Third share to Hannah the wife of John Elliot Beginning at a stake which is the Bounds of the second share: then running Easterly on s[d] second share to the s[d] thirds to a stake which is also a Bounds of the s[d] second share then Northerly on s[d] thirds about four rods and a Half to a stake which is a Corner Bounds of the s[d] thirds: then westerly to the s[d] way to a stake then southerly on s[d] way about four rods and an half to the place where it first began, one Quarter of an acre be it more or Less —

4[ly] The fourth share to John Jones Beginning at a stake which is the Bounds of the third share then running Easterly on the s[d] third share four rods and about two feet to a stake, then Northerly to the High way to a stake, then westerly on the s[d] way four rods and about two feet to the Corner of the land: then southerly on the High way to the place where it first began: one Quarter of an acre more or Less

5th & 6^{ly} The fifth & sixth shares to Daniel Jones Eldest son of the deceasd Beginning at a stake by the High way which is the Bounds of the fourth share & running southerly on the s^d fourth share till it comes to the third share where it is Bounded with a stake which is the Bounds of the fourth share then running easterly four rods and about two feet to a stake: then easterly on the forementioned third share & widows thirds four rods & about two feet to a stake: then Northerly to the High way to a stake by the fence: then westerly on the s^d way four rods and about two feet to a stake: then still westerly on the s^d way four rods and about two feet to the place where it first began: Half an acre more or Less —

7^{ly} The seventh share to Sarah the wife Ezekiel Flanders Beginning at a stake by the s^d way which is the Bounds of the sixth share & running southerly on the s^d sixth share to the forementioned thirds where it is Bounded with a stake the Bounds also of the s^d sixth share: then easterly on the s^d thirds four rods and a Half to a stake then Northerly to the way to a stake then easterly on the s^d way five rods and a Half to the place where it first began one Quarter of an acre more or Less —

8^{ly} The Eighth share to Judith Jones Beginning at a stake by the High way which is the Bounds of seventh share; & running southerly on the s^d seventh share to the widows thirds where it is Bounded with a stake a Bounds of the s^d seventh share: then running easterly on the s^d thirds five rods and an Half to a stake, then Northerly to the way or Christopher Goulds Land to a stake: then westerly on s^d way or Goulds Land six rods and a Half to the place where it first began one Quarter of an acre more or Less —

9^{ly} The Ninth & Last share to Mehetabel Jones widow of the deceasd in the Right of her daughter Miriam that is deceasd: Beginning at a stake the Bounds of the Eighth share & then running southerly on the Eighth share to the s^d thirds then easterly on the s^d thirds about six rods and a Quarter to a stake another Bounds of the s^d thirds, then Northerly also on the s^d thirds to the s^d Christopher Goulds Land where it is Bounded on a stake: which is another Bounds of the s^d thirds: then westerly on the s^d Goulds Land about seven rods and a Half where it first began; one Quarter of an acre more or Less —

2^ly The second division set off & Bounded as followeth viz:

1st The first share to Mehetabel widow of the deceasd in the right of her daughter Miriam deceasd in the orchard Bounded as followeth viz: Beginning at a stake in the orchard standing by the forementioned Christopher Goulds orchard; which is a Bounds of the widows thirds in the orchard; and from s^d stake running Northerly on s^d Goulds orchard till it comes to Powow River (so called): then westerly or south westerly by the s^d River to a stake standing on the Rivers Brink: then southerly to the s^d thirds in the s^d orchard where it is Bounded with a stake & stones; then easterly on the s^d thirds about four rods to the place where it first began: Half an acre more or Less

2^ly The second share to Samuel Jones in the above mentioned orchard; Beginning at a stake & stones by the s^d thirds which is the Bounds of the first share: then running Northerly on the s^d first share to the s^d River where it is Bounded on a stake which is a Bounds of the first share; then south westerly, on the s^d River to the s^d thirds then Easterly on the s^d thirds about four rods to the place where it first began: Half an acre more or Less —

3^ly The Third share to Moses Jones in the deceasds Land on the River Bounded as followeth viz: Beginning on the High way & at the River by the Bridge & from thence running Northerly on the River to a stake: then southerly to the High way to a stake; then Easterly about twelve rods to the place where it first began Half an Acre & ten rods more or Less —

4^ly The fourth share to Hannah now the wife of John Elliot: Beginning at a stake by the s^d High way which is the Bounds of the third share: then running Northerly on the s^d third share till it comes to the river: then still Northerly on the river to a stake: then southerly to the forementioned High way to a stake then easterly on the s^d High way about five rods to the place where it first began Half an acre & ten rods be it more or Less —

5^ly The fifth share to Judith Jones Beginning at a stake by the s^d High way which is a Bounds of the 4th share: and then running Northerly on the s^d fourth share till it strikes the River then Northerly on the River till it Comes to the great Rock (so Called) in the turn of the River: (which said great Rock is a Bounds of the deceas'ds Land on that side of the River) and then from s^d great Rock running westerly (or South Westerly) on ten acres of the Deceasds Land sold by order of Court since his death about two Rods to a stake then southerly to the forementioned High way, then Easterly on s^d way about five rods to the Bounds first mentioned; Half an acre & ten rods more or Less —

6 The sixth share to John Jones Beginning on the s^d High way at a stake which is a Bounds of the fifth share; & from thence running Northerly on the s^d 5th share to the forementioned ten acres to a stake the Bounds of the fifth share: & then westerly or south westerly on the s^d ten acres about five rods & three Quarters to a stake; then southerly to the s^d High way to a stake: then Easterly on s^d way about four and a Half rods to the place where it first began; Half an acre and ten rods be the same more or Less —

7^ly The seventh share to Sarah now the wife of Ezekiel Flanders Beginning on the s^d High way at a stake the Bounds of the sixth share then running Northerly on the s^d sixth share to the Land formerly sold as aboves^d to a stake the Bounds also of the 6th share; then running as the Last mentioned westerly (or south westerly) on the Land sold as forementioned about six rods and a Quarter to a stake then southerly to the s^d High way to a stake; then easterly on the s^d way about five rods to the place where it first began: Half an acre & ten rods more or Less —

8th & 9^ly The Eighth & Ninth shares to Daniel Jones Eldest son of the deceasd Beginning at the s^d High way, at a stake which is the Bounds of the seventh share & running Northerly on the s^d seventh share to the Land sold as aboves^d where it is Bounded on a stake which is the Bounds of the seventh share: then running westerly (or south Westerly) on the Land formerly sold as forementioned till it comes to a stake standing by the fence which is between the deceasds s^d Land and a piece of Land now in the possession of Joseph Jones: and then easterly on s^d Joseph Jones's s^d Land till it strikes the forementioned High way and then still easterly on the s^d way to the place where it first began one acre & twenty rods more or Less —

In Testimony of all foregoing we do hereunto set our hands the 28th day of July Anno Domini 1761

Jeremy Webster
William Rowell
Richd Collins

SAMUEL HADLEY   1759   HAMPSTEAD

In the name of God Amen: this Second day of May: 1759: I Samuel Hadley of the Town of Hampstead in the Province of New Hampshire in New England yeoman * * *

Imprimis I Give and bequeath to Judith my Dearly beloved Wife the Improvement of all my Real & Personal Estate so long as she remains my widow: and when she shall Marry another man my will is that she have the improvement of only one third of my Estate after my funeral Charges and other Debts are paid

Item I Give and bequeath to my two Sons namely Samuel & Jonathan all my Real Estate & my Right in a saw mill & also all my Husbandry Tools and all my Creatures not invadeing their mothers Right as above Exsspressed: my said son Samuel to have my fire lock: and in all other respects my said two sons to be Equal and to pay Equal to their sisters

Item I Give and bequeath to my Seven Daughter namely

Dorothy Abigail Sarah Judith Ruth Hephszibah Elenar; one Hundred pounds old tenor to Each to be paid by my two said sons; my said son Samuel to pay one Hundred pounds old tenor to my Daughter Abigail when he is Twenty two years old; further my said son Samuel to pay to my Daughter Sarah one Hundred pounds old tenor when he is Twenty four years old; my will is that when my said son Jonathan is Twenty two years old he shall pay to my Daughter Judith one Hundred pounds old tenor: further it is my will that my said son Jonathan when he is Twenty four years old Shall pay to my Daughter Ruth one Hundred pounds old tenor: further it is my Will that my said son Samuel Pay to his sister Hephszibah when he is Twenty Six years old one Hundred pounds old tenor; again it is my Will that my said son Jonathan pay to my Daughter Elaner one Hundred pounds old tenor when he is Twenty six years old; also it is my will that my said two sons Samuel & Jonathan pay to my Daughter Dorothy one Hundred pounds old tenor Equally betwen them when Jonathan my said son is Twenty Eight years old; further it is my Will that if one of my said sons die without Heirs the surviveing son to have what is willed to them both he paying what is Wil'd to my said Daughters if it be not paid

Item I give to my above said Daughters all my Housel stuff Equally Divided betwen them after my wife have done with them: I hereby Constitute make and ordain Judith my wife my soul Executrix of this my Last will and Testament giveing her all that is due to me from any Person or Persons She paying my funeral Charges and Just Debts * * *

his
Samuel + Hadley
mark

[Witnesses] Eben^r Gile, John Beard, Daniel Little.
[Proved June 3, 1761.]

[Inventory, attested June 2, 1763; amount, £5686. 0. 0; signed by Edmund Sawyer and Edmund Morse.]

BENJAMIN HILLS   1759   CHESTER

In the Name of God Amen. The Second Day of May 1759. I Benjamin Hills of Chester in the Province of New Hampshire in New England Yeoman, being Aged & infirm in Body * * *

Imprimis I give & bequeath to Rebecca my dearly beloved wife, a Case of Draws One Feather Bed with the Cloaths & furniture & all the Peuter to her & her Heirs forever My riding Horse & Two Cows, & one Third part of my Dewilling house & Barn, & ye one Halfe of the income of my Homestead, with a Sufficiency of good firewood during her Natural Life to be carried on & procured Yearly by my Executor.

Item I Give to my well beloved Samuel Hills besides what I have Already given to him ye Sum of five Shillings

Item I give to my Well beloved Daughter Abigail Moody besides what I have already given her the Sum Seven Dollars or An Equivalent in Paper Currancy within one Year after my Discease to her & her Heirs for Ever

Item I give to My Well beloved Daughter Rebecca Hills besides what I have Already given to her the Sum of Seven Dollars or An Equivalent in paper Currency within Two Years After My discease to her and her Heirs for ever

Item I give to My well Beloved Daughter Johanah Hazeltine besides what I have Already given to her ye Sum of Ten Dollars or An Equivalent in paper Currency to her & her Heirs for ever to be paid within Three Years After my Discease

Item I give to my well beloved Son Abner Hills besides what I have already given to him All my remaining part of that Hundred Acre Lott which I purchased of Philemon Blake to him & his Heirs forever

Item I give to My Well beloved Daughter Hannah French besides what I have Already Given to her ye Sum of Ten Dollars or An Equivalent in paper Currancy within Four Years After my discease to her & Her Heirs for ever

Item I give to My well beloved Daughter Prudence Chase

besides what I have already given to her the Sum of Ten Dollars to be paid within five years After my discease

Item I give to My well beloved Son Moses Hills besides what I have Already given him All my Coopers Tooles to him & his Heirs for ever

Item I give My Wearing Apparels to My Sones Equally to be divieded Amongst them

Item I gve to My Daugters After My Wifes discease All my Household Stuff to be Equally dived Amongst them

Item I give to My well beloved Son Benjamin Hills whom I Constitute my Executor of this my last Will & Testament All my Other Estate as well real as personal whatsoever & wheresoever whether in possession or revesion or remainder by him freely & fully to be possess'd & Enjoyed for ever by him & his Heirs

* * *

Benjamin Hills

[Witnesses] Joseph Richardson, Nathan Long, John Ambros. [Proved May 25, 1763.]

[Bond of Benjamin Hills, with Nathan Long as surety, both of Chester, yeomen, in the sum of £500, May 25, 1763, for the execution of the will; witnesses, William Parker, Cutts Shannon.]

SAMUEL STINSON   1759   DUNBARTON

[Administration on the estate of Samuel Stinson of Starkstown, yeoman, granted to James McCalley of Litchfield, yeoman, and his wife, Jane McCalley, May 4, 1759.]

[Probate Records, vol. 21, p. 276.]

[Bond of James McCalley and Jane McCalley, with Thomas Russ of Derryfield, cordwainer, and Matthew Patten of Bedford as sureties in the sum of £2000, May 4, 1759, for the administration of the estate; witnesses, Hugh Sterling, John Hall.]

[Warrant, May 4, 1759, authorizing John Hall and Hugh Sterling, both of Derryfield, gentlemen, to appraise the estate.]

[Inventory, June 26-27, 1759; amount, £1722. 7. 0; signed by John Hall and Hugh Sterling.]

[Account of the administrators; receipts, £896. 7. 0, personal estate; expenditures, £1055. 1. 0; mentions "Sundry Expences Laying in & nursing &c with a Child since the decease of said Stinson being Very Ill Some time after . . . . Supporting the dec^{ds} Son John from Augt 19 1757 to Feby 10th 1760 being under seven years of age . . . . Ditto his Son Sam^{ll} born march 29th since his fathers Death to the above date"; allowed Feb. 18, 1760.]

ZEBULON PEASE   1759

[Phoebe Stevens, wife of Samuel Stevens of Newmarket, yeoman, acknowledges the receipt from her son, Samuel Pease, of £452. 0. 0 which came to her from the estate of her son, Zebulon Pease, May 7, 1759; witnesses, William Parker, David Sewall.]

[See estate of Nathaniel Pease, 1749, vol. 3, this series, p. 678.]

JOSEPH TIDD   1759   HOLLIS

In the Name of God amen the fifteenth Day of May: 1759 I Joseph Tidd of Holles in the Province of New Hampsheir Husbandman being bound into his majesties Sarvis * * *

Imprimis I Give and bequeath to and order that my Honored mother be Comfortably Supported out of my Estate in a Decent mannar so long as she shall need it —

Itim I Give to my well beloved Brother Benjamin Peirce all my wearing apparrill —

and after my mothers Decess my Will is that all the Remander of my Estate be Equally Devided betwen my Brother and Sister and I Do likewise Constitute make and ordain Samuell Jewett of Holles yeoman in the Province aforesaid my sole Executor * * *

Joseph Tidd

[Witnesses] Peter Wheeler, Sam¹ Cumings, Prudence Cumings Junr.

[Proved Jan. 16, 1760.]

[Inventory, Jan. 4, 1760; amount, £256. 2. 11; signed by Benjamin Abbott and Ezekiel Jewett.]

CALEB PHILBRICK   1759   EPPING

In the Name of God Amen the 16th Day of May 1759 I Caleb Philbrick of Epping in the Province of New Hampshire in New England Husbandman I being Well in Body * * *

Imprimis I give and bequeath to my beloved wife mary Philbrick the Incum of one half of my home Stead and the Best room in my House and also one half of my Barn So Long as She Remains my widow and also I give to my wife all my Parsenal estate at her Despossel

Item. I give & bequeath to my well bloved Son John Philbrick all my Land where My Son John Now Lives that I have not Despos'd off before by deed, escept two acres Which I Reserve for my Son Samuel —

Item. I give and bequeath to my well beloved Son Samuel Philbrick two acres of Land and Bounded as followeth Begining at the South westerly Coner of the Six acres I Sold him and run Northeasterly Binding on Said Six acers the Whole Bredth of my Land So far as will Contain two acres

Item. I give & Bequeath to my Son Jonathan Philbrick the one half of my home Stead according to Quantity & Quality and also one half of my Buldings —

Item. I give & bequeath to my well beloved Son Nathanieal Philbrick all my Land Lying between the Land of Joseph Avery and thomas Drakes and also I order my son Nathaniel to Pay to my Executors five Hundred Pounds old tenor —

Item. I give to my beloved son Elias Philbrick the one half of my home Stead according to Quantity & Quality and also one half of my Buldings and to Come in Porsession at the age of twenty one years

Itim I give and bequeath to my beloved Dafter Elenar fogg twenty five Pounds old tenor and to be Paid By my Executors or Executor

Item I give & bequeath to my beloved Dafter Abaigal Philbrick twenty five Pounds old tenor and also one good Cow and Like wist to be fited with goods at the Day of her marridge or at ye years of Eighteen as Well as her Sister Elenar was and to be Paid by my Executors —

Item I give and bequeath to my beloved Dafter Ruth Philbrick twenty five Pounds old tenor and also one good Cow and Like wise to be fited with goods at the Day of her marridge or at the age of Eighteen years as well as her Sister Elenor was and to be Paid by my Executors —

Item I give and bequeath to my beloved Dafter alley Philbrick twenty five Pounds old tenor and also one good Cow and Likewise to be fitted with goods at the Day of her marridge or at the age of Eighteen years and to be Paid by my Executors —

I Likwise Constitute make & ordain my Wife mary Philbrick and my Son Jonathan Philbrick Executors * * *

Caleb philbrock

[Witnesses] Joseph Chandler, Peter Robinson, Abraham Perkins.

[Proved Dec. 26, 1759.]

[Bond of Mary Philbrick and Jonathan Philbrick, yeoman, with Abraham Perkins and Joseph Chandler, yeomen, as sureties, all of Epping, in the sum of £1000, Dec. 26, 1759, for the execution of the will; witnesses, William Parker, Joseph Simes.]

STEPHEN OTIS 1759 MADBURY

In the Name of God Amen, this twenty Second Day of May 1759 I Stephen Otis of Madbury Weaver, being very Sick & weak in Body * * *

Imprimis I give unto my three eldest Sons (viz) Joshua Stephen and John Otis if living, to each the Sum of Forty Shillings to be paid out of my Estate by my Executor or Executors without fraud.

Item. I give & bequeath to my Wife Elizabeth Otis whom I constitute and ordain my sole Executrix of this my last will and Testament all my Estate, Real & Personal to be by Her enjoy'd during her widowhood after which tis my will it be divided between the Children born to me of Her Body (i.e.) to the one or more of which she is now pregnant if it prove a Son to have a Double Share but if it prove a Daughter to share equally with the One now living (viz) Susannah Otis. * * *

Stephen Otis

[Witnesses] Israel Hodgdon, John Hanson, Nathan Kidder. [Proved Aug. 29, 1759.]

[Bond of Elizabeth Otis, with John Hanson and Israel Hodgdon, both of Dover, husbandmen, as sureties, in the sum of £3000, Aug. 29, 1759, for the execution of the will; witnesses, Timothy Walker, Jr., David Sewall.]

JOHN McNEIL 1759 LONDONDERRY

[Administration on the estate of John McNeil of Londonderry, mariner, granted to James Caldwell of Londonderry, yeoman, May 28, 1759.]

[Probate Records, vol. 21, p. 286.]

[Bond of James Caldwell, with Matthew Thornton and Robert Clark, yeoman, as sureties, all of Londonderry, in the sum of £500, May 28, 1759, for the administration of the estate; witnesses, Matthew Reid, Samuel Emerson.]

[Warrant, May 28, 1759, authorizing Robert Boyes and James Ramsey, trader, both of Londonderry, to appraise the estate.]

[Inventory, attested Aug. 14, 1759; amount, £4732. 0. 0; signed by Robert Boyes and James Ramsey.]

[Account of the administrator; receipts, £2064. 12. 0; expenditures, £2175. 9. 10; mentions "Keeping of the Deceasts Child from Aprile 20th A D 1756 to March 20th 1761"; allowed Dec. 17, 1764.]

JONATHAN YOUNG   1759   ROCHESTER

[Administration on the estate of Jonathan Young of Rochester, yeoman, granted to his widow, Elizabeth Young, May 29, 1759.]

[Probate Records, vol. 21, p. 303.]

[Bond of Elizabeth Young, widow, with Richard Bickford of Rochester, husbandman, and James Kielle of Dover, as sureties, in the sum of £500, May 29, 1759, for the administration of the estate; witnesses, Cutts Shannon, David Sewall.]

[Warrant, May 29, 1759, authorizing James Place and Joseph Walker, both of Rochester, yeomen, to appraise the estate.]

[Inventory, Sept. 26, 1759; amount, £2579. 11. 0; signed by James Place and Joseph Walker.]

JOHN WATTS   1759   SALEM

[Elizabeth Watts renounces administration on the estate of her husband, John Watts of Salem, May 30, 1759, in favor of Samuel Watts of Haverhill, Mass.]

[Administration granted to Samuel Watts of Haverhill, Mass., yeoman, May 30, 1759.]

[Probate Records, vol. 21, p. 249.]

[Bond of Samuel Watts, with Samuel Little, Jr., of Plaistow, yeoman, and Cutts Shannon of Portsmouth, gentleman, as sureties, in the sum of £500, May 30, 1759, for the administration of the estate; witnesses, Samuel Penhallow, William Parker.]

[Inventory, April 26, 1759; amount, £2276. 4. 0; signed by Samuel Watts and Jonathan Page.]

[Account of the administrator; receipts, £2165. 15. 4, personal estate; expenditures, £1524. 2. 10; mentions "Support of the Children"; allowed May 27, 1761.]

Wee the subscribers a Committee apointed to Set off the Right of Dower or thirds to Elisabeth Watts Rellict To John Watts Late of Salem In the Province of New Hampshire yeoman Decs[d] and Have accordingly set off as followeth (Viz) Two Hundred and fifty Seven Pound seven shillings old tenor In Personal Estate allso The House and Barn and three acres of Land on the Easterly side of the Roade and Joyns on Land of obediah Eastman and James Gregg, and also Twelve acres of Land on the westerly side of the aboves[d] Roade Begining at a stake and stones a Bounds of moses Kelley's Land so Westerly By s[d] Kelleys Land to a Nother stake and stones By Dustons Land so Takeing Equal width at Each End so far as to contain the aboves[d] Twelve acres —

Dated at Salem y[e] 5th of Jana[r] 1762 —

        Obadiah Eastman
        Timothy Ladd
          Committee

[Additional account of the administrator; expenditures, £48. 4. 0; mentions "Funeral Charges for a Child"; allowed Aug. 29, 1764.]

PRISCILLA SMITH   1759   PORTSMOUTH

[Administration on the estate of Priscilla Smith of Portsmouth, single woman, granted to Martha Smith of Portsmouth, single woman, May 30, 1759.]

[Probate Records, vol. 21, p. 249.]

[Bond of Martha Smith, with Hunking Wentworth and George Jaffrey as sureties, all of Portsmouth, in the sum of £500, May 30, 1759, for the administration of the estate; witnesses, William Parker, Richard Harvey.]

[Warrant, May 30, 1759, authorizing Joseph Peirce and John Wendell, both of Portsmouth, to appraise the estate; mentions the administratrix as sister of the deceased.]

[Inventory, Oct. 10, 1759; amount, £80. 15. 0; signed by John Wendell and Joseph Peirce.]

DANIEL QUINBY   1759   BRENTWOOD

[Administration on the estate of Daniel Quinby of Brentwood, husbandman, granted to his widow, Hannah Quinby, May 30, 1759.]

[Probate Records, vol. 21, p. 276.]

[Bond of Hannah Quinby, with Joseph Judkins and Sinclair Bean, yeomen, as sureties, all of Brentwood, in the sum of £500, May 30, 1759, for the administration of the estate; witnesses, Samuel Dudley, Benjamin Veasey.]

[Warrant, May 30, 1759, authorizing Sinclair Bean and Samuel Dudley to appraise the estate.]

[Inventory, attested Aug. 27, 1759; amount, £1366. 12. 0; signed by Sinclair Bean and Samuel Dudley.]

JOHN WATTS   1759   PLAISTOW

In the Name of God amen this Eleventh Day of June Anno Domini 1759: I John Watts of Plastow in the Province of New Hampsh^r in New England yeoman: being aged * * *

Item I Give and bequeath unto Sarah my dear and well beloved wife all my Household stuff and Goods within doors to be at her disposall also the use & Improvement of one third part of all the Housing & Lands which I herein bequeath to my two sons Samuel & Nathaniel Dureing her naturall Life to be by her freely possessed & injoyed

Item I give and bequeath unto my well beloved son Samuel all the Housing and Lands where he now lives Lying in the Town of Haverhill in Essex adjoyning to Land of Jonathan Marbles Heirs on one side & Websters Land on the other side in full of his portion in my Estate he paying to my Daughters what I here in order him

Item I give and bequeath unto my well beloved son Johns Heirs the Farm whereon he dwelt adjoyning to Land belonging to the Heirs of Capt Pecker on the south & on all other parts on the Highway Leading to Londonderry & Land of other Persons: in full of his portion in my Estate

Item I give and bequeath unto my welbeloved son Nathaniel all my Land and Buildings in Plastow and Salem near Providence Brook so Called within fence & not Disposed of he paying what I shall hereafter appoint him it being in full of his Portion of my Estate

Item I give and bequeath unto my well beloved Daughter Sarah Clement one Hundred pounds old tenor New Hampshire Money which I order my said son Samuel to pay her within one year after my Deceas

Item I give and bequeath unto the Heirs of my well beloved Daughter Elizabeth Curriar one Hundred pounds money old tenor to be paid by my Executor in manner following to my grandaughter Hannah Curriar Sixty pounds old tenor when she shall be Twenty one years old: and to my four granson Nathaniel Dudly James Simeon: I order that as they arive to the age of Twenty one years that they have ten pounds old tenor paid to each of them by my Executor and if any of them die before they have received as above their part to be equally Divided to the survivers

Item I give and bequeath unto my well beloved Daughter Mehitabel Eastman wife of Obadiah Eastman one Hundred pounds money old tenor New Hampshire money which I will and order my said son Samuel to pay her within two full year after my Decease

Item I give unto my well beloved Daughter Mary Webster wife of Joshua Webster one Hundred pounds old tenor which I order my s^d son Nathaniel to pay her in one year and half after my Decease

all the remainder of my Estate Exsepting some Land that I shall hereafter mention after all my Just Debts and mine and my Wives funeral Charges is paid is to be Equally Divided between my two sons Samuel & Nathaniel

and I do hereby Constitute ordain & appoint my son Nathaniel to be sole Executor of this my Last Will & Testament I also impowr my Executor to sell about sixty Acres of Land that lyeth between my son in Law Eastmans Land and the Land I have given to the Heirs of my s^d son John and also adjoins to Land of Seth Patee: the money this peice of Land fetches what is not improved to pay my s^d son Johns Debts and for my support in my lifetime I will and order to be given to my said son Johns son when he is Twenty one years old and if he departs this life before that time to be equally Divided to the surviveing Children of my said son John * * *

John Watts

[Witnesses] Henry hall, Abigail + Annis, Daniel Little.
[Proved Jan. 4, 1760.]

[Inventory, attested Feb. 11, 1760; amount, £3623. 11. 0; signed by Tristram Knight and Jonathan Page.]

NICHOLAS MEADER   1759   DURHAM

In the Name of God, Amen, the Ninth Day of June Anno Domini one Thousand Seven Hundred & fifty Nine, I Nicholas Meader of Durham in ye Province of New Hamps^e in New-England Husbandman, being advanced in Years, * * *

Imprimis, I Give & Bequeath unto my Beloved wife Sarah Meader the free & full Use & Improvement of my Dwelling House & Barn, & ye Produce of that Division of my Homestead Land on which my S^d Dwelling House Stands, & also ye Produce of a Certain Piece of my mowing Land, beginning at a Certain Elm Tree which is ye Bound between my Land & my Brother Joseph Meaders Land, from thence Runing Easterly by ye Dividing line between my Land & my s^d Brothers Land Twenty Rods, from thence northerly to a large Rock lying upon ye Land near a Division line between my Land & my S^d Brothers Land, & from thence by ye Division line between my Land & my S^d Brothers Land to my Pasture Land, And also the Produce of all my Thatch Bed from ye head of the Creek down to a Certain Stone Set in ye Ground, with liberty to Dry or Cure s^d Thatch upon ye Land, ye use of which I have Given to my Son Daniel Meader, adjacent to S^d Thatch Bed. And also all ye Produce of my Salt Marsh from ye head thereof Down to ye Trench, & from thence by ye s^d Trench northerly to an heap of Stones. And also ye one half of ye Feed of my Pastures, both of ye uper and lower Pastures; and also ye use & Improvement of thirteen Acres of my Land lying at Wheelwrites Pond; for fire wood to Support her fire, ye s^d thirteen acres in that Part of my s^d Land which adjoyns to Joseph Stimson's Land, Runing from ye High Way across my Land to ye afores^d Pond, & of a Breadth Sufficient to Compleat thirteen acres, holding an equal Breadth in Every Part. All ye aforegoing articles which I have Assigned unto my s^d Wife, I Give & Allow for her Sole use & Improvement yearly & every year during ye Term of her Continuing my Widow, but in Case She Shall Marry, then my will is that She Shall have her Proper Dowry out of my Estate, as by Law established.

I also Give & Grant to my S^d Wife ye free & full use and Improvement of all my Household Goods, Beds & Beding, & also of all my farming Tackling and utensils, during ye afores'd Term of her Continuing my widow. I also Give to my S^d wife, to her own Disposal, my Saddle Horse & one Yoke of oxen, & also ye one half of ye Remaining Part of my live Stock of Cattle Sheep & Swine.

Item, I Give unto my Son Samuel Meader & to his Heirs & Assigns for ever, Ten Acres of Land Adjoyning to his Homestead Land, being Part of my forty Acres on which my Son, John Meader lives, ye s^d Ten Acres Lyes in a Strip Runing ye whole length of my S^d forty Acres, & as wide as to Compleat s^d Ten Acres; and also Six Acres of Land more Lying on the Westerly Side of Lamper-Eel River, being the Part of Land that fell to me in ye Hook Land So Call'd.

Item, I Give unto my Son John Meader ye free & full use & Improvement of my Thirty Acres of Land where he now lives; and also ye Produce of my Thatch Bed, begining at a Certain heap of Stones, lying near ye little Marsh, & from thence Runing down to ye Mill Dam, & also ye Produce of ye one half of my Salt Marsh lying below the Trench, During the Term of his Natural life.

Item I Give to my Son Daniel Meader ye Produce of all my Land, begining Twenty Rods from ye aforesd Elm Tree & from that Extent Runing down to ye Marsh Point; And also ye one half ye feed of my Pasture Land; and also ye use of Twelve Acres of my wood Land, at Wheelwrite's Pond, to Support his fire, During ye Term of his natural Life.

Item, I Give unto my Son David Meader & to his Heirs & Assigns for ever, my Dwelling House & Barn and that Division of Land which my S^d Dwelling-House Stands upon, & the one half of my Pasture Land, and also a Certain Piece of my mowing Land, begining at a Certain Elm Tree, being ye Bound between my Land & my Brother Joseph Meaders Land, & from thence Runing Easterly by ye Dividing Line between my Land & my s^d Brothers Land Twenty Rods, & from thence Northerly to a large Rock lying upon ye Land near a Division Line between my Land & my s^d Brothers Land, & from thence westerly by ye Division Line between my Land & my s^d Brothers Land to my Pasture Land. And also all my Thatch-Bed from ye Head of ye Creek down to a Certain Stone, Set in ye Ground, with liberty to Cure or Dry his Thatch, Yearly & every Year, upon ye Land ye use & Improvement of which I have Given to my Son Daniel Meader, during his natural life, which Land is Adjacent to S^d Thatch-Bed. And also my Salt Marsh from ye Head thereof down to ye Trench, & from thence Northerly by ye S^d Trench to an heap of Stones. And also ye one half of my Pasture Land, both of ye upper & lower Pastures. And also Thirteen Acres of my Land lying at Wheelwrites Pond, being that Part of my Land which adjoyns to Joseph Stimson's Land, Runing from ye High-Way across my Land to ye afores^d Pond & of a Breadth Sufficient to Compleat Thirteen Acres, holding an Equal Breadth in every Part, And also all my Household Goods Beds & Beding, & all my farming Tackling & utensils. But my Will is that my S^d Wife During ye Term of her Remaining my Widow, Shall have ye free & full use & Improvement, Profit & Income of all ye afore mentioned Articles, which I have herein Given to my s^d Son David & to his Heirs & Assigns for ever, as is before Expressed. I also Give to my S^d Son David all my Waring Aparril.

Item I Give unto my Grand-Son Thomas Meader & to his Heirs & Assigns for ever Thirty Acres of Land lying where his father John Meader now lives, & also my Thatch Bed begining at a Certain heap of Stones lying near ye little Marsh, & from thence Runing down to ye mill Dam, & also ye one half of my Salt marsh lying below ye Trench, ye use & Improvement Produce & Profit of which Land Thatch Bed & Salt Marsh I have herein given to his S^d father during ye Term of his natural life. But in Case my s^d Grand Son Thomas Meader Should not Survive his s^d father John Meader, then I Give unto my Grand Son Stephen Meader & to his Heirs & Assigns for ever all ye above mentioned Articles herein Given to ye s^d Thos Meader, to be Possess'd & Enjoy'd by him ye S^d Stephen Meader, after ye Decease of his S^d father, & by his Heirs & Assigns for ever.

Item, I Give unto my Grand-Son Mark Meader, the Son of Daniel Meader, & to his Heirs & Assigns for ever, all my Land, begining Twenty Rods from the afores'd Elm Tree & from that Extent Runing down to ye Marsh Point; And also ye one half of my Pasture Land both of ye upper & lower Pastures; and also Twelve Acres of my Wood Land lying at Wheelwrites Pond, The use & Improvement Produce & Profit of which Land, both mowing Pasturing & Wood Land, I have herein Given to his father Danl Meader during ye Term of his natural life; But after his Decease, to be Possess'd & Enjoy'd by his S^d Son Mark Meader & by his Heirs and Assigns for ever. And my Will is that my s^d Son Daniel Meader, & my s^d Grand Son Mark Meader Shall make & keep in good Repair ye Partition fence between the mowing Land & ye Pasture Land, begining at ye Elm Tree afores'd & Runing Northerly to a Certain heap of Stones being ye Bound between my Land & my S^d Brother Joseph's Land.

Item I Give to my Grand Daughter Lydia Roberts four Hundred Pounds, old Tenor, to be Paid her by my Said Son Samuel Meader, within ye Term of Six Months after my Decease.

And I do hereby Constitute make & Ordain my s^d Wife Sarah Meader to be my Executrix, & Thomas Tuttle of Dover in ye Province afores'd to be my Executor * * *

nicos meder

[Witnesses] William Laighton, Hatevil Laighton Jn^r, Tobias Laighton.

[Proved July 29, 1767.]

[Inventory, attested April 27, 1768; amount, £533. 1. 8; signed by Amos Peaslee and Silas Tuttle.]

PETER STEVENS   1759   PLAISTOW

[Administration on the estate of Peter Stevens of Plaistow, husbandman, granted to Tristram Coffin of Newbury, Mass., yeoman, June 12, 1759.]

[Probate Records, vol. 21, p. 256.]

[Bond of Tristram Coffin, with Peter Coffin, clerk, and Jeremy Webster, both of Kingston, as sureties, in the sum of £500, June 12, 1759, for the administration of the estate; witnesses, Daniel Treadwell, William Parker, Jr.]

[Warrant, June 12, 1759, authorizing Samuel Kimball, yeoman, and Nathaniel Cheney, cordwainer, both of Plaistow, to appraise the estate.]

[Inventory, attested Oct. 8, 1759; amount, £570. 4. 0; signed by Samuel Kimball and Nathaniel Cheney.]

[List of claims against the estate, May 31, 1762; amount £131. 2. 5; signed by Nicholas White and Thomas Follansbee.]

[Account of the administrator; receipts, £540. 4. 6; expenditures, £444. 7. 10; mentions a widow and two minor children; allowed Nov. 16, 1762.]

[Settlement of claims; amount of claims, £111. 2. 1; amount distributed, £95. 16. 8; allowed March 2, 1763.]

THOMAS MEAD   1759   PORTSMOUTH

In the Name of God Amen. The Last will and Testament of Thomas Mead of Portsmouth in the Province of New Hampshire Cooper. I Thomas Mead being Sick * * *

Item. I Give and bequeath unto my well beloved wife Hannah Mead, the whole of my Estate both Real and personal during her Natural life. But if she shall have Occation to use any part or the whole thereof, the same I give unto her, her heirs and assigns.

Item After the decease of said Wife, if any of my Estate shall be Remaining, the Real Estate to be divided between my Son Joseph and daughter Marga^t and my parsonal Estate to my daughter marga^t I give the Same to them as aforesaid to them their heirs and assigns —

Item. my will is that my Two Grand Children Joseph and ann Wilkinson shall be paid the Sum of Ten pounds old Tenor (at the present Value) Each to be paid by my Son Joseph and daughter marga^t the Boye to Receive his part at twenty one Years of Age, and the Girl at Eighteen

Item, I do Request, and hereby appoint m^r Benjamin Akerman of Portsm^o to be Sole Executor * * * I have hereunto Set my hand and Seal the thirteenth day of June, in the 32^d Year of his majesty's Reign annoque Domini One thousand Seven hundred and fifty nine —

Thomas Mead

[Witnesses] Richard Fitzgerald, Richard Shortridge, Joseph Akarman.

[Proved Sept. 26, 1759.]

ALEXANDER WALKER, JR. 1759 LONDONDERRY

[Administration on the estate of Alexander Walker, Jr., of Londonderry, trader, granted to Alexander Walker of Londonderry, yeoman, June 14, 1759.]

[Probate Records, vol. 21, p. 256.]

[Bond of Alexander Walker, with Samuel Rankin and Thomas Walker as sureties, all of Londonderry, in the sum of £1000, June 14, 1759, for the administration of the estate of his son, Alexander Walker, Jr.; witnesses, William Parker, David Sewall.]

[Warrant, June 14, 1759, authorizing Moses Barnett and James McGregore, gentlemen, both of Londonderry, to appraise the estate.]

[Inventory, attested Nov. 19, 1759; amount, £3286. 7. 7; signed by Moses Barnett and James McGregore.]

[List of claims against the estate; amount, £1557. 0. 6; signed by Moses Barnett and James McGregore; attested Feb. 2, 1761; also list of claims for which Alexander Walker, Sr., was surety; amount, £2199. 1. 6; signed by Alexander Walker, and attested June 2, 1761.]

[Bond of Samuel Barr and James McGregore, gentleman, both of Londonderry, with John Goffe of Derryfield and David Steele of Peterborough, yeoman, as sureties, in the sum of £500, June 8, 1769, for the administration de bonis non of the estate; witnesses, James Kielle, Ezekiel Greeley, John Parker, Samuel Hale, Jr.]

[Account of the administrators, May 30, 1770; nothing to administer; signed by both.]

GEORGE MITCHELL   1759   LONDONDERRY

[Guardianship of John Mitchell, minor, son of George Mitchell of Londonderry, granted to John Mitchell, Jr., of Londonderry, June 27, 1759.]

[Probate Records, vol. 21, p. 262.]

JOHN JONES   1759   DURHAM

[Administration on the estate of John Jones of Durham, yeoman, granted to Abigail Jones of Durham, widow, June 27, 1759.]

[Probate Records, vol. 21, p. 261.]

[Bond of Abigail Jones, with Hubbard Stevens and Joseph Stevens, both of Durham, tanners, as sureties, in the sum of £500, June 27, 1759, for the administration of the estate; witnesses, William Parker, John Mitchell, Jr.]

[Warrant, June 27, 1759, authorizing William Drew and Samuel Demeritt, both of Durham, yeomen, to appraise the estate.]

[Inventory, Nov. 26, 1759; amount, £9754. 11. 6; signed by William Drew and Samuel Demeritt.]

[Account of Ebenezer Jones and his wife, Abigail Jones, administratrix; receipts, £2829. 11. 6; expenditures, £1618. 7. 10; allowed Sept. 30, 1761.]

[Warrant, April 30, 1762, authorizing Benjamin Mathes, Joseph Sias, gentleman, Jonathan Woodman, yeoman, Joseph Atkinson, and Thomas Chesley, yeoman, all of Durham, to set off the widow's dower.]

Province of } Pursuant to a Warrant directed to us the New Hampshire } Subscribers by the Honble Richard Wibird Esqr Judge of the Probate of Wills for the Province afores^d To set off the one third part of the Real Estate of John Jones late of Durham in s^d Province Yeoman deceas'd unto Abigail Jones the Widow of the said Deceas'd —

We have accordingly set off and bounded the s^d Abigails part as follows — beginning at the North West corner of the land which belonged to the said John by Eli Clarks land and running South Seventy One degrees East thirty one Rods & a half — then Runing South three deg^{res} west Sixty Rods, then East four Rods, then South 3 Deg^s West fifty Seven Rods to Benjamin Jones's land, then South 86 Deg^s West forty three Rods by s^d Benjamin's land, then South 76 Deg^s West Seven Rods, then West Twenty four Rods to the Road, then North Ten Deg^s West fifty Six Rods by the Road to Clark's land then North Seventy five Deg^s East Sixty Rods by s^d Clarks land, then North four deg^{rs} East fifty four Rods to the first mention'd bound — the whole within s^d Boundarys is forty three Acres Excepting Two thirds of the orchard at the East End which is in the Above Boundaries —

And also we have set of to the s^d Abigail her third of the dwelling house it being that which was first built, joining on the north side of the new house, together with the Cellar under her part — Also one third of the Twelfth part of the Stream at Durham Falls &c — Also one third part of the Barn vizt the Southerly end. —

And Also we have agreed that all the possessors of the Estate of the s^d John Jones deceased shall have full liberty to pass and Repass thro' each other's land to and from their respective lotts & the buildings and Orchard —

Durham October 20th 1762

Benjamin Mathes
Joseph Atkinson
Thomas Chesle   } Committee
Joseph Sias
Jonathan Woodman

OLIVER SMITH   1759   EXETER

In Name of God amen This Fifth Day of July anno Domini 1759 I oliver Smith of Exeter in the province of Newhamp^r Gentelman being but Weak of body * * *

first I Give unto my beloved Wife Rachel and to her Disposel all The Houshuld Stufe which she brought to me when I marred her, and I Give to my said wife one Cow and that to be Keept sumer and winter During the naturall Life of my Said wife or so Long as she Remains my widow as I shall hereafter order & I Give unto my said wife the Use and improvement of the westerly End of my Dwelling House and my bead Room and the one Halfe of my Celler and fierwood for one fier haled to her Door and the wood to haled from my Place at Dear Hill (so Caled) and teen bushels of Corn one Hunderd waight of Pork one Hunderd waight of beafe Two Galons of Rum Two Galans of melases Four Barels of Cyder one bushal of Potaters one bushel of Turnaps & half a bushel of beans Six Pounds of sheeps wool Ten Pounds of flax from the swingel Two Pare of Shews & the use of my Garden & Clock all The Pertucklers to be Paid and Deliverd to my said wife yearly During her natural Life or so Long as Shee Remains my Widow and I Give unto my said wife fifty pounds old tener and to be Paid out of my money

Iti^m I Give unto my my Daughter mehetabel Lyford & to her Disposel The full one Halfe of all my Personall Estate both within Dors & with out not allready Desposed of, to her mother in this my Last will viz the one halfe of my Housel Goods & the whole of my Clock after her mothers Desceece or marrage and the one halfe of all my Stock of Catel Sheep horses & Swine & the one halfe of my Debts & money

And I Give unto my Said Daughter mehetabal The use and Inprovenent of all my Lands be the same more or Less Lying & being in the Parish of Brintwood & near Dear Hill (so Caled) During her naturall Life and Thin The said Lands to be Equaly Divided to & among the Children of my said Daughter mehetabel That Shall Survive There mother & to there heirs & assings My said Daughter or her Leguall Representives Paying and Delivering to my said wife The full one halfe Part of what She is to have yearly as a Leagsey During her naturall Life or so Long as shee Remains my Widow

Iti^m I Give unto my two Grandsons (viz) oliver Calfe and Jeremiah Caffe sons to my Daughter Ruth Calfe Deceased and to there Heirs & assings for Ever Equaly to be Divided between them all my Lands in Exeter or Stratham Caled my whomestead be the same more or Less With all my buldings standing on the same and allso all That seventeen acres & halfe of Land & medow Ground Which I Purchesed of John Folsom Laying in Exeter aforesaid & on the south side of Walls Cove (so Caled)

They my said Grand sons to Come into Possession Imeadetly at my Decease Exepting That Part of the Dwelling House and Garden which I Gave to my wife & That at her Decease or marrage and my will is That if Either of my said Grand sons should Die before he arive to the age of Twenty one years Leiving no Issue Lawfully begoten of his body Then his Surviving Brother Shall have his Part of my Real Estate and furthermore I Give to my said Grand sons above mentioned the full one halfe Part of all my Personall Estate both within Dors & without Equally to be Divided between them & There aunt Lightford Excepting my Clock and what I Shal Give to There Sister Elisabeth in my Last will and what I have Given to my wife in this my Last will and Like wise my Will is That my said Grand sons viz Oliver Calfe & Jeremiah Calfe Shall have free Liberty to Cut There fier wood for there fiers for Twenty years after my Decease on that Tract of Land in brintwood which I Gave to my Daughter mehetabel & to her Children my Said Grand sons oliver & Jeremiah Paying & Delivering unto there Grandmother as it shall becom Due the full one halfe Part of what I have Given her in this my Last will & Testenent and to Pay There sister Elisabeth her Legsecy as I shall order in this my Last will.

Iti^m I Give to my Grandaughter Elisabeth Calfe Daughter of Ruth Deceased The full one halfe Part of my Housel Stufe within Dores Exepting my Clock and what I have Given to her Grandmother and I Give unto my said Grandaughter Elisabeth Calfe Five Hunderd Pounds old tener as money is at This time and to be paid to her by my two Grand sons oldiver Calfe and Jeremiah Calfe Each to Pay to there sister Two Hundrd and fifty Pounds old ter & to be Paid in six month after They arive at the age of Twenty one years

Iti^m I Give unto Abraham Clark That Served his time with me fifty Pounds old tenor bills of Credit to be paid by my Executrix in one year after my Decease

Iti^m I Give unto my two Grandsons Oliver Calfe & oliver Smith Lightford and to There heirs & assings Eccquely to be

Divided between them according to Quantity & Quality all my Right in the Town of Gilmantown in the province afore said be the same more or Less

Iti^m I Give unto Ithiel Smith Son of Ithiel Smith Late of Brintwood Deceased and to his heirs & assings all my Right of Land in That Tract of Land Granted by Theador Atkisson Esqr and others to John Samborn & others & Layeth near Pemessewaseet (So Caled) in the Province afore said

Lastly I Do hereby Constitute and appoint My Wife Rachel to be sole Excu^x   *   *   *

Oliver Smith

[Witnesses] Abnar Thustin, Joshua Wilson, Theo: Smith.
[Proved June 25, 1760.]

[Bond of John Calfe of Exeter, yeoman, and Moses Lyford of Brentwood, tailor, with Abner Thurston, cordwainer, and Joshua Wilson, yeoman, both of Exeter, as sureties, in the sum of £1000, June 25, 1760, for the administration, with will annexed, of the estate; witnesses, William Parker, Solomon Loud, Jr.]

[Warrant, June 25, 1760, authorizing Theophilus Smith and James Leavitt, gentleman, both of Exeter, to appraise the estate.]

[Inventory, June 26, 1760; amount, £33,172. 11. 0; signed by Theophilus Smith and James Leavitt.]

[Account of the administratrix; receipts, £137. 0. 0 and personal estate; expenditures, £795. 11. 6; mentions "abigail Maintained 26 Weeks . . . . Hannah 104 weeks . . . . Jeremiah & oliver 416 weaks each & not 7 years old now"; allowed Oct. 28, 1761.]

[Probate Records, vol. 22, p. 235.]

NATHAN HUNT   1759   SANDOWN

Province of } To the Honnerd Richard Wibard Esqr Judge
Newhamp^r } of Probets of wills &c —

Sir my husband Being Ded and Left me with a famuely of small children and I my selfe not capebel To manige the setteling of the small Estate Left by my husband this is To Request of your Honner To grant a Leter of administration To Eben^r Stevens Esqr as he is the Bigest Credeter that I Know of To the Estat of the Decesed — and is so doing you will much oblige your most Humbel Sarvent

Kingston July the 18th 1759

    Ichabod Shaw
    Sarah Shaw

                                         her
                              Ledea X Hunt
                                         mark

[Administration on the estate of Nathan Hunt of Sandown, yeoman, granted to Ebenezer Stevens of Kingston July 25, 1759.]

[Probate Records, vol. 21, p. 274.]

[Bond of Ebenezer Stevens, with Daniel Peirce of Portsmouth and Samuel French of South Hampton, gentleman, as sureties, in the sum of £1000, July 25, 1759, for the administration of the estate; witnesses, none.]

[Warrant, July 25, 1759, authorizing Ichabod Shaw and Israel Dimond, both of Kingston, gentlemen, to appraise the estate.]

[Inventory, attested Oct. 10, 1759; amount, £1476. 12. 0; signed by Ichabod Shaw and Israel Dimond.]

[Additional inventory, March 12, 1761; amount, £310. 0. 0; signed as above.]

[Warrant, May 23, 1761, authorizing Ichabod Shaw of Sandown, Israel Dimond, Nathan Jones, Henry Morrill, and Moses Colby, all of Hawke, yeomen, to divide the real estate among the widow, Lydia Hunt, and the seven children.]

Province of } We the Subscribers being appointed By the
New Hamp[r] } hon[ble] the Judge of the Probate for said Province A Committee to view the Real Estate of Nathan Hunt late of Sandown in said Province Yeoman Deceased Intestate & to set off to Lydia the widow of said Deceased her Dower in said Estate & to Consider whither the remaining two thirds of said Estate may be divided among all the Children of said Deceased without prejudice to the whole, & if it cannot to appraise the Same Have proceeded & Set off to the said Lydia her Dower as follows viz beginning on Land possessed by Samuel Plummer then run[g] Southerly by said Plummers Land thirty three Rods to Land in Possession of Benj[a] Pilsbury thence westerly twenty Rods to a Stake & Stones, thence northerly fifty two Rods to a Stake & Stones at Angling Pond thence Easterly thirteen Rods to a Stake & Stones thence Southerly thirty eight Rods to a Stake & Stones thence Easterly five Rods to the Place where it first began —

We have also Considered the remaining two thirds & think it can not be divided among all the Children of Said Deceased without Prejudice to the whole & have therefore Appraised the same & think the Present Value thereof to be five hundred & forty pounds Old Ten[r] there being twelve Acres of the Same — Witness our Hands June 8th 1762

Ichabod Shaw }
Israel Dimond } Committee &c
Henry Morrill }

[Account of the administrator; receipts, £928. 17. 0; expenditures, £861. 17. 2; mentions "Support of Eliz[a] Hunt for three years being a minor under 7 years"; allowed June 30, 1762.]

ANN PACKER   1759   PORTSMOUTH

In the Name of God Amen I Ann Packer wife of Thomas Packer of Portsmouth in the Province of New Hampshire Esq[r]

By and with the Consent of my Said Husband having a Personal Estate in my Own Right & being my Own Property * * *

Imprimis If Providence shoud order it so that I shoud be left a Widow & Contract any Debts my Will is that Such Debts & my Funeral Charges be paid out of my Estate with all Convenient Speed after my Decease —

Item I Give & bequeath all my wearing apparel to my Daughters Elizabeth Wentworth Mehetabel Rogers & my Grand-Daughter Anna Peirce Equally to be Divided —

Item all the Residue of my Estate I give & Devise to my Sons John Daniel William Isaac and Jotham and my Daughters Elizabeth & Mehetabel & my Said Grand Daughter Anna Peirce Equally to be Divided without any Preference of One to the other

Item Lastly I hereby Constitute & Appoint my Son Daniel Rindge Sole Executor * * * In Witness whereof I have hereunto Set my hand and Seal the Thirty first Day of July Anno Domini 1759

Ann Packer

[Witnesses] James Stoodly Ju^r, John Clark, Joshua Brackett. [Proved Feb. 8, 1762.]

Know All Men By these Presents That I the within Named Thomas Packer for Divers good Causes & Considerations more Especially that Justice & Equity may be Done to the Children & Grand Child of my Said Wife within named and that neither I my Self nor any Person Claiming in my Right either by Decent as next of kin or by Purchase may have any Part Interest or Demand in & unto the Estate mentioned & Referrd to & bequeathed by the within Written Will & Testament or thereby Intended to be Dispos'd of Did freely Consent to & approve of making the same as therein Declared & to the full & Due Execution thereof and farther did advise my Said Wife to Dispose of the said Estate in such manner and form & to whomsoever she shoud See Cause — And I do by these Present fully Approve Ratify & Confirm the said last Will & Testament as within

Written & Executed & Every clause & article thereof And for my Self my Heirs Executors & admin^rs do hereby Grant Remise Release & forever Quit Claim to the within Named Devisees & Legatees Respectively all the Right Title Interest & Demand which I by Law have or Ought to have to the Estate Devised or Bequeathed to them in & by this Said Last Will & Testament of my Said Wife And that I my Heirs Executors or Admin^rs shall not & will not make any Objection or take any Exception to the Probate & full Allowance & Approbation thereof In Witness whereof I have hereunto Set my hand & Seal the thirty first Day of July Anno Domini 1759 —

Thos Packer

[Witnesses] James Stoodly Ju^r, John Clark, Joshua Brackett.

SAMUEL VARNEY   1759   DOVER

In the Name of God Amen ye twenty forth of ye 8mo one thousand Seven Hundred & fifty Nine I Samuel Varney of Dover In the Province of Newhampshire in Newengland Husbandman Being veary week in Body * * *

Item I Give To Mary My well Beloved wife all My Estate within Dores & without Dureing Hir widowhood Exclusive of ye above Debts & Nessesary Charges that Shall Arise on the Estate & what I Shall Bisstow on my two Daughtors Hereafter mentioned —

Item I Give to My Daughtor Sarah twenty & Seven Pounds Starling Money when Shee Shall arrive to the age of twenty years to Be Paid in Household Goods

Item I Give to My Daughtor Mary when Shee arrives to Eighteen years of age Thirty & two Pounds Starling Money to Bee Paid as above —

Item I Give unto My Seven Sons Solomon Timothy Samuel

Simeon Amus Shubel & Joseph — after the Deceas or marriage of My Wife all the Remaining Part of my Estate to Bee Equally Devided Between them.

I also Constatute Make and ordain My Eldest Son Solomon Varney Sole Executor * * *

Samuel Varney

[Witnesses] Silvanus Hussey, Danl Ricker, Samuel Richards. [Proved April 30, 1760.]

[Bond of Solomon Varney, with Paul Ricker and Samuel Richards as sureties, all of Dover, in the sum of £500, April 30, 1760, for the execution of the will; witnesses, William Parker, David Sewall.]

[Mary Varney, widow, expresses her satisfaction with the executorship of Solomon Varney June 25, 1760; witnesses, William Ham, Samuel Richards.]

[Guardianship of Samuel Varney, minor, son of Samuel Varney, granted to Nathaniel Varney of Dover, yeoman, Jan. 28, 1761.]

[Probate Records, vol. 22, p. 21.]

[Bond of Nathaniel Varney, with John Brewster and Jacob Chamberlain, both of Rochester, yeomen, as sureties, in the sum of £500, Jan. 28, 1761, for the guardianship of Samuel Varney; witness, Solomon Loud, Jr.]

[Guardianship of Amos Varney, minor, aged more than 14 years, son of Samuel Varney, granted to Joshua Varney Nov. 28, 1764.]

[Probate Records, vol. 23, p. 342.]

[Bond of Joshua Varney of Dover, with Joseph Lowe and Enoch Hoag, both of Portsmouth, as sureties, in the sum of £500, Nov. 28, 1764, for the guardianship of Amos Varney; witnesses, William Parker, Jr., William Vaughan.]

NATHAN COLBY   1759   CONCORD

[Hannah Colby, widow, and Nathan Colby, oldest son, request that administration on the estate of Nathan Colby of Rumford be granted to Timothy Walker, Jr., of Rumford, Aug. 24, 1759.]

[Administration granted to Timothy Walker, Jr., of Rumford, bricklayer, Aug. 29, 1759.]

[Probate Records, vol. 21, p. 278.]

[Bond of Timothy Walker, Jr., bricklayer, with John Noyes of Suncook and James Graves of Hampstead, gentlemen, as sureties, in the sum of £2000, Aug. 29, 1759, for the administration of the estate; witnesses, Israel Hodgdon, John Hanson.]

[Warrant, Nov. 29, 1759, authorizing Ezra Carter and George Abbott, yeoman, both of Rumford, to appraise the estate.]

[Inventory, Nov. 28, 1759; amount, £3022. 17. 0; signed by Ezra Carter and George Abbott.]

[Commission, Nov. 28, 1759, to Ezra Carter of Penacook and John Noyes of Bow, yeoman, to receive claims against the estate.]

[List of claims, June 12, 1761; amount, £2354. 3. 10; signed by Ezra Carter and John Noyes.]

[Account of the administrator; receipts, £2141. 0. 0; expenditures, £1522. 6. 9; mentions "maintaince of Children that are under Seven Years old at this time . . . . funeral Charge & the Charge of lying in after the Intestates Decease"; attested Aug. 6, 1761.]

[Settlement of claims; amount of claims, £2354. 3. 10; amount distributed, £618. 13. 3; allowed Nov. 25, 1761.]

WILLIAM PEAVEY   1759   PORTSMOUTH

[Administration on the estate of William Peavey of Portsmouth, mariner, granted to John Peavey of Portsmouth, carpenter, Aug. 27, 1759.]

[Probate Records, vol. 21, p. 276.]

[Bond of John Peavey, with Daniel Warner and Nathaniel Warner, merchant, as sureties, all of Portsmouth, in the sum of £2000, Aug. 27, 1759, for the administration of the estate; witnesses, George Libby, Thomas Wendell, T. Greenwood.]

SAMUEL PALMER, JR.   1759   HAMPTON

In the name of God Amen this twenty Seventh Day of August Anno Domini 1759 and in thirty third year of his Majestys Reign Georg the Second King over Grate Britain &c I Samuel Palmer Juner of Hampton in the Province of new Hampshier in new England Esqr * * *

first I give and bequeath to my Daughter Jane Knowls the wife of Samuel Knowls twenty five pounds in money old Tenor to be Paid to her by my son Samuel Palmer within two years after my Decease

Secondly I give and bequeath to my Daughter Anna Palmer one hundred Pounds in money old tenor to be paid to her by my Said Son Samuel Palmer within one year after my Decease I also give to my Said Daughter Anna Palmer one fether bed and furnituer belonging to it that was her own mothers and further it is my will that my Said Daughter Anna Palmer shall have Liberty to Live in and Improve the westerly End of my Dwelling house untill she is married and also have six bushels of Indian Corn and sixty pounds weight of Pork and forty Pounds waight of beef and four Cord of fier wood and the milk of one Cow all found and Provided for her yearly and every year by my said Son Samuel Palmer untill she is married and no Longer thirdly I give to my said Daughters Jane and Anna all the moveables of all sorts that was their own mothers to be equilly Devided between them excepting onely the bed and beding which I gave to my said Daughter Anna as afore said

fourthly I give and bequeath to my son the said Samuel Palmer my Dwelling house and barn saveing onely the Privilidg as afore Said that my said Daughter Anna Palmer is to have of Liveing in the westerly Room in my Dwelling house untill she is married I also give to my said son Samuel Palmer all my land where my Dwelling house is six acres more or less with all my land in the Pastour some time Called Palmers Pastour Joining westerly to land of Redmans Southly to land of the Dows Eastly on Land of the Palmers six acres more or less with all my land Laying in the nook so Called six acres more or less bounding northerly on the way that Leads to tucks mill westly on land of Jeremiah Moulton southly on Palmers Paster so called Eastly on land of Josiah Moulton Junr to gether with all other my land laying in the first Division of the five Divisions in said Hampton both on the northly and southely side of lettle River with all my marsh Called the spring marsh and my meadow in the old fresh meadow near the Beach and also all my huccle Berry marsh laying between tuck mill and the Beach all the Said Parcels of land marsh are laying in Hampton afore said I give to my said son Samuel all my stock of Cattle and husbandry Implements with all my moveables in my house which I have not here in other ways Disposed of as afore said it is my Will that my Said Daughter Anna Palmer shall have one seventh Part of the apples in my orchard yearly every year so long as she Remains un- marryed

all the Lands I have Laying in Hampton as afore said or else where I give to my said son Samuel Palmer and to his heirs and assigns for ever and I Do here by Constitute make and ordain my Said Son Samuel Palmer to be sole executor * * *

Samuel Palmer Junr Esq

[Witnesses] John Lamprey, Jonathan Lock, Robert Moulton 3ᵈ.

[Proved June 30, 1762.]

[Inventory, attested Nov. 24, 1762; amount, £5317. 0. 0; signed by John Weeks and John Lamprey.]

PHILIP REED   1759   PORTSMOUTH

[Administration on the estate of Philip Reed of Portsmouth, mariner, granted to Dorothy Reed of Portsmouth, widow, Aug. 29, 1759.]

[Probate Records, vol. 21, p. 285.]

[Bond of Dorothy Reed, with Mark Langdon, gentleman, and Samuel Griffith, shopkeeper, as sureties, all of Portsmouth, in the sum of £3000, Aug. 29, 1759, for the administration of the estate; witnesses, David Sewall, Benjamin Akerman.]

[Inventory, Sept. 13, 1759; amount, £5859. 19. 11; signed by Eleazer Russell and Samuel Penhallow.]

ENOCH GOVE   1759   HAMPTON FALLS

[Administration on the estate of Enoch Gove of Hampton Falls, yeoman, granted to his widow, Hannah Gove, Aug. 29, 1759.]

[Probate Records, vol. 21, p. 303.]

[Bond of Hannah Gove, with Jonathan Swett and Caleb Sanborn, gentlemen, as sureties, all of Hampton Falls, in the sum of £3000, Aug. 29, 1759, for the administration of the estate; witnesses, Meshech Weare, Susanna Sanborn.]

[Warrant, Aug. 29, 1759, authorizing Jonathan Swett, gentleman, and Nathaniel Gove, yeoman, both of Hampton Falls, to appraise the estate.]

[Inventory, Oct. 10, 1759; amount, £12,123. 2. 0; signed by Jonathan Swett and Nathaniel Gove.]

[Account of the administratrix; receipts, £3058. 18. 0, personal estate; expenditures, £838. 10. 3; mentions personal estate of the former husband of the administratrix and his children; allowed March 28, 1760.]

Province of New Hamps^r } We the Subscribers being Appointed a Committee by the Honourable Judge of Probate of Wills &c: for said Province To Divide the Real Estate of Enock Gove late of Hampton falls in said Province Yeoman Deceas'd Intestate Among the Widow and Children of said Intestate. We have accordingly made Division of said Estate Shewn to us by Hannah Gove Administratrix of said Estate As follows vizt

To the said Hannah Gove the Widow for her Dower and thirds in said Estate We have Divided and Set off The Easterly Lower Room in the Dwelling House, where the said Deceas'd did lately live and the Back Room Adjoyning thereto — And the Garrett Over said Easterly Lower Room, And One third of the Celler As the Same is now Parted: also a Small Piece of Land between the East End of the Dwelling House and the Country Road, also a Priviledge in the Yard before the House for laying of wood going to the well and Such like also One third of the Barn at the Easterly End as far as to the third Post and Beam And a Proportionable Priviledge in the Cow yard also a Small Piece of Land for a Garding between the Cow yard And Orchard As the Same is now in fence also about One third of the Orchard at the west End Marked in the Plan herewith annexed by the letter m. and Bounded by Stakes Set up at Each End: also all the Remainder of that Piece of Land lying to the Westward of the Orchard and Barn yard Containing about twenty Eight Acres and a half Marked in the Plan by the Letter A. Bounding Southerly by a Way Westerly Land of Jonathan Chase & Notherly By Lands of Abraham Dow, Jonathan Moulton & ye widow

French also we have Set off to her five acres out of that Piece of Land which lyes on the Easterly Side of the Countrey Road being the Second Share from the Road As Discribed in the Plan and is Bounded Westerly by a Share Set off to Enock Gove Easterly by a Share set off to Mary Gove by Stakes Set up at Each Corner, Notherly by a Way which goes into Halls farm so Called and is ten Rods and Eight links of a Chain in Wedth by Said Way, Southerly by a Strip of Land one Rod and a half in Wedth left for a way to Capt Pike's land And is Nine Rods and three quarters of a Rod in wedth at that End Also a Piece of Salt Marsh in Hampton Falls aforesaid Containing five acres and One hundred and Seven Rods lying by the Dock And Commonly Called the Dock Marsh, Also One acre at the Easterly End of another Piece of Marsh near Waltons Grist mill Marked in the Plan by the letter O. Provided Nevertheless that the Lower Room in the Easterly End of the Dwelling House is not so set off to the said Hannah But that the Sons Enock Gove and Nathan Gove to whom the other part of the House is Set off may have liberty of Passing thro' to go to the Celler as they may have Occasion —

And the Remainder of Said Real Estate we have Divided Among the Children of said Deceas'd as follows vizt:

To Eleazar Gove the Eldest Son we have Divided and set off two Shares in that tract of Land lying on the Easterly Side of the Countrey Road at the Southerly End thereof the first Share Containing Eight acres and One Quarter of an acre Bounding Southerly by Canes Brook so Called Westerly by the Countrey Road and is twenty four Rods and three Quarters of a Rod in wedth by the Road and thirty One Rods and a half in Wedth at the Easterly side to Stakes Set up And the Second Share adjoyning to the first Containing Six Acres And One Quarter of an acre being fourteen Rods and a half in Wedth at the Westerly End by the Road and twelve Rods and three quarters of a Rod at the Easterly End to Stakes Set up —

Also we have Set off to the Said Eleazar two Shares in the

Orchard at the Southeasterly Corner Marked in the Plan by the letters b. and c. Each Share being About two Rods and a half in wedth and about ten Rods in length as the Stakes are Set up. Also we have set off to the said Eleazar the One half of his fathers Right in the Tract of Land Granted to Ichabod Robie Esqr And Others by the Purchasers of the Right of John Tufton Mason Esqr. Also two shares in the Marsh Namely One Piece Called the Marston Piece Containing One acre and one quarter of an acre Marked on the Plan by the letter P. and one other piece being the Westerly part of that piece of marsh near Walton's Mill Containg one acre and One hundred Rods Marked in the Plan by the letters Q and R.

Also we have Divided and set off to Enock Gove Son of the said Deceas'd for his Share of that Piece of Land lying on the East Side of the Countrey Road vizt Eight Acres And One Quarter of An Acre at the Northwest Corner Bounding Westerly by the Countrey Road Notherly by the way into Halls farm And is 29 Rods and One Quarter of a Rod by said Way to a Stake Set up Bounding Easterly by a Piece set off to the widow and by a Stake at the Southerly End Also One Share in the Orchard Marked in the Plan by the letter k. being about ten Rods in length and two Rods & a half in wedth being the Second Share from the Notherly Side.

Also One Share in the Marsh lying at the Southeasterly Corner of a Piece of Marsh by Perkins River so Called Said Share Contains about one acre and Eleven Rods Marked in the Plan by the letter A being fifteen Rods and five links of a Chain in Wedth at the Southerly End And Seven Rods and five links at the Notherly End by the Creek

Also we have Divided And Set off to Nathan Gove Son of said Deceasd for his Share Part of that Piece of Land lying on the Easterly Side the Countrey Road vizt Seven acres and fifty five Rods at the Northeasterly Corner Bounding Easterly by land of Capt Pike Notherly by the way into Halls farm And is Eighteen Rods and three Quarters of a Rod in wedth at that End, Westerly by a Share Set off to Rachel Chase by Stakes Set up Southerly by a Strip of land left for a way to Capt Pike's land And is Eighteen Rods and a half in wedth at the Southerly End As Described in the Plan. Also One Share in the Orchard Marked in the Plan by the letter i being the Notherly Share Also One Share in the Marsh being part of that Piece of Marsh near Perkins's River aforesaid Said Share Contains about One acre and Eleven Rods Marked in the Plan by the letters D. and E. the Piece D. being Surrounded mostly by a Creek And the Piece E. is a Small Piece between the Creek and the Share Set off to William bounded by Stakes Set up.

Moreover we have Divided And set off to the abovenamed Enock Gove and Nathan Gove Between them As part of Each of their Shares The Shop by the Countrey Road near the Dwelling House And the Land on which it Stands Also All the Remaining part of the Dwelling House & Barn And Priviledge of a yard by the Door Cow yard well and Land About the House Except what is set off to the widow for Dower as beforementioned

Also we have Divided And Set off to William Gove Son of the said Deceas'd for his share Part of that Piece of Land lying on the Easterly Side of the Countrey Road vizt Six Acres and One Quarter of an acre Bounding Notherly by the way into Halls farm and is fourteen Rods in Wedth by said Way, Westerly by a Share Set off to Mary Gove by Stakes set up, Southerly by a Strip of land left for a way to Capt Pike's land And is thirteen Rods And Eight links of a Chain in wedth at the Southerly End Easterly by a Share Set off to Rachel Chase by Stakes Set up. Also we have Set off to the said William One half of his fathers Right in the Tract of Land Granted to Ichabod Robie Esqr And Others by the Purchasers of the Right of John Tufton Mason Esqr — Also One share in the Marsh being Part of that Piece of Marsh by Perkins's River aforesaid Said Share Contains about One acre and Eleven Rods Marked in the Plan by the letter F. being Nine Rods and a half in Wedth Bounding Westerly by a Share set off to Sarah Blake by Stakes Set up, Southerly by a

Creek, Easterly partly by Nathan and partly by Mary as the Stakes are Set up also One Share in the Orchard Marked in the Plan by the letter k. Running from South to North thro' the Orchard and bounded by Stakes Set up

Also we have Divided And Set off to Rachel Chase wife of John Chase ju^r Daughter of said Deceas'd for her Share Part of that Piece of Land lying on the East Side the Countrey Road Containing Eight Acres and One Quarter of an acre Bounding Notherly by the way into Halls farm And is twenty Rods and One Quarter of a Rod in wedth by said Way Westerly by a Share Set off to William by Stakes Set up Southerly by a Strip of land left for a way to Capt Pikes land And is Eighteen Rods And twenty one links of a Chain in wedth at the Southerly End: Easterly by a Share Set off to Nathan by Stakes Set up. Also One Share in the Orchard Marked in the Plan by the letter d. being about ten Rods in lengh and two Rods and a half in wedth Bounded by Stakes Set up Also one Share in the Marsh being part of that Piece by Perkins's River Said Share Contains about one acre and Eleven Rods Marked in the Plan by the letters I. and K. being ten Rods and three quarters of a Rod in wedth at the Notherly End And Eleven Rods and one quarter of a Rod in wedth at the Southerly End Bounding Easterly by a Share set off to Sarah Blake and westerly by a Share Set off to Mary Greenleaf by Stakes set up

Also we have Divided and set off to Margarett Greenleaf wife of Paul Greenleaf Daughter of said Deceasd for her Share Part of that piece of Land lying on the Easterly Side the Countrey Road, Said Share Containing Eight acres and One quarter of an Acre Bounding Westerly by the Countrey Road and is Eighteen Rods and Sixteen links of a Chain in wedth by Said Road, Southerly by a Share Set off to Hannah Brown by Stakes set up, Easterly by land of Capt Pike And is Seventeen Rods in Wedth by said Pike's land and Notherly by a Strip of Land left for a way to Capt Pike's land by Stakes Set up. Also One share in the Orchard marked in the Plan by the letter e. being about ten

Rods in length and two Rods and a half in wedth Bounded by Stakes Set up. Also One share in the Marsh being part of that Piece of Marsh by Perkins's River Said Share Contains One acre and twenty Rods marked in the Plan by the Letter L. being twelve Rods and a half in wedth at the Notherly End and twelve Rods and three Quarters of a Rod at the Southerly End Bounding Westerly by a Share Set off to Hannah Brown and Easterly by a Share Set off to Rachel Chase by Stakes set up —

Also we have Divided And set off to Sarah Blake wife of Jeremiah Blake Daughter of said Deceas'd for her Share Part of that Piece of Land lying on the Easterly Side of the Countrey Road, said Share Containing Eight Acres and one Quarter of An acre Bounding Westerly by the Countrey Road and is twenty Rods in wedth by said Road, Southerly by a Share set off to Eleazar by Stakes Set up, Easterly by land of Capt Pike and is twenty Rods in Wedth at the Easterly End Notherly by a Share Set off to Hannah Brown by Stakes set up Also One Share in the Orchard marked in the Plan by the letter f. being the fourth Share from the Notherly Side Bounded by Stakes Set up. Also One Share in the marsh Containing about one acre and Eleven Rods Marked in the Plan by the letters G and H. being ten Rods and a half in Wedth at Each End Bounding Easterly by a Share set off to William and Westerly by a Share set off to Rachel Chase by stakes set up.

Also we have Divided And set off to Hannah Brown wife of Jonathan Brown Daughter of said Deceas'd for her Share Part of that Piece of land lying on the Easterly Side of the Countrey Road said share Containing Eight Acres and One Quarter of an acre Bounding Westerly by the Countrey Road and is Eighteen Rods and a half in wedth by said Road, Southerly by a Share set off to Sarah Blake by Stakes set up, Easterly by land of Capt Pike and is Eighteen Rods and a half in wedth by said Pike's land, and Notherly by a Share Set off to Margaret Greenleaf by Stakes set up — Also One Share in the Orchard Marked in the Plan by the letter g. and is the third Share from the Notherly side Bounded by Stakes set up. Also One Share in the Marsh at the Westerly End of the aforesaid Piece by Perkins's River Containing two acres marked in the Plan by the letter M being twenty Six Rods & three quarters of a Rod on the Southerly Side and twenty two Rods and one quarter on the Notherly Side Bounding Easterly by a share set off to Margarett Greenleaf by Stakes Set up —

Also we have Divided And set off to Mary Gove Daughter of said Deceas'd for her Share part of that Piece of Land lying on the Easterly Side of the Countrey Road, Said Share Containing Eight Acres and One Quarter of an acre Bounding Notherly by the Way into Halls farm Eighteen Rods in wedth by said Way Westerly by a Piece Set off to the Widow by Stakes set up Southerly by a Strip left for a way to Pikes land and is Sixteen Rods and Eight links of a Chain in Wedth at the Southerly End Easterly by a Share Set off to William by Stakes set up — Also a Share in the Orchard Marked in the Plan by the Letter I. between the Share of William and that set to the widow also One share in the abovementioned Piece of Marsh Containing One Acre and Eleven Rods Marked in the Plan by the letters B & C. The Piece Marked B. lying between Enock's Share & the Creek And that Marked C. is a Small piece on the Notherly side the Creek Bounded by Stakes Set up. All which Several Shares Are Described and Marked in the Plans herewith annexed In Making which Division we have had Regard to the Quality as well as Quantity of Said Estate and made the Several Shares As Equal as we Could: and this we make as our Return Dated the tenth Day of March Anno Domini 1761. —

Meshech Weare
Jeremiah Lane

[Additional account of the administratrix; receipts, £2260. 18. 9; expenditures, £331. 10. 0; allowed Sept. 30, 1761.]

[Petition, June 12, 1804, for division of the widow's dower, she being recently deceased; signed by Nathan Gove, William Gove,

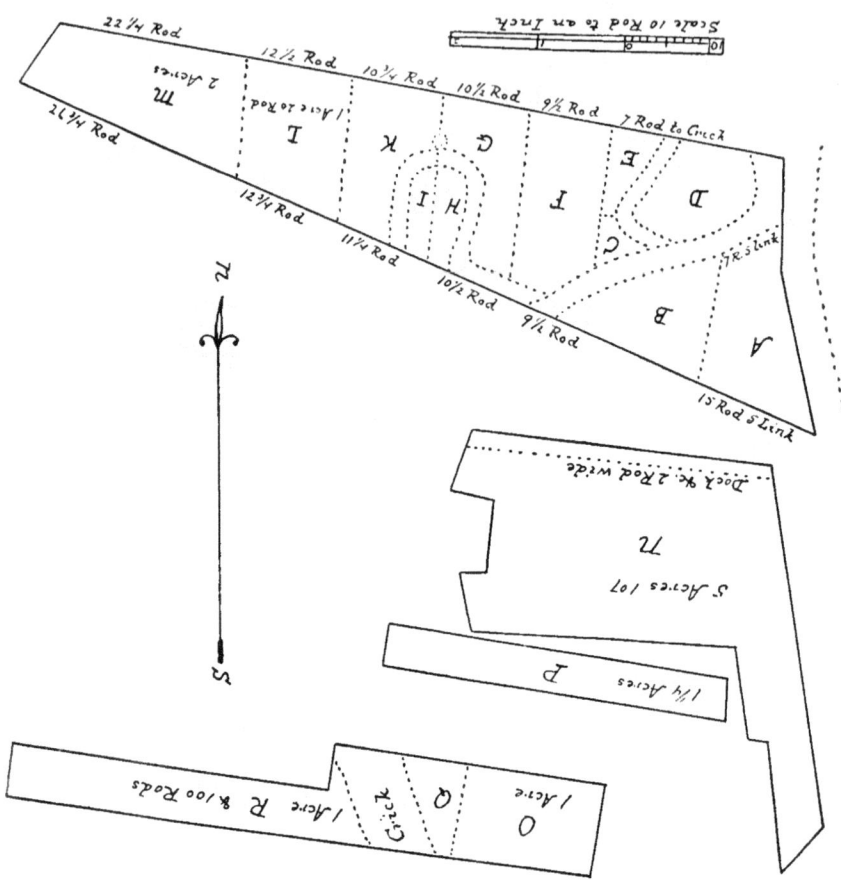

A Plan of the sundry pieces of marsh Belonging to the Estate of Lieuᵗ Enoch Gove Late of Hampᵗ falls Deceased which marsh is Divided Between the Several Heirs of said Deceased A to Enoch Gove B to mary Gove C to mary D and E to Nathan F to William G and H to Sarah Blake I and K to Rachel Chase L to Margᵗ Greenleaf M to Hannah Brown N to the widow O to the widow P to Eliazer Call'd the marston piece Containing 1¼ Acres Not measured therefore perhaps not in its proper shape Q and R to Eliezer.

Hampton falls Augᵗ 23: 1760.

Jer. Lane

NEW HAMPSHIRE WILLS

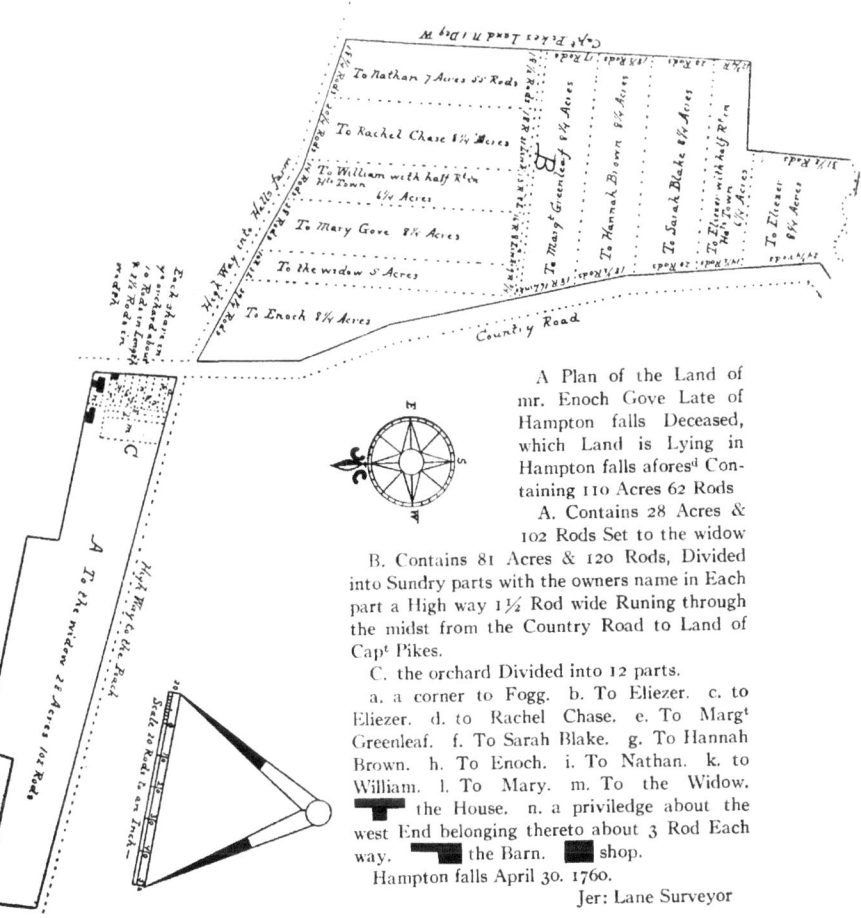

A Plan of the Land of mr. Enoch Gove Late of Hampton falls Deceased, which Land is Lying in Hampton falls afores[d] Containing 110 Acres 62 Rods

A. Contains 28 Acres & 102 Rods Set to the widow

B. Contains 81 Acres & 120 Rods, Divided into Sundry parts with the owners name in Each part a High way 1½ Rod wide Runing through the midst from the Country Road to Land of Cap[t] Pikes.

C. the orchard Divided into 12 parts.

a. a corner to Fogg. b. To Eliezer. c. to Eliezer. d. to Rachel Chase. e. To Marg[t] Greenleaf. f. To Sarah Blake. g. To Hannah Brown. h. To Enoch. i. To Nathan. k. to William. l. To Mary. m. To the Widow. ▬ the House. n. a priviledge about the west End belonging thereto about 3 Rod Each way. ▬ the Barn. ▬ shop.

Hampton falls April 30. 1760.

Jer: Lane Surveyor

and Joseph Philbrick in behalf of the rest of the heirs except Rachel Chase and Mary Perkins.]

[Commission, Sept. 17, 1804, to John Smith, Benjamin Dow, John Janvrin, Joseph Philbrick, all of Seabrook, and Simeon Rowe of Kensington to divide the widow's dower.]

Rockingham ss Pursuant to the above warrant We have set off the shares as follows (viz) — We have set off to Mary the Wife of Joseph Perkins one share containing one acre & one hundred and thirty rods & bounded as follows (viz) beginning at the westerly end of the Dower in the home place thence running easterly carrying the full wedth of said Dower fifteen rods & one half rod to a stake binding northerly on land of Benjamin Dow

We have set off to Hannah the wife of Thomas Chase one share containing one acre & one hundred & thirty rods, binding westerly on land set off to Mary the wife of Joseph Perkins, thence running easterly fifteen rods & one half rod to stakes & stones carrying the full wedth of said Dower

We have set off to Heirs of Elezer Gove one share containing one acre & one hundred & thirty rods binding westerly on land set of Hannah the wife of Thomas Chase, thence running easterly carrying the full wedth of the said Dower fifteen rods & one half rod to stakes & stones

We have Also set off to the aforesaid Elezer heirs one half share in the home place containing two acres & fourty rods binding westerly on land set off to the heirs of Sarah the wife of Jeremiah Blake thence running easterly carrying the full wedth of said Dower nine rods & one half rod to stakes & stones —

We have further set off to the aforesaid Elezer heirs one half share situate in Seabrook on the northerly side of the farm road so called binding Easterly on land of Paul Greenleaf & westerly on land of Enock Gove Jr the above half share contains about Five acres

We have set off to the heirs of Pegey the former wife of Paul Greenleaf one share containing Two acres & one half acre bounded as follows westerly on land set off to the heirs of Elezer Gove, thence running easterly carrying the full wedth of said Dower thirteen rods binding northerly four rods on land of Benj[a] Dow & nine rods on land of Timothy B. Lock to stakes & stones

We have set off to the heirs of Sarah the wife of Jeremiah Blake one share containing Three acres & fourty two rods binding westerly on land set off to Pagey the former wife of Paul Greenleaf thence running easterly carrying the full wedth of said Dower fourteen rods & one half rod to stakes & stones, the above shares binding southerly on a Highway with a stake & stones between each share

We have set off to Nathan Gove one share containing five acres & One hundred & twenty five rods binding westerly on land set off to the heirs of Elezer Gove thence running easterly Twenty five rods carrying the full wedth of the said Dower to stakes & stones binding southerly on a Highway northerly on land of Timothy B Lock in part & land of Enoch Gove in part

We have set off to William Gove one share containing Five acres & fifty two rods binding westerly on land set off to Nathan Gove thence running easterly carrying the full wedth of the said thirds binding southerly on a highway Thirty four rods & nineteen links to a stake & northerly on land of Enoch Gove Jr. twenty two rods to a stake

We have set off to the heirs of Enoch Gove all the Remainder part of the Twenty eight acres in the home place it being about four acres, together with all the building thereon, and all privileges to the same belonging

We have set off to Rachel Chase one share containing Five acres & two thirds of salt marsh it being the dock lot marsh (so called) Also one acre thach ground or flatts situate in Seabrook in the great flatts

Seabrook Octo[br] 2[d] 1804   Simon Rowe
                                       Benj[a] Dow } Committe
                                       Joseph Philbrick

ISAAC FOSS   1759   STRATHAM

In the Name of god Amen this thirtyeth Day of August Anno Domini one thousend Seven hundred and fifty nine. I Isaac foss of Stratham in the province of New Hampshir in New England gentelman, Being of Sound mind and memory But weak in body * * *

Imprimas I give and Bequeath to my Beloved wife Sarah foss the Southerly End of my house from top to Bottom to improve so Long as She Remains my widow & the improvement of my orcherd Before the house and a horse when She wants and the Keeping of one Cow and four sheep winter and summer and the Income of s^d Cow and Sheep and Sufficent firewood Cut fit for the fire at the Dore these to Be provided So long as She Remains my widow

Itam I give to my son thomas foss my Land that I bought of Nathanell write white & my Land I Bought of James Keneston & my Land I Bought of John pray Runing about North west from Sandy point Road to the River Except an acre of flats at the mouth of walls Creek: and my marsh I had of John wiggen and one half of my part of a Saw mill at wadleys falls So Called & one half of my Land at Notingham according to Quantity and Quality & one Chain & a pair or Set of Cart whoops & a pair of Steeres

Itam I give to my son Isaac Cole foss the Remainder of my land and marsh & flats in Stratham and Notingham not Before Disposed of and my Dwelling house that I now Live in Except that part my wife is to improve & the whole when She hath Done with it & my Barns on sd Land and the other half of my part of a saw mill at wadleys falls So Called & my oxen and two Cows and two heffers & my horse & my husbandry tooles & Implements Except what I gave to my son thomas foss

Itam I give to my son in Law Eliphelet wiggens fifteen pounds old tenor

Itam I give to my Daughter Sarah Burley one hundred and twenty pounds old tenor money to be paid in four years after my Decease

Itam. I give to my Daughter Comfort foss one hundred & twenty pounds old tenor money to be paid five years after my Decease and to Be fitted out as my other Daughters ware to Keep house withall at or Before the time She marries & a priviledg in the Rome with her mother while single

Itam I give to my Daughter Eleasebath foss one hundred and twenty pounds old tenor money to be paid six years after my Decease and to be fitted to Keep house as well as my other Daughters ware at or Before marrige Day and a priviledg in the Rome with her mother while single

and Lastly I give to my sons thomas and Isaac Cole all the Debts Due to me and if their be any thing not Deposed of I give it to my sd sons and order them to pay all my Debts Legecis and funerall Charges according to what thay Recive And I Do hereby Nominate and appoint my sd sons thomas foss and Isaac Cole foss to be Executors * * *

Isaac foss

[Witnesses] Ephraim Crockit, Cotton dockum, Daniel Samborn.

[Proved Nov. 25, 1761.]

[Administration on the estate of Isaac Foss of Stratham, testate, granted to Thomas Foss and Isaac Cole Foss, executors, Nov. 25, 1761.]

[Probate Records, vol. 22, p. 279.]

[Bond of Thomas Foss and Isaac Cole Foss, both of Stratham, yeomen, with Daniel Sanborn of North Hampton as surety, in the sum of £500, Nov. 25, 1761, for the execution of the will; witnesses, William Parker, Theophilus Smith.]

JOHN COTTON   1759   PORTSMOUTH

In the Name of God amen the thirtieth Day of August in the Year of our Lord 1759, I John Cotton of Portsmouth in the Province of New Hampshire Tanner being Weak in Body * * *

Item: I Give and bequeath unto my Son William Cotton his heirs and assigns forever the Sum of four pounds money New Tenor to be paid out of my Estate by my Executor within two Years after my Decease

Item: I Give and bequeath unto My Son John Cotton his heirs and assigns forever the Sum of four pounds Money New Tenor to be paid out of my Estate by my Executor within two Years after my Decease —

Item: I Give and bequeath unto my Daughter Mary Cotton her heirs & assigns forever the Sum of four pounds New Tenor and one feather Bed to be paid and Deliver'd out of my Estate by my Executor at a Convenient time after my Decease —

Item: I Give and bequeath unto my Daughter Martha Cotton her heirs and assigns forever the Sum of ten Shillings money new Tenor, One feather bed and one Large Oval Table to be paid and Delivered out of my Estate by my Executor a Convenient time after My Decease —

Item: I Give and Bequeath unto my Daughter Elizabeth Cotton her heirs and Assigns forever the Sum of twelve pounds money new Tenor and one Feather bed to be paid and Delivered out of my Estate by my Executor when she the Said Elizabeth shall arive at the age of Eighteen Years or on the Day of her Marriage which shall first happen —

Item: I Give and Bequeath unto My Daughter Abigail Cotton her heirs and assigns forever the Sum of twelve pounds money new Tenor and One Feather bed to be paid and Delivered out of my Estate by my Executor when the Said Abigail shall arive at the Age of Eighteen Years or on the Day of her Marriage which shall first happen —

Item: I Give and bequeath unto My Daughter Sarah Cotton her heirs and Assigns forever the Sum of Twelve pounds money new Tenor one Large Looking glass and a Chest of Draws, the Said Looking Glass and Chest of Draws I Will and order to be Sold to the best advantage by my Executor and the money that is raised thereby, and the Said twelve pounds New Tenor be all put out to use and the Principal and Intrest thereof to be paid unto the Said Sarah when she shall arive at the age of Eighteen Years or on her Marriage Day

And I Will and Order that my Dwelling-house and Land where I now live with all the privelidges and appurtenances thereof, with my Pasture and the whole of my Estate Both Real and personal Whatsoever and Wheresoever Not in this My Will disposed of, Be Sold by my Executor at a publick vendue and out of the Money that is raised thereby, I Will that all my just Debts funeral Charges Leagacies Necessary Charges and the Charges in Cloathing and Boarding My Minor Children until they shall be put out to an apprentice or Sarvice be paid, and the Remainder of What my Said Estate shall be Sold for after the payment of my Said Debts funeral Charges Leagacies Necessary Charges Cloathing and Boarding My Minor Children be taken from the Same I Give and Bequeath unto my Sons Clement Cotton and Joel Cotton their heirs and Assigns forever & the Same to be Divided Equally between the Said Clement and Joel Cotton their heirs and assigns both Principal and Intrest, (as I Desire the Money may be put to use as Soon as may be) and for the Same to be paid unto the Said Clement and Joel Cotton when they shall respectively arive at the age of Twenty One Years, by my Executor — And if one or More of my Said Children shall Decease before their Said Respective ages or Marriages I Will and Order that the Leagacy or Leagacies of the Deceased be equally Divided among My Serviving Children by my last Wife Bethiah I Also Will and order that those of my Children (that are in their Minority, and not as Yet put out) Be put out to Apprentice or Service Soon after my Decease by my Executor to places or people that my Children Consent to live with and my Executor shall approve of. And I Do hereby Nominate Constitute and appoint my Well beloved friend Mr Andrew Clarkson of Portsmouth in New Hampshire aforesaid Merchant to be My only and Sole Executor   *   *   *

John Cotton

[Witnesses] Thomas Bickford, Jos Clark, Deborah Mealcher. [Proved Sept. 26, 1759.]

[Warrant, Oct. 6, 1759, authorizing Eleazer Russell and Samuel Penhallow, merchant, both of Portsmouth, to appraise the estate.]

[Inventory, Nov. 6, 1759; amount, £2295. 15. 0; signed by Eleazer Russell and Samuel Penhallow.]

JOHN VENNARD   1759   NEWCASTLE

[Samuel Vennard renounces administration on the estate of his mother Sept. 10, 1759, in favor of his brother, William Vennard; witness, Joshua White.]

[Administration on the estate of John Vennard of Newcastle, mariner, granted to William Vennard of Newcastle, mariner, Sept. 10, 1759.]

[Probate Records, vol. 21, p. 286.]

[Bond of William Vennard, with Alcock Stevens, cooper, and Meshech Bell, innholder, as sureties, all of Newcastle, in the sum of £2000, Sept. 10, 1759, for the administration of the estate; witnesses, Samuel Parker, David Sewall. In this bond the name Elizabeth Vennard is changed to John Vennard as the deceased.]

JOHN GOVE   1759   HAMPTON FALLS

[Citation, Sept. 11, 1759, to Ruth Gove of Hampton Falls, widow, and Edward Gove, Jr., son of the deceased, to appear and take administration on the estate of her husband, John Gove of Hampton Falls, yeoman, deceased, intestate, more than six months, or to show cause why it should not be granted to Samuel Page, who married a daughter of the deceased.]

[Ruth Gove renounces administration Oct. 2, 1759; witnesses, David Gove, Martha Gove, Ebenezer Lovering.]

[Administration granted to Edward Gove of Hampton Falls, yeoman, Oct. 31, 1759.]
[Probate Records, vol 21, p. 315.]

[Bond of Edward Gove, Jr., with Nathaniel Gove and Ebenezer Lovering as sureties, all of Hampton Falls, yeomen, in the sum of £2000, Oct. 31, 1759, for the administration of the estate; witnesses, Ebenezer Stevens, David Sewall.]

[Guardianship of Patience Page, aged less than 14 years, granted to her father, Samuel Page of Kensington, Feb. 14, 1760.]
[Probate Records, vol. 21, p. 388.]

[Bond of Samuel Page, with Theophilus Page and Joseph Clifford as sureties, all of Kensington, in the sum of £1000, Feb. 14, 1760, for the guardianship of his daughter, Patience Page; witnesses, William Parker, Jr., Joseph Greeley, Jr.]

Province of New Hamps[r]
Whereas by an act of the General Assembly of said Province Entituled "An act for making Partition of Certain Lands therein Mentioned" Among Other things it is Enacted that there be five freeholders in this Province Appointed and Authorised they or any three of them to make Partition of said Lands Part of which Lands Referred to in said act are a Certain Piece of Land Situate in Hampton falls on the Notherly Side of the Road Commonly called the Mill Road near the Sawmill formerly Deacon Weare's Lying in Common And undivided between the heirs of John Gove Deceasd and the heirs of John Hobbs Deceas'd In Pursuance of which act we the Subscribers have undertaken to make Partition and Division of said Piece of Land having first given Due notice to all Parties Concerned agreeable to the Directions in said Act: And have Divided the Same as follows viz[t] The Whole Piece Containing Eleven Acres and Eighty two Rods, We have set off to the heirs of John Gove Deceas'd to

hold to them in Severalty five Acres on the Westerly Side, and to the heirs of the said John Hobbs Deceas'd the Remaining Six Acres and Eighty two Rods on the Easterly Side to hold to them in Severalty having Regard to the Quality of the Land in making said Division the bounds of said Division being a Stake set up at Each End — and the Easterly half set off to the heirs of said Hobbs we have Divided to and among said Heirs to Each to hold in Severalty as follows vizt That Share at the Notherly End marked in the Plan herewith annexed N° 1. Containing one hundred Rods of Land being Nine Rods in wedth we have set off to the heirs of Amos Towle Deceas'd, And the Second Share Marked in the Plan N° 2, Containing one hundred Rods of Land being Nine Rods in wedth we have set off to the heirs of James Towle Deceas'd. And the third Share marked in the Plan N° 3. Containing One hundred Rods of land being Nine Rods in wedth We have set off to Thomas Brown and Mehetable his wife in her Right. And the fourth Share Marked in the Plan N° 4. Containing One hundred Sixty four Rods of Land being fourteen Rods in wedth we have set off to Jonathan Towle And the fifth share marked in the Plan N° 5. Containing one hundred Sixty four Rods of Land being fourteen Rods in wedth We have set off to John Towle And the Sixth Share marked in the Plan N° 6. Containing One hundred Sixty four Rods of Land being fourteen Rods wedth we have also set off to the said John Towle. And the Seventh Share marked in the Plan N° 7. Containing one hundred and fifty Rods of Land being thirteen Rods in wedth we have set off to Jonathan Page and Mary his wife in her Right. And the Eighth Share marked in the Plan N° 8. Containing one hundred Rods of Land being the Share by the Mill Road aforesaid We have set off to Joseph Towle As set forth in the Plan herewith Annexed. And this we make as our Return Dated the twenty third Day of June Anno Domini 1760 —

          Meshech Weare
          Josiah Sanborn
          Jonathan Tilton

[Inventory, March 20, 1760; amount, £30,511. 12. 0; signed by Ezekiel Worthen and Ephraim Brown.]

[Warrant, Dec. 9, 1760, authorizing Meshech Weare, Ezekiel Worthen, gentleman, Abner Philbrick, Nathaniel Gove, and Jeremiah Lane, yeomen, all of Hampton Falls, to divide the real estate.]

Province of New Hamps^r

We the Subscribers being appointed by the Honourable Judge of Probate of Wills &c; for the Province aforesaid a Committee to Divide the Real Estate of John Gove Yeoman Late of Hampton Falls Deceas'd Intestate to and among the widow and Children of said Intestate Have Accordingly Divided the Same as hereafter Described, vizt there being Seven Children or Representatives of the said Deceas'd We have Divided the whole into Eight Shares allotting to the Eldest Son two Shares in the Same manner as we Should have made the Division had there been no third to have been set off to the Widow and then have Divided and Set off to the widow her third Part out of Each Respective Share the Division being made in this manner at the Special Request of Ruth Gove the widow of the said Deceas'd that her thirds might be so allotted that after her Decease Each Child's share might be Conveniently together: The Division is as follows

To Ruth Gove the widow of the said Intestate for her third part of what would be the Eldest Son's two shares if the whole were Divided among the Children, we have Set off the Westerly half of the Dwelling House where the said Ruth now lives, and a Piece of Land Containing one acre and fifty three Rods the Southwest Corner of the land on the North Side of the . . . . where the House Stands being twelve Rods and one quarter of A Rod in wedth by the Highway and the Easterly line passing through the middle of the House Bounded by Stakes set up as Described in the Plan by the letter O. also one third of the Largest Barn on the Southerly Side of the way at the Westerly End of said Barn, also a Piece of Land on the Westerly Side of the land which lies on the South Side of the Way Containing fourteen acres and one hundred & Seven Rods being twenty four Rods in wedth at the Southerly End and the Easterly line Passing through the Barn so as to take one third thereof at the westerly End Described in the Plan by the letter T. Bounded by Stakes Set up being Nineteen Rods in wedth on the Highway and from the highway Running South twenty five Degrees west Eight Rods passing through the Barn then on a Strait Course to the End of the twenty four Rods at the South End — Also a Piece of Marsh Containing two acres and a half of an acre lying on the Southerly Side of a Piece of Marsh by french's Creek so Called being Seven Rods and a half in Wedth Bounded by Stakes Set up and marked in the Plan by the letter m.

Also to the said Ruth for her third part of what Would be the Share of Daniel Gove one of the Sons of the Said Intestate if the whole were Divided Among the Children We have Set off A Piece of Land at the upper or Westerly End of the old Place so Called Containing Eight Acres and twelve Rods Described in the Plan by the letter C. being fifty two Rods And Eight links in length upon the Notherly Side from Jonathan Chase's land then Running Square across to the Southerly Side to a Pine Tree But not to Include one acre and a half at the Southwest Corner whereon an Orchard is Planted as marked in the Plan by the Letter D. also we have set off to the said Ruth One other piece of land Containing two acres and fifty three Rods part of that piece of Land which lyes on the notherly Side the way where the aforesaid Dwelling house is being Seven Rods And a half in wedth the Southwest Corner thereof being twenty two Rods and four links from the Southwest Corner of a Piece of land own'd by Edward Gove And is Bounded by Stakes Set up and Described in the Plan by the Letter M. and is fifty five Rods in Length. Also one Piece of Marsh at the Northeast Corner of the Halls farm Marsh Containing One acre and fifty four Rods lying in a triangular form Bounded by Stakes Set up Marked in the Plan by the letter a. Also we have Set off to the said Ruth for her third part of what would be the Share of Obediah Gove One of the Sons of the said Intestate if the whole were Divided among the Children A Piece of Land in Kensington on the Noth Side of the Road Called Stumpfield Road Containing Eleven acres & Seventy three Rods on the Westerly Side of the land where the said Obediah lives it being twelve Rods and Sixteen links in wedth Bounded by Stakes Set up, and Marked in the Plan by the Letter X.

Also we have Set off to the Said Ruth for her third Part of what would be the Share of Jonathan Gove One of the Sons of the said Intestate if the whole were Divided among the Children a Piece of Land at the upper End of the Long Pasture so Called Containing ten acres and twenty five Rods being twenty three Rods and a half in Wedth Bounded by Stakes Set up Marked in the Plan by the Letter H. also a Piece of Marsh Containing one acre and Seventeen Rods lying on the Notherly Side of a Piece of Marsh near Blackwater River so Called Bounded by Stakes Set up Marked in the Plan by the Letter i.

Also we have Set off to the said Ruth for her third Part of what would be the Share of David Gove one of the Sons of the Said Intestate if the whole were Divided Among the Children A Piece of Land lying on the Southerly Side of the Mill Road so Called Containing three acres and Sixty Rods being Seven Rods & ten links And a half in wedth And on the Westerly Side Seventy three Rods in length from the aforesaid Mill Road And on the Easterly Side Seventy Rods in length Bounded by Stakes Set up Marked in the Plan by the Letter K. which lyes on the west Side of the home farm

Also one other Piece of Land containing five acres and Eighty Eight Rods on the Notherly Side of the aforesaid Mill Road adjoyning to land of Jeremiah Gove on the west being Eleven Rods and Eight links in wedth Bounded by Stakes Set up, Marked in the Plan by the Letter P, also One acre of Marsh on the Southerly Side of a Piece of Marsh Southerly of Perkins River so Called being two Rods and Sixteen links in wedth marked in the Plan by the Letter t. Bounded by Stakes Set up. —

Also we have Set off to the said Ruth for her third part of what would be the Share of Ruth Green Daughter of Said Intestate if the whole were Divided Among the Children; A Piece of Land in Kensington Containing Six acres lying on the Southerly Side of Stumpfield Road so Called And on the Westerly Side of the Piece of Land which lyes there Bounded by Stakes Set up, Marked in the Plan by the Letter V. also a Piece of marsh in the Halls Farm Marsh so Called Containing one acre and one hundred And Six Rods Bounded by Stakes set up marked in the Plan by the Letter c. Also One Other Piece of Marsh Containing two acres and a half lying on the Notherly Side of a Piece of Marsh in Salisbury near the Place formerly Joseph Dow's being Nine Rods and Eight links in Wedth at the westerly End Bounded by Stakes set up Marked in the Plan by the Letter s.

Also we have set off to the said Ruth Gove for her third part of what would be the Share of Patience Page Grandaughter of the said Intestate her Mother one of the Daughters of said Intestate being Dead; A Piece of land Containing Eight acres lying on the Easterly Side of the land on the Southerly Side the way near the Dwelling House Adjoyning to land of Jonathan Chase being fourteen Rods and fourteen links in wedth at the Notherly End by the way, and fifteen Rods and Sixteen Links at the Southerly End Bounded by Stakes Set up marked in the Plan by the Letter Q. also a Piece of marsh Containing one acre and one hundred and Six Rods in the Halls farm Marsh so Called being Eight Rods in wedth Bounded by Stakes Set up Marked in the Plan by the letter d.

The Widows thirds being Set off as abovementioned in order that the Childrens Shares after her Decease might lye Conveniently together We have Divided the Remainder of said Real Estate Among the Children As follows vizt To Edward Gove the Eldest Son for his two Shares we have Set off a Piece of land where the Dwelling House is Containing Six Acres and one hundred and Seven Rods, with the Easterly half of the Dwelling House The Westerly line is twenty two Rods beginning by the way and Passing through the middle of the Dwelling House then Easterly Seven Rods then Notherly fourteen Rods and ten links then Easterly twenty five Rods and a half, then Southerly thirty Eight Rods to the aforesaid Road then Westerly by the Road to where it began Bounded by Stakes and Stones Marked in the Plan by the Letter N. Also a Piece of Land on the South Side the way — Containing twenty Seven Acres And fifty three Rods with two thirds of the Largest Barn thereon Bounding Westerly by a Piece Set off to the Widow Southerly by French's land, Easterly by a Piece Set off to Patience Page and Northerly by the way by Stakes set up Marked in the Plan by the Letter S. Also a Piece of Marsh Near Waltons Mill so Called Containing three acres and fifty two Rods Marked in the Plan by the Letter r. Also a Piece of Marsh by French's Creek so Called being the Notherly half of Said Piece of Marsh there lying being Seven Rods and a half in wedth Bounded by Stakes set up Marked in the Plan by the Letter n.

Also we have Set off to Daniel Gove for his Share a Piece of Land where the said Daniel now lives being part of the old Place so Called Containing fourteen acres and One hundred and four Rods at the Easterly End with the Dwelling House and Largest Barn thereon Bounded westerly by a Piece set off to the widow by a Stake at the Notherly Side and a Pine tree at the Southerly Side Notherly partly by land of Jonathan Gove and partly by a way and on the other sides partly by a Countrey Road partly by land of the widow Carr and partly by land of Edward Gove Described in the Plan by the letter B. Also a Piece at the Southwest Corner of the old Place Containing one acre and a half being twelve Rods in wedth and twenty two Rods in Length Described in the Plan by the Letter D. Also one other Piece of Land Containing four acres and One hundred and Seven Rods lying at the Southeast Corner of the farm where the Deceas'd lately liv'd Being fourteen Rods and fifteen links & a half in wedth at the Southerly End by the way and thirteen Rods in wedth at the Notherly End Bounded by Stakes set up Marked in the Plan by the Letter L. also a Piece of Marsh Containing two acres and a half on the Notherly Side of that piece South of Perkins River being Eight Rod in wedth marked in the Plan by the letter p. also a Small piece in the Halls farm Marsh Containing thirty Six Rods marked in the Plan by the Letter n.

Also we have set off to Obediah Gove for his Share a Piece of Land in Kensington Adjoyning to two acres whereon the said Obediah's House Stands on the Notherly Side of Stumpfield Road aforesaid Containing Sixteen Acres And One hundred And twelve Rods Bounding westerly by a Piece set off to the widow for her thirds Southerly by the aforesaid Road and at the Southeast Corner by two acres belonging to said Obediah where his house Stands And on the other sides by lands of Other Persons And is Marked in the Plan by the Letter W. also a Piece of Marsh near Waltons Mill Containing about one acre Called the Island Marked in the Plan by the letter k. also half an acre near Browns Rocks on the Southerly side of the Piece of marsh there marked in the Plan by the letter q.

Also we have Set off to Jonathan Gove for his Share A Piece of Land part of the long Pasture so Called Bounding westerly by a Piece set off to the widow for her thirds Southerly by the way and on the other Sides by lands of Others Marked in the Plan by the letter G also one other Piece at the Easterly Corner of the Long Pasture so Called Marked in the Plan by the Letter F. both Pieces Containing twenty Seven acres and fifteen Rods — also half an acre of Marsh near Brown's Rocks so Called being the Middle half Acre Marked in the Plan by the letter g. Also a Piece of Marsh Near Blackwater River so Called Containing two acres and thirty five Rods Bounding Notherly by a Piece set off to the widow for her thirds by Stakes set up and is Marked in the Plan by the letter j. Also we have Set off to the said Jonathan the Small Barn on the old Place so Called to be by him taken off of said Place within twelve months from this Date

Also we have set off to David Gove for his share a Piece of Land on the North side the mill Road so Called Containing Eleven acres and four Rods Marked in the Plan by the letter E. Bounding westerly by a piece set off to the widow for her thirds, Southerly by the way and on the other Sides by lands of Others, also one other Piece on the Southerly Side of the said Mill way Containing Seven acres and thirty five Rods Bounding westerly by a Piece set off to the widow for her thirds and is Seventy Rods in length on the Westerly Side Notherly by the way And on the other sides by the Shares of Others As Marked in the Plan by the Letter J. Also a Small Piece of marsh near Browns Rocks so Called Containing half an acre marked in the Plan by the letter f. Also a Piece of marsh South of Perkins River so Called Containing one acre and a half Marked in the Plan by the letter o. Bounding Southerly by a Piece set off to the widow for her thirds by Stakes set up, and Notherly by a Piece set to Edward Also we have Set off to said David the Small House in which he now lives And the Small Barn on the South side the way he to take off said house and Barn within twelve months from this Date or to forfeit them

Also we have set off to Ruth Green for her Share a Piece of Land in Kensington on the Southerly Side of Stumpfield Road so Called Near where Obediah Gove lives Containing Nine acres Marked in the Plan by the Letter U. Bounding Notherly by said Road, Westerly by a Piece set off to the Widow for her thirds by Stakes set up and on the Other sides by lands of Others. Also one Other Piece in Hampton falls on the Southerly Side the Mill Road so Called Containing Seven Acres Bounding Notherly by said Road, Easterly by land of Jonathan Weare And others twenty Eight Rods and on the Other Sides by Shares Set off to others by Stakes set up As Marked in the Plan by the letter I. Also a Piece of Marsh in the Halls farm Marsh so Called Containing three Acres and fifty four Rods marked in the Plan by the letter v. Bounding westerly by a Piece Set to the widow for her thirds by Stakes set up. and on the other Sides by marsh of

Others. also a Piece of flatts near the Beach Called three Acres marked in the Plan by the letter k. also a Piece of marsh in Salisbury Containing one acre and a half Marked in the Plan by the letter l. Bounding Notherly by a Piece Set off to the widow and on the other Sides by Marsh of Others.

Also we have set off to Patience Page for her Share a Piece of Land in Halls farm Containing thirteen Acres and thirty four Rods Marked in the Plan by the letter A. with a Piece of Marsh adjoyning thereto Containing five acres and fifty four Rods marked in the Plan by the letter e. Also a Piece of Land on the South Side of the way that goes by the House where the Deceas'd lately lived Containing Eight Acres marked in the Plan by the letter R. Bounding Notherly by said way Easterly by a Piece set to the widow for her thirds by Stakes set up and Westerly by a Piece set off to Edward. Also we have set off to said Patience the House on the old Place Called the Mill House, to be Removed off of said Place within twelve months from this Date or Else to be forfeited

To All Which Several Shares after the widows Decease the Perticular Parts set off to her out of Each Share are to be annexed —

And this we make As Our Return Dated this thirtieth Day of June Anno Domini 1761 —

Meshech Weare
Abner Philbrick
Jeremiah Lane

Each ones share Including with them the widdow's Thirds

	whole upland acres	Rods
To Edward, N, O, Eight acres S, T, 42	50	00
To Daniel B C D 24 acres 32 Rods, L M 7	31	32
To Obadiah W X 28 acres 25 Rods	28	25
To Jonathan F G H 37 acres 40 Rods	37	40
To David E P J K 27 acres 27 Rods	27	27

To Ruth I 7 acres U 9 V 6	22	00
To Patience A 13 acres 34 R Q R 16 acres	29	34
upland	224	158
	whole	marsh
	acres	Rods
To Edward m, n five acres r 3 acres 52 R	8	52
To Daniel a 1 acre 90 Rods. p. 2 acres & half	4	10
To Obadiah h. one acre. q. half an acre	1	80
To Jonathan 3 acres 22 R. i. j. and g half an acre	3	102
To David f. half an acre. o. Two acre & half	3	00
To Ruth b, c five acres k one l, s. four	10	00
To Patience d. e seven acres	7	00
marsh	37	84
upland	224	158
Land & Marsh Total	262	82

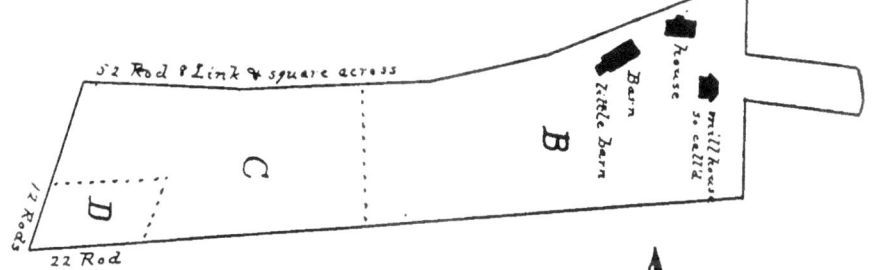

B. The Old place so call'd with C & D contains Twenty four Acres & 32 Rods

B. To Daniel as part of his share 14 acres 104 Rod
C. To the widow. 8 acres & 12 Rods
D. To Daniel whereon his own orchard stands 1½ Acre
E. To David Eleven acres & 4 Rods
F. G. To Jonathan 27 acres & 15 Rods
H. To the Widow Ten Acres & 25 Rods
I. To Ruth wife of David Green 7 acres
J. To David Seven acres & 35 Rods
K. To the Widow Three acres & 60 Rods

472   NEW HAMPSHIRE WILLS

 k. To Ruth flatts, call'd 3 Acres Equel to one
 l. To Ruth in Salisbury one acre & half
 m. To the widow 2 acre & 80 Rods by Frenches creek, call'd
 n. To Edward 2 acres & 80 Rod by Frenches creek
 o. To David one acre & half south of Perkins River, call'd
 p. To Daniel 2 acres & half,
south of Perkins River
 s. To the widow Two acres &
half in Salisbury
 u. To the widow one acre

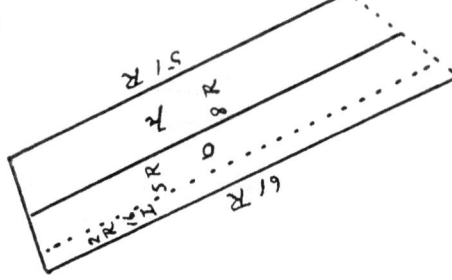

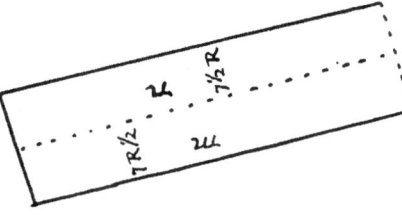

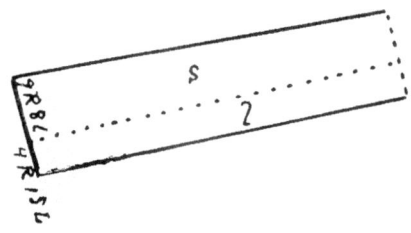

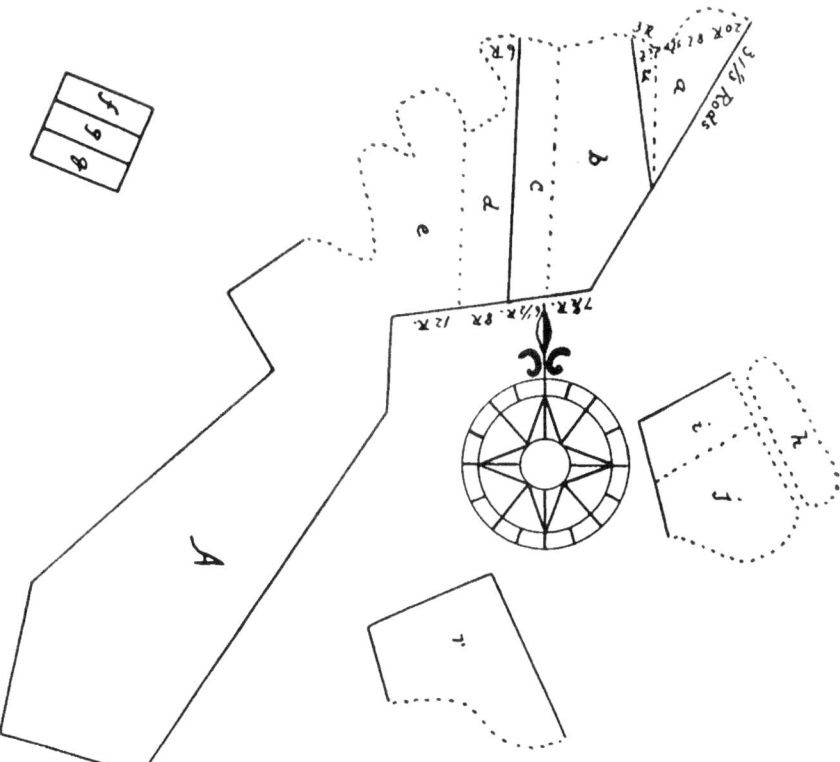

Province of New Hampshire } A Plan of the Estate of John Gove Late of Hampton falls Deceased Intestate with the Division thereof Lying in Sundry pieces both upland and Marsh and is Included within Black Lines Except by Creeks & Rivers in the marsh; Lines of Division between the Children of said Intestate a fine black Line, and the Widows Third part set off upon Each ones share with a prick'd Line. Each ones share of upland Discribed to them by Capital Letters as A. B. C. &c. of marsh by Small Letters of the alphabit as a. b. c. &c.

Hampton falls may 4th 1761.

p^r Jeremiah Lane Surveyor

A. In Halls farm so call'd containing 13 Acres & 34 Rods and is set to Patience, Daughter of Saml Page &c as part of her share

a. To the widow which contains 1 acre & 54 Rods
b. To Ruth Three Acres & 54 Rods.
c. To the Widow one acre 106 Rods.
d. To the widow one acre 106 Rods.
e. To Patience Five acres 54 Rods.
f. To David half an acre, at Browns Rocks so call'd
g. To Jonathan half an acre, at Browns Rocks.
q. To Obadiah half an acre, at Browns Rocks.
r. To Edward Three acres & 52 Rods near Waltons mill.
h. To Obadiah one acre, call'd the Island.
i. To the widow one acre & 17 Rods, at Black water River
j. To Jonathan Two acres & 35 Rods, at Black water River
u. To Daniel 36 Rods

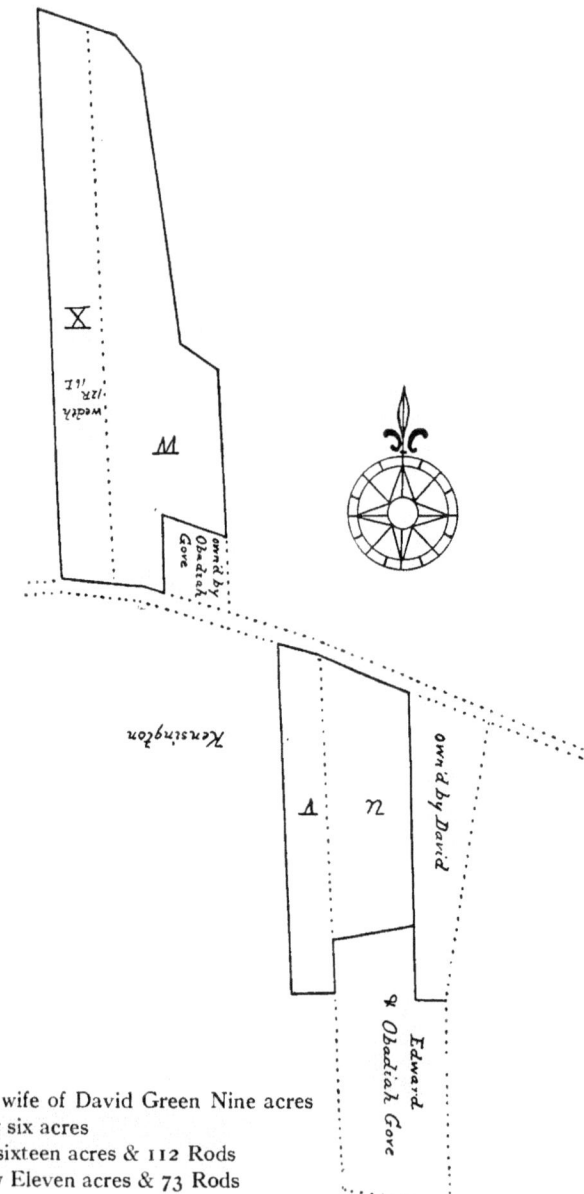

U. To Ruth the wife of David Green Nine acres
V. To the widow six acres
W. To Obadiah sixteen acres & 112 Rods
X. To the widow Eleven acres & 73 Rods

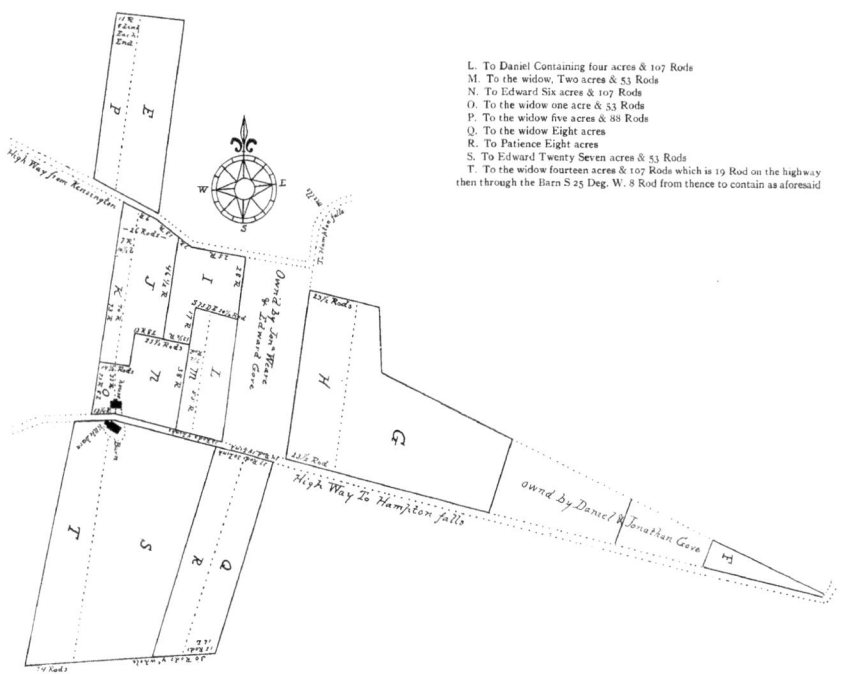

L. To Daniel Containing four acres & 107 Rods
M. To the widow, Two acres & 53 Rods
N. To Edward Six acres & 107 Rods
O. To the widow one acre & 53 Rods
P. To the widow five acres & 88 Rods
Q. To the widow Eight acres
R. To Patience Eight acres
S. To Edward Twenty Seven acres & 53 Rods
T. To the widow fourteen acres & 107 Rods which is 19 Rod on the highway then through the Barn S 25 Deg. W. 8 Rod from thence to contain as aforesaid

[Bond of Theophilus Page of Kensington, yeoman, with Ezekiel Worthen of Kensington, gentleman, as surety, in the sum of £500, April 13, 1770, for the guardianship of Patience Page, aged less than 14 years, daughter of Samuel Page, his son; witnesses, Benjamin Eastman, Enoch Worthen.]

JONATHAN AMBROSE 1759 NOTTINGHAM

In The Name of God amen This fourteenth Day of September Anno Domini 1759 I Jonathan Ambrose of Nottingham in the province of New hampshire Joyner being now Sick of a feavour and being apprehensive of the near approach of death * * *

I Give and bequeath to my Son Natthaniel Ambrose twenty Shillings old ten^r to be paid when he Comes to the age of twenty one years, by my Executer hereafter named.

Item I give to my Son Samuel Ambrose twenty Shillings old ten^r when he Comes to the age of twenty one years, to be paid by My Executer hereafter named.

Item I give unto my daughter Abigail Ambrose twenty Shillings old ten^r to be paid to her at the age of Eighteen years old by my Executer hereafter named.

Item I give to my Daughter hannah Ambrose twenty Shillings old ten^r to be paid to her at the age of Eighteen years.

Item I give to my Daughter Mary Ambrose twenty Shillings old ten^r to be paid to her at the age of Eighteen years.

Item I give to my daughter Rebecka Ambrose twenty Shillings old ten^r to be paid to her at the age of Eighteen years

Item As it appears that my wife is like to have another Child tho yet unborn I give unto it twenty Shillings old ten^r (if it lives) to be paid at twenty one years of age if a son and at Eighteen if a daughter —

Item I give and bequeath unto my well beloved wife Abigail and to her heirs and assigns forever, all my lands and Buildings laying and being in Exeter or Elsewhere and also I give unto my

Said wife all my movables both within doors and without, with my Cattle and Swine and likewise my tools belonging to my trade to be at her disposal for the bring up my Children Except what is before disposed of to be paid to my Children Above named

finally I do make and ordain my honoured father in law Samuel Goodhue of Hollis Gen^t to be Sole Executer * * *

his
Jonathan + Ambrose
Mark

[Witnesses] Benjamin Butler, Robert Harvey, Martha her + Huchinson. mark

[Proved May 23, 1760.]

[Abigail Ambrose, widow, consents to the executorship of her father, Samuel Goodhue of Hollis, May 23, 1760; witnesses, Daniel Grant, Sarah Bickford.]

[Bond of Samuel Goodhue, with John Hutchinson of Nottingham and Nicholas Doe of Newmarket, yeomen, as sureties, in the sum of £500, May 23, 1760, for the execution of the will; witnesses, Thomas Bradford, Mary Wendell.]

[Guardianship of Nathaniel Ambrose, minor, aged more than 14 years, granted to Richard Bartlett April 18, 1769.]

[Probate Records, vol. 25, p. 369.]

[Bond of Richard Bartlett of Pembroke, physician, with Aaron Whittemore of Pembroke, husbandman, and John Goffe of Derryfield as sureties, in the sum of £100, April 18, 1769, for the guardianship of Nathaniel Ambrose, living in Pembroke; witnesses, Samuel Hale, Jr., Jotham Odiorne.]

JOSEPH DAVIS　　　　　1759　　　　　CHESTER

[Administration on the estate of Joseph Davis of Chester, cordwainer, granted to Matthew Thornton of Londonderry Sept. 15, 1759.]

[Probate Records, vol. 21, p. 328.]

[Bond of Matthew Thornton, with James Ewins, yeoman, and William Wallace, cordwainer, as sureties, all of Londonderry, in the sum of £500, Sept. 15, 1759, for the administration of the estate; witnesses, Thomas Christy, Joseph Smith.]

[Warrant, Sept. 15, 1759, authorizing Samuel Emerson and Jonathan Hall, yeoman, both of Chester, to appraise the estate.]

[Inventory, Sept. 19, 1759; amount, £273. 5. 0; signed by Samuel Emerson and Jonathan Hall.]

[Guardianship of Abigail Davis, Sarah Davis, Samuel Davis, Nathan Davis, and Hannah Davis, minors, less than 14 years old, children of Joseph Davis, was granted to Benjamin Davis of Newbury, Mass., July 10, 1761.]

[Essex County, Mass., Probate Records, vol. 338, p. 253.]

[Bonds, one for each ward, of Benjamin Davis, joiner, with Edmund Davis of Newbury, Mass., cordwainer, and John Choate, Jr., of Ipswich, Mass., blacksmith, as sureties, in the sum of £1000 on each bond, July 10, 1761; witnesses, Daniel Davis and Daniel Appleton.]

[Essex County, Mass., Probate Files.]

[Guardianship of Daniel Davis, minor, more than 14 years old, son of Joseph Davis, was granted to Edmund Davis of Newbury, Mass., July 10, 1761.]

[Essex County, Mass., Probate Records, vol. 338, p. 253.]

[Bond of Edmund Davis, cordwainer, with Benjamin Davis of Newbury, Mass., joiner, and John Choate, Jr., of Ipswich, Mass., blacksmith, as sureties, in the sum of £1000, July 10, 1761; witnesses, Daniel Davis and Daniel Appleton.]

[Essex County, Mass., Probate Files.]

HANNAH SHERBURNE 1759 NEWCASTLE

In The Name of God Amen, I Hannah Sherburne of New Castle in the Province of New Hampshire Widow, * * *

Item, I give and bequeath unto my Grandson Thomas Odiorne of Greenland in the Province aforesaid Shopkeeper, and to my Grand daughter Elizabeth Odiorne who now lives with me All that my part Share Right & Title of in and to, the Dwelling House where I now live in New Castle aforesaid, together with the Land & appurtenances thereto belonging, To Hold to them the said Thomas Odiorne and Elizabeth Odiorne and their Heirs as Tenants in Common, and not as joint Tenants To the only proper Use and Behoof of them the said Thomas Odiorne and Elizabeth Odiorne and their Heirs for Ever, Save and Except a peice of Salt Marsh Containing by Estimation One Acre and an Half or thereabouts adjoining to Land of my Son Noah Sherburne, and which he rented of me at halves, Which said last mentioned peice or Parcell of Salt Marsh so reserved as aforesaid I do hereby give unto my aforesaid Son Noah Sherburne of New Castle aforesaid Husbandman, for and during the Term of his naturall Life, And after his Decease, I give the same to the said Thomas and Elizabeth Odiorne & their Heirs for Ever as Tenants in Common as aforesaid. Item I give unto the said Elizabeth Odiorne One Cow, One Calf and two Sheep, also the Bed and Bedding, which I now lie on, All the Furniture of my Chamber as it now stands, all my Wearing Apparell Outside and Inside, One large Pewter Soup Dish Six Pewter Plates, and my little Kettle. Item I give unto my Daughter Katherine Odiorne of Portsmouth in the Province aforesaid Widow, my large Bible and a Pewter Dish, for her life, and at her Decease, I give the same to the said Thomas Odiorne. Item I give and bequeath to my Daughter Hannah Blunt Wife of John Blunt of New Castle aforesaid Mariner, my Desk and Set of White Curtains Item I give and bequeath unto my Daughter Mary Randall Wife of James Randall of New Castle aforesaid Mariner, my great Iron Kettle Item I give to my Grandson Ebenezer Odiorne of Portsmouth Chairmaker and to his Heirs for Ever All my Right in & to Lands in Epsom in the Province aforesaid   Item I give unto the said Thomas Odiorne, my large Looking Glass in the Hall of my said Dwelling House And I do hereby Nominate and appoint the said Thomas Odiorne Executor and residuary Legatee of and under this my Will, and desire that he may be Guardian of the Body and Estate of his said Sister Elizabeth Odiorne untill She shall attain the age of Twenty One Years, or be married * * *   In Witness whereof I have hereunto Set my Hand and Seal this Seventeenth day of September Anno Domini 1759.

The Mark of + Hannah Sherburne
[Witnesses] Mark Langdon, Geo: Janvrin, Samuel Aris.
[Proved Jan. 26, 1763.]

JOSIAH BATCHELDER   1759   HAMPTON FALLS

In the Name of God Amen the twenty Second Day of September in the year of Our Lord Christ one Thousand Seven hundred And fifty nine, I Josiah Bachelder of Hampton falls in the Province of New Hampshire in New England Yeoman * * *

Item I Give and Bequeath to my well beloved wife Sarah the Use Income and Improvement of One third part of all my Lands In Hampton whether Upland Salt Marsh or meadow And One third Part of my Dwelling House and Celler and of my Barn for her to Improve During her Natural life if she Sees Cause; I also Give her to be at her own Disposal One third part of all my Stock of Creatures and of all my moveables without Doors of what Sort soever, And of all my Houshold Goods within Doors; And the Remaining two thirds of all my Stock of Creatures and moveables without Doors I Give to my two Sons Nathanael And David Equally Divided between them. And the Remaining two thirds of All my Houshold Goods within Doors I Give to my said Wife to Dispose of Among all my Children According to her Discretion, And if no such Disposal shall be made by her In her lifetime Then I Give one half of said two thirds to my Daughter Healey, And the Remainder Equally among all my Sons

Item I Give and Bequeath to my Son Nathanael Bachelder one half of all my Lands and Buildings in Hampton of what Sort soever (Excepting one Acre and a half of marsh lying in a Bend of Taylors River so Called which I have Given to my Sons Elisha and Reuben as hereafter mentioned; and the Improvement my wife is to have) what I have here Given to my Said Son Nathanael my meaning is that he shall hold the Same in the following manner Namely To him During his Natural life, And if he shall Dye without Issue lawfully Begotten of his Body then the Same shall go to my Son David Bachelder his heirs and assigns. But if my Said Son Nathanael shall have Issue Lawfully begotten of his Body then to hold the Same to him the said Nathanael his heirs and assigns.

I also Give to my said son Nathanael his heirs & assigns One half as to Quantity and Quality of what land I own in the Eighty Acre Division so Called in the Township of Chester in the Province aforesaid which is half a Lott laid out to the Original Right of Philip Towle and one Lott which I boughtof Michael Dearbon, my said Son Nathanael to have one half of said Lott and half, Also One half of a Certain Piece of Land which I have lying in the Township of Kingstown in the Province aforesaid Containing About Sixty Acres lying at the upper or westerly End of the Lott Nº 1 in the two hundred acre Grants so Called Bounding on Exeter line Westerly, And Land of Jonathan Swett Easterly. I Also Give to my said Son Nathanael One half of all my Right in the Township of Chichester in said Province, And I Order him my Said Son Nathanael to Pay to his Sister Sarah Healey Six Pounds Sterling or Equivalent thereto In any Bills of Publick Credit; to be paid her within two years after my Decease —

Item I Give and Bequeath to my Son Elisha Bachelder to him his heirs and assigns One half of a Certain tract of Land which I have lying in Kingstown aforesaid being part of the Lotts N° 1, and N° 2, In the two hundred Acre Grants so Called, my said Son Elisha to begin at the Lower or Easterly Side of Land Owned by Capt Richard Nason, And thence to go Eastwardly so far as to take One half that tract of Land which I there have lying below or to the Eastward of said Nason's land. I Also Give to my said Son Elisha his heirs and assigns one half of all my lands in the Township of Chester aforesaid Except what I have given In this my will to my Sons Nathanael And David. I also give to my said Son Elisha his heirs and assigns one half of All my Right in the tract of Land Granted to Ichabod Robie Esqr and Others by the Purchasers of the Right of John Tufton Mason Esqr

Item I Give and Bequeath to my Son Reuben Bachelder to him his heirs and assigns the Eastwardly half of that tract of Land which I have lying in Kingstown aforesaid, the Westerly half whereof I have Given to my son Elisha. Also the half of all my Lands in the Township of Chester aforesaid Except what I have Given to my sons Nathanael and David; Also one half of all my Right In the tract of Land Granted to Ichabod Robie Esqr And others by the Purchasers of the Right of John Tufton Mason Esqr

Item I Give and Bequeath to my Sons Elisha & Reuben abovenamed One Acre and a half of marsh lying in a Bend of Taylors River so Called at the Northeasterly part of my meadow there which is part of my home Place to be Equally Divided between them, Each to hold One half thereof in Severalty to him his heirs And Assigns —

Item I Give And Bequeath to my Son David Bachelder to him his heirs and assigns, On half of all my Lands and Buildings In Hampton of what Sort soever (Excepting that in the Bend of Taylors River which I have Given to my sons Elisha And Reuben; And the Improvement which my wife is to have) Also I Give and Bequeath to my said Son David his heirs and assigns the one half as to Quantity and Quality of what Land I own in the Eighty Acre Division so Called in the Township of Chester aforesaid, the Other half whereof I have Given to my Son Nathanael as abovementioned; also One half of the Piece of Land in Kingstown aforesaid Containing about Sixty Acres as above Described the Other half whereof I have Given to my Son Nathanael, Also One half of all my Right in the Township of Chichester aforesaid the other half whereof I have Given to my Son Nathanael And I Order my Said Son David to pay to his Sister Sarah Healey within two years after my Decease Six Pounds Sterling or Equivolent thereto in Bills of Publick Credit.

Item I Give and Bequeath my wearing Apparell to my Sons, Nathanael, Elisha, Reuben, and David Equally Between them—

Item I Give and Bequeath to my Daughter Sarah Healey twelve Pounds Sterling or Equivolent thereto in Bills of Publick Credit to be Paid her within two years after my Decease by my Sons Nathanael and David Equally between them as before Ordered

Lastly I Do by these Presents Constitute and Appoint My Sons Elisha Bachelder and David Bachelder to be Executors

* * *

Josiah Bachelder

[Witnesses] Meshech Weare, Sam[ll] Shaw, Joseph Bachelder. [Proved Oct. 31, 1759.]

[Elisha Batchelder of Kingston declines executorship of the will in favor of his brother, David Batchelder, Oct. 29, 1759.]

[Warrant, Oct. 31, 1759, authorizing Meshech Weare and Joseph Batchelder, husbandman, both of Hampton Falls, to appraise the estate.]

[Inventory, Dec. 24, 1759; amount, £47,795. 6. 0; signed by Meshech Weare and Joseph Batchelder.]

HANSON MESERVE 1759 PORTSMOUTH

In the Name of God Amen The twenty Seaventh day of September anno Domine One thousand Seven hundred and fifty nine —

I Hanson Meserve of Portsmouth in ye Province of New Hampshire Mariner * * *

Item I Give unto my Beloved Brother Georg Meserve of Portsmouth aforesaid Merchant all that my Farm in Portsmouth aforesaid now in the occupation of John Hight, and all my Lands in that Township or Tract of Land Calld Allens Town in Said Province and all that that was my Late Honourd Father Nathaniel Meserve Mansion house in Said Portsmouth with ye Garden Warehouse and all the Privileges and appurtenance thereunto belonging of what kind or Nature Soever and all my Personal and Real Estate whot soever and wheresoever it is or may be found I giv unto my Said Brother George Meserve To Have & to hold to him his heirs and assigns forever and I do hereby Constitute and appoint my Said Brother George Meserve Executor * * *

Hanson Meserve

[Witnesses] D Peirce, Saml Hale, Will^a Earl Treadwell.
[Proved Dec. 31, 1762.]

JOHN CUTT 1759 PORTSMOUTH

[Administration on the estate of John Cutt of Portsmouth granted to his son, John Cutt of Portsmouth, cooper, Oct. 2, 1759.]

[Probate Records, vol. 21, p. 304.]

[Bond of John Cutt, with Samuel Cutt, merchant, and James Dwyer, truckman, as sureties, all of Portsmouth, in the sum of £1000, Oct. 2, 1759, for the administration of the estate; witnesses, William Parker, James King.]

[Warrant, Oct. 2, 1759, authorizing Eleazer Russell and Samuel Penhallow, merchant, both of Portsmouth, to appraise the estate.]

[Inventory, Jan. 26, 1760; amount, £7228. 7. 0; signed by Eleazer Russell and Samuel Penhallow.]

[Account of the administrator; receipts, £3578. 7. 0; expenditures, £1682. 13. 1; allowed Jan. 20, 1761.]

[Additional inventory, Feb. 25, 1761; amount, £1662. 0. 0; lands in Chester; signed as above.]

[Appraisal of the real estate, March 7, 1761, at £10,990. 0. 0; signed by Hunking Wentworth, John Hart, Daniel Rogers, Joseph Alcock, and Stephen March. Order of court, June 30, 1761, settling the real estate on the only son, John Cutt.]

[Receipt, April 18, 1761, from Jacob Mills to his brother, John Cutt, for $1000, part of his wife's portion of the estate of her father, John Cutt.]

[Additional account of the administrator; receipts, £1983. 8. 11; expenditures, £986. 3. 2; allowed June 24, 1761.]

JAMES STEVENS   1759   PORTSMOUTH

In the Name of God Amen, The Last will and Testament of James Stevens, I James Stevens of Portsmouth in the Province of New Hampshire being Weak in Body * * *

Item, To Mary my beloved wife and to her heirs and assigns I give my Negro woman named Flora, (and I desire my said wife to Sell her so that she may go and live at Gloster in the County of Essex) all the Estate that was her's at the time of her Intermarriage with me (Except a Suit of Curtains) my Best bed bedsed Curtain Rods Curtains and Vallins, my worst Bed, Six leather Chairs, one Great leather Chair, a Haretine Easey Chair,

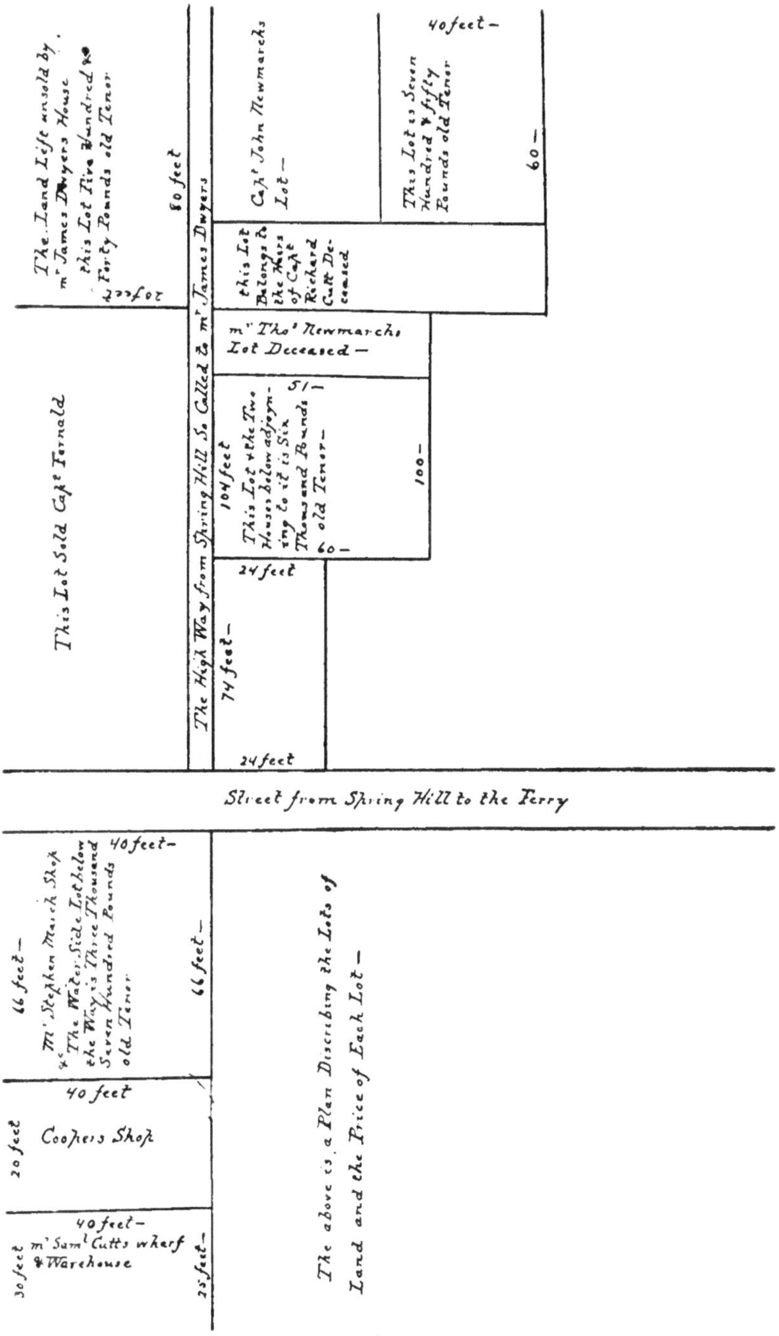

NEW HAMPSHIRE WILLS

[Plan diagram with the following labels:]

- The Land Left unsold by mr James Dwyers House this Lot Five Hundred & Forty Pounds old Tenor
- 80 feet
- 20 feet
- 40 feet —
- Capt John Newmarchs Lot —
- This Lot is Seven Hundred & fifty Pounds old Tenor
- 60 —
- this Lot Belongs to the Heirs of Capt Richard Cutt Deceased
- This Lot Sold Capt Fernald
- mr Thos Newmarchs Lot Deceased —
- The High Way from Spring Hill So Called & mr James Dwyers
- 104 feet
- 51 —
- This Lot w:th the Two Houses below adjoyning to it is Six Thousand Pounds old Tenor
- 100 —
- 60 —
- 24 feet
- 74 feet —
- 24 feet

Street from Spring Hill to the Ferry

- 40 feet —
- 66 feet —
- mr Stephen March Shop & The Water Side Lotbelow the Way is Three Thousand Seven Hundred Pounds old Tenor
- 66 feet —
- 40 feet
- Coopers Shop
- 20 feet
- 30 feet
- 40 feet —
- mr Saml Cutts wharf & Warehouse
- 25 feet —

The above is a Plan Discribing the Lots of Land and the Price of Each Lot —

my Great Silver Tankard, one Silver Spoon, one Silver Porringer, three Silver Teaspoons, one Cow my little Looking Glass and one third part of all the Residue of my parsonal Estate herein not particularly disposed off, also unto my said wife during her natural Life I give Two thirds of the Income of my Real Estate in Gloster in the County of Essex, my Desk Closestool and bedpan

Item, To my son Samuel James Stevens and to his heirs and assigns I give my Silver pepper box one Silver Spoon; my desk, Close Stool and Bed pan after my wife decease; with one third part of my parsonal Estate not herein particularly given away —

Item. To my Daughter Susanna James, her heirs and assigns, I give one Silver Porringer one Silver Spoon one bed and bedsteed and one third part of my parsonal Estate not herein particularly given away —

Item. To my Daughter Elizabeth, the wife of Jacob Elwell, her heirs and assigns I give my Chest of Drawers, she having already what more I designd for her.

Item. To Elizabeth Littlehale that now lives with me, and her heirs and assigns I give my second best bed beding for the Same, Second best Curtains Vallins bedsted & Curtain Rods; my little Silver Tankard one Silver Porringer one large Silver Spoon and Two Silver Tea Spoons —

Item I appoint my Brother William Stevens and Mr James Stoodley Junr to be Executors of this my last will and Testament, and desire them to Receive the third part of the income of my Estate in Gloster that is not herein before mentioned and lay out the Same in Repairing the Same, during the time of my wife's natural Life and immediately after the decease of my said Wife I order the said Estate at Gloster to be sold and hereby authorise my Executors (or the Survivour if one dies before the Same is finished) to Sell the Same and the money that shall be Raised by the Sale thereof Togather with what of the third part of the Rent Remaining unlaid out as aforesaid (if any there be) shall be divided among all my Children in Such manner as the Law directs as in Interstate Estates, viz Two Shares to my Son & a Single Share to Each of my Daughters, and I farther order and desire my Executors to Sell My Great looking Glass Great Brass Kettle and high Candle Stick and the money Raised by said Sale to be Improved to defray the Expences of my Funeral * * * and in Confirmation hereof I have here unto set my hand & Seal this fourth day of october in the Thirty third Year of his majesty's Reign annoque Domini 1759 —

James Stevens

[Witnesses] Clem^t Jackson, John Shackford, Cutts Shannon. [Proved Oct. 23, 1759.]

[Warrant, Oct. 23, 1759, authorizing Eleazer Russell and Cutts Shannon, gentleman, both of Portsmouth, to appraise the estate.]

[Inventory, Oct. 23, 1759; amount, £2872. 7. 0; signed by Eleazer Russell and Cutts Shannon.]

[Account of James Stoodley, executor; receipts, £2891. 2. 1, personal estate; expenditures, £3096. 16. 0; mentions "Expences of the two Brothers of the Deceas'd while at the Funeral"; allowed April 27, 1768.]

[Additional account of James Stoodley, surviving executor; receipts, £106. 6. 8; expenditures, £84. 9. 1; allowed Dec. 12, 1769.]

TIMOTHY COTTON   1759   PORTSMOUTH

[Administration on the estate of Timothy Cotton of Portsmouth, joiner, granted to Mary Cotton of Portsmouth, widow, Oct. 30, 1759.]

[Probate Records, vol. 21, p 309.]

[Bond of Mary Cotton, with John Elliot, glazier, and Gregory Purcell, merchant, as sureties, all of Portsmouth, in the sum of £500, Oct. 30, 1759, for the administration of the estate; witnesses, George Libby, David Sewall.]

PETER RUSSELL 1759 LITCHFIELD

In the Name of God Amen: I Peter Russel of Litchfield In the Province of New Hampshire Gentleman Being Sensiable of my Approaching Dissolution * * *

Item my Will is and I do hearby Bequeath unto my Beloved wife Deborah whome I Likewise Constitute and ordain Sole Executor of this my Last will and Testament for her maintenance and support after my Decease During her Natural Life the one full Third part of the Improvemet of my Real Estate and one half of my house with one Third part of my Barn with one Third part of my household furnture with one Third part of my stock and Husbandry Utensills

Item my will is and I do Give unto the Heirs of my son Peletiah Rusell Deceased five Shillings Starling which is his or there full pard or Portion out of my Estate to be paid within one year after my Decease

Item I Give and Bequeath unto My Daughter Rachel five Shillings Starling which is her full portion out of my Estate to be paid within one year after my Decease which is her full part out of my Estate

Item I Give and Bequeath unto my Daughter Rebackah three Pounds five Shillings Starling mony to be paid within one Year after my Decease which is her full part out of my Estate

Item I Give and Bequeath unto my Daughter Phebe four Pounds Starling mony to be paid within one Year after my Deceas which is her full part out of my Estate

Item I Give and Bequeath unto my Daughter Deborah five Shillings Starling mony to be paid within one Year after my Decease which is her full part out of my Estate

Item I Give and Bequeath unto my Daughter Hannah four Pounds Starling mony to be paid within one Year after my Decease which is her full part out of my Estate

Item I Give and Bequeath unto my Daughter Sarah four Pounds Sterling mony within one Year after my Deceas which is her full part out of my Estate

Item my will is that my four sons (viz) Peter Russell Jun[r] Joseph Russel James Russell & Thomas Russell Have the Remainder of my Estate Real and Personal in Equal Propotion

Item my will is that all my Just Debts and Duties that I do owe In Right to any Person or Persons whatsoever Shall be well and Truly paid together with all the Leagusies Before mentioned within the Term of one Year after my Decease by Executor Before Mentioned Together with a Desent Burial to be paid out of my Estate by my Executor

Item my will is that at the Decease of my wife her Thirds Shall be Equaly Devided Between my four sons (viz) Peter Joseph James & Thomas with my Six Daughters (viz) Rachel Rebackah Phebe and Deborah Hannah and Sarah in Equal Propotion * * *

In Testimony whereof I have hereunto Set my hand and seal this third day of November in the Thirty third Year of his Majestyes Reign Anno Q Dom. 1759

Peter Russell

[Witnesses] william Patterson, William mcQuesten Junier, James Underwood.

[Proved Nov. 28, 1759.]

[Bond of Deborah Russell, with James Nahor and William Reed, gentlemen, as sureties, all of Litchfield, in the sum of £1000, Nov. 28, 1759, for the execution of the will; witnesses, John Harvell, John Cochran.]

MARY MESERVE   1759   PORTSMOUTH

[Administration on the estate of Mary Meserve of Portsmouth, widow, granted to Joseph Jackson of Portsmouth, housewright, Nov. 5, 1759.]

[Probate Records, vol. 21, p. 328.]

[Bond of Joseph Jackson, with James Dwyer, innholder, and George Janvrin, mariner, as sureties, all of Portsmouth, in the sum of £3000, Nov. 5, 1759, for the administration of the estate; witnesses, Joseph Simes, Mary Wendell.]

SIMEON COLE   1759   DURHAM

[Administration on the estate of Simeon Cole of Durham, yeoman, granted to Abner Clough of Nottingham, yeoman, Nov. 16, 1759.]

[Probate Records, vol. 21, p 351.]

[Bond of Abner Clough, with Ezekiel Greeley of Londonderry and Nathaniel Thompson of Durham, husbandmen, as sureties, in the sum of £2000, Nov. 16, 1759, for the administration of the estate; witness, David Sewall.]

EBENEZER PIERCE   1759   HOLLIS

[Bond of Elizabeth Pierce, widow, and Eleazer Stearns, both of Hollis, with Ebenezer Ball of Hollis, husbandman, and Zachariah Shattuck of Monson as sureties, in the sum of £500, Nov. 26, 1759, for the administration of the estate of Ebenezer Pierce of Hollis; witnesses, Rachel Lovewell, Jonathan Lovewell.]

[Inventory, Nov. 7, 1759; amount, £2736. 7. 4; signed by Benjamin Blanchard, Jr., and Francis Worcester, Jr.]

[Account of Eleazer Stearns and his wife, Elizabeth Stearns, administratrix; receipts, £1243. 7. 4, personal estate; expenditures, £841. 8. 8; mentions "maintaince of Mary daughter of said Deceased under seven years old 297 weeks"; allowed Sept. 19, 1765.]

[Guardianship of Mary Pierce, aged less than 14 years, daughter of Ebenezer Pierce, granted to John Hale Oct. 8, 1765.]

[Probate Records, vol. 23, p. 558.]

[Bond of John Hale, with Samuel Cummings and Samuel Hobart as sureties, all of Hollis, in the sum of £300, Oct. 8, 1765, for the guardianship of Mary Pierce; witnesses, Samuel Hale, Ebenezer Pierce.]

We the subscribers Set of to Elizabeth Stearns late widow & Relict of Ebenezer Peirce of Holles in the Province of New Hampshire D^d her Dower, or one full third part of her said Husbands Real Estate lying & being in Holles, being in two pieces Containing Eleven Acres & sixty one pole, be the same more or less, One piece lying on the East side of the Road Containing one Acre & eleven Rods bounded as follows, beginning at a stake & Stones, about one Rod north of the House, thence East Seventeen Degrees South Ten Rods to a Stake & Stones, thence South Fifteen degrees west Thirteen Rods & an half till it comes to land lately owned by Richard Peirce to a Stake & Stones, Thence Westerly by said Peirces land to the Road, Thence Northerly by said Road to the first Bound Mentioned Together with the House well &c which is on this Piece. —

The Other piece lying on the west side of the Road, Containing Ten Acres & Fifty Rods, Bounded as follows beginning at a Stake & Stones, being the Southeast Corner of the Premises, bounding on land lately owned by Richard Peirce, Thence Westerly by said Peirces land Twenty six Rods to a Stake & Stones, Thence North nine degrees East Fifty Rods untill it comes to land owned by Timothy Cook to a Stake & Stones, thence Easterly by said Cooks land to the Road, thence Southerly by said Road to the first Bound mentioned. — The Barn Stands on this piece, & the Widow is to have only the East end as far as the Floar way, with priviledge of the Floar to pass & repass & to thrash grain &^{c}, allowing the Heirs liberty of the other part of the Barn, & yard room to the Road also liberty for the heirs to pass

& repass through the last mentioned piece of Land, on the north side next said Cooks, where it will be the least damage, they putting up the fences &c —

Holles April 15th 1766   Sam[ll] Cumings
Samuel Hobart
Stephen Powers

[Additional account of the administrators; receipts, £13. 8. 0; expenditures, £3. 11. 0; allowed June 27, 1766.]

MOSES TRUSSELL   1759   PLAISTOW

[Bond of Jane Trussell, widow, with John Mills and Thomas Williams, both of Hampstead, yeomen, as sureties, in the sum of £500, Dec. 6, 1759, for the administration of the estate of Moses Trussell of Plaistow, yeoman; witnesses, Daniel Little, Edmund Sawyer.]

[Inventory, attested March 3, 1760; amount, £1895. 5. 0; signed by Edmund Sawyer and Edmund Morse.]

[Guardianship of Jacob Trussell, minor, aged more than 14 years, son of Moses Trussell, granted to Jonathan Carlton June 2, 1763.]

[Probate Records, vol. 23, p. 46.]

[Bond of Jonathan Carleton of Plaistow, gentleman, with Joseph Blanchard of Merrimack as surety, in the sum of £500, June 2, 1763, for the guardianship of Jacob Trussell; witnesses, John Hale, Thomas Westbrook Waldron.]

[Warrant, Jan. 27, 1764, authorizing Edmund Sawyer, Edmund Morse, John Mills, Bartholomew Heath, and Nathan Goodwin, all of Hampstead, to appraise the real estate for settlement on the oldest son; returned at £800 Feb. 20, 1764, signed by Edmund Sawyer, Edmund Morse, and John Mills.]

[Warrant, April 12, 1764, authorizing Edmund Sawyer, Edmund Morse, and John Mills to set off the widow's dower.]

Province of } To the Honble Richard Wibird Judge of
Newhampshire } Probate &c for said Province

In obedience to a warrant from your Hon^r to us Directed For that purpose We have sot off to the widdow Jane Trussell her thirds of the Real Estate of Moses Trussell Deceas^d as Directed in Said warrant which is Bounded as followeth (Viz)

Begening at the South Easterly Corner of Land now in Possession of Joseph Hadley of Hampstead thence Runing Southerly By the Highway that Leads from Hamp^d to Plastow about twelve Rods to a stake and stons Thence westerly aboute Sixty Rods to a stake and stons Thence Northerly aboute fourty Rods to the westerly Corner of Said Hadleys Land then Runing By S^d Hadleys Land as that Runs to the Bounds first mentioned Encluding the Buildings on the Same

Plastow June ye 11th 1764   Edmund Sawyer
          Edmund Morss
          John mills

[Account of the administratrix; receipts, £1145. 5. 0, personal estate; expenditures, £590. 7. 8; mentions "Suport of a Child under Seven years 112 weeks"; allowed June 21, 1764.]

BENJAMIN WILLIAMS   1759   DANVILLE

In the Name of God Amen this Nineteenth Day of December one thousand Seven hundred fifty nine I Benjamin Williams of Newbury in the County of Essex and Province of the Massachusets bay in New England Husbandman * * *

Imprimis I Give to my beloved Wife Jemima all my houshold Goods wereing apperrel & Provision in the house I give her also the Improvment of all my Estate both real and personal four years from this time provided She take the care of & bring up my children till the four years be Expired & after the S^d four years are Expired my will is that She Should have the Imprment of one third part of all my Estate during her natural life I also Give to this my wife five acres of land in Newbury which lays by Indian river so called and I do constitute & ordain this my wife the Sole Executrix of this my last will & testament and it is my will that She pay all my Just debts and funeral charges and receive all that is due to me

Item I give to my Daughter Abigail four pounds to be paid by my Son Thomas in four years from this time besides what I have Given her before

Item I give to my Daughter Mary thirty Pounds to be paid to her by my Sons Thoms and Joseph Equly between them, in four years from this time

Item I Give to my Son Thomas the one half of all my Estate both real and parsonal which is not otherwise disposed of when he Shall arive to the age of twenty one years or when his mothers four years Improvment are Ended: this I give him provided he Shall pay to his Sister Abigail four Pounds his Sister Mary fifteen pounds his Sister Jemima twenty Six pounds twelve shillings & Eight pence and to his brother Benjamin twenty five pounds at Such times as I have Given it to them

Item I Give to my Son Joseph the other half of all my Estate when his mothers four years Improvment are Ended this I Give to this my Son provided he Shall pay to his Sister Mary fifteen pounds his Sister Sarah twenty Six pound twelve Shillings & Eight pence and to his Brother Benjamin twenty five Pounds at Such times as I have given it to them in this my will

Item I give to my Daughter Jemima twenty Six pounds twelve Shillings & Eight pence to be paid to her at the age of twenty one years or at marrage which Shall first happen by my Son Thomas

Item I Give to my Daughter Sarah twenty Six pounds twelve Shillings and Eight pence to be paid to her by my Son Joseph when She Shall arive to the age of twenty one years or at Marrage which Shall first happen

Item I Give to my Son Benjamin fifty Pounds to be paid to him by my Sons Thomas and Joseph Equilly between them when he Shall arive to the age of twenty one years * * *

Benjamin Willems

[Witnesses] Abner Sawyer, Caleb Moody Ju^r, Edmund Bayley.
[Endorsed] not provd filed Augt 1766

[Administration on the estate of Benjamin Williams of Hawke, cooper, granted to Jemima Williams, widow, Aug. 27, 1766.]
[Probate Records, vol. 24, p. 280.]

[Bond of Jemima Williams, widow, with Jonathan Blake and Israel Dimond, yeomen, as sureties, all of Hawke, in the sum of £500, Aug. 27, 1766, for the administration of the estate; witness, William Vaughan.]

[Inventory, filed Dec. 3, 1766; amount, £479. 11. 4; signed by Samuel Webster and Henry Morrill.]

[Account of the administratrix; receipts, £235. 7. 4, personal estate; expenditures, £127. 17. 10. 2; allowed July 29, 1767.]

Province of } We the Subscribers Being appointed a
New Hampsh^r } Committee By the Honble Judge of Probate of wills &c for said Province to Divide & set off to Jemima Williams of Hawke widow & Relict of Benjamin Williams late of Hawke yeoman Deceas^d Intestate her Dower which happens to her of the Real Estate of the said Deceased, Being one full third Part: Likewise the other Two Thirds to be Divided among the Children of said Intestate Pursuant to the above trust we found the said Intestate when he Died to be siezed of sixty six acres and three Quarters of an acre of Land in Hawke aforesaid which we Proceeded to sett off and Divide in the Following manner (viz) Leaving one Third Part of said Land on the North and the other third part on the south the widows Thirds Lying in the middle and to be sixteen Rods on the High-way and to Run west that width the whole Length of said Land Containing Twenty Two

acres and twenty Rods Likewise one Third part of the House and Barn and a Third part of the Income of the orchard Likewise one Third part of a Coopers shop on said land and then sett off & Divided the other Two Thirds to the Children being seven in Number in the following manner (viz) Eleaven acres and twenty Rods on the North side of said Land to Thomas williams the Eldest Son it Being Two Shares Then five acres and an Half and Ten Rods to Mary the wife of Dudley Kindrick & Likewise the Same Number of acres to Jemima Williams which Contains the one Third part on the North side of the widows Then the other Third part on the south of the widows; Sett off to Joseph Williams one share Being five acres and an Half & fifteen Rods adjoining to the widows then one share to Abigail the wife of Stephen moulton one share to Sarah Williams & one share to Benjamin Williams all the above shares or Pieces are Bounded at Each End with stakes and stones — and Likewise Evry one of them their share in the Buildings —

Dated at Hawke aforesaid this Twelfth Day of December Annoque Domini 1767

          Henry morrill
          Israel Dimond
          Phineas Sanborne

JONATHAN DOW   1759   PLAISTOW

[Mary Dow renounces administration on the estate of her husband, Jonathan Dow of Plaistow, who "Died Intestate Some time about the month of June last having no Child of full age", Dec. 19, 1759, in favor of Nathaniel Bartlett of Plaistow; witnesses, Enoch Bartlett, Katharine Bartlett.]

[Administration granted to Nathaniel Bartlett, yeoman, Dec. 26, 1759.]

[Probate Records, vol. 21, p. 352.]

[Bond of Nathaniel Bartlett, with Daniel Annis of New Hopkinton and John Webster of Penacook, yeomen, as sureties, in the sum of £1000, Dec. 26, 1759, for the administration of the estate; witnesses, William Parker, Cutts Shannon.]

[Warrant, Dec. 26, 1759, authorizing Moses Stevens and John Green, both of Plaistow, yeomen, to appraise the estate.]

[Inventory, Jan. 28, 1760; amount, £5532. 5. 0; signed by John Green and Moses Stevens.]

[Account of the administrator; receipts as per inventory; expenditures, £361. 13. 2; allowed May 27, 1761.]

[Warrant, June 24, 1761, authorizing Nicholas White, Samuel Little, William Ayer, gentleman, Moses Stevens, and Thomas Cheney, yeomen, all of Plaistow, to set off to John Cooper and his wife Mary her dower in the estate of her former husband, Jonathan Dow.]

Province of } Plastow January ye 22: 1762
Newhamp^r } By order of ye Honble Judg of Probate of wills &c the subscribers have set of to John Cooper of Plastow yeoman & mary his wife her Dowry which Happened to Her out of the estate of her former Husbon Jonathan Dow Late of Plastow Disceast buted & bounded as followeth (viz) Begining at ye high way at a stake & stones about ten Rods southerly of Land belonging to Capt Ayers thence southwesterly about Sixty Poles to a small white oack mark^t with stones about it thence North westerly about fifty Poles to a small wallnut tree mark^t thence south westerly about thirty Poles to a stake by John ayers Land thence on ye Line on s^d ayers Land to Sawyers & by Sawyers to ye highway thence Notherly by ye Rode to ye bounds first mentioned In Cluding in s^d Dowry ye one halef of the house & barn with ye Privilidges there to belonging

moses stevens
Thomas Cheney
William Ayer

[Guardianship of Phoebe Dow, Nathan Dow, and William Dow, aged less than 14 years, children of Jonathan Dow, granted to Samuel Kimball Nov. 24, 1762.]

[Probate Records, vol. 22, p. 500.]

[Guardianship of Mary Dow, minor, aged more than 14 years, daughter of Jonathan Dow, granted to Samuel Kimball Nov. 24, 1762.]

[Probate Records, vol. 22, p. 500.]

[Bond of Samuel Kimball of Plaistow, yeoman, with Benjamin Scribner of Brentwood and James Bly of Plaistow, yeomen, as sureties, in the sum of £1000, Nov. 24, 1762, for the guardianship of Mary Dow; witnesses, Daniel Gilman, 3d, John White.]

[Bond of Samuel Kimball, with the same sureties, in the sum of £1000, Nov. 24, 1762, for the guardianship of Phoebe, Nathan, and William Dow, aged less than 14 years, children of Jonathan Dow; witnesses, the same.]

[Additional account of the administrator; receipts, £1081. 9. 0; expenditures, £1613. 17. 2; mentions "allowance to the Widow for bring^g up two of the deceased children Since may 1762"; allowed Dec. 29, 1762.]

[Guardianship of Phoebe Dow, minor, aged more than 14 years, daughter of Jonathan Dow, granted to William Ayer May 17, 1763.]

[Probate Records, vol. 23, p. 78.]

[Bond of William Ayer, with Ebenezer White as surety, both of Plaistow, in the sum of £500, May 17, 1763, for the guardianship of Phoebe Dow; witnesses, William Parker, John Wentworth.]

[Account of Samuel Kimball as guardian of Nathan Dow and William Dow, minors, children of Jonathan Dow; receipts, £10. 6. 6; expenditures, £56. 8. 0; allowed April 30, 1766.]

[Probate Records, vol. 24, p. 196.]

Provence of } To The Honarabel John wintworth Esq' Judg
Newhamsher } of Probets for Said Provence —

In a Bedence to the order of the Governor Council & assembley we have attended the service of Deviding the Estate of Jonathan Dow Late of Plastow Decest and have Divided of to Nathan & william a Bout fourteen ackers and a half of Land alowing the Eldest Son a Dubel Share (it is Bounded as followeth) Beginning at a stake & stones By the Rhode Being a Bounds of Cap' william ayer Land thence Runing southerdly by the Rhode Ten Rhods to a stake and stones that is a Bounds of there mothers thurds thence westerdly By there mothers Land about fifty eight Rhods & half to a stake and stones Thence Norlwesterdly By there mothers Land a Bout thurty eight Rhods & half to a small tree marked which is a Bounds of there Sisters Land thence Noarth Earsterly or Earsterly By there Sisters Land about fifty Rhods to a stake and stones By Land of Cap' ayer thence By ayer Land South Earsterly a Bout thurty three Rhods to a stake and stones thence By ayer Land Earsterdly or Southeasterly about Eighteen Rhods to the furst Bounds mentioned — we Give it as our appinion that it is there parts of Said Land —

Plastow august 8–1766 —

Jonathan Carleton
Daniel Poor
Humphery Noyes

[Additional account of Samuel Kimball as guardian of Mary Dow, Nathan Dow, William Dow, and Phoebe Dow, children of Jonathan Dow; receipts, £64. 1. 5¾; expenditures the same; allowed May 25, 1768.]

[Probate Records, vol. 25, p. 171.]

JAMES FRENCH 1759 SALEM

[Mary French, "being his Heir," renounces administration on the estate of James French of Salem Dec. 25, 1759, in favor of Capt. Jacob Bayley; witnesses, Abner Bayley, Hannah Pattee.]

[Administration granted to Jacob Bayley of Hampstead, gentleman, May 9, 1760.]

[Probate Records, vol. 21, p. 431.]

[Bond of Jacob Bayley, with James Dwyer of Portsmouth, innholder, and James Carr of Goffstown, yeoman, as sureties, in the sum of £500, May 9, 1760, for the administration of the estate; witnesses, William Parker, Solomon Loud, Jr.]

JONATHAN BURBANK 1759 HOPKINTON

[Administration on the estate of Jonathan Burbank of New Hopkinton, gentleman, granted to his widow, Ruth Burbank, Dec. 26, 1759.]

[Probate Records, vol. 21, p. 352.]

[Bond of Ruth Burbank, with Daniel Annis of New Hopkinton, and James Cochran of Londonderry, yeomen, as sureties, in the sum of £1000, Dec. 26, 1759, for the administration of the estate; witnesses, William Parker, Cutts Shannon.]

[Warrant, Dec. 26, 1759, authorizing Peter Howe and John Putney, both of New Hopkinton, yeomen, to appraise the estate.]

[Inventory of the estate of Capt. John Burbank, March 19, 1760; amount, £5847. 11. 2; signed by John Putney and Peter Howe.]

[Commission July 1, 1761, to Ezra Carter of Bow and Timothy Clements of New Hopkinton, yeoman, to receive claims against the estate.]

[Commission, July 25, 1764, to Henry Lovejoy of Bow and Asa Foster of Pembroke, gentlemen, to receive claims against the estate.]

DANIEL LESLIE   1759   LONDONDERRY

[Administration on the estate of Daniel Leslie of Londonderry, yeoman, granted to his widow, Hannah Leslie, Dec. 26, 1759.]

[Probate Records, vol. 21, p. 352.]

[Bond of Hannah Leslie, with James Cochran of Londonderry and Daniel Annis of New Hopkinton, yeomen, as sureties, in the sum of £1000, Dec. 26, 1759, for the administration of the estate; witnesses, William Parker, Cutts Shannon.]

[Warrant, Dec. 26, 1759, authorizing James McGregore and William Rankin, both of Londonderry, yeomen, to appraise the estate.]

[Inventory, attested March 12, 1760; amount, £10,265. 2. 0; signed by James McGregore and William Rankin.]

[Account of the administratrix; receipts, £2325. 2. 0, personal estate; expenditures, £4032. 9. 10; mentions "maintaing 3 of the dec^d Children under the age of 7 years one 156 Weeks & still under age one 117 one 24"; allowed Nov. 12, 1762.]

[Bond of Alexander Leslie, cordwainer, with James Cochran and Jonathan Cochran, yeomen, as sureties, all of Londonderry, in the sum of £500, April 25, 1778, for the administration de bonis non of the estate; witnesses, Dinah Cochran, Samuel Allison.]

JONATHAN CRAM   1759   HAMPTON FALLS

In the Name of God Amen This twenty Ninth day of December in the year of Our Lord Christ One Thousand Seven hundred fifty nine I Jonathan Cram of Hampton falls in the Province of New Hampshire in New England Yeoman   *   *   *

Item I Give and Bequeath to my well beloved wife Elizabeth the Use Income and Improvement so long as she shall Remain my Widow, of the Southerly part of my new House as far As the Partition between the Rooms, Also of the Celler Under the Same, And of One half of my Barn that is on the South Side of my House, And of One half of my Orchard on the West Side of Exeter Rode, And also of One half of my Land where I now live on the Westerly Side of Exeter Road Containing about One hundred Acres in the whole And also of two Cows and My Horse and Six sheep out of my Stock of Creatures, And also of One half of all my moveables within Doors: All That is here mentioned that my wife is to have the Improvement of so Long as she Remains my Widow at her Decease or time of marrying Again shall go to my two Sons Nehemiah And Jonathan my Executors Excepting the moveables. And further I give and Bequeath to my said Wife One third part of all my Moveables within Doors for her to use and Dispose of As she shall think proper what I have here given my said wife is so to be understood that she Release Any Other Demands on my Estate —

Item I Give and Bequeath to my Son John Cram to him his heirs And assigns a Piece of Land where he now lives in Chester in the Province aforesaid it being one half of An Hundred Acre Lott so Called Number 18 Also one half of an hundred Acre Lott so Called in Chester aforesaid Number 16, being the Southerly half of said Lott Also One third Part of half a Right which I own in the Township of Chichester in the Province aforesaid.

And I Order him my said Son John to Pay to my Son Ebenezer when he shall Come to the Age of twenty years One yoke of three year old Steers, One Cow one three year old heifer, a Horse five Sheep, two Chains, a Cops and Pin. And I further Order my Said Son John to Pay to my Son Joseph when he shall Come to the Age of Twenty years, One yoke of three year old Steers, five Sheep And One Chain.

Item I Give And Bequeath to my Two Sons Nehemiah Cram And Jonathan Cram to them their heirs and Assigns Equally Divided between them As to Quantity and Quality All my Home Place where I now live on the westerly Side of Exeter Rode Containing About one hundred Acres be the Same more or Less with the Buildings thereon Excepting the Improvement of any part thereof Otherwise ordered in this my will for the term of such Improvement I Also Give to my said two Sons Nehemiah and Jonathan in manner aforesaid, One Other Piece of Land in Hampton falls aforesaid Containing About thirty five Acres Adjoyning to Land of Capt Row And Philimon Blake, Also One Other piece of Land in Hampton falls aforesaid on the East Side of Exeter Rode Containing About twenty three Acres Adjoyning to land of Benjamin Cram on the Northerly Side, Also one other piece of Land in Hamptonfalls aforesaid Containing About twenty Acres near Taylors River so Called Adjoyning to land of Benjamin Moulton, Also One Other Piece of Land lying in Kensington in the Province aforesaid at a Place called Grassy Swamp Adjoyning to land of Col^o Peter Gilman Also a Piece of Salt Marsh in Hampton falls aforesaid Containing About two Acres and a half, Also all my Husbandry And Carpentry Tools, And All my Stock of Creatures not Otherwise Disposed of in this my will all these to be Equally Divided Between my said two Sons Nehemiah And Jonathan And I Do hereby order them to pay to my Son Joseph Cram when he shall arrive, at the age of twenty years, One Cow, one three year old heifer One Horse one Chain and one Cops and pin. I Also Order them to find and Provide for my Daughter Mary Cram five Cord of Good firewood Halled to the Door and Cut fit for the fire yearly so Long as she shall live unmarried, also one Barrill of Cyder and to let her have Out of the Orchard Apples Sufficient for her use Winter And Summer

Item I Give and Bequeath to my Son Ebenezer Cram to him his heirs and assigns An Hundred Acre Lott so Called in Chester in the Province aforesaid Number 22, also One Cow, one Horse, five Sheep, one yoke of three year old Steers one three year old heifer two Chains and One Cops and pin to be paid him by my Son John as before ordered in this my will

Item I Give and Bequeath to my Son Benjamin Cram his heirs

and assigns An hundred Acre Lott of Land in Chester aforesaid Number 20, in the Second Range of Lotts, Also One Cow, One Horse, five Sheep, One Yoke of three year old Steers One three year old heifer two Chains and One Cops and Pin to be paid him when he shall Arrive at the Age of twenty years by my Son Nehemiah Cram whom I hereby order to pay the Same

Item I Give And Bequeath to my Sons Joel Cram and Joseph Cram their heirs and Assigns Equally Divided between them An hundred Acre Lott so Called in Chester aforesaid Number 112, Also three Quarters of an hundred Acre Lott in Chester aforesaid Number 113, Also three quarters of An Eighty Acre Lot so Called in Chester aforesaid Number 100, Also I Give to Each of them One Cow, One Horse, five Sheep One Yoke of three year old Steers, one three year old heifer two Chains, and One Cops and pin to be Paid them as they Respectively Arrive at the age of twenty Years, Joel to be paid by my Son Jonathan, And Joseph to be paid by my Sons John Nehemiah And Jonathan as before ordered in this my will.

Furthermore I do hereby Give all my wearing apparel to my four Sons Ebenezer Cram Benjamin Cram Joel Cram And Joseph Cram to be Equally Divided between them

Item I Give And Bequeath to my Daughter Mary Cram One hundred Pounds old Tenor to be paid her by my Executors within One year after my Decease, also One third part of All my Moveables within Doors at my Decease, Also the Use of One fire Room Namely at the North End of my new House and half the Celler under the Same so Long as she Remains Unmarried Also firewood Cyder and Apples to be Provided by my Sons Nehemiah and Jonathan and Deliverd her As before Ordered so long as she shall Remain Unmarried. I Also Give her one Cow And a two year old heifer And four Sheep And the Cow is to be kept for her winter and Summer by my said Sons Nehemiah and Jonathan if my said Daughter shall Desire it so long as she Remains Unmarried

Item I Give and Bequeath to my Son Nehemiah Cram my

Great Bible Also half a Sixty Acre Lott so Calld in Chester aforesaid

Item I Give One half An Original Right which I have in the Township of Chichester in the Province afores'd Equally between my three Sons John, Nehemiah and Jonathan. And I Give my Clock to my Son Jonathan, what is here mentioned in this place of part of a Right in Chichester to my Son John Intends the Same as was before mentioned to him

Item If there be Any Lands belonging to me not mentioned in this my will I Give the same to my Sons Nehemiah And Jonathan Equally between them also my Right in the old Sawmill so Called in Hampton

Item I Give and Bequeath to my four Sons Ebenezer Benjamin Joel And Joseph all my Houshold goods not before Disposed of Equally between them

Lastly I Do by these presents Constitute and appoint my Sons Nehemiah Cram and Jonathan Cram to be Executors * * *

Jonathan Cram

[Witnesses] Meshech Weare, Jonathan Tilton, Nathan Tilton. [Proved May 28, 1760.]

[Elizabeth Cram, widow, renounces her legacy and claims dower May 28, 1760; witnesses, Jonathan Tilton, Joseph Shaw.]

[Warrant, May 28, 1760, authorizing Theophilus Smith of Exeter and John Sherburne of Kensington to appraise the estate.]

[Inventory, June 5, 1760; amount, £50,803. 14. 6; signed by Theophilus Smith and John Sherburne.]

[Guardianship of Ebenezer Cram, minor, aged more than 14 years, son of Jonathan Cram, granted to John Cram of Chester Oct. 29, 1760.]

[Probate Records, vol. 21, p. 512.]

[Guardianship of Joel Cram and Joseph Cram, minors, aged

more than 14 years, children of Jonathan Cram, granted to Jonathan Cram of Hampton Falls Oct. 29, 1760.]

[Probate Records, vol. 21, p. 513.]

[Guardianship of Benjamin Cram, aged less than 14 years, son of Jonathan Cram, granted to Nehemiah Cram of Hampton Falls Oct. 29, 1760.]

[Probate Records, vol. 21, p. 513.]

[Bond of Jonathan Cram, yeoman, with Theophilus Smith of Exeter and John Cram of Chester, yeoman, as sureties, in the sum of £500, Oct. 29, 1760, for the guardianship of Joel Cram and Joseph Cram; witnesses, William Parker, Cutts Shannon.]

[Bond of John Cram of Chester, yeoman, with Theophilus Smith of Exeter and Jonathan Cram of Hampton Falls, yeoman, as sureties, in the sum of £500, Oct. 29, 1760, for the guardianship of Ebenezer Cram; witnesses, William Parker, Cutts Shannon.]

[Bond of Nehemiah Cram, yeoman, with Theophilus Smith of Exeter and John Cram of Chester, yeoman, as sureties, in the sum of £500, Oct. 29, 1760, for the guardianship of Benjamin Cram; witnesses, William Parker, Cutts Shannon.]

[Guardianship of Joseph Cram, minor, aged more than 14 years, son of Jonathan Cram, granted to Nehemiah Cram of Hampton Falls Feb. 25, 1767.]

[Probate Records, vol. 24, p. 346.]

[Guardianship of Joel Cram, minor, aged more than 14 years, son of Jonathan Cram, granted to John Cram of Raymond Feb. 25, 1767.]

[Probate Records, vol. 24, p. 346.]

[Bond of John Cram of Raymond, with Nehemiah Cram of Hampton Falls and Simon Sanborn of Hampton as sureties, in the sum of £500, Feb. 25, 1767, for the guardianship of Joel Cram; witness, William Vaughan.]

[Bond of Nehemiah Cram, with John Cram and Simon Sanborn as sureties, in the sum of £500, Feb. 25, 1767, for the guardianship of Joseph Cram; witnesses, William Vaughan, William Parker.]

SAMUEL AYERS   1760   PORTSMOUTH

[Administration on the estate of Samuel Ayers of Portsmouth, barber, granted to Jacob Lavers, joiner, and Samuel Frost, mariner, both of Portsmouth, Jan. 1, 1760.]

[Probate Records, vol. 21, p. 358.]

[Bond of Jacob Lavers, joiner, and Samuel Frost, mariner, with Charles Hight, sailmaker, and John Wendell, merchant, as sureties, all of Portsmouth, in the sum of £500, Jan. 2, 1760, for the administration of the estate; witnesses, Joseph Simes, Eliza Wibird.]

[Inventory; amount, £2091. 9. 0; signed by John Shackford and Joseph Peirce; no date.]

[Warrant, April 5, 1762, authorizing Eleazer Russell and Samuel Penhallow, merchant, both of Portsmouth, to receive claims against the estate.]

[List of claims, Oct. 26, 1762; amount, £10,380. 7. 4; signed by Eleazer Russell and Samuel Penhallow.]

PETER FASSETT   1760   GOFFSTOWN

[Administration on the estate of Peter Fassett of Goffstown granted to James Carr of Goffstown, yeoman, Jan. 4, 1760.]

[Probate Records, vol. 21, p. 358.]

[Bond of James Carr, with John Goffe of Derryfield and Moses Barron of Bedford, gentleman, as sureties, in the sum of £500, Jan. 4, 1760, for the administration of the estate; witnesses, William Parker, John Langdon, Jr.]

[Warrant, Jan. 4, 1760, authorizing John Goffe of Bedford, gentleman, and Job Kidder of Goffstown, yeoman, to appraise the estate.]

[Inventory, attested Jan. 25, 1760; amount, £49. 12. 9; signed by John Goffe and Job Kidder.]

WILLIAM PARKER   1760   LITCHFIELD

[Administration on the estate of William Parker of Litchfield, rope-maker, granted to his brother, Thomas Parker of Litchfield, gentleman, Jan. 19, 1760.]

[Probate Records, vol. 21, p. 358.]

[Administration on the estate of William Parker granted to his widow, Mehitabel Parker, and Thomas Parker of Litchfield, Feb. 7, 1760.]

[Probate Records, vol. 21, p. 385.]

[Bond of Mehitabel Parker and Thomas Parker, with William Richardson of Pelham and Richard Nason of Hampton Falls, gentlemen, as sureties, in the sum of £1000, Feb. 7, 1760, for the administration of the estate; witnesses, Thomas Westbrook Waldron, John Chamberlain, Thomas Bixby, Samuel Gibson.]

THOMAS WYMAN   1760   PELHAM

In the Name of God amen the Nineteenth Day of January one Thousand Seven Hundred and Sixty and in ye Thirty third year of his Majestys Reign: I Thomas Wyman of Pelham in the Province of Newhampshire Husbandman Being very Sick and weak in Body * * *

Item My will further is: I Give to my only Surviving Son Thomas Wyman Ju^r all the lands I now Possess in the Town of Pelham wheresoever the same may be found: viz my homstead or house Lots Containing about Sixty acres more or less allso

Beaver Brook meadow with the upland adjoyning thereunto about Thirty nine acres more or less: allso one hundred acres at a Place Called Chandlers farme more or less being quantity for quallity as the same may be Butted and Bounded: and Divided with Capt William Richardson: allso all my Buildings Standing on any of the above said lands: allso all my Stock of Cattle my horse and hogs Excepting one red Coullared Cow which I give to my Daughter Sibbell Wyman: allso I further Give to my said son Thomas all my working Tools of husbandry allso all my other Movable Estate without and within Doors of Every sort Excepting that Part of household stuff or Movable Estate which I have lately sold to my Daughter Sibbell Wyman by a Bill of sale Some time before I made this Will: the whole that I have Given to my said son Thomas: I Likewise Give it to his Lawfull heirs:

Item my will further is: I Give to my Daughter Lucy Stearns or to her Lawfull heirs with what I have allready Given her: the sum of one hundred Pounds passable money according to the old Tenor to be Paid to her out of my Estate by my Son Thomas Wyman or his lawfull heirs at or before the End of two years from my Discease

Item My will further is I Give to my Daughter Sibbell Wyman or to her Lawfull heirs: with what I have allready Given together with the within mentioned Cow: the Sum of three hundred Pounds Passable money according to the old tenor: to be Paid to her out of my Estate by my said Son Thomas Wyman or his lawfull heirs at or before the End of one year from my Decease:

Item I Constitute and ordain my Son Thomas Wyman Ju^r above mentioned and Mr John Butler of Pelham in said Province Husbandman to be my Executors * * * In Witness whereof I have here unto Set my hand and Seal the Day and year above Written

his
Thomas + Wyman
mark

[Witnesses] James Sherburne, Eleazar Whiting, William Wyman.

[Proved Feb. 13, 1760.]

[Bond of Thomas Wyman, Jr., and John Butler, with James Sherburne and William Wyman as sureties, all of Pelham, in the sum of £1000, Feb. 13, 1760, for the execution of the will; witnesses, William Parker, Jr., William Parker.]

[Account of the executors; receipts as by inventory; expenditures, £1056. 14. 4; allowed June 17, 1761.]

JAMES JOHNSON   1760   CHARLESTOWN

[Administration on the estate of James Johnson of Number Four, gentleman, granted to his widow, Susanna Johnson, Jan. 25, 1760.]

[Probate Records, vol. 21, p. 384.]

[Bond of Susanna Johnson, with Isaac Parker, gentleman, and John Hastings, Jr., yeoman, as sureties, all of Charlestown, in the sum of £1000, Feb. 1, 1760, for the administration of the estate; witnesses, William Heywood, Silvanus Hastings.]

[Inventory, April 5, 1760; amount, £219. 10. 0; signed by John Hastings, Jr., and William Heywood.]

[Account of Susanna Hastings, administratrix; receipts, £229. 16. 7¾; expenditures, £573. 19. 5½; mentions "Cash paid Jos: Morse which he lent Capt James Johnson when in Captivity"; allowed May 16, 1774; signed by John Hastings, Jr., and Susanna Hastings.]

DANIEL CARTY   1760   EXETER

[Anna Carty renounces administration on the estate of her husband, Daniel Carty, in favor of her father-in-law, John Carty, Jan. 29, 1760; witnesses, Nathan Rowe, Noah Emery.]

[Administration on the estate of Daniel Carty of Exeter, yeoman, granted to his father, John Carty of Exeter, yeoman, Jan. 29, 1760.]

[Probate Records, vol. 21, p. 362.]

[Bond of John Carty, with Nathaniel Folsom, gentleman, and Jeremiah Smith, yeoman, as sureties, all of Exeter, in the sum of £500, Jan. 29, 1760, for the administration of the estate; witnesses, William Parker, John Langdon, Jr.]

DANIEL LEAVITT   1760   EXETER

[Administration on the estate of Daniel Leavitt of Exeter, laborer, granted to Daniel Tilton of Exeter, trader, Jan. 30, 1760.]

[Probate Records, vol. 21, p. 383.]

[Bond of Daniel Tilton, with Theophilus Smith of Exeter and John Dow of Epping, yeoman, as sureties, in the sum of £1000, Jan. 30, 1760, for the administration of the estate; witnesses, William Parker, John Langdon, Jr.]

[Account of the administrator; receipts, £102. 0. 0 "Cash rec^d of Capt Saml Gerrish for Wages as an artificer in the Kings works"; expenditures, £51. 0. 0; allowed Feb. 25, 1761.]

[Guardianship of Daniel Leavitt, aged less than 14 years, granted to Nathaniel Healey Feb. 22, 1769.]

[Probate Records, vol. 25, p. 365.]

[Bond of Nathaniel Healey of Kensington, with Benjamin Moulton and Jeremiah Lane, both of Hampton Falls, yeomen, as sureties, in the sum of £500, Feb. 22, 1769, for the guardianship of Daniel Leavitt, son of Daniel Leavitt; witnesses, Samuel Hale, Jr., Stephen Swett.]

JEREMIAH DRESSER   1760   CONCORD

[Administration on the estate of Jeremiah Dresser of Rumford, yeoman, granted to his widow, Mehitabel Dresser, Jan. 30, 1760.]

[Probate Records, vol. 21, p. 384.]

[Board of Mehitabel Dresser, with Ephraim Worthen of Rumford, yeoman, and Nehemiah Lovewell of Dunstable, gentleman, as sureties, in the sum of £1000, Jan. 30, 1760, for the administration of the estate; witnesses, William Parker, John Langdon, Jr.]

ANDREW DOE   1760   NEWMARKET

[Administration on the estate of Andrew Doe of Newmarket, husbandman, granted to Samuel Doe of Newmarket, gentleman, Jan. 30, 1760.]

[Probate Records, vol. 21, p. 383.]

[Bond of Samuel Doe, with Thomas York of Durham, yeoman, and Zachariah Foss of Portsmouth, innholder, as sureties, in the sum of £500, Jan. 30, 1760, for the administration of the estate; witnesses, William Parker, John Langdon, Jr.]

BENJAMIN YORK   1760   DURHAM

[Administration on the estate of Benjamin York of Durham, yeoman, granted to Thomas York of Durham, yeoman, Jan. 30, 1760.]

[Probate Records, vol. 21, p. 384.]

[Bond of Thomas York, with William Drew of Durham, yeoman, and Samuel Doe of Newmarket, gentleman, as sureties, in the sum of £500, Jan. 30, 1760, for the administration of the estate; witnesses, William Parker, John Langdon.]

[Warrant, Jan. 30, 1760, authorizing Thomas Young and Robert Smart, yeoman, both of Newmarket, to appraise the estate.]

[Inventory, attested April 30, 1760; amount, £1578. 4. 3; signed by Thomas Young and Robert Smart.]

[Account of the administrator; receipts, £1577. 0. 0, personal estate; expenditures, £425. 13. 4; mentions "Two Years looking after & Tending the dec^d and his wife"; allowed Nov. 25, 1761.]

SAMUEL SMITH   1760   EXETER

[Dolly Smith renounces administration on the estate of her husband, Samuel Smith of Exeter, yeoman, "Lately Dyed (in the Army)", in favor of her father, Theophilus Smith of Exeter, Jan. 26, 1760; witnesses, James Thurston, Benjamin Boardman, Theophilus Smith, Jr.]

[Administration granted to Theophilus Smith of Exeter Jan. 30, 1760.]

[Probate Records, vol. 21, p. 385.]

[Bond of Theophilus Smith, with Daniel Tilton of Exeter, trader, and Joshua Neal of Stratham, gentleman, as sureties, in in the sum of £1000, Jan. 30, 1760, for the administration of the estate; witnesses, William Parker, John Langdon, Jr.]

[Warrant, Jan. 30, 1760, authorizing Ephraim Robinson and Noah Emery, both of Exeter, gentlemen, to appraise the estate.]

[Inventory, April 30, 1760; amount, £2356. 5. 0; signed by Ephraim Robinson and Noah Emery.]

JOHN MESERVE   1760   PORTSMOUTH

[Administration on the estate of John Meserve of Portsmouth, rope-maker, granted to his widow, Sarah Meserve, Jan. 30, 1760.]

[Probate Records, vol. 21, p. 383.]

[Bond of Sarah Meserve, with Luke Mills, mariner, and Samuel Waters, joiner, as sureties, all of Portsmouth, in the sum of £1000, Jan. 30, 1760, for the administration of the estate; witnesses, John Pickering, Samuel Ham.]

[Warrant, Jan. 30, 1760, authorizing Eleazer Russell and Samuel Penhallow, shopkeeper, both of Portsmouth, to appraise the estate.]

[Inventory, Feb. 4, 1760; amount, £4240. 4. 0; signed by Eleazer Russell and Samuel Penhallow.]

[Warrant, April 27, 1761, authorizing Eleazer Russell and Samuel Penhallow, merchant, both of Portsmouth, to receive claims against the estate; another warrant of the same date appoints Andrew Clarkson and William Knight, both of Portsmouth, merchants.]

[List of claims, Feb. 1, 1762; amount, £9589. 8. 10; signed by Eleazer Russell and Samuel Penhallow.]

[Warrant, Feb. 15, 1762, authorizing Eleazer Russell, Samuel Penhallow, and John Griffith, all of Portsmouth, shopkeepers, to set off the widow's dower.]

Province of New Hampshire } We the Subscribers appointed a Committee By the Hon[ble] Richard Wibird Esq Judge of the Probate of Wills &c for said Province to set off to Sarah Meserve Widow Relict of John Meserve Late of Portsmouth Ropemaker Deceas'd her Dower of the Real Estate of said Deceas'd Pursuant thereto by Estimation according to the best of our Judgment We set off and hereby do report to have set off to the said Sarah Meserve for her Dower, the Mansion

House & Land & Buildings thereon, Bounded Southerly on the Street to Islington, Westerly on the street to the Bridge, Northerly & Easterly on the Land of Doctor John Ross Late of Portsmouth Deceas'd —

Given under our hands Portsmouth May the 14th 1762 —

Eleazer Russell
Saml Penhallow
John Griffeth

[Additional inventory, Sept. 1, 1762; amount, £419. 16. 3; signed as above.]

PEARSON BROWN   1760   HAMPTON FALLS

[Administration on the estate of Pearson Brown of Hampton Falls, yeoman, granted to Samuel Gerrish of Dover, gentleman, Feb. 1, 1760.]

[Probate Records, vol. 21, p. 385.]

[Bond of Samuel Gerrish, with Philip Johnson of Greenland and Alexander Todd of Landonderry, gentlemen, as sureties, in the sum of £1000, Feb. 1, 1760, for the administration of the estate; witnesses, William Parker, Nathaniel Adams.]

CHARLES STONEMAN   1760   PORTSMOUTH

[Administration on the estate of Charles Stoneman of Portsmouth, joiner, granted to his widow, Esther Stoneman, Feb. 4, 1760.]

[Probate Records, vol. 21, p. 385.]

[Bond of Esther Stoneman, with Joseph Abbott, laborer, and John Savage, farmer, as sureties, all of Portsmouth, in the sum of £500, Feb. 4, 1760, for the administration of the estate;

witnesses, Elizabeth Wibird, Mary Wendell.]

[Warrant, March 7, 1760, authorizing Richard Evans and Daniel Davis, both of Portsmouth, to appraise the estate.]

[Inventory, March 8, 1760; amount, £475. 10. 0; not signed.]

SAMUEL CLIFFORD   1760   KENSINGTON

In The Name of God Amen I Samuel Clifford of the Parish of Kensington in the Province of Newhampshire in Newengland Yeoman * * *

1ly   I Give and Bequeath to my Well beloved Wife Sarah Clifford the improvement of the east end of my Dwelling house and the one halfe of my orchard and the Improvement of all my moveables Within Doars During her Widowhood and no longer and at her Death or Day of marriage the house orchard and moveables to go to those that I Give them to in this my Will — and I Give my sd wife two Cows to improve her Widowhood and to be Keept winter and Sumer by my son Samuel Clifford and at her Death I Give Said Cows to my son Samuel Clifford and I Give my Said wife twelve Bushels of Indian Corn one Bushel of Rye two Bushels of wheet two Bushels and a halfe of mault two hundred weight of pork one hundred weight of Beef Eight pound of sheeps wool five pound of Cotten wooll Six pound of flax from the Coome and five Cord of wood at the Doar Cut fit for the fier all and every article which I have given my Said wife I order my son Samuel Clifford to provide for his mother yearly and every year so long as Shee Continues my Widow and no longer But if my Son Samuel Should Refuse to provide for his mother as is above exprest then my Said wife Shall have Liberty By this my will to Enter into possession of all my estate During her widowhood

2ly   I Give and Bequeath forever unto my son Benjamin Clifford the one halfe of my land laying in the Parish of Eppin be y^e

whole fifty acres more or less he haveing had a large Portion Given him by Deed from his father

3ly I Give and Bequeath to my Son Joseph Clifford three pound money old tenor Bills of Credit to be paid to him by my Son Samuel Clifford within one year after my Decease he having had his portion by Deed Before

4ly I Give and Bequeath to my four Daughters namely abigail Carr Sarah Prescott Rachal Prescott and hannah Palmer all my Brass Iron puter Beads and Beading in or Belonging to my house Excepting one Bead and Beading Belonging to Said Bead and I Give my Said Daughters all my Chasts and Chairs Excepting my newest Great Chair all and every article to be Equally Divided between my Said four Daughters at my wives Decease and not till then

5ly I Give and Bequeath to my Son Samuel Clifford forever the east end of my Dweling house the one halfe of my Barn and my orchard only his mother is to improve as is Before mentioned and I Give my Said son all my Stock of Creatures of all Sorts whatsoever and newest Greate Chair and one Bead and the Beading Belonging to Said Bead and I Give my Said son Samuel Clifford forever all my land laying in the Parish of Kensington be the Same forty four acres more or less laying in the first West Division So Called and in the Second Range — and I Give my Said son all my Implyments of husbandry and all my Wearing Cloaths and all my money by me or Due to me and if their be any thing that I have not Desposed of in this my Will I Give it or them to my Executor — and I Do Constitute and Appoint my son Samuel Clifford to be my Executor * * *

In Witness Whereof I the s^d Samuel Clifford have hereunto Set my hand and affixt my seal This Eighth Day of february: anno: Domini 1760 and in the thirty third year of the Reign of King George the second &c   Samuel Clifford

[Witnesses] Simon Clifford, Theophilus Page, Ezekiel Dow.
[Proved April 27, 1763.]

[Warrant, April 27, 1763, authorizing Theophilus Page and Benjamin Brown, Jr., husbandman, both of Kensington, to appraise the estate.]

[Inventory, attested Aug. 28, 1763; amount, £11,000. o. o; signed by Theophilus Page and Benjamin Brown.]

JOHN HOLMES 1760 PORTSMOUTH

[Administration on the estate of John Holmes of Portsmouth, shipwright, granted to Jeremiah Holmes of Portsmouth, shipwright, Feb. 8, 1760.]

[Probate Records, vol. 21, p. 385.]

[Bond of Jeremiah Holmes, with Benjamin Holmes, mariner, and James Holmes, shipwright, as sureties, all of Portsmouth, in the sum of £500, Feb. 8, 1760, for the administration of the estate; witnesses, William Parker, Lydia Parker.]

SAMUEL LOVERING 1760 KINGSTON

[Administration on the estate of Samuel Lovering of Kingston, yeoman, granted to William Lovering of Kingston, yeoman, Feb. 11, 1760.]

[Probate Records, vol. 21, p. 388.]

[Bond of William Lovering, with John Thorne, yeoman, and Josiah Bartlett, physician, as sureties, all of Kingston, in the sum of £500, Feb. 11, 1760, for the administration of the estate; witnesses, William Parker, Jr., Nathan Rowe.]

EBENEZER JOSE 1760 PORTSMOUTH

In the Name of God Amen I Ebenezer Jose of Portsmouth in the Province of New Hampshire in New England Cooper being at Present in an ill State of bodyly Health * * *

Imprimis I give & bequeath to my beloved Son Ebenezer Jose & to his heirs & assigns the moity or one half of all my Estate Subject nevertheless to such Conditions restrictions & reservations as are herein after mentioned & not otherwise —

Item — I give & bequeath to my beloved son Michael Dennis Jose & to his heirs & assignes one moity or half Part of my Estate afores^d Subject nevertheless to such Conditions & reservations and ristrictions as are herein after Expressed & not otherwise

Item — I give & bequeath to my beloved Daughter Joanna Jose Two Hundred Pounds of the Value of the Present Currency of the old Tener So called One Hundred Pounds to be paid her by my Son Ebenez^r Jose the other Hundred Pounds thereof to be paid her by my Son Michail Dennis Jose and each respectively to Pay the Same within one Year after they respectivly arrive at the age of Twenty one Years or their coming into the Possession of the respective Legacies above s^d which soever Shall last happen (if Personaly Demand by her) & not otherwise and this is one of the Conditions mentioned in the respective Legacys bequeathed them above —

Item My Will is & I hereby give & bequeath unto my beloved wife Margret Jose the whole & Sole Improvement of my now Dwelling House & the Land whereon it Stands togeather with all the Gardens out Houses and also all the Furniture Household Stuff & Utensells therein or thereunto belonging; to have & to hold the same during the Time She Continues my Widow & no longer and then to revert to my Said Sons as above mentioned & this also is one of the Conditions & reservations made in the respective Legacys given to my Said Sons as above mentioned —

Item My Will is That it case it should happen that either of my Said Sons should Die before he arives at the age of Twenty one Years that the Survior Shall Have Hold & Enjoy the Legcy herein before bequeathed to such son so Dying & the Said Survivor in this Case to Pay to his Sister Joanna Four Hundred Pounds (old Tenor as afore s^d) to be paid her at Such Period &

on Such demand as is before in this will mentioned for the Payment of One Hundred Pounds by my aforesaid sones respectivly & this to be in Lieu of the s^d Two hundred Pounds before mentioned & in full of all her Demands by Virtue of this my Will —

Lastly I do hereby also nominate Constitute & appoint my beloved Wife Margret Jose Executrix & my much respected Brother Cap^n Joseph Hixon Executor of this my Will & Testament hereby revoking & Disannulling all others by me Excecuted in Testamony whereof I have hereunto Set my hand & Seal this 20th Day of Feb^{ry} One thousand Seven hundred & Sixty —

Ebenezer Jose

[Witnesses] Niel Lamont, Theodore Atkinson Junr, Richard Servan.

A Codicil to be Annext to & taken as Part of my Last Will & Testament.

Whereas I Ebenezer Jose of Portsmouth in New Hampshire in New England have Executed a last will and Testament Bearing Date the 20th Day of February Instant in which I have Disposed of & order'd the Settlement of my Real & Personal Estate but made therein no Particular Disposition of my Estate that Desended to me from my Father Richard Jose late of Portsmouth Decease'd & as I have not in my said will order'd what Part of my Estate shou'd be Disposed of for the Payment of my Just Debts & Funeral Expences or for the Repayment of such Debts as may be Contracted in my sickness. I do by these Presents order & Direct that what ever may be my Part share or Portion coming & belonging to me from my said Fathers Estate shall be Disposed of for the Paym^t of such Debts & Funeral charges & I hereby Impower and Desire my said Executors to sell & Dispose of the same and Apply the neat Proceeds thereof as there shall be occation to answer the Ends aforesaid Dated at Portsm^o the 26th Day of Feb^{ry} 1760

Ebenezer Jose

[Witnesses] Theodore Atkinson Junr, Abraham Crusey, Richard Servan.
[Proved March 26, 1760.]

EBENEZER HINSDALE   1760   DEERFIELD, MASS.

In the Name of God Amen I Ebenezer Hinsdale of Deerfield in the County of Hampshire in the Province of the Massachusetts Bay in New England Esqr being very infirm and Weak in Body, But of Sound and perfect Mind and Memory (Blessed be God) Do this Twenty Third Day of February in the Year of our Lord one Thousand Seven hundred and Sixty make and Publish this my last Will and Testament * * *

And my real Estate and Personal Estate I dispose in the following manner, That is to say I give to my worthy and beloved Wife Abigail all my Personal Estate of every sort wheresoever the same is or may be at the Time of my decease to have and to hold s^d personal Estate to her the s^d Abigail her Executors Administrators and Assigns forever.

Also I give to my said wife all my real Estate lying and being within the Township of Deerfield afores^d and the District of Greenfield, To have and to hold s^d real Estate to her my said Wife during the Term of her Natural Life and no longer   And to the Natural and lawfull begotten Children of my Brother Samuel Hinsdale who shall be living at the time of my said wifes Decease Born or that shall be Born I give three Ninth Parts of all my s^d real Estate in Deerfield and Greenfield aforesaid to be taken immediately upon my s^d Wife's decease and not before, And to have and to hold the s^d three Ninth Parts to said Children in the following manner and Proportion to wit in case said Children shall be all male or all Female It is my will Intent and meaning that said three Ninths shall be equally divided to and among them and that each of said Children shall hold one such equal Part and Share to him or Her and his or her Heirs and assigns forever; But in case it shall so happen that some of said Children shall be Male and some Female It is my Will and meaning that Each and every Male of said Children shall take and have a share and Portion double to the share and Portion of the Female of said Children and that the shares of the males shall be equal the one to ye other and that the shares of the Females shall be Equal the one to the other and that Each one of them both Male and Female shall have and hold their respective Shares to him and her, and to his and her Heirs & assigns forever respectively.

Also to the natural Children of my Brother John Hinsdale deceased, who shall be living at the Time of my said Wife's Decease I give two ninth Parts of all my said Real Estate in Deerfield and Greenfield aforesaid to be taken immediately on my said Wife's decease and not before, and to have and to hold the said two ninth Parts to said Children in the following Manner and Proportion, That is to say in case such Children shall be all Male or all Female It is my Will and meaning that s^d two ninth Parts shall be equally divided between them, and that each of said children shall hold one such equal Part and Share to him or her and his or her Heirs and assigns forever, But in case some of said Children shall be Male and some Female It is my will and meaning that each and every Male among said Children shall take and have a Portion and share double to the share and Portion of the Female among said Children and that the Shares of Each male shall be equal the one to the other & the Share of Each Female shall also be equall the one to the Other, and that Each one of them both Male & Female Shall have and hold their Respective Shares to him & her & his & her Heirs and assigns Forever Respectively.

And to the Natural and lawfull begotten Children of my Brother Elijah Williams Esqr who shall be living at the Time of my said Wife's decease, Born or that shall be Born I give Four Ninth Parts of all my s^d real Estate in Deerfield and Greenfield aforesaid to be taken immediately after my said Wife's decease, and not before, and to have & to hold the four Ninth Parts to them s^d Children in the following Manner and Proportion that is to say in case such children shall be all Male or all Female, It is my will that s^d four Ninth Parts shall be equally divided between them and that Each of said Children shall hold one such equal Part & Share to him or her and his or her Heirs and assigns Forever But in Case some of said Children shall be Male and some Female It is my Will and meaning that Each & every Male of said Children shall take and have a Portion and Share Double to the Portion and Share of the the Female among said Children and that the shares of Each Male (if there be more than one) shall be equal the one to the other, and that the Shares of the Females (if there shall be more than one) shall be equall the one to the other and that each one of them both Male and Female shall have and hold their respective Shares to him and her and his & her Heirs and assigns Forever respectively

Also I give to my s^d Wife Abigail all the residue of my Real Estate wheresoever the same lies and is Situate either in this or any other Province or Colony in America to have and to hold the said Residue to her the said Abigail Heirs and assigns forever to her Sole use & disposal forever

Also in Case Darius Hinsdale the Son of my Brother Samuel Hinsdale shall be liberally Educated and shall be sent for such Education to Harvard Colledge in Cambridge in New England; I give to said Darius Twenty Pounds Sterling Money of Great Britain to be paid to him immediately on his being entred and Admitted a Student of s^d Colledge, & in case s^d Darius shall continue a Student of said Colledge one year I give to him another Sum of Twenty Pounds Sterling to be paid to him at the Expiration his s^d First year & in case he shall continue a Student at said Colledge two years I give him another Sum of Twenty Pounds Sterling to be paid at the End of said Second year, And in Case he shall continue a Student there three years I give him s^d Darius another Sum of Twenty Pounds Sterling to be paid to him at the End of his Third Year, And in case he shall continue a Student of said Colledge Four Years and shall at the end of said Four years be Honoured with the Degree of Bachelor of Arts, at said Colledge I give him said Darius other Twenty Pounds Sterling to be paid immediately after his being Admitted to Said Degree.

Also in case my Hon^d Mother shall out live her present Husband Mr George Beale I give to her my said Mother an annuity of Forty Shillings Sterling to be paid to her every Year during her Natural Life from and after her said Husband's decease.

And I hereby order that in case It should so happen that all my Personal Estate besides and Exclusive of all Wearing apparrell and all my Household Furniture and Utensils, of all Sorts and all such Husbandry Implements & Utensills as my Executor shall Judge Necessary for her own use; Shall not Extend and be Sufficient to pay and satisfy all the Just Debts which I shall owe at the Time of my decease, I say I Order that my Executrix herein after Named shall Sell so much of any of my Lands either in New Hampshire or this Province according to her discretion as shall be necessary & Sufficient together with my Personal Estate Exclusive of the Wearing apparrell Household stuff and Husbandry Implements aboves^d to make Moneys Enough to pay my s^d Debts Notwithstanding the above demises of the Remainder of my Estate in my Lands in Greenfield & Deerfield after ye Expiration of my Wife's said Term there in to the Children of my Brethren above named, and in that case I fully authorize and Impower my Executrix herein after Named to make Sale of so much Land as aboves^d and to make and Execute all Such Deeds, and Instruments as shall be proper & Needfull effectually to convey such Land to ye Purchaser.

But if my Personal Estate exclusive of all Wearing apparrell & all my Household Stuff and all such Husbandry Utensills as abovesaid, shall be fully sufficient to pay my Just Debts; In that Case It is my will and Intent that none of my Lands or Real Estate either in Deerfield or Greenfield should be Sold to pay Debts But that my Personal Estate not herein before Excluded and Excepted shall be improved & disposed to that Purpose and it was my true meaning in the foregoing Gift and Bequest thereof to my Said Wife that She should have the same so charged —

And Lastly I hereby make and appoint my s^d Wife Abigail sole Executrix * * *

Ebenezer Hinsdale

[Witnesses] Joseph Hawley, Thomas Williams, Moses Severance.

[Proved in Massachusetts Feb. 17, 1763, and in New Hampshire March 2, 1763.]

[Inventory, filed March, 1764; amount, £119. 10. 10; personal estate; signed by Peter Evans and Daniel Shattuck.]

ALEXANDER PARK   1760   WINDHAM

[Bond of Joseph Park, with Robert Park and Alexander Park as sureties, all of Windham, yeomen, in the sum of £500, Feb. 26, 1760; for the administration of the estate of Alexander Park of Windham, yeoman; witnesses, John Cochran, Robert Boyes.]

[Warrant, Feb. 26, 1760, authorizing John Cochran and Samuel Morrison, both of Windham, gentlemen, to appraise the estate; mentions Joseph Park as son of the deceased.]

[Inventory, March 8, 1760; amount, £4270. 1. 0; signed by Samuel Morrison and John Cochran.]

ABIJAH FOSTER   1760   NEW IPSWICH

[Administration on the estate of Abijah Foster of New Ipswich, yeoman, granted to his widow, Mary Foster, March 1, 1760.]

[Probate Records, vol. 21, p. 423.]

[Bond of Mary Foster, with Samuel Kenney, yeoman, and Timothy Heald, gentleman, as sureties, all of New Ipswich, in the sum of £1000, March 1, 1760, for the administration of the estate; witnesses, Asa Bullard, Martha Brooks.]

[Inventory, March 19, 1760; amount, £140. 11. 7. 2; signed by Ephraim Adams and Benjamin Adams.]

[Guardianship of Samuel Foster, minor, aged more than 14 years, son of Abijah Foster, granted to Aaron Kidder of New Ipswich April 25, 1760.]
[Probate Records, vol. 21, p. 549.]

[Bond of Aaron Kidder, with John Dutton and Ichabod Howe as sureties, all of New Ipswich, yeomen, in the sum of £500, April 25, 1760, for the guardianship of Samuel Foster; witnesses, Francis Fletcher, Peter Fletcher.]

ELISHA JACKSON 1760 PORTSMOUTH

[Administration on the estate of Elisha Jackson of Portsmouth, mariner, granted to Daniel Jackson of Portsmouth, gentleman, March 3, 1760.]
[Probate Records, vol. 21, p. 395.]

[Bond of Daniel Jackson, gentleman, with Simeon Akerman, boat-builder, and Richard Hart, shopkeeper, as sureties, all of Portsmouth, in the sum of £500, March 3, 1760, for the administration of the estate of his son-in-law, Elisha Jackson; witnesses, William Frost, William Parker.]

[Warrant, March 3, 1760, authorizing John Griffith and Thomas Hatch, both of Portsmouth, to appraise the estate.]

[Inventory, May 23, 1760; amount, £797. 17. 0; signed by John Griffith and Thomas Hatch.]

[Guardianship of Hannah Jackson, minor, aged more than 14 years, daughter of Elisha Jackson, granted to William Pearne May 8, 1762.]

[Probate Records, vol. 22, p. 346.]

[Bond of William Pearne, mariner, with George Boyd, mariner, and Ebenezer Odiorne, turner, as sureties, all of Portsmouth, in the sum of £500, May 8, 1762, for the guardianship of Hannah Jackson, daughter of Elisha Jackson, blockmaker; witnesses, Samuel Aris, Joseph Lowe.]

[Guardianship of Hannah Jackson, minor, aged more than 14 years, daughter of Elisha Jackson, granted to Joseph Lowe of Portsmouth, tinman, Dec. 2, 1767.]

[Probate Records, vol. 25, p. 46.]

[Bond of Joseph Lowe, with Thomas Chadbourne, blacksmith, as surety, both of Portsmouth, in the sum of £500, Dec. 2, 1767, for the guardianship of Hannah Jackson; witnesses, Peter Pearse, Robert Parkes.]

[Account of William Pearne, guardian; receipts, £296. 13. 4; expenditures, £1983. 5. 0; mentions "boarding Schooling & Cloathing the said Ward from the 4th day of January 1755 till the 2^{d} day of February 1763"; allowed Jan. 31, 1770.]

PHILIP McCARGIN 1760 HAMPSTEAD

[Petition of Dinah Robertson, Hampstead, March 8, 1760, for the appointment of John Muzzey of Hampstead as guardian of her son, Philip McCargin, aged less than 14 years.]

[Guardianship of Philip McCargin, aged less than 14 years, son of Philip McCargin of Hampstead, yeoman, granted to John Muzzey of Hampstead March 28, 1760.]

[Probate Records, vol. 21, p. 408.]

[Bond of John Muzzey, with Peter Eastman and Stephen Johnson as sureties, all of Hampstead, in the sum of £1000,

March 28, 1760, for the guardianship of Philip McCargin; witnesses, William Parker, Solomon Loud, Jr.]

GEORGE WARREN   1760   PORTSMOUTH

[Administration on the estate of George Warren of Portsmouth, blacksmith, granted to his widow, Elizabeth Warren, March 21, 1760.]

[Probate Records, vol 21, p 400.]

[Bond of Elizabeth Warren, with Robert Hart and John Pendexter, butchers, as sureties, all of Portsmouth, in the sum of £500, March 21, 1760, for the administration of the estate; witnesses, William Parker, Solomon Loud, Jr.]

[Administration on the estate of George Warren granted to his widow, Elizabeth Warren, and George Warren of Portsmouth, blacksmith, May 28, 1760.]

[Probate Records, vol 21, p 448.]

[Bond of Elizabeth Warren and George Warren, yeoman, both of Portsmouth, with John Pendexter of Portsmouth, yeoman, and Thomas Leighton of Newington, husbandman, as sureties, in the sum of £3000, May 28, 1760, for the administration of the estate; witnesses, David Sewall, George Seward.]

[Warrant, May 28, 1760, authorizing Eleazer Russell and Thomas Peirce, gentlemen, both of Portsmouth, to appraise the estate; the same document was issued under date of March 21, 1760.]

[Inventory, Aug. 27, 1760; amount, £2675. 8. 0; signed by Eleazer Russell and Thomas Peirce.]

[Account of the administrators; receipts, as per inventory; expenditures, £20. 19. 7½; allowed Oct. 29, 1766.]

DANIEL BURDITT 1760 MALDEN, MASS.

These may Certify that I Joanna Burditt Earnestly Desire that m^r Thomas Burditt of malden may be Guardian of my only Child Joanna Burditt who is about four years old

her
Joanna × Burditt
mark

[Middlesex Co., Mass., Probate Files.]

[Bond of Thomas Burditt of Malden, Mass., cordwainer, with Thomas Burditt of Medford, Mass., leather dresser, as surety, in the sum of £500, March 24, 1760, for the guardianship of Joanna Burditt, daughter of Daniel Burditt of Dunstable; witnesses, Andrew Bordman and David Green.]

[Middlesex Co., Mass., Probate Files.]

[Bond of Jonathan Green, gentleman, with Joanna Burditt, widow, as surety, both of Malden, Mass., in the sum of £500, Nov. 28, 1763, for the guardianship of Joanna Burditt, minor, in her ninth year, daughter of Daniel Burditt of Malden, Mass.; witnesses, Andrew Bordman and Ebenezer Stedman.]

[Middlesex Co., Mass., Probate Files.]

AMOS MAIN 1760 ROCHESTER

In ye Name of God Amen the twenty fourth Day of March one Thousand Seven Hundred & Sixty I Amos Main of the Town of Rochester in ye Province of New Hampshire in New-England Clerk being very weak in Body * * *

Imprimis I give & bequeath to my dearly beloved Wife Elizabeth ye produce of the one Third of My Homestead during her widowed, & if she marries again then the Improvement of one Third of My Homestead during her Natural Life.

Item I give and bequeath to My Said dearly beloved wife all my Houshold goods to be disposed of by her when she pleases among her Daughters

Item I give & bequeath to my S^d dearly beloved Wife My Negro man Pomp to her, her Heirs, & assigns, and also my Gelding Horse & my mare.

Item I give & bequeath to my S^d beloved Wife three Cows, & all my Hiefers, to her Her Heirs & assigns.

Item I give & bequeath to My Said beloved Wife ye Improvement of two or three Acres of My Homestead, where she pleases for planting.

Item I give & bequeath to Said beloved wife & My Unmarried daughters ye use of one half of My dwelling House, which half she pleases, so long as she & they or any of them remain Unmarried.

Item I give & bequeath to My beloved Son Josiah all my Homestead (excepting half an Acre, which I shall hereafter dispose off for a Burying place, & a few rods wch I shall hereafter Mention, out of ye lot which was originally John Busseys & ye produce & improvement of part thereof as afore Said, together with ye buildings thereon standing and all ye appurtenances & priviledges thereunto belonging excepting ye use of part of Sd House as above Said, To Him his Heirs & assigns for ever.

Item I give and bequeath to My S^d beloved Son Josiah My Home lot, which is Called ye Ministers lot, which fell to me by Virtue of my being ye first Settled Minister in Said Town of Rochester, to him his Heirs & assigns for ever.

Item I give & bequeath to My Said beloved Son Josiah ye Marsh in ye Lot called ye Ministers Lot in ye Second Division of lands in S^d Rochester to him his Heirs and assigns for ever, with ye priviledge of passing too & from S^d Marsh as he shall have occasion.

Item I give & bequeath to My S^d beloved Son my Oxen & Steers for ye common use of ye family

Item I give and bequeath to My Said beloved Son Josiah, My Stallion Horse & one Cow

Item I give and bequeath to My S^d beloved Son Josiah ye whole of My third division lot which belongd to ye Ministers right or lot before Mentiond, to him his Hiers & assigns for ever.

Item I give and bequeath to My beloved daughter Mary Seventy Acres of land in ye Second Division of lands in S^d Rochester, which I bought of Mr John Wood, which originally belong'd to John Bussey, to Her, Her Heirs & Assigns for ever.

Item I give & bequeath to My beloved Daughters Elizabeth & Lydia Two thirds of ye Lot of Land in ye Second Division in S^d Rochester which I bought of Jonathan Church, to be equally divided between them, to them their Heirs & assigns for ever.

Item I give & bequeath to My beloved Daughters, Hannah, Abigail & Mercy ye whole of My Lot in ye Second Division of Rochester afrs^d belonging to ye Ministers right before Mentioned, excepting ye Marsh before Mentioned, to be equally divided between them, to them their Heirs & assigns for ever

Item It is My Will that My Said beloved Son Josiah receive all My Outstanding Debts, & that he pay all my lawfull debts out of ye Same So far as they will go: & if they are not enough to discharge all my debts, then its my will that my Said Son take or Sell so Much of My lands in S^d Rochester, as yet not bequeathed as shall be Sufficient to discharge S^d outstanding Debts, & what remains of My Unbequeathed lands in Said Rochester, after My Said debts are discharged, I give & bequeath to all My afore Said Daughters, to be equally divided between y^m to them their Heirs & assigns for ever

Item I give and bequeath to My beloved Grand Son Amos main Hayes a Certain parcell of land belonging to ye Lot I bought of S^d John wood, which originally belong'd to S^d John Buzzey, y^t is to say ye Home lot, begining by ye main road y^t passes thro' ye first Division of lands in S^d Rochester Joyning to ye northeasterly Corner of Wentworth Hayes land, running by S^d Road Northwesterly four rods then taking ye four rods in width, running Southwesterly by S^d Wentworth Hayes land till Said Wentworth Hayes's tan pits are included and no farther, to him his Heirs & assigns for ever, only ye S^d Wentworth Hayes to have ye Improvement thereof, during his natural life.

Item I give & bequeath one half acre of land Square, Joyning to ye South-west Corner of ye Burying place by ye Meeting House in S^d Rochester for a Burying place for My family forever

Item I give and bequeath My whole Library to My S^d Wife & Children to be equally Divided between y^m to y^m their Heirs & assigns

Item I do hereby constitute make & ordain My S^d Son Josiah My Sole Executor * * *

Amos Main

[Witnesses] Charles Baker, Is^a Libby, Paul Libby.
[Proved April 30, 1760.]

[Inventory, July 28, 1760; amount, £5580. o. o; signed by Edward Tibbetts and Isaac Libby.]

JONATHAN GARLAND   1760   HAMPTON

In the name of God Amen this twenty fifth Day of march Anno Domini 1760 in the thirty third year of his Majestys Reign Georg the second King over Grate Britain &c I Jonathan Garland of Hampton in the Province of new Hampshier in new England Cordwainer * * *

1 I give and bequeath to the Children of my son Jonathan Garland Deceased twenty shillings in money old tenor —

2nd I give and bequeath to my son Joseph Garland twenty shillings in money old tenor —

3^{ly} I give and bequeath to my Daughter Abigail Marston the wife of David marston twenty shillings in money old tenor —

4^{ly} I give and bequeath to my Daughter Sarah Tucke the wife of Benjamin Tucke twenty shillings in money old tenor —

5th I give and bequeath to my Daughter Rachel Johnson the wife of Benjamin Johnson twenty shillings in money old tenor —

6th I give and bequeath to my Daughter Mary Garland one fether bed and beding belonging to one bed and furnituer of it and one Cow and also it is my will that my said Daughter Mary shall have so much Puter and brass and Iron and wooden furnituer for the furnishing a house as either of her Sisters that are married had of me all to be provided for her by my son Samuel Garland: further it is my will also that my said Daughter Mary shall have liberty to live in the westly Room in my Dwelling house so long as she Remains unmarried

7th I Give and bequeath to my son the said Samuel Garland my Dwelling house Saveing onely the liberty for my said Daughter Mary to live in the westly Room of my Dwelling house as afore said. I also give and bequeath to my afore said son Samuel Garland my barn and all my buildings in Hampton with all my land and marsh and meadow Ground that I have laying in said Hampton to gether with all my Right in the town ship of Chichester in the Province afore Said with all my thatch Ground laying at the Cross Beach. I also give to my said son Samuel all my stock of Cattle and husbandry Implements that is I give to my said son Samuel Garland all my estate Real and Parsonal to him and to his heirs and assigns for ever which I have not here in other ways Dispoised of, and it is my will that my said son Samuel garland Shall Pay my afore said Leaguses Just Debts and funeral Charges. I Do Like wise Constitute make and ordain my said son Samuel Garland to be sole executor * * *

Jonathan Garland

[Witnesses] Samuel Dow, Samuel Palmer 3d, Jonathan Dow. [Proved May 28, 1760.]

[Warrant, May 28, 1760, authorizing Samuel Palmer and Deacon Joseph Philbrick, both of Hampton, to appraise the estate.]

[Inventory, July 28, 1760; amount, £6948. 5. 0; signed by Samuel Palmer and Joseph Philbrick.]

SAMUEL HAINES   1760   GREENLAND

[Administration on the estate of Samuel Haines of Greenland, yeoman, granted to his widow, Anna Haines, March 26, 1760.]

[Probate Records, vol. 21, p. 400.]

[Bond of Anna Haines, with Joshua Jenness of Rye, yeoman, and Benjamin Parker of Portsmouth, shopkeeper, as sureties, in the sum of £1000, March 26, 1760, for the administration of the estate; witnesses, William Parker, Theodore Atkinson, Jr.]

[Warrant, March 26, 1760, authorizing Richard Jenness, 3d, of Rye and John Folsom of Greenland, yeoman, to appraise the estate.]

[Inventory, attested May 28, 1760; amount, £5319. 5. 0; signed by Richard Jenness, 3d, and John Folsom.]

PETER URIN   1760   SALEM

[Administration on the estate of Peter Urin of Salem, yeoman, granted to his widow, Ruth Urin, March 27, 1760.]

[Probate Records, vol. 21, p. 412.]

[Bond of Ruth Urin, with Peter Merrill, blacksmith, and Isaac Clough, Jr., yeoman, as sureties, all of Salem, in the sum of £500, March 27, 1760, for the administration of the estate; witnesses, Edward Clark, Amos Merrill.]

[Warrant, March 27, 1760, authorizing John Hall and Edward Clark, both of Salem, to appraise the estate.]

[Inventory, May 15, 1760; amount, £1959. 5. 0; signed by John Hall and Edward Clark.]

WILLIAM HOPKINS   1760   PORTSMOUTH

In the Name of God amen The Twenty Seventh Day of March in the Year of our Lord Christ 1760, I William Hopkins of Portsmouth in the Province of New Hampshire Blockmaker being weak and low in Body * * *

Item I Give and Bequeath to My beloved Wife Elizabeth Hopkins, her heirs and assigns forever My Dwelling House and the Land thereto belonging with all the appurtenances thereof. Also the whole of My Estate both real and personal Wheresoever and Whatsoever after My just Debts and funeral Charges is payed out of the Same as aforesaid

And I the Said William Hopkins Do hereby Constitute Make and Ordain My Said Wife Elizabeth Hopkins Sole Executrix * * *

William Hopkins

[Witnesses] Israel True, Thomas Bickford, Hannah Bickford. [Proved Nov. 25, 1761.]

[Bond of Elizabeth Hopkins, with Thomas Bickford, schoolmaster, and Titus Salter, merchant, as sureties, all of Portsmouth, in the sum of £500, Nov. 25, 1761, for the execution of the will; witnesses, William Parker, Ichabod Libby.]

JONATHAN THING   1760   BRENTWOOD

In the Name of God Amen I Jonathan Thing of Brentwood In ye Province of New Hampshire in New England Yeoman, being weak of Body * * *

Item I Give Devise and Bequeath to my well Beloved Sons Jonathan Thing and John Thing their heirs and assigns forever all my Lands to be Equally Divided between them Immediately after my Decease

Item I Give and bequeath to my Son Jonathan Thing the Dwelling house that he now lives in and ye one half of my Barn, and my will is y^t my Son Jonathan Thing aforesd Should have his part of my Whome place on ye Westerly Side of Sd Place

Item I Give and Bequeath to my Son John Thing my Now Dwelling House and ye one half of my Barn, and my will is y^t my Son John Thing aforesd Should have his part of my whome place on ye Easterley Side of Sd place

Item I Give to my well Beloved Daughter Elizabeth Thing ye Sum of Two Hundred and fifty Pounds old Tenor money when She arives at ye age of Eighteen Years, to be paid by my two Sons aforesd

Item I Give to my well beloved Daughter Mehetable Thing ye Sum of two Hundred and fifty Pounds old Tenor money to be paid by my two Sons before mentioned when She arives at ye age of Eighteen Years

Item I Give to Each of my Daughters aforementioned (Viz) Elizabeth Thing and Mehetable Thing a Cow and Calf Immediately after my Discease and also to Each of my Sd Daughters a pair of Sheep

Item I Give to my Sd Daughters Elizabeth Thing and Mehetable Thing all my Indoor Moveables Excepting my wearing Apparrel, which I Give to my two Sons before mentioned

Item My Will is y^t my two Daughters be brought up by my two Sons aforesd at their Cost and Charge till they arive at ye age of Eigteen Years

Item I Give Devise & Bequeath to my two Sons aforesd Viz Jonath Thing and John Thing all ye Rest of my Stock and all my out Door moveables to be Equally Divided between them after My Decease

Item I Give and Bequeath My Pew in Brentwood meeting house to be Equally Divided between my four Children Namely Jonathan Thing John Thing Elizabeth Thing & Mehetable Thing

Finally I Do hereby Constitute Ordain and appoint My Trusty and Well beloved Sons Jonathan Thing and John Thing to be Executors * * * in Witness whereof I have hereunto

Set my hand and Seal this Twenty Seventh Day of March Anno Domini 1760 and in ye Thirty Third Year of his Majestys Reign
Jonathan Thing

[Witnesses] Nathaniel Trask, Gilman Lougee, Edward Thing. [Proved April 30, 1760.]

[Warrant, April 30, 1760, authorizing Samuel Dudley and Abraham Clark, both of Brentwood, to appraise the estate.]

[Inventory, attested May 27, 1760; amount, £12,245. 0. 0; signed by Samuel Dudley and Abraham Clark.]

[Guardianship of Elizabeth Thing, minor, aged more than 14 years, daughter of Jonathan Thing of Brentwood, granted to Jonathan Cram of Brentwood June 25, 1760.]

[Probate Records, vol. 21, p. 460.]

[Bond of Jonathan Cram, yeoman, with Jeremiah Rowe, yeoman, and Moses Lyford, tailor, as sureties, all of Brentwood, in the sum of £500, June 25, 1760, for the guardianship of Elizabeth Thing; witnesses, Solomon Loud, Jr., William Parker.]

DAVID CORLISS 1760 SALEM

[Administration on the estate of David Corliss of Salem, yeoman, granted to his widow, Hannah Corliss, March 28, 1760.]

[Probate Records, vol. 21, p. 407.]

[Bond of Hannah Corliss, with Peter Merrill, blacksmith, and Isaac Clough, Jr., as sureties, all of Salem, in the sum of £500, March 27, 1760, for the administration of the estate; witnesses, Edward Clark, Amos Merrill.]

[Inventory, April 3, 1760; amount, £1681. 5. 0; signed by John Hall and Edward Clark.]

[Petition of Hannah Corliss, June 30, 1762, for licence to sell real estate, stating that "the demands against the said Estate amounts to the Sum of about 730 £ old Tenor besides Two young Children at the time the dec[d] went into the army one of which was Sickley and lived only about four months after the father, and one Child the adm[x] was big with at the time the dec[d] went away which Child was only one month old at the time of his decease"; licence granted the same date.]

[Account of the administratrix; receipts, £1681. 5. 0; expenditures the same; mentions "maintaining 3 Children of the dec[d] to this time being under age in the whole being 372 weeks, one only 4 years old now"; allowed June 7, 1763.]

DAVID MORRISON 1760 LONDONDERRY

[Bond of John Morrison, yeoman, with Abram Morrison, cooper, and Alexander Craige, weaver, as sureties, all of Londonderry, in the sum of £500, March 29, 1760, for the administration of the estate of David Morrison of Londonderry, yeoman; witnesses, Robert Wallace, Hugh Young.]

[Warrant, March 29, 1760, authorizing Robert Wallace, gentleman, and Hugh Young, yeoman, both of Londonderry, to appraise the estate; mentions John Morrison as a brother of the deceased.]

[Inventory, April 12, 1760; amount, £3868. 5. 0; signed by Robert Wallace and Hugh Young.]

WILLIAM HAINES 1760 GREENLAND

In the Name of God Amen I William Haines of Greenland in the Province of New Hampshire Gen[t] being under Indisposition of Body * * *

Item I give & Bequeath to Mary my beloved wife the use & Improvement of the Room in my Dwelling House where we usually Sit the Chamber over it the Bed Room we lodge in the Dairy Room & the Poarch leading to the Well During her Life I also give her to her own Disposal all my Houshold Goods & moveables within Doors meaning my Furniture & utensils of housekeeping I also give her my weaving Loom with all the Geer & Tackle thereto belonging I also give her two Milch Cows & the keeping of the same Winter & Summer & the Calves till they shall be three months old Yearly During her Life I also give her Eight cord of Good Merchanable Cord wood to be hal'd to her Door Yearly During her Life & Cutt fit for her fire & Eight Bushels of Corn, a Bushel of Good wheat two Bushels of malt three Barrels of Cyder, one hundred pounds weight of good Pork & the same quantity of good Beef five pounds of Sheeps wool & three pounds of Cotten wool all & every of said particulars to be provided & delivered to her Yearly at her House afores^d I also give her my Saddle horse which I usually Ride & my part of the Horse Chair & tackling which I have with my Son William —

Item I give to my Son Matthias twenty acres of Land more or Less where he now lives bounded South Easterly by the Road leading to Hampton on the South West by the Way leading from said Road to John Langs on the North West by Land of said Langs & on the North East by a Fence which parts said Twenty Acres more or less from my other Lands said Fence running up to the Country Road I also give him all my part share & interest in the undivided Lands in the Town of Epsom in said Province & one half part of my Right title & Interest in the Stream & Sawmill at Greenland aforesaid on the Road leading to Stratham at the place called the great Bridge & one half of an acre of thatch ground Lying in the Parish of Rye all which premises I devise to him my said son his Heirs & Assigns forever —

Item I give & Devise to my son William his Heirs & assigns all my salt Marsh & Thatch ground in Greenland afores^d and all other my lands and Buildings & all Real Estate in Greenland with the Reversion & Remainder of the Buildings aforesaid devised & given to the use of my Wife besides what I have given to his Brother Matthias as afores^d I also give my said son William all the Residue & remainder of my personal Estate which is not Disposed of in this my last will & I order him to provide for his mother all the particulars herein before given to her as aforesaid & in Defalt of his so Doing then She shall hereby have full power & authority to enter upon & take the profits of any part of my Real Estate herein given to the said William to the full Value of what he shall fail of providing & Delivering to her Yearly as afores^d

Item I give & Devise to my Son David the Bed & Beding which he has of mine in his possession as also the Chains Sled & other Utensils which he already has in his hands & for some time has had & I also Confirm to him his Heirs & assigns all that Land which I have given him by Deed already Executed all which I intend to be his full part & all that he shall have of my Estate —

Item I give & devise to my Son John that five hundred pounds which I let him have to pay for the Land he purchased of Dudley Ladd & Nathaniel Ladd & the Smiths anvil & other Tools which I let him have with the Shop I built for him & half an acre of thatch ground in the Parish of Rye all which he has already in his hands & possession to his Heirs & assigns forever

Item I give to Patience Lock & Jonathan Lock the Children of my Daughter Sarah Lock the late Wife of Jonathan Lock besides what I have already given her in her life time the Sum of fifteen pounds vizt to each Seven pounds Ten Shillings of the old Tenor or other Bills of Credit or money equal to so much old Tenor as it now passes to be paid within two Years after my Decease to be paid by my Son William —

Item I give & bequeath my Grand Children John & Margaret Johnson the Children of my Daughter Margaret Deceas'd the Sum of fifteen pounds old Tenor as aforesaid that is Seven pounds ten Shillings each to be paid by my Son William within four Years after my Decease —

Item I give & bequeath to my Daughters Mary Johnson & Elizabeth Jones each Fifteen Pounds old Tenor as afores[d] besides what they have already had to be paid by my Son William within four Years after my Decease

Lastly I Constitute & Appoint my Son William to be Sole Executor * * * In Witness whereof I have hereunto Sett my hand & Seal the first Day of April Anno Domini 1760 & in the thirty third year of his Majesties Reign

Wiliam Haines

[Witnesses] Abraham Johnson, John Lang, Ebnezor Johnson Jur.

[Proved Feb. 10, 1761.]

[Bond of William Haines, yeoman, with Matthias Haines, gentleman, as surety, both of Greenland, in the sum of £1000, Feb. 10, 1761, for the execution of the will; witnesses, William Parker, Solomon Loud, Jr.]

SAMUEL SEAVEY   1760   RYE

In the name of God amen the first day of Aprail, one thousand Seven Hundred and Sixty I Samuel Sevey of Rye in the Province of New Hampshire Husbandman Being Very Sick & Week in Body * * *

Imprimis I Give & Bequeath to my well Beloved wife Abagail Sevey one cow and all my house hold Goods to her dispose amongst my Children for Ever also one third of all the income of my Estate and one third of my house with fire wood Conveant for her to be found by my Executor for and duering her Life time

Itam I Give and Bequeath to my well beloved Son Ithamy Sevey the one halfe of my Right of Land in Jenness town to him & to his Heirs and assigns for Ever

Itam I Give and Bequeath to my well beloved Son Samuel Sevey Ju[r] that house & Barn where he now Lives also the Land he improves by Said house also the one halfe of my Land in Jennes town to him & to his heirs & assigns for Ever.

Itam I Give and Bequeath to my well beloved Son Henry Sevey the one halfe of my Land in the town Ship of Epsom to him and to his Heirs and assigns for Ever

Itam I Give and Bequeath to my well beloved Son Jonathan Sevey the one halfe of my Land in the township of Epsom to him and to his Heirs and Assigns for ever also one hundred pounds new tenor bills to be paid him by my Executore

Itam I Give and Bequeath to my well beloved Son Moses Sevey and to his Heirs and assigns for Ever all my Estate Real & Persnal where So Ever & what So Ever not other ways Disposed of in this my Last will

Itam I Give to my Grandson Sam[l] Sandborn ten pounds New tenor to be paid him by my Executor when he is twenty one years old & if he Should dye befor then to be paid to his Brother Nathaniel Sandborn

Itam I Give and Bequeath to my Grand Son Nathaniel Sandborn ten pounds New tenor to be paid him by My Executore when he Comes to the age of twenty one years and if he Shall dye before he Comes to the age of twenty one years then to be paid to his Brother Sam[l] Sandborn

Itam I Give unto my three Daughters twenty Pounds New tenor Bill Each of them namely Abagail Clifford Mary Connor and Mehetable Blue to be paid them by My Executour with in one mounth after my Decease

Lastly I do by these Presents Constitute and appoint my Son Moses Sevey to be my Sole Executor * * *

Samuel
his + Marke
Sevey

[Witnesses] Francis Lock, Henry Dow, Rich[d] Jenness 3[d].
[Proved Sept. 30, 1761.]

[Warrant, Sept. 30, 1761, authorizing Francis Locke and Samuel Jenness, both of Rye, yeomen, to appraise the estate.]

[Inventory, Nov. 5, 1761; amount, £7720. 0. 0; signed by Francis Locke and Samuel Jenness.]

JOHN MATTOON   1760   NEWMARKET

[Administration on the estate of John Mattoon of Newmarket, mariner, granted to Hubartus Mattoon of Newmarket, blacksmith, April 2, 1760.]

[Probate Records, vol. 21, p. 463.]

[Bond of Hubartus Mattoon, with Jacob Fowler of Newmarket, tailor, and John Dudley of Exeter, trader, as sureties, in the sum of £1000, April 2, 1760, for the administration of the estate; witnesses, Amos Seavey, Cutts Shannon.]

SAMUEL PERHAM   1760   NEW IPSWICH

[John Perham, aged and infirm, states that he is grandfather of the children of Samuel Perham, and requests that his son, Lemuel Perham of Dunstable, may administer the estate, and be appointed guardian of the five children under 14 years of age; dated Littleton, (Mass.), April 3, 1760.]

[Administration on the estate of Samuel Perham of New Ipswich, yeoman, granted to Lemuel Perham of Dunstable, Mass., yeoman, April 15, 1760.]

[Probate Records, vol. 21, p. 412.]

[Bond of Lemuel Perham of Dunstable, Mass., with Thomas Lund and Oliver Woods, husbandmen, both of Dunstable, N. H., as sureties, in the sum of £500, April 15, 1760, for the administration of the estate; witnesses, Phineas Lund, Jonathan Lovewell.]

[Warrant, April 15, 1760, authorizing Reuben Kidder, gentleman, and Joseph Bates, husbandman, both of New Ipswich, to appraise the estate.]

[Inventory, May 23, 1760; amount, £474. 6. 0; signed by Reuben Kidder and Joseph Bates.]

Province of Newhampshire Newipswich Janna^r ye 2^d 1761

To The Right Honorable Richard Wibert Esqr Judge of Probates —

Sir this is to Inform you that m^r Sam^{ll} Perham of this place & wife Died Last March and Left Seven Children the youngest was about nine months old and five of ye youngest of S^d Children have no Guardeen: —

Your Humble Petisioners prayeth that you would grant (if Such a thing may be) that Lemuel Perham may no Longer administer on ye Estate of ye Deceas^d for he has Taken no Care to pay anything for keeping S^d Children and hath Taken ye Chief of ye Stock into his own hands which he might have Sold for the Support of ye Children which he Refused and Tels those which have the Children that they must keep them or provide places for them which they cannot by Reason of there being no money for their Support and there is no body to Let them out for any Term of Time the oldest of s^d five is Eleven years old and ye administrator has paid Towards Cloathing S^d Children Eighteen Shillings and Sixpence in Sterling money, the most of s^d Children Remain at the places that in pity they ware taken to when their parents ware Sick — We therefore Desire that your Honour would be pleased to Consider us in our Difficulties as an Infant Plantation and be plased to Give a Letter of administration to Capt Reuben Kidder and of Gaurdeenship for he appears a man of Truth and fidelity and we make no Doubt he will Take faithfull Care of ye poor fatherless and motherless Children that we as an Inhabitants may not be at ye Cost to Bring them up when we Believe there is Estate Enough to pay all ye Debts and Bring up s^d Children if Prudently managed —

But if Such a thing may not be as to put in a new Administrator y[r] Petisioners pray you would by some means Releive us from these Difficulties and you'l greatly Oblige y[r] Humble petisioners and Servants —

Oliver Procter	Benj[a] King
Jonas Woolson	Isaac Appleton
John Dutton	John Chandler
Eben[r] Bullard	John Dutten Ju
Joseph Bates	Joseph Kidder
Ephraim Adams	Benjamin Adams
Joseph Stevens	

[Guardianship of Mary Perham, Lydia Perham, Sarah Perham, Asa Perham, and Elizabeth Perham, aged less than 14 years, children of Samuel Perham, granted to Reuben Kidder of New Ipswich, yeoman, Jan. 20, 1761.]

[Probate Records, vol. 22, p. 7.]

[Bond of Reuben Kidder, with Joseph Blanchard of Merrimack and Samuel Hobart of Dunstable, gentleman, as sureties, in the sum of £1000, Jan. 20, 1761, for the guardianship of Mary, Lydia, Sarah, Asa, and Elizabeth Perham; witnesses, Hercules Mooney, William Parker.]

[Guardianship of Samuel Perham and Amos Perham, minors, aged more than 14 years, children of Samuel Perham, granted to Benjamin Adams of New Ipswich, yeoman, Feb. 24, 1761.]

[Probate Records, vol. 22, p. 30.]

[Bond of Benjamin Adams of New Ipswich, yeoman, with Joseph Cotton, boat-builder, and John Elliot, glazier, both of Portsmouth, as sureties, in the sum of £1000, Feb. 24, 1761, for the guardianship of Samuel and Amos Perham; witnesses, William Parker, Solomon Loud, Jr.]

[Warrant, June 6, 1761, authorizing Jonathan Lovewell and Jonathan Loud, gentleman, both of Dunstable, to receive claims against the estate.]

[List of claims, March 22, 1762; amount, £373. 7. 11; signed by Jonathan Lovewell and Jonathan Lund.]

[Account of the administrator; receipts, £412. 13. 3; expenditures, £139. 4. 2; mentions children, Samuel Perham, Amos Perham, Lydia Perham; allowed May 5, 1762.]

[Settlement of claims; amount of claims, £373. 7. 11; amount distributed, £273. 9. 1; allowed May 22, 1762.]

AARON KIMBALL   1760   HOPKINTON

In The name of God Amen: I Aaren Kimball of new Hoepkintown so Caled In the proviance of new hampshear in new England yamman * * *

secondly I Hearby Appoint my Beloved wife Susanah Kimball Executer of this my last will — And

I Hearby Give to my wife Susanah Kimball all my personal Estate Also I Give unto my beloved wife above said all the Improvement of my Homestead that is alredy under Improvement so long as She Remains my Widow

thirdly I Give unto my sun Abel Kimball a fourty acher lot He now lives on

Fourthly I Give unto my suns timothy Kimball and Abraham Kimball all my home stead Containing by Estemation Eighty achers also I Give to my sd suns Timothy and Abraham Kimball a forty acher lot of land laying by land of Jotham How all sd land to be Eaqualy Devided

fiftly I Give unto my sun Samuel Kimball a second Devishon lot of land Containing by Estemation Eighty achers which lot I purchesed of Jotham How

Sixthly I Give unto my three yongest suns Aaron Kimball nathaniel Kimball and Phinias Kimball all my lands and medow in the township of the above said hopkintown that I have not alredy Disposed of and In Case one or more of my three yongest suns Decese Before thay arive to the age of twenty one years then he or thay that survive is to have the whole

Seventhly I Give unto my Daughter Elisabeth How five pounds old tennor to be payed By my suns timothy and Abraham Kimball in two years after my Decease:

8ly I Give unto my Daughter mary How Fifty pounds old tennor to to Be payed by my suns timothy and Abraham in one year after my Deceas

9ly I Give unto my Daughter Susannah Kimball one hundred and fifty pounds old tennor to be payed By my suns timothy and Abraham at the age of Eighteen

10ly I Give unto my Daughter Ruth Kimball one hundred and fifty pounds old tennor to be payed By my Suns timothy and Abraham above said at the age of Eighteen

The Above Leageses to be payed Eaqualy by the above said Timothy Kimball and Abraham Kimball in money at the Same Value as it is at this Day

In testemony of all which I have Hear to Set my Hand and seal this fifth Day of Aprill anno Domini one thousand seven Hundred and sixty and in the thirty third year of His majesties Reign

Aron kimball

[Witnesses] Nathan Kimball, Samuel kimball, Benj[a] Gage.
[Proved Aug. 27, 1760.]

[Inventory, Nov. 20, 1760; amount, £14,514. 14. 6; signed by Ezra Carter and Matthew Stanley.]

JOSEPH MERRILL   1760   STRATHAM

In the name of God amen the Sixteenth Day of april 1760 — Joseph merril of Stratham in the province of newhempshir in new England Shoomaker Being well in Body * * *

Imprimis I Give and Bequeath to Charity Merril my beloved wife the norwest End of my Dweling house and one third of my

Seler & twenty Rods of Land near my Dweling house and the Liberty of water at my well So Long as She Lives my widow and my executor hear after named shall provide for my said wife three Cord & a half of fier wood a year yealy So Long as she Lives my widow: and I Give to my Said wife the income of one Cow & two Sheep So Long as she Lives my widow and my Said wife to tak her Chois of my Cows and Sheep and my Executor hear after named shall keep said Cow and sheep sumer and winter so Long as she Lives my widow and I give to my Said wife fifteen bushels of Ingin Corn & fifteen pounds of Flax a year yearly So Long as She Lives my widow from the Swilgle and I give to my said wife two Cyder Barrals and to be fild with good cyder and apals for my wifes own use and fifty pound of Beef a year yearly as She Lives my widow and I give to my Said wife one Swine and to be parstred by my Executor hear after named so long as she Live my widow and all to be paid and Dun by my Executer hear after named for my widow that is above writen yearly So long as She Remains my widow and if my Said wife Shold marry again then She is to quit all these things above writen and to have only hir thirds of my Estate

Itim I Give to my Beloved Son Joseph merril five pounds in money or pasable Bills of Credit old tener to be paid out of my estate by my Executor hear after named with in two year after my Decease I have given to my Son Joseph merril formerly what I thought was proper for him

Itim I Give to my beloved Son Dainel merril five pounds in money or passable bill of Credit old tener to be paid out of my Estate by my Executor hear after named with in two year after my Decease I have Given to my Son Dainel merril formerly what I though was proper for him

Itim I Give to my beloved Son James merril five pounds in money or passable bills of Credit old tener or one half of my wearing Close which the Said Jaims pleases to be paid by my Executer hearafter named with in two three mounths after my Decease

Itim I Give to my beloved Daughter Elizabath Lavitt five pounds in money or passable Bills of Credit old tener and my handiorns to be paid by my Executor hear after named within two year after my Deceas

Itim I Give to my Granson Josiah Lavitt Sixteen Dolers or the Valey of it in marchentable pay to be paid by my Executor hearafter named to be paid to the Said Josiah when he Coms to be one and twenty years of age if then Living outherwas for to Return to my Son Benjamin one half and the outher to my Daughter Elizabath Lavitt

Itim I Give to my Beloved Daughter Ester merril fifty pounds of money or passable Bills of Credit old tener and a Cow and Calf and a Brass kittel and Still and kulinder and two Sheep to be paid by my Executer and Deliverd that is my Executor hear after named is to pay the Said Ester the fifty pounds & Deliver the outher things above menshened to the above Said Ester when she is of Eighteen years of age and the Bed that the said Ester Lies on

Itim my Will is that my Wife shall have the houshold goods that she Brough with her and one half of all the houshold goods that we have got together since we ware marrid, and my Son Benjamin merril shall find my said wife a hors for her to Ride on So long as she Lives my widow and if my said wife shold marrey again then She is to quit all these things above written

Itim I Give to my beloved Son Benjamin Merril the East end and back part of my Dweling house and Barn and I Give all my Land in Stratham to my son Benjamin merril and his Heirs & assings for Ever, and I give all my Cattel and Sheep and hors & Swine to my son benjamin merril that are not gifen away befor and my Said Son Benjamin is to have my shop & tools with all my Uetensels for husbandtri of what nater or kind so ever & the bed & beding that he now Lies upon and my gun & Loome & sadil & Bridel & Cyder Barrils & malt Barrils & a Iorn Kittel to be my said Benjmin merril and I ordar my son Benjamin merrill to pay all my honest Debts and all the Legeses above mensined in my will & give me & my wife a Deaseant burel my will is that my Son Benjamin merril is to have one half of my Close I Likewise Constitut and make & ordain my Said Son Benjamin merril my Sole Executor * * *

Joseph merrill

[Witnesses] Jacob Low, Thomas Moore Jun., William Moore Junr.

[Proved March 27, 1771.]

[Bond of Benjamin Merrill, with William Moore, 3d, and Jacob Lowe as sureties, all of Stratham, in the sum of £500, March 27, 1771, for the execution of the will; witnesses, Samuel Hale, Jr., Joseph Boyd.]

PHINEAS STEVENS   1760   CHARLESTOWN

[Administration on the estate of Phineas Stevens of Charlestown, gentleman, granted to his widow, Elizabeth Stevens, April 16, 1760.]

[Probate Records, vol. 21, p. 488.]

[Bond of Elizabeth Stevens, with John Hastings, Jr., and William Heywood, yeomen, as sureties, all of Charlestown, in the sum of £500, April 16, 1760, for the administration of the estate; witnesses, Benjamin Bellows, Samuel Hunt.]

[Warrant, April 16, 1760, authorizing Isaac Parker and John Hastings, Jr., both of Charlestown, to appraise the estate.]

[Inventory; attested Dec. 27, 1760; amount, £347. 3. 0; signed by Isaac Parker and John Hastings.]

[Warrant, May 8, 1761, authorizing Isaac Parker, Samuel Hunt, gentlemen, John Hastings, Jr., William Heywood, and Stephen Farnsworth, yeomen, all of Charlestown, to divide the real estate.]

Province of } Agreable to the Warrant Exhibited to us
N. Hampshire } y" Subscribers by y" Judge of the Probate of wills, for the Dividing of y" Estate of Capt Phinehas Stevens Late of Charlestown Deceas'd finding the Real Estate to be £93. 10 — Sterling Money of Great Britton after the Debts being paid, of which Sum we have set of to y" widow Elizabeth Stevans Relect to y" Intestate £31 in Land & three & four pence in Money being her Dower or thirds of y" above £93. 10. Viz 2 three acre Lotts N° 36 & 37 in the first Division of Interval at £21 — also 1 six acre Lott N° 41 in y" fourth Division of Interval at £10 — Making £31 —

The Remainder of y" Real Estate being Sixty two pounds Ten shillings Lying Ill Convenient for a Division we Judge it best to be Settled upon Saml Stevens the Eldest son to the Intestate upon his paying to Each of y" Heirs y" sum of six pounds four shilling & Eight pence Sterling Money Viz. To Willard, & Simon, Enos, Mary, Phinehas Catharine Prudence & Solomon Stevens being all Heirs to the Deceas'd Allowing Saml Stevens to be Equal to two of y" other Heirs and three shilling & four pence Sterling to y" widow makes in y" whole £62 — 10 —

The Estate that is to be Settled on s^d Saml Stevens is as follows Viz —

3 5 acre Lotts N° 61 : 62 & 63 in y" Second Division of Interval at £54 —

1 6 Acre Lott N° 32 in y" fourth Division D^o £8. 10 — £62. 10 —

Charlestown y" 25th august 1761 Isaac Parker }
Wm Heywood } Com^{tte}

JONATHAN HUBBARD 1760   CHARLESTOWN

[Administration on the estate of Jonathan Hubbard of Charlestown, gentleman, granted to Benjamin Bellows of Walpole April 16, 1760.]

[Probate Records, vol. 21, p. 412.]

[Bond of Benjamin Bellows of Walpole, with Theodore Atkinson and Daniel Peirce, both of Portsmouth, as sureties, in the sum of £500, April 16, 1760, for the administration of the estate; witnesses, Theodore Atkinson, Jr., Joseph Weeks.]

[Warrant, April 16, 1760, authorizing Isaac Parker, gentleman, and John Hastings, Jr., both of Charlestown, to appraise the estate.]

[Inventory, attested Aug. 26, 1760; amount, £98. o. 3; signed by Isaac Parker and John Hastings, Jr.]

[List of claims against the estate; amount, £99. 11. 8; not signed.]

[Bond of Amos Whitney, gentleman, with Zachariah Emery, yeoman, as surety, both of Townsend, Mass., in the sum of £500, Oct. 16, 1761, for the guardianship of Jonathan Hubbard, minor, in his fifteenth year, son of Jonathan Hubbard; witnesses, Eleazer Green, Jr., and Abel Lawrence.]

[Middlesex Co., Mass., Probate Files.]

[Guardianship of Samuel Hubbard, minor, aged more than 14 years, son of Jonathan Hubbard, granted to Benjamin Bellows March 11, 1765.]

[Probate Records, vol. 23, p. 442.]

[Bond of Benjamin Bellows of Walpole, with Samuel Stevens and Simeon Olcott, gentleman, both of Charlestown, as sureties, in the sum of £1000, March 11, 1765, for the guardianship of Samuel Hubbard; witnesses, John Holt, Benjamin Bellows, Jr.]

JOSEPH WOOD   1760   CHARLESTOWN

[Administration on the estate of Joseph Wood of Charlestown, yeoman, granted to Benjamin Bellows of Walpole April 16, 1760.]

[Probate Records, vol. 21, p. 412.]

[Bond of Benjamin Bellows, with Theodore Atkinson and Daniel Peirce, both of Portsmouth, as sureties, in the sum of £500, April 16, 1760, for the administration of the estate; witnesses, Theodore Atkinson, Jr., Joseph Weeks.]

[Warrant, April 16, 1760, authorizing Isaac Parker, gentleman, and John Hastings, Jr., yeoman, both of Charlestown, to appraise the estate.]

[Inventory, attested Aug. 26, 1760; amount, £61. 10. 3; signed by Isaac Parker and John Hastings, Jr.]

[List of claims against the estate; amount, £53. 5. 8.]

DORCAS WARD   1760   PORTSMOUTH

[Administration on the estate of Dorcas Ward of Portsmouth, widow, granted to Henry Sherburne of Portsmouth, gentleman, April 17, 1760.]

[Probate Records, vol. 21, p. 413.]

[Bond of Henry Sherburne, with John Pendexter, butcher, and John Gunnison, tailor, as sureties, all of Portsmouth, in the sum of £500, April 17, 1760, for the administration of the estate; witnesses, William Parker, Solomon Loud, Jr.]

[Inventory, April, 1760; amount, £2182. 1. 3; signed by Samuel Sherburne and Thomas Peirce.]

[Account of the administrator; receipts, £2172. 3. 3; expenditures, £994. 17. 0; mentions "Expense for Nahum a Son Shoes &c his board &c. from March 29, 1760, to march 31, 1762 being 104 weeks he having been kept School during that time . . . . nursing negro Woman in her Sickness"; allowed March 31, 1762.]

[Additional account; receipts, £1177. 6. 3; expenditures, £497. 6. 3; mentions "Eight Munths Board of Nahum from first of April till Last of Nov^r"; allowed June 27, 1764.]

[Additional account; receipts, £771. 18. 0; expenditures, £123. 18. 3; mentions Nahum Ward, son of the deceased; allowed Aug. 31, 1769.]

[Guardianship of Nahum Ward, minor, aged more than 14 years, son of Nahum Ward, granted to Noah Parker of Portsmouth, gunsmith, Oct. 30, 1765.]

[Probate Records, vol. 24, p. 23.]

[Bond of Noah Parker, with George Gains and Edmund Davis, joiners, as sureties, all of Portsmouth, in the sum of £500, Oct. 30, 1765, for the guardianship of Nahum Ward; witnesses, Richard Wibird Penhallow, William Parker.]

JACOB GALE   1760   KINGSTON

In the Name of God Amen: the 22^d day of April 1760 I Jacob Gale of Kingstown in the Province of New Hamps: in New England, Inn holder; being now Sick in Body * * *

Imp^s I Give and Bequeath unto Susanna my now dearly beloved wife the one third part of all my personal estate to her, her Hiers & Assigns for ever, & to be at her dispose; Likewise I Give to my s^d wife Dureing he Natural Life the One Third part of my Real Estate, and my dwelling House and Barn I Give to her only so Long as she remains my widow —

And I do hereby Constitute make & ordain my s^d wife & my son Daniel to be sole Executors of this my Last Will & Testament —

And my Will is that my Executors pay all my Honest debts; and gather & Collect all my debts that are due to me —

Further I Give to my s^d wife Susanna, & my s^d Son Daniel my Said Executors the remaining two thirds of my Estate; by them to be enjoyed & Improved; for the Support of my younger Children until they & Each of them arrives to the age of fourteen years; and hereby will & order them to take Care of &

provide for each of them until they arrive to that age; and then viz: when my youngest Child Liveing Shall be fourteen years old, my will is that the s^d two thirds of my Estate both Real & personal be divided to & among my Children in the following manner viz: my sons Jacob, Daniel, Eliphalet, Amos, Eli, Benjamin, John Collins & Stephen be all Equal in all their parts & shares (Saveing & Excepting the s^d Amos) whose share or part my will is that it shall be ten dollars Less than one of the other sons; and my Daughters viz: Susanna now the wife of Nathanael Bachelder, & Mary, shall be Equal in their shares or parts but their shares or parts to be but Half so much as the sons; And I haveing furnished my s^d daughter Susanna for House keeping in order for marrying &c to the amount of 200 Dollars which is to be allowed towards her part and so I Give & Bequeath the s^d two thirds of my Estate to my s^d Children as abovementioned to be divided among them viz: the s^d Sons to be Equal in their shares or parts: (Saveing & Excepting Amos) as bovementioned whose part is to be Ten Dollars Less than another share and a daughters share or part to be but Half so much as a sons and so my s^d Daughters in that proportion to be Equal, allowing & Includeing the above mentioned sum which she has already receiv'd, it being deliver'd to her in January 1757: And then the other remaining Third with the Dwelling House & Barn I will at the Decease of s^d wife to be divided to & among my s^d Children in the forementioned proportion; only without Exception viz my s^d sons to be Equal therein, and my s^d Daughters also to be Equal; tho but Half So much as a son: and so my s^d Children my s^d Estate in the forementioned Manner; To Have And To Hold to them their Hiers & assigns forever; And further I Will & order that the forementioned Division of my s^d Estate at Each of the Seasons there of be made & Set off to my s^d Children by five of the Selectmen for the Town of Kingstown, (or within the Town of s^d Kingstown) that shall then be in the office of Select men, or the Major part of them * * *

Jacob Gale

[Witnesses] Jeremy Webster, Daniel Rowell, William Witcher. [Proved June 16, 1760.]

[Warrant, June 16, 1760, authorizing Jeremy Webster and William Parker, both of Kingston, gentlemen, to appraise the estate.]

[Amos Gale, son of Jacob Gale, makes choice of his mother, Susanna Gale, as his guardian Jan. 21, 1761; witnesses, Jeremy Webster, Daniel Gale.]

[Guardianship of Amos Gale, minor, aged more than 14 years, son of Jacob Gale, granted to Susanna Gale of Kingston Jan. 28, 1761.]

[Probate Records, vol. 22, p. 18.]

[Bond of Susanna Gale, widow, with Jeremy Webster and Daniel Gale, yeoman, as sureties, all of Kingston, in the sum of £500, Jan. 28, 1761, for the guardianship of Amos Gale; witness, Solomon Loud, Jr.]

[Guardianship of Eli Gale, minor, aged more than 14 years, son of Jacob Gale, granted to Nathaniel Batchelder March 14, 1763.]

[Probate Records, vol. 22, p. 542.]

[Bond of Nathaniel Batchelder, yeoman, with Jeremy Webster and William Parker as sureties, all of Kingston, in the sum of £500, March 14, 1763, for the guardianship of Eli Gale; witnesses, John Elliot, Jonathan Currier.]

THOMAS EASTMAN   1760   DANVILLE

In the Name of God Amen I Thomas Eastman of Hawke in Province of New Hampshire being bound abroad in the Expedition against Canada   *   *   *

Item. I give & bequeathe to my Brother obadiah Eastman his heirs & Assigns Seven hundred pounds Old Ten^r as money now is vizt Dollars at Six pounds a piece to be paid him in one Year after my Decease by my Executer hereafter named —

Item I give & bequeath to my Brother Ebenezer Eastman Seven hundred pounds old Ten^r as money now is, when he shall arrive to the age of twenty one years to be paid him by my Executor hereafter mentioned.

Item I give & bequeath to my Sister Sarah Eastman One hundred pounds Old Ten^r as money now is to be paid her by my Executor when she arrives to the age of Eighteen Years —

Item I give & bequeath to my Sister Mary Eastman One hundred pounds old Ten^r to be paid her by my Executor when she arrives to the age of Eighteen Years, as the money now is —

Item I give & bequeath to my Brother Edward Eastman his heirs & Assigns for ever all the residue of my Estate both real & personal wherever the same is or may be found with all Debts & monies that at the time of my Decease may be due & justly coming to me

My will further is that if my said brother Ebenezer Should die before he is twenty one years of age that the money herein given him shall be equally divided between my said Sisters Mary & Sarah & paid to them accordingly — or if either of my said Sisters should die before they are respectively eighteen years of age that what is given them be paid the Survivor —

& I hereby Constitute & appoint my said Brother Edward Eastman Sole Executor * * * In Witness whereof I have hereunto set my hand & Seal the 24th Day of April Anno Domini one thousand Seven hundred & Sixty —

Thomas Eastman

[Witnesses] Elizabeth Parker, Eliphalet Coffin, W Parker.
[Proved Dec. 23, 1760.]

[Bond of Edward Eastman, yeoman, with Thomas Wadleigh, yeoman, and Thomas Welch, innholder, as sureties, all of Hawke, in the sum of £1000, Dec. 24, 1760, for the execution of the will; witnesses, Elizabeth Parker, William Parker.]

[Guardianship of Ebenezer Eastman, minor, aged more than 14 years, son of Thomas Eastman, granted to Jonathan Fifield, Jr., of Hampton Falls, yeoman, March 17, 1761.]

[Probate Records, vol. 22, p. 50.]

[Bond of Jonathan Fifield, Jr., with Thomas Wiggin, gentleman, and Joseph Fifield, yeoman, both of Stratham, as sureties, in the sum of £500, March 17, 1761, for the guardianship of Ebenezer Eastman; witnesses, Richard Nelson, Cutts Shannon.]

JOSHUA NEAL   1760   STRATHAM

In the Name of God Amen, the twenty fourth Day of April, in the year of our Lord God one Thousand Seven Hundred and Sixty I Joshua Neal of Stratham in the Province of New Hampshire Gentleman, being weak in Body * * *

Imprimis. I give and Bequeath unto Abigael, my well Beloved wife the whole Use and improvement of all my Home place where I now Dwell both House and Land; and also the use & improvement of one third part of my Land & Buildings at my Farm where I formerly Dwelt; and also the use & improvement of all my Household Goods, During her Natural Life; also I give to my Said wife one Cow, and all my Sheep, and all the Swine at my Door, and all the Provisions I now have in my House, and all the Money I Shall have by me at my Decease; and Two Hundred Pounds in Money of the old Tenor to be paid her out of my Estate within twelve Months after my Decease; and also Six Cords of wood per year yearly During her Natural Life to be Delivered to her Equally by my Executors hereafter Named.

Item. I give unto my two Grand Daughters vizt Elizabeth Griffith and olive Griffith their Heirs and Assigns, Two Hundred Spanish Mill'd Dollers; or so much of other Money as Shall be Equal to two Hundred Dollers, to be Equally Divided between them, and paid to them when they Shall come to the age of twenty one Years, or Marriage Day, And in Case that Either of them Shall Die before She Arrives to that Age or Marriage Day that the whole Sum be paid to the Surviving one if it Arrives to the Abovesaid time. And in Case that Neither of them Shall Arrive to that Age or Marriage Day, My Will is that Said Sum be paid to my two Daughters Anna Veazey and Abigael Cate or to their Heirs, Equally to Each.

Item I give Unto my Grandson Stephen Cate his Heirs and Assigns All my Home place where I now Dwell both House and Land and he to come into Possession thereof at the Age of twenty one years, if my Said wife has Done with the improvement thereof by that time, also I give Said Stephen my Gun, to be Deliver'd to him at the Age of twenty one years.

Item. I give to my Grandson Joshua Veazey his Heirs and Assigns one Hundred Spanish Mill'd Dollers, or so much other Money as Shall be Equal thereunto, to be paid out of my Estate when he Shall Arrive to the Age of twenty one Years.

Item. I give unto my two Daughters their Heirs and Assigns vizt Anna Veazey and Abigael Cate, (after all my Debts and Legacies, and Funeral Charges are paid) all the Remainder of my Estate both Real and Personal, whatsoever & wheresoever which I have not given away as aforesaid, to be Equally Divided between them.

And further my Will is, and I do hereby Constitute Appoint and Ordain my two Sons in Law vizt Thomas Veazey and Samuel Cate my Sole Executors * * *

Joshua Neal

[Witnesses] Samuel Veasey, Samuel Leavitt, Saml Lane.
[Proved May 28, 1760.]

[Bond of Thomas Veasey and Samuel Cate, both of Stratham, yeomen, with Hubartus Neal of Newmarket, gentleman, and Samuel Leavitt of Straham, yeoman, as sureties, in the sum of £5000, May 28, 1760, for the execution of the will; witnesses, David Sewall, Samuel Lane.]

ROBERT MASON   1760   DURHAM

In the Name of God Amen —

the Twenty fifth day of april in the year of our Lord one Thousand Seven hundred and Sixty I Robert Mason of Durham in newhampshire in newengland husbandman being Sick and in a Low Condition * * *

Item I give and bequath my Daughter mary mason five Shillings to be paid to her when she arives to the age of Eighten years by my Said Executrex —

Item I give and bequath to my Daughter Temprance mason five Shillings to be paid her by my Executrex when she a rives to the age of Eight years

Item I give and bequath to my Son Lemuel mason five shillings to be paid by my Executrex when she Coms to be Twenty one years of age —

Item I give and bequath unto my Loveing wife Susana mason all the Remaining part of my Estate in the Town of Durham both Real and personal to her and her hairs and assigns for Ever To have and To hold —

and I do hereby make ordain and appoint my Said Loveing wife Susana mason my Sole Executrex * * *

                                          Robert Mason

[Witnesses] John Adams, Thomas young, Josiah Hilton.
[Proved May 28, 1760.]

[Inventory, June 18, 1760; amount, £1523. 4. 0; signed by Thomas Young and Walter Bryent.]

JAMES WHITING   1760   HOLLIS

[Claims of James Whiting, April 26, 1760, against the estate of his father, James Whiting of Hollis, deceased; amount, £257. 18. 0; mentions "my brother . . . . Doct^r Hall for his Bill for visits and medicines for the Deceased & wife when sick";

claimant desires "Administration may not be Granted to any other person as I am an heir and the bigest Creditor and being obliged to go in the war desire the Adm^n may rest untill I return next fall if Providence admit of it."]

JOSEPH PERKINS 1760 HAMPTON FALLS

In the Name of God Amen this Twenty Ninth day of April anno domini one Thousand Seven Hundred & Sixty: I Joseph Perkins of Hampton falls in the Province of New Hampshire in New England yeoman being Sick and weak in body * * *

Secondly. I Give and Bequeth unto my well beloved wife Elesebeth Perkins my Riding Beast I also give my wife the one third Part of all my Land and marsh which in Right that doth to me belong for her to use and Improve as Long as she shall Remain my widow I also Give my said wife all my houshold goods within doors for her use and Improvment and for her to dispose of to my Children as She Shall See fit

3dly I Give and Bequeth unto my Son Benjamin Perkins & his heirs for Ever that twelve acres of up Land Laying on the falls River Eastward of my Dwelling house which twelve acres of Land I Bought of Abraham Dow: I also Give my Said Son Benjamin four Acres of Salt marsh Laying in hampton falls at a Place Called Perkens Neeck to be the East End of my marsh there I also order my Son David Perkins to Deliver to my Said Son Benjn one good Cow when he Shall Come to the age of twenty one years I also order my Said Son Benjn Shall be Put out to Som Sutable Trade at Convenant age: I order my Executor here after Named shall Improve what I have given My Son Benjn in this my will untill he the Said Benjn Shall Com to the Age of Twenty one years: —

4^{thly} I Give unto my Daughter Lydia Swain wife to william Swain of Hampton falls Junour Twenty Pounds old tenor to be Leavid out of my Estate and and be Paid within one year after my Decease: to be Paid by my Executor here after Named:

5thly I Give and Bequeth unto my Daughter Sarah Perkins Two Hundred Pounds old tenor in money or houshold goods to be Leavid out of my Estate and to be Paid by my Executor within two years after my Decease to be money or goods which Shall Then best Sute him to Pay: — but and if She Shall marry within two year after my Decease then he my Executor Shall Pay her the money or goods on her marrage;

6thly I Give and Bequeth unto my Daughter Hannah Perkins Two Hundred Pounds old Tenor in money or houshold goods to be Leavid out of my Estate and to be Paid her by My Executor hereafter Named when She Shall Come to the age of Eighteen year: to be money or goods which Shall best Sute my Executor at that time: I also order my said Daughter Hannah Shall be Brought up on my Estate until She Shall Come to the age of Eighteen year: by my Executor here after Named

7thly and Lastly I make and ordain my Son David Perkins Soal Executor to this my will: I Give and bequeth unto him my Son David he Paying and Preforming what I have ordered him to Pay and Preform in this my will to him and to his heirs and assigns for Ever all my whole Estate which I have Not Disposed of alreaddy in this my will as Land marsh Buildings Cattle Sheep and Swine with my Impliments of Husbandry or husbandry tools or any Estate or Part of Estate whatsoever with Those Parts I have given of my Estate to my wife the Improvment of for a Term of time when the time of her Improvment is out * * *

Joseph Pearkins

[Witnesses] John Pierce, Ebenezer Tucker Jun, Abner Philbrick.

[Proved June 24, 1761.]

[Warrant, June 24, 1761, authorizing Jonathan Fifield, Jr., and Henry Roby, both of Hampton Falls, yeoman, to appraise the estate.]

[Inventory, Aug. 3, 1761; amount, £10,178. 0. 0; signed by Henry Roby and Jonathan Fifield.]

JONATHAN SANBORN 1760   KINGSTON

In the Name of God Amen this 7th Day of may 1760 I Jonathan Sanborn of Kingston in the Province of New Hampshire in New England Yeoman   *   *   *

Imp^s I Give & Bequeath unto Hannah my now well Beloved wife the one half of my home Place that is to say as I have Before Disposed of one half of what was formerly my home Place by Deed I Give to my said wife one half of the Remainder with one third Part of the House & Barn standing on said Place for her use & improvement so Long as she Remains my widow: further I Give & Bequeath to my said wife two Cows two sheep & one swine to her her Hiers and assigns forever also all the Household stuff that she Brought with her to me that shall be found in being at my Discease also the Priviledge of Cutting a Load of hay yearly on my Land in the mill Pond meadow so Called so Long as she Remains my widow

Item I Give & Bequeath to my well Beloved son Timothy Sanborn his Hiers & assigns forever all the Residue of my Land when he now Lives; Forty acres I have already Given him the said Timothy by Deed and the Residue of my Land there I hereby Give to him his hiers & assigns as above mentioned: and also the one twelfth Part of the saw mill in s^d Town Called the Little River saw mill it being the Lower mill on the said Little River in said Town also the one half of my Pew in the meeting house in said town

Item I Give & Bequeath to my well Beloved son Samuel Sanborn his Hiers and assigns forever all the Residue of my Land in the Seventh Lott in the Division of the two Hundred acre Grants so Called in the Parish of Sandown in Said Kingston viz all the Residue of my Land in said Lott over and above what I have Before this instrument Given to him the said Samuel Sanborn with the one half of my Right & Intrest in the saw mill on said Lott where the said Samuel now Lives (Commonly Called Deerfield mill) and the said half of my Right & Intrest in the Prividge of the Stream & other Priviledges & appurtenances there to Belonging: He Paying the Legacies hereafter mentioned

Item I Give & Bequeath to my well Beloved Daughter Love now the wife of Reuben Clough one Hundred Pounds Equal to what is Called the old tenor to be Paid as followeth viz one moiety at the End of one year and the other moiety at the End of two years after my Discease and to be Paid as above said by my son Samuel Sanborn the one half of Each Payment to be made in marchantable Lumber and the other half in Passable Bills of Cred^t of the afors^d old tenor or other money or Passable Bills Equivalent she having already had her Portion out of my Estate

Item I Give & Bequeath to my well Beloved son wooster Sanborn his Hiers & assigns forever all the Residue of my Land in Brentwood in the Province afors^d which I Purchased of Maj^r Daniel Gilman of Exeter (that is to say) all the Residue of my Land there over and above what I have Before Given him my said son wooster by Deed, with all the Priviledges & appurtenances thereto Belonging; with the other half of my Right & Intrest in the forementioned saw mill Commonly Called Deerfield mill with the other half of the Priviledge of the Stream & the other half of my Right & Intrest in all the Priviledges & appurtenances there to Belonging —

Item I Give & Bequeath to my well Beloved Daughter Joanna now the wife of Robert Crafford, her hiers & assigns one Hundred Pounds Equal to that which is now Called the old tenor to be Paid the one half in one year after my Discease the other half in two years after my Discease The one half of Each Payment to be made in Good marchantable Lumber and the other half in Passable Bills of the old tenor or in other Money or Passable Bills Equivalent Fifty Pounds of which sum to be Paid as above mentioned by my son Samuel Sanborn and the other fifty Pounds to be Paid as above said by my son Jonathan Sanborn she the said Joanna having also had her Portion out of my Estate —

Item I Give & Bequeath unto my well Beloved son Jonathan

Sanborn his hiers & assigns forever all the other half of my Homestead Living being Situate in Kingston it being Part of the Little River Mill Grant so Called with the one half of the Buildings thereon the other half of my said Homestead Living I have Before this Instrument Given my said son Jonathan by Deed But it is to be understood here that I have in this my Last will Given one half of the Remainder of my said Homestead Living to my said wife for her use & Improvement so Long as she Remains my widow; and so my said son Jonathan is not to Come into Possession of her part till her marriage after my Death or her Decease and then my said son Jonathan his hiers & assigns to Come into the Peaceable Possession & Enjoyment thereof with the Remaining Part of my Right or Intrest in the Little River saw mill so Called with the stream & Dam & all Priviledges and appurtenances thereto Belonging which I have not Disposed of by this my Last will: And also my meadow in trickling falls mill Pond so Called being about ten acres more or Less as it is Laid out & Bounded also a small Piece of Land which I Purchased of Richard Long Lying Near the Cramberry meadow (so Called) in said Town also about fifteen acres of Land be the same more or Less which was Laid out to the Right of my Honor[d] Father Jonathan Sanborn Esq[r] in the upper west Devision Next to Chester and in the seccond Range of Lotts in said Devision also one half of a Right or share in the Common & Undevided Lands in said Kingston also the other half of my Pew in the meeting House in said Town I also Give to my said son Jonathan and his hiers and assigns all the Rest of my Estate Both immovable as Lands &c where Ever situated & moveable as Cattle sheep &c & implements for work &c and all other of my Estate of what Name or Nature soever which I have not Disposed of by this my Last will & testament He paying the Legaices here in Before mentioned —

And I Do further will & ordain that my two sons Samuel & Jonathan Pay the Beforementioned Legacies as Beforementioned —

And I Do hereby Constitute make & ordain my said son Jonathan to be sole Executor * * *

Jonathan Sanborn
his

[Witnesses] Amasa + Dow, Josiah Bartlett, Parmenas Watson.
Mark

[Proved June 25, 1760.]

[Inventory, July 3, 1760; amount, £9667. 8. 0; signed by Jeremy Webster and William Parker.]

JAMES FRENCH   1760   SALEM

[Administration on the estate of James French of Salem, yeoman, granted to Jacob Bailey of Hampstead, gentleman, May 9, 1760.]

[Probate Records, vol. 21, p. 431.]

BENJAMIN WALTON   1760   AMHERST

[Administration on the estate of Benjamin Walton of Amherst, yeoman, granted to John Harvell of Litchfield, yeoman, May 13, 1760.]

[Probate Records, vol. 21, p. 432.]

[Bond of John Harvell, with Jonathan Lovewell of Dunstable and William Richardson of Pelham, gentleman, as sureties, in the sum of £500, May 13, 1760, for the administration of the estate; witnesses, William Parker, Solomon Loud, Jr.]

[Warrant, May 13, 1760, authorizing William Read, gentleman, and James Underwood, yeoman, both of Litchfield, to appraise the estate.]

[Inventory, June 26, 1760; amount, £1025. 10. 0; signed by William Read and James Underwood.]

JOHN SAYLOR 1760 NASHUA

[Administration on the estate of John Saylor of Dunstable, yeoman, granted to William Greenleaf of Boston, Mass., merchant, May 17, 1760.]

[Probate Records, vol. 21, p. 432.]

[Bond of William Greenleaf, with William King and Thomas Bradford, both of Portsmouth, merchants, as sureties, in the sum of £500, May 17, 1760, for the administration of the estate; witnesses, Simon Hobbs, Benjamin Ingalls.]

[Inventory, May 5, 1760; amount, £348. 3. 1; signed by John Swallow, Timothy Read, and Philip Ullerick.]

[Administration de bonis non granted to David Fick Jan. 5, 1764.]

[Probate Records, vol. 23, p. 159.]

[Bond of David Fick of Salem, Mass., sugar refiner, with William Torrey and Henry Appleton, both of Portsmouth, merchants, as sureties, in the sum of £10,000, Jan. 5, 1764, for the administration of the estate; witness, William Vaughan.]

[Inventory of the real estate in New Hampshire, Nov. 12, 1764; amount, £266. 10. 0; signed by Enoch Hunt, Stephen Powers, and David Nevin.]

[License to the administrator, David Fick of Dunstable, yeoman, April 13, 1767, to sell real estate.]

[Warrant, April 13, 1767, authorizing Jonathan Lovewell and Robert Fletcher, yeoman, both of Dunstable, to receive claims against the estate.]

[Power of attorney from David Fick of the Northern Liberties, Philadelphia, Pa., sugar refiner, to James Lovell of Boston, Mass., merchant, July 2, 1768, to settle his account as administrator.]

[Account of the administrator; receipts, £32. 6. 0; expenditures, £30. 6. 0; allowed May 29, 1772.]

[List of claims against the estate; amount, £151. 4. 3½; signed by Jonathan Lovewell and Robert Fletcher, and attested May 26, 1772.]

[Settlement of claims; amount of claims, £151. 4. 3½; amount distributed, £2. 0. 0; allowed May 29, 1772.]

EBENEZER GROW   1760   GREENLAND

In the Name of God Amen I Eben^r Grow of Greenland in the Province of New Hamp^r Blacksmith going into the army & as tis uncertain whither I shall return again or not * * *

Imprimis I give & bequeath unto my Brother Isaac Grow One Broad Cloth Coat Jacket & Breeches, one Shirt, one pair of Stockens one Castor Hatt & one Wigg all which are now in a Chest in the Hands of Mr Joshua Pickerin also I give him my s^d Bro^r all my wages except fifty pounds which is given to Bro^r Elijah.

Item I give & bequeath unto my two Sisters Hannah and Sarah Grow One hundred & fifty pounds old Tenor Equally Divided between them both which is let out at Interest & the Notes in the Hands of Mr Joshua Pickerin Junr of s^d Greenland —

Item I give unto my Brother Elijah the Sum of fifty pounds old Tenor out of my Wages — & herely Constitute & appoint Mr Joshua Pickerin my Sole Executor * * *

In Witness whereof I have hereunto Set my hand & Seal the 20th Day of May 1760 —

                                       Ebenezer Grow

[Witnesses] John Sherburn haines, Thos Odiorne, Thomas piper.

[Proved March 31, 1762.]

ELISHA WINSLOW		1760		KINGSTON

[Administration on the estate of Elisha Winslow of Kingston, gentleman, granted to Jonathan Downing of Kingston, yeoman, May 21, 1760.]

[Probate Records, vol. 21, p. 433.]

[Bond of Jonathan Downing, with Elisha Swett and Francis Batchelder, yeomen, as sureties, all of Kingston, in the sum of £500, May 21, 1761, for the administration of the estate; witnesses, William Parker, Abigail Parker.]

[Administration granted to Jonathan Moulton Oct. 27, 1763.]

[Probate Records, vol. 23, p. 89.]

[Bond of Jonathan Moulton of Hampton, with Joseph Wright of Salem, gentleman, and Benjamin Blake of Epsom, husbandman, as sureties, in the sum of £500, Oct. 27, 1763, for the administration of the estate; witnesses, John Hale, Samuel Hobart.]

[Inventory, Nov. 5, 1764; amount, £620. 0. 0; signed by John Moulton and William Parker, Jr.]

[List of claims against the estate; amount, £146. 16. 8; signed by Jonathan Greeley and William Parker, Jr., and attested March 27, 1767.]

[Account of the administrator; receipts, £35. 2. 0; expenditures, £13. 17. 0; allowed Sept. 19, 1767.]

[Settlement of claims; amount of claims, £146. 16. 8; amount distributed, £21. 5. 0; allowed Oct. 1, 1768.]

SAMUEL NEAL		1760		NEWMARKET

[Administration on the estate of Samuel Neal of Newmarket, yeoman, granted to his widow, Catherine Neal, May 28, 1760.]

[Probate Records, vol. 21, p. 447.]

[Bond of Catherine Neal, with Hubartus Neal, gentleman, and Walter Neal, husbandman, as sureties, all of Newmarket, in the sum of £5000, May 28, 1760, for the administration of the estate; witnesses, Richard Jenness, 3d, David Sewall.]

[Warrant, May 28, 1760, authorizing Capt. Winthrop Hilton and Peter Folsom, both of Newmarket, to appraise the estate.]

[Inventory, attested Aug. 28, 1760; amount, £10,385. 10. 0; signed by Winthrop Hilton and Peter Folsom.]

JABEZ EATON   1760   HAMPTON FALLS

[Bond of Sarah Eaton, widow, with Jacob Smith, yeoman, and Abner Hoyt, husbandman, as sureties, all of Hampton Falls, in the sum of £3000, May 28, 1760, for the administration of the estate of Jabez Eaton of Hampton Falls, gentleman; witnesses, Meshech Weare, Giles Merrill.]

[Warrant, May 28, 1760, authorizing Richard Smith, gentleman, and Daniel Felch, yeoman, both of Hampton Falls, to appraise the estate.]

[Inventory, attested Oct. 28, 1761; amount, £12,956. 5. 0; signed by Richard Smith and Daniel Felch.]

[Warrant, July 7, 1762, authorizing Meshech Weare, Richard Smith, Daniel Felch, Tristram Collins, and Jeremiah Lane, tailor, all of Hampton Falls, to divide the real estate.]

[Account of the administratrix; receipts, £1406. 5. 0, personal estate; expenditures, £860. 8. 8; allowed May 30, 1764.]

Province of New Hampsh^r } By Order of the Honble Richard Wibird Esqr Judge of the Probate of Wills &c for Said Province To us the subscribers, to Divide the Real Estate of Jabez Eaton Late of Hamptonfalls in the Province aforesaid Yeoman Deceased Intestate, among the Widow & children of Said Intestate as the Law Directs &c. We have as follows (viz)

Firstly We have Set off to Sarah Eaton widow Relict of Said Intestate as her Dower & third part of said Estate, a piece of Land where the House stands Containing two Acres with Orchard thereon, Bounded as follows (viz) Westerly on a share of Orchard Set to Joshua Eaton hereafter named, the south westerly Corner Bounds of said two acres being stake & stones put Down by the fence six rods & Ten Links of the chain from the Southwest Corner of said Orchard, thence runing by the Highway before the House Twelve rods & a quarter to stake and stones by the fence & runing from said Highway Northerly Down to the Creeck where it is also Bounded, at the Northwest Corner with a small maple tree standing Down the Bank being Six Rods & Ten Links of the chain from the fence which runs from the Highway Down to said Creek at the West End of the orchard, & from said maple Easterly Twelve Rods & a quarter to an Elm tree spotted on three sides which piece of Land is mark'd in the Plan hereto annexed with the Letter W. We have also set to the said Sarah the East half of the Dwelling house so far as to the middle of the Chimney throughout from Top to Bottom, also the West End of the Barn so far as the middle of the Barn floor also the Priviledge of the Barn yard belonging thereto We have also set to the said Sarah a piece of Land in the place call'd the Carr pasture Containing Ten acres & one hundred & thirty two Rods being the westerly side of said pasture which piece of Land is mark'd in the aforesaid Plan with the Letter P. Also a piece of Land lying before the house on the Southerly Side of the highway call'd the Barn Lott Containing Five acres & one hundred & twelve rods which piece of Land is mark'd in the Plan with the Letter N. Also a Piece of Land in the place Call'd the great Pasture Containing three acres & one hundred & forty rods Lying at the Southwest Corner of said Pasture being fourteen Rods and a half wide at the South End where we have put Down stake and stones by the fence & Runing Northerly Forty five Rods being thirteen Rods & a quarter wide at the North End where is also stake & stones which piece of Land is mark'd in the Plan with the Letter M. Also a piece of Land in the place Calld the Brown place Containing fourteen acres & one hundred and thirty six rods, the south westerly corner Bound being stake and stones put Down at the corner of the fence and the Northwesterly Corner Bound a stake at the south westerly Corner of the Field & Bounded Northerly on said field as the fence now stands allowing a Drift way for passing and repassing to the marsh where the way now is by said fence which piece of Land is mark'd in the Plan with the Letter D. We have also set to the said Sarah a piece of Marsh Containing Four Acres and Seventy Eight Rods which piece of marsh is Call'd the mill Island piece and is mark'd in the aforesaid plan with the Letter (i) Also a piece of marsh Containing two Acres being the Northerly side of the piece of marsh Call'd the Sanborn marsh & we have set a stake at Each End for the Southerly Bounds of Said two acres which piece of marsh is mark'd in the plan with the Letter (f)

Secondly We have Set off to Samuel Eaton Eldest Son of the Said Intestate for his Double Share of said Estate A Piece of Land Containing Sixty Rods being part of that call'd the Brown place and is the piece on which the Old house stands which is Call'd the Brown house together with said house which piece is mark'd in the aforesaid Plan with the Letter Q. Also A piece of Land Lying before Said old house on the southerly side of the Highway Containing Eight Acres & one hundred & fifteen Rods being the Northerly part of the field belonging to the aforesaid Brown place and is Bounded as follows (viz) begining at a stake by the fence at the upper End of the orchard which stake is about two Rods from the Northwesterly Corner of said orchard from thence runing on a strait line through the Orchard Easterly Down to the Edge of the Marsh which is about Ninty Rods to a Stake set up at the Edge of said marsh about twelve Rods South from the fence and from thence to said fence then Bounded Northerly on said fence, Land of Jonathan Walton & the highway which piece is Described in the aforesaid Plan by the Letter

B. Also a piece of Land Containing Ten Acres & Ninty two Rods, Nine acres & twelve Rods of which is the Westerly Side of the aforesaid Brown place, being fourteen Rods wide at the North End where there is a stake set up, & Ten Rods wide at the South End at which Ten Rods we have also set a stake with stones around the same & one acre & a half of Said Ten Acres & Ninty two Rods is the South Easterly Corner of the piece calld the great Pasture being Forty five Rods in length and five Rods & Eight Links of the chain in wedth at Each End where we have put Down stake & stones both of which pieces are included in one and are accordingly set forth in the plan as but one piece which is there Described by the Letter H.

We have also Set to the Said Samuel a piece of Marsh call'd the Close Containing Four acres & Seventy three Rods mark'd in the Plan with the Letter (k)

Thirdly We have Set off to Paul Eaton for his share the west half of the Dwelling house so far as to the middle of the Chimney throughout, also a strip of Land at the backside of the same & at the West End Joyning thereto half a Rod wide together with the Priviledge of the yard before Said house belonging thereto and also the priviledge of the Well

We have also set to the said Paul a Piece of Land where the Barn stands Containing three acres Bounded as follows (viz) Westerly on Land Set to the widow aforesaid Begining at the aforesaid widows South Easterly Bounds which is stake & stones by the highway & Runing by said way sixteen Rods & a half to stake & stones by the fence & Runing Northerly to the Creek where it is bounded on the west side with an Elm tree before mentioned which is spotted on three sides from thence Easterly Sixteen Rods & a half to a black oak tree spotted on three sides which piece of Land is Described in the aforesaid Plan with the Letter V. we have also set to the said Paul the East End of the Barn so far as to the middle of the Barn floor: also a piece of Land in the place call'd the Car Pasture Containing Five acres Lying on the Easterly side of said pasture being Eleven Rods and ninteen links of the chain wide at Each End where we have put Down stake & stones which piece of Land is mark'd in the Plan with the Letter O. Also a piece of Land lying in the place calld the great Pasture Containing two acres & a quarter Lying on the westerly side of the aforesaid acre & a half set to Sam¹ in said great pasture as aforesaid the westerly Bounds of which are its Easterly Bounds & from then Runing Westerly Eight Rods to stake & stones at Each End which piece of Land is mark'd in the Plan with the Letter L. we have also set to the said Paul a Piece of marsh Lying in Salisbury at the place call'd the wood side medow Containing one acre lying on the southerly side of said Piece of marsh being four Rods & two thirds of a Rod wide at Each End where we have set Down stakes which piece of marsh is mark'd in the Plan with the Letter (a).

Fourthly We have Set off to Sarah Eaton for her share a Piece of Land in the home place Containing four acres Bounded as follows (viz) Westerly on a share set to Paul aforesaid which Easterly Bounds are the Westerly Bounds for the Said Sarahs four acres from thence Runing Easterly Twenty three Rods at Each End to stake & stones by the highway, & to a black burch at the North End spotted on three sides which piece of Land is mark'd in the Plan with the Letter T. also a Piece of Land in the aforesaid Brown place So call'd Containing five acres & a half Bounded as follows (viz) Easterly on Land set to the widow, in part and part on Land of Trustram Collins, being Six Rods & a half wide at the South End where we have Set Down stake & stones, & seven Rods at the North End from the North Westerly Corner Bound of the aforesaid widows share before mentioned, to a stake by the highway fence, allowing the Priviledge of Passing & Repassing through the North Easterly Corner of said share where the way now goes which share is mark'd in the Plan with the Letter E. also we have set to the said Sarah a piece of marsh Containing one acre & one hundred and thirty six Rods being the southerly side of the piece Call'd the Sanborn Marsh to a stake set Down at Each End which piece of marsh is mark'd in the Plan with the Letter (e) also one other piece of marsh Lying in Salisbury aforesaid being part of the piece of marsh Call'd the wood side as aforesaid Containing one acre Lying on the Northerly side of the aforesaid acre set to Paul aforesaid the Northerly Bounds of which is its southerly Bounds from which Runing Northerly five Rods at Each End to stakes there set Down which piece of marsh is mark'd in the Plan with the Letter (b)

Fifthly We have set off to Jabez Eaton for his share a piece of Land in the aforesaid home place Containing four acres and a half Bounded Westerly on the share Set to Sarah aforesaid from thence Runing Easterly the whole wedth of said home place thirty three Rods on the highway to a stake set Down by the fence, & twenty Seven Rods on the North side by the Creek to a Black oak tree standing up the Bank spotted on three sides which piece of Land is mark'd in the Plan with the Letter S. Also a piece of Land Lying on the south side of the highway over against said four acres & half being part of the place Call'd the great Pasture aforesaid Containing five acres & thirty two Rods being the North Westerly part of Said great pasture, Bounded Westerly on Land of Benjamin Eaton, southerly on Land set to the aforesaid widow as part of her Dower, thirteen Rods & one third part of a Rod to stake & stones, Northerly on the highway twelve Rods and two thirds of a Rod to a stake by the fence Easterly on the share set to Joshua aforesaid, which piece of Land is Described in the Plan by the Letter K. Also a piece of Land Containing half an acre which is the upper End of the orchard by the aforesaid Dwelling house, with orchard thereon Lying in a strip from the highway to the aforesaid Creek three Rods & five links wide to stake & stones at Each End which is mark'd in the Plan with the Letter Y. Also a piece of marsh in Salisbury aforesaid being the Northerly part of the piece of marsh calld the wood side Bounded Northerly on the Ditch, Easterly on the River, being Ten Rods & three quarters on said River to a stake and thirteen Rods and a half wide at the West

End where is also a stake put Down in the marsh, the south side being on a strait Line from stake to stake Containing two acres & one hundred & twenty Eight Rods which piece of marsh is mark'd in the Plan with the Letter (d).

Sixthly We have set off to Joshua Eaton for his share a piece of Land Containing four acres & Seven Rods being the Easterly End of the aforesaid home place Bounded Westerly on the share set to Jabez aforesaid whose Easterly Bounds before named are the Westerly Bounds of the said four acres & seven Rods from which Bounds to contain all that lies Easterly from them of said home place which piece of Land is mark'd in the plan with the Letter R. Also a piece of Land Lying on the southerly side of the highway being the North Easterly part of the place Call'd the great pasture aforesaid Bounded Westerly on the aforesaid share Set to Jabez the Easterly Bounds of which are its Westerly Bounds, Bounded Northerly on the aforesaid highway twelve Rods & two thirds of a Rod, & southerly on Paul aforesaid and part on the aforesaid Samuel thirteen Rods & a third part of a Rod, & Easterly on the said Samuel taking half the wedth of the aforesaid place call'd the great pasture Containing five acres & a half which piece of Land is Described in the plan by the Letter I. Also a piece of Land with orchard thereon Containing half an acre being part of the aforesaid orchard by the Dwelling house Bounded Westerly on the aforesaid share of orchard set to Jabez whose Easterly Bounds are its westerly Bounds being three Rods and five links wide at Each End & throughout Bounded Easterly on the share of orchard set to the aforesaid widow whose before named Westerly Bounds are its Easterly Bounds which piece is mark'd in the Plan with the Letter X. Also a piece of marsh in Salisbury aforesaid being part of the piece calld the wood side aforesaid Containing two acres & sixty two Rods Bounded Northerly on the Share Set to Jabez aforesaid Easterly on the River ten Rods & three quarters to a stake, & being thirteen Rods & a half wide at the West End where is also a stake set Down in the marsh & Runing on a strait line from stake to stake which piece of marsh is markd in the Plan with the Letter (c).

Seventhly. We have Set off to Abigail Eaton for her share a Piece of Land Containing five acres & twelve Rods being part of the piece of Land Call'd the Brown place Bounded Westerly on the share set to Samuel aforesaid Northerly on the aforesaid highway seven Rods to a Stake by the fence Southerly on a highway six Rods & Runing on a strait line from stake to stake, which piece of Land is markd in the plan with the Letter G. Also a piece of Land Containing five acres & Sixty Rods being the South Easterly part of the field belonging to said Brown place Bounded Southerly on the fence the whole length of said fence So far as it goes strait, which is about fifty Rods Westerly on a share set to Mary Eaton hereafter named Runing from the upper End of said strait piece of fence Northerly about square twelve Rods to a stake by the Edge of a Ditch, from thence on a strait line about fifty five Rods to a stake which stands twenty two Rods North from the lower End of the aforesaid strait piece of fence which piece of Land is markd in the Plan with the Letter A. Also a piece of marsh Joyning partly on said piece of Land Containing two acres & Seventeen Rods the North Westerly Bound of which marsh is a stake set Down thirteen Rods North of said lower End of the aforesaid strait piece of fence & from said stake Easterly about square is another stake which is by the Ditch & is the North Easterly bound of said piece of marsh from thence following the Ditch & fence &c to the aforesaid stake which piece of marsh is markd in the Plan with the Letter (g)

Eighthly We have Set off to Mary Eaton for her share a piece of Land Containing four Acres & one hundred & thirty four Rods being the South Westerly part of the Field in the aforesaid Brown place Bounded as follows (viz.) begining at a stake by the highway which stake is the South Westerly Corner Bounds of the aforesaid Samuels Share in said field and from said stake southerly as the fence goes six Rods then westerly with the fence by said highway to the Corner of said field which is about Eleven Rods then South Easterly about Seven Rods as the fence goes to a stake set up at the Corner of said fence which stake is the North Easterly Corner Bound of the Share set to Sarah aforesaid from thence Easterly as the fence of the field goes to the Corner which is about forty Rods then Northerly by the fence to the Corner then to the aforesaid stake set by the Ditch for the aforesaid Abigails Northwesterly Corner Bounds, from thence on a strait line thro' the orchard to the stake first mentioned which piece of Land is markd in the Plan with the Letter C. Also a piece of Land in the aforesaid Brown place Containing five acres & Nineteen Rods Bounded Westerly on the aforesaid Abigails Share Northerly on the highway Seven Rods to a stake by the fence & southerly on a highway Six Rods to stake and Stones by the fence from thence on a strait line Northerly to the aforesaid stake by the highway which piece is markd in the Plan with the Letter F. Also a piece of marsh being part of said Brown place Containing two acres & seventeen Rods Bounded Westerly on Samuel aforesaid in part & part on Abigail aforesd to the aforesaid stake set for the Northwesterly Bound of the said Abigails marsh & southerly on said Abigails Marsh to the stake by the Ditch aforesaid Easterly on said Ditch & Northerly by fence &c to the stake for the aforesaid Samuels North Easterly Bounds, which piece of marsh is mark'd in the Plan with the Letter (h)

thus have we Divided the Real Estate of Jabez Eaton aforesaid and this we make as our Return thereof. Dated at Hampton falls December 29th 1763

                Tristram Collins ⎫
                Richard Smith ⎬ Committee
                Jeremiah Lane ⎭

A Plan of the Real Estate of Jabez Eaton Late of Hamptonfalls Deceased Intestate, as it is Divided among the Widow & Children of said Intestate Said Estate both Lands & Marsh are Included within Black lines, Except by Rivers & Creeks are prick'd: Division lines between shares are prickd lines the shares of upland are mark'd with Capital Letters as A. B. C. &c. the marsh with small Letters as a. b. c. &c. A Con-

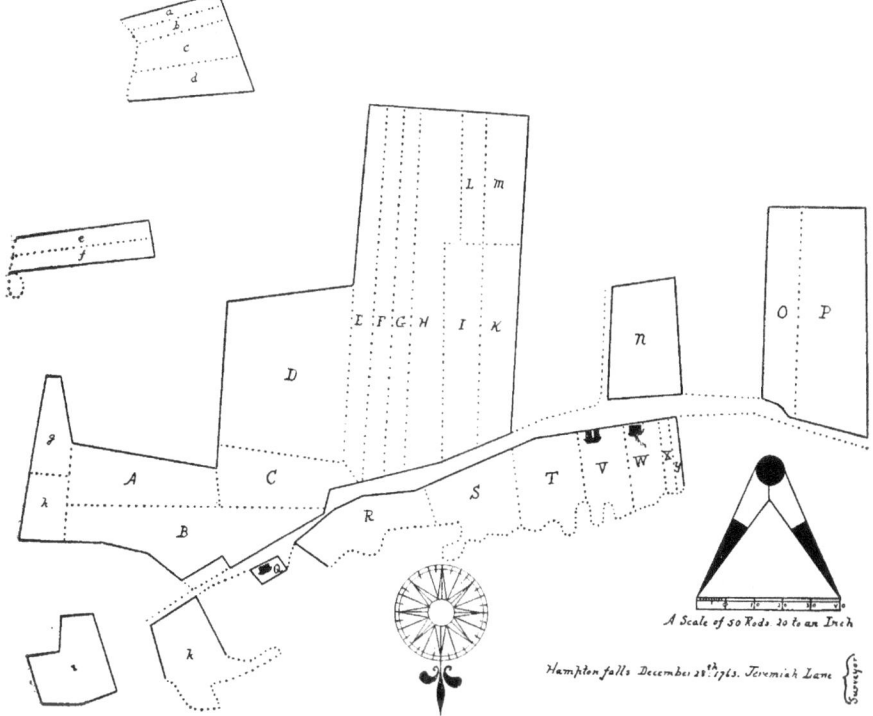

tains 5 Acres & 60 Rods B. 8 Acres & 115 Rods C. 4 A. 134 R. D. 14 A. 136 R. E. 5 A. 80 R F. 5 A. 19 R. G. 5 A. 12 R. H. 10 A. 92 R. I. 5 A. 80 R. K. 5 A. 32 R, L. 2 A. 40 R. M. 3 A. 140 R. N. 5 A. 112 R. O. 5 Acres. P. 10 A. 132 R. Q 60 Rods. R. 4 A. 7 R. S. 4 A 80 R. T 4 A. V. 3 A. W. 2 A. X 80 R y. 80 R. Marsh. a 1 Acre b. 1 A. c 2 A. 62 R. d. 2 A 128 R. e. 1 A 136 R. f. 2 A. g. 2 A 17 R. h. 2 A 17 R. i. 4 A 78 R. k. 4 A 73 R.

JOHN HOBBS   1760   HAMPTON

Province of New Hamps^r } Whereas by An Act of the General Assembly of said Province Entituled "An Act for making Partition of Certain lands therein mentioned" among other things it is Enacted that there be five freeholders in this Province Appointed And Authorised they or any three of them to make Partition of said Lands, Part of which Lands Referred to in said act are Certain Lands in Hampton Lying in Common among the Heirs of John Hobbs late Deceas'd And Others —

In Pursuance of which Act we the Subscribers have Undertaken to make Partition and Division of Said Lands as follows (having first given Due Notice to all Parties Concern'd Agreeable to the Direction in said act:) Namely A Piece of Land in Hampton near Lobbs Hole so Called Containing in the whole twenty five Acres and one hundred forty four Rods lying in Common between the heirs of John Hobbs Deceas'd and the heirs of Amos Towle Deceas'd On the Southerly Side of a Certain highway we have Divided and sett off the westerly half to the heirs of the said Amos Towle Deceas'd to Hold in Severalty and the Easterly half to the Heirs of the said John Hobbs Deceas'd to hold in Severalty the Bounds of said Division being a Stake and Stones on the Notherly Side by the aforesaid highway, and on the Southerly Side a Small Pine Spotted and a heap of Stones as Described in the Plan herewith annexed: and the Easterly half of said Piece of Land we have Divided to and among the Several heirs of the said John Hobbs Deceas'd to hold to Each of them in Severalty as follows vizt The Easterly Share marked in the Plan N° 1 we have set off to John Towle Containing One Acre and Ninety Nine Rods of Land the Bounds between that & the Second Share being at the Notherly End a Stake and Stones by the aforesaid highway, and at the Southerly End a Birch Tree Standing in the Corner of the fence And the Second Share marked in the Plan N° 2 we have Set off to the Said John Towle he having a Double Share; said Second Share is five Rods and a half in wedth at Each End and Contains the like Quantity of Land the Bounds between that and the third Share being at the Notherly End a Stake and Stones by the aforesaid highway and at the Southerly End a Knotch in the fence and the third Share Marked in the Plan N° 3 being five Rods and a half in wedth at Each End Containing the like Quantity of Land we have sett off to Thomas Brown and Mehetable his wife in her Right The Bounds between the third and fourth Shares being at the Notherly End a Pine bush Spotted by the aforesaid Way and at the Southerly End a Knotch in the fence. And the fourth Share marked in the Plan N° 4 being Six Rods in wedth at each End Containing the like Quantity of Land we have sett off to Joseph Towle the Bounds between the fourth and fifth Shares being at the Notherly End a Small pine bush Spotted by the aforesaid highway and at the Southerly End a Small Alder Spotted. And the fifth Share marked in the Plan N° 5 being Six Rods and one quarter in wedth at Each End Containing the like Quantity of Land we have sett off to Jonathan Towle, the Bounds between the fifth and Sixth Shares being at the Notherly End a Stake by the aforesaid way, and at the Southerly End a knotch in the fence. And the Sixth Share marked in the Plan N° 6, being Six Rods and one quarter in Wedth at Each end Containing the like Quantity of Land we have sett off to the heirs of James Towle Deceas'd the Bounds between the Sixth and Seventh Shares is at the Notherly End a Pine bush Spotted And at the Southerly End a Pine Stump Spotted. And the Seventh Share marked in the Plan N° 7, being Six Rods and a quarter and two links of a Chain in wedth at Each End Containing the like Quantity of Land we have sett off to Jonathan Page and Mary his wife in her Right the Bounds between the Seventh and Eighth Shares being at the Notherly End a Stake and Stones by the aforesaid way and at the Southerly End a knotch in the fence. And the Eighth Share marked in the Plan N° 8, being Six Rods and a half in wedth at Each End Containing the like Quantity of Land we have Set off to the heirs of Amos Towle Deceasd. And this we make As Our Return Dated the twenty third Day of June Anno Domini 1760 —

                        Meshech Weare
                        Jonathan Tilton
                        James Leavit

Province of } Whereas by an Act of the General Assemby New Hamps[r] of said Province Entituled "An Act for making Partition of Certain Lands therein Mentioned" Among Other things it is Enacted that there be five freeholders in this Province appointed and authorized they or any three of them to make Partition of said Lands Part of which Lands Referred to in said act are a Certain Piece of Land in Hampton lying in Common among the Heirs of John Hobbs late Deceas'd and the heirs of Amos Towle late Deceas'd near the House of Jonathan Towle in Hampton and a Certain Piece of Land in Kensington at the Cedar Swamp lying in Common Among the heirs of John Hobbs late Deceas'd and Thomas Brown, and a Piece of Land in North Hampton lying in Common with the heirs of Amos Towle late Deceasd and Others In Pursuance of which Act we the Subscribers have Undertaken to make Partition and Division of said Lands having first given Due Notice to all Parties Concernd agreeable to the Directions in said act And have Divided Said Lands as follows viz[t] That Piece of Land in Hampton near Jonathan Towles house Containing four acres and Eight Rods of Land in the whole Bounding Southerly by the Countrey Road and Eastwardly by a way which goes by Jonathan Towles House we have Divided between the heirs of John Hobbs Deceas'd and the heirs of Amos Towle Deceas'd to Each to hold in Severalty And have set of the Southerly half next the Countrey Road to the heirs of the said John Hobbs Deceas'd And the Notherly half to the heirs of said Amos Towle Deceas'd, the Bounds being a Stake and Stones set up. And the Southerly half of said Piece of land we have Divided to and among the Several heirs of the said John Hobbs Deceas'd to hold to Each of them in Severalty as follows viz[t]. We have set off the Southerly

Share next the Countrey Road marked in the Plan Nº 1 to Jonathan Towle: and the Second Share marked in the Plan Nº 2 to John Towle: And the third Share marked in the Plan Nº 3 to John Towle: and the fourth Share marked in the Plan Nº 4 to the heirs of James Towle Deceas'd: And the fifth Share Marked in the Plan Nº 5 to Thomas Brown and Mehetable his wife in her Right: And the Sixth Share marked in the Plan Nº 6 to the heirs of Amos Towle Deceasd: And the Seventh Share marked in the Plan Nº 7 to Jonathan Page and Mary his wife in her Right: And the Eighth Share marked in the Plan Nº 8 to Joseph Towle, all which Several Shares have the same quantity of land and are of the Same wedth being three Rods and Eight links of a Chain in wedth And are Divided by Parellel lines Across said lott and Stakes set up at Each Division as Described in the Plan herewith annexed. — That Piece of Land in Kensington at the Cedar Swamp lying in Common among the heirs of John Hobbs Deceas'd and Thomas Brown we have Divided between the said heirs and said Thomas Brown and have Set off to the said Thomas Brown to hold in Severalty ten acres at the Southerly End of said Lott: And to the said heirs ten Acres and One Half of an Acre to hold in Severalty at the Notherly End of Said Lott making the Division Equal having Regard to Quantity and Quality — the Bounds of said Division are a Black burch tree Spotted Standing by the fence on the westerly side And a Stump of a tree Standing by the fence on the Easterly Side Spotted. And the Notherly half of said Piece of Land we have Divided to and among the Several heirs of the said John Hobbs Deceasd to hold in Severalty as follows vizt that Share next to Thomas Brown's marked in the Plan Nº 1 Running Across the Lott being Sixteen Rods And a half in wedth we have Set off to Joseph Towle: the Second Share marked in the Plan Nº 2 being Sixteen Rods and Eleven links of a chain in wedth we have set off to Jonathan Towle the third Share marked in the Plan Nº 3 being Sixteen Rods and ten links of a chain in wedth we have set off to Jonathan Page and Mary his wife in her Right:

the fourth Share marked in the Plan N° 4 being Sixteen Rods and nine links in wedth we have set off to the heirs of James Towle Deceas'd: the fifth Share Marked in the Plan N° 5 being Sixteen Rods and Eight links in wedth We have set off to the heirs of Amos Towle Deceasd: The Sixth Share marked in the Plan N° 6 being Sixteen Rods and Seven links in wedth we have Set off to John Towle The Seventh Share marked in the Plan N° 7 being Sixteen Rods and Six links in wedth we have set off to John Towle: all the foregoing shares Contain Equal quantity of Land: And the Eighth Share marked in the Plan N° 8 being Eighteen Rods in wedth we have set off to Thomas Brown and Mehetable his wife in her Right said Share being Larger than the Other by Reason of the Quality of the Land The Bounds between the Seventh & Eighth Shares being a hemlock tree Spotted on the East Side and the bounds between the other Shares being Stakes set up by the fence on the East Side And Running Parellell lines across the Lott. That Piece of Land in North Hampton lying by the Countrey Road near Simon Page's in Common between the heirs of Amos Towle Deceas'd and Others Containing Sixteen acres and twenty Rods in the whole we have Divided And Set off to the Said heirs of Amos Towle Deceas'd to hold in Severalty two acres on the Notherly Side of Said piece of Land being five Rods and two links of a Chain in wedth at Each End and is bounded by Stakes set up at Each End, this being the Proportion belonging to said heirs And all other Shares being before Setled. And this we make as our Return Dated the twenty third Day of June Anno Domini 1760. —

       Meshech Weare
       Jonathan Tilton
       Reuben Gove Dearborn

Province of Newhampshire } Whereas by an Act of the General assembly of Said Province Entituled an act for making Partition of Certain Lands therein Mentioned Among other things it is Enacted that there be five freeholders in this

Province appointed and Authourized they or any three of them to make Partition of Said Lands Part of which Lands Referred to in Said Act are a Certain Peice of Land in Hampton Lying in Common among the Heirs of John Hobbs Late Deceased And

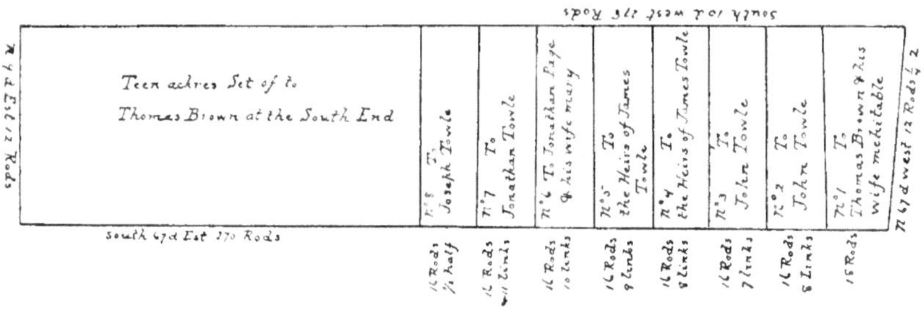

the wedth of Each mans Part is set against the same

This is a trew Plan of a Lot of Land Lying in Kensingtown Next to South Hampton Line Near the house of Philip Dows Surveyed for the Commity appointed by the General assembly to Divide Said Lot of Land by me

Benjamin Leavitt

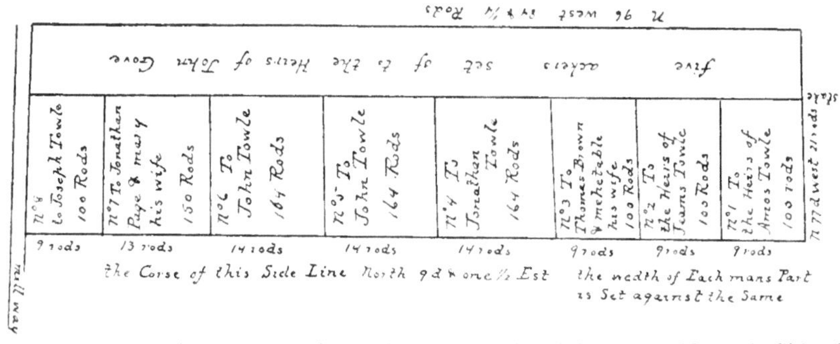

This is a Trew Plan of a Lot of Land in Hampton falls lying on the Northely Side of the Roade Commonly Called the mill Roade Near the Saw mill formerly Deacon wears Surveyed for the Committe appointed by the General assembly to Devide Said Lot of Land By me

Benjamin Leavitt

the Heirs of amos Towle Late Dec^d Near the House of Jonathan Towle in Hampton & a Certain Peice of Land in Kensington at the Cedar Swamp Lying in Common Among the Heirs of John Hobbs Late Dec^d & Thomas Brown And a Peice of Land in North hampton Lying in Common with the Heirs of Amos Towle

Late Dec^d & others In Pursuance of which Act we the Subscribers have undertaken to make Partition & Division of Said Lands having first Given Due Notice to all Parties Concerned Agreeable to the Directions in Said Act & have Divided Said Lands as

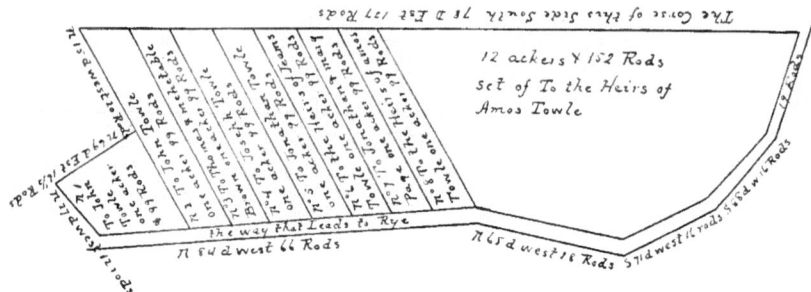

This is a Trew Plan of a Peas of Land in Hampton Town at a Plase Called Lobshole, Laying the Est Side of the Roade that Leads to Rey Near the house of Zeckariah Batchelders Survayed for the Committe appointed by the General Assembly to Devide said Peas of Land by me

Benjamin Leavitt

This is a Trew Plan of a Pease of Land in Hampton Town the North side of the Roade that Leads to Portsmouth Near the house of Jonathan Towle his Barn Stands on Said Land Survayed for the Committe appointed by the Generel assembly to Devide Said Peas of Land By me

Benjamin Leavitt

follows Viz — that Peice of Land in Hampton near Jonathan Towles House Containing four Acres & Eight Rods of Land in the whole Bounding Southerly by the Country Roade & Eastwardly by a way which goes by Jonathan Towles House we have Divided between the Heirs of John Hobbs Deceased And the Heirs of Amos Towle Dec^d to Each to Hold in Severalty And have Set off the Southerly half next the Country Road to the Heirs of the Said John Hobbs Dec^d & the Northerly half to the Heirs of Said Amos Towle Dec^d the bounds being a Stake And Stones Set up. And the Southerly half of Said Peice of Land we have Divided to & among the Several heirs of the Said John Hobbs Dec^d to Hold to Each of them in Severalty as follows Viz We have Set off the Southerly Share next the Country Roade marked in the Plan N° 1 To Jonath Towle And the Second Share marked in the Plan N° 2 To John Towle. And the third Share marked in the Plan N° 3 to John Towle And the Fourth Share marked in the Plan N° 4 to the Heirs of James Towle Dec^d And the fifth Share marked in the Plan N° 5 to Thomas Brown & mehitable his wife in her Right. And the Sixth Share marked in the Plan N° 6 to the Heirs of Amos Towle Dec^d And the Seventh Share marked in the Plan N° 7 to Jonathan Page & mary his wife in her Right And the Eighth Share marked in the Plan N° 8 to Joseph Towle all which Several Shares have the Same quantity of Land & are of the Same wedth being three Rods & Eight Links of a Chain in wedth & are Divided by Parellel Lines Across Said Lot & Stakes Set up at Each Division As Described in the Plan herewith annexed That Peice of Land in Kensington at the Ceder Swamp Lying in Common Among the Heirs of John Hobbs Dec^d & Thomas Brown we have Divided between the Said Heirs & Said Thomas Brown And have Set off to the Said Thomas Brown to hold in Severalty ten Acres at the Southerly End of Said Lott And to the Said Heirs ten Acres & one half of an Acre to Hold in Severalty at the Northerly End of Said Lott making Division Equal haveing Regard to Quantity & Quality the Bounds of Said Division are a Black Burch Tree Spotted Standing by the fence on the Westerly Side & a Stump of a tree Standing by the fence on the Easterly Spotted. And the Northerly half of Said Peice of Land we have Divided to & among the Several Heirs of the Said John Hobbs Dec^d to hold in Severalty as follows Viz that Share next to Thomas Brown's marked in the Plan N° 1, Running Across the Lott being Sixteen Rods & a half in wedth we have Set off to Joseph towle the Second Share marked in the Plan N° 2 being Sixteen Rods & Eleven Links of a Chain in wedth we have Sett off to Jon^a Towle The Third Share marked in the Plan N° 3, being Sixteen Rods & ten Links of a Chain in wedth we have Sett off to Jonathan Page & mary his wife in her Right. the fourth Share marked in the Plan N° 4. being Sixteen Rods & nine Links in wedth we have Sett off to the Heirs of James towle Dec^d: the Fifth Share Marked in the Plan N° 5. being Sixteen Rods & Eight Links in wedth we have Sett off to the Heirs of Amos towle Dec^d the Sixth Share marked in the Plan N° 6. being Sixteen Rods & Seven Links in wedth we have Sett off to John Towle. The Seventh Share marked in the Plan N° 7. being Sixteen Rods & Six Links in wedth we have Sett off to John Towle All the foregoing Shares Contain Equal quantity of Land: And the Eighth Share marked in the Plan N° 8. being Eighteen Rods in wedth we have Sett off to Thomas Brown & Mehitable his wife in her Right Said Share being Larger than the Other by Reason of the Quality of the Land the Bounds between the Seventh & Eighth Shares being a hemblock tree Spotted on the East Side And the Bounds between the Other Shares being Stakes Set up by the fence on the East Side And Running Parellel Lines Across the Lott That Peice of Land in Northampton Lying by the Country Road near Simon Page's in Common between the Heirs of Amos Towle Dec^d And Others Containing Sixteen Acres And twenty Rods in the whole We have Divided & Sett off to the Said heirs of Amos Towle Dec^d to hold in Severalty two Acres on the Northerly Side of Said Peice of Land being five Rods & two Links of a Chain in wedth at Each End & is bounded by Stakes Set up at Each End this being the Proportion belonging to Said heirs & all other Shares being before Settled And this we make as our Return Dated the twenty third Day of June Anno Domini 1760

         Meshech Weare
         Jonathan Tilton
         Rheuben Gove Dearbon

[Probate Records, vol. 24, p. 365.]

WILLIAM MACK   1760   LONDONDERRY

In the Name of God amen this 17 Day of Jun Ann Dom 1760 I William Mack of Londonderry in the Province of New hampshire In Newingland Wever Being sike of Bodey * * *

Imprimas I Give and bequeth to Shusanna Mack my Well beloved Wife the one third of all my Reall and Personall Estat During hir Naterall life

Itam I Give and Bequeth to My sone John Mack all the Rest of my Reall and Personall Estat and his Mothers third of the Reall Estate at hir deseas He Paying the following Legeses to wit —

I alow my sone Robert Mack to be Mentained During his naterall Life by my Wife Susanna and My sone John of My Estate. —

Itam I alow to My Daughter Martha Mack one hundred Pound old tenor In six years from this deat at the Reat of six pound per Dollor —

Itam I allow to My Daughter agnes one hundred Pounds old tenor at the same Reat in Eight years from this Deat —

Itam I alow my sons arsbald William and James to be Mentained and scooled out of my Personall Estat till they arive Respectivly to the age of Eight years and then I alow my Wife to bind Each of them till they arive to the age of Eighteen years to such treads as they shall Chows and When they Respectivly arive at the age of twintey one Years Each to Reseve out of my Estat the sume of twintey Spanish Milled Dollors or that velue of what Corencey Pases in this Province at that time —

finely I ordain & appoint my Wife Shusanna Mack my soll Executrix of this my Last Will and testment Disilowing and Desinolling all formor and other Wills and bequethments and alowing this and No other to be my Last Will and testment and I alow John Barnat and Robert Wallace to be over sears with full Power to see that this my Last Will and testment be Duley Executed by my Exe[r]

                                                             his
                                        William + Mack
                                              mark

[Witnesses] Thomas Jemeson, John Barnett, Robert Wallace.
[Proved June 24, 1761.]

[Warrant, June 2, 1761, authorizing Samuel Fisher and Thomas Wallace, both of Londonderry, yeomen, to appraise the estate.]

[Inventory, June 20, 1761; amount, £4101. 16. 0; signed by Samuel Fisher and Thomas Wallace.]

WILLIAM HILL   1760   MADBURY

In the Name of God Amen I William Hill of Madbury in the Province of New Hampshire Yeoman being in health * * *

Item I give and bequeath to Patience my Wife all my household goods or Furniture of my house within Doors and half the Produce of my Homestead & my farm at Free Town in Madbury aforesaid during the time she shall Remain my Widow to be Deliverd as hereafter is mentioned these bequeasts to be in Lieu of her Dower which if she shall Demand notwithstanding these gifts to her then these bequests shall be wholly Void — I give her also half my Dwelling house as she shall chuse during said Term

Item I give & Devise my Son Benjamin all my Farm & Land at a place called Free Town in said Madbury to have and to hold to him his Heirs & Assigns and order him to deliver to his Mother Yearly one half the Produce of said Land during the time of her Widowhood as aforesaid and in Default thereof I give her full power to Enter & take the said Land into her own Possession and to hold the same during the time aforesaid —

Item I give and Devise my Homestead Farm and all the Land thereto belonging to my son Robert to hold to him his Heirs & assigns and order him to pay and Deliver one half the Produce thereof to his mother Yearly as aforesaid and in Default thereof I hereby give her Power to Enter & hold the said Land as aforesaid I also Reserve for her use during the said time of her Widowhood one half my Dwelling house Cellar & thro-out viz that half she shall chuse during said Term I also give to my said son Robert my flats or Thatch ground at or near James Bunkers neck so called — and all my Out Lands to him his Heirs & assigns as aforesaid —

Item give to my Daughter Abigail the Wife of James Jackson Fifty pounds old Tenor having heretofore given her Sundry things —

Item I give & bequeath to my Daughter Sobriety four hundred pounds old Tenor the said Legacies to be paid by my two Sons jointly according to the Present Value thereof —

Item all the Rest of my Estate not herein before mentioned I give Devise and bequeath to my said Sons jointly & to their Heirs & assigns and I also Constitute & appoint my Said Sons joint Executors * * *

In Witness whereof I have hereunto Set my hand & Seal the 20th Day of June Anno Domini 1760 —

William Hill

[Witnesses] Meshech Drew, Paul Drew, Theophilus Hardy. [Proved June 24, 1761.]

[Bond of Benjamin Hill and Robert Hill, with Meshech Drew as surety, all of Madbury, in the sum of £500, June 24, 1761, for the execution of the will; witnesses, Cutts Shannon, Solomon Loud, Jr.]

EPHRAIM MARSH   1760   LONDONDERRY

In the Name of God Amen I Ephraim Marsh of Londonderry within the Prov^{ce} of Newhamp^{re} in New Engl^d being weak in body * * *

Item I order my dear Wife the Income of my real Estate and the use of the Utentials for Husbandry and household Furniture during the Time of her Widowhood she keeping the Family together till the younger Children are of Age

Item I leave to my Son Ephraim a Division of Land In Goffes Town so called as also two hundred Pound Old Ten[r] to be payd him by my Exac[r] in a Year after my Decease with what he has already got

Item I order my Daughter Abigal Fifty Pounds old Tenor to be payd in a Year after my Decease wth what she has already got

Item I leave to my Three Daughters Hannah and Ruth and Phebe two Hundred Pounds Old Ten[r] Each Hannahs to be payd within a Year after my Decease and the other two in Sixteen months

Item I leave my real Estate on wch I dwelt to my Two Sons Samuel and John to be divided between them in equal Shares they to enter on the Possession of their respective Shares as soon as they are out of their Minority and my Dear Wife from thence forward enjoying her Widows Dower or Right of thirds my said two sons enjoying what personal Estate is then remaining out of doors & my wife the remainder

Item I order that in Case it should please divine Providence that an aditional Charg Should arise by long sickness or otherwise during my Life and other means should not be found to defray it that then so much of my real Estate should be sold as may be suff[t] to that end

Finaly I appoint my Dear Wife Hannah to be the Sole Exac[r] * * *

Signd Seald Published and declard this 27th Day of June 1760

Ephraim Marsh

[Witnesses] John Moor, James MacGregore, Margaret M[c]gregore.

[Proved Nov. 7, 1760.]

[Inventory, attested Feb. 2, 1761; amount, £6759. 10. 0; signed by James Wilson and James McGregore.]

[Account of the executrix; receipts, £2759. 10. 0, personal estate; expenditures, £1515. 2. 2; allowed Oct. 30, 1765.]

EPHRAIM TIBBETTS 1760 DOVER

In the Name of God Amen I Ephr^a Tibbets of Dover in the Province of New Hampshire in New England Yeoman being Aged & Infirm in body * * * I Give and Bequeath to my Eldest Son Ephraim Tibbets all that Tract of Land Lying on ye westerly Side of ye Main Road that leads from Cochecha to Hiltons Point, that is to Say all the Land that I own Lying between Said Main road & Dirty Lane (So Called) together with my Dwelling House Barn orchard and all other the appurtenances thereto belonging and also one whole right or Share in the Swamp or ox pasture to him the S^d Ephraim his heirs & assigns forever he & they Carefully Complying with the following Conditions (vizt) that he pays out unto my Daughter Judeth Tuttle Ten Pounds old Tenor within Six months after my Decease & also my funeral Charges & Just Debts if any & also that he grants free & full Liberty to my Son Samuel Tibbets to Dewell with him in my Said house if he See Cause untill he arive to the age of Twenty one years. Item I Give & Bequeath unto my Son Samuel Tibbets the whole of my Lower field Lying between Said Dirty Lane & Back river be ye Same more or less with the Orchards thereon and also one whole right or Share in the Swamp usually Called the ox pasture to him the S^d Saml his heirs & assigns forever, and all the Rest & Residue of my Estate Real & Personal or of whatsoever Name Nature or kind I Give to my Two Sons Ephr^a & Saml Tibbets to be Equally Divided between them, provided that he my Said Son Saml return home from the army in which he is now gone and if he Don't returne home from ye Army & live untill he Arive to the age of Twinty one years then in Such Case I Give & Bequeath ye whole I have here Given him my S^d Son Saml both real & personal to my Son Ephr^a Tibbets, whom I Do Constitute & appoint Sole Exec^r * * * In Witness whereof I have hereunto Set my hand & Seal this Twenty Eighth Day of June 1760 and in the Thirty third year of his Maj^{tes} Reign

Ephraim Tebbets

[Witnesses] Alex^r Caldwell, Sarah Caldwell, Abigail Thomas. [Proved April 30, 1761.]

[Warrant, April 30, 1761, authorizing Howard Henderson and Alexander Caldwell, both of Dover, mariners, to appraise the estate.]

[Inventory, July 4, 1761; amount, £4008. o. o; signed by Howard Henderson and Alexander Caldwell.]

INDEX

NAMES OF PLACES

Alder Meadow 319
Allenstown 483
Amesbury, Mass. 53, 60, 63
      369, 371, 401, 402
Amherst 323, 353, 398, 400, 566
    (Souhegan West). 137, 323, 353, 398
Andover, Mass. 291
Angling Pond 437
Atkinson 11

Back River 241, 593
Barnstead 233
Barrington 79, 208, 275, 276
Bass Creek 109
Beaver Brook 509
Bedford 26, 27, 38, 284, 285, 353
      368, 369, 375, 388, 414, 507, 508
    (SouheganEast) 38, 369
Beech Plain 192
Berwick, Me. 92, 221, 287
Billerica, Mass. 165
Blackwater 306, 309, 311
Blackwater River 230, 465, 468
Boar's Head 172
Boar's Marsh 260
Boscawen (Contoocook) 43
Boston, Mass. 144, 191, 293, 329, 567
Bow 157, 177, 228, 236
      237, 390, 391, 441, 500
Bradford, Mass. 8
Brattleborough, Vt. 388
Brentwood . . 74, 96-98, 105, 114, 115, 145
      166, 167, 175, 186, 194, 204, 222
      223, 225, 226, 242, 243, 289, 301
      320, 321, 334, 349, 350, 356, 421
      433-435, 498, 535-537, 564
Brown's Rocks 468, 469
Buckstreet (Pembroke) 177, 390, 391
Bunker's Neck 591
Burnt Swamp 117

Candia 267
Cane's Brook 446
Canterbury 42, 43, 213, 287
      309-311, 383
Cedar Swamp 196, 365, 582
      583, 585, 587
Charlestown 510, 550-553
    (Number 4) 510
Chester.... 9-11, 22, 23, 60, 152, 153, 168
      169, 182, 205-207, 221, 222, 229
      230, 262, 263, 270-272, 277, 301
      302, 324-326, 341, 348, 349, 369
      375, 393, 396, 413, 414, 477, 480-
      482, 484, 502-506, 565
Chichester ... 261, 480, 482, 502, 505, 533
Clam Banks 119
Close 573
Cocheco (Dover) 305, 306, 593
Concord 13, 76, 441, 512
    (Penacook) 236, 441, 497
    (Rumford) ... 13, 15, 17, 76, 441, 512
Concord, Mass. 165
Contoocook (Boscawen) 43
Crankway 270
Crowley's Falls 223

Danville 493, 556
    (Hawke) 115, 436, 495, 556, 557
Deer Hill 206, 433
Deerfield 128, 129
Deerfield, Mass. 521, 522, 524
Derryfield (Manchester).... 38, 121, 179
      247, 276, 368, 369, 374
      414, 415, 430, 476, 507
Dirty Lane 593
Dock Marsh 446, 455
Dover 28, 30, 34, 35, 47, 64, 65, 67
      78-80, 95, 96, 160, 162, 240, 280
      286, 291, 292, 304-307, 315, 316
      339-341, 353, 359, 373, 403, 404

INDEX

Dover, *continued.*
    418, 419, 439, 440, 515, 593, 594
    (Cocheco)............305, 306, 593
Dracut, Mass.....................239
Dry Pines.......................80
Dublin........................240
Dunbarton.....................414
    (Starkstown)................414
Dunstable (Nashua)...52, 58, 81, 91, 137
    143, 209-211, 238-240
    246, 335-337, 389, 512
    529, 543, 545, 566, 567
Dunstable, Mass..........333, 336, 543
Durham.....27, 28, 35, 40, 41, 69, 78-80
    184-186, 227, 315, 359, 368
    381-384, 386, 424, 430, 431
    490, 512, 560
Durham Falls................185, 432

Ellins's Point....................102
Epping........18, 60, 108, 109, 124, 138
    145, 158, 159, 175, 189, 190, 225
    256, 266, 267, 270, 271, 282, 283
    301, 334, 335, 416, 418, 511, 516
Epsom......228, 362, 479, 539, 542, 569
Exeter.........18, 37, 38, 51, 52, 86, 97
    115, 119, 120, 130, 132, 138, 145
    151, 160, 167, 169, 170, 175, 176
    185-187, 189, 197, 205, 206, 232
    242, 243, 268-270, 279, 280, 282
    283, 289, 334, 335, 342-344, 350
    356, 357, 360, 361, 386, 432, 433
    435, 480, 502, 503, 505, 506, 510
    511, 513, 543, 564
Exeter River.............115, 116, 206

Falls River...........230, 270-272, 561
Falmouth, Me.....................55
Fan..............................16
Fitzwilliam.....................240
Fort William Henry...............57
Framingham, Mass..................6
Freetown......................590
Fremont (Poplin)................115
French's Creek..............464, 467
Fresh Marsh Creek...........253, 254

Getchell's Rocks.............192, 193
Gilmanton..............107, 186, 435
Glade...........................89
Gloucester, Mass.............484, 486
Goffstown..............123, 285, 374
    388, 500, 507, 508, 592
Gouges Wigwam.................119
Grassy Swamp..................503
Great Hill......................187
Great Plain......................16
Great Swamp....................16
Greenfield, Mass.........521, 522, 524
Greenland...1, 3, 4, 35, 54-56, 76, 77, 83
    85, 115, 195, 196, 199, 204, 226
    227, 229, 245, 249-251, 253, 327
    356, 357, 360, 361, 363-365, 392
    393, 397, 478, 515, 534, 538, 539
    541, 568
Groton, Mass....................373

Hall's Farm.............446-449, 451
    464, 466, 468-470
Hampstead....9, 11, 12, 70, 122, 123, 143
    152, 153, 169, 234, 235
    261, 320, 327, 334, 411
    441, 492, 493, 527, 566
Hampton.....6, 18, 56, 74, 75, 89, 93-95
    97, 120, 131, 133, 171, 172, 212-
    214, 216, 226, 260, 264, 302, 358
    442, 443, 479-481, 505, 506, 532
    533, 539, 569, 580, 582, 585, 586
Hampton Falls..20, 22, 110, 111, 116, 118
    120, 131, 151, 170, 173, 222, 229-
    232, 270-273, 301, 303, 353, 354
    357, 358, 367, 444-446, 460, 461
    463, 469, 479, 482, 501, 503, 506
    508, 511, 515, 558, 561, 562, 570
Haverhill, Mass......12, 25, 61, 174, 196
    199, 259, 290, 325, 326
    366, 419, 420, 422
Hawke (Danville).115, 436, 495, 556, 557
Hilton's Point...................593
Hinsdale.......................388
Hittytitty Brook.................164
Hogpen........................302
Hollis.....81, 83, 111, 112, 143, 144, 148

INDEX

Hollis, *continued.*
149, 282, 283, 289, 336-338
415, 456, 476, 490, 491, 560
Hook......................382, 425
Hopkinton..............195, 500, 546
 (New Hopkinton).497, 500, 501, 546
Hornswoods....................383
Huckleberry Marsh..........261, 443
Hudson..................150, 182, 346
 (Nottingham West)...150, 166, 182
183, 237, 238, 346, 347

Ipswich, Mass..............51, 52, 477
Islington................208, 275, 515

Jennesstown (Warner)........541, 542
Johnson's Creek...................80

Keeneborough....................242
Kensington..........73-75, 87, 90, 114
115, 131-133, 135, 149, 151, 160
170, 171, 205, 206, 273, 281, 301
303, 304, 355, 392, 454, 461, 465
466, 468, 469, 475, 503, 505, 511
516-518, 582, 583, 585
Kingston..17, 18, 38-40, 49, 50, 60, 61, 96
97, 103-106, 115, 117, 130, 133
138-140, 145-149, 189, 191-194
196, 199, 226, 266, 278, 281, 297
298, 300, 303, 318-320, 354, 355
369, 371, 401, 406, 428, 436, 480-
482, 518, 554-556, 563, 565, 569
Kittery, Me..............196, 199, 253

Lampereel River..........270, 271, 425
Lee.........................126, 127
Litchfield.........38, 181, 247, 284, 353
374, 414, 488, 489, 508, 566
Little Boar's Head............171, 172
Little Harbor....................196
Little Hill......................230
Little River...........93, 119, 171, 186
260, 383, 443, 563, 565
Littleton, Mass...................543
Littleworth...................66, 67
Lobbs Hole......................580

Londonderry.......22, 26, 29, 48, 49, 75
87, 95, 121, 122, 144-147, 162
165, 168, 169, 179-182, 204, 205
237, 238, 259, 260, 323, 324, 326
333, 341, 360, 372-375, 389, 390
394, 395, 397, 398, 418, 419, 422
429, 430, 477, 490, 500, 501, 515
539, 589-591

Madbury..........79, 80, 418, 590, 591
Malden, Mass....................529
Manchester..................121, 276
 (Derryfield)...38, 121, 179, 247, 276
368, 369, 374, 414, 415, 430, 476, 507
Mason......................338, 373
 (Number 1)..................373
Medford, Mass...................529
Meredith (New Salem)............157
Merrimack.........41, 58, 151, 165, 166
239, 240, 353, 389, 492, 545
Merrimack River...............16, 43
Methuen, Mass..................8, 366
Middle Plain.....................16
Middleton, Mass..................57
Mill Island......................572
Monadnock No. 7 (Stoddard).......240
Monson......................57, 490

Nantucket, Mass..................173
Nashua...............52, 91, 137, 209
238, 246, 335, 389, 567
 (Dunstable)......52, 58, 81, 91, 137
143, 209-211, 238-240
246, 335-337, 389, 512
529, 543, 545, 566, 567
New Boston......................95
New Hopkinton (Hopkinton).......497
500, 501, 546
New Ipswich.............173, 174, 282
525, 526, 543-545
New Salem (Meredith)............157
New Salem (Salem).............8, 237
Newbury, Mass..........55, 85, 90, 266
289, 428, 477, 493, 494
Newcastle...............45, 196, 311
348, 380, 460, 478

INDEX

Newington............77, 232, 233, 249
   273, 274, 387, 528
Newmarket........29, 30, 46, 47, 67, 68
   123, 137, 138, 158, 185, 186, 189
   227, 256, 323, 357, 359, 360, 415
   476, 512, 513, 543, 559, 569, 570
Newton.....53, 54, 61, 62, 369, 371, 406
Nook..........................443
North Hampton........44, 45, 171, 172
   176, 178, 249, 251, 260, 264, 312
   327, 364, 457, 582, 584, 585, 588
   (North Hill)................260
North Hill (North Hampton).......260
North River....................383
Nottingham........6, 7, 68, 71-73, 123-
   129, 131, 133, 176, 184, 189, 190
   227, 228, 281, 302, 319, 349, 350
   362, 367, 383, 456, 475, 476, 490
Nottingham West (Hudson)....150, 166
   182, 183, 237, 238, 346, 347
Number 1 (Mason)...............373
Number 2 (Wilton)............57, 183
Number 4 (Charlestown)...........510

Palmer's Marsh..................260
Partridge Point..................241
Pelham..........150, 163, 167, 168, 237
   346, 347, 508-510, 566
Pembroke...............390, 476, 500
   (Buckstreet).........177, 390, 391
   (Suncook).................14, 441
Pemigewasset River...............435
Penacook (Concord)......236, 441, 497
Perkins Neck....................561
Perkins River.....447-451, 465, 468, 469
Perrystown (Sutton)...............69
Peterborough....................430
Philadelphia, Pa..................567
Pickering's Neck..................208
Pine Island.....................215
Plaistow........8-11, 19, 21, 25, 49, 58
   60, 163, 165, 168, 169, 174, 205
   234, 235, 243, 245, 247, 249, 264
   265, 268, 277, 290, 291, 330, 334
   349, 400, 420, 422, 428, 492, 493
   496-499

Poplin (Fremont).................115
Portsmouth.............5, 6, 8, 21, 29
   30, 36, 37, 41, 42, 47, 48, 70, 71
   78, 85, 86, 99-103, 105, 114, 120
   154, 156, 183, 184, 191, 195-198
   208, 209, 211, 212, 220, 221, 239
   249, 253-255, 274-276, 289, 292-
   296, 311, 315, 329-332, 342, 351
   352, 357-360, 367, 368, 373, 375-
   377, 386, 387, 392, 395, 420, 421
   428, 429, 436, 437, 440, 442, 444
   457, 459, 460, 478, 479, 483, 484
   487, 489, 490, 500, 507, 512, 514-
   516, 518, 520, 526-528, 534, 535
   545, 552-554, 567
Powow River.................61, 409
Providence Brook................422

Quarter Mile....................273

Raymond.......................506
Ring Swamp.....................93
Rochester..........28, 51, 67, 178, 287
   288, 304, 306, 316, 340, 384, 404
   406, 419, 440, 529-532
Rumford (Concord).........13, 15, 17
   76, 441, 512
Rye......45, 46, 102, 154, 170-172, 196
   249-252, 364, 396, 534, 539-542

Sagamore Creek..................208
Salem.....8, 70, 163, 165, 178, 179, 220
   238, 259, 264, 267, 268, 328, 329
   367, 419, 420, 422, 499, 534, 537
   566, 569
   (New Salem)................8, 237
Salem, Mass....................567
Salisbury, Mass...279, 466, 470, 574-576
Salisbury and Amesbury Dist........53
Salmon Falls................308, 310
Sanborn Marsh...............572, 574
Sandown....................261, 320
   325, 326, 436, 437, 563
Sandy Point....................456
Sargent's Island................89, 93
Scarborough, Me.................329

INDEX 599

Scotland Road.................300
Seabrook....................454, 455
Sheffield's Grant................66
Simonds's Grant................227
Somersworth.......30, 69, 79, 91, 92, 96
  220, 277, 280, 283, 286-288, 304
  306-308, 310, 315-317, 349, 373
Souhegan East (Bedford).......38, 369
Souhegan West (Amherst).........137
  323, 353, 398
South Hampton.......53, 69, 77, 78, 90
  91, 139, 141, 142, 192-195, 279
  301, 369, 370, 401, 402, 406, 436
Spicket River....................164
Spring Marsh................260, 443
Spruce Swamp...............214, 215
Starkstown (Dunbarton)..........414
Stoddard........................240
  (Monadnock No. 7)............240
Stratham.......18, 30, 31, 33, 34, 37, 85
  106-110, 157, 158, 204, 226, 227
  249, 282, 283, 343, 344, 356, 381
  390, 391, 433, 456, 457, 513, 539
  547, 549, 550, 558, 559

Suncook (Pembroke)..........14, 441
Sutton (Perrystown)..............69
Swain's Creek...............271, 272

Taylor's River....271, 272, 480, 481, 503
Tolend..........................64
Tower Hill Pond................327
Townsend, Mass.................552
Towwow, Me....................287
Trickling Falls.......194, 298, 299, 565
Tuck's Mill Pond.................93

Wadleigh's Falls..............227, 456
Wall's Cove....................433
Wall's Creek...................456
Walpole....................551, 552
Warner (Jennesstown)...........541
Westford, Mass.................247
Wheelwright's Pond.........424-427
Wilton.....................57, 183
  (Number 2)...............57, 183
Windham......75, 87, 257-259, 341, 525

York, Me....................54, 249

NAMES OF PERSONS

Abbott, Benjamin........112, 114, 116
    George....................17, 441
    Joseph.........................515
    Thomas..................290, 291
Adams, Benjamin.....274, 349, 526, 545
    Elizabeth.................143, 212
    Ephraim.........91, 210, 526, 545
    Jacob..........................210
    John...........................560
    Jonathan.................146, 147
    Joseph.........................274
    Mary......................148, 149
    Nathaniel................315, 515
    Sarah (Smith)............146, 147
    William...................148, 149
    Winborn.......................315
Aiken, Edward................181, 398
    James...............285, 286, 325
    John...........................325
    Nathaniel......................398
Akerman, Benjamin...208, 209, 429, 444
    Elizabeth......................208
    Hannah........................208
    Joseph.........................429
    Josiah....................208, 209
    Mary..........................208
    Nahum...................208, 209
    Sarah.........................208
    Simeon.............208, 209, 526
Alcock, Joseph..........5, 48, 296, 484
Alld, John......................137
Allen, John...................54, 327
    Jonathan..................57, 84
    Mary (Cate)...................84
    Priscilla.......................57
    Robert...................144, 145
Allison, Elizabeth................398
    Samuel........................501
Ambrose, Abigail................475

Ambrose, *continued*.
    Abigail (Goodhue)............475
    Hannah.......................475
    John..........................414
    Jonathan................475, 476
    Mary.........................475
    Nathaniel...............475, 476
    Rebecca......................475
    Samuel.......................475
Ames, David......................29
    Sarah (m. Hilton).............29
    Stephen..................81, 112
        148, 149, 282, 283
Anderson, James.............179, 180
    James, Jr......................179
    Jane.....................181, 182
    Janet....................179, 180
    John....................179–182
    Matthew.................181, 182
    Robert........................179
    Samuel.......................390
Annis, Abigail....................423
    Daniel.............497, 500, 501
Appleton, Daniel.................477
    Henry........................567
    Isaac........................545
Apthorp, Henry..................395
Archdeacon, Peter................330
Aris, Samuel.................479, 527
Armour, Andard..................329
    Gain...............257–259, 341
    Janet (Gilmore)..........257, 258
    Jean.........................258
    Mary.........................258
Atkinson, Joseph.........368, 431, 432
    Theodore........244, 435, 552, 553
    Theodore, Jr.............520, 521
        534, 552, 553
Atwell, John.................337, 338

INDEX

Austin, Benjamin....................95
  Benjamin, Jr...................95
  John..........................16
  Joseph...................304, 403
  Nathaniel..........241, 242, 403
  Samuel........................96
Avery, Joseph.....................417
Ayer, John...................196, 497
  William..................497-499
Ayers, James................397, 398
  John..........................41
  Mary (Jenkins)................76
  Samuel..................397, 507
  William.................397, 398

Babb, Joshua................351, 352
  Philip...................156, 351
Bagley, David............61, 62, 369
  Dorothy (m. Morrill)..........62
  Henry......................62, 63
  Jonathan......................62
  Orlando..........60-62, 192, 266
  Sarah (m. Sargent)............63
  Thomas........................62
Bailey, Jacob...............143, 566
  Joseph.......................144
Baker, Benjamin...........10, 11, 60
  Charles.............66, 308, 532
  Lydia (Wentworth)............287
  Moses........................267
  Otis.................65, 67, 280
  Sarah........................287
Balch, Andrew...........178, 220, 329
  Caleb........................178
Ball, Ebenezer....................490
Ballou, see Blue.
Banfill or Banfield, John.......36, 212
Barker, Benjamin..................31
  Ebenezer.....................128
  Ephraim......................110
  Ezra.........................128
  William.......................33
Barnes, Joseph....................274
Barnett, John.........169, 260, 589, 590
  Moses....87, 274, 372, 374, 375, 430
Barr, John................49, 75, 341

Barr, *continued.*
  Samuel.............29, 49, 75, 147
    162, 260, 341, 342, 373-375, 430
Barrett, Nathan...................333
Barron, Moses..........369, 388, 507
Barry, Simon......................396
Bartlett, Enoch...................496
  John.........................190
  Joshua, Jr..............298, 299
  Josiah..............278, 279, 297
    300, 318, 518, 566
  Katharine....................496
  Nathaniel........119, 400, 496, 497
  Richard......................476
  Thomas.......................127
Batchelder, Abigail............24, 355
  Benjamin................132, 369
  Cornelius....................116
  Daniel.......................355
  David....................479-482
  Ebenezer................149, 354
  Elisha...................480-482
  Elizabeth..........23, 24, 68, 355
  Ephraim.................131-134
  Francis......................569
  Hannah...................68, 355
  Isaiah......................23, 24
  Jethro........................68
  John....................131, 135
  Jonathan...................67, 68
  Joseph......22, 131, 132, 134, 482
  Joshua..................114, 115
  Josiah.............111, 132-134
    170, 222, 303, 479, 482
  Margaret................131, 132
  Mary......22-25, 68, 114, 116, 355
  Mercy........................149
  Nathan.............131, 132, 193
  Nathaniel..........114, 131-135
    479-482, 555, 556
  Page......................22, 23
  Phineas......................149
  Reuben..................480-482
  Samuel.............114, 134, 149
  Sarah............68, 132, 149, 479
  Sarah (m. Beede).........115, 116

Batchelder, *continued.*
    Sarah (m. Healey)........480, 482
    Stephen....................171
    Susanna.....................24
    Susanna (Gale)..............555
    Thomas.....132, 134, 318, 319, 354
    Timothy................133, 134
    William.................68, 116
Bates, Joseph.................544, 545
Bayley, Abner.................268, 499
    Edmund.....................495
    Jacob...................499, 500
    Mary.......................268
Beal, —— (Hinsdale).............524
    George.....................524
Bean, Elizabeth (Bridgham).........40
    Enoch.......................96
    James...105, 186, 187, 225, 356, 357
    Jeremiah....................37
    Joseph..............193, 369, 370
    Mary (Judkins)..............224
    Ruth.......................356
    Sinclair....................421
Beard, John....................412
Beck, John......................86
Bedel, Abial..................237, 238
    Dorothy..................237, 238
    Elizabeth (Kelly).........237, 238
Beede, Daniel............204, 321, 323
    Phineas....................115
    Sarah (Batchelder).......115, 116
Bell, John.....................147
    Meshech....................460
    Shadrach.................246, 348
    Thomas.....................348
Bellows, Benjamin........388, 550–553
Bennett, William...............329
Bergin, John................357, 360
Bernard, Samuel................279
Berry, Eleanor..................250
    Francis.............249, 251, 252
    James..................249–253
    Joseph..................251, 252
    Richard.................249, 252
    Stephen.....................51
    William.................249–252

Bestow, Hannah (Jackson).....331, 332
Bickford, Abigail................161
    Dependence.................315
    Elizabeth...................161
    Elizabeth (Leavitt)..........106
    Ephraim....................162
    Hannah.....................535
    John................51, 160, 161
    Jonathan...............161, 305
    Joseph.....................286
    Joseph, Jr..............162, 406
    Judith.....................160
    Martha (m. Tibbetts).........161
    Phoebe (Varney)............406
    Richard....................419
    Sarah......................476
    Thomas.....103, 212, 332, 460, 535
Bixby, Thomas...................508
Blair, Ann (Clendenin)............372
    David......................372
    Elizabeth..................372
    Frances....................372
    William................372–374
    William, 3d.................374
Blaisdell, Jonathan............63, 266
    Moses......................232
    Ralph......................266
    Ralph, 3d...................61
Blake, Benjamin.................569
    Israel......................120
    Jeremiah...........450, 454, 455
    Jonathan...................495
    Mary...............118, 120, 148
    Mary (Rowe)................117
    Philemon...........208, 413, 503
    Samuel.....................243
    Sarah (Gove).....448–450, 454, 455
Blanchard, Augustus..............238
    Benjamin.....82, 143, 144, 337, 338
    Benjamin, Jr.....144, 336, 338, 490
    Caesar.....................239
    Hannah.....................238
    James..................238, 240
    Jonathan.........238, 240, 246, 359
    Joseph.............166, 174, 238
            239, 353, 492, 545

INDEX

Blanchard, *continued.*
  Joseph, Jr. 58, 151
  Jotham 151, 238
  Katharine 238, 240
  Nathan 57, 58
  Rebecca 239
  Rebecca (m. Minot) 238
  Richard 44
  Sarah 238
  Thomas 91
  Thomas, Jr. 91
Blazo, William 392
Blodgett, Ebenezer 346
  Jeremiah .346
Blood, Elnathan 246
  Josiah 144
Blue, Mehitabel (Seavey) 542
Blunt, Hannah (Sherburne) 478
  John 478
Bly, James 498
Boardman, Andrew 165, 247, 529
  Benjamin .513
  Stephen 158
Boyd, Anna .398
  George 311, 527
  Joseph 550
  Robert 49
Boyes, Robert 95, 419, 525
  Thomas 285, 286
Boynton, Joshua 338
  Samuel 204
  Sarah 204
Brackett, Benning 227, 228
  Elizabeth 226, 228, 229
  George 227–229
  James 4, 56, 57, 226
             227, 229, 245, 246, 364, 366
  John 226, 228, 229, 362, 363
  Joshua 226, 228, 438, 439
  Martha 4
  Mary 226, 228
  Pay 227
  Samuel 227
  Thomas 226
Bradford, Thomas 476, 567

Brewster, John 440
  Joseph 311
Bridgham, Elizabeth (Choate) 38–40
  Elizabeth (m. Bean) 40
  Jacob 39
Brooks, Martha 526
  Micah 138
Brown, ——— 93
  Abel 279
  Abraham 334, 335
  Anna (Buswell) 20
  Arthur 197, 200
  Benjamin 401, 518
  Benjamin, Jr. 518
  Elisha 230, 231
  Enoch 53, 54
  Ephraim 463
  Ezekiel 18, 159, 267, 334, 335
  Hannah (Gove) 449, 450
  Jedediah 229–231
  Jeremiah 229, 231
  John 274
  Jonathan 230, 231, 450
  Joseph 251, 253, 364, 366
  Marmaduke 22
  Mary 229, 231
  Mehitabel 462, 581
                  583, 584, 587, 588
  Michael 355
  Nathan 115
  Pearson 515
  Samuel 235, 371
  Simeon 297, 298
  Thomas 230, 462
                  581–585, 587, 588
Bruce, Elizabeth 368
  Elizabeth (m. Lane) 368
  William 28, 368
Bryent, Robert 364
  Walter 30, 560
  Walter, Jr. 186
Bullard, Asa 526
  Ebenezer 545
Bunker, James 591
Burbank, John 500
  Jonathan .500

Burbank, *continued.*
  Ruth........................500
Burbeen, Paul....................17
Burditt, Daniel..................529
  Joanna.......................529
  Thomas.......................529
Burge, Ephraim...................83
Burleigh, David.................381
  Joseph, Jr...................189
  Josiah.......................138
  Sarah (Foss).................456
  Thomas.......................362
Burnham, Jeremiah...........184, 381
  Jeremiah, Jr.................385
  Joshua.......................127
  Meriel.......................315
  Winthrop.....................315
Burns, George...............346, 348
Burnside, David.................162
Buss, Hannah (m. Horney).....292-296
  Joseph..............292-294, 296
  Lydia....................292-296
  Mary.........................294
Bussey, John................530, 531
Buswell, Anna (m. Brown)..........20
  Deliverance (m. Clifford)......20
  Judith.....................20, 21
  Mary (Worthen)..................20
Butler, Benjamin.................476
  John....................509, 510
  Joseph.............168, 346, 390
Butterfield, Elizabeth...........210
  Ephraim......................183
  John......................52, 246
  Mary.........................246
  Thomas..................246, 247
  William......................333
Buzzell, Samuel..................130
  William......................130

Caldwell, Alexander.........241, 242
              286, 404, 406, 594
  James...............375, 418, 419
  Sarah........................594
Calfe, Elizabeth.................434
  Jeremiah................433, 434

Calfe, *continued.*
  John................297, 300, 435
  Oliver..................433, 434
  Robert........................14
  Ruth (Smith)............433, 434
  William..................39, 297
Campbell, David..................390
  Henry........................181
  Robert...................22, 179
Canney, Benjamin........240, 241, 304
  Elizabeth....................162
  Ichabod......................304
  John.........................241
  Joseph.......................241
  Martha (m. Meader)...........240
  Rose....................240, 241
  Susanna (m. Hanson)..........240
  Thomas..................240-242
  William......................241
Carleton, Jeremiah................41
  Jonathan...10, 11, 13, 265, 492, 499
Carr, ———....................24, 25
  Abigail (Clifford)...........517
  James..............374, 500, 507
  Moses.......70, 92, 280, 284, 307
  Sanders......................138
  Widow........................467
Carter, Ephraim..................195
  Ezra........15, 237, 441, 500, 547
Carty, Anna......................510
  Daniel..................510, 511
  John....................510, 511
Casman, John.....................192
Cate, Abigail.....................83
  Abigail (Neal)...............559
  Comfort (m. Seavey)...........84
  Eleazer.......................37
  James..........................2
  Joshua..................83-85, 204
  Lydia (m. Haines).............84
  Margaret (m. Johnson).........84
  Martha (m. Thing).............84
  Mary (m. Allen)...............84
  Rachel....................83, 84
  Samuel....35, 36, 107, 156, 197, 559
  Sarah.....................83, 84

Cate, *continued.*
   Stephen....................559
   Tucker..................83, 84
   William, Jr..................37
Caverly, Hannah................275
   Margaret....................275
   Mary (m. Nelson)............275
   Moses...................275, 276
   Nathaniel...................275
   Sarah.......................275
   Thomas.....................275
   William....................275
Chadbourne, Hannah.............352
   Thomas............377, 380, 527
   William....................240
Chaddock, Abra..............283, 284
   William....................283
Chaffin, David..................383
Challis, Dorothy.............369, 370
   Enoch..................369–371
   John........................53
   Lydia......................371
   Lydia (m. Varnum).......371, 372
   Peleg................369, 371
   Sarah......................371
   Thomas....................371
Chamberlain, Jacob..............440
   John....................41, 508
Chandler, ———...............509
   John.......................545
   Joseph............175, 190, 417
   Sanborn....................213
Chapman, ———..............250
   Widow.....................251
Chase, Abigail...............237, 238
   Andrew.....................34
   Anna..................31, 32, 34
   Dudley......................31
   Ezekiel....................346
   Hannah (Gove)..............454
   Henry......................348
   Jacob....................23, 25
   James..................165, 166
   John........................13
   John, Jr...................449
   Jonathan.........445, 464, 466

Chase, *continued.*
   Love....................30–34
   Mary.......................31
   Nathan....................266
   Nathaniel..................165
   Prudence (Hills)............413
   Rachel (Gove).......448–450, 455
   Roger..................237, 238
   Ruth...................237, 238
   Sarah (m. Piper)..........31–34
   Thomas...........30, 31, 33, 454
Cheney, Nathaniel...............428
   Thomas....................497
Chesley, Jonathan.............2, 359
   Mary (Weeks)..............2–4
   Thomas...........185, 431, 432
   Thomas, Jr..................28
Childs, Richard...............40, 41
Choate, Abigail..................40
   Amni......................299
   Anna.......................40
   Benjamin...............297–300
   Elizabeth...................40
   Elizabeth (m. Bridgham).....38–40
   John, Jr...................477
   Jonathan.................38, 39
   Ruth......................297
   Ruth (m. Judkins)...........298
   Ruth (m. Sleeper)........297, 300
   Simeon....................299
Christy, Thomas.................477
Church, Jonathan................531
Churchill, Elizabeth (Jackson)...331, 332
   John......................332
Cilley, Benjamin.............318, 320
   Joseph............189, 281, 367
Claggett, Wyseman...354, 386, 395, 403
Clark, Abraham..............434, 537
   Daniel.............106, 362–364
   Ebenezer................362, 363
   Edward.........165, 178, 534, 537
   Eli.......................431
   Enoch...........55, 245, 246, 249
      251, 253, 360, 361, 363–365
   George....................395
   Greenleaf...........361, 363, 365

Clark, *continued.*
   John............48, 110, 121, 181
                      333, 341, 438, 439
   Joseph............23, 25, 327, 361
                      362, 364–367, 460
   Mary...........360, 361, 364, 365
   Phyllis......................363
   Robert.......29, 182, 324, 375, 419
   Samuel......................108
   Satchell.....................356
Clarkson, Andrew......103, 330, 459, 514
Clary, William...................174
Clay, Jonas..................262, 263
Clement, Daniel..................261
   Sarah.......................261
   Sarah (Watts)................422
Clements, Abigail.................316
   Abner...................316, 317
   James....................315–317
   Job......................316, 317
   John......................70, 317
   Ruth........................70
   Sarah...................316, 317
   Shuah......................316
   Timothy....................500
Clendenin, Ann (Blair)............372
   Robert......................373
   William.....................145
Clifford, Abigail (Seavey)..........542
   Abigail (m. Carr).............517
   Benjamin....................516
   David...................105, 106
   Deliverance (Buswell)..........20
   Hannah (m. Palmer)..........517
   Israel........................21
   Joseph..................461, 517
   Rachel (m. Prescott)..........517
   Samuel..................516, 517
   Samuel, Jr................74, 171
   Sarah......................516
   Sarah (Towle)...............213
   Sarah (m. Prescott)..........517
   Simon......................517
   William....................216
Clough, Abner....................490
   Ann (French)................301

Clough, *continued.*
   Isaac, Jr..................534, 537
   Jeremiah....................44
   Love (Sanborn)..............564
   Rachel (French).............301
   Reuben.....................564
   Theophilus..................194
   Winthrop...................301
   Zaccheus........115, 116, 175, 263
Coburn, Nathan..................338
Cochran, Agnes...................284
   Dinah......................501
   James..................500, 501
   Jane (m. Moore)..........323, 324
   John..............259, 489, 525
   Jonathan...................501
   Joseph..................284, 285
   Margaret...................284
   Margaret (m. Steele).........285
   Mary......................284
   Ninian.....................26
   Peter......................323
   Samuel.................284, 398
   Thomas.....................95
Coffin, Abner....................227
   Eliphalet................371, 557
   Moses...............137, 138, 256
   Peter...............194, 227, 428
   Tristram...................428
Cogan, Stephen..................186
Colburn, Thomas.................346
Colby, Benaiah....................60
   David.......................50
   Hannah....................441
   Maria (Emmons)..............50
   Moses......................436
   Nathan.....................441
   Theophilus..................320
   Willoughby.................175
Colcord, Samuel..................319
Cole, Samuel......................8
   Simeon.....................490
Coleman, Abigail (Huntress).......233
   Deliverance (Swett)..........173
   Huldah (Swett)..............173
   Phineas....................233

Collins, Joseph ... 406
   Richard ... 77, 78, 401, 406, 411
   Tristram ... 570, 574, 578
Conant, Abel ... 83
   Catherine ... 81, 83
   Josiah ... 81–83
   Widow ... 144
Connor, Benjamin ... 280
   David ... 391
   Mary (Leavitt) ... 280
   Mary (Seavey) ... 542
   Meribah ... 138
   Samuel ... 391
Cook, Timothy ... 491, 492
Cooper, John ... 497
   Mary (Dow) ... 497
   Moses ... 266
Copp, Susanna ... 178
Corliss, David ... 537
   Hannah ... 537
Cotton, Abigail ... 458
   Bethiah ... 459
   Clement ... 459
   Elizabeth ... 458
   Joel ... 459
   John ... 457–459
   Joseph ... 114, 368, 545
   Martha ... 458
   Mary ... 458, 487
   Sarah ... 458, 459
   Timothy ... 487
   William ... 458
Coultes, John ... 41
Craige, Alexander ... 538
   Andrew ... 22, 23, 222, 277, 349
   Robert ... 182
   Thomas ... 29
Cram, Benjamin ... 503–506
   Daniel ... 173
   Ebenezer ... 502–506
   Elijah ... 301
   Elizabeth ... 501, 505
   Joel ... 504–506
   John ... 502–507
   Jonathan ... 321, 501–506, 537
   Joseph ... 502–507

Cram, *continued*.
   Mary ... 503, 504
   Nehemiah ... 502–507
Crawford, Joanna (Sanborn) ... 564
   Robert ... 564
   William ... 326, 341
Creighton, Ann ... 342–344
   Thomas ... 342
Crimbel, Charles ... 314
Critchett, Ann ... 225
   Elias ... 68
   Thomas ... 21, 223, 225
Crockett, Elizabeth ... 352
   Ephraim ... 457
   Jonathan ... 352
   Joshua ... 197
Crockford, Daniel ... 99, 100
   Isabella ... 99
   Isabella (m. Noble) ... 99, 100
Crombie, John ... 374
   John, Jr. ... 374
Cromett, Elizabeth (Davis) ... 383
Cross, Nathan ... 237
Crossett, James ... 182, 349
Crusey, Abraham ... 521
Cummings, Bridget ... 338
   Caleb ... 337, 338
   Ebenezer ... 338
   Eleazer ... 150
   Elizabeth ... 338
   Ephraim ... 168
   Jane ... 333
   Jerathmeel ... 333
   John ... 182
   Jonathan ... 151
   Joshua ... 337, 338
   Larned ... 337, 338
   Leonard ... 333
   Lucy ... 335, 336, 338
   Lucy (m. Kendall) ... 336, 337
   Martha ... 150
   Philip ... 337, 338
   Prudence, Jr. ... 416
   Rachel ... 333
   Rebecca ... 338

Cummings, *continued.*
  Samuel................81, 82, 112
                114, 148, 151, 282, 283
                336-338, 416, 491, 492
  Sarah........................182
  Silas.........................333
  William.............182, 335-338
Cunningham, John..............48, 49
  Robert........................48
Currier, Ann (m. Marble).........244
  David...................244, 245
  Dudley......................423
  Eliphalet....................193
  Elizabeth (Watts)............422
  Ezra....................192-194
  Hannah......................422
  James.......................423
  Jeremiah....................194
  John........191-194, 243, 245, 402
  Jonathan....................556
  Judith..................192, 194
  Mary...............192, 194, 244
  Nathaniel...................423
  Rachel......................244
  Rhoda..................192, 194
  Ruth...................191, 194
  Samuel........90, 91, 195, 401, 403
  Sarah.......................244
  Sargent.............194, 195, 220
  Sego........................191
  Simeon......................423
Cushing, ———.................64, 65
Cutt, John.............5, 114, 483, 484
  Samuel......................483

Dame, Hannah...................352
Daniell, Eliphalet..................35
Darling, John................148, 354
Davis, Abigail....................477
  Amos.......................334
  Benjamin...............334, 477
  Daniel......381, 382, 385, 477, 516
  Edmund.................477, 554
  Elizabeth...............381, 382
  Elizabeth (m. Cromett).......383
  Ephraim....47, 78, 79, 381, 385, 386

Davis, *continued.*
  Francis.............383, 385, 386
  Hannah.....................477
  James....................78, 384
  John........................184
  Joseph..................255, 477
  Moses.......................334
  Nathan......................477
  Obadiah.....................382
  Phoebe.................384, 385
  Ruth........................334
  Samuel.................347, 477
  Sarah..............382, 384, 477
  Thomas...........47, 78, 382-386
  Timothy....................221
  Zerviah................384, 385
Deane, Thomas....................87
Dearborn, ———..............93, 326
  Abraham....................245
  Jonathan....................264
  Levi......55, 178, 251, 364, 366, 392
  Margaret (Fifield)............104
  Michael.....................480
  Peter.......................104
  Reuben G............314, 584, 588
  Sarah (Leavitt)..............264
  Simeon..................55, 249
  Thomas.....................267
Demeritt, Job.....................28
  Samuel......................431
Dennett, John....229, 364, 369, 375, 381
  Joseph......................157
Dickey, Samuel...................122
Dimond, Israel.......436, 437, 495, 496
  Reuben.................401, 403
Dinsmoor, Abraham..........282, 283
  Asa....................282, 283
  Hannah.....................282
  John...................282, 329
Doak, John......................162
Dockum, Cotton.................457
Doe, Andrew....................512
  Nathaniel....................68
  Nicholas....................476
  Samuel.....................512
Dole, Hannah...................330

INDEX

Dole, *continued.*
   Parker........................330
   Stephen..................248, 249
Dolloff, Martha (Leavitt)..........106
Douglas, Patrick...................95
Dow, ———........................443
   Abraham............205, 445, 561
   Amasa..................138, 566
   Benjamin............335, 454, 455
   Charity..................249, 252
   Daniel......................220
   Ebenezer....................190
   Ezekiel...............74, 207, 517
   Hannah..................91, 246
   Hannah (m. Jenness)..........93
   Henry...................249, 542
   Jeremiah..................93–95
   John...........175, 205, 335, 511
   Jonathan.............21, 74, 132
                 171, 496–499, 533
   Joseph......................466
   Judith (Worthen)..............20
   Mary............94, 496, 498, 499
   Mary (m. Cooper)............497
   Nathan..............74, 498, 499
   Nathaniel................220, 264
   Noah.....................93, 94
   Phoebe..................498, 499
   Richard............163, 179, 367
   Samuel......................533
   Sarah (m. Johnson)............93
   Simon.....................93–95
   Timothy......................21
   William.................498, 499
Downing, Jonathan................569
   Josiah, Jr....................234
Downs, Gershom................30, 51
   John.........................30
   Margaret (m. Walker).........51
   Nathaniel....................92
   Priscilla....................295
Drake, ——— (Lunt)..............55
   Abraham.....................57
   Nathaniel....................57
   Robert.......................57
   Simon......................190

Drake, *continued.*
   Thomas.....................417
   William......................22
Draper, Joseph..................7, 75
Dresser, Jeremiah.................512
   Mehitabel...................512
Drew, Abigail..................78–80
   Elijah........................80
   Francis....................78, 80
   Joseph....................78–80
   Mesheeh....................591
   Paul........................591
   Tamson...................78–80
   Tamson (m. Hayes).........79, 80
   William.................431, 512
Drought, Robert...................99
Drown, Jonathan.................381
Drury, Gershom..................282
Dudley, Biley....................167
   Elizabeth....................242
   Hannah (Leavitt)............106
   James.............105, 225, 226
   John........................543
   Jonathan................242, 243
   Mary (m. Watson)...........242
   Mercy (m. Thing)............242
   Nicholas....................166
   Samuel...98, 167, 242, 243, 421, 537
   Sarah (m. Leavitt)...........242
Duncan, George..................260
Dunlop, James...................342
Durgin, Daniel....................54
   Francis.....................109
Durrell, Joseph.................31, 33
Dustin, ———...................420
   John........................234
   Jonathan....................204
   Obadiah.....................70
   Sarah...................204, 205
Dutton, John.................526, 545
   John, Jr.....................545
Dwinell, Abigail..................110
   Amos.......................110
   Anna.......................111
   John........................144
   Molly.......................111

Dwinell, *continued.*
  Susanna...................111
Dwyer, James......29, 95, 483, 490, 500

Eady, Anthony..................258
Eakens, Thomas.................318
Eastman, Benjamin..............475
  Ebenezer................557, 558
  Edward..................138, 557
  Joseph..................104, 354
  Mary........................557
  Mehitabel (Watts)............423
  Obadiah...................70, 163
      165, 205, 420, 423, 556
  Peter.......................527
  Richard.....................237
  Samuel......................104
  Sarah.......................557
  Shuah (Fifield)..............104
  Thomas.............43, 556–558
  Timothy.....................104
  William...................9, 158
Eaton, Abigail..............577, 578
  Benjamin....................575
  Jabez..........570, 575, 576, 578
  Joshua.............571, 575, 576
  Mary........................577
  Paul....................573–576
  Samuel......373, 572–574, 576–578
  Sarah......570–572, 574, 575, 578
  Theophilus..............261, 262
Ela, Edna (Little)................248
Elkins, ———...................214
  Thomas.......................50
  Widow.......................172
Elliott, Ephraim.................104
  Hannah (Jones).........407, 409
  John...................352, 369
      407, 409, 487, 545, 556
  Jonathan....................190
Ellsworth, Jeremiah..............243
Elwell, Elizabeth (Stevens)........486
  Jacob.......................486
Emerson, Caleb..................248
  Daniel...............81, 83, 112
  Joseph......................144

Emerson, *continued.*
  Moses............79, 80, 185, 186
  Nathaniel...............222, 324
  Samuel...............23, 25, 153
      222, 263, 264, 324, 327, 375, 477
  Solomon..................79, 80
  Stephen.................122, 152
Emery, Anthony..................46
  Joshua.....................291
  Noah............18, 19, 38, 86
      115, 120, 176, 232, 280, 282, 283
      335, 342, 346, 350, 351, 510, 513
  Zachariah..................552
Emmons, Joseph..................49
  Maria........................49
  Maria (m. Colby).............50
  Samuel..............49, 50, 193
Estes, Elijah....................307
Etheridge, Nathaniel..............318
Evans, Peter....................525
  Richard.................103, 516
  Samuel......................99
Evers, Ann (Harford)............291
Ewins, James....................477
Eyre, see Ayer.

Fabyan, Elizabeth (Huntress)......233
  Samuel.................233, 249
Farley, Samuel.............112, 148
Farnsworth, David...............338
  Stephen....................550
Farrington, Stephen...............16
  Stephen, Jr..................17
Farwell, Eleazer.................333
Fassett, Peter...................507
Felch, Daniel...................570
Fellows, Elizabeth (Rowe).........207
  Joseph...................96, 97
  Nathaniel..........86, 292, 294
  Ruth (Rowe)................207
Ferguson, John 168
Fernald, John.....8, 17, 18, 27, 29, 30, 35
      37, 38, 46, 47, 49, 51–53, 58, 70
      75, 77, 78, 81, 96, 105, 114, 377
Fick, David....................567
Fifield, Edward.................354

INDEX

Fifield, *continued.*
   John............104, 192-194, 279
   Jonathan, Jr..............558, 562
   Joseph..............103, 104, 558
   Margaret (m. Dearborn).......104
   Samuel...............39, 40, 104
   Sarah..................103, 104
   Sarah (m. Stevens)............104
   Shuah (m. Eastman)...........104
Fisher, Samuel.......179-182, 398, 590
Fiske, Amos......................82
   Ebenezer..................18, 175
Fitzgerald, Richard...............429
Flagg, Eleazer................111, 112
   Hannah...................111, 112
   John..........................111
   Jonas..............111, 148, 149
Flanders, ———...................16
   Abigail......................322
   Ezekiel..................408, 410
   Hannah......................221
   Jeremiah..................77, 78
   Jonathan....................127
   Mary....................320-323
   Mehitabel............77, 321, 322
   Onesiphorous............321, 322
   Philip.......................221
   Rhoda......................322
   Samuel..................320-322
   Sarah (Jones)............408, 410
   Thomas.....................386
Fletcher, Francis..................526
   Gershom....................247
   John...................210, 333
   Peter.......................526
   Robert.................567, 568
Fogg, Abner......................249
   Daniel..................170-172
   Eleanor (Philbrick)...........417
   Hannah.................170-172
   James.......................355
   Jeremiah...........170, 171, 355
   Samuel.....................279
   Sarah..................172, 355
   William.....................129
Follansbee, Thomas...............428

Follansbee, *continued.*
   William.................325, 326
Folsom, Elizabeth (Sanborn).......256
   Ephraim....................186
   John.............56, 57, 250, 251
              253, 364, 380, 433, 534
   Nathaniel............87, 342, 346
              376, 377, 380, 511
   Peter...................360, 570
Footman, Francis.................382
Forbush, Benoni..................353
   Mary.......................353
Ford, John...................127, 129
Foss, Comfort....................457
   Elizabeth...................457
   Isaac...............227, 456, 457
   Isaac C..................456, 457
   Sarah......................456
   Sarah (m. Burleigh)...........456
   Thomas.................456, 457
   Zachariah...................512
Foster, Abijah................525, 526
   Asa....................393, 500
   Mary...................525, 526
   Samuel.....................526
Fowler, Jacob....................543
Fox, Mary (Sanborn)..............256
Freese, Jacob.................175, 267
French, ———....................467
   Ann (m. Clough).............301
   Anna (m. Roby).............301
   Deborah.................140, 141
   Eleazer.....................210
   Ezekiel.................139, 140
   Green..................139, 141
   Hannah.................140-142
   Hannah (Hills)..............413
   Henry..................139-141
   Jacob......................301
   James............141, 499, 566
   Jane (m. Winslow)...........301
   Jemima (m. Sanborn).........301
   Joseph.........58, 142, 401, 403
   Mary..............139-142, 499
   Mary (m. Peavey)...........301
   Moses......................142

French, *continued.*
 Nathaniel....................278
 Rachel (m. Clough)...........301
 Reuben...............139, 140, 142
 Ruth....................139, 141
 Samuel...53, 139-142, 301, 338, 436
 Samuel, Jr............139, 141, 142
 Thomas......................323
 Widow.......................446
 William.....................301
Frost, George....................380
 Samuel......................507
 William.....................526
Furber, Mary (Stoodley).......376, 377
 Nathaniel...................332

Gage, Benjamin..................8, 547
 Daniel..................163, 168
 Deborah.......................8
 John, Jr.................67, 78
 William.......................8
Gains, George............295, 296, 554
Gale, Amos..................555, 556
 Benjamin....................555
 Daniel..............229, 554-556
 Eli....................555, 556
 Eliphalet...................555
 Jacob..................554-556
 John C......................555
 Mary........................555
 Stephen.....................555
 Susanna................554, 556
 Susanna (m. Batchelder)......555
Gardner, John....................156
Garfield, Benjamin...............388
 Eunice......................388
Garland, Abigail (m. Marston)....532
 Jacob.......................318
 Jonathan...............532, 533
 Joseph.................271, 532
 Mary...................532, 533
 Rachel (m. Johnson).........532
 Samuel......................533
 Sarah (m. Tuck).............532
Garvin, James.........69, 308, 310, 311
Gault, Elizabeth.................393

Gault, *continued.*
 Matthew....................393
 Samuel.....................393
Gerrish, John.................85, 86
 Prudence (Horney).........85, 86
 Samuel..................511, 515
Gibbs, Jonathan....................6
Gibson, John.....................44
 Samuel.....................508
Giddings, John...................130
 Zebulon....................360
Gilchrist, Alexander..........285, 286
 William....................334
Gile, Asa........................127
 Ebenezer................70, 412
 Sarah (Nealey).............128
Gillis, Hugh.....................26
Gilman, Abigail..............105, 106
 Andrew.................166, 167
 Anna (m. Leavitt)..........167
 Antipas....................186
 Caleb..................269, 270
 Constantine................361
 Daniel.........85, 278, 368, 564
 Daniel, 3d.................498
 Deborah................359, 360
 Dorothy (Sherburne)..196, 199, 202
 Eliphalet..................130
 Jacob......................105
 James..................130, 360
 Jeremiah...............166, 167
 John..............335, 350, 390
 John, Jr......120, 167, 335, 350, 351
 John M.....................106
 Jonathan........106, 132, 138, 176
 Mary...................278, 279
 Nicholas...............350, 351
 Peter..........106, 197, 202, 503
 Samuel.................189, 357
 Stephen................106, 278
 Theophilus.........342, 346, 350
 Timothy....................359
Gilmore, Agnes (m. Gilmore)......258
 David......................258
 James..................257-259
 Janet (m. Armour).......257, 258

INDEX

Gilmore, *continued.*
    Margaret................257, 258
    Margaret (m. Stewart).........258
    Mary (m. McAdams)..........257
Glidden, Elizabeth................115
    John........................170
    Jonathan................186, 187
    Richard......................119
Glines, Ann........................42
    Elizabeth.....................43
    Israel........................42
    James........................43
    John......................42-44
    Mary......................42, 43
    Nathaniel.....................43
    Richard....................43, 44
    William....................43, 44
Godfrey, Abigail..................327
    Hannah (Redman)............261
    Joseph..............204, 321, 323
    Nathan......................261
    Simon.......................327
Goffe, John........38, 232, 247, 369, 374
              388, 430, 476, 507, 508
    Sarah.......................247
Goodhue, Abigail (m. Ambrose).....476
    Samuel......................476
Gooding, James.................46, 47
    Robert........................47
    Susanna......................47
    Susanna (m. Palmer)...........47
    Zerviah.......................47
Goodwin, Daniel........39, 220, 369, 370
    David........................39
    James........................47
    Nathan......................492
Gookin, Elizabeth................377
    Love.........................55
    Nathaniel...............377, 380
Gordon, Abigail (Judkins)..........224
    Abigail (m. Roberts)..........188
    Benjamin................188, 189
    Benoni......................187
    Daniel..................186, 187
    Dinah (m. Magoon)...........188
    Hannah (m. Smith)...........188

Gordon, *continued.*
    James.......................187
    Nathaniel.......145, 160, 188, 189
    Thomas.............186, 187, 189
    Timothy....................187
Goss, Deborah....................84
    Nathan.......................84
    Nathaniel......................5
    Richard.......................5
Gould, ———......................61
    Abigail (m. Pike).............402
    Christopher....77, 78, 402, 408, 409
    Esther......................373
    Joseph...................90, 402
    Nehemiah...................373
Gove, Daniel.......21, 464, 467, 470, 471
    David..........461, 465, 469-471
    Edward.461, 464, 466, 467, 469-471
    Edward, Jr................460, 461
    Eleazer......446, 447, 450, 454, 455
    Enoch...........444-448, 451, 455
    Enoch, Jr................454, 455
    Hannah.................444-446
    Hannah (Worthen)............20
    Hannah (m. Brown).......449, 450
    Hannah (m. Chase)...........454
    Jeremiah....................465
    John...............460, 461, 463
    Jonathan..........20, 21, 127, 129
             354, 465, 467, 468, 470, 471
    Margaret (m. Greenleaf)...449-451
    Martha.....................461
    Mary.............446, 448, 449, 451
    Mary (m. Perkins)............454
    Nathan.........446-449, 451, 455
    Nathaniel............110, 111, 353
                444, 445, 461, 463
    Obadiah.............465, 468-471
    Peggy (m. Greenleaf)......454, 455
    Rachel (m. Chase) 448-450, 454, 455
    Ruth............460, 461, 463-466
    Ruth (m. Green)......466, 469, 471
    Sarah (m. Blake)..448-450, 454, 455
    William.........448, 449, 451, 455
Graham, Arthur..................389
    Eleanor.....................389

Graham, *continued.*
  Hugh........................390
Grant, Daniel...............335, 476
Graves, Benjamin................189
  Elizabeth......................73
  Jacob..........................74
  James..................122, 357, 441
  John........................73-75
  William......................74, 75
Gray, Samuel....................353
Greeley, Ezekiel............78, 430, 490
  Jonathan..........49, 50, 63, 569
  Joseph......................98, 99
  Joseph, Jr............193, 281, 461
  Richard...................150, 394
  Samuel.................150, 166, 237
  Samuel, Jr......150, 166, 183, 237
Green, Daniel C.................231
  David...................135, 529
  Eleazer, Jr...................552
  John.................173, 290, 497
  Jonathan.................318, 529
  Nathan........................303
  Peter.........................373
  Ruth (Gove).........466, 469, 471
Greenfield, Samuel...............261
Greenleaf, Margaret (Gove)....449-451
  Paul............231, 449, 454, 455
  Peggy (Gove)............454, 455
  William.......................567
Greenwood, Thales.........71, 99, 442
Greer, Mary (Nutt)...............182
Gregg, James....................420
Griffin, Isaac...............147, 148
  Mary.....................147, 148
Griffith, Elizabeth...............558
  Gershom.......................56
  John........102, 105, 514, 515, 526
  Mary (Lunt)................56, 57
  Olive.........................558
  Samuel...................86, 444
Grouard, James...................71
Grove, Alice (Jenkins)............76
Grow, Ebenezer..................568
  Elijah........................568
  Hannah.......................568

Grow, *continued.*
  Isaac.........................568
  Sarah.........................568
Gunnison, John..................553

Hackett, Ephraim.................44
Hadley, Abigail..................412
  Anna.........................327
  Daniel.......................328
  David........................328
  Dorothy......................412
  Eleanor......................412
  Elizabeth....................328
  Esther.......................328
  Hannah..................327, 328
  Hepzibah.....................412
  Jonathan................411, 412
  Joseph.............327, 328, 493
  Judith..................411, 412
  Mary.........................328
  Nehemiah.....................348
  Ruth.........................412
  Samuel.............328, 411, 412
  Sarah........................412
  Susanna......................328
Haines, Abner....................55
  Anna.........................534
  David........................540
  Elizabeth (m. Jones).........541
  John........108, 250, 252, 253, 540
  John S.......................568
  Joseph..................250, 251
  Lydia (Cate)..................84
  Margaret (m. Johnson)........540
  Mary.........................538
  Mary (m. Johnson)............541
  Matthias.......392, 393, 539-541
  Samuel...................36, 534
  Sarah.........................55
  Sarah (Whidden)...............36
  Sarah (m. Locke).............540
  William.....249, 392, 393, 538-541
  William, Jr................56, 249
Hale, Benjamin................9-11
  Ebenezer......................9
  Enoch........................240

Hale, *continued.*
   Hannah 9, 10, 295
   Henry 183
   John 83, 337, 338, 491, 492, 569
   Mary 8, 10, 11
   Mary (m. Noyes) 9
   Samuel 6, 359, 387, 483, 491
   Samuel, Jr. 130, 240
                    430, 476, 511, 550
   Sarah 9–11
   Thomas 8–11, 174, 277, 349
Haley, Stephen 264
Hall, Henry 423
   John 121, 122, 163
         220, 281, 329, 414, 415, 534, 537
   John, Jr. 163, 165, 179, 220
   Jonathan 477
   Joseph 64, 76, 241
   Mary (Hazelton) 325
   Ralph 163, 165
   Samuel 220
   Thomas 122, 277
Ham, Betty (Roberts) 308, 311
   Ephraim 99, 100
   George 156
   John 308
   Patience (Harford) 291
   Robert 376, 377, 380
   Samuel 514
   William 440
Hamblett, John 347
   Joseph 168
   Josiah 168, 347
Hamilton, Samuel 357
Hanson, Benjamin 306
   Daniel 92
   Ebenezer 92
   Ephraim 79, 315, 404, 406
   George 66, 305, 306
   Hannah 305, 306
   Humphrey 306
   Isaac 66, 91, 92, 304, 306
   Isaac, Jr. 92
   John 92, 418, 441
   John B. 315, 381

Hanson, *continued.*
   Joseph 66, 162
          242, 304, 315, 403, 404, 406
   Joseph, Jr. 65, 67, 304
   Lydia (m. Watson) 305
   Rose 306, 307
   Sarah 91, 92, 306
   Susanna 304, 306
   Susanna (Canney) 240
   Tobias 305, 306
Hardy, Biley 130
   Dudley 130
   Love 184–186
   Mary 130, 184–186
   Nathaniel 184–186
   Robert 130
   Samuel 381
   Sarah 184–186, 381
   Theophilus 184–186, 591
Harford, Ann (m. Evers) 291
   Betty (m. Mace) 291
   Elizabeth 291
   Elizabeth (m. Nethersell) 291
   Joseph 291
   Patience (m. Ham) 291
Harriman, Joseph 21
   Mary (Page) 59
   Stephen 174
Harris, Ebenezer 246
   William 269
Hart, Daniel 377
   David 380
   George 71
   John 353, 387, 388, 484
   John, Jr. 387
   Richard 526
   Robert 528
   Samuel 293, 357
   Thomas 304, 307, 330
Harvell, John 489, 566
Harvey, Francis 123
   John 127, 129
   Richard 421
   Robert 73, 189, 367, 476
   William S. 388
Hastings, John 550

Hastings, *continued.*
    John, Jr..........510, 550, 552, 553
    Silvanus....................510
    Susanna (Johnson)............510
Hatch, Thomas....................526
Haven, Samuel.........6, 197, 200–203
Hawley, Joseph...................525
Hayes, Amos M...................531
    Ichabod.......................66
    Paul........................79, 80
    Samuel......................79, 80
    Tamson (Drew)..............79, 80
    Wentworth...................531
Hazeltine, Henry.................265
    Joanna (Hills)................413
Hazelton, Belle..................326
    Deacon......................325
    Ephraim.................324, 327
    James.......................326
    John....................324–326
    Mary........................324
    Mary (m. Hall)...............325
    Samuel......................325
    Thomas..................324, 327
Heald, Timothy..................526
Healey, Nathaniel............120, 511
    Nathaniel, Jr..........120, 133, 173
    Sarah (Batchelder).......480, 482
Heard, Samuel, Jr................292
Heath, ———......................25
    Bartholomew.............265, 492
    Miriam......................277
    Richard.................174, 277
    Sargent......................53
Henderson, Howard........79, 80, 594
Hewitt, James....................274
Heywood, William........510, 550, 551
Hicks, Joseph....................359
Hight, Charles...................507
    John........................483
Hildreth, Levi...................168
Hill, ———.......................253
    Abigail (m. Jackson)..........591
    Benjamin................590, 591
    Jacob.......................326
    Joshua...................85, 204

Hill, *continued.*
    Patience....................590
    Reuben.....................127
    Robert..................590, 591
    Samuel.....................237
    Sobriety....................591
    William.................590, 591
Hilliard, Benjamin............302, 303
    Elizabeth...................302
    Hannah.....................302
    Huldah (Moulton)........135, 136
    Jonathan................301–304
    Joseph......................301
    Joseph C.............136, 303, 304
    Mary....................301–303
    Mercy...................302–304
    Nannie......................302
    Rachel (m. Sanborn)..........302
Hills, Abigail (m. Moody).........413
    Abner.......................413
    Benjamin................413, 414
    Dorcas......................150
    Ezekiel..................150, 183
    Hannah (m. French)..........413
    Henry......................150
    Joanna (m. Hazeltine)........413
    Moses......................414
    Prudence (m. Chase)..........413
    Rebecca....................413
    Samuel.............150, 166, 413
Hilton, Edward................29, 323
    Josiah........29, 231, 273, 323, 560
    Martha (Weeks)..............2–4
    Mary.......................323
    Sarah (Ames)................29
    Winthrop..........2, 158, 360, 570
Hinsdale, ——— (m. Beal)........524
    Abigail.............521, 523, 525
    Darius..................523, 524
    Ebenezer................521, 525
    John........................522
    Samuel..................521, 523
Hixon, Honor (Horney)............85
    Joseph...................85, 520
Hoag, Enoch.................306, 440
    John........................185

INDEX 617

Hoag, *continued.*
  Nathan..............53, 54, 204
Hobart, David...........81, 137, 338
  Samuel...................83, 167
        337, 338, 491, 492, 545, 569
Hobbs, Anna (Simonds)............57
  Benjamin..................44, 45
  Hepzibah......................88
  Humphrey.....................57
  James..............167, 220, 284
  John....................461, 462
        580, 582, 583, 585-587
  Joseph.......................45
  Mary.........................45
  Mercy........................44
  Nathaniel.................44, 45
  Nehemiah.....................89
  Noah......................88-90
  Patience.....................87
  Patience (Towle).........213, 216
  Samuel....................88-90
  Simon.......................567
  Stephen...............87, 89, 90
Hodgdon, Caleb..................305
  Israel..................418, 441
  Joseph..................127, 129
  Mary (Nealey)...........128, 129
  Shadrach.....................80
Hogg, John...87, 153, 169, 281, 304, 320
Hoit, Jonathan...................32
Holland, John, Jr...............282
Holmes, Benjamin................518
  James.......................518
  Jeremiah....................518
  John........................518
Holt, John......................552
Honey, Gideon....................91
  Hannah.......................91
Hook, Dyer.................115, 116
Hooker, William............212, 332
Hopkins, David..................145
  Elizabeth...................535
  John........................260
  William.....................535
Hopkinson, Jonathan..............22
Horne, George...................373

Horne, *continued.*
  Isaac.......................280
  Nathaniel....................96
Horney, Betty....................85
  David.....................85, 86
  Gilbert......................85
  Hannah....................85, 86
  Hannah (Buss)...........292-296
  Honor (m. Hixon).............85
  John.........................85
  Mary.........................85
  Peter........................52
  Prudence (m. Gerrish)......85, 86
Houston, Alexander..............395
  Hannah......................389
  John........................389
  Noah........................389
  Samuel......................395
Howe, Elizabeth (Kimball).......547
  Ichabod.....................526
  Jotham......................546
  Mary (Kimball)..............547
  Peter.......................500
Hoyt, Abner.....................570
  Benjamin....................371
  Daniel..................189, 190
  Jacob........................13
  Judah.......................190
  Micah.......................371
  Richard.....................335
  Samuel......................371
Hubbard, Jeremiah............17, 130
  Jonathan................551, 552
  Samuel......................552
Huckins, Meribah (Jackson).......28
  Robert.......................28
Hunking, Mark..............211, 386
Hunt, Elizabeth.................437
  Enoch....................81, 567
  Lydia...................436, 437
  Nathan..................436, 437
  Samuel......................550
Huntoon, Daniel.................323
  Joanna......................323
  John........................104
  Josiah..................29, 323

618   INDEX

Huntoon, *continued.*
  Nathaniel 318
Huntress, Abigail (m. Coleman) 233
  Elizabeth (m. Fabyan) 233
  George 233
  John 234
  Joseph 233, 234
  Mary 233, 234
  Samuel 232–234
  Solomon 233
  William 233, 234
Hussey, Silvanus 291, 440
Hutchinson, Abigail 225
  Daniel 167, 168
  John 225, 476
  Martha 476
  Nathan 57

Ingalls, Benjamin 567
  Eldad 248, 249
  John 235, 248
Innes, Samuel 391

Jackson, Abigail (Hill) 591
  Benjamin 27, 28
  Clement 86, 295, 487
  Daniel 368, 526
  Dorothy 331, 332
  Dorothy (m. Whipple) 331
  Elisha 526, 527
  Elizabeth 254
  Elizabeth (m. Churchill) ... 331, 332
  Ephraim 331, 332
  Ephraim, Jr. 332
  Hannah 527
  Hannah (m. Bestow) 331, 332
  James 591
  Jeffry 331
  Johnson 331
  Jonathan 254
  Joseph 253, 331, 489, 490
  Joshua 211
  Margaret 254
  Mary 27, 253, 254
  Mary (m. Monson) 331, 332
  Meribah (m. Huckins) 28

Jackson, *continued.*
  Nathaniel 211, 253, 255, 276
  Richard 253–255
  Samuel 211, 253–255
  Sarah 254
  Thomas 253
  William 27, 28, 331, 332
Jaffrey, George 421
James, Israel 18
  John 288
  Susanna (Stevens) 486
Jameson, Thomas 590
Janvrin, George 479, 490
  John 454
Jaques, Daniel 8
Jeffry, James 36
Jenkins, Alice (m. Grove) 76
  Hannah (Whidden) 36
  Mary 76
  Mary (m. Ayers) 76
  William 36, 76, 77
Jenness, Francis 159
  Hannah (Dow) 93
  Joshua 534
  Nathaniel 93
  Richard, Jr. 46
  Richard, 3d 154, 156, 170–172
    249–251, 253, 364, 366, 397, 534
                            542, 570
  Samuel 542, 543
Jewell, Barnes 401
  Dorothy 401
  Joseph 401, 402, 406
  Mark 184
  Samuel 61
Jewett, Ezekiel 416
  Jonathan 397
  Samuel 416
  Stephen 83
Johnson, Abraham 541
  Benjamin 532
  Dorothy (Smith) 290
  Ebenezer 249, 250
  Ebenezer, Jr. 541
  James 36, 510
  John 163, 165, 168, 328, 334

Johnson, *continued.*
    Jonathan....................337
    Margaret....................540
    Margaret (Cate)...............84
    Margaret (Haines).............540
    Mary (Haines)................541
    Nathan...........57, 361, 363, 366
    Noah....................336, 389
    Obadiah.....................290
    Peter........................93
    Philip.......................515
    Rachel (Garland).............532
    Sarah (Dow)..................93
    Stephen..............123, 153, 527
    Stephen, Jr................152, 153
    Susanna.....................510
    Susanna (m. Hastings).........510
    Thomas.............169, 264, 265
    William.....................364
Jones, Abigail................430, 431
    Abigail (m. Jones).........431, 432
    Ann (Whidden)................36
    Benjamin....................431
    Daniel..........401, 406, 408, 410
    Ebenezer....................431
    Elizabeth (Haines)............541
    Evan........................164
    Hannah (m. Elliott).......407, 409
    Jacob.......................402
    John.....36, 407, 410, 430–432, 540
    Jonathan............401–403, 406
    Joseph......................411
    Judith..................408, 410
    Mehitabel...........401, 408, 409
    Miriam..................408, 409
    Moses...................407, 409
    Nathan......................436
    Samuel..........402, 403, 407, 409
    Sarah (m. Flanders).......408, 410
    Stephen................28, 69, 101
    Timothy............327, 356, 357
    William......................92
Jose, Ebenezer...............518–520
    Joanna......................519
    Margaret................519, 520
    Michael D...................519

Jose, *continued.*
    Richard.....................520
Judkins, Abigail (m. Gordon)......224
    Anna.......................223
    Benjamin...................298
    Joel...................222, 225
    John....................50, 115
    Jonathan................224, 226
    Joseph.........222–225, 357, 421
    Mary (m. Bean).............224
    Rebecca....................224
    Rebecca (m. Lord)...........224
    Ruth (Choate)...............298
    Samuel..................223–225
    Sarah...................223–225
    Zachariah...............224, 226

Keene, Samuel...................326
Kelly, Elizabeth (m. Bedel)....237, 238
    Joseph..................237, 238
    Judith......................178
    Mary....................237, 238
    Moses......................420
    Richard.....................178
    Ruth....................237, 238
    William.....................178
Kelsey, James............124, 126, 319
    Robert..................350, 351
Kendall, Ebenezer................336
    Lucy (Cummings).........336, 337
Kendrick, Dudley.................496
    Mary (Williams)..............496
Kennedy, William.................357
Kenney, Samuel..................526
Kennison, Waldron................229
Kenniston, James.................456
Kent, John...................234, 235
Kezar, John......................153
Kidder, Aaron...............174, 526
    Benjamin............38, 368, 369
    Benjamin, Jr.................369
    Job........................508
    John................38, 368, 369
    Joseph.....................545
    Nathan.....................418
    Reuben.............174, 544, 545

620   INDEX

Kielle, James 34, 35, 86, 307
     315, 341, 353, 419, 430
Kimball, Aaron 546, 547
 Abel 546
 Abraham 546, 547
 Caleb 170, 175
 Ebenezer 234
 Elizabeth (m. Howe) 547
 Esther (m. Wheeler) 164
 Hannah (m. Wheeler) 164
 Jemima 163
 Jemima (m. Webster) 163
 Joanna 37
 John 347
 Jonathan 69, 370
 Joseph 189, 234, 235
 Mary (m. Howe) 547
 Nathan 547
 Nathaniel 546
 Patty 235
 Phineas 546
 Richard 163-165
 Robert 269, 270
 Ruth 547
 Samuel . . 291, 428, 498, 499, 546, 547
 Sarah 234, 235
 Susanna 546, 547
 Thomas, Jr. 37
 Timothy 546, 547
King, Benjamin 545
 James 483
 William 567
Knight, John 10, 11, 13, 265
 John, Jr. 395
 Joseph 289
 Nathaniel 10, 12
 Tristram . 245, 277, 278, 290, 330, 423
 William 42, 514
Knowles, Jane (Palmer) 442, 443
 Joseph 45
 Samuel 170-172, 442

Ladd, Alice 334
 Daniel 334, 335
 Dudley 540
 Elizabeth 39

Ladd, *continued.*
 John 39
 Josiah 185
 Nathaniel 186, 335, 540
 Timothy . 165, 244, 245, 290, 330, 420
 Trueworthy 39, 40
Lamont, Neil 520
Lamprey, John 95, 444
Lamson, Samuel 137, 400
Lancey, William 137
Lane, Elizabeth (Bruce) 368
 Jeremiah 451, 463
       470, 511, 570, 578
 John 368
 Joshua 213
 Samuel 107, 559
Lang, Abigail 105
 Benjamin 396
 Catherine 101
 Daniel 101-103
 John 396, 539, 541
 Mark 396, 397
 Martha 101
 Molly 396
 Moses 101, 102
 Nathaniel 101
 Robert 102, 105
 Ruth (Sherburne) 392
 Sarah 101
 Susanna 395, 397
 Susanna (m. Yeaton) 396
 Thomas 396
 William 395-397
Langdon Ann (Sherburne) . . 196, 199, 202
 John 38, 51, 52, 58, 367, 386, 513
 John, Jr. 335, 507, 511-513
 Joseph 154, 156, 197, 202
 Mark 183, 195, 274, 444, 479
 Samuel 37, 197, 200-203
Larabee, Elizabeth (Weston) 400
Lavers, Jacob 373, 507
Lawrence, Abel 552
 David 18, 19, 190, 338
 Jeremiah 143
 William 373
 Zachariah 112, 114

Lear, Walker................154
Leavitt, Abigail..............107
   Anna (Gilman)............167
   Benjamin..................37
   Captain...................99
   Daniel............166, 167, 511
   Elisha...................356
   Elizabeth................356
   Elizabeth (Merrill)..........549
   Elizabeth (m. Bickford).......106
   Ephraim..............106, 107
   Gilman...................167
   Hannah (m. Dudley).........106
   James..............213, 215, 216
               282, 283, 435, 582
   Jeremiah...............37, 279
   John.....................106
   Jonathan.............106, 107
   Josiah...................549
   Martha...................107
   Martha (m. Dolloff).........106
   Mary.............167, 264, 279
   Mary (m. Connor)...........280
   Moses....................264
   Samuel..........30, 106, 107, 559
   Sarah....................106
   Sarah (Dudley).............242
   Sarah (m. Dearborn).........264
   Sarah (m. Wadleigh).........106
   Stephen...............107, 167
   Susanna..................107
Lee, Joseph..................333
   Margaret.................144
Leighton, Hatevil, Jr............427
   Sarah...................404
   Solomon.................404
   Thomas..................528
   Tobias...................427
   William..................427
Leslie, Alexander..............501
   Daniel...................501
   Hannah..................501
Lester, John..................261
Lewis, William..........99, 100, 103
Libby, Abigail (Titcomb).........340
   Benjamin................341

Libby, *continued.*
   George........70, 330, 358, 442, 487
   Ichabod..................535
   Isaac....................532
   Jeremiah.........69-71, 211, 221
   Jeremiah, Jr..............70, 71
   John......................71
   Paul....................532
   Sarah....................70
Liggett, Catherine (m. McConechey) 394
   Effie (m. Smith)............394
   James...................394
   John....................394
   Samuel..................394
Light, Deborah................86
   Ebenezer.................151
   John.....................86
Litch, William................349
Little, Benjamin...............153
   Captain..................57
   Daniel..........25, 49, 234, 235
               330, 412, 423, 492
   Edna (m. Ela).............248
   Ezekiel..................248
   George...............247, 248
   Joseph............248, 249, 330
   Mary....................277
   Samuel.............11, 13, 497
   Samuel, Jr.............401, 420
   Thomas...25, 169, 235, 247, 277, 278
Littlehale, Elizabeth............486
   Hannah..............167, 168
   Isaac................167, 168
Livermore, Matthew............86
   Samuel...............368, 373
Locke, Edward................321
   Francis...............542, 543
   Jonathan.............444, 540
   Margaret.................281
   Patience.................540
   Sarah (Haines)............540
   Timothy B................455
   Ward....................281
Long, Ebenezer.............49, 286
   John....................395
   Nathan..................414

622 INDEX

Long, *continued*.
   Richard....................565
Longfellow, Jonathan......129, 197, 230
Lord, Esther.....................52
   Hannah.....................52
   Jonathan............51, 52, 342
   Rebecca (Judkins)............224
   Thomas.....................51
Loud, Jonathan..............283, 545
   Solomon....................315
   Solomon, Jr....60, 69, 123, 189, 237
         393, 435, 440, 500, 528, 537
         541, 545, 553, 556, 566, 591
Lougee, Edmund...............51, 52
   Gilman.....................537
   Joseph...............51, 52, 170
Love, John.......................95
Lovejoy, Henry..................500
Lovell, James....................567
Lovering, Ebenezer...............461
   Moses...................175, 176
   Samuel.....................518
   William....................518
Lovewell, John..............211, 333
   Jonathan............91, 137, 143
      210, 211, 246, 247, 333, 336, 346
      389, 490, 543, 545, 546, 566–568
   Nehemiah..........137, 389, 512
   Rachel.....................490
   Zaccheus................239, 336
Lowe, Jacob................381, 550
   Joseph.................440, 527
Lund, Ephraim...............52, 338
   Jonathan...............246, 546
   Phineas................210, 543
   Rachel......................52
   Thomas......52, 210, 211, 246, 543
   William....................210
Lunt, ——— (m. Drake)...........55
   Abraham....................54
   Daniel...................54–57
   Henry......................55
   James....................55, 57
   Job........................55
   John.....................55, 57
   Love......................128

Lunt, *continued*.
   Mary.......................54
   Mary (m. Griffith).........56, 57
   Mary (m. Wingate).........55, 57
   Samuel..................55, 57
Lyford, Biley....................145
   Mehitabel (Smith)........433, 434
   Moses..................435, 537
   Oliver S...................434
Lynn, Agnes....................182
   Joseph................22, 23, 182
   Nathaniel..................182
Lyon, Ebenezer..................137

McAdams, James.................258
   Janet......................257
   John.......................257
   Margaret...................257
   Mary (Gilmore).............257
   Samuel.....................257
McAllister, David................397
   John.......................397
McCalley, James.................414
   Jane.......................414
McCargin, Dinah (m. Robertson)...527
   Philip..................527, 528
McCarrell, Ann..................182
McClintock, Samuel..............362
McConechey, Archibald...........394
   Catherine (Liggett)..........394
   Janet (m. Orr).............26, 27
   John......................26, 27
   Martha....................26, 27
   Mary......................26, 27
   Samuel....................26, 27
McCrillis, John..............123, 367
   John, Jr...................367
Mace, Betty (Harford)............291
McFee, John....................178
McGregore, David.................48
   James..........181, 430, 501, 592
   Margaret...................592
Mack, Agnes....................589
   Archibald..................589
   James......................589
   John.......................589

Mack, *continued.*
   Martha....................589
   Robert....................589
   Susanna...................589
   William...................589
McKeen, Samuel................389
McMurphy, Alexander.....29, 277, 395
   Jane......................394
   John.......................29
   Robert....................394
McNeil, Abraham...............121
   Elizabeth.................121
   Janet.....................121
   Jean.................121, 122
   John......................418
   Mary......................121
   Richard...................121
   Robert....................121
   William...................121
McQuesten, William, Jr............489
Magoon, Dinah (Gordon)..........188
Main, Abigail...................531
   Amos.................529, 532
   Elizabeth.............529, 531
   Hannah....................531
   Josiah...............530-532
   Lydia.....................531
   Mary......................531
   Mercy.....................531
   Pomp......................530
Mann, Mary....................341
   Nathan....................341
Mannering, John..................5
   Sarah......................5
Marble, Ann (Currier)............244
   Jonathan..................422
March, Clement.................36
   Joseph................79, 110
   Paul..................249, 289
   Stephen.................5, 484
Marcy. See also Massey.
   Daniel....................164
Marsh, Abigail..................592
   Ephraim..............591, 592
   Hannah....................592
   John.................150, 592

Marsh, *continued.*
   Phoebe....................592
   Ruth......................592
   Samuel....................592
   Thomas....................150
Marshall, Comfort...............3, 4
   Daniel....................237
   George........2, 3, 41, 42, 211, 255
   John.....2, 3, 99, 100, 112, 209, 332
   Margaret..................3, 4
   Thankful (Weeks)...........2, 3
   William..............261, 262
Marston, ———................447
   Abigail (Garland)...........532
   Anna......................177
   Daniel...............176-178
   David................177, 532
   Mary.......................57
   Mehitabel..................45
   Miriam....................177
   Roby.................176, 177
   Samuel...............176-178
   Sarah................176-178
   Simon.............57, 177, 178
   Theodore..................177
   William............74, 75, 260
Martin, Elizabeth............211, 212
   John......................387
   Nolar.....................211
Mason, Esther (Weymouth).......373
   John....................7, 373
   John T.........302, 447, 448, 481
   Lemuel....................560
   Mary......................560
   Mary (Nealey)..........125, 126
   Robert....................560
   Susanna...................560
   Temperance................560
Massey. See also Marcy.
   Daniel............163, 165, 220
Mathes, Benjamin.....35, 359, 431, 432
   Valentine............34, 315, 381
Mattis, John....................16
Mattoon, Hubartus..............543
   John......................543
Mead, Hannah..................428

INDEX

Mead, *continued.*
  Joseph.....................429
  Margaret...................429
  Thomas................428, 429
Meader, Daniel.............424–427
  David..................425, 426
  John...................425, 426
  Joseph............424, 425, 427
  Mark.......................427
  Martha (Canney)............240
  Nicholas...............424, 427
  Samuel.................425, 427
  Sarah..................424, 427
  Stephen................426, 427
  Thomas.................426, 427
Melcher, Deborah................460
Melvin, Abraham.................262
  Benjamin...............262, 263
  Elizabeth...................262
  Jean.......................263
  John.......................263
  Lydia......................263
  Mary...................262–264
  Patrick.................262, 263
  Sarah......................263
Mendum, Nathaniel..............191
Merrill, Abel............10, 346, 347
  Abraham...................121
  Amos..................534, 537
  Benjamin...............549, 550
  Charity....................547
  Daniel.................347, 548
  Eliphalet.......195, 279, 401, 406
  Elizabeth (m. Leavitt)........549
  Esther.....................549
  Giles......................570
  Isaac......................347
  James.............114, 115, 548
  James, Jr...................356
  John...................236, 237
  John, Jr....................236
  Joseph..........391, 547, 548, 550
  Joshua......................10
  Nathaniel...........164, 165, 347
  Peter..................164, 178
                220, 367, 534, 537

Merrill, *continued.*
  Phineas..................32–34
  Rachel.....................346
  Rebecca...............346, 347
  Samuel................346, 347
  Samuel, Jr.............346, 347
Meserve, George......289, 386, 387, 483
  Hanson....................483
  Henry.....................387
  Jane..................387, 388
  John......................514
  Mary..................388, 489
  Nathaniel..........289, 387, 483
  Nathaniel, Jr..............386
  Sarah..............386, 387, 514
  Sarah (m. Wheeler)..........387
Mills, Jacob....................484
  John...................122, 152
              348, 349, 395, 492, 493
  Luke...................208, 514
  William....................348
Minot, James...............238, 239
  Rebecca (Blanchard).........238
Mitchell, George................430
  John......................430
  John, Jr...............430, 431
Moffatt, John...................289
Monson, Mary (Jackson)......331, 332
Moody, Abigail (Hills)...........413
  Caleb, Jr..................495
Mooney, Hercules...........368, 545
Moore, ———.................253, 254
  Agnes.....................324
  Daniel......................27
  James......................27
  Jane (Cochran).........323, 324
  John............38, 285, 369, 592
  John, Jr...................286
  Margaret...................247
  Mary......................324
  Robert....................324
  Samuel......240, 247, 324, 348, 374
  Thomas, Jr................550
  William....................27
  William, Jr................550
  William, 3d................550

Morgan, Abiah..................159
   Anna........................159
   Benjamin....................159
   Betty.......................159
   Elizabeth...................159
   Hannah......................159
   Reuben......................159
   Susanna.....................159
   Timothy.................158, 159
Morrill, Aaron...................133
   Abner.....90, 91, 141, 195, 401, 406
   Benjamin....................141
   Dorothy (Bagley).............62
   Ephraim.....................322
   Ezekiel......................44
   Henry...........436, 437, 495, 496
   Jacob........................62
   John........................168
   Joseph..................350, 351
   Levi........................167
   Thomas.......................90
Morrison, Abram..................538
   David.............71, 73, 267, 538
   Ebenezer....................267
   James........73, 87, 128, 129, 319
   John.............87, 266, 267, 538
   Margaret..................72, 73
   Mary...................266, 267
   Mary (m. Perkins)............267
   Mary (m. Ray)................71
   Samuel..............87, 258, 525
   Sarah (m. Simpson)............72
   Thomas......................87
   William..................73, 319
Morse, Abigail...................266
   Abner.......................266
   Edmund.............412, 492, 493
   Jacob.......................266
   Joseph......................510
   Mary........................266
   Ruth........................266
   Sarah.......................266
Moses, George......................8
   James.......................102
Moulton, Abigail.................221
   Abigail (Williams)...........496

Moulton, *continued.*
   Abraham................135, 136
   Benjamin...............503, 511
   Daniel......................260
   Dorothy (m. Page)........135, 136
   Elizabeth..............135, 136
   Ezekiel......................75
   Huldah (m. Hilliard)......135, 136
   Jeremiah....................413
   John........................569
   Jonathan........326, 358, 445, 569
   Jonathan, Jr.................18
   Joseph..................221, 376
   Joseph, Jr..................364
   Josiah, Jr..................443
   Mary...................135, 136
   Nehemiah....................172
   Noah.........................46
   Reuben......................171
   Robert, 3d..............95, 444
   Stephen.....................496
   William......................45
Muchmore, Nathaniel.............351
Murphy, John................331, 332
Muzzey, Daniel..................163
   John....122, 123, 152, 153, 320, 527

Nahor, James....................489
Nason, Captain..................302
   Richard......118, 232, 303, 481, 508
Neal, Abigail...................558
   Abigail (m. Cate)............559
   Anna (m. Veasey)............559
   Catherine...............569, 570
   Hubartus................559, 570
   John........................110
   Joshua..............31, 107, 356
                   513, 558, 559
   Samuel......................569
   Walter......................570
Nealey, Andrew..............125, 127
   Jane (m. Sanborn)........125, 126
                      128, 129
   John....................123, 127
   Joseph..................125-129
   Margaret............123, 124, 126

626 INDEX

Nealey, *continued.*
    Margaret (m. Norris)......128, 129
    Mary (m. Hodgdon).......128, 129
    Mary (m. Mason).........125, 126
    Matthew........123, 124, 126, 127
    Sarah......................126
    Sarah (m. Gile)...............128
Nelson, Deliverance...........154, 156
    George.....................156
    James..................156, 386
    John....151, 154, 156, 295, 381, 386
    Jonathan...................235
    Mary (Caverly)..............275
    Matthew................154, 156
    Richard....................558
Nesmith, Arthur..............259, 260
    John, Jr....................144
    Margaret................259, 260
Nethersell, Elizabeth (Harford).....291
Nevin, David....................567
Newman, Benjamin...............261
    Patience (Redman)...........261
Newmarch, Benjamin.............114
    Joseph..............243, 348, 380
    Sarah......................114
    Thomas....................114
Newton, John....................17
Nichols, Ebenezer................399
    Mehitabel (Weston)...........400
Noble, Isabella (Crockford).....99, 100
    James......................329
    John........................99
    Moses.......................71
Norris, James......18, 19, 124, 126, 190
    Margaret (Nealey)........128, 129
Norton, John....................397
    Jonathan...................397
Noyes, Humphrey.............11, 499
    John...................393, 441
    Mary (Hale)..................9
    Stephen.....................12
Nudd, Abigail................313, 314
    Abigail (Thomas).............313
    James..................147, 314
    Martha.................313, 314
Nute, James.....................80

Nutt, David.....................263
    Jane.......................182
    John.......................182
    Mary......................182
    Mary (m. Greer).............182

Ober, Anna..................328, 329
    John.......................329
    John, Jr....................328
Odell, William...................400
Odiorne, Ebenezer............478, 529
    Elizabeth...............478, 479
    Jonathan...................387
    Jotham....................476
    Katharine (Sherburne)........478
    Thomas..361, 364, 366, 478, 479, 568
Odlin, John..............130, 282, 357
Olcott, Simeon..................552
Ordway, John...................401
    Nathan.................369, 370
    Nehemiah..................142
Orr, Alexander.................26, 27
    Janet (McConechey)........26, 27
Osgood, Anna (m. Stickney).........14
    Benjamin.................14-17
    Elizabeth (m. Webster).........14
    George.....................13
    Hannah..................13-17
    James...................13-17
    John....................14-17
    Lucy.......................13
    Phyllis.....................14
    Richard Hazzen............14-17
    Samuel.....................15
Otis, Elizabeth..................418
    John.......................418
    Joshua.....................418
    Stephen...................418
    Susanna...................418

Packer, Ann (Rindge).........437, 438
Page, Abigail..................18, 19
    Asa........................12
    David...................18, 354
    Dorothy (Moulton).......135, 136
    Elizabeth...................194

INDEX 627

Page, *continued*.
  Francis......................119
  Hepzibah (Towle)...........213
  Jabez.......................50
  James......................136
  John................18, 136, 216
  Jonathan........12, 216, 245, 420
      423, 462, 581, 583, 587, 588
  Joseph....................58-60
  Mary..58, 60, 462, 581, 583, 587, 588
  Mary (Towle)...............213
  Mary (m. Harriman)..........59
  Moses...................59, 245
  Onesiphorous...............354
  Patience.461, 466, 467, 470, 471, 475
  Samuel.............460, 461, 475
  Simon..................178, 584
  Theophilus....74, 461, 475, 517, 518
  Thomas....................216
  Timothy....................59
  William....................194
Paine, John.............292-294, 296
Pallet, Jane.....................57
  Joseph.....................57
Palmer, Anna................442, 443
  Barnabas...................51
  Daniel.................390, 391
  Elizabeth (m. Thurston).......390
  Hannah....................391
  Hannah (Clifford)............517
  Jane (m. Knowles)........442, 443
  John......................391
  Joseph.................390, 391
  Mehitabel..................391
  Samuel..........95, 442, 443, 533
  Samuel, Jr...............442, 443
  Samuel, 3d...............95, 533
  Sarah..................390, 391
  Susanna (Gooding)............47
  Thomas....................296
Park, Alexander.................525
  Joseph....................525
  Robert....................525
Parker, Abigail.............315, 569
  Benjamin..................534
  Catherine..................347

Parker, *continued*.
  Elizabeth..........239, 267, 557
  Isaac..............510, 550-553
  John..............115, 121, 123
      130, 387, 388, 430
  Lydia................10, 11, 518
  Mary......................342
  Mehitabel..................508
  Nathaniel...............129, 144
  Noah......................554
  Oliver....................240
  Samuel..160, 186, 268, 315, 376, 460
  Thomas..........38, 239, 353, 508
  Thomas, Jr..................359
  William....................6, 8
    10, 11, 18, 22, 27, 29, 30, 35, 37
    41, 46, 51, 53, 54, 60, 69, 70, 75
    77-81, 87, 92, 95, 104, 107, 110
    114, 115, 123, 127, 130, 133, 138
    145, 148-150, 153, 160, 162, 165
    167, 170, 171, 178, 183, 185, 186
    189, 191, 195, 197, 200, 201, 204
    205, 208, 211, 220, 222, 226, 229
    231, 235, 237, 238, 243, 245, 249
    255, 259, 262-264, 267, 268, 270
    273, 274, 276, 277, 279-284, 286
    289, 292, 293, 301, 304, 307, 312
    314, 315, 318-321, 327, 329, 330
    332, 334, 335, 342, 347, 349, 352
    355, 357, 360, 364, 367, 369, 373-
    375, 380, 381, 391, 393, 401, 403
    406, 414, 415, 418, 420, 421, 429
    431, 435, 440, 457, 483, 497, 498
    500, 501, 506-508, 510-513, 515
    518, 526, 528, 534, 535, 537, 541
    545, 553, 554, 556, 557, 566, 569
  William, Jr...........38, 115, 121
    123, 136, 169-171, 175, 238, 267
    279, 281, 304, 354, 355, 371, 375
    406, 428, 440, 461, 510, 518, 569
Parkes, Robert...............37, 527
Parkhurst, Joel..................333
Parsons, William................142
Pattee, Hannah.............268, 499
  Seth...................205, 423
Patten, Elizabeth................284

Patten, *continued.*
  John.........................26
  Matthew.....38, 277, 284, 369, 414
  Samuel...............27, 284, 353
Patterson, James..................146
  Peter.................48, 121, 122
  Rachel (Smith)..............146
  William.....................489
Pattinson, James..................234
  Joseph...............47, 48, 133
  Mary.........................47
  Thomas.....................274
Paul, James..................162, 205
  Margaret....................162
Peacock, Mary....................261
Pearne, William..................527
Pearse, Peter....................527
Pearson, Martha........342, 344, 345
  William.................191, 293
Pease, Nathaniel..................415
  Phoebe (m. Stevens)..........415
  Samuel......................415
  Zebulon.....................415
Peaslee, Amos....................427
  Daniel................8, 60, 163
  Elizabeth...................166
  Joseph....................53, 54
  Moses.....................53, 54
  Rebecca.....................166
Peavey, Anthony..................301
  John........................442
  Mary (French)...............301
  William.....................442
Pecker, Captain..................422
  Elizabeth....................25
  Hannah.......................25
  James........................25
  John.....................16, 25
Peirce, Anna.....................438
  Daniel..................41, 329
    352, 436, 483, 552, 553
  Joseph..................421, 507
  Nathaniel....................41
  Thomas......99, 100, 211, 528, 553
Pendexter, John..........148, 528, 553
Penhallow, John..................387

Penhallow, *continued.*
  Richard W..................554
  Samuel................41, 86, 99
    100, 103, 184, 191, 255, 289, 293
    329, 330, 332, 352, 376, 387, 388
    420, 444, 460, 484, 507, 514, 515
Perham, Amos...............545, 546
  Asa.........................545
  Elizabeth...................545
  John........................543
  Lemuel..................543, 544
  Lydia...................545, 546
  Mary........................545
  Samuel..................543-546
  Sarah.......................545
Perkins, Abraham...18, 19, 124, 126, 417
  Benjamin....................561
  David...................561, 562
  Elizabeth...................561
  Hannah......................562
  John.....................30, 267
  Jonathan....................281
  Joseph..231, 303, 359, 454, 561, 562
  Lydia (m. Swain)............561
  Mary (Gove).................454
  Mary (Morrison).............267
  Sarah.......................562
  Sarah (Wiggin)..............108
  William.....................373
Perryman, Nicholas..............120
Peters, Willett.................235
Pettengill, Benjamin.............12
Philbrick, Abigail..........45, 46, 417
  Abner..........354, 463, 470, 562
  Alley.......................417
  Caleb...................416, 417
  Daniel.......................46
  Eleanor (m. Fogg)...........417
  Elias.......................417
  Hannah.......................46
  John........................416
  Jonathan.........46, 82, 416, 417
  Joseph...........46, 454, 455, 533
  Joses....................45, 46
  Mary....................416, 417
  Nathaniel...................417

Philbrick, *continued.*
   Priscilla.................251, 252
   Reuben......................46
   Ruth.......................417
   Samuel.....................416
   Sarah.......................46
   Tryphena....................46
Philbrook, Caleb................392
   Mary.......................392
   Robert T.....249, 251, 252, 361, 362
Philpot, James..................307
Pickering, John.............115, 514
   Joshua...............56, 57, 568
   Joshua, Jr...............364, 568
   Winthrop....................77
Pierce, Benjamin................415
   Ebenezer...............490, 491
   Elizabeth..................490
   Elizabeth (m. Stearns).....490, 491
   John.......................562
   Mary..................490, 491
   Richard....................491
Pike, Abigail....................90
   Abigail (Gould).............402
   Captain................446-451
   Daniel.....................317
   James.................317, 334
   John...........138, 308, 310, 311
   Mary......................256
   Thomas.....................90
Pillsbury, Benjamin..............437
Pinkham, Jonathan...............178
Piper, Benjamin..................68
   John......................158
   John L..................31, 33
   Jonathan....................33
   Samuel, Jr.................158
   Sarah (Chase).............31-34
   Thomas....................568
Place, James....................419
Plummer, Elizabeth (Titcomb).....340
   John..................304, 340
   Samuel.....................437
Pollard, James..................247
Pomeroy, ———................388
   Mehitabel..................388

Poor, Daniel......60, 245, 290, 291, 499
Pottle, Simon....................18
   William, Jr.............107, 110
Powers, Anna...................143
   Francis....................144
   Peter......................143
   Stephen................143, 149
          336-338, 492, 567
   Whitcomb..................336
Pray, John.....................456
Prentice, Reuben................165
Prescott, Abigail (m. Whidden)....367
   Abraham....................90
   Benjamin...........207, 264, 289
   Elisha.................232, 273
   Jeremiah...........159, 270-273
   John...................271-273
   Jonathan...........151, 271, 367
   Joseph.................271-273
   Nathaniel..............271, 272
   Rachel (Clifford)............517
   Samuel......118, 120, 151, 270-273
   Sarah (Clifford).............517
   Stephen....................303
   William............270, 272, 273
Presson, Edward...........23, 25, 182
Pritchard, Christopher............348
Proctor, James...........106, 226, 318
   Oliver.....................545
Purcell, Gregory.................487
Purington, Zaccheus..............291
Purmort, Hannah................335
   John..............38, 243, 280, 335
Putnam, Jacob..................183
Putney, Henry..................173
   John......................500
   Martha................173, 174

Quimby, Daniel.................421
   Hannah....................421
Quint, Jonathan.................274

Ramsey, James..................419
   John......................182
Rand, John.....................396
   Lucia.....................396

Rand, *continued.*
   Rachel....................396
   Thomas....................133
Randall, Benjamin..............348
   James......................478
   Mary (Sherburne)............478
   Miles...........184, 359, 368, 381
   Samuel.....................317
   Samuel, Jr..................317
   Simon......................184
Rankin, Samuel..................429
   William....................501
Ray, David......................72
   Mary (Morrison).............71
   William...................71, 72
   William, Jr..................72
Read, Timothy...................567
   William....................566
Redman, ———...................443
   David...................260, 261
   Hannah (m. Godfrey).........261
   John............260, 261, 349–351
   Joseph..................260, 261
   Patience (m. Newman).......261
   Sarah...................350, 351
   Tristram................260, 261
Reed, Dorothy...................444
   Philip...............41, 105, 444
   Robert.....................353
   William....................489
Reid, Matthew..............145, 419
Reynolds, James.................373
Richards, Benjamin.......174, 277, 278
   Samuel.....................440
Richardson, Amos...........168, 347
   Ebenezer...................150
   Joseph.....................414
   Sarah......................183
   Seth.......................183
   Susanna....................183
   Timothy.....................81
   William................163, 167
         168, 237, 508, 509, 566
Ricker, Daniel...................440
   Ebenezer...................288
   Mercy......................288

Ricker, *continued.*
   Paul......................440
Rindge, Ann (m. Packer).......437, 438
   Daniel.....................438
   Elizabeth (m. Wentworth).....438
   Isaac......................438
   John.......................438
   Jotham.....................438
   Mehitabel (m. Rogers).........438
   William....................438
Ring, Seth........................6
Roberts, Abigail (Gordon).........188
   Betty......................308
   Betty (m. Ham)..........308, 311
   David...................264, 265
   Francis.................307–311
   Joanna..................264, 265
   John....................308, 311
   John C.....................310
   Joseph..........35, 66, 79, 80, 307
   Keziah.....................286
   Love....................308, 309
   Lydia......................427
   Molly...................308, 310
   Sarah...................308, 311
   Stephen....................286
   Timothy....................286
Robertson, Dinah (McCargin)......527
Robinson, Alice...................97
   Ephraim.............38, 97, 175
         279, 280, 335, 513
   James......................98
   John.......................165
   Jonathan............97, 98, 391
   Peter......................417
   Timothy....................286
Roby, Anna (French).............301
   Daniel.....................301
   Hannah (Shedd)...............53
   Henry......................562
   Ichabod.....273, 302, 447, 448, 481
   John........................22
   Samuel......53, 130, 222, 247, 264
Rogers, Daniel................6, 484
   James......................65
   Mehitabel (Rindge)..........438

Rogers, *continued*.
   Samuel..................266
   Samuel, Jr................266
Rolfe, Benjamin..........15, 145, 149
Rollins, Ichabod.......30, 308, 310, 311
   Noah....................234
Ross, John....................515
Rowe, Apphia..................205
   Benjamin....206, 207, 232, 273, 274
   Caleb..................206, 207
   Captain...................503
   Charles...................232
   Daniel....................117
   Elizabeth (m. Fellows).........207
   Elizabeth (m. Taylor).........117
   Ephraim...................207
   Jane (m. Swett)..............207
   Jeremiah................206, 537
   John................117, 206, 207
   Jonathan................205–207
   Joseph....................205
   Judith....................232
   Mary (m. Blake).............117
   Mehitabel..............116, 117
   Moses....................206
   Nathan................117, 232
                     259, 510, 518
   Paine..............116, 117, 120
   Rachel....................273
   Robert..............99, 116, 117
                    119, 205–207, 272
   Ruth.....................392
   Ruth (m. Fellows)............207
   Simeon...................454
   Simon....................455
   Winthrop........133, 135, 206, 207
Rowell, ———................61
   Aaron..................325, 326
   Daniel....................556
   Job......................279
   John.....................175
   Joseph...................163
   Rice..................127–129
   Sarah.................175, 279
   William............63, 406, 411
Rundlett, Charles...............323

Rundlett, *continued*.
   Jonathan.............18, 19, 267
Russ, Thomas..................414
Russell, Deborah............488, 489
   Eleazer.............41, 42, 86, 99
      100, 184, 191, 329, 330, 332, 352
      387, 444, 460, 484, 487, 507, 514
                          515, 528
   Hannah................488, 489
   James..................301, 489
   Joseph....................489
   Olive.....................247
   Pelatiah................247, 488
   Peter..................488, 489
   Peter, Jr..................489
   Phoebe................488, 489
   Rachel................488, 489
   Rebecca...............488, 489
   Samuel...................317
   Sarah.................488, 489
   Thomas...................489

Salter, Titus...................535
Sanborn, Abner.................302
   Abraham..................151
   Benjamin...............256, 318
   Caleb...........110, 232, 358, 444
   Daniel..........98, 115, 314, 457
   Dorothy..................151
   Ebenezer..............178, 249
   Edward................137, 138
   Elisha.................98, 99
   Elisha, Jr..................98
   Elizabeth..............137, 153
   Elizabeth (m. Folsom).........256
   Enoch.................171, 172
   Ezekiel...................137
   Hannah...................563
   Israel....................256
   Jane (Nealey)....125, 126, 128, 129
   Jemima (French)............301
   Jeremiah..................90
   Jethro....................153
   Joanna (Crawford)...........564
   John...............256, 354, 435
   Jonathan....137, 138, 318, 563–566

Sanborn, *continued.*
   Joseph 29, 256, 271
   Josiah 216, 462
   Love (m. Clough) 564
   Mary (m. Fox) 256
   Matthew N. 129
   Nathan 301
   Nathaniel 542
   Peter 50
   Phineas 115, 116, 496
   Priscilla 392
   Rachel (Hilliard) 302
   Reuben 272, 301, 353
   Samuel 50, 542, 563–565
   Simon 506, 507
   Susanna 444
   Timothy 563
   Tristram 192
   Tristram, Jr. 104
   Worcester 564
Sanders, Avery 366
   William 70
Sargent, Aaron 69
   Charles 69
   Edward 318
   John 8
   Moses 63
   Nathaniel 348, 380
   Nathaniel P. 25, 290, 291
   Sarah (Bagley) 63
   Zebediah 69
Satchell, John 391
Saunders, Oliver 237, 238
Savage, John 515
Sawyer, ——— 497
   Abner 495
   Edmund 412, 492, 493
   Joshua 11
Saylor, John 567
Scales, James 44
Scammon, Richard 65, 67
Scribner, Benjamin 498
   Joseph 169
   Joseph, Jr. 169
   Lydia 169
Searles, Daniel 210

Searles, *continued.*
   John 210, 211
   Lydia 209
   Mary 210, 211
   Samuel 209–211
Seavey, Abigail 541
   Abigail (m. Clifford) 542
   Amos 543
   Comfort (Cate) 84
   Henry 542
   Ithamar 541
   Jonathan 542
   Mary (m. Connor) 542
   Mehitabel (m. Blue), ... 542
   Moses 542
   Samuel 541, 542
   Samuel, Jr. 541
Secomb, Simmons 297, 300
Senter, John 333
   Samuel 333
Servan, Richard 520, 521
Severance, Elizabeth 97
   Ephraim, Jr. 97
   Jacob 97
   Moses 525
Sewall, David 54, 71, 75, 85
   105, 138, 143, 145, 153, 162, 183
   184, 189, 195, 197, 204, 205, 211
   212, 222, 226, 245, 249, 255, 256
   264, 274, 289, 292, 312, 318, 320
   321, 327, 329, 330, 341, 352, 367
   373, 386, 397, 415, 418, 419, 429
   440, 444, 460, 461, 487, 490, 528
                      559, 570
Seward, George 367, 368, 375, 528
Seymour, Ann 183
   Henry 41, 183
Shackford, John 71, 154, 156, 184
   209, 293, 367, 368, 375, 386, 487
                         507
   William 65, 67, 154
                      156, 315, 341
Shannon, Cutts .. 17, 30, 48, 49, 56, 60, 78
   120, 165, 169, 189, 209, 255, 267
   276, 277, 294, 304, 349, 352, 354
   357, 358, 368, 414, 419, 420, 487

INDEX   633

Shannon, *continued.*
    497, 500, 501, 506, 543, 558, 591
    Richard C....................104
Shattuck, Daniel................525
    Zachariah...................490
Shaw, Benjamin.................6, 7
    Caleb...................136, 304
    Esther.......................6, 7
    Ichabod................436, 437
    John......................7, 304
    Joseph...............98, 99, 505
    Joshiah.......................97
    Malachi......................273
    Mehitabel (Weare)............358
    Moses.......................281
    Samuel......................482
    Sarah.....................7, 436
    Susanna.......................7
Sheafe, Jacob...........105, 289, 386
    Thomas.....................377
Shedd, Hannah.................52, 53
    Hannah (m. Roby).............53
    John......................52, 53
Sheffield, ———............305, 306
Shepard, Benjamin...........350, 351
    Daniel.......................69
    John...........40, 44, 45, 58, 353
    John, Jr....................400
Sherburne, Ann (m. Langdon).......196
                      199, 202
    Dorothy (m. Gilman)..196, 199, 202
    Hannah.................478, 479
    Hannah (m. Blunt)...........478
    Henry.......154, 195-199, 202, 553
    James...................347, 510
    John...............183, 195-200
                  202, 355, 392, 505
    Joseph..................191, 293
    Katharine (m. Odiorne).......478
    Mary (m. Randall)............478
    Mehitabel...................191
    Nathaniel...............191, 392
    Noah........................478
    Ruth (m. Lang)..............392
    Samuel......195, 197-201, 386, 553
    Thomas......................35

Shortridge, Richard..............429
Sias, Joseph..............78, 126, 127
                   184, 381, 431, 432
Simes, Joseph.........71, 418, 490, 507
Simonds, Anna (m. Hobbs).........57
    Joseph.......................57
Simpson, Andrew............127, 129
    Andrew, Jr...................73
    Elizabeth....................72
    John.....................72, 380
    Sarah........................72
    Sarah (Morrison).............72
    Thomas.....7, 72, 123, 184, 319, 367
Slade, Samuel....................301
Sleeper, Benjamin................276
    Ebenezer........130, 131, 321, 323
    Edward.....................138
    John.........96, 213, 225, 226, 318
    Ruth (Choate)...........297, 300
    William.................297, 300
Sloane, David...................338
Smart, Joseph...................227
    Robert......................513
Smith, Abigail............97, 290, 435
    Abraham.................90, 148
    Adam.......................262
    Andrew.................146, 147
    Ballard.....................290
    Benjamin........38, 290, 291, 369
    Daniel..................145, 189
    Dolly.......................513
    Dorothy....................290
    Dorothy (m. Johnson).........290
    Ebenezer.....................3
    Effie (Liggett)...............394
    Elias.......................239
    Elizabeth...............145, 146
    Hannah..................97, 435
    Hannah (Gordon)............188
    Israel.......................96
    Ithiel......................435
    Jabez....................75, 343
    Jacob...............110, 111, 570
    Jane........................96
    Jeremiah............97, 435, 511

Smith, *continued*.
    John 75, 110, 170
                                     175, 185, 394, 454
    Jonathan 96, 226
    Joseph 47, 185, 189, 357
                                     381, 385, 386, 477
    Margaret (Weeks) 3, 4
    Martha 421
    Mehitabel (m. Lyford) 433, 434
    Nathaniel 145, 146, 187
    Nicholas 349, 350
    Oliver 96, 97, 432, 435
    Priscilla 421
    Rachel 432, 435
    Rachel (m. Patterson) 146
    Richard 570, 578
    Ruth (m. Calfe) 433, 434
    Samuel 18, 19, 389, 513
    Samuel, Jr. 43
    Sarah (m. Adams) 146, 147
    Sargent 290
    Susanna 146
    Theophilus 31, 52, 86, 145
        146, 151, 170, 269, 283, 289, 343
        344, 350, 356, 435, 457, 505, 506
                                          511, 513
    Theophilus, Jr. 513
    Thomas 97
    William 146, 147, 371
Spaulding, Asa 165
    Joseph 333
    Reuben 237
    Stephen 237
Stackpole, Philip 220
    Samuel 220
    William 284
Stanley, Matthew 547
Stark, Archibald 276
    Eleanor 276
    Henry 276
    Isabel (m. Sterling) 276
    Jean (m. Stinson) 276
    John 276
    Samuel 276
    William 276
Stearns, Eleazer 490

Stearns, *continued*.
    Elizabeth (Pierce) 490, 491
    Lucy (Wyman) 509
Stedman, Ebenezer 529
Steele, David 430
    Henry 189
    James 285
    John 170
    Margaret (Cochran) 285
Sterling, Hugh 414, 415
    Isabel (Stark) 276
Stevens, ——— 281
    Aaron 17
    Alcock 460
    Anna 152
    Benjamin 104, 123
    Catherine 551
    David 122, 123, 381
    Ebenezer 39, 40, 49, 60
        63, 104, 121, 194, 279, 436, 461
    Elizabeth 550, 551
    Elizabeth (m. Elwell) 486
    Enos 551
    Flora 484
    Hubbard 79, 186, 359, 431
    James 484, 487
    John 96, 153
    Joseph 431, 545
    Mary 122, 484, 551
    Moses 21, 30, 70, 79, 92
        265, 307, 317, 334, 349, 364, 497
    Nehemiah 152
    Peter 428
    Phineas 550, 551
    Phoebe (Pease) 415
    Prudence 551
    Samuel 415, 551, 552
    Samuel, Jr. 486
    Sarah 282
    Sarah (Fifield) 104
    Simon 551
    Solomon 551
    Susanna (m. James) 486
    Thomas 61
    Timothy 153
    Willard 551

INDEX 635

Stevens, *continued.*
  William....................486
Stevenson, Abraham..............382
Stewart, John................258, 259
  Margaret (Gilmore)...........258
  Robert.......................53
  Sarah...................258, 259
Stickney, Anna (Osgood)...........14
  Moses.......................353
  Wade........................353
Stiles, Samuel.....................28
Stimson, Joseph..............424, 426
Stinson, Jean (Stark).............276
  John........................415
  Samuel..................414, 415
Stokell, Robert...................209
Stoneman, Alexander..............332
  Charles.....................515
  Esther......................515
  Mary........................332
Stoodley, Elizabeth...............376
  James...................376, 377
  James, Jr................264, 270
    279, 280, 334, 438, 439, 486, 487
  John........................376
  Jonathan................375-377
  Mary........................375
  Mary (m. Furber)........376, 377
Straw, Lawrence..................193
  Samuel......................402
Sullivan, John............186, 317, 386
Sutton, Richard...................176
Swain, Abigail...............118, 119
  Caleb...................120, 272
  John................118-120, 271
  Jonathan....................119
  Lydia (Perkins).............561
  Martha......................118
  Nathan......................119
  Stephen.....................118
  William.................118, 119
  William, Jr.................561
Swallow, John....................567
Swett, Anna.......................97
  Benjamin.......17, 96, 97, 173, 297
  David.......................230

Swett, *continued.*
  Deliverance (m. Coleman).....173
  Elisha................39, 40, 569
  Huldah (m. Coleman).........173
  Jane (Rowe).................207
  Jonathan...............111, 173
    207, 358, 444, 445, 480
  Joseph......................207
  Josiah......................207
  Mehitabel...................207
  Sarah.......................207
  Stephen.....................511

Taggart, James.................48, 122
  Janet........................48
  John.........................48
Tallant, Hugh....................346
Tarbell, Samuel..................338
Tarbox, Leod.....................333
  Noah........................333
Tate, Joseph.....................373
Taylor, Anna.................175, 176
  Catherine...............175, 176
  Elizabeth (Rowe)............117
  John................175, 176, 178
  Joseph..............175, 176, 269
  Mercy.......................303
  Timothy.....................389
  William.................269, 270
  Willoughby..............268, 269
Thing, Benjamin...................87
  Edward......................537
  Elizabeth...............536, 537
  John....................535, 536
  Jonathan........115, 116, 535-537
  Martha (Cate)................84
  Mehitabel...................536
  Mercy (Dudley)..............242
Thom, John 259
  William.....................259
  William, Jr.................259
Thomas, Abigail..............312, 594
  Abigail (m. Nudd)...........313
  Benjamin................312, 314
  Elisha..................313, 314
  James.......................313

Thomas, *continued.*
   Jonathan....................312
   William.....................313
Thompson, Agnes.................75
   Barbara....................374
   Benjamin........162, 210, 374, 375
   Dorothy (Young)............319
   Ebenezer........185, 381, 385, 386
   James..................294, 374, 375
   Janet......................374
   Nathaniel...................490
   Samuel......................75
   Thomas....................319
   William.....................75
Thorndike, Joshua................220
Thorne, John....................518
Thornton, Matthew..........144, 181
                239, 419, 477
Thurston, Abner......282, 283, 289, 435
   Elizabeth (Palmer)............390
   James............52, 289, 343, 513
   Moses..................109, 282, 283
   Samuel..................282, 283
   Stephen....................390
Tibbetts, Edward.................532
   Ephraim................241, 593
   Judith (m. Tuttle)............593
   Martha (Bickford)............161
   Peter......................341
   Samuel....................593
Tidd, Joseph.................415, 416
Tilton, Daniel.....87, 335, 342, 511, 513
   Jonathan................215, 216
             462, 505, 582, 584, 588
   Joseph..........132, 133, 151, 207
   Josiah......................148
   Nathan....................505
   Sherburne...............133–135
   Timothy....................133
Titcomb, Abigail (m. Libby).......340
   Ann....................339, 341
   Benjamin...................340
   Daniel..................339–341
   David......................340
   Elizabeth (m. Plummer).......340
   Enoch......................340

Titcomb, *continued.*
   John....................339, 341
   Mary......................340
   Sarah (m. Wingate)...........340
Todd, Alexander.................515
   Andrew.....................48
Tolford, John...................169
   Major......................325
Torrey, William..........387, 388, 567
Towle, Alice....................204
   Amos...............462, 580–588
   Benjamin...............212–216
   Caleb......................276
   Caleb, Jr....................276
   Ebenezer...................204
   Elisha..................212–216
   Hepzibah (m. Page)..........213
   Jacob......................212
   James...462, 581, 583, 584, 587, 588
   John....462, 580, 583, 584, 587, 588
   Jonathan....462, 581–583, 585–588
   Joseph......462, 581, 583, 587, 588
   Mary (m. Page)..............213
   Patience (m. Hobbs)......213, 216
   Philip......................480
   Rebecca...................212
   Sarah......................212
   Sarah (m. Clifford)...........213
   Tabitha (m. Tuck)...........213
Traill, Robert....................22
Trask, Nathaniel.................537
Treadwell, Catherine.............376
   Daniel.....................428
   Jacob.....................8, 276
   Mary......................376
   Nathaniel..............376, 380
   Nathaniel, Jr................377
   Samuel....................376
   William E.....48, 105, 276, 289, 483
Trefethen, Abraham................5
True, Abraham..............124, 126
   Israel......................535
Trussell, Jacob..................492
   Jane...................492, 493
   Moses.................492, 493
Tuck, ———....................443

Tuck, *continued.*
   Benjamin...................532
   Jonathan...................216
   Sarah (Garland).............532
   Tabitha (Towle).............213
Tucker, Benjamin................320
   Ebenezer, Jr................562
   John........................104
Tuckerman, John.................311
   Nathaniel...................311
Tuttle, Elijah........241, 242, 305, 403
   Judith (Tibbetts)...........593
   Silas.......................427
   Thomas......................242
Twombly, William................162
Tyng, ———......................347

Ullerick, Philip................567
Underhill, John..........22, 23, 349
Underwood, James...........489, 566
   Mary........................151
   Phineas.....................151
   Timothy.....................247
Urin, Peter.....................534
   Ruth........................534

Vance, William..................373
Varney, Amos....................440
   Benjamin....................404
   Elijah......................404
   Elizabeth...................404
   Humphrey....................404
   James..................403, 404
   Joseph......................440
   Joshua......................440
   Lydia.......................404
   Mary...................439, 440
   Mordecai....................404
   Moses..............403, 404, 406
   Nathaniel...................440
   Peter.......................404
   Phoebe.................403, 404
   Phoebe (m. Bickford)........406
   Samuel.................439, 440
   Sarah.......................439
   Shubael.....................440

Varney, *continued.*
   Simeon......................440
   Solomon............404, 439, 440
   Timothy.....................439
Varnum, Lydia (Challis).....371, 372
   Peter.......................371
Varrell, Susanna................186
Vaughan, Anna...................329
   Elliott...............183, 196, 329
   William.................23, 77, 80
      107, 110, 133, 149, 158, 178, 182
      235, 259, 267, 317, 358, 375, 440
          495, 506, 507, 567
Veasey, Anna (Neal).............559
   Benjamin................98, 421
   Jonathan.................98, 99
   Joshua......................559
   Samuel.................249, 559
   Thomas...............31–34, 559
Vennard, Elizabeth..............460
   John........................460
   Samuel......................460
   William.....................460

Waddell, James.............168, 169
   John...................168, 169
   Margaret (m. Wilson)....168, 169
Wadleigh, Ann...................106
   Joseph.............106, 334, 355
   Joseph, Jr.............135, 355
   Philip......................334
   Sarah (Leavitt).............106
   Thomas......................557
Waite, Phineas..................373
Walden, Jacob..............377, 380
Waldron, George........154, 197, 351
   Thomas W..........95, 178, 291
      292, 315, 353, 359, 404, 492, 508
Walker, ———.....................76
   Alexander..............429, 430
   Alexander, Jr...............429
   Elizabeth....................76
   Isaac........................76
   Joseph..................51, 419
   Joseph, Jr...................51
   Margaret (Downs)............51

INDEX

Walker, continued.
- Robert................284–286
- Thomas....................429
- Timothy............16, 236, 237
- Timothy, Jr...15, 374, 406, 418, 441

Wallace, James..................179
- John.......................324
- Robert.................179, 182
  360, 398, 538, 589, 590
- Robert, Jr..................182
- Thomas...........182, 398, 590
- Thomas, Jr..................182
- William............250–252, 477

Wallingford, Ebenezer............70

Walton, ———......446, 447, 467, 468
- Benjamin...................566
- George....................234
- Jonathan...................572

Ward, Dorcas...................553
- Nahum.................553, 554

Warner, Daniel..............195, 442
- Nathaniel..................442

Warren, Benjamin...............349
- Elizabeth..................528
- George....................528

Waters, Samuel...........41, 42, 99
  100, 255, 368, 514

Watkins, Andrew................380
- Jane......................380

Watson, Benjamin................78
- David......................67
- Dudley.....................64
- Isaac...................64–66
- Joanna..................65, 66
- John........................2
- Jonathan...................69
- Joseph.................67, 340
- Lydia (Hanson)..............305
- Mary (Dudley)...............242
- Nathaniel..................229
- Nicodemus.................328
- Parmenas..................566
- Samuel.............34, 64, 65

Watts, Elizabeth............419, 420
- Elizabeth (m. Currier).......422
- John........25, 419, 420, 422, 423

Watts, continued.
- John, Jr....................25
- Mary (m. Webster)..........423
- Mehitabel (m. Eastman)......423
- Nathaniel..............422, 423
- Samuel......25, 419, 420, 422, 423
- Sarah.....................422
- Sarah (m. Clement).........422

Weare, Deacon..................461
- Elizabeth..................358
- John...................87, 162
- Jonathan...................469
- Joseph....................160
- Mary..................160, 358
- Mehitabel.............357, 358
- Mehitabel (m. Shaw).........358
- Meshech........21, 92, 110, 111
  118, 120, 173, 215, 216, 231, 232
  273, 303, 358, 444, 451, 462, 463
  470, 482, 505, 570, 582, 584, 588
- Nathaniel..........160, 357, 358

Webster, ———..................422
- Abel......................143
- Abigail....................166
- Andrew....................358
- Daniel....................324
- Ebenezer..................193
- Elizabeth..................90
- Elizabeth (Osgood)...........14
- Israel.....................60
- Jemima (Kimball)............163
- Jeremy...........39, 40, 49, 50
  60, 63, 78, 90, 148, 194, 266, 297
  300, 318, 319, 369, 370, 401, 406
  411, 428, 556, 566
- John..22, 163, 222, 237, 268, 290, 497
- John, Jr....................245
- Joshua....................423
- Samuel....................495

Wedgewood, Jonathan.............45

Weed, David...................322
- Leander...................321
- Orlando................320, 321

Weeks, Caesar....................4
- Comfort.....................1
- Comfort (m. Weeks)..........2–4

Weeks, *continued.*
  Hannah..................... 1, 3
  John......... 1-4, 45, 213, 264, 444
  Joseph.................. 552, 553
  Joshua................. 1, 2, 4, 5
  Margaret (m. Smith).......... 3, 4
  Martha (m. Hilton)........... 2-4
  Mary....................... 245
  Mary (m. Chesley)............ 2-4
  Mary (m. Wiggin)............ 246
  Matthias.................. 55, 56
  Neptune...................... 2
  Samuel............... 68, 77, 137
  Sarah....................... 56
  Thankful (m. Marshall)....... 2, 3
  Walter........... 2, 245, 246, 397
  Walter, Jr.................. 245
  William...... 1-5, 56, 229, 250, 262
Welch, David.................... 96
  Samuel...................... 96
  Thomas..................... 557
  William..................... 47
Wells, Thomas... 122, 152, 153, 324, 326
  Thomas, Jr.................. 325
Wendell, John............. 421, 507
  Mary............... 476, 490, 516
  Thomas................. 315, 442
Wentworth, Bartholomew.......... 69
  Benjamin............. 69, 287, 288
  Ebenezer............... 21, 22, 69
  Elizabeth.................... 95
  Elizabeth (Rindge)........... 438
  Ezekiel.............. 95, 280, 288
  Gershom................. 286-288
  Hunking........... 22, 48, 71, 115
                 154, 196, 293, 296, 358
                 375, 376, 387, 421, 484
  John..... 69, 277, 303, 307, 349, 498
  John, Jr.................... 133
  Jonathan........... 308, 310, 311
  Lydia (m. Baker)............. 287
  Mark.................... 69, 295
  Mark H................ 173, 395
  Paul....................... 288
  Rebecca..................... 21
  Samuel........... 21, 22, 196, 280

Wentworth, *continued.*
  Sarah.............. 280, 287, 288
  Thomas................. 288, 349
  William........... 30, 69, 284, 291
West, Love..................... 41
  Mary....................... 349
  William..................... 41
Weston, Daniel............. 399, 400
  Ebenezer............... 398-401
  Ebenezer, Jr............ 399, 400
  Elizabeth (m. Larabee)........ 400
  Hepzibah................... 400
  Isaac.................. 400, 401
  Mehitabel (m. Nichols)........ 400
  Ruth....................... 398
  Southrick.................. 400
  Tabitha.................... 400
  Thomas..................... 400
Weymouth, Esther (m. Mason)..... 373
  Samuel..................... 373
Wheeler, Abner............. 267, 268
  Benjamin, Jr................ 163
  Esther (Kimball)............ 164
  Hannah (Kimball)........... 164
  Jonathan............... 267, 268
  Nehemiah................... 387
  Peter...................... 416
  Sarah (Meserve)............. 387
  Solomon............ 297, 298, 300
  Stephen.................... 164
  William................ 259, 268
Whidden, Abigail (Prescott)....... 367
  Ann (m. Jones)............... 36
  Elizabeth................... 36
  Hannah (m. Jenkins).......... 36
  James.................. 367, 386
  John..................... 35-37
  Joseph...................... 37
  Mary........................ 36
  Michael.................... 386
  Michael, Jr.............. 71, 255
  Samuel................... 36, 37
  Sarah (m. Haines)............ 36
Whipple, ———.................. 387
  Dorothy (Jackson)........... 331
Whitcher, Benjamin.......... 124, 126

Whitcher, *continued*.
    William....................556
White, Ebenezer................498
    James.......................290
    John........................498
    Joshua......................460
    Nathaniel W.................456
    Nicholas................428, 497
    William......................49
Whiter, Joseph..................142
Whiting, Eleazer.............346, 510
    James.......................560
    Joseph......................211
Whitney, Amos..................552
    James.......................333
Whittaker, Daniel............243, 244
Whittemore, Aaron...............476
    Abigail.....................393
Whittier, Abner................53, 54
Wibird, Eliza................507, 516
    Richard.....................200
    Thomas......................195
Wiggin, Andrew...........30, 47, 158
    Andrew, 3d..................246
    Anna........................157
    Bradstreet..............157, 158
    Chase..............157, 158, 391
    Coker...................157, 158
    Comfort.................157, 158
    Eliphalet...................456
    Henry.......................109
    John........................456
    Jonathan..........31, 33, 34, 107
    Joseph..................108, 110
    Joshua........................2
    Martha..................157, 158
    Mary........................109
    Mary (Weeks)................246
    Nancy.......................158
    Samuel......................107
    Sarah (m. Perkins)..........108
    Simon..................107–110
    Susanna............107, 109, 110
    Thomas.............109, 158, 558
    Thomas, Jr..................158
    Winthrop................157, 158

Wilkins, Timothy................165
Wilkinson, Ann..................429
    Joseph......................429
Willard, Oliver.................388
Willey, Theodore.................51
    Theodore, Jr.................51
Williams, Abigail...............494
    Abigail (m. Moulton)........496
    Benjamin..........54–56, 493–496
    Elijah......................522
    Jemima.................493–496
    John........................337
    Joseph.................494–496
    Mary.................54–56, 494
    Mary (m. Kendrick)..........496
    Sarah..................494, 496
    Thomas.........492, 494–496, 525
Wilson, ———....................360
    Benjamin....................360
    James.....48, 75, 145, 260, 341, 592
    John...................168, 341
    Joshua...........95, 343, 344, 435
    Margaret (Waddell)......168, 169
    Thomas..............49, 95, 263
Winchester, Ebenezer..............6
Wingate, Aaron..................305
    John.............45, 55, 150, 391
    Joshua.........35, 57, 307, 404, 406
    Mary (Lunt)................55, 57
    Moses...............65, 67, 305
    Paine..................31, 33, 34
    Sarah (Titcomb).............340
Winsley, Samuel....96, 97, 130, 131, 278
Winslow, Elisha.................569
    Jane (French)...............301
    Samuel......................301
Wood, John......................531
    Joseph......................552
Woodbury, Ebenezer..............329
    Ephraim.....................220
Woodman, John...................320
    Jonathan........368, 382, 431, 432
    Joshua......................192
    Joshua, Jr..............298, 299
    Nathaniel...................259
Woods, Oliver...................543

Woolson, Jonas...............545
Worcester, Francis..........143, 144
  289, 337, 338
  Francis, Jr...............81, 144
  336, 338, 490
  Jesse.......................289
  Noah........................82
Worth, Joseph.................173
Worthen, Enoch................475
  Ephraim....................512
  Ezekiel................463, 475
  Hannah (m. Gove)............20
  Judith (m. Dow).............20
  Mary (m. Buswell)...........20
  Moses.......................20
  Samuel...................19–21
  Thomas......................19
Wright, Benjamin........81, 137, 282
  Joseph............165, 179, 569
  Joshua......................81
Wyman, Lucy (m. Stearns).......509
  Sybil.......................509

Wyman, *continued*.
  Thomas.................508, 509
  Thomas, Jr............508–510

Yeaton, Ann....................295
  Francis............308, 310, 311
  Susanna (Lang).............396
York, Benjamin................512
  John.........................47
  Susanna......................47
  Thomas......................512
Young, Aaron..................318
  Dorothy....................318
  Dorothy (m. Thompson)......319
  Elizabeth..................419
  Hugh.......................538
  James......................105
  John..................318, 319
  Jonathan..............318, 419
  Joseph.................64, 123
  Moses......................318
  Richard.......4, 5, 84, 85, 158
  Thomas........29, 30, 68, 513, 560

Milton Keynes UK
Ingram Content Group UK Ltd.
UKHW040058180324
439604UK00007B/1107